Egyptians on Crete, p. 74

ANCIENT CIVILIZATIONS

Cover design by Vito Fiorenza

MAINSTREAMS OF CIVILIZATION

VOLUME I: ANCIENT CIVILIZATIONS

PREHISTORY TO THE FALL OF ROME

Carlton J. H. Hayes and James H. Hanscom

VOLUME II: MEDIEVAL AND EARLY MODERN TIMES

THE AGE OF JUSTINIAN TO THE EIGHTEENTH CENTURY

Carlton J. H. Hayes and Frederick F. Clark

VOLUME III: MODERN TIMES

THE FRENCH REVOLUTION TO THE PRESENT

Carlton J. H. Hayes, Margareta Faissler, and Judith Walsh

PREHISTORY TO THE FALL OF ROME

ANCIENT CIVILIZATIONS

CARLTON J. H. HAYES
JAMES H. HANSCOM

MACMILLAN PUBLISHING CO., INC.
NEW YORK
COLLIER MACMILLAN PUBLISHERS
LONDON

THE AUTHORS

Carlton J. H. Hayes

Late Seth Low Professor Emeritus of History, Columbia University

James H. Hanscom

Professor of Social Studies, New York University

ACKNOWLEDGMENTS

The poem on page 342 is from the *Greek Anthology*, translated by William Corry, London, George Allen, 1905. The quotation on page 224 is from *The Greeks*, by H. D. F. Kitto, Penguin Books, Inc., paper, 1951, page 95. The quotation in the caption on page 336 is from *Art in the Western World*, by David M. Robb and J. J. Garrison, Rev. Ed., Harper, 1942, page 449.

MACMILLAN PUBLISHING CO., INC.
866 THIRD AVENUE, NEW YORK, N.Y. 10022
COLLIER MACMILLAN CANADA, INC.

Printed in the United States of America
ISBN 0-02-185580-3

Printing: 2 3 4 5 6 7 8

Contents

MAPS:

USING DOCUMENTS (and Prehistoric Evidence):

ANCIENT CIVILIZATIONS

Prologue

Here is a history of ancient times and man's earliest civilizations. These civilizations, covering some four thousand years in time, were created in north Africa and Eurasia, the great stretch of land that extends from the Atlantic Ocean to the Pacific. Today Eurasia is divided into Europe, Asia, and the Middle East. In the Middle East arose man's first civilization, the Mesopotamian, after many thousands of years had passed following man's first appearance on earth.

Why study ancient history? One answer is that the contributions of ancient men were unique. They created civilizations from a series of basic steps without precedent. Among these were learning to plant, to live together in villages, to specialize in occupation. These were gigantic steps in the development of man. Once civilization arose, why did some men organize themselves into authoritarian kingdoms while others developed self-governing city-states? Why did ideas about life after death develop, and how did they differ among different peoples? Why did such different civilizations arise once the basic steps were taken? Ideas such as creating city-states and imagining a life after death were first originated by ancient men. They set patterns of thought we follow, with variations, today. How and why did they do this?

History poses many questions. In order to answer them, the historian has to select carefully from the mass of material at his disposal. "History is . . . the record of what one age finds worthy of note in another," said the Swiss historian Jacob Burckhardt. Such a definition recognizes an essential fact. Although history, broadly speaking, is the record of everything men have thought, said, and done in the past, it is obviously impossible to record everything. Obviously also, we do not know everything, even if we could record it. So the historian selects what he believes to be the most significant material at his disposal. His selection, however, may not coincide entirely with that of other historians. It may well differ from the histories written in other generations by men who saw things from another perspective. It may change as new material comes to light. History, then, is a record of events whose selection and significance is subject to the interpretations of those who call themselves historians.

The historian sees trends and developments that shed light on what came before and what happened after. Only when events have been organized into meaningful patterns, however, can they illuminate the past and the future. To be able to think about his material more easily, the historian categorizes it. The largest of these categories concern politics (how men govern themselves), economics (how men produce, distribute, and consume goods and services), society (how men deal with each other, individually and in groups), and culture (how men express their thoughts, feelings, ideas in art, literature, philosophy). How the earliest men dealt with the concerns of these categories—the mistakes they made, the successes they had—is the subject of ancient history.

Finally, and of great importance, ancient history, like all history, provides us with experience we cannot have ourselves. This experience is indirect. It comes through knowledge rather than participation. Nevertheless, it enables us to make better decisions about events affecting our lives in the present and future; it helps us to understand more clearly attitudes, interests, and values of the society we live in; it makes it possible for us to deal more successfully with societies of other peoples who have interests and values different from our own. Without experience there can be no awareness. Without awareness there can be no understanding. History, then, gives us knowledge of experience we cannot have ourselves and which, even though indirect, helps us to understand both ourselves and others.

As you begin your study of the ancient world, you might consider the words of the Roman statesman Marcus Tullius Cicero (106–43 B.C., page 390). He said, "History is the witness of the times, the light of truth, the life of memory, the teacher of life. . . ." You will discover whether these words are true. You will see how men, isolated, alone, reach out to communicate with each other, and then build villages and cities, great empires and states that exchange ideas. You will note how in so many instances ancient men lived lives that are so different from our own yet so alike in ways you may not have thought of. When you have considered all these things, you may wish to make your own definition of the significance of history and of the ancient world.

PART 1

Beginnings

Earth existed for billions of years before man appeared. Man has existed for only a tiny fraction of time in earth's history. Yet, whereas man's history as a civilized being has covered only some five thousand years, the early stage of his development lasted for hundreds of thousands of years in the period known as the Stone Age.

The great landmark in the Stone Age was the development of agriculture, or food planting. This most fundamental of all human revolutions brought marked changes into man's pattern of life. From being a food hunter, always on the move and dependent on the environment, man became a food producer, settled in villages, where he gradually learned to gain control over his environment. The population increased from the regular food supply. New inventions were made. Man made images to worship and to appease the gods he thought were in the wind, the thunder, and the water, and gradually these images took on his own likeness. Social groups emerged, and specialization of occupation appeared. By the end of the New Stone Age man was prepared to take the great step into civilization.

The study of ancient man, in the vast ages before he was civilized, is one of the most modern areas of research. The great questions about who ancient man was, how he developed, how he lived, and why he did what he did, are in large measure unanswered.

Every day in different parts of the world, evidence of the ancient past comes to light. What we do not know, however, is still much more than what we do know. So the student of ancient man must be always alert to the latest discoveries. He must always be ready to rethink his conclusions in the light of new information.

1

Man and His Past

Each person is his own past. At any moment the mind and the body are the totals of what one thought and did this morning, yesterday, and in all the days and years back to one's beginning. And beyond that, one is the past of one's ancestors through physical heredity and of other people long dead through inherited customs, traditions, and ideas.

What personal experience is to the individual, that is, a past that gives him greater understanding, history is to mankind. But experience has no meaning or usefulness for those who cannot recall it. In the same way, history can have no meaning unless the great experiences of groups, of nations, or of all mankind are remembered. And to be remembered longer than the lifetime of those involved, the experience must be transmitted, or passed on, from one generation to the next.

TRANSMITTING EXPERIENCE

In order to pass on experience one must have speech, so man's first and most difficult task was to develop language. Without the aid of words and precise ideas, man could not organize his personal memory, and he could not tell his experiences and his ideas to others. With speech, individuals could exchange thoughts, and group traditions followed. Such traditions could then be transmitted orally from old to young.

Genealogies (family relationships), sagas (tales of heroes and their adventures), moral precepts and rules of behavior ("Thou shalt"), taboos (warnings of things dangerous or forbidden—"Thou shalt not"), legends of ancient happenings, and myths of superhuman beings—all these are known to have been transmitted orally from generation to generation, sometimes for centuries without alteration. Two thousand years ago the Druids of Britain transmitted their beliefs orally, and when the last Druid trained in the lore died, the details of their beliefs were lost forever.

CLARIFYING TIME

Man found, however, that to organize his experience and to transmit stories of events from earlier times, he had to make reference to time. The reality of time *as it relates to human life* was and is difficult to understand. It may be measured by some mechanical device in terms of units such as minutes, hours, days, weeks, years. But in relation to daily life, one hour is not the same to two different people. For one person the hour drags and seems endless; for another the same hour races by. The holidays so slow in coming may seem to gallop once they are here; so in relation to human reaction the duration and passage of time cannot be recorded in a meaningful way. To say that one civilization lasted five thousand years and another lasted one thousand does not tell us which was richer in terms of human experience.

Man, however, needed to organize time so that he could remember events in the order in which they happened. He therefore invented time measures.

The rising and setting of the sun served as the unit of the day. When a larger measure was needed, the apparent growth and waning of the moon was used. To tell the "months" apart, man identified them by descriptive names. The American Indians, for example, had a "Planter's Moon," a "Hunter's Moon," and a "Harvest Moon." Some early men stopped at this point. Their traditions might hark back to "many moons ago," but this could mean anything—years, centuries, or eons.

Some early men noted that the moon's development from crescent to full was repeated twelve or thirteen times during the cycle of the seasons. Others noticed that different conditions repeated themselves regularly—the lengthening and shortening of the daylight hours, the appearance of certain groups on the horizon at sunset or sunrise, the rising and falling of the Nile in Egypt, the regular changes in the seasonal winds and rains in India, the recurrence of planting and harvesting seasons. From some or all of those cycles came the concept of the year as a measure of time.

To identify the different years, they were named. One year might become known as "The Year of No Harvest," another as "The Year of the Earthquake," a third as "The Year of the Coming of the Strangers." The name would then be expressed in a simple picture, and lists of the pictures were kept to help transmit the tradition.

The oldest example of such a list or calendar known today is the Palermo Stone, so called because of its present location in the museum of Palermo, Sicily. It is a list some five thousand years old, covering Egyptian year-names and kings for about seven hundred years.

THE INVENTION OF THE CALENDAR

As time went on, men in many societies made lists of rulers, and years were identified as the first, second, or whatever year of a certain king's reign. This *regnal* calendar system has continued through history in governments headed by emperors, kings, caliphs, and popes. The Assyrians kept lists of officials (*limma*) plus records of eclipses of the sun and moon. The Roman Republic dated its laws by the chief Roman executives, the consuls. Modern republics, such as the United States, never follow this practice because it might seem to suggest that the President is a ruler in the royal sense.

The Romans also identified the year by reference to the founding of Rome. The destruction of Carthage, for example, was recorded as taking place during the consulate of Scipio Aemilianus and in 607 A.U.C. (*Anno Urbis Conditae*, Year of the Founding of the City).

The Greeks also used two systems, identifying a year by the name of the chief magistrate, the archon, or by reference to the Olympic Games, which were held every fourth year, or by both.

In more modern times, similar calendars have been invented. Muslims date their era from the year of Muhammad's flight from Mecca to Medina, so their dates are identified for us in the west with the letters A.H. (*Anno Hejirae*, Year of the Flight).

The Christian calendar is based on the birth of Jesus, although the estimated date of this event is considered to be wrong by three to seven years. The early Christians did not use this system. It was not until several hundred years after Jesus' birth that Christians determined to date their calendar from his birthday.

Christians have since used the A.D. (*Anno Domini*, in the year of the Lord) calendar so widely that today in much of the world, including non-Christian areas, the A.D. letters are omitted as unnecessary.

In the Christian calendar the years before the birth of Christ are counted backward from the year 1 A.D. and are labeled B.C. (before Christ). According to the Christian calendar the traditional date of the founding of Rome was 753 B.C. (the year 1 in the old Roman calendar), and the Greek Olympics were first held in 776 B.C. (the first year of the first Olympiad according to ancient Greek reckoning).

When it is noted that the year 1 in the Jewish calendar corresponds to 3761 B.C. and the year 1 in the Chinese calendar to 2697 B.C., it might be thought that these calendars were in existence before these dates. Actually, the beginning dates are estimates. Just as the Christians in the fourth century A.D. counted back to the birth of Christ, so Jewish leaders of about 360 A.D. counted back to a traditional date for the beginning of the world. Thus the Christian and Jewish calendars have actually been used for about the same length of time. In the same manner the Chinese counted back to the time they believed their calendar system had come into existence.

Since there is no calendar accepted by all nations and religions, events are often dated according to two or three systems, as was the Roman and Greek custom. A recent Thanksgiving Day proclamation by a state governor was dated three ways—by the Christian year, by the founding of the state as a colony in America, and by the independence of the United States. Thus the year of Caesar's murder could be identified as 709 A.U.C. (Roman), 44 B.C. (Christian), 3717 (Jewish), 2653 (Chinese), the first year of the 183rd Olympiad (Greek), and 1845 before the founding of the United States. Or, to use a calendar that is always in the back of our minds, how many years ago?

THE MODERN HISTORIAN AND THE PAST

Knowledge of the past comes from many sources—from written records and also from knowledge revealed by sciences developed in the last century or so. New sciences of some importance to the historian are *anthropology*, the study of man's physical and cultural development; *archaeology*, the discovery and study of material remains; *geology*, the study of rock and earth formations; *philology*, the study of languages and written records; *sociology*, the study of conditions and change in groups; and *psychology*,

An archaeological dig. Archaeological excavations in the sands of Nubia, Sudan, revealed the wall of a buried building and on the wall the painting of an angel. The wall, it turned out, belonged to an early Coptic Christian church.

the study of human behavior. Archaeologists have found and studied caves, ruins, and tombs containing bones of and objects—artifacts—made and used by early man. From these bones and artifacts scientists have discovered facts and made deductions about the history and culture of man for periods when writing did not exist, or when written records were lost, or when an existing record was in a language not yet translated.

It used to be customary to use the word "history" to mean only that part of the human past that could be learned from writings and inscriptions. The story of the eras before writing was invented was called "prehistory."

The phrase "unrecorded history" was preferred by some writers because it could apply equally to the period before writing was in existence and to the many cases after its invention when records were lost or the ability to read them was lost. Thus many older historians omitted the prehistoric because it was not history as they defined it.

More and more, however, the word history is being used for the whole human story, regardless of the source of information. In this usage the term prehistoric is not distinct from historic but is one part of it. We will use prehistory in this sense in this book.

CHANCE AND THE SURVIVAL OF RECORDS

Various unplanned conditions or events have helped preserve some ancient ruins, artifacts, and writings for modern use. Because the Egyptians hated the ruler Ikhnaten for tampering with their religion, they abandoned his capital, Akhetaten, after he died. The desert winds and sands buried it.

Because the people of the Middle East hated and feared the mighty Assyrian city of Nineveh, after its overthrow no one could be persuaded to live on the site. Even thieves developed a superstitious fear of the place. As a result the ruins, including the great library, lay covered until modern times by a mound of earth.

The eruption of the volcano Vesuvius in 79 A.D. buried two small Roman cities, Pompeii and Herculaneum. Much of Pompeii has been excavated in modern times to reveal many facts about city life in Roman times that would otherwise be unknown. The work at Herculaneum has gone more slowly. Unlike the tons of ashes that buried Pompeii, rivers of liquid mud and lava flooded over its sister city and hardened into airtight rock. The rock covering has made excavation extremely difficult and costly, but it has also preserved precious art treasures and many Greek and Roman manuscripts. Two thirds of this town still lies buried and nobody knows what long lost classics still wait in the stony darkness of two thousand years.

Over three thousand years ago a landslide covered the entrance to an Egyptian royal tomb. So, although other tombs were pillaged centuries ago, the tomb of the teenaged pharaoh Tutankhamen kept its marvels until the twentieth century.

These are only a few examples of chance preservation of the past.

CHANCE AND THE RECOVERY OF THE PAST

Sometimes knowledge of the past is recovered only by chance.

Digging a trench at Rosetta in Egypt in 1800, a French soldier unearthed a slab inscribed with one text in three kinds of writing. This accidental discovery made it possible for experts eventually to solve the mystery of the long-unreadable Egyptian inscriptions, because one of the three languages was known to experts.

In 1819, British army officers on a hunting trip in India accidentally found caves at Ajanta covered with magnificent Buddhist wall paintings fifteen hundred years old. Similarly, by mere chance Angkor, the ancient capital of the Khmer civilization, deep in the Cambodian jungle, and the amazing twenty-thousand-year-old cave paintings of prehistoric man in the Pyrenees mountains were stumbled upon by men in search of other things.

INSPIRATION AND THE RECOVERY OF THE PAST

Sometimes it is not pure chance but inspiration combined with good luck that helps searchers on the trail of the past. Nineteenth-century scholars were generally agreed that Homer's tale of the Trojan War was fiction, although some speculated about where Troy would have been, if it had been. Heinrich Schliemann, a retired German merchant, had loved the story of Troy from boyhood and was convinced the city had existed. Disregarding the opinions of the scholars, he financed his own expedition to Turkey in the 1870's. Using Homer as his only guide, he selected a hill, dug, and there was Troy. Then Schliemann traveled to Mycenae, in Greece, where, again according to Homer, the great king Agamemnon had lived. There, in a place that had been only an unimportant village in more recent times, Schliemann found the buried ruins of the king's palace and graves with royal dead.

If Homer's tales were true, Greek legends might be also. The legends of a mighty king Minos on the island of Crete and his Labyrinth, in which lived a monster called the Minotaur, led the Englishman Sir Arthur Evans to Knossos. He spent his fortune and the remaining years of his life making excavations in Crete. As a result, today we can walk through the unearthed ruins of the Labyrinth, sit on the little stone throne of Minos (note photo,

Tutankhamen's tomb. A clutter of objects met the astounded gaze of Howard Carter and Lord Carnarvon when they entered the small four-room tomb of Tutankhamen. Among the objects in the antechamber, below, were animal-shaped couches and white oblong boxes containing animal offerings. On the left were two dismantled gilt chariots. Other objects included the folding stool of possibly Nubian workmanship, various boxes and chests, vases and chairs. Twice thieves had briefly entered the tomb, shifted around its contents, perhaps stole some, and then fled for unknown reasons. Priests resealed the tomb.

page 113), see the sun and shadow sweep across the paved area where perhaps Theseus danced before Ariadne, and wonder how much of the story of the monster is true. The discoveries of Schliemann and Evans revealed to us civilizations whose very existence had been forgotten.

Not long after the first of these discoveries, new-found inscriptions gave evidence of still another lost civilization, the Hittite, on the Anatolian plateau in present-day Turkey. Subsequent excavations have proven the existence of these people. Historians now know of four ancient civilizations in the eastern Mediterranean, where only a century ago they had thought there were but two. The picture of the ancient world, consequently, has been profoundly changed.

ARCHAEOLOGISTS—DETECTIVES OF THE PAST

Although accidental discoveries make exciting headlines, most of the great accomplishments of archaeology result from the painstaking work of scientists called archaeologists. Archaeology is the study of material remains—that is, things, such as bones, buildings, campsites, tools, weapons, and art objects from past ages. The accomplishments of archaeology involve painstaking study, long and toilsome drudgery, clear reasoning, and the cooperation of scholars of many nations.

Even a spectacular discovery such as that of the tomb of the young pharaoh Tutankhamen was the result of all these factors. Frenchmen, Germans, and scholars of other nationalities had established the names of the dynasty, or family of kings, to which Tutankhamen belonged. Others had found and explored the robbed and deserted tombs of the dynasty, all of which were in one valley near modern Luxor in Egypt. Two Englishmen, Howard Carter and his patron, Lord Carnarvon, reasoned that the one missing tomb must be there too. For three years Carter moved ton after ton of rubble without finding a sign that his reasoning was correct. Then one day he exposed the doorway to a tomb; and in the dust on the floor of the outer chamber were footprints from over 3,000 years ago.

These experts in bones and stones and pottery and fabrics and graves and tools come from many countries, and as often as not their work takes them halfway around the world on the trail of the past.

PHILOLOGISTS—DETECTIVES OF LANGUAGE

When the archaeologist has dug up the past and has interpreted his findings as best he can, there is still much that the historian wants to know. One may find a ruin and prove that it was some kind of shrine, possibly to a god whose image was found inside. But this information does not tell us what the worshipers in that shrine believed. Archaeology may deduce that an excavated building was a schoolroom. It cannot always tell us what the pupil learned there, or why the school was maintained or at whose expense.

At this point the philologist, the scientist of language, becomes essential. He must decipher the unknown languages, read the clay tablets, the parchment scrolls, the papyrus rolls, if the historian is to do his work.

The success of the philologist, like that of the archaeologist, is built on the contributions of scholars in many countries. One brilliant success of philology came a little over a century ago, when English, French, and Swedish scientists used the Rosetta Stone (above, page 8, and photo, page 72) to solve the mystery of ancient Egyptian writing. Since then the translation of Egyptian records has gone on, and for many years to come we shall have to adjust our ideas of life in Egypt in the light of more and more evidence.

A second great success came in the mid-nineteenth century, when, with the aid of an inscription on a cliff at Behistun, Iran, the languages of ancient Assyria and Babylonia were deciphered. Like the continuing Egyptian translations, these from Mesopotamia, the region of the Tigris and Euphrates rivers, add to and alter our understanding of the early civilizations of the Middle East.

A third success came early in the twentieth century, when the mystery of Hittite inscriptions in ancient Anatolia was partially solved.

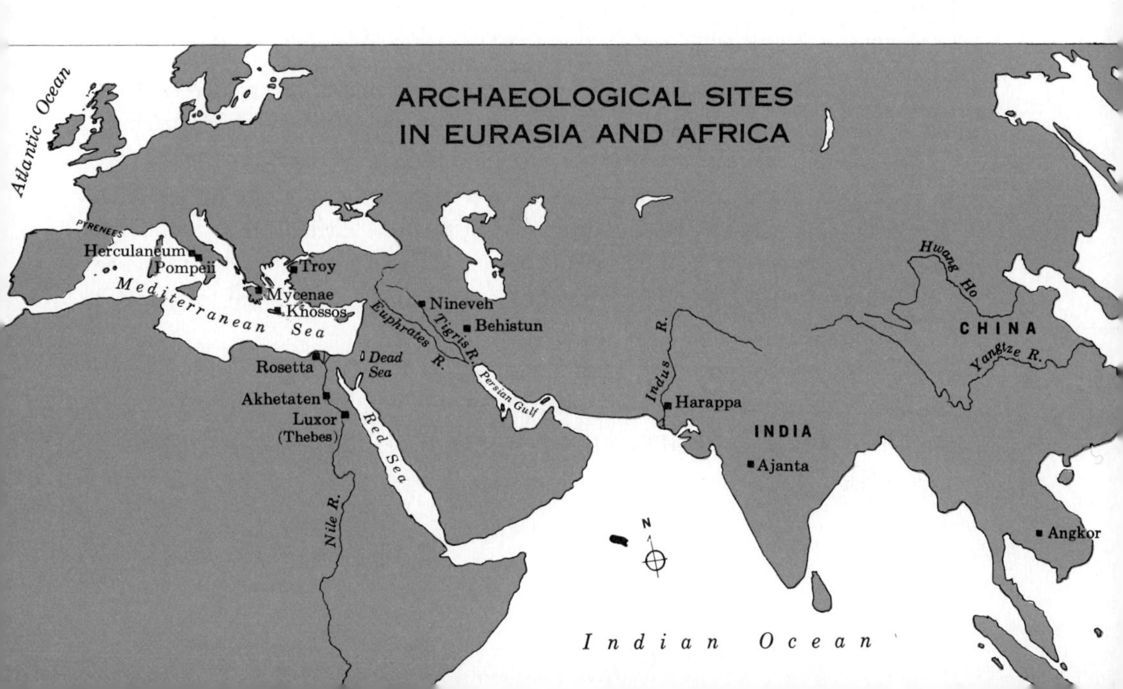

The latest achievement came in the 1940's with the first reading of one of the three early Cretan scripts. First translations are only now becoming available. A few names of places, a few names of gods, lists of supplies collected when the threat of invasion hung over the land—that is all thus far. But there are dedicated students at work, and it is not unreasonable to believe that one day the names of people and the great events in their lives will be uncovered and that the thoughts of the Cretans whose faces we have seen on the ruined palace walls will live once more in the memory of man.

The four great successes of philology mentioned above have revolutionized ancient history. But the puzzles facing the language detectives are far from solved, and future finds by archaeologists will pose new puzzles for philologists and in turn new understandings for historians.

KEEPING AN OPEN MIND

From what we have been saying, it is clear that ancient history is a very *modern* subject. Although it concerns people and ways of living of long ago, what we know about it and what we understand about it are constantly being increased and improved. The history student, therefore, like the science student, must be alert to the possibility of error in judgments based on evidence that changes even as we study it. When we find a person or event being given different dates, for example, we must note on what the different estimates are based. Books written about Egypt a century ago, by authors with access to only a few material remains and very limited translations of ancient writings, dated some ancient persons and civilizations a full thousand years earlier than do recent studies.

In most cases the revision of dates and of interpretations of personalities and events reflect increased knowledge or the introduction of better research techniques. However, just because a book is the latest does not necessarily mean that it is the most reliable. Newness does not always mean progress. The claims of writers must be examined critically. "Criticism" in this sense does not mean finding fault; rather, it means thoughtful consideration and evaluation of material. So one reads history thoughtfully, critically, with an open mind.

Valuable contributions to man's understanding of himself come from a study of human experience in the past, even though one realizes that the conclusions may be tentative and not final.

A NOTE TO THE STUDENT

At the end of each chapter, you will find questions and activities. They are intended to help you review the text and broaden your understanding of its meaning.

To be able to work with the questions and activities with ease, the following method should be used. It will help you bring the text into focus. It will help you retain what you have read longer and will lead to reading faster with greater understanding.

First, skim through the whole assignment as quickly as possible, without interruption. Do not linger over hard words or separate items. The idea is to get an overview of the chapter's contents.

Second, start again from the beginning now that you know what the subject of the chapter is and what its main points are. This time read carefully. Note new *words*. If a word is unfamiliar, or if you cannot guess its meaning from the way it is used, consult the dictionary. Mastering a new word will help you to proceed faster with your reading in the future. Notice the names of *people*, *groups*, and *individuals*. Associate the person or group with something else, for example, an event, a time, a place. Notice *places*. Locate them immediately by using a map. It is surprising how quickly "place knowledge" grows, and how much more interesting history is when you know where it occurred. Notice *time*. Relate it to incidents and people. Dates by themselves are only numbers, but when people, place, and time are associated, each helps to place the other in order. Try to picture the events. A "flood" is not just a word; it is homes swept away, people drowning; a "battle" is not just a term; it is noise, bravery, cowardice, hope, fear, death. Visualizing what you read is one of the surest ways to fix it in your mind. Then think about *causes*. Why did something happen? What lay behind it? Think, finally, what the *significance* and *importance* of the event or person may be. Was the event important to people living then or to those who came later? Did it have important consequences?

In this second step you use the questions that historians ask: who, what, where, when, why. Now you are prepared to take step three.

Third, test yourself on the questions and activities at the end of each chapter. See if you can recall the principal ideas and themes of the assignment in terms of specific people, places, and events. You will find that after following the first two steps, you will be able to take part in the activities and answer the questions at the end of each chapter with ease and confidence.

People, Places, and Terms

Heinrich Schliemann
Sir Arthur Evans
Howard Carter
Lord Carnarvon

Eurasia

genealogy

saga
taboo
regnal calendar
A.H.; A.D.; B.C.
anthropology
archaeology
philology
artifact

history
prehistory
unrecorded history
dynasty
decipher
sociology
psychology
geology

Mastering the Reading

1. In what ways is a nation's history similar to personal experience? Why was speech important to man's development? What were some of the forms man used to transmit his experiences before writing was invented? Why did man need to measure time?
2. What are some of the unplanned conditions or events that have helped to preserve records, shelters, and belongings of ancient man? What is the precise difference among *preservation*, *discovery*, and *recovery* of remnants?
3. What factors are responsible for the successes of archaeologists in digging up the past? What are four successes of philologists which have occurred in the last century and a half?

Interpreting the Text

1. Why is time difficult to record in a meaningful way even though we have units with which to measure it? Think of a specific event in your life that illustrates your answer.
2. Why is ancient history often called the newest or most modern history? What problems does this present to the historian? to you?

Exploring Beyond the Text

Ancient Words in Modern English. Although English is Germanic in origin, over 60 per cent of our words come from Latin, directly or indirectly, and many come from Greek, Hebrew, Arabic, Sanskrit, and Persian. Keep a glossary noting the derivation of new words and their present-day meanings. Some of the most important ones will be called to your attention.

The Greek word *logos* appears in English constantly as the ending *-logy*. Look up the meaning of *-logy* along with *archae* in *archaeology* and *anthropos* in *anthropology*.

2

The Old Stone Age

Man's beginnings are a mystery. Scientists are detectives, seeking clues, interpreting scattered bits of evidence, suggesting theories that could explain the evidence, and then strengthening or changing the theories in the light of new evidence as it is found. Naturally, as in any mystery where evidence is scanty or incomplete, there will be various theories. Historians will disagree and debate over the meaning of the evidence. As was said in Chapter One, we must keep an open mind with respect to conclusions in history. This becomes more and more important as we go further back into the past and have to reason from fewer and fewer facts.

THE GEOLOGICAL BACKGROUND

The earth is variously estimated to be two, three, and four billion years old. (Billion is here used according to American and French practice—one billion = one thousand million—and not as in Britain and Germany where one billion = one million million.)

Geologists divide the earth's story into several time periods. Only the last three, the Pliocene, the Pleistocene, and the Holocene, concern us in our search for early man.

THE PLIOCENE

Let us assume that the earth is four billion years old. During the Pliocene, which lasted many millions of years and which ended about one million years ago, the earth's crust formed and reformed, rose and fell many times in many places, before it became as it is today. At some time between seven and one million years ago, in the last Pliocene period, a great crumpling of the crust thrust up great mountains in a giant wrinkle across the earth. From west to east that upheaval produced the Atlas range of North Africa, the Sierras and Pyrenees of Spain, and the Alps, the Balkans, and the Carpathians of Central Europe. Climbing higher as we move eastward, we find the Caucasus in southeastern Europe, the Elburz in Iran, the Hindu Kush in Afghanistan, and the Himalayas of northern Pakistan and India. There, on the "roof of the world," the great chain embraces the plateau of Tibet, which is actually higher than the mountains in many places. The highland wrinkle moves northeast through the Tien Shan and the Grand Altai to the Stanovoi in northeastern Siberia. Jumping into Alaska, the great mass turns north and south, and we have the Rocky Mountain Highland in North America and the Andes in South America. Some of the mountains, the Himalayas for example, seem to be rising still.

The emergence of the great wall of mountains across the earth naturally changed the climates of the land masses. Central Asia, for example, was cut off from the rain-bearing winds from the Indian and Pacific oceans and became desert.

The Pliocene period ended with this major reshaping of the earth.

THE PLEISTOCENE AND THE HOLOCENE

The Pliocene passed into the Pleistocene at some point between a half million and a million years ago and lasted until about twenty thousand years ago. Four times during the Pleistocene the northern continents of the earth were buried under great masses of ice and snow. These periods are called the Ice Ages. When glacial, or icy, conditions prevailed in the north, the regions near the equator had pluvial, or rainy, periods. Each glacial-pluvial age lasted more than a hundred thousand years. Equally long periods of warming and drying occurred in between. These are called Interglacials. The First Ice Age and the First Interglacial Age were the earliest; the latest Ice Age was the fourth. Today we are living in the Fourth Interglacial, which geologists have named the Holocene Period (see chart, page 48).

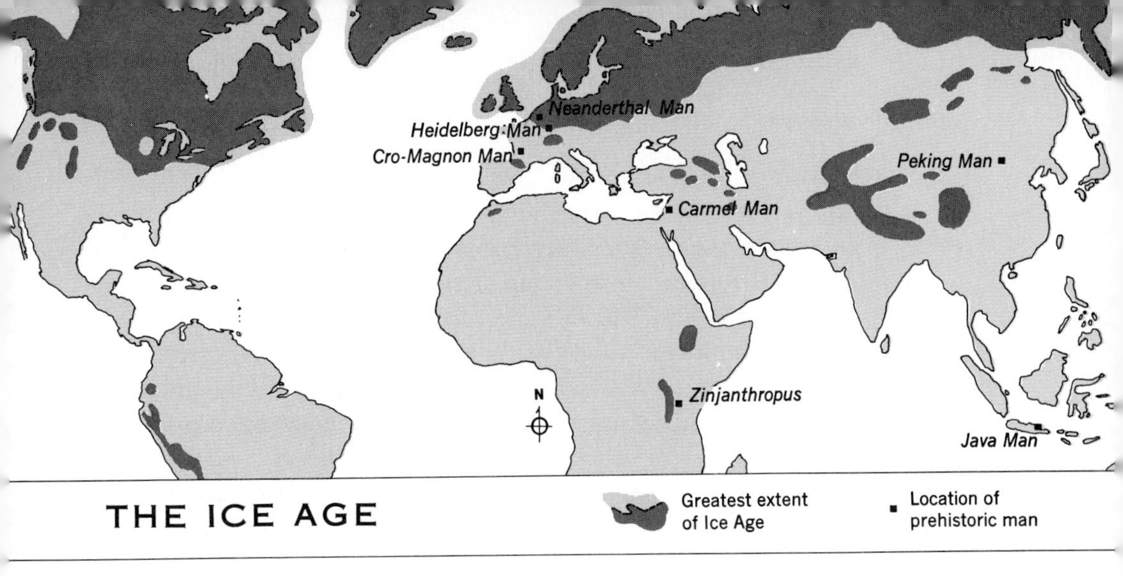

THE ICE AGE

The ice from the Fourth Ice Age is still receding. During the times of greatest glaciation vast amounts of water were locked up in the form of ice. Ocean levels fell as much as 300 to 600 feet. During the interglacial periods, the oceans rose correspondingly. With the melting glaciers, Niagara began to pour over its falls between twelve and twenty thousand years ago. Great lakes still cover much of Canada, Scandinavia, and Siberia, while Greenland remains largely buried under the ice. As the earth slowly warms, the lakes and the ice will one day, many thousands of years from now, disappear. Already the formerly rainy, grassy plains of Africa, Arabia, India, and the southwest United States have turned into deserts as the rains of the Fourth Ice Age have vanished or have shifted farther north.

THE COMING OF MAN

At some point in the Pleistocene man first appeared. When this happened is unknown, but it must have been between 400,000 and 800,000 years ago, depending on how long one determines the Pleistocene to have lasted. In 1959 a skull fragment (Zinjanthropus) was found in East Africa. Tested by new methods of determining age, it was considered to be possibly 1,750,000 years old. If this discovery is supported by more evidence in years to come, the beginning of the age of man will not only be pushed back a full million years beyond present estimates but will be moved out of the Pleistocene entirely. Such a change would affect everything we have concluded about earliest man.

EARLIEST MAN'S APPEARANCE

What did earliest man look like and how did he live? Naturally we would like to know, but these questions are matters of guesswork. From a few bones scientists create reconstructions of how they think the whole man looked. They give us a picture of a creature with a very low forehead and a very large jaw with teeth something like those of an ape and something like those of a human who walked in a stooped position. These ideas are probably close to the truth, but as to skin color, eye color, amount of body hair, shape of fingernails or claws, and other such matters, one person's guess is as good as another's. Diappointing as it may be, the circumstances surrounding the beginnings of mankind can only be conjecture. It is little less than a miracle that anthropologists are beginning to be able to tell us a little about when he appeared and where he lived. More than that we may never know, because the evidence has to have survived perhaps more than a million years, and its discovery rests strongly on chance.

LOWER, OR EARLY, PALEOLITHIC MAN

Paleoliths are stone weapons or tools. We can now distinguish between the oldest and crudest and the later and more skillfully made. The former we call lower paleoliths because they represent a lower or cruder level of skill and were found at a lower level of digging. Lower paleoliths were made by man between the Second and the Third Ice Ages, roughly three or four hundred thousand years ago. Paleoliths have given their name to a period of man's development. The Paleolithic period is also called the Old Stone Age.

We know, from finding their bones, that men who made the simple chipped flint stones that we call paleoliths lived in South, East, and North Africa, in the widely separated islands of England and Java, and in especially large numbers in China.

THE DEVELOPMENT OF LANGUAGE

Scholars believe that during the Lower Paleolithic period man's language abilities were greatly developed. They are, of course, guessing. But this guess seems reasonable in the light of the large groups of skeletons found together in the caves near Peking, China, belonging to the man whom scientists have labeled *Sinanthropus pekinensis* (the Chinese Human from Peking or, as he is more familiarly called, Peking Man; see map, page 19).

Early men. Several examples of heads of early men as anthropologists think they might have looked. From bottom to top: Zinjanthropus, Paranthropus (early Pleistocene), Peking Man, Neanderthal, and Cro-Magnon. To make these constructions, anthropologists must work from a few fragments and much imagination, which may or may not be verified by later discoveries. Zinjanthropus was recreated from his cranium; Paranthropus consisted of a skull and parts of the lower jaw; Peking Man, Neanderthal, and Cro-Magnon were modeled from complete skulls.

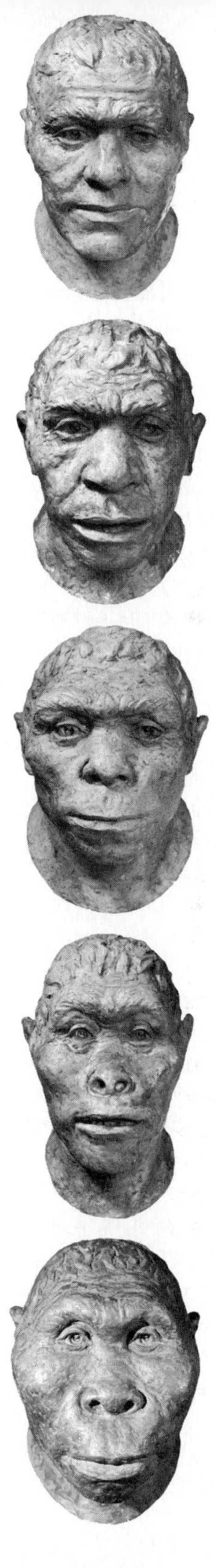

Group existence in caves provide an opportunity to exchange ideas about making weapons, about the nature and use of fire, and possibly about the purpose of cannibalism. All these things were part of Peking Man's life. Cannibalism was apparently not due to food shortages. Possibly, therefore, it had a religious meaning as it does among some cannibal tribes of modern times. (It must be remembered, in other connections as well as this one, that trying to understand ancient people from our knowledge of modern tribes is risky. Modern primitives [page 54], that is, people without writing who live simple lives close to nature, may have been influenced by more sophisticated neighbors or ancestors. Such influences, obviously, could not have affected primitives in the earliest times.)

As man developed words, his ideas sharpened and he began to think more clearly. As he thought more clearly, he further improved his words. Language and thinking thus interact on each other and improve each other. The first value, then, of the invention of language was to aid in the improvement of man's thinking.

The second value of improving language was that it enabled man to hand on his knowledge to his children. When the experience of one generation could be handed on or transmitted to the next generation, the younger generation had a head start in knowing about the problems of life and the solutions to those problems. In other words, human experience began to be cumulative. It was added to by each generation instead of dying out with each individual, as it does with animals.

TOOLS AND THE USE OF FIRE

Two distinct kinds of Lower Paleolithic stones show that separate peoples discovered how to make better weapons. One group lived in Africa, the other in Asia near the Pacific. The African group learned to chip away the outside of a piece of flint until the central core was left as the completed tool. These people, called the Core Culture people, perfected a heavy all-purpose pear-shaped hand axe. This name is misleading. Though a hand axe was probably used for digging roots, skinning animals, and scraping furs, it was never used as an axe. Because hand axes are found all the way from Africa to Britain, we know that the Core Culture people wandered across whole continents in the Lower Paleolithic Age. Eastward they reached India.

At the peak of each Ice Age the Core Culture people seem to have retreated to Africa. Because they lived in the open country, their skeletal remains are rare. However, as it seems probable these people were ancestors of *Homo sapiens* (thinking man—ourselves), great attention is being paid today to East Africa where the Core Culture is thought to have originated.

The second way invented by early man to shape flint was to strike off a big flake and work it into a tool for cutting and scraping. It differed from a core tool by having a flat side where the flake had split off from the parent stone and a rounded side from the original outside of the parent. Flake-toolmakers lived in East Asia, in Java, and in Burma. We can trace them across India and into Europe by the remains of their tools.

The Core people, wandering north and south, and the Flake people, moving east and west, passed through Palestine. It is not known whether both groups were there at the same time. If they were, modern man may have emerged from the mixing of the two.

Every improvement in tools has meant that man has made a more efficient adjustment to his surroundings, whether for peace or war. Better spear points mean more success in killing game or fish and in fighting with other men. Better scrapers mean more efficient preparation of animal skins to cover the body against the cold.

Archaeological finds of ashes alongside human skeletons indicate that in this period man had discovered how to use fire. Fires at the mouths of caves were obviously built for protection and to keep out intruding wild animals; those in the cave interior were for warmth. Whether man cooked his food at this time is not known.

THE BEGINNINGS OF SOCIAL ORGANIZATION

The cooperation necessary to fight large animals and to preserve existence must have encouraged the development of social or group organization and this led to the earliest form of the tribe (page 35). Then the give-and-take of ideas and the sharing of problems and solutions must have strengthened the feeling that the group was important. Mankind has always needed at least a small social unit—the family—in order to protect the infant humans. Now, an increased awareness of the value of the group seems to have appeared.

Nothing ever changed for the people living in the Lower Paleolithic Age. Climatic differences from an Ice Age to an Interglacial Age and then back to the ice again were spread over 200,000 years. So were the developments in language, tools, and social organization. But looking back on those slow moving centuries, we can see that the changes were of as great an importance to man as those of any age to follow.

UPPER, OR LATE, PALEOLITHIC MAN

After the Third Ice Age, man's tools, both core and flake varieties, further improved. The core hand axe in particular became lighter and more beautifully shaped, and its users spread again over eastern and northern Africa, southern and western Europe as far north as England, and eastward through Palestine into India. Human skeletal remains are more numerous, so it is known that these ancestors of *Homo sapiens* had thinner skulls than earlier men and high unapelike foreheads, but a somewhat smaller brain capacity than modern man.

The flake users in Europe were represented by two types, possibly related. The earlier, and perhaps the ancestor of the second, is called Heidelberg Man because his remains were first found near that German city (see map, page 19). He differed from modern *Homo sapiens* by having a sloping brow instead of a forehead, a sloping jaw instead of a chin, and very massive teeth. He was followed by Neanderthal Man (named after the Neander Valley [thal] in Germany, where he was first discovered) who was also apelike. Both these men were probably hairier than modern man, which may have helped them survive glacial cold.

By the time the ice came the fourth time, Neanderthal Man had progressed enough to survive the ice by living in caves. Since the caves protected his bones, we know much more about his physical characteristics than about those of the men who lived before him. He had beetling brows, prominent teeth, and a lot of hair. It must be remembered, however, that in spite of such characteristics, Neanderthals were men, not apes. They had the skills of men and some of their emotions.

During or just after the Fourth Ice Age, Neanderthal Man was burying his dead, and remains from burials added to the evidence that would survive to the present time. Because of burial remains it is now possible to trace Neanderthal Man in many parts of Europe and the Middle East. He also lived in a few sites in Africa and Asia, although there is no evidence at the present time of any Upper Paleolithic contacts between eastern Asia and the western continents.

At one time it was thought that Neanderthal Man was completely destroyed when *Homo sapiens* appeared. The discovery in Palestine of Carmel Man, who possessed characteristics of both Neanderthal and *Homo sapiens*, has made this theory very unlikely. Whether modern man is descended from Carmel Man or from him and other varieties of men is a problem for future study.

About twenty thousand years ago many changes took place on earth. The horse, cow, reindeer, beaver, elephant, rhinoceros, bear, lion, and other creatures appeared in their modern forms, along with unmistakably rational man (*Homo sapiens*). At this time, several kinds of men inhabited the earth.

As the ice slowly retreated, game animals increasingly abounded in Europe. That continent also became the scene of great cultural activity. Neanderthal Man vanished completely, and with him went all traces of the flake culture. Modern man became the only type of human being on earth.

THE MEN OF CRO-MAGNON

One kind of *Homo sapiens* to appear some 25,000 years ago was the Cro-Magnon, named after the locality in southern France where his bones were first identified (see map, page 19). Cro-Magnons certainly were men of splendid physique. They were six feet tall, broad-shouldered, and deep-chested, with broad foreheads, wide eyes, and bigger brains than twentieth-century men.

At first it was thought that the men of Cro-Magnon were ancestors of white Europeans and had wiped out the Neanderthals. Now we are not sure. They may or may not have direct descendants in parts of Europe. They may have been a branch line with no heirs among later people. Just where they belong in man's family tree is not certain. They certainly did not spring into the world abruptly, although when they appeared still remains a mystery. Nor did they suddenly wipe out their Neanderthal neighbors. Evidence is accumulating to indicate that for some time they must have lived beside them and eventually may have mixed with them to some degree.

NEW TOOLS

Not only did *Homo sapiens* look different from his predecessors, but he was smarter. His tools demonstrate his advance. They included longer, thinner, sharper blades and quantities of *microliths* (tiny stones). The small, sharp points used as darts in blowguns and as arrowpoints were savagely effective weapons against animals and other men. In earlier times men had had spears; now they had harpoons, which gave them the ability to kill at greater distances. They also made daggers. With these new weapons, the newcomers took over the hunting grounds and cave homes of the vanishing Neanderthals.

In addition to flint daggers and microliths, the men of the Upper Paleolithic made other weapons and objects out of ivory, bone, and reindeer horn. Bone spear-throwers made it possible to hurl the wooden-shafted spears with their bone or stone heads much farther. Horn spear-straighteners enabled hunters to straighten their wooden shafts for reuse after impact had bent them out of shape. Although we do not know when clothing was first worn, it is certain that the Upper Paleolithic man had begun to shape his garments. He used ivory and bone pins and needles. Whistles were also made out of bone, but whether for magic, music, religion, hunting, or communication purposes is uncertain.

CAVE ART

Men of the Upper Paleolith were artists. This fact is important to us today because it tells us something about men living at that time. First, art is created for a purpose; it requires thought. Man was advanced enough at this stage in his development to consciously create forms and shapes with meaning. Art, therefore, gives us a glimpse into man's thinking. Second, the drawings and paintings and the images in clay, stone, and wood sometimes tell us what the objects in the environment were like. They tell us, for example, that some men lived at the time of the woolly mammoth, and art, therefore, helps us date the men. Finally, the art of ancient man helps us gauge the progress of his manual dexterity, that is, his skill in using tools. Manual dexterity reflects the development of his brain and his increasing intelligence.

Late Paleolithic man made small clay statuettes of men, women, and animals and beads and pendants of shell, ivory, bone, and colored stone. But his most interesting venture into art was in the paintings in the midnight depths of some of his caves. Southern France and the Spanish Pyrenees are the scene of one such group of paintings by the men of Cro-Magnon. Another, and distinct, type extends in spots from eastern Spain to the southern part of Africa.

The earliest of such cave paintings were simple outlines filled in with solid color. But later the artist shaped the cave wall or ceiling into figures in low relief (slightly raised against their background), tinted in shades of yellow, brown, red, and black to emphasize the contours of the figure. Most paintings are of animals killed for food, although the lion and tiger,

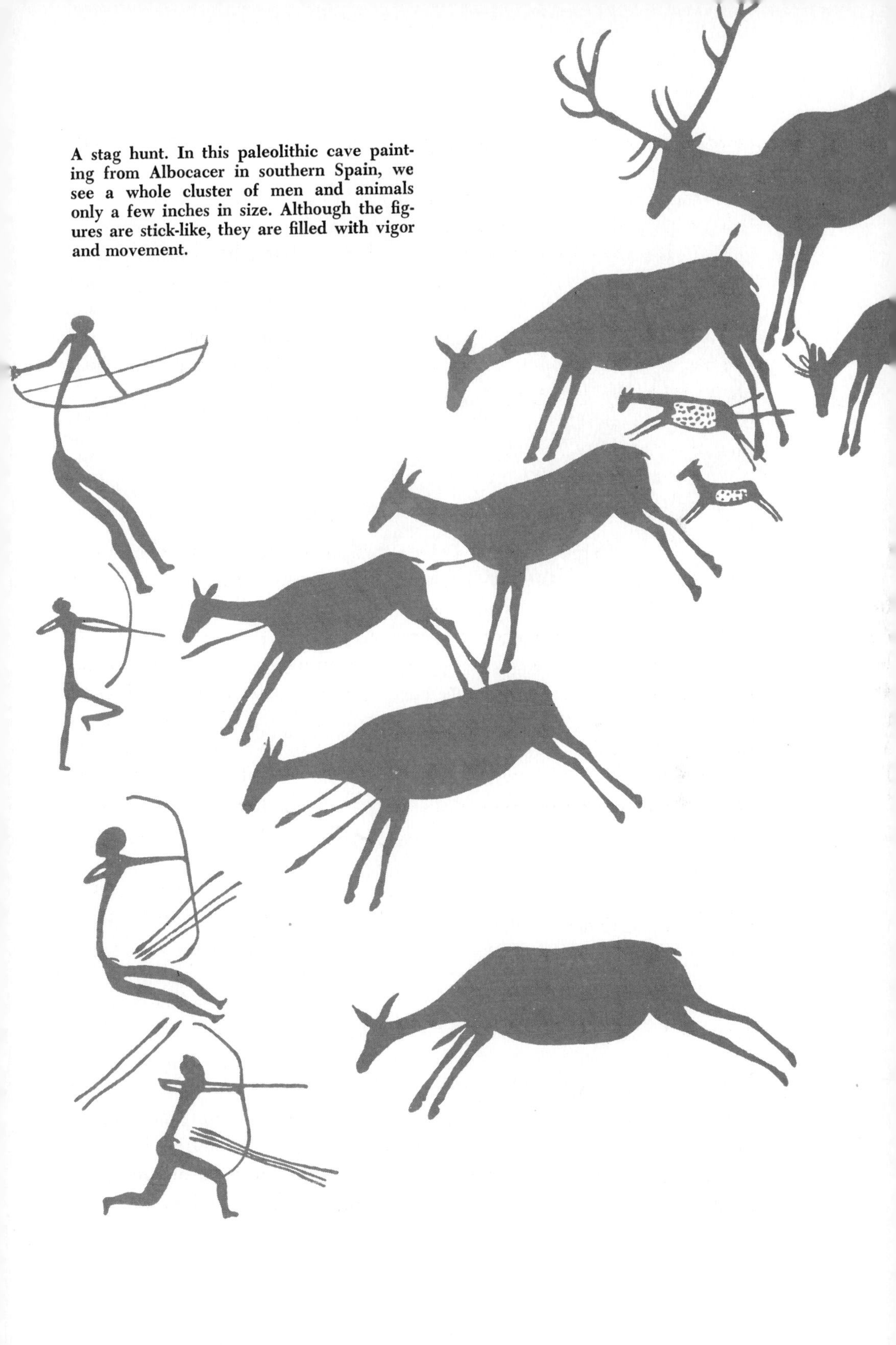

A stag hunt. In this paleolithic cave painting from Albocacer in southern Spain, we see a whole cluster of men and animals only a few inches in size. Although the figures are stick-like, they are filled with vigor and movement.

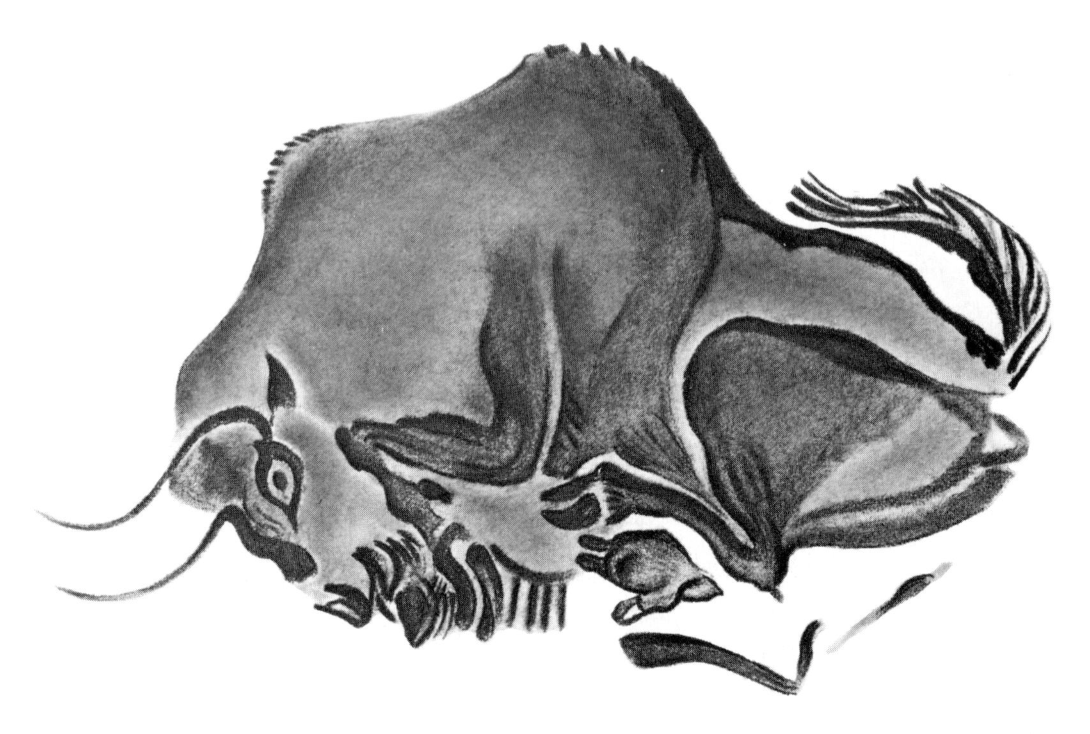

A bison. This paleolithic painting is in the cave of Altamira in northern Spain. Unlike the stick-like figures from Albocacer, the bison and other animals at Altamira are full of dignity and form. The differences between the paintings in northern and southern Spain have not been explained. The paleolithic artists used mineral substances—manganese, red and yellow ochre—for paints, a large flat bone for a mixing palette, and reeds and bristles for brushes.

which they did not eat, are also shown. Some scholars think that these paintings were created as aids for hunting; others, that they were created for religious purposes. But whatever the paintings meant to those who made them, we must remember that without the help of a written word we are guessing about the intentions of men with lives, experiences, and knowledge different from our own who lived perhaps thirty thousand years ago.

THE RACES OF MAN

Properly used, the word *race* refers to a very large group of people of the same physical type. In an individual's immediate family, not all the brothers and sisters will be physically alike. Nevertheless, many may be enough alike for there to be a "family resemblance." Usually this resemblance does not consist of a single feature but of a combination of features that makes it possible to identify a child at a glance with a certain family. For example, many of the children of the X family are tall, thin, big-boned, snub-nosed, blue-eyed, broadheaded, wide-mouthed, with pale, freckled skin, reddish curly hair, and with unusually large chins, hands, and feet. Such a combination leads the visitor to say, "You must be one of the X children." In very ancient times, when a few families lived together in a separate group apart from others, repeated intermarriage among the same families produced certain combinations of traits that again made it possible to identify individuals as belonging to one nation or tribe instead of another. Thus there came to be an Asian type, a European type, an African type. The conditions needed for such types to develop are (a) isolation for (b) a long period of time, with (c) inbreeding. These three circumstances caused the development of the large groupings we call race, or, to use a term modern scholars prefer, racial stocks. Thus the combination of straight black hair, a nose with a low base, an eye with a pronounced fold, a skin pigmented from pale gold to brown, and other such traits are identified as the Mongoloid or yellow race. So also we speak of a Caucasian or white race and of a Negroid or black race. Note that race is based on physical characteristics that can be recognized on sight. It has nothing to do with mental ability, blood-types, or other characteristics that call for scientific identification.

Racial identifications are often confused with linguistic ones because a particular group of humans may be the only ones to use a particular language. But obviously a language can be adopted by peoples other than its original speakers, and in the course of time one language may be spoken by peoples of widely different racial identifications. Think of the diversity of people who speak English around the world today.

Sometimes certain customs or costumes are identified with a given race. They are part of the group's culture. But, like language, cultural characteristics can be adopted by many kinds of people other than the originators.

Language and cultural traits thus confuse the usage of the term race.

As soon as migration brought racial types into contact with each other, physical mingling and crossbreeding, occurring side by side with mixing of languages and cultural adaptation made the term race less and less accurate. The Bronze Age is probably the latest period when the term race can be used meaningfully, and even then we know that much crossbreeding had already gone on. After 1000 B.C. racial strains and distinct language groups can be seen only vaguely. In any Iron Age group, the Hellenes (Greeks) for example, the language had elements of many origins, and the physical national type of Hellene did not conform to any strict racial type. In modern times the mixture of physical types makes the term race even more meaningless, and hence the need for, and partial acceptance of, a new phrase, *racial stock*, which indicates origins rather than pure physical types.

❦ ❦ ❦

Man's life on earth began during the Old Stone Age. Long eons of time had passed, however, before man appeared. Not until the geological age known as the Pleistocene, some million to half a million years ago, do historians believe that man emerged, and it took him more eons to become *Homo sapiens*, or modern man.

During the long period of time between his appearance and the end of the Old Stone Age, man made enormous advances. He learned how to communicate with other men, how to fashion tools, and how to use fire. While he was making these great intellectual advances, he also developed the rudiments of a social organization. In the age ahead his social organization would prepare him to become a food producer settled in villages rather than a food hunter, forever on the move.

People, Places, and Terms

Sinanthropus
Heidelberg Man
Neanderthal Man
Cro-Magnon Man
Carmel Man
Homo sapiens

Peking
Palestine
Neander Valley

Heidelberg

Pliocene
Pleistocene
Holocene
Ice Age
pluvial
glaciation
glacial
interglacial

reconstruction
Paleolithic
paleoliths
primitives
race
racial stock
ethnic
modern
microlith
manual dexterity

Mastering the Reading

1. What physical and climatic features are typical of all Ice Ages, glacial and interglacial?
2. In which geological period are ancient men known to have existed? What evidence do we have to support possible earlier dates? Why are the theories about the beginnings of man only guesswork?
3. What four major developments were made by man during the Lower Paleolithic period? Why were they important?

4. What changes in man's abilities and way of life marked the transition to the Upper Paleolithic? What characteristics distinguished Neanderthals from apes and other primates?
5. How is *race* best defined? Why is it difficult to classify people by race today? How do language and culture confuse race classification?

Interpreting the Text

1. In what ways are tools a useful guide to man's technical and intellectual development?
2. What physical aspects, mental abilities, and skills are associated with *Homo sapiens* and not with earlier men?

Exploring Beyond the Text

1. During the Fourth Glacial Age was your area under glacial or pluvial conditions? How do you know? Are there any geological or geographic conditions in your area now that can be explained by the area's condition in the Fourth Glacial Age?
2. Much discussion about ancient man is naturally concerned with his tools; for a tool is an extension of man, a substitute for part of a man's body. List all parts of the body for which each of the following is a substitute: claw hammer, pliers, saw, pick-axe, and screwdriver. Think of more complicated tools and the parts of the body for which they are substitutes (i.e. scissors, computer). What conclusions can be drawn about tools and man's brain?
3. *Ancient Words in Modern English.* Learn to recognize both parts of each of the following words. One of these has a part you met in Chapter 1. Do you recognize it? Add these words and their meanings to your glossary:

Sinanthropus *Homo sapiens* paleolithic

3

The New Stone Age

During the Old Stone Age, man was a food hunter, wandering from place to place as the wild plants and fruits were eaten up, or as the fish in a given stream or lake vanished, or as the herds of wild animals moved to new feeding grounds.

About ten thousand years ago man entered on a series of changes that eventually made him a food producer instead of a food hunter. First he discovered how to plant seeds and then how, by selecting the best of each crop, to improve the food value of the plant. This was the beginning of farming. Next, instead of following the wild herds of sheep and goats, man tamed, or domesticated, them and became a herdsman.

Agriculture required man to settle down. He had to guard his crops from wild animals and nomadic, or wandering, tribes. He had to protect his animals. Herding, however, permitted man to remain a nomad. Thus, two ways of life existed. A herding, or pastoral, tribe continued a nomadic life based on guiding the herds and flocks from place to place as grass and water supplies were used up. Such a tribe might plant a few crops and trust to luck that the crops would still be there when the tribe returned from its migration.

The second way of life, the one that led to civilization, was followed by tribes that settled down. These tribes created the first villages. They faced new problems, such as planning storehouses for their food, building walls for the village, or constructing a central fort to protect them in case of attack from other tribes. Settling in one place led to many changes: a new social organization to regulate the lives of those living together permanently in one place, the creation of a surplus of food to feed those who did not farm, and new physical needs that led to such inventions as pottery and furniture of a simple kind.

These changes affected every phase of life so profoundly that taken together they made what is called the Neolithic Revolution. The Neolithic Revolution included not only farming and herding, the development of village life, and the invention of pottery, but also another important change, improvement in the making of stone tools and weapons. These improved stone objects are called *neoliths*, or new stones. From them scholars have named this stage of man's development the Neolithic period. The Neolithic period and the previous transitional period together are the New Stone Age.

Obviously the Neolithic Revolution did not occur in all places at the same time. As we shall see, it spread outward from its place of origin to regions farther and farther away until it had encompassed the whole earth.

THE MESOLITHIC TRANSITION

Great and lasting changes in history never come as sharp breaks with the past. There are always stages when the old is passing away but the new has not yet fully arrived. The transitional stage between the Paleolithic and the Neolithic is called the Mesolithic (Middle Stone) Age, and covers, roughly, the period 8000 to 6000 B.C.

THE SETTING

A highland area stretches from the Atlantic to India. This highland area was formed during the great upheaval of the earth that occurred during the late Pliocene period (page 18). Mountains rise above a plateau in Africa, Arabia, Iran, and India. Three great river systems occupy low valleys ranging in height from 1500 feet down to sea level. The first of these great river systems is the Nile in Egypt; the second is the Tigris and Euphrates in Mesopotamia; and the third is the Indus on the Indian subcontinent (see map, page 95). The highland area is broken into by the Mediterranean Sea, the Red Sea, the Persian Gulf, the Black Sea, and the Caspian Sea.

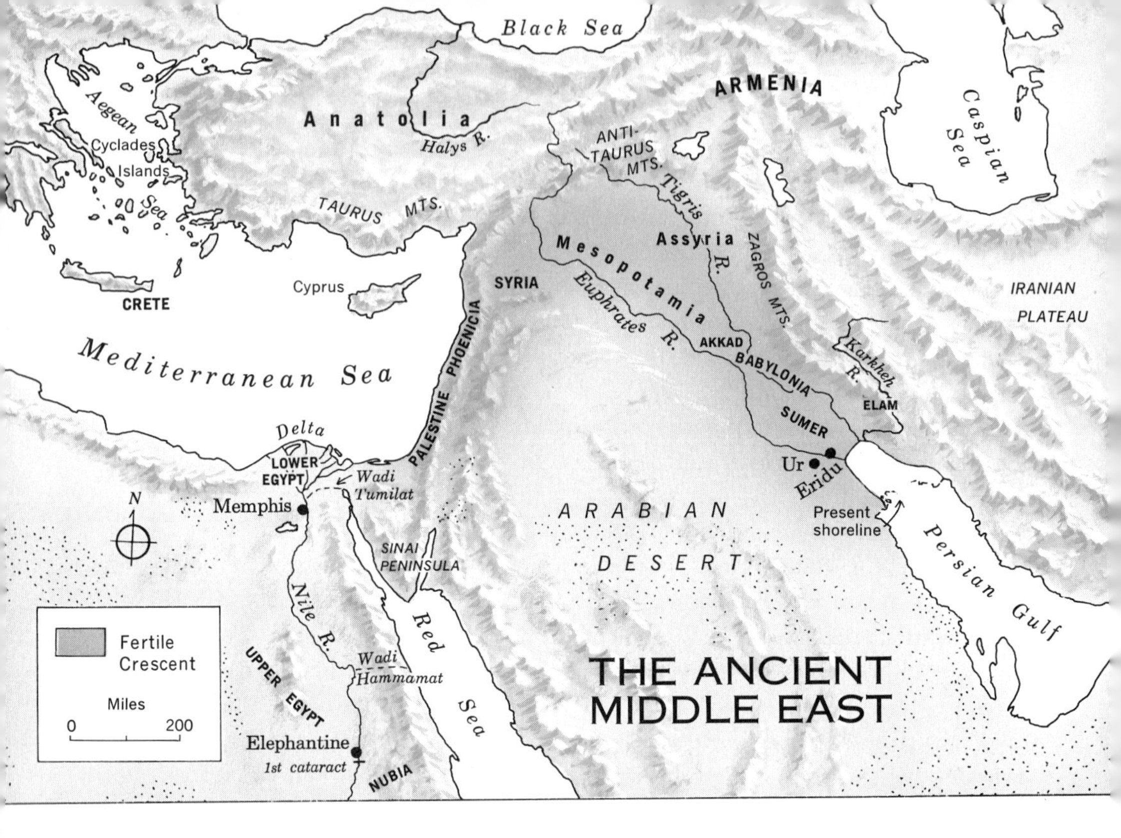

In the last six thousand years the highland area has become the largest continuous hot, dry region on earth, with great expanses of desert wastes. But twenty thousand years ago, as the Fourth Ice Age closed, these conditions did not exist. Ice still covered northern Europe, and separate glaciers clutched the Alps and the Pyrenees. The Atlantic winds, which today bring rain to northern Europe, blew across the regions south of the glaciers. As a result, today's deserts were then rich plains covered with grass and trees.

In the center of the highland area, mankind first entered the transitional Mesolithic phase. This region is called the Middle East. The Middle East includes northeastern Africa (Egypt) and western Asia. Another name for western Asia, and one that will appear in this book, is the Near East. In ancient times the Near East was made up of Phoenicia and Palestine along the coast, Syria and Mesopotamia inland, Persia (Iran) to the east, and the plateau of Anatolia (Asia Minor) to the north.

THE NATUFIANS

Near Mt. Carmel, in Lebanon (ancient Phoenicia), have been found the remains of a people believed to have lived in the transitional period between the Old and the New Stone ages. They were discovered in the Wadi en-Natuf and so were given the name Natufian. Other remains of these people have since been discovered elsewhere (see map, next page).

At the present time not too much is known about the Natufians because they are a discovery of recent years. We do know that during the two or three thousand years that the Mesolithic period lasted, the Natufians remained hunters and fishermen. They still practiced the magic rites inherited from their Paleolithic forebears, and they still lived in caves or out in the open as in the Old Stone Age. But they were learning new ways. They domesticated the dog, and they planted grains and fruits. The beginning of domestication of animals and the beginning of cultivation were signs of the Neolithic Age just ahead.

SOCIAL ORGANIZATION

It is believed that man first identified himself as a member of a small, immediately related group we can call the family and then of a larger group, including less closely related members, called the clan. Clan members were in turn part of a large group made up of many clans, the tribe. A tribesman was entitled to share in the common property of the tribe, in the hunting and fishing grounds and, later, during the Neolithic period, in the grazing and farming lands. As an adult the tribesman could own such personal possessions as weapons, tools, ornaments, and clothing.

In some tribes, relationships were determined in relation to the father, and inheritance was from the father to the son. This was a *patrilineal* (father-related) society. In other tribes inheritance was through the mother, and the mother's relatives were considered more closely related to, and therefore more responsible for, the child than the father's. Such tribes or clans are called *matrilineal* (mother-related).

The clans and tribes were regulated by the decisions of the elder members of the families acting as a council. Leadership rested in chiefs. Usually there was a special chief for war. Another outstanding leader of the tribe was the man wise in the lore of magic and religion.

Since theoretically all members of a clan were related by blood, they all claimed a common ancestor, and many tribes had a sacred totem, or emblem, of that ancestor. Often the totem was taboo, that is, it could not be eaten, touched, or looked at because it was associated with the spirit of the clan ancestor. At other times, perhaps on holy days with proper ceremony, if the totem was edible, it might be the principal food.

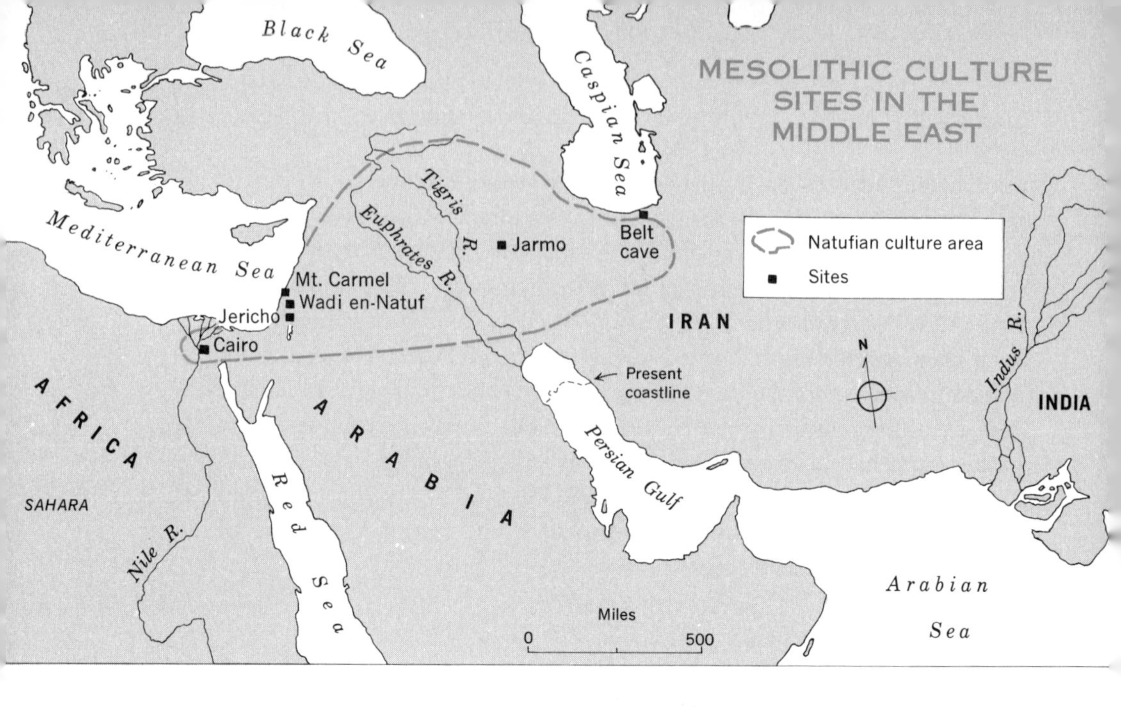

Magic was an essential part of life. With magic, hostile forces or difficult situations could be more successfully controlled. Before the men went on a deer hunt, pictures of deer were drawn and arrows stuck in them. It was believed that such a ritual would cause the real arrows and real deer to act in accord with the picture, or "in sympathy" with it.

The social organization of the tribe and the practices the tribe followed had undoubtedly existed in much the same form during the Paleolithic Age. They developed during the Mesolithic period and were the foundation upon which Neolithic man built.

THE NEOLITHIC REVOLUTION

During the sixth millennium (6000–5000) B.C. the retreat of the great glaciers of the Ice Age continued. It became increasingly important for man in the Middle East to remain close to water supplies. The change in environment, coupled with the slowly changing ways of living that resulted, stimulated man to make the further changes of the Neolithic Revolution.

FARMING

The outstanding development of the Neolithic period was man's realization that food could be obtained by planting. Agriculture enabled man to settle down, and this was the first step on the road to civilization. Agriculture also enabled man to have a regular food supply. This greatly increased the population.

Among Neolithic crops, first in importance was grain developed from native grasses. At least two kinds of millet—barley and wheat—were the first grains man cultivated. A second group of foods included beans, peas, lentils, and vetch. Figs, dates, peaches, apples, plums, and grapes composed a third group of foods. By the end of the Neolithic period the olive, valuable both as a food and for its oil, which was used in cooking and to protect the human skin, had been enlisted in the service of mankind.

Goats and sheep made up man's first herds. Dogs aided in guarding them. As the Neolithic period continued, other domesticated animals included pigs, donkeys, cows, and oxen.

NEW TOOLS

In earlier Paleolithic and Mesolithic times man shaped his stone tools and weapons by chipping them. Mesolithic man also shaped bone by working it with stone knives. Around 6000 B.C. man got the idea of grinding stone as well. At the same time he used harder stones, like granite. Such stones not only took a sharper, stronger cutting edge but could also be resharpened by grinding when they became dull. An axe of such hard stone could cut a tree without falling to bits as a piece of flint would do.

For tilling the ground, man invented the hoe. With his new instrument he was able to break the soil into crude chunks, making it easier to plant his crops. For some two thousand years small plantings were made with the help of the hoe. Then, in Egypt, the plow was invented by lengthening the hoe handle and tying it to a yoke fastened to the horns of an ox. To use an animal in addition to the tool was another major advancement. With animal strength to pull it through the ground, a larger blade than that of the hoe could be managed. Plowing was deeper. Larger fields could also be farmed, so more food was produced.

For reaping his grain, man invented a knife with a slotted bone handle into which a series of stone points were fitted. The bone handles were often beautifully carved in the shapes of animal heads, indicating that the not-so-pressing survival tasks left time for artistic expression.

One of man's greatest inventions was the wheel. Mesolithic man had sometimes dragged people or possessions from place to place on sleds, but that was hard and slow. Sleds were still used through the Neolithic Age in the Middle East, but the wheeled cart appeared beside them in Mesopotamia. In the first carts the axle was rigidly fastened to the wheels and turned with

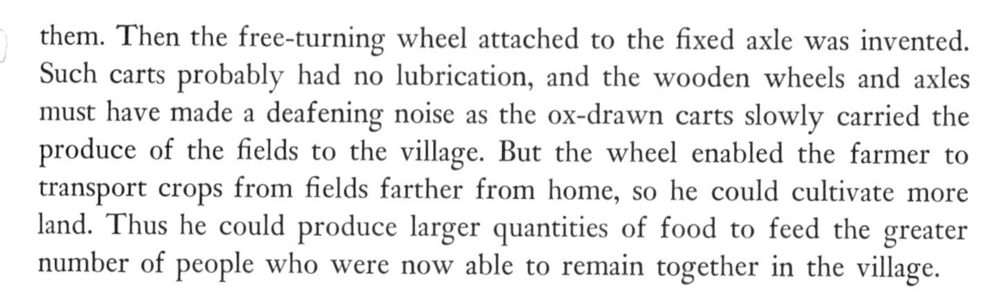

them. Then the free-turning wheel attached to the fixed axle was invented. Such carts probably had no lubrication, and the wooden wheels and axles must have made a deafening noise as the ox-drawn carts slowly carried the produce of the fields to the village. But the wheel enabled the farmer to transport crops from fields farther from home, so he could cultivate more land. Thus he could produce larger quantities of food to feed the greater number of people who were now able to remain together in the village.

THE FIRST VILLAGES

The care of his crops obliged man to settle down in permanent locations. He became a community dweller in a village by building his house near those of others for mutual protection from wild animals or marauding tribesmen. The oldest village to be identified by archaeologists was at Jericho, in Palestine, and it is believed to date from 8000 B.C.

The earliest houses were mud and wattle huts. Such houses were round and had a single room. Later, houses were built of wood, stone, mud bricks dried in the sun, or pisé (clay mixed with straw or dung and trodden in water, then dried in the sun). Mud and pisé houses were usually rectangular.

Jericho. A view of the diggings around the oldest village we know. Jericho is believed to be 10,000 years old. The famous walls that Joshua brought tumbling down were from thousands of years later, about 1400 B.C. In the background, above, is an Arab refugee village.

These later houses had more rooms, and outbuildings appeared for the animals, who had presumably shared the same quarters with their masters.

The center of life in the home was the hearth, usually placed in the center of the room under a hole in the roof through which smoke could escape. A stone or brick oven stood on this spot, and sometimes a stone seat lay alongside it. Beds were mattresses of straw.

Community life led to the need for community enterprises. Granaries, created by the united villagers for the common use, were built to store the crops, showing that ownership of the food supplies rested in the village and not in private hands. Here was a carry-over into Neolithic life of the Old Stone Age custom of sharing food. Sanctuaries for religious rites and shrines for community worship appeared in many Neolithic villages. Inside were devotional objects, such as tiny images of the Mother Goddess.

Another community enterprise was the community grave area surrounded by stone slabs. Community graves were usually used for the burial of chieftains, for in most Neolithic communities the dead were buried in family tombs or by the hearth.

As the Neolithic period advanced and villages became wealthy in surplus foods and goods, they found it necessary to defend their property from hungry marauders. In the very late Neolithic period an important community project was the erection of walls to surround the entire village. As early as 8000 B.C. the first village of Jericho was protected by a great stone wall with towers large enough to contain inner stairways. Outside the fortifications, a ditch 9 feet deep and 27 feet wide was dug out of the solid rock that underlay the village.

Finally, in villages located in swampy areas or along rivers such as the Nile and the Tigris and Euphrates, an important community project was to dig canals to drain the swamps in wet weather and irrigate the fields, and to build embankments along the rivers to prevent the flooding of the land during the rainy season. Such a project called for more social cooperation than man had previously found necessary and for the appointment of leaders with power to enforce rules of work.

THE BEGINNING OF SPECIALIZATION

Village life gradually developed the need for different occupations. As life became more complex, new needs arose. Not all men tended the fields, hunted, or were warriors. Some grew skilled in producing the artifacts or objects necessary in a more settled community. They were the forerunners of artisans.

Late Neolithic clay pots. Antelopes, ibexes, flamingoes, and aloe trees decorate predynastic vases from Egypt. Pots from northern Egypt were buff gray and pale pink with red line decorations, above; those from southern Egypt were red with white decoration. These jars are believed to imitate earlier jars made in stone.

Even though there were specialists in the Neolithic villages, each family still knew the basic crafts, such as basketry. Baskets woven from reeds and grasses were used for carrying grains from the fields. Since one idea leads to another, men found that packing the baskets with damp mud made it possible to carry liquids. The discovery that the mud lining could stand by itself if baked led to the invention of pottery. Grain could be stored more safely in pots. Such valuable liquids as grape juice and olive oil could be preserved, and meat could be cooked without losing its nourishing juices.

Once the potters learned how to bake, designs and colors were preserved. Although Neolithic potters had no other intention than to meet their own needs, they left a priceless aid to archaeologists and historians. By analyzing the clay, the glazes, and the designs, modern students have been able to trace groups and their customs and techniques from place to place and have established sequences of cultures where no written records exist.

Man spun his first thread with the New Stone Age spindle whorl and wove his first cloth on Neolithic looms. Flax was spun and woven into linen in Egypt by 1400 B.C. Wool was woven in the Middle East. For a long time, however, leather remained more common for Neolithic garments than the newer cloths.

Metalworking was invented in the Neolithic period. Man began to shape those metals he found in a natural state. Copper was such a metal, as were silver and gold. Gold may have been the first metal to catch man's eye. It is found in a pure state, and while searching for flint man was probably attracted by its glinting yellow beauty. Later, as he came to realize that gold does not rust, he associated it with eternal things like the sun and used it for such important religious purposes as masks to cover the faces of dead chieftains.

We do not know how or when man discovered that heated metal can be shaped more easily than cold (smelting) or that melted metal can be poured into molds and will harden into the shape of the mold (casting). But once these discoveries were made, perhaps about 3500 B.C., they were among the many signs that man had left the Neolithic era and had entered that of civilization.

RELIGION

Many practices are assigned to the Neolithic period only because they were already in existence when written records started. So it is with man's earliest beliefs. There is no way of knowing how long they existed in any specific form.

Neolithic man apparently observed certain rites in connection with the spring and autumn equinoxes, when day and night are equal in length, and with the summer and winter solstices, the longest and shortest days of the year. We do not know what associations he built around them or whether they were celebrated in connection with his agricultural seasons or his worship of the sun. Whatever the reason, those times of the year became so sacred to mankind that the great religions of historic civilizations found it easier to adapt them than to forget them. The historic religions simply gave them new meanings to fit their own teachings.

Neolithic man apparently had deeply rooted ideas about the earth as the Great Mother of all living creatures. Her earliest symbols included the tree, both pine and fig, the serpent, certain birds, such as the dove, owl, and raven, and certain animals, such as the cow, pig, bear, and later the horse. Turning his eyes to the stars, Neolithic man saw the Great Mother there in many forms: the Great Bear, or the Great Serpent, the Mother of Grain—constellations named in the New Stone Age and still called by those names today.

Neolithic religion differed from modern religion in several ways. Indeed, the phrase Neolithic religion, is really using a modern term—religion—in an ancient context. This is deceiving. Neolithic man did not have a religion in the modern sense at all. First, the worship of the Great Mother was not monotheism, that is, the belief that one god or goddess is single and supreme. All the facets of life and the forces of nature had names, and these names identified divine realities. Birth, death, hunger, fear and love; moon, sky, wind, sun, and rain; lions, falcons, serpents; and so on in endless number were godlike too. Such belief is called polytheism, for it sees gods in all the different aspects of nature.

Second, in Neolithic times there was no clearly defined creed that had to be accepted if one was to be a member of the religious group. The religious group was not in any way distinct. It was made up of the tribe or village as a whole.

Finally, Neolithic man would have been unable to understand the modern idea that religion is separate from daily life, that worship is to be practiced only in a special building one day a week. Neolithic man felt a unity in nature, the divine, and material things; and he believed that the mysterious forces of the universe could be influenced by his behavior. His whole life reflected this: the ceremonials he conducted, the clothes and jewelry he wore, the music he played, the art he created.

In the Old Stone Age man had directed some of his magical rites at the hunt in order to increase the chances of catching game. These same rituals were practiced in Neolithic times, but they were redirected toward agriculture and the ceremonies attending the planting and the harvest. Rituals to make the rain fall or to affect the flooding of the river were among the most important, and in Mesopotamia and Egypt the rainmaker was the most influential member of the tribe.

Head of an image. A late Neolithic baked-clay sculpture from south Anatolia, about seven thousand years old. Its face is masklike but nonetheless discernible—an unusual phenomenon in so early a piece. Possibly the head was set up on a post to serve as an object of worship.

WARFARE

Man had competed with animals and other men for food in the Old Stone Age, and now he competed for the new grazing fields and croplands. Neolithic villages were in great peril from attack. If Jericho (page 38) is at all representative, massive fortifications surrounded some of the later villages. The houses, granaries, herds, and tools of the villagers must have looked very inviting to wandering peoples still living in an Old Stone Age culture or to those anxious to add to their own goods.

Weapons consisted of darts, spears, arrows, and axes made of the harder stones that could be ground. That ancient weapon of the hunter, the sling, continued to be used throughout the whole Neolithic period and appeared later in the armies of civilized men. In trained hands the slingshot could kill at three hundred feet, and stones were supplemented by clay bullets baked in great numbers.

THE NEOLITHIC REVOLUTION AND CULTURE LAG

When new ideas or inventions appear in a society, they will spread in two ways, downward through that society and outward to other peoples. Both processes take time, for people are slow to make changes that mean giving up methods that are well known and trusted and may even threaten their survival. We can call this lag, or delay, in the spread of a cultural object or idea a *culture lag*.

Since the Neolithic Revolution produced fundamental changes in man's way of life, it took some four thousand years before it was accomplished in the regions where it began. By that time much of it was already spreading outward to other peoples in adjoining regions.

CULTURE ZONES

About 4000 B.C. the cultural regions of the world were roughly as follows: In the Middle East, from the Nile River to the Caspian Sea, Neolithic life was coming to an end, and man was on the verge of developing his first civilizations. Around this central zone of true Neolithic life was a belt of land where the Neolithic Revolution was under way but was only partly completed. This zone spread outward across North Africa along the Sahara Desert to the Atlas Mountains; on the other side of the Middle East it stretched from the Caspian Sea into Siberia and was moving slowly toward China and into India. Around this second zone of incomplete Neolithic change lay a third region in which man was still living in the Old Stone Age. This region included central Africa, northern Europe, eastern Asia, and America.

These concentric zones, that is, bands about the same center, will appear, with variations, throughout ancient history. As the innermost area rises to a higher and higher cultural level, the surrounding areas also rise but to a lesser degree, and there will still be a lag in the spread of the central cultures to the men on the outskirts.

Because of the existence of culture zones and because of the culture lag, we cannot use a term like neolithic with a specific date unless we specify a particular place. The Middle East was neolithic, for example, in 6000 B.C., Britain was neolithic in 2000 B.C., while parts of America were neolithic when Columbus arrived.

❦ ❦ ❦

Man began to master his environment more effectively than previously in the Middle East in the period 8000 B.C. to 4000 B.C. We call this period the New Stone Age, and it includes the Mesolithic transition and the Neolithic Revolution. From being a wandering hunter searching for food, man became a villager producing it. His habitation changed from caves that he found on his wanderings to houses that he built. Villages arose slowly and gradually became more orderly, with streets and community buildings such as granaries and shrines. Skills became more specialized, although specialization was not complete. Surpluses of food allowed new social groups to develop. Extra food, tools, and ornaments made trade with other villages possible. This further stimulated revolutionary changes in human ways of living.

In defense of his own property man learned to fortify, and in attacks on his neighbors' villages he improved his fighting tools and techniques. Community work on canals and dikes and maintaining the village shrine further encouraged him to act as part of a group for the common good. His love of beauty found outlets in carving wood, bone, ivory, and stone, in modeling clay images (though they were primarily for religious purposes), and in shaping and decorating pottery.

In Neolithic communities man laid the foundations on which civilizations would rise.

People, Places, and Terms

Natufians

Nile River
Tigris River
Euphrates River
Indus River
Middle East
Egypt
Mesopotamia

food hunter

river system
clan
food producer
nomadic
nomad
domesticate
pastoral
migration
Mesolithic
Neolithic
tribe

totem
specialization
monotheism
polytheism
cult
Great Mother
culture lag
culture zone
patrilineal
matrilineal
solstice

Mastering the Reading

1. What have been some major physical and climatic changes in the highland area that stretches from the Atlantic to India? What effect did this have on the migration of animals and man?
2. What were five major developments made by food hunters in the Neolithic period? What is the importance of the Natufians in an understanding of the Neolithic Revolution?
3. How were Mesolithic men socially organized? What was the relationship among the different social units?
4. What new crafts, inventions, and techniques were developed as a result of settled conditions and why?
5. How do new ideas or inventions spread?

Interpreting the Text

1. How "revolutionary" was the Neolithic Revolution? What aspects of man's culture in the Neolithic Age were still the same as they had been in the Paleolithic Age?
2. Compare the way a pastoral tribe lived with the way a settled, farming tribe lived. What conflicts might have arisen between them?

Exploring Beyond the Text

1. In order to understand some of the problems of Neolithic man as he settled in the Middle East, try to read about life in a desert region or interview someone who has lived in a desert area. Guide your investigation with a few good questions: How can people stand 125° heat? How does one dress? What is the source of the water supply? What grows in the desert?
2. Make a chart listing the basic activities performed by men in the periods that you have studied so far—Lower Paleolithic, Upper Paleolithic,

Mesolithic, and Neolithic. Include the way men in each of the particular periods performed each of these activities. What patterns do you see? Are there some activities which change more than others? If so, why?

3. *Ancient Words in Modern English.* Parts of each of the following words are frequently found in other combinations. Look up the meanings and derivations of any words or parts of words with which you are unfamiliar. Add these words and their meanings to your glossary:

mesolithic	Mesopotamia	monotheism
neolithic	Mediterranean	polytheism

Working with the Map

In this chapter you have been introduced to the Middle East and to the bodies of water in the area that will be referred to frequently. Study the map carefully and try to picture the area in your mind. Practice for a while and then try to draw a free-hand map.

Looking Back to Beginnings

Hundreds of thousands of years were spent by mankind in the kind of life which we call the Old Stone Age. Progress was so slow in those years that it seems to us that early men were living in times that were almost changeless. But very slowly, gains were made in physical adaptation and in mastering the environment. More rapid change characterized the New Stone Age. In this period of development, which began only about ten thousand years ago, man learned to control his environment in a limited way, and social changes were introduced as man became a settled dweller in villages.

In the Old Stone Age and in the New Stone Age, man's life is called primitive to distinguish it from the more socially developed civilized societies that appeared later. To classify both Stone Ages as primitive, however, must not obscure the fact that very great differences existed between them. In the Old Stone Age, man was completely at the mercy of his environment and had to find his food, clothing, and shelter where chance permitted. In the New Stone Age, man became a food producer, a settler in permanent locations, and the inventor of political, social, and economic customs.

The domestication of animals and, above all, the enlargement of the food supply through planting, revolutionized man's existence. These developments enabled him to live in larger groups and then to specialize in his work. Such changes in turn led to civilization.

Some Questions to Answer

1. "Man is both a biological and a social animal." What are the functions performed by man as a biological animal? What are the functions or activities performed and practiced by men in groups no matter how primitive or advanced the men are?
2. Define the word culture in its broadest sense, as it applies to any society or group, despite their stage of development. What are some other ways in which we use the word culture in a restricted sense?
3. What constitutes your environment? How does environment influence culture? How does culture change environment?

Using Evidence from Prehistoric Times

Imagination, as well as careful study, is the key to unlocking the history of the past in the vast stretch of time before writing was invented. This period is often called prehistory. Some aspects of life in prehistoric times can be reconstructed with great certainty, some with less, and on some aspects we can only use our imagination. On the latter, even the opinions of scholars who have spent their lives studying this subject will differ. Let us begin with examples illustrated in your text on pages 27 and 28.

Cave Paintings. The Stag (Deer) Hunt is a paleolithic cave painting in southern Spain. Of what facts can we be certain, based on this drawing? For example, it is clear that these prehistoric people hunted deer with bows and arrows. Of what else can we be certain? Now, turn to the use of your imagination. Why did these prehistoric artists draw pictures of a deer hunt? Was it for some kind of religious reason? Was it to bring good luck in hunting? Was it simply to help tell a story?

Now, look at the painting of a bison from a cave in northern Spain. Bison disappeared from Europe about 10,000 years ago. The Altamira cave in which this painting appears existed long before that event; hence we know these paleolithic artists must have seen bison and probably hunted them. We can reconstruct the

BEGINNINGS

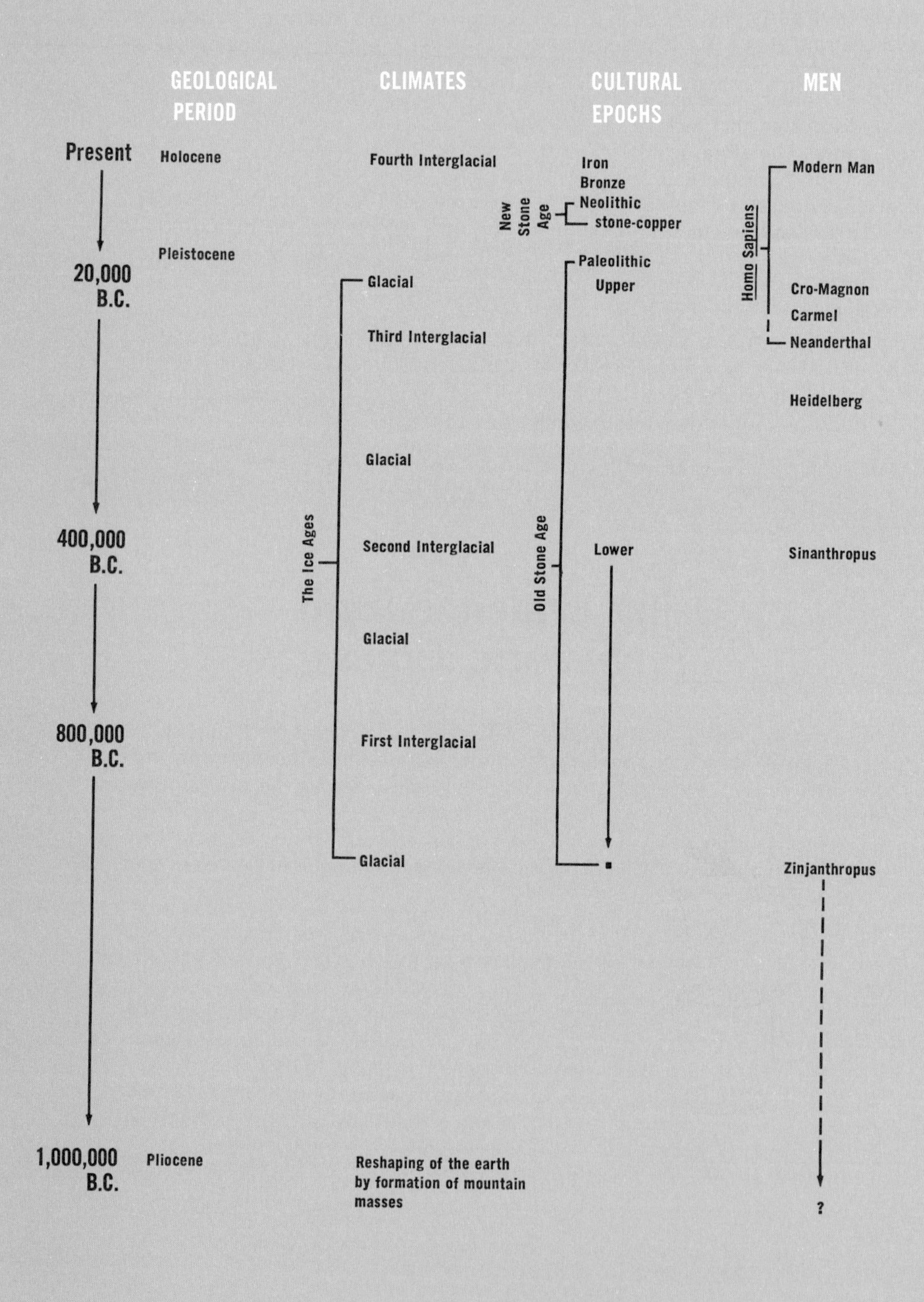

GEOLOGICAL PERIOD
CLIMATES
CULTURAL EPOCHS
MEN
Present
Holocene
Fourth Interglacial
Iron
Bronze
New Stone Age
Neolithic
stone-copper
Modern Man
Homo Sapiens
Pleistocene
20,000 B.C.
Glacial
Paleolithic
Upper
Cro-Magnon
Carmel
Third Interglacial
Neanderthal
Heidelberg
Glacial
400,000 B.C.
The Ice Ages
Second Interglacial
Old Stone Age
Lower
Sinanthropus
Glacial
800,000 B.C.
First Interglacial
Glacial
Zinjanthropus
1,000,000 B.C.
Pliocene
Reshaping of the earth by formation of mountain masses
?

artists' methods and materials, but when we try to understand the intent and purposes of this painting, we must use our imagination. And, as the text states, "we are guessing about the intention of men . . . who lived perhaps thirty thousand years ago."

Tools. Humans have used tools made of stone for over a million years. Scholars have discovered that techniques of making tools changed and improved during that period. Therefore, scholars study the tools prehistoric people left behind for clues about both the time they were made and how they were used. Two examples of prehistoric tool-making techniques are shown below. Which one developed first? Explain your answer.

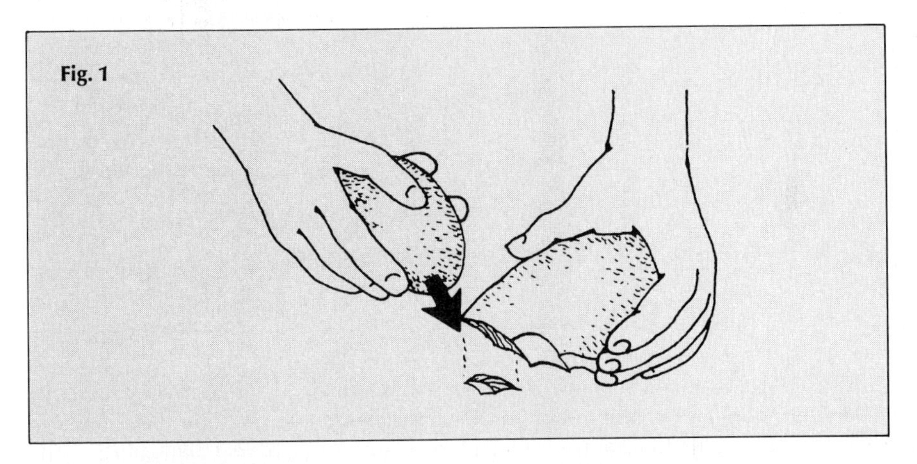

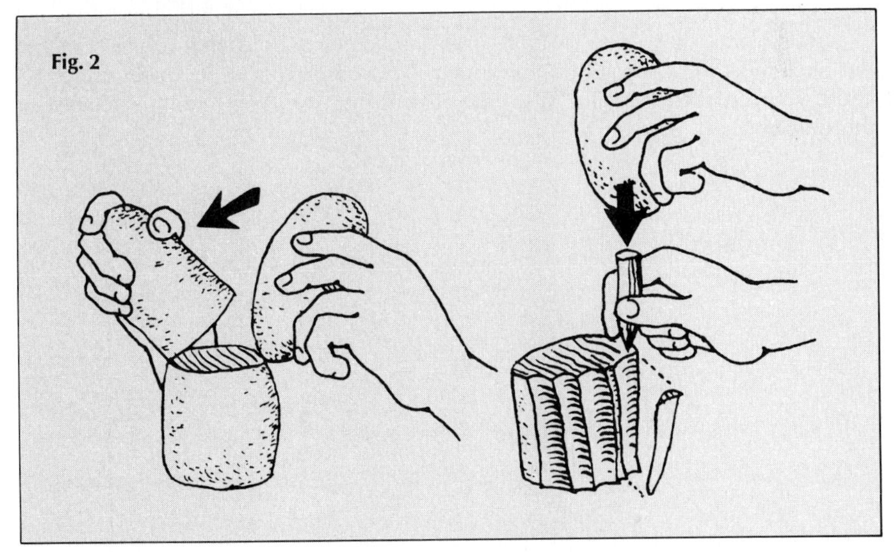

The uses of a tool are sometimes fairly easy to reconstruct. The tool (Figure 3 below) is small, less than two inches long. What was it probably used for? The tool (Figure 4) is considerably larger, and it can be hand-held very comfortably. Only one of its sides is sharp. What could it have been used for? If you find this last question difficult to answer, you should also know that from other evidence we are certain that the people who used this tool wore the skins of animals.

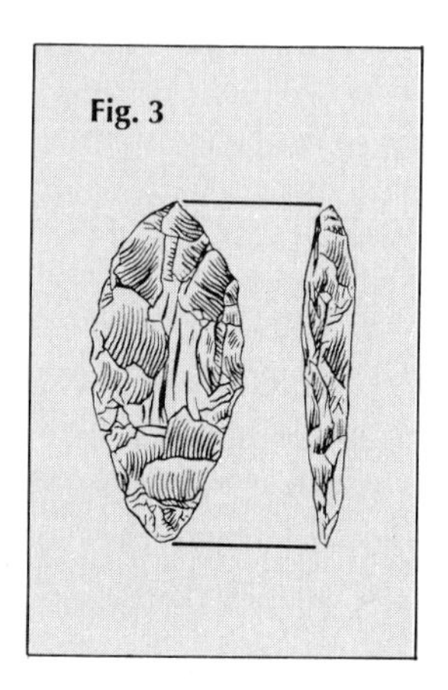
Fig. 3

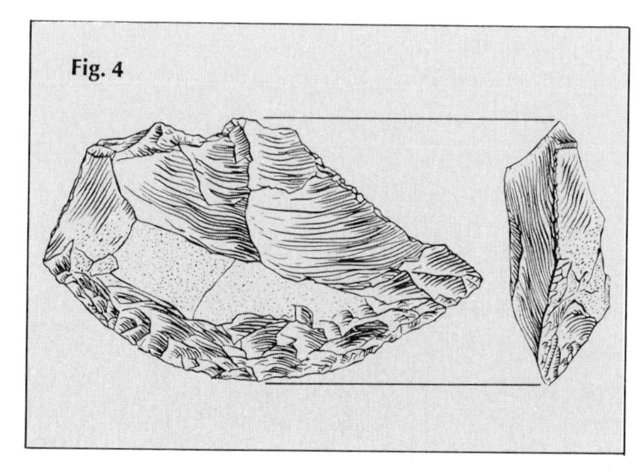
Fig. 4

Now, imagine that you have discovered the site of a hunting camp used by paleolithic humans. Furthermore, you have discovered a flat stone that served as a seat for the toolmaker and small pieces of stone left from making tools. The fossils of charred bones also are found near the remains of a fire. Discolored soil in certain places shows you that it has replaced posts or poles that rotted long ago but once must have supported a dwelling. How much of the life of these people could you reconstruct? What you have read in the text may help you to answer this question.

PART 2

First Civilizations

3600-1000 B.C.

Between 3500 and 3000 B.C., in the valleys of the Tigris, Euphrates, and Nile rivers, men first became civilized. Not long after, civilization also developed along the banks of the Indus River in the Indian subcontinent.

The use of the metal copper marked the transitional period between the New Stone Age and civilization. This period is therefore called the Copper-Stone Age. The discovery of copper was followed by the invention of bronze. Bronze has given its name to the first era of man's civilized history.

In the Bronze Age, early civilized people struggled with the fundamental problems facing men living together in large groups: how they should govern themselves, how they should feed and occupy themselves, how they should better their existence and perhaps continue it in the next world. As men moved beyond their own river valleys, they encountered each other, and trade and large-scale war were born. And in the Bronze Age, for the first time in history, individuals are known: men—and women—whose portraits we have, whose personalities as well as deeds were recorded.

In the Bronze Age, civilizations flourished not only in the Middle East and India but also in Crete and China. In these Bronze Age civilizations, men faced for the first time almost all the problems that modern men encounter.

4

Civilization Begins: The Copper-Stone Age

3600–2800 B.C.

When man gave up nomadic food hunting and settled in primitive food-producing villages with farms and herds, the change was so great that we speak of it as the Neolithic Revolution. A second change, equally revolutionary, followed in Egypt and Mesopotamia. This was the Urban Revolution, so called because it was based on the development of the first cities.

In the fertile valleys, crops became plentiful, so a surplus of food existed. This in turn supported a greatly increased population, and the Neolithic villages grew larger. Freed from the necessity of growing their own food, people in the villages were able to pursue special occupations. Some governed, others were priests or warriors, still others were craftsmen. The villages became cities. The beginnings of specialization were seen in Neolithic times, but its growth and development were a natural result of the problems facing people living together in urban masses.

PRIMITIVE CULTURE AND CIVILIZATION

At this point it might be worthwhile to pause a moment to consider two terms that have been used and will be used again in discussing ancient history. The terms are *primitive* and *civilized.*

Primitive and civilized describe kinds of human culture. (Culture is the way of life of a people, including all their skills and techniques.) Primitive and civilized do not describe whether men are happy or unhappy in their primitive or civilized state, or whether they are morally good or evil. The terms, therefore, are not used to praise or blame. They are used merely to describe.

What we will see is that the difference between the primitive and the civilized lies in the nature of their cultures.

THE CHARACTERISTICS OF A PRIMITIVE SOCIETY

A primitive group controls a small area of land. If the tribe is nomadic, it will occupy a few miles of pasture land in one season and perhaps migrate to another locality for the next season. If the tribe is settled, it may control a single small river valley, while across the hills in the next valley another tribe will live.

A primitive group is illiterate. Writing systems are found necessary only by more complex societies than those at the primitive level. Simple systems of pictograms (page 64) may exist in a primitive society, but there is no body of written literature. The legends of the past are transmitted orally, and it is amazing how accurately such traditions can be preserved over many centuries.

A primitive society blends religion, warfare, and daily life into a social organization in which a few leaders stand out. There may be separate leadership for war and religion. A close unity among gods, men, and nature is felt by primitive groups. This unity expresses itself in customs that represent an ancient and admirably successful adaptation of the group to its particular natural environment.

The primitive economy is based on the nomadic tribe or the agricultural village, and trade is by barter.

THE CHARACTERISTICS OF A CIVILIZED SOCIETY

The first characteristic of a civilized society is the city as a political, social, and cultural entity. The very word *civilization* comes from the Latin *civis,* meaning citizen of the *civitas,* city.

Agriculture exists in a civilized society. In fact, agriculture was the principal institution of every civilization of ancient times. Agriculture also exists in a primitive society, but in a civilized society the farmlands and the farm villages are subordinate to the city. The people of the farmlands reflect the culture of the city to a greater or lesser degree depending on their wealth and on the communications existing between the farming areas and the city.

A civilized society is large in population. A primitive society may be large or small. The Egyptian Old Kingdom, for example, had from one to several million people instead of the few thousand who lived in the same territory in earlier times.

A civilized society controls a large territory. The size of the territory will grow greater or smaller along with the ups and downs of the civilization's history, but at all times it will include many more square miles than a primitive society. Before Egypt was united, many small tribal groups occupied the land. Following unification, one people, the Egyptians, occupied the Nile Valley, the Nile delta, and other territory beyond.

The institutions of a civilization are so developed that they can be studied separately from one another. In other words, we can make separate studies of Egyptian government, Egyptian economy, Egyptian arts, Egyptian science, and so on. In a primitive society these institutions are so intermingled that one cannot be treated separately from the others.

Civilizations are literate. They have writing systems to keep their records and to transmit their literature, history, science, and everything else pertaining to their way of life.

A civilization understands the use of metals and is capable of extracting them from the native ores. Primitive groups may use metals, such as gold, that are found in a natural state and can be shaped easily, but generally primitive man will depend on tools and weapons of wood or stone that can be fashioned directly from nature.

Thus it is evident that when we say that one society is primitive and another is civilized, we are not saying which is better, or happier, or best adjusted for the welfare of its people.

There are two other words we might consider at this point. These words are *savage* and *barbarian* and are sometimes used by historians to mean the most primitive as opposed to the partly civilized. This usage differs, however, from the everyday use of these words by people who are not well educated or, who use them as labels for behavior that differs from their own and that, therefore, they do not like.

FROM NEOLITHIC TO CIVILIZED SOCIETY

Perhaps by about 5000 B.C. Neolithic men had settled close to the Nile in Egypt and to the Tigris and Euphrates in Mesopotamia. In the next fifteen hundred years, three Neolithic cultures appeared in turn in Egypt, and a similar sequence of Neolithic cultures existed in Mesopotamia. In each case the succeeding culture was able to adjust better to its problems than had its predecessor.

THE GEOGRAPHIC SETTING

The highlands of the Middle East, where the Neolithic Revolution took place, dip on the west into the valley of the twin rivers, the Tigris and the Euphrates. As the earth slowly warmed following the Fourth Ice Age, deserts appeared around and between these rivers. Steadily, as the years passed, the Arabian peninsula dried up, and the northern part jutted like a great bay window into the grasslands of Syria. In time the desert bay became such a dead waste that travelers from Mesopotamia to Egypt were obliged to go north and west on the Euphrates and then turn south into Syria and follow the Mediterranean shore to Egypt. This route makes a curve shaped like the crescent moon, so it was named the *Fertile Crescent* (see map, page 34).

The river valleys were originally very dangerous. Man had to learn to overcome the problems that life along them entailed. The delta areas, flat

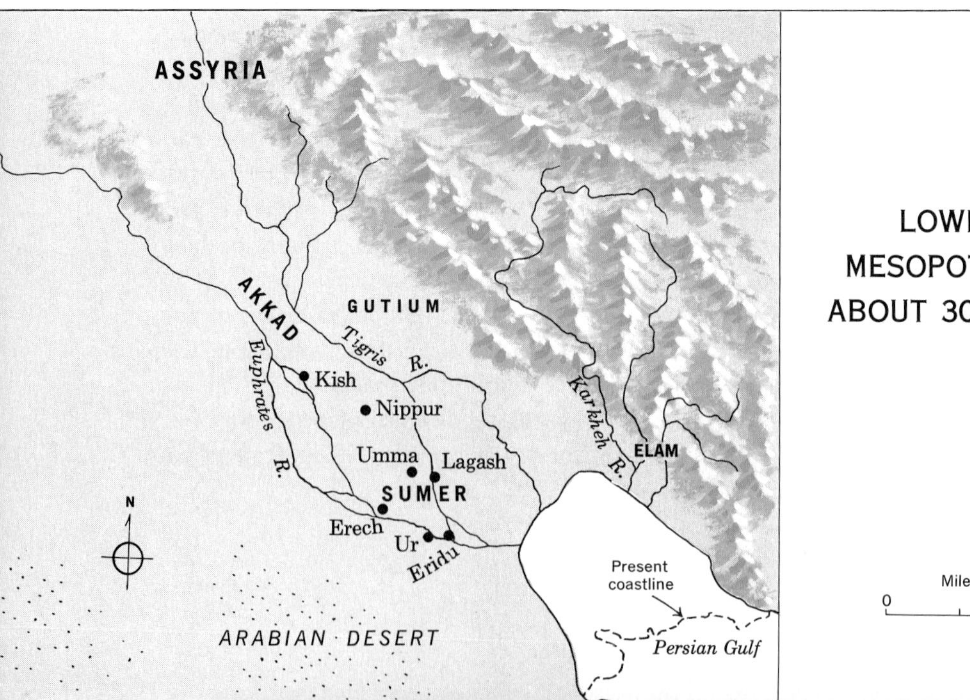

LOWER MESOPOTAMIA, ABOUT 3000 B.C.

muddy plains near the sea, were swamps completely drowned by the slightest rise of the rivers. Delta farms and villages were continually undermined as the flooding rivers cut and recut changing channels through the mud. A safe location one day was often the river bottom the next. Another hazard arose from the wild animals that competed with man for the river waters as the plains nearby turned into deserts. In the river swamps lurked the terror of poisonous snakes. Death from snake bite was so common that it became a principal object of man's magic and medicine.

The delta lands, however, were inexhaustibly fertile because they were built up of topsoil carried by the rivers from the upstream highlands and were refertilized each year by fresh silt deposits. Channels were alive with fish, and the reed swamps teemed with birds. So man settled in the valleys despite their perils and gradually developed the first civilized societies.

LOWER MESOPOTAMIA: CITY-KINGDOMS

In the lower reaches of the Tigris and Euphrates rivers there existed a delta plain of deep rich mud. It was made up of the topsoil of mountains to the north, which had been washed down by the rivers for many thousands of years. Naturally there were no stones in this soil, and its fertility was practically inexhaustible. The broad flat plain was about the size of New Jersey, and to the east of it there was a much smaller one where the Karkheh River came down from the hills of Elam to the Persian Gulf. Throughout history the three rivers have built the plain farther and farther into the Persian Gulf. The ruins of the city of Eridu, which was a seaport in 3500 B.C., are now 150 miles from the present seashore. It must be remembered, therefore, that although their remains are inland today, the first cities were located very near the sea.

Mesopotamia is the land "between the rivers." This is the meaning of the name given by the Greeks to the fertile plain watered by the Tigris and Euphrates rivers. The Euphrates is the longer river, the Tigris more dangerous because its flood course is unpredictable. In ancient times, after following a long path from the mountains of Armenia, the rivers entered the Persian Gulf separately, not together as they do today.

Mesopotamia is divided into several parts. The northern area was ancient Assyria, a rough country of hills and stones where wandering tribes pastured their sheep. Farther south lay Babylonia, divided in turn into Akkad in the north and the delta plain called Sumer.

North of Mesopotamia were the mountains of Armenia and the mountains separating the Fertile Crescent from the plateau of Anatolia. To the east lay the land of Elam, to the south were the barren wastes of the Arabian Desert, where more nomadic tribes wandered with their flocks, and to the west the grasslands of Syria bordered on the mountains and valleys of coastal Palestine and Phoenicia (see map, page 34).

The geography of Mesopotamia played an important role in influencing the outlook and history of the Mesopotamians. Natural barriers existed only on the north. From the hill country of Assyria, from the mountains of Elam, and from the deserts of Arabia, hungry tribes looked at the watered fields of the people living in the river valley of the Tigris and Euphrates and wanted them. Invasions and immigrations were increasing, warfare was constant. To make matters more difficult, the flooding of the rivers, so necessary to irrigate the fields, was unpredictable. It depended on the winter snows in the mountains of Armenia, and it was affected by landslides in the gorges of the tributary rivers and the accumulation of silt. Unexpectedly the river might change course or overflow without warning. Instead of a beneficial irrigation, disaster resulted. Fields were wiped out, homes and flocks disappeared. About 4000 B.C. an especially frightful calamity occurred. The entire delta plain was swept by a river flood so great that it left a bed of clay eight feet thick over the countryside. Farms, villages, animals, men, perished except in the two or three towns that stood on the highest mounds.

The discovery in 1929 of evidence of this flood was of great interest to Bible students. It gave some substance to the legend of Noah and the Ark, a legend already known to duplicate in many details a Mesopotamian legend of a world flood.

Life was not secure for the ancient Mesopotamians. They looked up to the heavens fearfully, never knowing whether a hostile tribe might sweep down from the hills killing them all or cut off their water supply from a spot farther up the river. They did not know when the river might suddenly go on a rampage and drown them or disappear entirely. Still, for all the uncertainties, food was plentiful, animals and fish abounded and grains grew easily, and it was possible not only to grow enough to live but also to produce a surplus. So the fertility of the land led to the growth of the first cities of the ancient Middle East and to the organization of these cities into self-contained units called city-states, or, to use the term more accurately, city-kingdoms. The first of these city-kingdoms were in the delta plain of Sumer.

THE SUMERIANS

At some time between 4000 B.C. and 3000 B.C. strangers called Sumerians came into the delta plain of the Tigris and Euphrates. From them the plain took its name of Sumer (Shinar in the Bible). The evidence of their bones shows that they were different from the Natufians and later Neolithic peoples of the Middle East. Their own legends said that they had come to Sumer "from the sea." The Hebrew tradition said that they had come from "the east into the plain of Shinar." It seems probable that they had come from some region beyond the mountains to the north and perhaps had first passed through Elam to the seacoast, after which they turned north into Sumer. This route would reconcile both legends with the hypotheses of archaeology.

Sumerian statuettes. Huge eyes staring intently, arms raised and hands clasping offertory vessels in ritual gestures, these twelve statuettes, the largest about 30 inches high, were found together beneath the floor of a Sumerian temple-sanctuary at present-day Tell Asmar, Iraq. They date from the early two thousands B.C. Some scholars believe they are deities. Others believe they are priests. Others think they represent the members of a family who, according to custom, placed them at the feet of the temple god to worship on their behalf. Such statuettes were common, but this group is remarkable for the way it conveys to us the uncertainty and intensity of the relationship of the Mesopotamians to their gods.

The new arrivals mixed with the survivors of the preflood people of the plain, and from the union arose an inventive, energetic culture that took the great step into civilization. There is debate over whether the Sumerians brought improved methods of farming, the potter's wheel, and the art of molding metals from their earlier home, or whether these were the achievements of the preflood people, or whether they were accomplished by the united Sumerians and preflood folk. Whatever the case, after perhaps one thousand years and by 3000 B.C., cities and civilization existed in Sumer.

SUMER'S CITIES

The early cities of Sumer have long since crumbled into rubble mounds, but from excavations and the descriptions of the Greek historian Herodotus, who visited Mesopotamia two thousand years later, in the fifth century B.C., we can imagine Sumer at its height.

As far as the eye could see the flat land stretched away, muddy when wet, raising clouds of dust when dry. Lines of green meant a canal; broader green patches marked the courses of the sluggish rivers. Date palms, olive groves, grape vines, wheat and barley fields, grazing sheep, goats, and cows showed that the soil was rich. And when the endless flatness became wearisome, the traveler's eyes would seek a hill against the sky. But it would not be a hill. As one came closer, a city took shape. It had narrow streets and temples set in open spaces. It had a great city wall with giant gates guarded by soldiers. Within the great wall stood another ring of walls, and from the center of the second ring a mighty temple tower, the *ziggurat,* soared skyward in three broad bands of colored brick: black, white, and blue. Lines of priests, some naked with their oiled skins shining in the blazing sun, others in colored robes, could be seen passing up and down the flights of steps that led to the temple built far above at the top of the tower. In some cities, trees and bushes were planted on the terraces up the ziggurat's sides. How the water to irrigate this shrubbery was raised to the upper levels is not known.

A thousand years later the houses were two-storied, and built around central patios, but we cannot assume that the first city houses, which must have been much simpler, were the same. We do know that from the earliest period they were built of sun-dried brick and that they were built of the same material throughout Sumerian history, for stone and timber were obtainable only through trade.

Between the towns a complex system of canals served the double purpose of draining off excess water after flooding and bringing water to the fields for irrigation. In the towns gold and copper objects, cast in molds, were plentiful, and writing was fully developed.

By 3000 B.C. several cities were prospering on the Sumerian plain. Among them were Ur, Erech, Nippur, Kish, Lagash, and Umma. Whether or not kings ruled is uncertain. Sumerian legend says that it was in the period after the great flood that "kingship descended from the gods." Historically we are sure of kings in Sumer only after 2700 B.C., although there is some evidence from religious records of their earlier existence.

It seems likely that the earliest rulers were not only the leaders who organized the work needed to build and maintain the canals and control the irrigation but that these same leaders were also mediators between the people and their gods. In a country where disaster could strike so suddenly and where the welfare of the people was so closely tied to a beneficial flood, the need to placate gods that seemed so capricious to the Sumerians gave rise very early to a powerful priest class. In time the priests needed assistants, and so a government by priests, or *theocracy*, came into being. In return for their services the priests were supported by the people who toiled as farmers. Later, as the need arose for a military leader to defend the city from attack by other cities, a separation of powers between leaders seems to have occurred. But the historical record is scant, and we can only guess at such developments.

The priests were not only the intermediaries between the citizens and their gods, and the persons trained in canal maintenance and irrigation supervision, but they were also the custodians of the accumulated reserves of food and goods (see below), and were specialists in the mysterious magic of writing, with all the power it gave over the gods (page 65). Clearly the priests of Sumer were the persons on whose shoulders the civilization of Sumer rested.

SUMERIAN RELIGION

Although the Sumerians believed in many gods of nature, and several ziggurats, each dedicated to a different god, were built in the largest cities, generally the Sumerians in each city called themselves the "children" or "servants" or "people" of one particular god and believed that their well-being depended on keeping that god's good will. The chief structure in each city, therefore, was the ziggurat, the home of the patron god of that city while on earth. At the top of the ziggurat was a welcoming temple, while a second shrine at ground level served as his abode. Other rooms

The Ziggurat of Ur. Over the remains of the ziggurat, at present-day Muqayyar, Iraq, an artist has drawn a reconstruction of the temple as it looked when complete. The ziggurat's form was intended to facilitate the god's descent from heaven. The earliest shrines of the Sumerians, however, were single-room rectangular structures. The ziggurat did not develop into its typical stepped-tower form until the end of the Sumerian period, about 2000 B.C.

included kitchens and dressing rooms. In the lower stages of the ziggurat or in adjoining buildings were the great supply rooms where the "people of the god" stored their extra food, clothing, and tools. These were in the care of the priests, who had the responsibility of guarding them and rationing them out to the people in times of need. In other buildings around the ziggurat, but still within the temple enclosure, were the working rooms of the priestly scribes, who kept all the records of the city, and working rooms for weavers and metalworkers or other craftsmen.

The Sumerians believed that the gods formed a council like a council of chiefs on earth, in which each god had his rank or place. In this council the vote of a single member was outweighed by that of the council as a whole. This explained to the Sumerians why a good and obedient city might suffer disaster, for the vote of the city's particular god could be overruled by the council.

Although she never held the position of the head of the council of gods, the Mother Goddess of the earth probably had the strongest hold on the people's affections. She was called Inanna or Ishtar. In a sacred marriage celebrated each year, she married the king to assure the fertility of the earth for the coming farming season. At the annual festival in each city the king represented Tammuz, Ishtar's husband. The king's marriage to a priestess representing the goddess was believed necessary to renew the vegetation and the productivity of the soil in the springtime. Tammuz (or Dumu-zi), "the faithful son of the waters that come forth from the earth," was thought to die each year and go to the land of darkness and death from which ordinary mortals never returned. Through the ritual hymns of Ishtar we can follow the bereaved wife as she descends into the world of death to seek Tammuz, whose autumnal passing had been observed by ceremonies of sorrow and wailing all over Sumer. After giving up, one by one, all the beauties of the land as bribes to the guardians at the various doorways of death, Ishtar rescues Tammuz and brings him back to the living earth, and spring is born anew. By this myth the Sumerians explained the sequences of seasons, the periods of food growing, and the idleness of nature in winter. It is interesting to note that in the death and resurrection of Tammuz the Sumerians did not see a hope of overcoming death for themselves. In later times and other lands an association between what happened to the god and what happened to man after death was made, but to the Sumerians the place of the dead was in the Land of No Return.

SUMERIAN ARITHMETIC

The Sumerians, along with the Egyptians, were the earliest mathematicians of the ancient world.

Continual flooding of the farmlands surrounding the cities erased property markings. This made it necessary to resurvey the fields to reestablish boundaries and led to the development of geometry and arithmetic. The Sumerians invented a number system that was followed by many later people and is used in the United States today. At first, like all primitive people using their fingers or toes, they counted up to ten. Instead of then using ten as their basic unit and, for instance, multiplying ten by ten, they multiplied six by ten, making sixty their next unit. Then they alternated between six and ten as multipliers, arriving at a sequence of 10, 60, 600, 3,600, 216,000, and so on. Now half of ten is five, and five divided into sixty gives twelve, so twelve became another key unit to the Sumerians. Since thirteen could not be arrived at by multiplying or dividing tens and sixes, they did not use it and it became unlucky, as it is to us today. We still divide a minute into sixty seconds, an hour into sixty minutes, a year into twelve months, so a little of Sumerian culture is with us every day.

SUMERIAN WRITING

About 3500 B.C. the people of lower Mesopotamia near the sea and those living in the hills of Elam, which rise just to the east of the Tigris and Euphrates delta lands, entered the first stage leading to writing by drawing *pictograms*. Pictograms are simplified pictures of objects, such as an eye to represent the eye. The pictograms of all early systems naturally looked alike in most instances because the objects drawn, such as arrows, have little variation.

As the pictograms became standardized in each society, definite ideas came to be associated with them. A snake did not represent merely the animal but also carried the idea of hidden danger. Such a symbol is called an *ideogram*.

When ideograms are further developed to represent their sounds, they become *phonograms*. Thus a pictogram of a ball might in time become the ideogram for anything that bounces, and later still the same design could become the phonogram for the sound *ba*.

As pictograms were altered into phonograms, all likeness to actual pictures was lost. In Sumer each syllable became a design of large and small wedges made by sticking the point of a bamboo stick or bone into the wet clay. This kind of writing is called *cuneiform* (wedge-form from the Latin *cuneus*, wedges). Sumerian cuneiform is hard to learn to read because it has 560 different syllable combinations of wedge marks. This served to restrict the knowledge of writing to a small number of people.

In the muddy plain of Sumer there was no stone and a shortage of wood. Of clay, however, there was an ample supply. Clay was the material on which the Sumerians left their records.

The baked tablets of the Sumerians and their successors are so hard as to be imperishable. Hundreds of thousands of them exist, many recovered from libraries established by the kings, and the translation of all those found, and yet to be found, will go on into the distant future, making clearer bit by bit the history of the peoples of the Fertile Crescent.

To sign their records and letters, the Sumerians made beautifully carved seals from hard stone. The seals carried the name of a person or, if the signature was that of a ziggurat priest, the symbol of a god. Some of the

A cylinder seal (right) and its impression. A hunting scene in the mountains decorates the seal of Balu-ili the Cup Bearer (his signature appears on the upper left-hand corner of the impression). Seals were in continuous use in Mesopotamia for some 3,000 years. They had both everyday and mythological themes. The subject matter was usually stylized into a repetitive decorative pattern, sometimes without, sometimes with action, such as in this example from the Akkadian period of Sumerian history.

seals were inscribed on the flat side of an otherwise oval stone, and a hole was bored through the upper part of the seal, which made it possible to carry the seal on a string around the neck. Such seals were sometimes made of semiprecious stone such as chalcedony. The Sumerians also carved small cylinders with inscriptions or symbols or pictures. By rolling the cylinder seal on the damp clay tablet a continuing impression could be made.

In all early civilizations writing was regarded as magical. To be able to write a name was thought to give the writer magical power over the person or thing named. In many early societies writing was guarded as a priestly secret, and it was taboo to say or write the names of special gods or kings. In Egypt the people spoke of "Pharaoh," *Per-aa*, meaning Great House, not of "King" So-and-so.

Cuneiform writing was used by the Sumerians for a thousand years, and for two thousand more by the peoples that followed them in the Middle East. As a result, the later people knew Sumerian literature and mythology, and so the ideas of the Sumerians were kept alive long after they themselves had passed away.

EGYPT: THE FIRST UNIFIED STATE

From the far distant mountains of Ethiopia in East Africa and from Uganda in central Africa, the Nile flows north to the Mediterranean, making a narrow ribbon of green vegetation through brown deserts that crowd in on both sides. On its way to the sea cataracts, or waterfalls, interrupt the river's path. There are six, numbered First, Second, Third, . . . from north to south. The First Cataract, at present-day Aswan or ancient Elephantine, was for a long time the southern boundary of ancient Egypt. It represented the farthest point to which the river boats could sail without being unloaded and hauled overland. Subsequently the Egyptians expanded their territory south into the regions of Africa between the First and Fourth cataracts, the land of Nubia and Kush (modern Sudan).

THE NILE AND THE LAND OF EGYPT

Without the Nile there would have been no Egypt. As the Greek historian Herodotus put it, "Egypt is the gift of the river." Without the Nile's overflow and the silt it deposited over the land, Egypt would have remained part of the deserts that enclose it on either side.

The ancient Egyptians did not know why the river overflowed or even where it came from. Its source remained a mystery until about a hundred years ago, when an Englishman, John Speke, discovered that it started on its 4,145-mile journey to the sea from Lake Victoria in Uganda. This Nile, called the White Nile because of its milky-colored waters, is joined at Khartoum in the Sudan by the clear waters of its primary tributary, the

The Nile. On the great river that is central to the existence of Egypt, feluccas, or river boats, sail north. On the lower right is a village with beehive-shaped houses, and mosques. In the background is the desert that continuously presses on the cultivated land.

Blue Nile, which rises in the mountains of Ethiopia, ancient Abyssinia. From June to September the waters of the Blue Nile are swelled by heavy rainfall and the melting of the Ethiopian snows. This causes the level of the river to rise and eventually to overflow its banks. Until the building of the High Dam at Aswan in the 1960's, the river flooded annually from June to December.

The Nile was central to the civilization of the ancient Egyptian. In its waters and on its banks teamed the fish and wildlife that not only supplied food but also provided hours of amusement in hunting and fowling. Over its waters, which flowed north, the peasant, courier, and soldier could move easily between all parts of the kingdom; when he wished to return upstream, he merely raised his sails, for the prevailing winds blew south. The river was bounded either by the cliff of the valley through which the river flowed or by the sands of the desert, and it never changed its course or overflowed unpredictably. Regularly, surely, the river rose, flooded, or fell. The peasant named the seasons of the year from its rhythm: Seed Time, Flood Time, Harvest Time.

In ancient times the Nile emptied into the Mediterranean through several different branches that formed a steamy, marshy triangular delta. During the Ice Ages two outlets had also been formed to the Red Sea: the Wadi Hammamat in the south and the Wadi Tumilat in the north. The Wadi Hammamat was dry by historic times, but its bed served as an overland route and its walls as a quarry. The Wadi Tumilat was last dredged during Roman times and is now dry, but when it was kept free of silt during times of prosperity, ships could pass from the Mediterranean up the Delta, over to the Red Sea, and on to the east.

Ancient Egypt consisted of the six-hundred-mile valley from the First Cataract at Elephantine north to the Mediterranean. Upper Egypt, upstream, the valley, was clear and dry, and the sun blazed across the sky day after day. Lower Egypt, downstream, the Delta, was more humid with occasional rain, but it was very fertile. In Upper Egypt the cultivated land stretched out on both sides of the river to a maximum width of seven miles. The distinction between the cultivated land and the desert was so sharp that one could stand with a foot in each. The Egyptians called their land *Kemet*, the Black Land, distinguishing it from the Red Land, the surrounding deserts.

To the ancient Egyptian, life was good. Blessed with fertile soil nourished by a river whose rhythm was constant, defended by natural frontiers of desert and sea, he was amply supplied with food and the natural resources

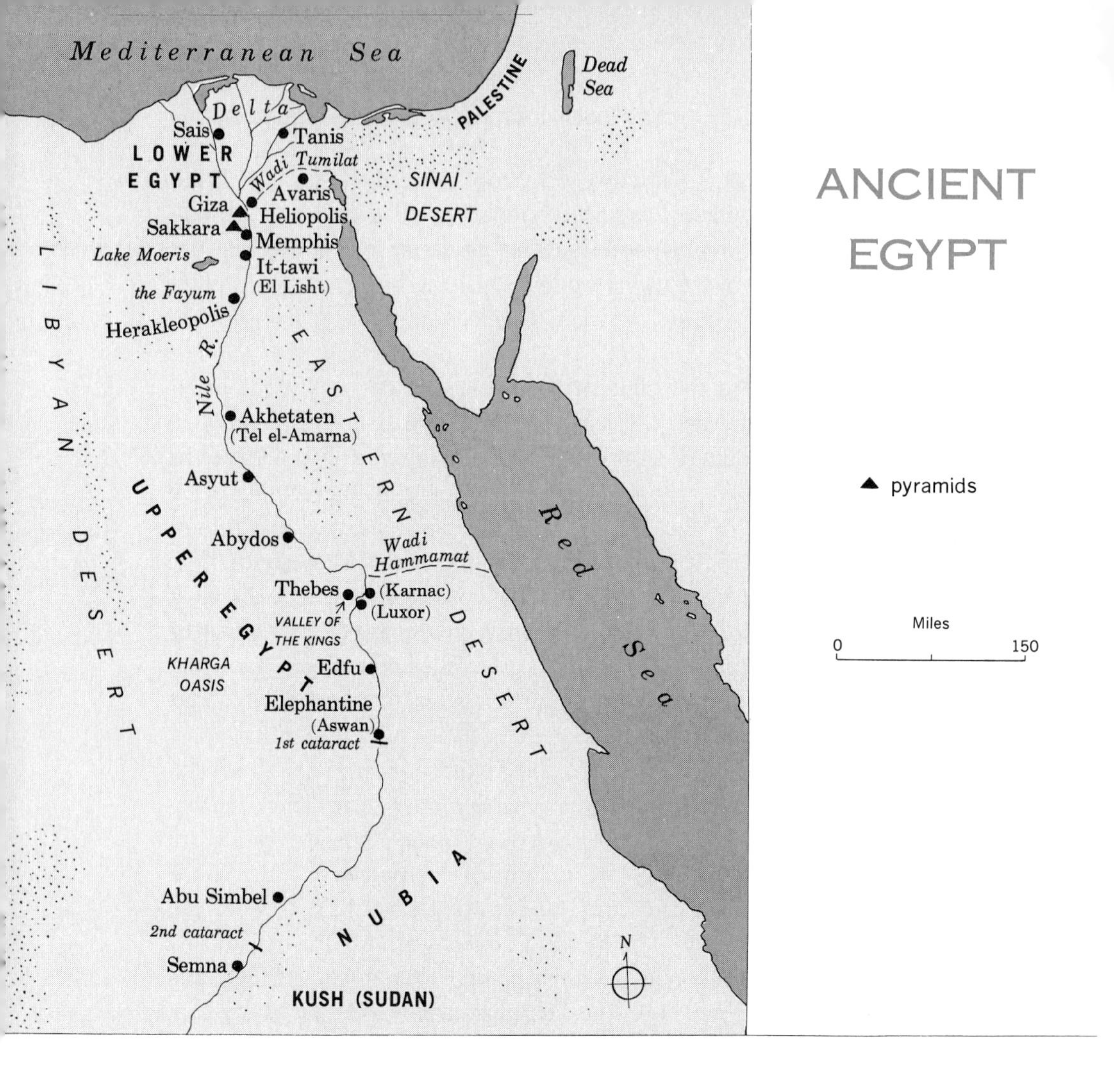

needed for civilization to grow. He was warmed by a sun that rose every day, shone in splendor, and sank in a blazing ball behind the flat horizon only to rise once again uninterrupted by storm or rain. Egypt was never-changing, secure, serene, beautiful in the sparkling clearness of the day and the velvety blackness of the star-studded night, and its civilization reflected the stability of its environment.

PREDYNASTIC EGYPT

During the period 3600–3200 B.C., life in the Nile Valley was undergoing a number of changes that eventually led to the rise of civilization. Scholars refer to this period as *predynastic* because it immediately preceded the founding of Egypt's dynasties, or families of kings.

From about 5000 B.C. Egypt had been the site of a sequence of Neolithic cultures, each more developed than the one before it. During the second Neolithic culture in the Nile Valley (c. 4000 B.C.) the donkey was introduced as a beast of burden. It was brought into Egypt by newcomers from Libya who worshiped a goddess of whose name we know only the letters N T. This goddess carried a spear, and her clothing included a goatskin bib around her neck. She was a goddess of the underworld, as was shown by the great serpent that accompanied her, and she was the patroness of war and of the peacetime craft of weaving. We will meet her later again in other countries to which her worship spread (page 73). The Libyan men wore their hair in a long side lock curling over one shoulder and they wore peculiar loin cloths instead of the kilts worn by other early Egyptians. These facts are significant because they are the key to tracing the migration of some of these people to another land, Crete, as we shall see later in the chapter.

Between 3500 B.C. and 3000 B.C. Egyptian life showed the influence of two groups of strangers from Asia. First, Semitic migrants appeared from Arabia. The Semites, as they are called, made little change in the life of the Neolithic Egyptians with whom they mingled. They were followed by a group from the eastern Mediterranean, probably from Syria or the lands to the north. The second group introduced new grains and the grape vine.

There were many other signs of growth and change in predynastic Egypt. Boats were invented to sail the Nile. They were made of bundles of reeds tied together and propelled by oars. Trade was greatly expanded, bringing in new materials. The beautiful blue lapis lazuli used in jewelry for the kings and images of the gods came all the way from distant Baluchistan (modern Pakistan), probably by way of Sumer and then along the Fertile Crescent route. Images of the gods, formerly fashioned in pottery, were made of metal cast in molds.

The gods the Egyptians were to worship in historic times were taking form. Like most primitive peoples, the Neolithic Egyptians identified each clan or tribe with an animal totem. This totem had magical associations for the people, who regarded it as their ancestor or as their protector. The tribal totems became the gods of the first cities. One of the most important was the hawk-falcon, Horus. Two other animals, the cobra and the vulture, also appeared in earliest times. In historic Egypt the vulture and the cobra were depicted on the king's headpieces to represent Upper and Lower Egypt, while the falcon Horus represented the king himself (see photograph, page 84).

THE FIRST UNIONS

Historians believe that sometime around 3400 B.C. the villages of Lower Egypt formed a union. At about the same time, it is thought, the villages of Upper Egypt also joined together. The rivalry that seems to have existed between the two areas led to warfare, and at one time Lower Egypt conquered Upper Egypt as far south as the First Cataract. We do not know how long the conquest lasted, but it did not produce a lasting union. Around 3200 B.C., however, a chieftain of Upper Egypt marched north. He conquered the Delta lands and unified Egypt. Egyptian tradition identifies the conqueror as Menes and counts him as the founder of the First Dynasty and the builder of a capital city, Memphis, near the junction of the upper valley and the Delta.

The stele or palette of Narmer. Left, King Narmer, identified by many scholars as Menes, conquers his foe, Lower Egypt. Right, the king defeats his foreign enemies, symbolically lined up with their heads at their feet. We do not know the meaning of the animals with twisted necks, but portraying fantastic animals was Mesopotamian. The palette, dated about 3200 B.C., shows the king wearing the white crown of Upper Egypt on the left, and the red crown of Lower Egypt on the right. The union of the Two Lands, therefore, has been effected, and this stele probably commemorates that great achievement. The stylization of the palette with several artistic devices used throughout Egyptian history—different levels for the action, the figures portrayed either full-faced, sideways, or from above, the stance of the king—are seen here for the first time, fully developed at this very early date.

THE ARCHAIC PERIOD: DYNASTIES ONE AND TWO, 3200–2800 B.C.

The chronology of the dynasties of Egypt has come down to us from fragments of a list that was compiled by Manetho, an Egyptian priest who lived around 300 B.C. He divided Egyptian rulers into thirty dynasties, and for convenience modern historians have continued to use his classifications. There is, however, disagreement on the dates of the first two dynasties. For the present we can say tentatively that the First Dynasty lasted from 3200–2900 B.C. and the Second came to an end about 2800 B.C.

The union of Egypt under the kings of the First and Second Dynasties was one in name only. In the middle of the Second Dynasty the shaky union of the two kingdoms collapsed into a civil war, which lasted through the reigns of several kings. Royal monuments and tombs were destroyed by the rebels. The ninth and last king of the Second Dynasty finally pacified the country and left it stable and firmly united.

Very little knowledge exists about Egyptian society under the first two dynasties. It is known that there were three distinct social classes: the nobility, probably descended from the tribal chiefs of Neolithic days, who claimed as their own the former tribal estates; the artisans; and the peasants. The great mass of the people were in the last category and were employed primarily in agriculture. They also worked in the mines and quarries, in military service, and at building temples, palaces, and tombs. The social system was not rigid in early Egypt. A man's career depended on his natural abilities and the favor of the king. This flexibility in allowing a skillful craftsman to advance to important positions in the government endured for perhaps two or three centuries.

In the days of the First and Second Dynasties the tomb of a king or a great noble consisted of a pit about twelve feet deep enclosing a series of brick rooms. The central room was used for the burial, and the others were filled with the personal belongings of the dead person. The pit was roofed with heavy timber, on top of which was a thick layer of crushed stone and earth. On top of this, at ground level, was built a *mastaba*, a rectangular structure of bricks. The goods placed in the mastaba were less valuable than those buried in the pit beneath. The outer walls of the mastaba were built up to a height of twenty to twenty-five feet and were painted with bright colors to imitate the mats and carpets that hung in people's homes. An enclosure wall separated the mastaba from the rows of graves of the owner's servants, killed so they could serve him in the other world. This practice ended during the Second Dynasty. Thereafter, small carved figures replaced human beings as servants to the dead.

Writing. By 3000 B.C. writing in Egypt had been perfected. In Sumer the earliest use of writing was for business records, such as inventories and bills of sale. In Egypt writing was primarily for religious purposes and was carved on stone or inscribed on a kind of paper that the Egyptians made from papyrus reeds.

The Egyptian system of writing is called *hieroglyphic,* and the symbols are called *hieroglyphs* from the Greek for "sacred carvings." Hieroglyphics is a combination system. It has ideograms (𓁹 eye), phonograms representing groups of consonants as well as single words (𓏌 nw = pot), and phonograms representing single consonant sounds (𓏏 t). After a word was written, a final sign, the determinative, was added at the end just to make sure the meaning was clear. For example the ancient Egyptian name for Egypt was Kemet: 𓆎𓅓𓏏𓊖 𓆎=*km*; 𓅓=*m*; 𓏏=*t*; 𓊖= the determinative: the sign for a village with crossroads dividing it into quarters.

Hieroglyphics remained in use for religious and royal records throughout Egyptian ancient history, although later the Egyptians invented two simplified systems of writing, hieratic (priestly) and demotic, which were used

The Rosetta Stone. The great French scholar Jean Champollion used the inscriptions on this stone to decipher hieroglyphics. The discovery of the stone was an accident. In the late eighteenth century, French soldiers in Egypt were digging in the Rosetta branch of the Nile Delta, where they uncovered a black stone covered with writing. Scholars determined that the writing was hieroglyphics (top), an unknown language that turned out to be demotic (center), and Greek (bottom). Champollion correctly guessed the three inscriptions said the same thing in three different languages. As he knew Greek, he checked the symbols enclosed in circles called cartouches (which scholars knew denoted the king's name) against the corresponding word in Greek and so matched off the symbols. Knowledge of hieroglyphics had been lost since the first centuries A.D.

for everyday purposes. For some reason the Egyptians never took the step of using only the consonant (alphabetic) signs exclusively, though they had 24. Nevertheless, the Egyptian alphabet signs had great influence on the formation of the Semitic alphabet script, which is the basis of our own.

In developing hieroglyphics the Egyptians produced signs for the consonants but never bothered to develop any for the vowels. For one who knew the language it was enough to write DG for the reader to know that *dog* was meant. (DD TH DG DG THT HL N TH GRDN?) As a result, modern historians must guess at the missing vowels in ancient Egyptian words. Many use Greek spelling after 300 B.C. For the city MNFR, for example, we accept the Greek *Memphis*. For the god SR, we use the Greek *Osiris*. But we must remember that they are Greek spellings and not Egyptian. When there is no Greek model, the historian uses his own judgment. Was TTMS Thotmes, Tutmoses, Tatmusa, Atithimese? Students will find variant spellings for Egyptian names in the different books they read.

CIVILIZATION BEGINS IN CRETE

Four hundred miles northwest of the Egyptian delta lies the island of Crete. African Libya is two hundred miles to the south, and the mainland of Asia is two hundred miles to the northeast (see map, page 134). Crete lies directly on the line of volcanic and earthquake disturbance that runs east and west through the Mediterranean, and from the beginning the Cretans worshiped the god of the deep sea, who tossed the earth much as an angry bull tosses a man on its horns.

Men of neolithic culture first reached the island between 6000 and 5000 B.C. They settled in the mountains that dominate the Cretan landscape, and in mountain caves they made their first homes, worshiped tiny female idols, and buried their dead.

Most of the early Cretans were small slender people, probably of Libyan descent, although some skeletal remains suggest the broader head and stockier bone structure of the people of Asia. Like neolithic people everywhere, they were organized in clans and tribes.

About 3200 B.C. a large number of newcomers reached southern Crete. Their religious symbols—the trident, the double axe, the shield shaped like the numeral 8—were those of the Delta tribes of Lower Egypt. The Libyan goddess N T, with her spear, snake, spindle, and goatskin bib, came with them, and she remained one of their chief deities. Other evidences of the newcomers' Egyptian or Libyan origin was the soldiers' custom of training their hair in a long lock curled over one shoulder and their use of a peculiarly shaped loin cloth instead of a kilt. It seems likely that these people may have been fleeing from Menes's conquest of Lower Egypt (page 70). They mixed with the Neolithic Cretans of the mountains to form the Cretans of civilization.

The population of the island increased slowly. Men came down from the mountains to build their houses in valleys and along the sea coast. Single village settlements joined together into small towns along the eastern and southern coasts facing the Fertile Crescent and Egypt, with both of which the Cretans traded. The first civilized Cretans naturally turned to the sea, becoming the first naval people in history. Their long narrow ships with slim oars sailed north to the Cyclades Islands for marble, lead, and copper and south to Egypt for ivory.

As the Cretans moved slowly from neolithic to civilized life, writing was invented, pottery was made and painted, copper was smelted. The search for metal ores led to the founding of many new settlements. Perhaps the stimulus for writing and the techniques of painting came from Egypt and the Fertile Crescent, but from its very earliest days it was clear that Cretan civilization was not going to be a second-hand copy of either of the other two. Cretan writing resembled neither hieroglyphics nor cuneiform. Artistic designs were those suggested by sea creatures or by flowers or animals native to Crete. Cretan artists were endlessly inventive with new designs and forms as long as Cretan civilization lasted, and they had a special love of, and flair for, objects on a small scale (page 133).

While the coastal people were moving into civilization, the mountain areas remained neolithic in culture, and mountain caves continued to be used for religious shrines.

Crete was near enough to the continents of Asia and Africa to receive migrations of settlers from both and yet far enough away from them to be able to work out its own ideas without interference. Because of its nearness to the Greek mainland, Crete is considered to be part of the continent of Europe. It is interesting to note that of the first civilizations developed by man, one was in Asia, one was in Africa, and one was in Europe.

❦ ❦ ❦

In 2800 B.C. a bird's eye view of the world would have shown three civilizations lying side by side, the more developed and fully urbanized Egyptian and Sumerian and the younger Cretan. The three were surrounded by a zone of neolithic culture that had spread outward from its original home in the Middle East to southern Spain, northern France, southern Britain, eastern Sicily, southern Italy, Greece, and Central Europe and to northern China, Japan, and India. Beyond the zone of neolithic life, the rest of mankind still struggled to find food in the Old Stone Age way.

People, Places, and Terms

Sumerians	Assyria	civilized	artisan
Egyptians	Babylonia	Urban Revolution	delta
Cretans	Armenia	literate	cataract
Libyans	Elam	institution	hieroglyphics
	Upper Egypt	ziggurat	pharaoh
Nile River	Lower Egypt	mastaba	theocracy
Arabian Desert	Memphis	pictogram	savage
Fertile Crescent	Crete	ideogram	barbarian
Palestine		phonogram	hypothesis
Persian Gulf	primitive	cuneiform	

Mastering the Reading

1. In what ways are Sumerian origins and early accomplishments clouded in mystery? What gains had the early Sumerians made by 3000 B.C.?
2. What was the significance of the following to Sumerian life: the ziggurat, 60 seconds, Council of the Gods, priests, Tammuz and Ishtar?
3. In what specific ways was Egypt a "gift" of the Nile? In what ways may geography have influenced the outlook of the Sumerians? the Egyptians?
4. In what ways was Cretan culture like that of Egypt and the Fertile Crescent, and in what ways was it distinctly Cretan?

Interpreting the Text

1. How did villages enable men to specialize? How did specialization lead to cities?
2. What reasons can you think of to explain why the Egyptians united but the Sumerians did not?

Exploring Beyond the Text

1. Present a report on Jean Champollion's efforts to crack the code of hieroglyphics.
2. Philologists have translated the Sumerian clay tablets. Read some of the translations. What could a political scientist, a sociologist, and a child psychologist learn about Sumerian life from these tablets?

5

Civilization Flowers: The Early Bronze Age

2800–2000 B.C.

During the eight centuries following 2800 B.C., Egypt and Sumer rose to new heights in the arts of civilization. In Egypt the period was one of stability and continuity in government and society. In Mesopotamia several peoples ruled the land between the Tigris and Euphrates, each absorbing and then building on the cultural attainments of the talented Sumerians.

During the same period another river valley people, those living along the Indus River in what is now Pakistan, took their place beside civilized man. Their civilization seems to have arisen abruptly and to have ended just as abruptly. At the same time, in Crete and the Aegean civilization was moving forward, while in Europe and China Neolithic culture was spreading and developing.

The end of this period seems to teach a new and alarming lesson. Although man may make gains in improving his condition, he can also lose his hard-won victories. Permanence is not a mark of civilization.

THE INVENTION OF BRONZE

One of the ways in which civilizations differ from primitive cultures is in using metal tools instead of stone ones. We have seen that the first metal so used was copper. The use of copper was followed by the invention of bronze, an alloy, or mixture, harder than copper and therefore more serviceable for tools and weapons. Precisely where and when this discovery was made is not yet known. It is likely that coppersmiths in Egypt, Sumer, and Crete could not help noticing that copper ore contained traces of other minerals, such as nickel or tin. This suggests that the discovery that tin and copper make the strongest combination may have been made in more than one place. It is certain that by 2500 B.C. civilized people were using the new mixture of copper and tin to make bronze.

The use of bronze gave its name to a new age in man's development. This age lasted from about 2800 B.C. to approximately 1000 B.C., when iron ore, discovered and worked perhaps as early as 1500 B.C. by the Hittites, replaced copper as the primary metal in civilization. Iron, unlike bronze, is plentiful and cheap. Once the knowledge of how to smelt it became widespread, every village smith in both civilized and neolithic communities could use it. The widespread use of iron inaugurated another new age in the history of man.

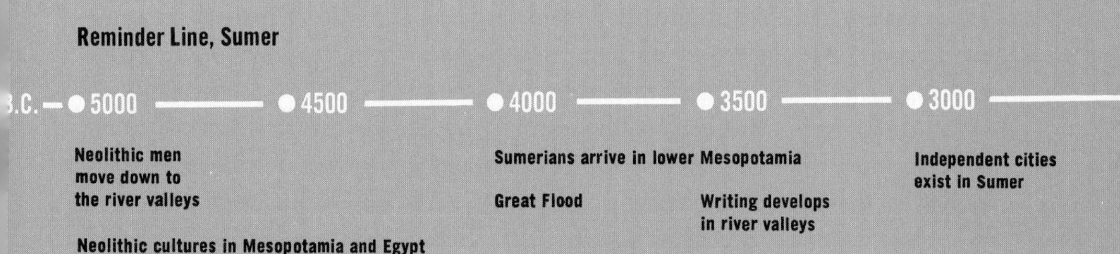

EARLY DYNASTIC SUMER AND UNION IN MESOPOTAMIA

By 2800 B.C. the plain of Sumer had turned into a land of divided city-states struggling with each other for supremacy. Chief among the contenders were the cities of Ur, Kish, Erech, and Lagash. About 2700 B.C. hereditary royal families (dynasties) had established themselves, and Ur became the predominant city. This period of Mesopotamian history, known as Early Dynastic Sumer, was followed by the unifications of Sargon and Ur-Nammu. These unifications did not last, and the city-states of Sumer were eclipsed by the spread of civilization to new centers farther north.

SUMERIAN GOVERNMENT

The government of each city seems to have rested in an assembly of all free males and a group of elders bound together by allegiance to the city's chief god. Actions by the assembly required unanimous agreement. Such a system could not work swiftly, and often, of course, unanimity was impossible to achieve. To meet emergencies such as war, flood, or famine, a temporary single ruler, the *lugal,* was appointed. At the end of the emergency the lugalship ended, and power was returned to the assembly and the elders. After 2800 B.C., as the cities increased in size and warfare between them became more common, the cities found themselves in conditions of continual emergency. Under these conditions an important political change took place. One-man rule became permanent in Sumer.

The chief priest of the city's god was often the person chosen to be ruler. This was a logical choice because he was already the head of an economic organization involving many of the citizens. In such cases he was called not *lugal* but *ensi,* a religious title reminding the people that he was the god's "tenant-farmer," presumably having the god's support in his rule.

Whether the ruler was the civilian *lugal* or the priestly *ensi,* he acquired his governing post through his position as agent of the assembly or agent of the god. Although the supreme power came to be handed down from father to son, the inheritance was not based on the concept of the family's right to kingship. Instead, it seemed to the Sumerians to have been an expression of the god's will to the inheritor, which passed more easily from father to son than from stranger to stranger. After 2700 B.C. lugalships and ensiships remained in certain families, and Sumer became a land of dynastic rulers.

OCCUPATIONS IN ANCIENT SUMER

Each ziggurat community controlled lands outside the city walls and formed a self-contained economic and social unit. Within each community were officials, priests, merchants, craftsmen, farmers, herdsmen, fishermen, and slaves. Everyone had a job and responsibility within his community. Blind people worked in the fruit orchards. Soldiers worked during peacetime as carpenters, bricklayers, gardeners, fishermen, or harvesters. Prisoners of war were held by the priests rather than by private individuals, and they worked as porters, or gardeners, or in other jobs alongside the citizens. Women had legal equality with men in Sumer and had important tasks to fulfill. They were assigned work on the farms outside the walls and were cooks, brewers of beer, and makers of wine inside the city. Many of the young people were apprenticed to the craft unions or guilds, which taught them their particular arts and crafts. Slave girls assisted the women and cared for the animals.

Each person had his or her assigned tasks. Each then shared in the products and produce of the community.

Another important and valuable part of the economic unit of the city-states was the large animal population. Oxen and donkeys were used to pull plows, carts, and chariots. Goats and sheep were raised for wool, hides, and milk, and pigs were raised for their meat.

BURIAL CUSTOMS OF THE SUMERIANS

The Sumerian rulers were buried beneath the courtyards of their houses. Dynastic graves at Ur have revealed the dead man's bodyguard, his male and female attendants, and in one case 68 women robed in all their finery, the oxen still yoked to the royal chariots, all lying in neat rows outside the royal burial chamber. Daggers, helmets, bowls, statues, and other objects of great magnificence, many made of gold, lay in the tombs with dishes of copper, silver, alabaster, marble, and volcanic glass, and harps, gameboards, and other objects decorated with mosaics of semiprecious jewels. Food and drink were also placed near the dead ruler for his use in the afterlife.

From the royal grave at Ur clothing of the dead attendants reveals that they were persons of importance, not slaves. There was no disarray or disturbance of the skeletons. This seems to suggest that death was voluntary. In one burial a lady of the court had apparently been late for the ceremony. Still rolled up in her pocket was the blue hair ribbon she had not had time to put on, a hair ribbon unrolled by an archaeologist 4,800 years later.

The practice of many peoples at a certain stage of their culture is to kill the servants and retainers of their chiefs on the death of the ruler. They believe that the dead chieftain would thus be assured of the service and attention in the world of the dead that he was accustomed to receive in that of the living. In Sumer this practice seems to have been adopted during the Early Dynastic Period, but it was given up at the end of that era, about the same time, roughly, as in Egypt (page 71).

Two objects from the Royal Cemetery at Ur. Left, a helmet. Right, a bull's head decoration on the top of a lyre. The helmet, made of gold, imitates a wig, with the details of the hair carefully modeled. The inside of Sumerian helmets was lined with cloth and held in place by thongs passing through holes along the lower edge. The bull, curiously wearing a beard, is made of gold leaf over a wooden core; his hair and beard are of lapis lazuli. Both objects show the admirable skill of the Sumerians in making small objects.

Although the practice of human sacrifice existed in Early Dynastic Sumer, it was restricted to royal burials. Commoners and nobles were buried with weapons, ornaments, and food but with no human companions.

END OF EARLY DYNASTIC SUMER

About 2500 B.C. the city of Ur lost the predominance it had acquired over the other Sumerian cities. Leadership passed to other cities, among them Lagash and Umma. Eventually, about 2400 B.C., all were conquered and brought into union by Sargon of Agade.

UNION OF SUMER AND AKKAD UNDER SARGON (SHARRU-KINU)

The unity the cities of the Sumerian plain had never achieved, indeed, had even struggled against through the first centuries of their existence, was imposed on them forcibly from the outside. The man who achieved their unification was Sharru-kinu, better known by the Greek version of his name, Sargon. He was probably a Sumerian since his early career was as a minor official in Kish, but he left the delta plain, and upriver in the region of Akkad, he founded the city of Agade, about 2350 B.C.

The people of Akkad were for the most part Semites from Arabia who had given up their nomadic lives in the desert to settle in the fertile river valley. From their contacts with the cities of Sumer, they learned the arts of civilization, retaining only their Semitic language but writing it in Sumerian cuneiform. Sargon's conquest of Sumer was the first of many steps in spreading Sumerian culture throughout the Fertile Crescent.

For 160 years Sargon and his descendants ruled the united kingdom of Sumer-Akkad. It was a period of prosperity, a growing population, and flourishing business at home.

The businessmen of Sumer-Akkad kept abreast of the expanding economy by inventing bookkeeping and devising new banking techniques, including credit, loans, and interest. Trade involved many contacts with foreign people. From the seaports of Sumer merchants sailed with their cargoes to India, and to them came ships from the civilization in the Indus Valley. From the upriver centers in Akkad boats carried goods up the Euphrates as far as the Anatolian plateau, from which point caravans of donkeys continued north into the neolithic regions of Armenia and Anatolia, or westward to Syria. Semitic Akkadian became the language of everyday life and business in the Fertile Crescent, and cuneiform became familiar throughout the Middle East. The ancient Sumerian speech was used only in religious rituals. The growing body of new literature, which included tales of heroes, mythology, dictionaries, grammars, and books on astronomy and medicine, were written in Akkadian.

END OF THE UNION OF SUMER-AKKAD

In spite of the unity imposed on them by Sargon's dynasty, the old cities of Sumer remained fiercely individualistic and continually plotted to recover their ancient independence. They seized such opportunities as the death of a king and the succession of a new one to erupt into civil war. At the same time the prosperity of Sumer-Akkad excited the desires of the uncivilized tribes of the neighboring peoples of Arabia and of Assyria, who used every disturbance within Mesopotamia as an opportunity to infiltrate the valley. From the east came a succession of attacks by the tribes living in the hills. Elam had never accepted Sumerian or Akkadian rule. Finally, a revolt within Sumer-Akkad in 2180 B.C. coincided with attacks by the Elamites and other hill tribes. The Sargonid dynasty was overthrown, and the union of Sumer-Akkad fell apart.

SUMER'S LAST GREAT DAYS: THE THIRD DYNASTY OF UR

About 2075 B.C. the city of Ur expelled its conquerors and brought Sumer, Akkad, and Elam under its sway. At no other time in its long history was Ur so important. The Third Dynasty of Ur was founded by Ur-Nammu, a great soldier and a great ruler famed for his justice and his good works. His dominions equaled those of Sargon two centuries earlier and stretched from the Persian Gulf to the Mediterranean Sea along the Fertile Crescent. His dynasty lasted about 125 years, until 1950 B.C. At that time, caught between eastern and western invaders, among them tribesmen from Arabia, Ur was overwhelmed and its last king carried off as a captive.

In the century that followed, political chaos reigned in the Fertile Crescent. Population dwindled, invaders ran roughshod over the land, and the economy and society were reduced to the lowest point in a thousand years. Just as in Egypt at the same time (page 93), civilization seemed in danger of perishing.

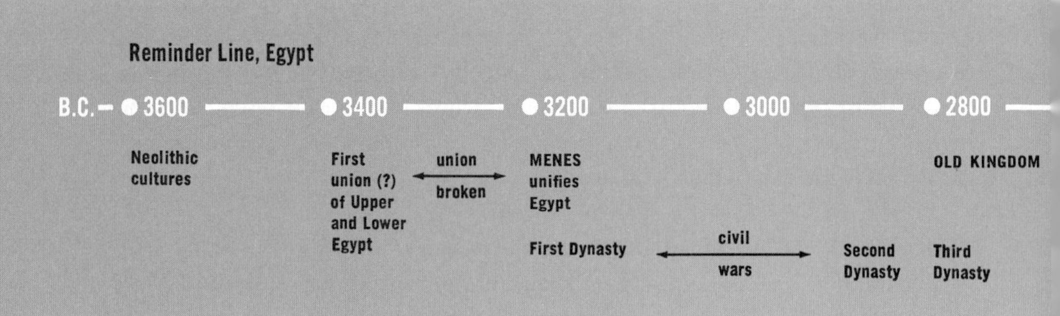

EGYPT: THE OLD KINGDOM, C. 2800–2200 B.C.

The six centuries following 2800 B.C. in Egypt are known as the Old Kingdom. This period is also called the Pyramid Age, because at this time the Egyptians built those remarkable tombs we call pyramids to house their dead kings. The term is not quite accurate, however, as pyramids were built for several centuries after the Old Kingdom had collapsed.

The Old Kingdom includes Dynasties Three to Six. During these dynasties a full flowering of the growth in the first two dynasties took place. The Old Kingdom established the pattern of life that lasted for the next 2,500 years. It worked out a theory of government and forms of administration, religious beliefs, and artistic conventions that were so right to Egyptian thinking that no need was seen later to improve them. During the Old Kingdom communications were established with people living in surrounding lands, and trade extended as far north as Phoenicia, as far east as the Red Sea coast to the land of Punt, probably modern Somalia, and south to beyond the Second Cataract of the Nile.

With the Sixth Dynasty came a gradual collapse of government. The king lost control of his nobles, and this resulted in a general weakening of Egyptian civilization and a period of upheaval that lasted for a couple of centuries, a time known as the First Intermediate Period, or Feudal Age.

THE KINGSHIP AND THE GOVERNMENT

The king in ancient Egypt held a very special place in the lives and minds of the people. He was accepted as "a god by whose dealings one lives, the father and mother of all men, alone by himself, without equal." These are the words of the great noble Rekhmire, vizier (first minister) to King Thutmose III, who lived some fifteen hundred years after the unification of the Two Lands. Let us look at them more closely.

The king is "a god . . ." Upon creation, so the Egyptians believed, Egypt was ruled by a god. This god came to be identified as Re. After a while Re decided to return to heaven, but he did not abandon Egypt; he left his son, who had an Egyptian mother, to rule in his place. His son, Horus, was not merely the representative of a god but was a god himself, the Son of Re.

The king "is a god by whose dealings one lives . . ." Leadership in the river valleys arose from the need to regulate the annual flood. Without the Nile, life in Egypt could not have existed. The function of the king was to preside over the waters of the river by conducting the rituals that would insure a beneficial overflow. As a god, the king had influence with his relatives in heaven and could make sure the flood was not too high and not too low.

The king is ". . . the father and mother of all men . . ." The king of Egypt was ruler of all men, foreigners as well as Egyptians. Surrounding peoples were expected to acknowledge this, and scenes painted on the walls of the tombs show tribute offered to the king from allies as well as from subject peoples.

Horus. The king is represented as the hawk-god Horus. He wears the double crown of the Two Lands: the white crown of Upper Egypt within the Red Crown of Lower Egypt. The sacred cobra or uraeus curves over the crown. The god stands over the hieroglyphics of two of his names: on the left, his coronation name, Kakhepere (Ka 𓂓 , Kheper 𓆣 , Re 𓇳); and on the right, his birth name, Senwosret.

Lastly, the king is ". . . alone by himself, without equal." The god who ruled Egypt naturally owned all the land and everything in it. He controlled all the products of mines, quarries, workshops. He was chief priest, head of the government, commander-in-chief of the army. To carry out his duties he appointed officials to act for him, but they were deputies only.

Finally, the king was the personification of the divine order that existed since the beginning. The divine order was made visible through the workings of truth, justice, and order, which the Egyptians called *maat*. *Maat* could be overthrown by evil, but its restoration was necessary for the state to function properly.

The king, then, had no equal throughout Egypt. He was the god in whose hands lay the welfare of the land. The king coordinated nature (the Nile) and society (the government and the economy) and established *maat* for the well-being of the people. Without the king the Egyptian state could not exist, never had existed, and, as we shall see, fell into disorder when the kingship weakened.

We would very much like to be able to explain how the theory of divine kingship originated, to know exactly how the divinity of the king evolved. But we do not. All we can deduce is that the idea suited the Egyptian temperament, for it lasted throughout Egyptian history, and that it had its origins far back in the centuries before Egypt became civilized. Before unification, each province (*nome*) of Egypt had been ruled by its local god as king. The king embodied the attributes of the particular totem-divinity with which the nome was associated. One of these divinities was the hawk, Horus. Horus had been the totem of the clan of Upper Egypt that came north with Menes when Egypt was unified. He was now identified as the son of Re who had been left behind to rule in his father's place. To complicate matters further, the king was identified not only with Horus but also with the god of the underworld, Osiris (page 87), as well as with the god of the sun, Re. Although all these identifications may be confusing to us, they represented to the ancient Egyptian the totality of the divine kingship in heaven, on earth, and in the underworld.

The Duties of the King. To the king, alone without equal, fell the government of the kingdom. Daily he consulted with his officials about ruling the land. He kept a close watch on the irrigation projects and officiated at the opening of new ones. He knew how many jars of wheat and bolts of linen were collected in taxes and how much copper, gold, and turquoise was mined in Sinai. The caravans of donkeys moving up the Nile into the Sudan, the land of Kush, to trade for ebony, ivory, ostrich feathers, and fragrant gums were sent at his command. He was informed of the expeditions by sea to the land of Punt and of those returning from Phoenicia and Palestine with cedarwood, wine, and precious oils and resins to embalm the dead. The king supervised the storage of the products in his warehouses and their distribution in time of need.

As commander-in-chief of the army, the king personally led his troops in battle. During the Old Kingdom fighting seems to have been limited to punitive raids to control the border tribes: the Nubians of the south, the Libyans of the west, and the Asiatics, as the people of western Asia were called. As chief priest, the king was the mediator between heaven and earth, but priests conducted ceremonies and honored the gods in his name and offered sacrifices of food and wine.

As head of the government the king controlled the administration, although he was assisted by his officials. The greatest officials were the viziers, or chief ministers, one for Upper and one for Lower Egypt. Below the viziers was a hierarchy of lesser officials, and scribes. At first the vizier was the king's brother or another close member of his family, but later the post fell to the great nobles, and toward the end of the Old Kingdom it became hereditary.

Harvest scene from the tomb of Menna, Scribe of the Fields of the Lord of the Two Lands. At the upper left, the fields are measured by a rope knotted at regular intervals. Boys hold the supplies of the scribes and workers. The scribes (wearing shirts) take down the measurements. To the right, a couple brings refreshments. On the lower register, a horse and chariot wait to take away the produce of the fields. Workers collect the grain as scribes note down the amounts. To the right, Menna receives wine. The scene is typical of many that were carved or painted on the walls of tombs throughout Egyptian history, except that during the Old Kingdom the horse and chariot were unknown in Egypt; this painting is from the later New Kingdom. Note the two levels of the action and the figures portrayed half sideways, half fullface, as in the palette of Narmer.

THE NOBLES

The nobles had many functions. At any moment one might be sent north or south to act as governor (nomarch) of a province (nome). Others served as judges, supervised expeditions to quarry stone from Elephantine and the Wadi Hammamat, or led military expeditions into Sinai. When not occupied with state business, a noble retired to his country estate, where he passed his days supervising the activities of his peasants hunting in the marshes, boating, fishing, and relaxing with his family. His house was spacious, airy, and gaily painted, and often it had a garden and a pool in which lotus blossoms floated and fish swam, a cool oasis in the hot desert land. When guests came to dinner, they were entertained by musicians playing the harp and lyre. Women wore heavy beaded necklaces, rouged their cheeks, and lined their eyes with kohl, a substance that not only made their eyes look bigger but during the day also protected them from the blinding sun. On top of their black wigs they set small cones to perfume the air as the night passed in laughter and talk.

THE ROLE OF WOMEN

In ancient Egypt women were free to appear in public and were highly respected. Each man had only one wife, as did the king, although Pharaoh also had a large harem. Land was held in the woman's name and was passed on to her eldest daughter. Royal inheritance also passed through the daughter, and a new king married the old king's daughter to confirm his claim to the throne. This was the primary reason for the Egyptian custom of intermarriage in the royal family (see chart, page 124), but this custom does not seem to have been followed by the people.

RELIGION IN THE OLD KINGDOM

The tribal gods of Egypt were worshiped by the Egyptians as long as their civilization lasted. Two nontribal gods were also important. One was Re, and the other was Osiris. They represented the two great natural forces that most influenced the life of the ancient Egyptian, the sun and the water.

Re was the god of the sun. It is possible that his worship was introduced from Asia by immigrants from the Fertile Crescent. Instead of human or animal representation, his symbol was the obelisk, a tall, slender column pointing skyward. Sometimes, but not always, the obelisk was carved from a single stone. Because it weighed many tons, it was difficult to transport from the quarry to the place of erection, but the Egyptian engineers solved the problem by using wooden ramps over which they slid the obelisk to a waiting barge on the Nile.

The importance of Re to the royal family was indicated in the Fourth Dynasty when the pharaohs Khaf-re and Menkau-re incorporated the name of Re into their own names. Beginning with the Fifth Dynasty (c. 2500 B.C.), the title Son of Re became the fifth of the official Great Names of the king and was so used for two thousand years. As time passed, Re was identified with Amon, a local god of Thebes, and he eventually became Amon-Re, the king of the gods.

The increased importance of the sun god, Re, meant a decreasing importance of older gods associated with the stars, particularly those around the North Star. Henceforth, the east, where the sun rose, and the west, where the sun set, became sacred regions: the east of birth and the west of death, where the king would reign with Re in the afterlife. Egyptian villages were usually on the east bank of the Nile, while the pyramids and mortuary temples and cemeteries were all on the western side, the "land of the dead."

While the pharaohs were looking up to the sun and calling themselves Sons of Re, another god was gaining favor, especially among the poorer classes. He was Osiris, the Great Green One, the personification of the life-giving Nile waters, and the Great Black One, who represented the fertile soil where grain miraculously sprang from seemingly dead seeds. Legend told that Osiris had lived in far distant times, that he had been murdered by his brother Set, and that his body had been cut up and scattered around Egypt to be reassembled and brought back to life by his sister-wife, the goddess Isis. But Osiris did not return to earth. Instead he became a judge of the dead in the underworld. As time passed, the Egyptians blended the legends of Osiris with those of Horus, making Horus the son of Osiris and Isis and his father's avenger. (Remembering that Horus was the son of Re, we mustn't get confused. One figure blending different roles was perfectly acceptable to the Egyptians.) The coffins of kings showed the king carrying the insignia of Osiris or represented as Osiris, wearing a royal crown and carrying either a royal scepter or the flail of the grain harvester and the crook of the shepherd and bound in mummy wrappings.

During the Old Kingdom Re was more important than Osiris; his priesthood at Heliopolis gained great importance, and royal riches were showered on his temples.

THE BELIEF IN THE AFTERLIFE

The Egyptians believed firmly that life after death existed, and that it was in all respects a duplicate of life on earth. During the Old Kingdom, only the king could hope for immortality, but in later periods the nobles and even ordinary men could share in it and live ever after in the Fields of Contentment.

In order to make life after death an exact duplicate of the world of the living, the Egyptians believed that the dead should be reminded of all the details of daily life. For a wealthy nobleman this meant having around him in his tomb all the objects from his earthly career as well as all the people, including servants, slaves, craftsmen, and workmen, from his estate. Scenes from daily life were depicted on the walls. Tiny images in lifelike poses of artisans, farmers, and craftsmen were grouped about to answer the dead man's call and were called "answerers."

The Pyramids. The royal attempt to outwit time and death produced the pyramids, one of the most astounding architectural phenomena of history. Much of the great wealth and power of the Old Kingdom rulers were devoted to building these great tombs. To understand why this was possible, it must be remembered that to the people the deathlessness of the pharaoh meant that as a god he would watch over them forever and that they would share in the good fortune he magically created. The king mobilized the farmers, who could not work in the fields during flood time, and he fed and clothed them in return for the labor that it seems they gave willingly to insure royal immortality.

The pyramids followed logically from the step of enlarging the mastaba and then placing another smaller one on top of it to give it greater grandeur. This was the idea of Imhotep, vizier to King Zoser of the Third Dynasty. Imhotep was a man of genius who, as architect, sage, writer, and physician, was immortalized by succeeding ages. He built the Step Pyramid and the complex of buildings surrounding it at Sakkara, close to Memphis, for King Zoser. He built in stone, and his were the first monumental stone buildings in the world. Instead of straight sides rising to a point, the Step Pyramid grows in a series of layers, each smaller than the one below. This led directly to the final pyramid form, which was devised by simply building up with less sharply defined levels.

The finest of the pyramids was the Great Pyramid of the Fourth Dynasty ruler King Khufu, or Cheops, as the Greeks called him. It covers thirteen acres of ground and contains 2,300,000 limestone blocks, each weighing at least two and a half tons, some as much as fifteen tons. They were dragged into place up earthen ramps, which were dismantled when the pyramid was finished. The whole mass was faced with more limestone, smooth and white, and the tip of the pyramid was covered with electron, a mixture of silver and gold that, gleaming in the sun, could be seen for miles over the land. The finished tomb towered nearly five hundred feet in the air.

A Pyramid at Giza and the Sphinx. For three thousand years the pyramids of Egypt and the man-beast known as the Sphinx have intrigued and impressed visitors. In the first millennium B.C., the ancient Egyptians themselves were tourists in their own land. They visited the great monuments to their long-dead kings and carved their initials in the stone to record their visit.

Adjoining each pyramid was a mortuary temple containing life-sized statues of the king. Constant religious ceremonies kept the dead ruler supplied with food and drink. The burning of incense accompanied the chanting of magical incantations and provided occupation for great numbers of priests. Eventually the expense of the original building was dwarfed by the cost of the temple upkeep, which over the centuries contributed to the drain on Egypt's economy.

Near the pyramid of Khafre lies the famous Great Sphinx, a statue 187 feet long in the form of a crouching lion with a human head. It is believed to be a portrait of Khafre. The Sphinx was the largest portrait head in the world until modern times, when the Americans carved the faces of four of their presidents on Mount Rushmore.

As eternal homes for the pharaohs, the pyramids were failures. Grave robbers found their secret entrances and looted them. Their gleaming façades were quarried away for buildings of a later time. Their temples were abandoned when the government was no longer able or willing to maintain the vast armies of priests needed to attend them, their treasures were stolen, and they were abandoned to the jackals until the windblown desert sands finally left them heaping mounds whose function was forgotten.

Mummification. Believing that the body would be needed in the next world, the ancient Egyptians perfected the art of preserving it for what they hoped would be eternity. Mummification was a long and complicated process. In the later New Kingdom it took seventy days to prepare a pharaoh for burial. Organs and brains were removed and stored in jars in the tomb. The shell of the body was treated with special oils, the cavities were packed with spices, and then the body was tightly wrapped in linen bands. Pitch, gums, and other substances were poured over each layer of bandages so that the whole hardened into an airtight mass. At first mummification was reserved for the king, but it was later adopted by the great nobles and others wealthy enough to afford it.

Because of mummification the Old Kingdom Egyptians discovered many things about the human body unknown to other ancient peoples, such as the Sumerians, whose religion forbade mutilating the dead. Egyptian knowledge of the body may have been the primary reason for the excellent reputation of Egyptian physicians in the ancient world.

LITERATURE AND ART IN THE OLD KINGDOM

Art in the Old Kingdom was primarily religious. Literature too had an important religious function. Inscribed on the walls of the pyramids were religious and magical inscriptions, including parts of ancient kingly rituals from Neolithic and predynastic times. There were also a great number of magical spells. These inscriptions instructed the pharaoh how to answer when he was examined by the gods sitting in judgment on him and to make his ascent into the sky, where he would take his place in the boat of Re, which is the sun sailing across the heavens. So the pharaoh may be absolutely certain of success in seeking immortality, he is even instructed to devour all the gods in order to acquire their different powers. These inscriptions, which scholars call the Pyramid Texts, reveal to us many Egyptian beliefs about the world of the dead and the afterlife.

In art the conventions that guided the Egyptian artist for centuries took their final form. Balance in design was perfected as a permanent characteristic of Egyptian painting and sculpture. Sculpture in the round portrayed the pharaoh and the nobles frontally, well balanced, sometimes

Menkaure and his Queen. This portrait of the king who built the third of the great pyramids at Giza, and his queen, is carved in gray-green slate of great hardness. Both figures stride forward, the queen's arm circling her husband's waist. Yet the figures seem immobile. They are solid and impersonal. Such a rendition, however, effectively suggests the eternal quality of the god-king who lives forever. The webbing between the figures and their limbs was a device used to strengthen the sculpture.

standing, sometimes seated, in every case designed to reflect the dignity and responsibility of the sitter. The hard stone in which the artist sculpted reflected the immortality of the king, and the stability and continuity of the Egyptian world view and of the king who represented it. The practice of drawing the human head and body in profile but showing both shoulders henceforth distinguished Egyptian drawings and carvings in relief from those of all other peoples. The relative importance of various people in the same picture was shown by making more important people larger. Thus a pharaoh might be drawn ten times larger than the farmers in the same design, while the queen was perhaps half the size of her husband and five times larger than her servants.

Like all Mediterranean people, ancient or modern, the Egyptians loved to be surrounded by color. In the Old Kingdom certain colors became standard for use on wall pictures and statues. Statues of green stone were painted with reddish-brown flesh tints. If the stone was naturally reddish-brown, the face and hands were left unpainted but the eyes, hair, ornaments, and clothing were colored. If the stone used for an inscription was of unusual beauty, the base and back pillar were usually left in natural tones, but the engraved characters were filled in with blue. In the standardization of colors, men were darker, usually reddish, and women were light. Cretans and Asiatics were usually tan or reddish, Libyans were white, and Negroes were black.

DECLINE OF THE OLD KINGDOM

The Old Kingdom did not come to a sudden end. Looking back we can see that the ninety-year reign of the Sixth Dynasty pharaoh Pepi II was the last great one of the Old Kingdom and that its great length seems to have weakened the country. By 2200 B.C. a serious decline had set in. The provincial nobility had increased in power and prestige. Great estates that once belonged to the king had passed into the hands of the bureaucracy and, through inheritance, had been broken into smaller and smaller units. The nobles claimed hereditary rights in governmental activities. No longer were they willing to pay the taxes to maintain the vast tomb and temple construction and upkeep. Each noble tried to rule in his own right, and a complete collapse of the central authority resulted. Raids by Nubians from the south into Upper Egypt and by desert nomads from Arabia and Libya into Lower Egypt coincided with clashes between powerful provincial magnates. The government was helpless to crush the rebellions or to oust the foreigners.

THE FIRST INTERMEDIATE PERIOD, C. 2200–2000 B.C.

During the time of troubles Egypt was in turmoil. Tombs were robbed, temples were destroyed, the statues of the kings were defaced and overthrown. The irrigation system collapsed, and famine followed. Foreign trade vanished. Several dynasties of kings tried to rule from Memphis while competing princes claimed control of Upper Egypt. We hear of a Seventh and Eighth Dynasty in the north and a Ninth and Tenth in the south, but they were dynasties in name only.

Men looked back to the Old Kingdom and wrote tales of the wonders of its great days. Many turned to religion for solace, and in the worship of Osiris they found hope of immortality for others besides the pharaoh. All men hoped for a future "good King" who would come to save the country and reestablish *maat*.

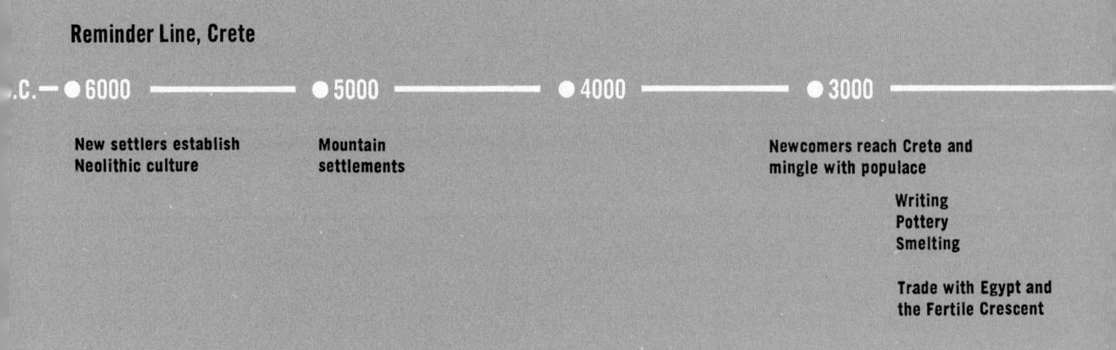

CIVILIZATION IN CRETE

Life in Crete seems to have continued along peaceful lines. The growth of total population and the increase in the number of towns was greatest in eastern Crete where, as before, sea trade with Asia and Egypt were of primary importance. The chief port was Mochlos, whose peninsula connection with Crete lasted some time longer before an earthquake turned it into a separate island. From eastern Crete the sailors voyaged to Sicily and southern Italy, where they introduced their pottery, the use of copper and gold, and their agricultural skills to the Neolithic tribesmen.

Some time after 2600 B.C. the Messara Plain in southern Crete, facing Egypt, became Crete's greatest farming region and produced a surplus of grain crops. The first towns in north-central Crete appeared, but they were not yet so important as the thriving ports of the east or the grainlands of the south.

By 2000 B.C. disorders overseas caused the eastern ports of Crete to lose much of their trade, and with their economic decline they ceased to be the leading centers of Cretan civilization. Their political importance was taken over by new urban centers in central Crete; Knossos and Mallia rose on the north coast, and Phaistos on the south.

In the mountains of central Crete, Neolithic tribes continued their old way of life. Clan organization came to an end, however, as urban life became the accepted pattern, even in such primarily farming regions as the Messara plain.

INDIA'S FIRST CIVILIZATION

Man's fourth civilization arose between 2500 B.C. and 1500 B.C. on the Indus River in the regions of Sind and Baluchistan in modern Pakistan. At its peak, about 2100 B.C., this civilization occupied almost all the territory of present-day western Pakistan.

Only in the last few years have archaeologists given serious attention to the Indus civilization. The sites were discovered in the 1870's but their rubble was promptly used by Indian workmen to build the new railroads. Not until the 1920's were the sites systematically investigated.

Both the birth and death of this civilization were aided by the arrival of strangers from the northwest. The first were of the Mediterranean type who had settled earlier in Egypt, Crete, and the Middle East. It seems probable that they had originated on the Iranian plateau or in Afghanistan. There they advanced from a Neolithic culture toward civilization and then spread east into the Indus River Valley, mingling with and ruling over the native population. From figurines recovered from the ruins we know that some of the native people were Negroes of a stock that in prehistoric times lived in southern Asia and on the islands of the western Pacific.

The strangers who put an end to the Indus Civilization are a mystery at present. It has been suggested that they were an Indo-European tribe called the Aryans, because Aryan hymns tell of attacks on cities with great fortresses that scholars believe might be those of the Indus. The Aryans, however, were charioteers, and the use of chariots was not widespread at the time of the first attacks on the Indus cities. It would seem, then, that

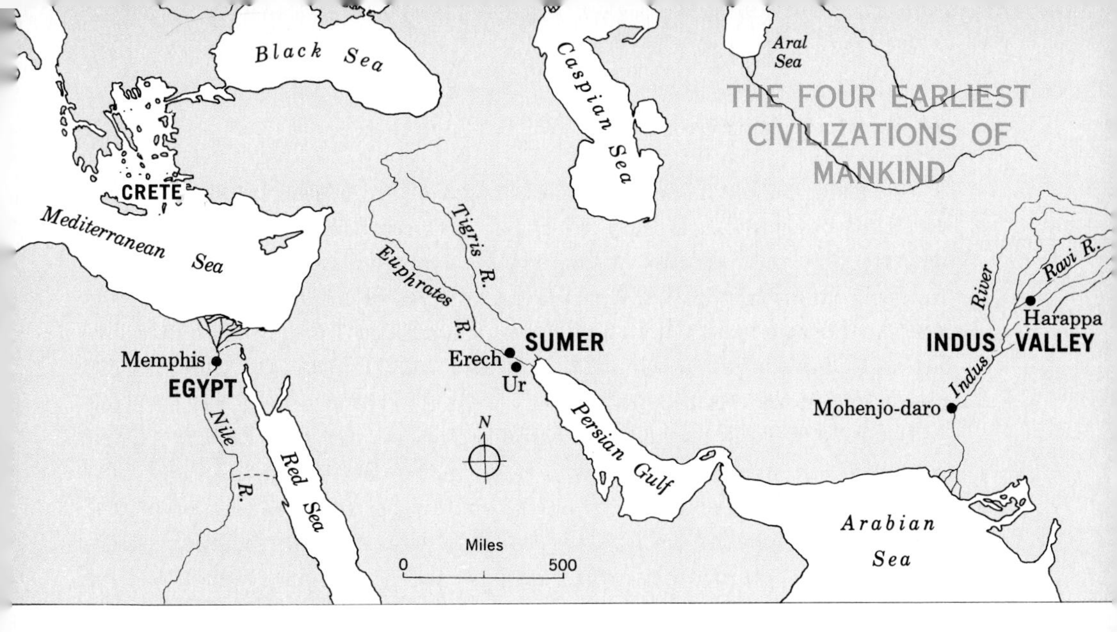

Aryans probably did not appear in India until after the strangers we are seeking here.

We know very little of the origins of the Indus Valley civilization. Because we cannot translate its writing, whatever the beautiful seals covered with script might tell us remains for future students to learn. That strangers were present at the beginning of the Indus civilization merely underscores the point that it is possible that this civilization began abruptly. Perhaps it did not arise by evolution out of primitive cultures preceding it on the same land, as happened in the earlier civilizations to the west, Egypt, Sumer, and Crete.

INDUS VALLEY CITIES

Forty or more settlements of varying sizes have been found in the Indus River region. Chief among them were two large cities, Mohenjo-daro and Harappa. These cities were carefully laid out. Indeed, they were the best-planned cities in the ancient world. They were built according to a design of broad straight avenues criss-crossed by narrower streets at right angles to the avenues. Underneath ran brick-lined sewers connecting with indoor toilets and baths on the ground floor of each house. Covered manholes in the streets gave access to repairmen.

The cities had large pools, but whether they were used for general bathing or had some religious use is not known. Strangely, no temples or tombs of a ruling class have yet been found. Cemeteries certainly existed, but the remains in them are all of ordinary people, judging by the objects discovered in them.

The Indus people made many tiny images of the Mother Goddess of the earth. They show a kinship to those of Crete and Sumer-Akkad and indicate that the worship of the goddess was widespread in very early times. In addition, the Indus people had images of a god unknown to the west—a horned male with three faces, surrounded by animals. He is believed to be a possible forerunner of the later Hindu god Shiva in his appearance as Lord of the Beasts.

The most striking object in each Indus city was the great brick fort that rose up in the middle of the town. They are a puzzle to archaeologists. Do they indicate that the whole city lived in fear of attack and had built the citadels as a place of refuge? Or do they indicate that the rulers were afraid of the people they were ruling? Such questions cannot yet be answered.

INDUS VALLEY LIFE

The educated guesses of talented scholars have played an important part in reconstructing the civilization of the Indus Valley people. The principal occupation was farming in the lands that lay around the cities. During this early period the land produced wheat, barley, melons, peas, dates, and the first cotton grown anywhere in the world. Like the civilizations to the west, the people of the Indus Valley had tame dogs, cats, and pigs, and the earliest known hens. Undomesticated animals included humped cattle, water buffalos, and possibly elephants, whose tusks supplied the ivory on which the Indus people carved beautiful circular seals with chisel and drill. The seals also show wild animals, such as apes, tigers, crocodiles, and many birds, such as the parrot, that are native to the region. They have led scholars to believe that the climate then was like that of the north of India today.

Pottery figurines were baked in kilns, as were the millions of bricks needed for houses and fortresses. Baking was essential because sun-dried brick would not have survived the torrential downpour of the Indian monsoon.

Trade was next in importance to farming. Boats were used for internal transport over hundreds of miles of river, and in the days of Sumer, Sargon, and later of Ur-Nammu, ships sailed as far as Mesopotamia, where Indus seals have been recovered. The Indus people also traded with Egypt, Troy, Afghanistan, and southern India. They bought gold, turquoise, lapis lazuli, copper, and an imitation jade, which they made into jewelry that they then exchanged, along with pearls, ivory combs, and cotton, for more raw materials.

THE DECLINE OF THE INDUS CIVILIZATION

Having made a bold and successful beginning and having established a thriving and sophisticated city life, the civilization of the Indus people began to show a decline about 2000 B.C. Arts and crafts do not show the skill and workmanship of earlier times. They became shoddy and poorly executed; trade with other peoples seems to have fallen off; repairs on city edifices were carried out carelessly. An internal decay within the civilization itself took place. At the same time attacks by unknown invaders began, coinciding with attacks on the Egyptians and Mesopotamians.

At first only the outlying villages and smaller towns were lost to the newcomers. The situation then worsened, and a curtain descends on the scene. The history of the next three hundred years is unknown except that at some time toward the end of that period the two dominating cities of Harappa and Mohenjo-daro were conquered. The slaughtered dead were left to lie in the streets until their skeletons were brought to light some 3500 years later. The newcomers apparently burned, looted, and passed on. By 1500 B.C. the last traces of civilization in the Indus Valley were erased, and northern and western India had returned to a primitive state for the next several hundred years. It is thought that an offshoot of the Indus civilization may have made its way into central India, but only a hint of this is evident now.

THE NEOLITHIC REVOLUTION REACHES EUROPE AND CHINA

Through the expansion of trade, which brought the advances of the civilized centers to surrounding areas, Neolithic culture spread steadily throughout Europe and Asia in the eight centuries following 2800 B.C. By 2000 B.C. only the northern lands from Norway east to the Pacific Ocean remained in the Old Stone Age.

More advanced neolithic groups occupied the Upper Danube Valley, the plains north of the Black and Caspian seas, and the British Isles. They were also found in northern China and there laid the basis for the civilization that was to grow in the next millennium (*mille*—thousand; *annum*—year).

NEOLITHIC CHINA

During the period 2800–2000 B.C. neolithic changes spread into northern China. From central Asia farming villages with wattle and mud huts, goats, sheep, pigs, cattle, and wheat farming using the hoe appeared in the valley of the Yellow River (Hwang Ho). Whether also by introduction from the west or by separate invention in China, the potter's wheel and the art of painting pottery appeared. Mud bricks were probably made, and perhaps copper was in use. Irrigation was developed, and the gods of nature were worshiped.

The Chinese did not abandon Old Stone Age ways completely as the Neolithic Revolution went on. Burial customs, for example, remained unchanged.

While neolithic culture was spreading into northern China from the northwest, a variant form of it was also spreading up the seacoast from southeast Asia. The second neolithic culture was based on fishing and the sea. Stone tools were ground and pottery was handmade, but rice was farmed instead of wheat, and netmaking and canoe building were highly important crafts unknown to the northern Chinese. There is some evidence, though not enough to be absolutely certain, that the building of houses on poles and the tattooing of the body were also features of this culture.

In time the two neolithic cultures in China met and blended into one. Its double origin gave to the civilization that grew out of it a character somewhat different from the cultures of Europe and western Asia.

❦ ❦ ❦

The period 2800–2000 B.C. was one of the most important in ancient history. Two civilizations flourished, a third continued to grow, and a fourth was developed, though it collapsed. Many tribes passed from the Old Stone Age into the New Stone Age, the most important of which were those of China in the extreme east. At the end of this period the partial collapse of the civilized areas coincided with the attacks and migrations of many restless, uncivilized peoples.

People, Places, and Terms

Sargon	Aryans	Hwang Ho	pyramid
Ur-Nammu			sphinx
Asiatics	Sumer	alloy	mummy
Imhotep	Akkad	lugal	*maat*
Khufu	Indus Valley	ensi	vizier
Amon	Mohenjo-daro	divine kingship	millennium
Re	Harappa	obelisk	mortuary

Mastering the Reading

1. By whom and how was the leadership of a Sumerian town shared? How was a ziggurat community organized? What do their burial customs tell us about Sumerian beliefs in an after-life? about their skill as craftsmen? about Sumerian social organization?
2. In what ways was Sargon a good king at home and abroad? How did Sumer-Akkad differ culturally from the earlier Sumer?
3. What was the role of the king in ancient Egypt? What can the pyramids tell us about Old Kingdom religion, art, and government? How did the nobles contribute to the development of the Old Kingdom and to its decline?
4. In what ways were the Indus Valley cities different from the cities of other civilizations of the period? How did these cities thrive? What is the mystery surrounding their origin and disappearance?

Interpreting the Text

1. What are some artistic techniques that are associated specifically with Sumer? with Egypt? with the Indus civilization?
2. In what ways did the Egyptian religion reflect the climate and geography of Egypt?
3. How did the power of an ensi differ from that of a pharaoh? Why?
4. About 2000 B.C. semi-barbaric tribes overthrew or disturbed the civilized areas to some degree. How do you account for this in each area?

Exploring Beyond the Text

1. Art serves a different purpose in different societies. Read about Egyptian tomb paintings and the techniques used. Then prepare a lecture on the purpose of art from the point of view of an Egyptian artist. Include in your lecture how the Egyptian point of view differs from your own.
2. Create an imaginary conversation between Khufu and his architect as they discuss the design of the Great Pyramid. Reveal religious beliefs, engineering and architectural developments, and other cultural aspects of the Old Kingdom.

Working with the Map

Examine the map of the four civilizations. Where did their paths cross? What products in particular did each want from the other?

6

Attack and Revival: The Middle Bronze Age

2000–1600 B.C.

The civilizations of Mesopotamia and Egypt that arose so splendidly only to disintegrate around 2000 B.C. moved forward to new glory and strength after a period of readjustment to the eruptions of tribes from the border lands. Sumer-Akkad was absorbed into a larger Mesopotamian state called Babylonia, which became the first empire as well as the largest and most powerful state the Fertile Crescent had yet seen. Egypt revived during the Eleventh and Twelfth Dynasties of the Middle Kingdom to reach a peak of prosperity based on agriculture and trade. A new state arose in Anatolia, while on the island of Crete prosperity developed a brilliant culture that influenced the Achaeans, a people who settled on the mainland of Greece. In the Far East, China progressed from Neolithic culture to that of city-states. Only India did not share in this recovery.

NEW LANDS AND NEW PEOPLES

Around 2000 B.C. waves of migrant tribes swept down into the civilized centers and spread out into territories that had been Neolithic in the third millennium B.C. One such group pushed north from the Arabian desert to settle in northern Mesopotamia and in that area of the eastern Mediterranean occupied by Palestine and Syria. They were Semites, the ancestors of the Babylonians, Phoenicians, Hebrews, and Arameans. Another group, the Indo-Europeans, was a very large collection of tribes related by language. They were the forebears of many peoples who settled in Europe, the Middle East, and over the Iranian plateau to India.

THE INDO-EUROPEANS

The name "Indo-European" was invented by modern scholars for those peoples speaking closely related languages who lived from India to western Europe.

The original Indo-European homeland lay somewhere between central Europe and Western Asia. While the Indo-Europeans were still living as

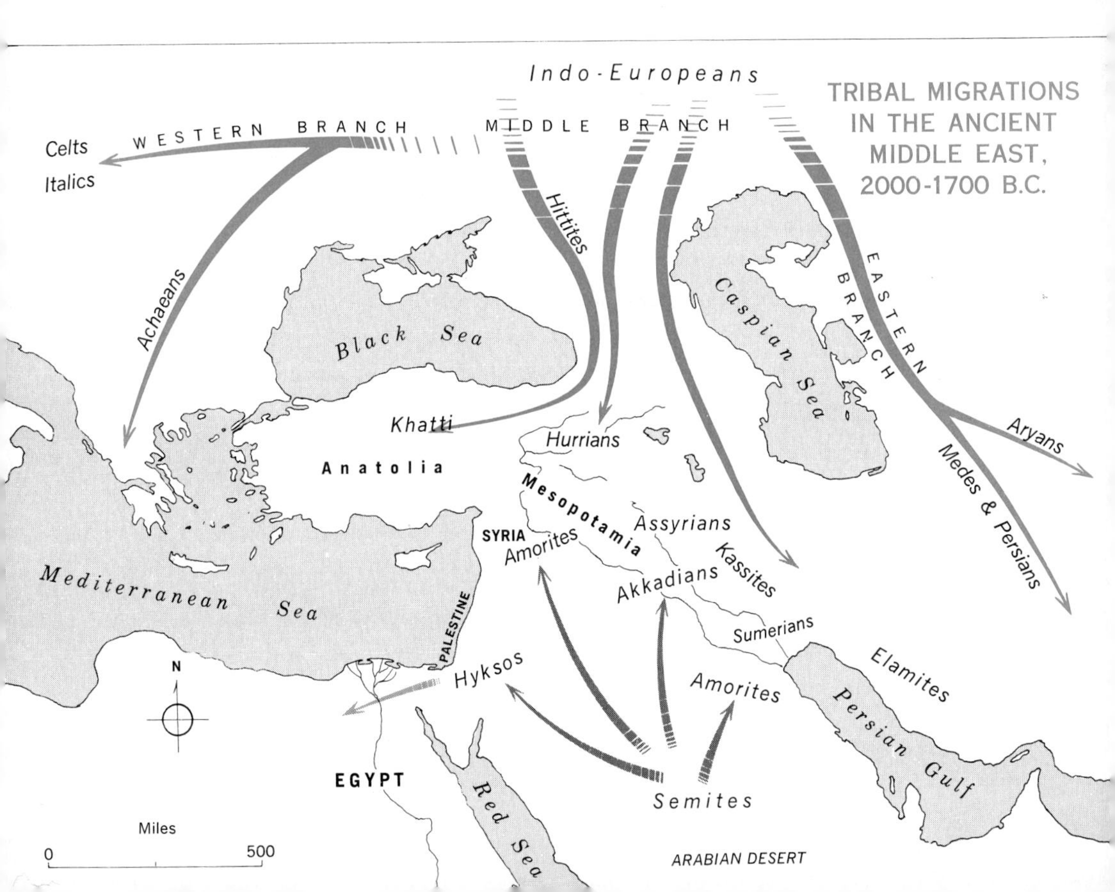

one people, they were partly nomadic and partly agricultural in their way of life. Sheep and cattle were domesticated, perhaps after contact with the more advanced peoples of the Fertile Crescent. They were the first people to use and tame the horse, which became identified with the Mother Goddess of nature. Horse worship was carried by the Indo-Europeans into many countries. Indo-European society was usually patrilineal, monogamus (one spouse, not many), and warlike. Chiefs were military leaders. They were buried under mounds, called by archaeologists *barrows*, and with them were buried battle-axes of stone and of copper. In the tombs of some of the greater chiefs were gold and silver weapons acquired through trade.

In prehistory, the Indo-European tribes had divided into three main branches, each of which in turn subdivided several times.

The western branch established a center reaching from the Black Sea west into the valley of the Danube. From this branch are descended the Celtic, Italic, and Hellenic (Greek) peoples, and later the Germanic. The first of this group to play a role in civilization were the Hellenic Achaeans.

The middle branch is the least known group. These people appear in history moving along the west coast of the Black Sea and through the Caucasus mountains on its east coast. We will meet them as the Hittites in Anatolia (Asia Minor). Culturally they were closely related to western Indo-Europeans.

Around 2000 B.C. another group, warriors apparently without wives, invaded the highlands southwest of the Caspian Sea and settled among the native Hurrians. After some centuries they formed the kingdom of Mitanni, whose great days came about 1450 B.C., when Egypt was an ally and Mitannian princesses married pharaohs (page 121). Others of the warriors became the overlords of the Kassites and the other peoples native to the mountains overlooking Mesopotamia. Still another group moved into southern Palestine, mixing along the way with native groups and the Semites to form the Hyksos (page 111), who swept into Egypt around 1750 B.C.

The eastern branch of the Indo-Europeans was based on the lands from the Baltic to the prairie lands north and east of the Caspian Sea. Several groups entered the plateau of Iran, where they formed the tribes of the Medes and the Persians (page 171), and the branch known as Aryans (page 281) invaded India at a time still undetermined. In Europe, the Slavs and the Balts are also descended from this eastern branch.

Not all the Indo-European peoples became civilized. Many remained north of the civilized centers. We will meet them as the Celts and Germans (see above), who settled in Europe, and as nomadic tribes with various names—Cimmerians, Scythians, Sakas—who lived north of the Danube River and across the steppes of central Asia to the borders of China.

The barbarian peoples had much to learn from civilization. The learning, however, was not all one way. They contributed new ideas, new methods and techniques, new blood to enrich the life of those with whom they mingled. Proving excellent pupils, they adapted what they brought to what they learned, as the civilizations of the Hittites and the Greek Achaeans were the first to show.

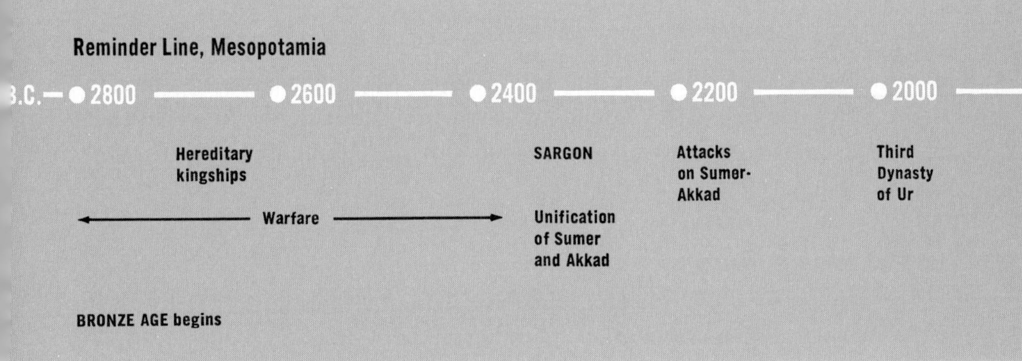

MESOPOTAMIA AND THE AMORITE EMPIRE OF BABYLON

In the Mesopotamian valley of the Tigris and Euphrates, civilization, which we have seen move northward by the addition of Akkad to Sumer, moved into northern Mesopotamia and by 1800 B.C. had spread over the land henceforth to be known as Babylonia.

THE BABYLONIAN EMPIRE AND HAMMURABI

Around 2000 B.C. Semitic tribes from Arabia known as Amorites were on the move, entering Syria and Mesopotamia. Many settled in Sumer-Akkad, where they established the little village of Babylon. Under the Amorites, Babylon grew into a large city with temples and palaces.

The sixth Amorite king, Hammurabi, extended Babylonian territory and had conquered Babylon's neighbors by 1750 B.C. Sargon had previously controlled some of this territory, but Hammurabi governed an empire that

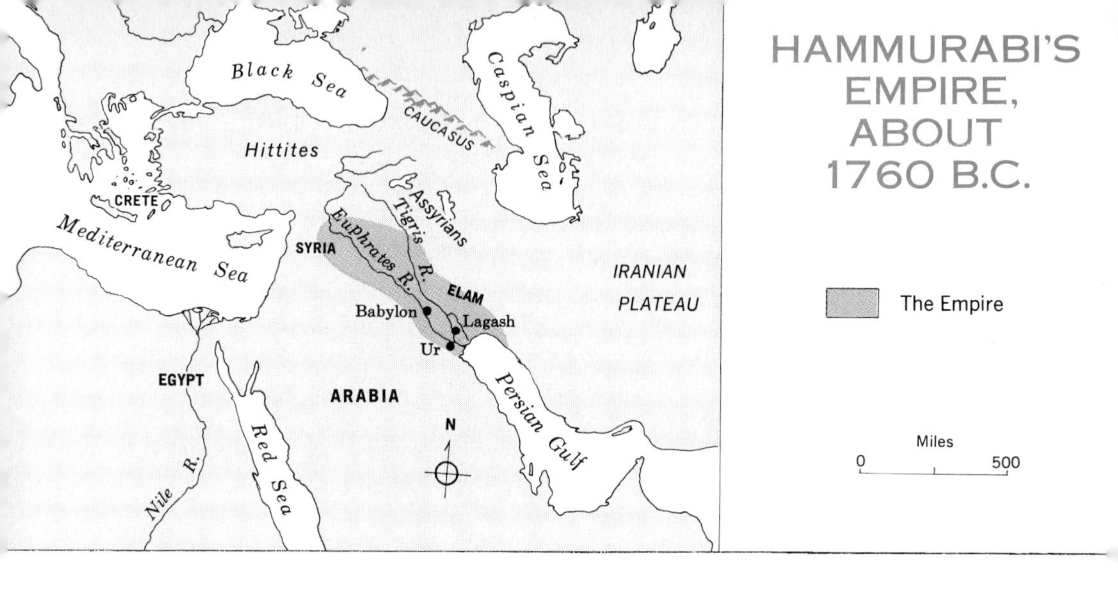

encompassed the Fertile Crescent from Elam to Syria. The fame of Babylon became so great that after Hammurabi the name Babylonia was used instead of Sumer-Akkad for lower Mesopotamia and the adjoining Euphrates and Tigris Valley.

HAMMURABI'S CODE OF LAWS

For centuries before Hammurabi, laws had multiplied in the different cities of Sumer. The arrival of the Semites in the Euphrates Valley made it necessary to reissue the old Sumerian laws in the Akkadian language. Hammurabi ordered a committee of experts to examine all the laws, to remove contradictory ones, to organize the remainder, and to revise them in line with the needs of the time. Finally he ordered them made public in such a way that all might know what was lawful and what was not. Hammurabi therefore was not the inventor but the codifier of the great collection of laws that bears his name.

Until recently the great code of laws created by Hammurabi was thought to be the oldest such code in the world. Now we know of an earlier legal code, that of Ur-Nammu of the Third Dynasty of Ur, and still more ancient ones probably existed. But the code of Hammurabi will always be of major importance because it reveals much of the complex life of the people of Babylonia after 1800 B.C.

A picture carved at the top of the stone column of the laws discovered in 1901 shows the god Shamash seated on a mountain top handing the tablets of the law to Hammurabi. The people were thus reminded that breaking the laws inscribed on the stone would be an offense against the gods as well as against the king.

The stele of Hammurabi. Standing in an attitude of respect before the seated god, Hammurabi receives the laws from Shamash, who holds in his hand the rod and circle, symbols of his power. The setting of the scene is the mountains, not the Mesopotamian plain. Below the figures, 282 laws are recorded on the seven-foot black basalt column.

The laws are clearly stated, as are the punishments for breaking them. Right is right, wrong is wrong, and the code seems to echo the old tribal law of an "eye for an eye and a tooth for a tooth." The code covered slavery, marriage and divorce, medicine, banking and safe deposits, labor regulations, military service, farming, commerce, building debts, and inheritance. In each instance the rights and duties of all parties were made clear. In Hammurabi's Babylonia the severity of the punishment varied according to the class of the person who committed the crime. Punishments were equal within classes, but not between. The noble who knocked out the eye of another noble had his eye knocked out, but if he knocked out the eye of a commoner, he paid a fine. Social responsibility, however, was also greater the higher one's position. Nobles paid in kind for offenses against each other; commoners usually paid money. Slaves suffered the most. If a slave merely knocked a commoner down, he suffered mutilation.

Whether the Babylonian courts were as severe as the law allowed is uncertain. Nevertheless, the code Hammurabi created was superior to anything man had produced before and was to remain man's greatest legal achievement for the next two thousand years. Many nations made collections of their laws, but until the code of Roman law prepared for the Emperor Justinian about 550 A.D., there was none to equal Hammurabi's in clear organization and in the detailed coverage of the legal problems of a society.

BABYLONIAN WRITINGS

The literature of Babylon included prayers, hymns, and epic poems. Many concerned heroes and myths of the gods. Some of the tales, such as the one of the hero who built a great ship and in it survived the flood, were long remembered by the Hebrews and appear in the Bible under Hebrew names. Others, such as the epic of Gilgamesh, in which the hero, who was based on a real figure who had lived in Sumer, underwent testing and trial in his search for immortality, were preserved later in the literature of the Greeks and the Romans. Gilgamesh, for example, appears a thousand years later as the Greek hero Herakles (Hercules). The love story of Ishtar and Tammuz and the story of the death and resurrection of Tammuz (page 63) were among the most popular of the tales of the older gods.

Babylonian medicine was primarily herbal and magical. Medical writings were devoted to information about the use of herbs as cures for illness, and particularly to spells and charms that were believed to have a magical effect in treating the sick.

Many writings were devoted to divination, the practice of prophesying from present signs what is to happen in the future. Two methods of divination were widely accepted in Babylonia and from there spread throughout the whole ancient world during the next two thousand years. One was astrology, the study of the movements of the stars, moon, and sun in relation to each other. The principle of "As above, so below" taught that unity existed between the heavenly bodies and the affairs of man on earth and that the events to come on the earth were foreshadowed in the heavens. The second method of divination was to seek signs of coming events among men in the organs, particularly in the liver, of animals sacrificed in religious ceremonies. During all animal or bird sacrifices, the liver was carefully examined by the priests for unusual swellings or discoloration. Clay models of the liver were then made, and sections of it were marked to indicate the kind of event involved, the place on earth where it would occur, and so on. These models were kept for reference in each temple.

THE DECLINE OF BABYLON

The great Amorite Empire of Babylon began to deteriorate in its economy, arts, and crafts. Babylon fell before invaders from outside its borders soon after 1600 B.C., when the Hittites from Anatolia (page 112) captured it. State affairs called the Hittite leaders back to their own country, so they abandoned Babylon, leaving it in ruins. From the mountains to the east of Mesopotamia the Kassites swept down into the valley and permanently occupied the region from Babylon to the sea. For the next five centuries they remained in control. They lived in other cities of Babylonia, however, and the ruins of Babylon remained empty until after 1000 B.C., when the city was reoccupied and entered a new phase of its history.

Reminder Line, Egypt

.C.— ● 2800 —— ● 2600 —— ● 2400 —— ● 2200 —— ● 2000 ——

OLD KINGDOM
Dynasties 3-6

Imhotep
Step Pyramid ——→ Pyramids

Pepi II

Raids from surrounding tribes

FIRST INTERMEDIATE PERIOD
Dynasties 7-10

EGYPT: THE MIDDLE KINGDOM, C. 2000–1800 B.C.

Slowly the people of the Nile Valley struggled out of the political, economic, and social disorders that had brought the Old Kingdom to an end. After nearly two hundred years of turmoil, a new dynasty arose that reestablished the kingship and repelled attack. This new period of prosperity, the Middle Kingdom, lasted some two hundred years until invaders and internal weaknesses again brought collapse.

RECOVERY UNDER THEBAN PRINCES

During the twenty-first century B.C. Egypt was reunited by a vigorous ruler of the southern city of Thebes. Thebes had been a small, unimportant town during the Old Kingdom. It was located well up the river in Upper Egypt, far removed from the center of government (see map, page 60). During the chaos of the First Intermediate Period, Theban princes nominally recognized the rulers of Herakleopolis south of the Delta. Gradually the Theban princes extended their sway over the territory of the southern kingdom, south from Thebes to Elephantine and north to Abydos. Finally, they drove out the Nubians. By 2040 B.C. Mentuhotep, a ruler of the Eleventh Dynasty, had defeated the rulers at Herakleopolis and had established his sway over all of the Two Lands. This strong ruler, who governed Egypt for nearly fifty years, established his capital at Thebes. He acknowledged the supremacy of the local Theban god, Amon, who was gradually elevated in importance by association with Re.

During both the Eleventh and Twelfth Dynasties, Middle Kingdom Egypt had a stable, centralized government. It enjoyed a revived and expanded trade that extended into the Sudan, Syria and Mesopotamia, and the Aegean.

It created a literature unsurpassed in later times and art objects of beautiful workmanship that give a vivid picture of the prosperous life of the times. The kings maintained their control primarily through their strong personalities, their success in extending Egyptian influence through trade and control over border territories, and creating the wealth that made Egypt the envy of its neighbors. During the Twelfth Dynasty, the capital was removed to It-Tawi, modern El Lisht.

THE ELEVENTH AND TWELFTH DYNASTIES

Politically, the king did not regain the absolute authority he had held during the Old Kingdom. The nobles no longer acted only in the name of the pharaoh as they had done during the Pyramid Age. They acted on their own authority, retaining the rights they had acquired during the time of troubles to govern, tax, and control labor in their individual provinces. The king was, in many instances, no more than an equal among equals. The pharaohs tried again to centralize the government, but by the time the king had succeeded in reducing the power of his nobles to that of crown officials, the Middle Kingdom was drawing to an end in political confusion and invasion.

The sixth pharaoh of the Twelfth Dynasty, Amonemhet III (c. 1840 B.C.), ruled for 46 years, and during this long period he concentrated his efforts

A portrait of King Senwosret III of the Twelfth Dynasty. The squarish features and flat modeling of the face suggest the possible Nubian descent of the Middle Kingdom pharaohs. Senwosret wears the *nemes*, a striped wig covered with linen or leather, worn only by the ruler.

on internal development. One of the great achievements of his reign was the conversion of a great area of swamplands into a rich farming region. This area, known as the Fayum, was about fifty miles south of Memphis adjoining the Nile (see map, page 68). By dredging out the center of the Fayum, the overflow of the Nile, which had previously created worthless swamps, was collected in a new lake. Lake Moeris was a pleasure center for fishing and boating as well as a reservoir for the irrigation ditches of the Fayum. The Fayum greatly increased the cultivable land of Egypt. Amonemhet III sent expeditions to work the mines of Sinai and to bring back timber from Syria and Phoenicia. Trade also flourished with Cretans and other island people, for pottery from the faraway Aegean has been discovered at Abydos.

Egypt's borders in the north and south were secured by strings of forts. These extended to Semna just below the Second Cataract in Kush (the Sudan), the southern boundary of the Middle Kingdom; the northeastern frontier was guarded by a fortified barrier known as The Wall of the Princes (see map, page 121). Expeditions were sent to the western frontier against Libyan raiders and to the eastern front against the Asiatics. Troops were also sent south, beyond the Third Cataract, in order to establish commercial relations with the natives.

Egypt was rich and prosperous within its borders during the Middle Kingdom. Traders spread reports of its power and strength as they traveled through the Middle East—reports which could not have encouraged Egypt's enemies. Egypt obtained the enviable reputation of being a country not only of wealth and luxury but also of might.

THE LITERATURE OF THE MIDDLE KINGDOM

The Middle Kingdom was the golden age of Egyptian literature. Prose and poetry covering rolls of papyrus have been discovered carefully buried in tombs. Tales of adventure were very popular. One of the most famous concerns Sinuhe, an army officer who deserts during a civil war and has a series of adventures in Syria before being pardoned and allowed to return to Egypt. Another, *The Story of the Shipwrecked Sailor*, is the tale of an Egyptian seaman who tells his master about bravery under harrowing conditions. Other prose works included maxims on how to lead a good life and mythological tales that recounted the very human adventures of the gods, such as *The Outwitting of Re by Isis* and *The Struggles of Horus with Set.* In poetry, love songs were sung to the accompaniment of the lyre, and other lyrics honored the pharaoh or were recited at festivals and funerals.

Egyptian literature reflected the practical and confident nature of the ancient Egyptian. The regular rhythm of his life gave him security and a faith in the things of this world. His difficulties arose from his dealings with other men, not from capricious gods or an unexplainable environment. Even life after death was possible if the proper spells and incantations were available for the journey into the underworld. Such spells were carefully compiled by scribes. They were laboriously written on the lid of the coffin of every person rich enough to afford one, and so received the name of Coffin Texts.

The hieroglyphics of the Middle Kingdom were beautifully executed and colored. The style of writing was elegant and sophisticated, the model for good prose and poetry long after the Middle Kingdom had passed away.

MIDDLE KINGDOM ART

The art of the Middle Kingdom is a tribute to the skill and craftsmanship of the ancient Egyptians. Especially fine work was produced in the minor arts, such as the detailed, skillfully carved and colored tomb objects created for the pleasure and comfort of the rich in the next life. These objects reflect a refined and elegant taste, expressive of the age. Jewelry of gold, silver, lapis lazuli, and other semiprecious stones consisted of necklaces, rings, bracelets, hair ornaments; little figures of animals, boats, and men were carved of wood and painted. There were hippopotamuses of faience (crushed quartz pebbles), covered with the foliage of their Nile environment, and gaming and cosmetic sets of painted ivory, all perfectly matched.

Two tomb objects. On the right, a boat; on the left, a little faience hippopotamus. Such objects, of everyday possessions and surroundings, reveal the life of Middle Kingdom Egyptians in some detail. The boat carried the master, seated under a canopy for protection from the hot Egyptian sun, on a round of duties. The boat was guided by the oars in the back and propelled by the rowers on a windless day. At the front stands a look-out, and behind him is the mast of the sail, now missing.

Monumental sculpture decreased in quantity, although the unsurpassed skill of Egyptians in stoneworking produced superb portraits of the pharaohs that reveal in careworn faces the heavy tasks facing great rulers. Although all the kings built and rebuilt on old and new sites, very little architecture remains. Pyramids were smaller, and other buildings were made of brick and rubble rather than stone.

CHANGES IN RELIGION

Since the end of the Old Kingdom, the funeral rites formerly reserved for the pharaoh had been taken over first by the great nobles and then by anyone wealthy enough to afford the expensive ceremonies. In this democratization of the royal religion, the god who gained the greatest following among the people was Osiris. Whereas the hope of resurrection had formerly been associated only with the king, now every man began to dream of it for himself.

The legendary site of the tomb of Osiris was at Abydos. During the Middle Kingdom it became a universal practice to make a pilgrimage there to take part in the annual festival that reenacted the death and resurrection of the god (page 88). It became a common custom to identify all dead persons as the "Osiris So-and-so." Funeral statues show the dead one bound in mummy wrappings imitating the image of Osiris.

At the same time that the worship of Osiris was spreading throughout Egypt, the god Amon was gaining in royal favor. The pharaoh Amonemhet I (c. 1990 B.C.) had bolstered the importance of Amon by installing a permanent priesthood in the god's temple in Thebes to pray for the welfare of the king and of Egypt.

DECLINE OF THE MIDDLE KINGDOM

After 1800 B.C. Egypt weakened once more, and the Middle Kingdom came to an end in internal disorder and external attack that recalled the conditions under which the Old Kingdom had collapsed. In 1780 B.C. Egypt was divided; the Thirteenth Dynasty held weak sway over Upper Egypt at the same time that the Fourteenth tried to control lower Egypt. Official records ceased, the economy collapsed, and arts and crafts suffered.

By 1750 B.C. the outlying lands in Palestine and Sinai began to fall to invaders whom the Egyptians called Hyksos. In the absence of records these people remain a mystery to us. Some seem to have been composed of a people called the Hurrians, who had settled along the upper Euphrates.

Others were Indo-European warriors. Still others were Semites from Arabia with whom the Indo-Europeans had mingled and who joined the host in the hope of looting the wealthy cities of the Nile. The Hyksos had been moving into Egypt over a period of years, but their number seems suddenly to have increased. The victories of the invaders were due partly to the internal weakness of the Egyptians and partly to the use of war chariots drawn by horses. The introduction of the horse as a military weapon points to the presence of Indo-European warriors. The Egyptians, like all civilized people up to this time, had only the tiny donkey to pull their chariots.

The second breakdown of the Egyptian state that followed is usually called the Second Intermediate Period. It lasted some two centuries while the hated invaders, whom the Egyptians refused to mention in their records, ruled the Two Lands.

ANATOLIA AND THE HITTITES

Anatolia (Asia Minor and present-day Turkey) is a wild and rugged land, totally surrounded by mountains that cut it off on the east from the plains of Syria. It has a difficult climate with extremes of heat and cold, and it is subject to earthquakes. In ancient times land for farming was limited, and the terrain was better suited to herding. The area was, however, rich in the resources desirable to ancient peoples. Timber was plentiful and metals abundant, including copper, tin, lead, iron—undiscovered until the Hittites arrived—as well as silver and gold, both separately and in the combination known as electron. Animals provided wool and hides. These resources attracted settlers, who had entered Anatolia by 7000 B.C.

In the years 2100–2000 B.C. the Halys Valley and the surrounding highlands in north central Anatolia were settled by a people who called themselves Khatti. They may have been Asiatics, related to the Hurrians who were expanding from along the Euphrates into southern Anatolia at that time.

About 1900 B.C. an Indo-European tribe swept south through the Caucasus mountain passes and then turned west (see map, page 101), passing to the north of the Euphrates, slaying the people, and burning the villages. The path of destruction was so severe that archaeologists have no difficulty tracing it 3,800 years later. These people marched north to the Halys River and conquered the Khatti nation, making their city of Hattusas the capital of a new state, which the Egyptians called "Kheta" and which we call "Hittite." The Hittites formed the first great state of Asia Minor. Between 1600 and

1200 B.C. they conquered the Mitanni, who had settled in northern Mesopotamia, and contested Egyptian control of Syria.

HITTITE CIVILIZATION BEGINS

The conquering Indo-European warriors quickly adapted themselves to living in towns. From the conquered Khatti and from traders bringing goods and ideas from Egypt, Crete, and the Fertile Crescent, they learned the ways of civilized men. Their own writing system was hieroglyphic, but the designs were original and showed no relationship to the hieroglyphs of Egypt. The Hittites also learned to write in cuneiform, which they used in trading with the Fertile Crescent countries.

Politically the Hittite nation was a national federation of ten small states based on cities whose locations are not yet established. All recognized the overlordship of the Hittite Great King, who reigned in Hattusas (see map, page 131). The federation was the accomplishment of Labarnas, the first Great King. His son made Hattusas (present-day Borghaskoy) the capital and took from it his own name of Hattusilis. These two Great Kings established control over lands in western Anatolia (Arzawa) and the Hurrian lands along the upper Euphrates. The third Great King, Mursilis, marched down the Euphrates to Babylon, which he destroyed (page 106), bringing Hammurabi's empire to an end. Called home by disorders there, Mursilis was assassinated, and the Hittite kingdom fell into a state of anarchy that lasted for over a century. The Hittite period of glory was yet to come.

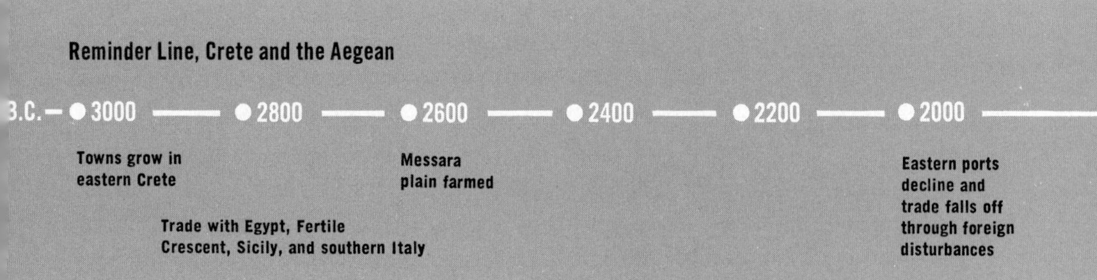

CRETE AND THE AEGEAN

After 2000 B.C. events or conditions in Crete as yet unknown led to the rise in power of local princes or petty kings, and the island was divided into small states. Royal palaces were erected at Knossos and Mallia in the north and at Phaistos in the south, indicating that the center of activity had shifted away from the earlier civilized eastern end of the island.

Royal power grew, and there was an increase of population during that prosperous, peaceful period. The 135 hieroglyphic signs of the first Cretan writing system were reduced to ninety and were written in a script called Linear A, still untranslated. During the 1600's B.C. the commercial ties of Crete with Egypt and the Near East ceased because of the activities of the Hyksos and the Hittites. Cretan traders turned north and became influential at Mycenae, Tiryns, and Pylos on the Greek mainland (see map, page 134). These cities had been founded by descendants of Indo-European invaders called Achaeans (see map, page 101) at the end of the third millennium B.C.

Several times the Cretan cities were destroyed by violent earthquakes. But the Cretans refused to be dismayed and always rebuilt with such determination that around 1600 B.C. the palace at Knossos became the most splendid that Crete ever knew.

The great palace at Knossos was an architectural wonder. Standing four stories high, it was built on a sloping hill and was arranged so that the main entrances and the great courtyard were on the third level. It contained about eight hundred small rooms, corridors, stairways, and air shafts, which also served to admit light to the interior rooms. Toilets and bathrooms with running water adjoined the apartments. The walls of this city-in-one-building were of gleaming white gypsum and polished limestone ablaze with color—red columns and blue and green borders. The walls were decorated with brilliant scenes painted on the wet plaster, called frescoes. In earlier years the scenes were from nature and wild life. Crocus, myrtle, lilies, bluebirds, partridge, monkeys, and flying fish were painted in a realistic style that had no parallel in the ancient world except where Cretan artists were employed on the Greek mainland or perhaps in Egypt when Ikhnaten built his new capital city (page 125). Human figures were introduced in the later Knossian palace, redecorated following new earthquakes and after the Achaeans began to exert their influence on Crete. Activities from everyday life portrayed religious festivals, sports, games, and dancing.

The palace at Knossos reflected the brilliant culture that existed on Crete during these centuries. The island was governed by what seems to have been a priest-king ruling from the palace, which served not only as administrative center and royal residence but also as a religious shrine

The Palace at Knossos. Right, the so-called throne room of Minos, and left, a room in the palace. The palace's running water and sewerage system still worked when excavated while the wonderful frescoes of sea and human life that decorated the palace walls continue to dazzle and impress us.

(page 133). Surrounding the king were wealthy landowning nobles. They formed a court that was enlivened by music played on lyres, flutes, and a form of bagpipe, where dancing, boxing, and bull-baiting (page 133) were favored activities. Women were as free to participate in social life as were men. Merchants and craftsmen lived in cities connected by roads, while tenant-farmers called serfs supported the population by toiling on the land.

NEOLITHIC CHINA MOVES INTO CIVILIZATION

Between 2000 and 1600 B.C. civilization in China grew out of the neolithic foundations already laid there.

The population increased, and the size and number of villages grew and developed, in some cases into small city-kingdoms. Princes or petty kings claimed divine relationships to the gods, and their elaborate burials were attended by human sacrifice similar to that much earlier in Egypt and Sumer. Bronze was introduced to take the place of copper, pottery, and wood. Writing passed quickly from the pictographic to the ideographic stage and showed no similarity to the writing symbols of other peoples.

In its earliest civilization China duplicated the experience of Egypt and Sumer. It is interesting to note, however, that no trace of any large-scale migration from the Fertile Crescent has ever been found. The appearance of western ideas in China may be due to simultaneous invention or to the influence of a small number of traders who carried the culture of the Middle East eastward, or to the passage of civilized ideas from tribe to tribe across central Asia. We do not know.

In their legends the Chinese tell of five "emperors" who invented the wheeled cart, writing, the use of metals and jade and other stones, the weaving of silk, the building of houses and temples of brick, the science of astronomy, and the system of musical notation. The five emperors, according to legend, were followed by the first dynasty of Chinese rulers, the Hsia. Whether or not the five emperors and the Hsia kings ever lived, the changes spoken of in these traditions apparently did occur between 2000 and 1600 B.C.

❦ ❦ ❦

Between 2000 and 1600 B.C. man learned more about controlling his environment. The loss of one civilization (India) was offset by the beginnings of three others: the Hittite, the Achaean, and the Chinese. The experiences of Egypt and Babylon remind us, however, that although civilizations may attain great power and wealth, they cannot retain them without constant vigilance. Both these mighty civilizations were disrupted by the onslaughts of less advanced cultures.

People, Places, and Terms

Indo-Europeans
Semites
Amorites
Hammurabi
Kassites
Mentuhotep
Osiris
Hyksos
Hurrians

Khatti
Hittites
Achaeans

Babylon
Thebes
the Fayum
Anatolia
Hattusas

Knossos

divination
astrology
federation
monogamous
barrow
language family
epic

Mastering the Reading

1. Why should anthropologists think the Indo-Europeans had some common origin? What similar customs did they share?
2. What is known of the origin of the Semitic-speaking peoples? What imprint did the Amorites leave on Mesopotamian culture?
3. What can we learn from Hammurabi's Code about life in Babylonia?
4. How did the roles of the pharaoh and his nobles of the Eleventh and Twelfth Dynasties differ from those of the previous period?
5. What does Middle Kingdom literature reveal about Egyptian taste in style and content? What proof is there that the craftsmen were highly skilled? Who were the Hyksos and how did they manage to overthrow Egypt?
6. What is Anatolia like? Why should anyone fight to control it? Who settled there? How was the Hittite state organized?
7. What proof is there of peaceful progress in Crete while upheaval existed elsewhere? What was the function of a palace such as that at Knossos?

Interpreting the Text

1. In spite of barbaric attacks after 1750 B.C., what were some major milestones reached by people in the central zones of civilization by that time? What new materials, instruments, and technological knowledge had been attained?
2. What does *codification of the law* mean? Why is it considered an advance? To whom is it an advantage? What does it say about the power of the leaders?
3. What flaws in the Egyptian and Babylonian societies weakened them? What advantages did the Hyksos, the Hittites, and Kassites have over the people conquered?

Exploring Beyond the Text

1. Read some of Hammurabi's Code and debate the question, How just were the laws of Hammurabi's Code?
2. Compare the Osiris stories with the Gilgamesh Epic. What are the similarities? How does each reveal differences in thought about afterlife and resurrection?
3. Compare the wall paintings of Crete with the tomb paintings of Egypt. What differences exist in subject matter? in technique? What do they reveal about women, foreigners, and slaves in each society?

Working with the Map

Which Indo-European groups settled in areas with an advantageous location? with good resources? Which groups were not so fortunate?

7

Imperial Age of Bronze

1600–1200 B.C.

In the period 1600–1200 B.C. the world of the ancient Middle East drew together. In the previous four centuries, the techniques of civilization had changed Neolithic villages into city-states. Civilization had then spread along river valleys and over trade routes to unite different parts of the Fertile Crescent into Sargon's empire and Hammurabi's. It had drawn the Two Lands of Egypt into a united whole and had extended Egyptian influence up the Nile into the Sudan; it had spread to the Aegean and to the Greek mainland; it had moved into Asia Minor. It now encompassed the whole eastern end of the Mediterranean.

Ambassadors and legates traveled from court to court carrying on an international diplomacy and correspondence: arranging treaties, demanding protection and gold, relaying warnings, pleading for help. Hundreds of clay tablets written in the international language of the day, the cuneiform Akkadian, have been discovered at the pharaoh Ikhnaten's capital of Akhetaten, revealing to an astonished world a web of international relations. From the conquered to the victors, and among allies, goods were exchanged, booty brought home, and tribute paid. Routes led into Egypt from the Fertile Crescent. They extended through Syria and Palestine, across the Aegean, north into Anatolia and down the Euphrates. Such routes were traveled extensively by Asiatics moving into Egypt to trade or settle, by Egyptian commanders taking up their posts in garrison towns, by Cretan and Greek traders, and by envoys like the Babylonian Kassites sent to the Egyptian court of Amenhotep III to inquire why another Kassite bride was required when the king's sister had already been sent.

From 1600–1200 B.C. the Egyptians, the Hittites, and the peoples of Crete and the Greek mainland shared the most important roles in the expanding drama of the growth of civilization. Egypt, recovered from the occupation of the Hyksos, entered on a period of renewed strength and vigor in which it exploded into Syria-Palestine to make war on the Asiatics and to carry home tribute and booty. Egypt was the dominant power of the ancient Middle East for some three hundred years. Then the Hittites, building an empire of their own, successfully challenged Egyptian supremacy in Syria. Their success established a new balance of power, which was upset by the impact of migratory tribes that once again moved into the Mediterranean world around 1200 B.C. These tribes brought the Bronze Age to an end. They destroyed the Hittite civilization, isolated Egypt, cut off the thriving start of the Greeks, and gave rise to several small city-states in Syria and Palestine that played a short but important role during the following three hundred years.

Beyond the Mediterranean world, only China advanced in civilization during this period. The Shang era is the first for which archaeologists have records. Elsewhere, the world moved slowly into neolithic culture or remained paleolithic.

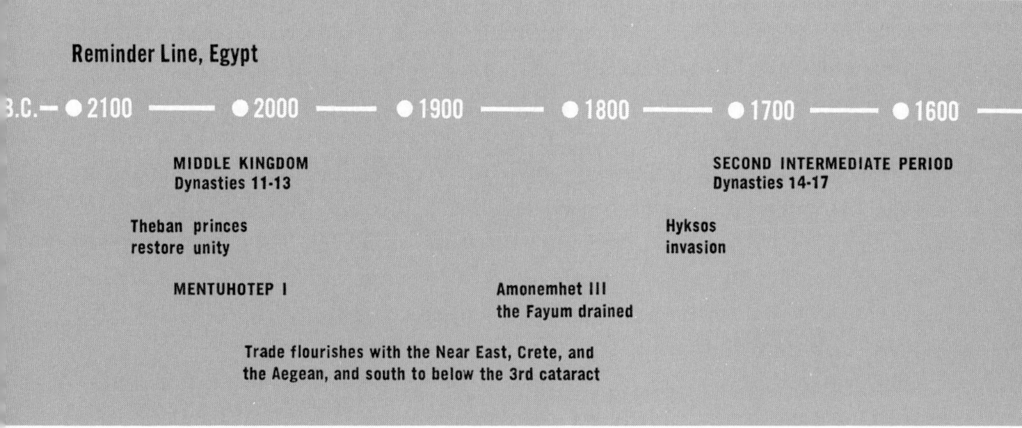

EGYPT: THE NEW KINGDOM, 1580–1085 B.C.

The Hyksos were in Egypt about two hundred years. They established a center of government at Avaris, in the eastern corner of the Delta (see map, page 68). While the Hyksos formed Dynasties Fifteen and Sixteen, tribute-paying Theban princes ruled Upper Egypt from Elephantine to Cusae, north of Asyut, waiting for the right moment to reassert native Egyptian control.

That moment came in the early 1500's B.C. The Egyptians began a war of liberation under Kamose, a ruler of the Seventeenth Dynasty of Thebes. The war was completed by his younger brother Ahmose, the founder of the great Eighteenth Dynasty of the New Kingdom or Empire Age. Ahmose took Avaris by siege and finally drove the Hyksos out of Egypt, pursuing them deep into Palestine.

EGYPT'S EMPIRE

The Egyptian eruption into Syria and Palestine in pursuit of the Hyksos reflected the energy of a newly invigorated people. They had a battle-trained army with high morale. Because their harvest was earlier, the Egyptians were ready to swoop down on their unsuspecting enemies just as they were gathering their crops. Most important of all, the target city-states of Syria-Palestine were not united. They played the game of favoring the winning side as soon as they could figure out which it was; and they changed alliances with the greatest of ease to promote their individual concerns.

Egypt's interest in Asia reflected an entirely new spirit among the Egyptians. In earlier days they had been content to remain secure within their own borders and to trade for the few things Egypt lacked. Now the Egyptians became an aggressive, militant people. Ahmose's successors were to turn the desire for expansion into an active foreign policy. The empire the Egyptians eventually controlled extended at its height from the Euphrates Valley to the Fourth Cataract of the Nile.

The first pharaohs following Ahmose recovered Nubia and made it into a province ruled over by an appointed viceroy, the "King's Son of Kush." Further ventures north into Palestine and Syria were largely raids for plunder, but these forays made a big impression. During the seventeenth and sixteenth centuries B.C. Egyptian influence there was dominant and remained so until the rise of the Mitanni.

The Mitanni, a mixture of Hurrian and other peoples ruled by an Indo-European aristocracy, inhabited the land around the great bend of the Euphrates. To the east lay the young nation of the Assyrians, and to the northwest was the rising empire of the Hittites. By 1470 B.C. the Mitanni had conquered the eastern Hittite territories, and Mitannian influence was rising, while Egypt's was falling.

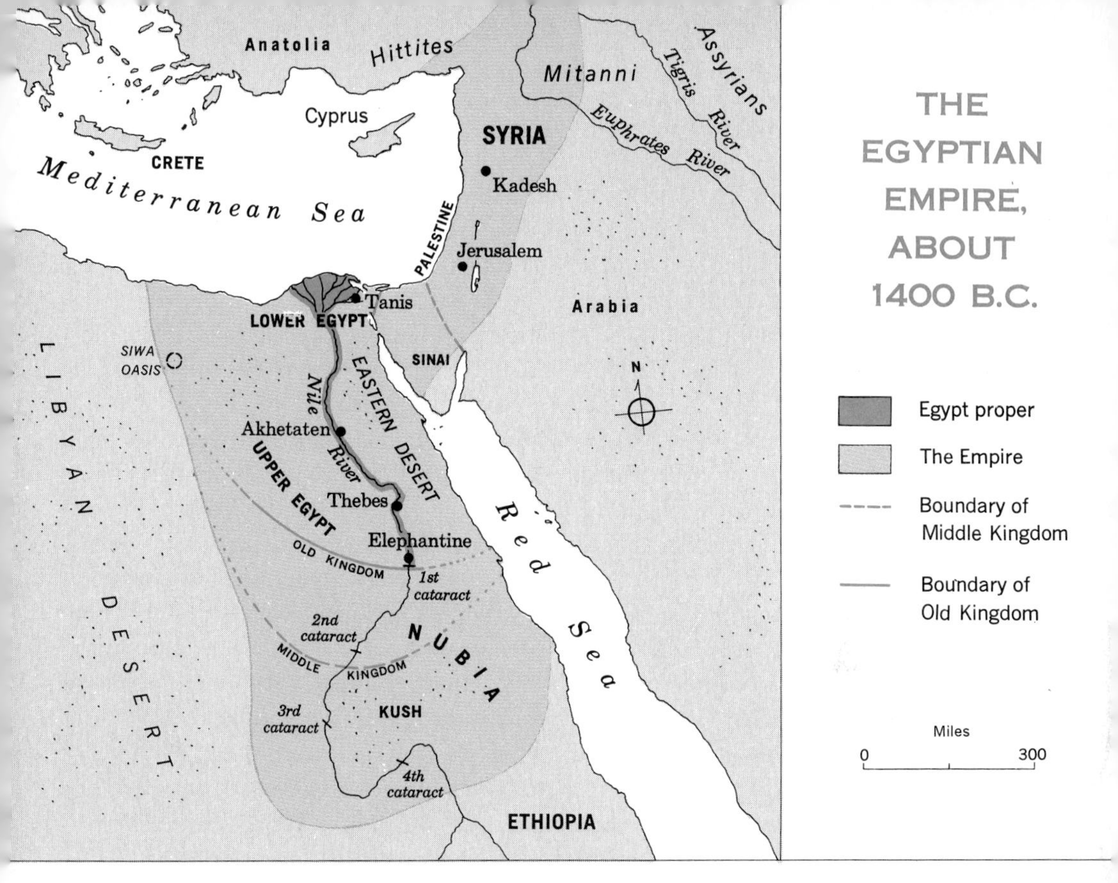

This state of affairs was arrested by Egypt's greatest warrior pharaoh, Thutmose III (1482–1450 B.C.). Ably leading Egypt's soldiers, he reestablished Egypt's position by seventeen campaigns over twenty years. His forces included not only an army but also a fleet, which used the Syrian coastal cities to launch attacks into the interior. The Mitanni were not completely checked, however, until the reign of Thutmose's successor, when the two powers entered into an alliance, and a Mitanni princess was sent to Egypt to grace Pharaoh's harem. Thutmose III commemorated his victories by raising splendid obelisks, four of which may now be seen in the cities of Rome, London, Paris, and New York (Cleopatra's Needle).

To consolidate their gains the Egyptians stationed commanders in garrison towns located at strategic points. The sons of local rulers were brought to Egypt, serving as hostages but educated along with the Egyptian royal children "to serve their (Egyptian) lord and stand at the portal of the (Egyptian) king"—hopefully upon their return home as well. At the height of the empire Egypt directly controlled Nubia and Kush as provinces, but the cities and princes of Syria and Palestine were only controlled indirectly, paying tribute and sending hostages as signs of their submission.

By the beginning of the 1300's B.C. the fortunes of the Hittites were reviving (page 131). Under the great king Suppiluliumas, the Hittites sacked the Mitanni capital. The pharaoh Ikhnaten, preoccupied with the worship of Aten (page 125), ignored pleas for help from the Mitanni and his other allies. The royal archives contain numbers of reports from the Egyptian military governors in army posts in Palestine and Syria telling of revolts by the vassal princes and of risings by the desert tribes. The governor at Jerusalem begged for more soldiers and supplies to put down attacks by a new desert people, the Apru (Habiru) who may have been related to the early Hebrews. All such reports were ignored in the councils of Pharaoh, who was too busy engineering his one-man religious revolution to find time to send aid to colonial outposts. The letters were filed unanswered, and rebellion and invasion outside Egypt itself grew steadily more serious. One by one Egypt's allies fell, and Syria came under the dominance of the Hittites. Finally the pharaoh Harmhab (c. 1325 B.C.), recognizing Egyptian weakness, signed a temporary truce with the Hittites.

By the end of the 1300's B.C. the great days of the Egyptian Empire were drawing to a close. One great century remained, but the spirit that had carried Egypt forward was waning.

THE EIGHTEENTH DYNASTY, A GOLDEN AGE, 1580–1319 B.C.

When Ahmose had succeeded in pushing out the Hyksos, he found himself master of a people whose spirit was solidly behind their new leader. The kingship was once again reestablished with power, force, and authority.

The New Kingdom rulers established themselves at Thebes and made the city into a great capital. They raised Amon-Re to be the supreme god. The temple of Amon at Thebes was the most splendid in the land. It eventually covered some 62 acres. Pharaoh after pharaoh added pylons (gateways), courtyards, halls, and shrines over a period of two thousand years. The great hypostyle hall (hall with columns) of the Twentieth Dynasty is 338 feet wide and 170 feet deep and has 136 columns in 16 rows. The central nave has twelve columns 79 feet high in two rows. Started in the Middle Kingdom (page 111), the Temple of Amon at Thebes represented the power and wealth of the Egyptian pharaohs and their empire.

Along with the worship of Amon-Re, that of Osiris continued throughout Egypt. The morality of the Osiris religion was debased, however, by the

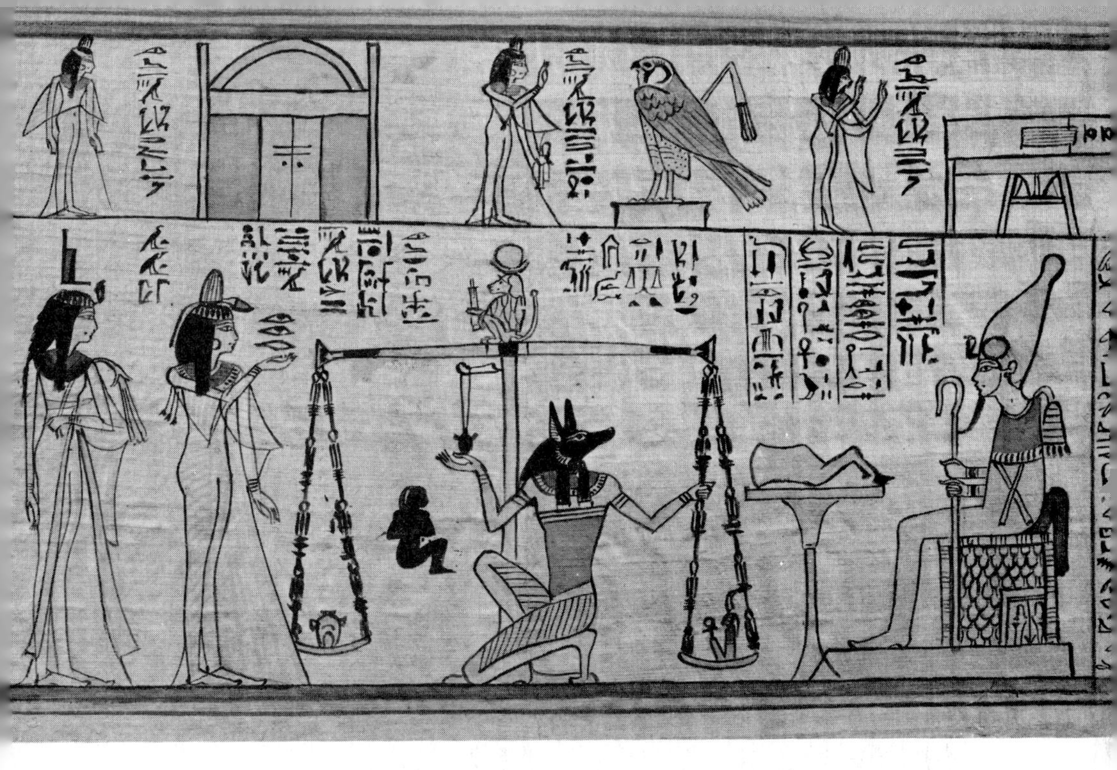

An illustration from the *Book of the Dead*. This collection of hymns, prayers, and chants enabled the deceased to successfully pass the judgment of the gods. Here the Princess Entiu-ny, guided by the goddess Isis, left, stands trial before Osiris, right. The jackal god Anubis is weighing her heart against the plume of the goddess of truth, Maat, and asking the princess to state that she did not murder, did not steal, did not lie. This is just one scene from a very long papyrus roll on which such prayers and scenes were written and then buried in the tomb.

use of the charms and spells in the *Book of the Dead* to fool the god into granting immortality to all, regardless of the goodness of their lives.

During the New Kingdom the pharaohs were buried in rock-cut tombs dug into the cliffs on the left bank of Thebes, the Valley of the Kings (see map, page 68). The tombs of the queens and those of the nobles, painted with scenes of everyday pleasures and duties (see photo, page 86), honeycombed the surrounding cliffs, while on the plain below great mortuary temples were raised to honor the god-pharaoh.

Trading was extensive. During the reign of Queen Hatshepsut (1504–1482 B.C.) trading with Punt was reestablished, and an expedition was sent to obtain the luxuries to which Egyptians had become accustomed. Its adventures are carved on the walls of the queen's beautiful step-terraced mortuary temple close to the Valley of the Kings. We see the precious myrrh trees, their rootballs carefully protected by baskets, safely transported to Egypt and then planted for the queen in the garden of her temple.

Queen Hatshepsut was the first great woman that we know of in history. On the death of her husband-brother Thutmose II, she assumed the regency since her nephew-stepson Thutmose III was still a child. But soon she forgot all about Thutmose and acquired for herself all the trappings and authority of Pharaoh. She wore the beard that dignified the king on state occasions and the headpiece that indicated his kingship. She wore the double crown. Indeed, her sex was a puzzle to her people as she was officially referred to as "His Majesty." Strong willed and ably assisted by Senmut, her architect and favorite, and unable as a woman to lead military expeditions, Hatshepsut made Egypt prosperous by encouraging trade and building and by stabilizing the administration. Her domination of her nephew, however, earned his undying hatred. Upon establishing himself in power, Thutmose III revenged himself by covering up or obliterating her name from all her monuments, and resuming the military campaigns.

The prosperity of the New Kingdom reached its climax under Amonhotep III (1412–1375 B.C.). During a long rule, while Egypt enjoyed years of peace and stability and the fruits of empire, Amonhotep established a court of luxury and splendor. He built temples and palaces, lavishing them with

EGYPTIAN DYNASTIC RELATIONSHIPS

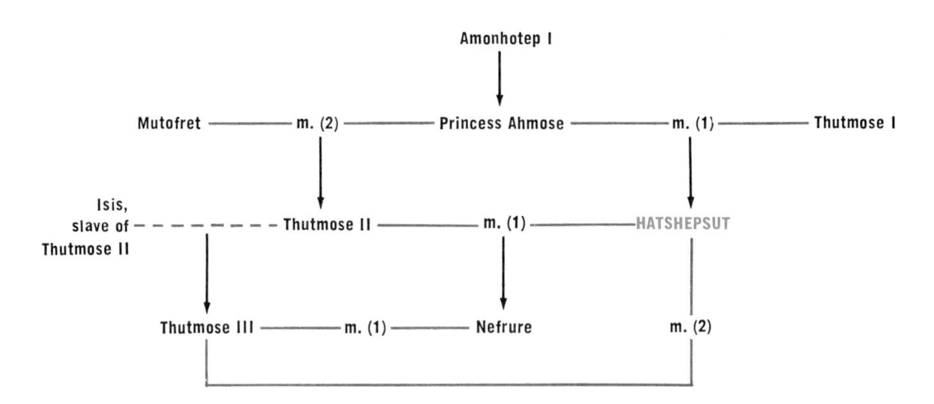

Heredity in ancient Egypt was through the female. A king, therefore, to secure the throne, had to marry the daughter of the previous king. Hatshepsut's marriages indicate how complicated relationships within one family could be. Hatshepsut was first *aunt* to Thutmose III because she was his father's half-sister (as well as his wife). Hatshepsut, secondly, became *mother-in-law* to Thutmose III when he married her daughter (who was also his own half-sister). Hatshepsut, thirdly, became *wife* to Thutmose III after the death of her husband, who was her half-brother and Thutmose III's father.

gold and silver. Out in the desert he constructed a large pleasure lake and a palace for his queen. "Numerous royal statues in granite of Elephantine, in quartz and every splendid and costly stone, established as everlasting memorials and shining in the faces of men like the morning sun" filled Thebes. Other gigantic statues showed the pharaoh seated with his favorite spouse, Tiy, a commoner whom he made Great Royal Wife. Tiy was the first queen to be named alongside her husband in official records. She was also the mother of one of Egypt's most remarkable pharaohs, Ikhnaten.

IKHNATEN (AMONHOTEP IV) AND THE DECLINE OF DYNASTY 18

In defiance of the people, the customs, and the long-established gods, Ikhnaten (1387–1366 B.C.) used the full power of a pharaoh to impose a new religion on Egypt. Born during the old age of Amonhotep III and Tiy, Ikhnaten had a head too large, a potbelly, and spindly legs. Possibly he suffered from tuberculosis, which caused curvature of the spine. The boy grew up at a court dominated by the luxury-loving companions of his father and the scheming politicians surrounding his intelligent mother. He was brought into the government as coregent in his early twenties and became pharaoh in his own right at thirty. Promptly he turned his back on everything associated with his childhood. Whether he was moved by physical or mental illness or whether his reforms were supported by older ideas or by the convictions of his wife, Nefertiti, is not known.

Ikhnaten closed the old temples, scandalizing and arousing superstitious fear among the people, and decreed the worship of a single god, Aten. Aten was intangible, unlike the other gods of Egypt, and he was symbolized by the rays of the sun. The king changed his own name from Amonhotep to Ikhnaten (spirit of Aten). He built a new capital city, Akhetaten, between Thebes and Memphis (modern Tel-el Armarna), and there the king decreed the abolition of the artistic conventions of the past. The new religion demanded new forms of expression. The result was that the palaces of the new capital were decorated with paintings and carvings strange by Egyptian standards. The pharaoh and his queen were portrayed relaxing with each other, eating, playing with their little daughters, enjoying themselves under the beneficent rays of the sun disc. Perhaps these scenes were the work of foreign artists, possibly from Crete, as there was constant exchange between Crete and Egypt at this period. There is nothing Cretan in the pictures of Ikhnaten, however, which exaggerate the deformities of the king almost to the point of caricature. Ikhnaten's art reflected a new spirit of naturalness and individuality that is entirely contrary to the

Ikhnaten and Nefertiti at Akhetaten. Right, the king and his wife play with three of their seven little daughters as the breezes blow and the rays of the Aton bless them. Such naturalistic art was far different from the formal poses customarily used to portray the god-king. The Egyptians did not understand Ikhnaten's art, nor did they accept Ikhnaten's idea that there was only one god. Left, Nefertiti, a painted limestone bust of the wife of Ikhnaten. It was found lying in the dust of a sculptor's studio at Akhetaten. The queen wears a crown and the elaborate necklace favored by ancient Egyptian women. *Nefer* meant *beautiful* in Egyptian.

formality and impersonality of traditional Egyptian art. It did not survive its founder.

Even before Ikhnaten's death (1366 B.C.), it was clear that his single-handed attempt to change the religion of a whole nation by force had failed, and with his successor the worship of Aten vanished overnight. The experiment at Akhetaten had lasted only 25 years. The priests were opposed, the populace did not understand, and the generals could not make war successfully with a pharaoh uninterested in empire. The ancient gods headed by Amon-Re were restored, the temples were reopened, and their sacrificial rituals resumed. Thebes became once more the capital, and Ikhnaten's city at Akhetaten was abandoned.

Short reigns by the young Tutankhamon (page 10) and the boy-king's widow, Ikhnaten's daughter Ankhsenamon, followed, and the Eighteenth Dynasty ended with them, in national turmoil and confusion. With the aid of the Amon priests a general named Harmhab seized the throne and reestablished law and order. Ikhnaten had so weakened the country that Harmhab was unable to muster the strength needed to drive the Hittites from the former Egyptian colonies in Syria, so he accepted the loss of the Egyptian posts in the Fertile Crescent and signed a treaty of peace with the Hittites (page 122).

THE NINETEENTH DYNASTY AND RAMSES II

A new dynasty began with Ramses I, who ruled for one year (1319 B.C.), and Seti I (1318–1299 B.C.), who advanced once more into Palestine and reconquered whatever parts of Syria were not claimed by the Hittites. His son Ramses II (1298–1231 B.C.) reigned 67 years. Ramses II became a legend. The length of his reign, his boastfulness—he had his exploits carved on temples all over Egypt—his harem, which seems to have been one of the largest in history, and the many battles he fought to restore Egypt's prestige in western Asia impressed the weaker generations that followed.

Ramses devoted the first twenty years of his reign to war with the Hittites. In 1294 B.C. he fought the battle of Kadesh, which his monuments celebrate as a great Egyptian victory. Unfortunately for Ramses' reputation, the Hittites claim Kadesh as a victory for themselves, and it is to be noted that after the battle the Hittites still remained in Syria. (Only the personal bravery of the pharaoh himself and of his troops saved the day.) Sixteen more years of struggle failed to alter the situation, so Ramses finally negotiated a nonaggression treaty with the Hittites. Egypt was to control south Syria, the Hittites north Syria. The settlement between the two empires not only ended the war between them but also stabilized the relations of their allies and brought peace to the Middle East for a generation.

The change from militarism to diplomacy abroad was paralleled by changes at home. Having by now outdone his predecessors in magnificent building at Thebes, largely by using his predecessors' monuments or replacing their names with his, Ramses built a new royal city far to the north in the eastern part of the Delta. At Per-Ramses he grew old amid pomp and ceremony. Luxury replaced strength at the court and in the country at large. As the Egyptians lost the warlike spirit that had characterized them for the past three centuries, it became necessary to hire more and more foreign troops to defend the country. The aging pharaoh kept the good will of the Amon priests by many gifts, which dangerously increased their already great power.

Warnings of new troubles came from the north. Uprooted peoples of the Aegean, joining forces with attacking migratory tribes, all collectively known as Peoples of the Sea, were on the move. From the western desert Libyan tribesmen were becoming ever more threatening. But no echoes of such dangers were allowed to reach the ears and ruffle the calm that shut in the old pharaoh at Per-Ramses. Egypt's last great century was drawing to a close.

EGYPT: THE EIGHTEENTH TO TWENTY-FIRST DYNASTIES

EIGHTEENTH DYNASTY 1580-1319 B.C.	
AHMOSE 1580-1545 B.C.	Completes the war begun by his brother Kamose, expels the Hyksos.
Ahmose's successors follow up his Asiatic victories; rise of the Mitanni	Egypt now uses bronze, new weapons, horse and chariot, all introduced by the Hyksos.
THUTMOSE II 1508-1504 B.C.	Nubia and Kush governed by an Egyptian viceroy.
HATSHEPSUT 1504-1482 B.C.	First woman to rule as Pharaoh. Commerce and trade encouraged; expedition to Punt; much building.
THUTMOSE III 1482-1450 B.C.	Restores and expands Egyptian prestige in western Asia; Palestine and Syria dependencies.
AMONHOTEP III 1412-1375 B.C.	Egyptian influence extended to fourth cataract of the Nile; empire at it greatest extent; Egypt at its peak in power and influence. Thebes a city of luxury and wealth.
AMONHOTEP IV-IKHNATEN 1387-1366 B.C.	Removes capital to Akhetaten where worship of one god, Aten, is instituted. Rise of the Hittites; loss of influence in western Asia.
TUTANKHAMEN 1366-1357 B.C.	Restores Amon and capital at Thebes; Ikhnaten's religious revolution fails.
HARMHAB 1353-1319 B.C.	Signs treaty with Hittites; restores order in Egypt.
NINETEENTH DYNASTY 1319-1200 B.C.	
RAMSES I 1319-1318 B.C.	Begins attempt to reconquer lands in western Asia lost to Hittites.
SETI I 1318-1299 B.C.	Fights in western Asia and regains some territory in Palestine and Syria.
RAMSES II 1298-1231 B.C.	Regains south Syria, leaves north Syria to the Hittites; famous for his boasting and for his building all over Egypt.
MERNEPTAH 1232-1222 B.C.	Struggles to arouse fighting spirit in Egypt and fend off attacks.
TWENTIETH DYNASTY 1200-1085 B.C.	
RAMSES III 1182-1151 B.C.	Repels invaders and saves Egypt.
RAMSES IV-XI 1151-1085 B.C.	Egypt in state of decline; internal weakness.
TWENTY-FIRST DYNASTY 1085-945 B.C.	
DIVISION OF EGYPT	Priests rule Upper Egypt from Thebes; Tanite kings rule Lower Egypt from Tanis.

END OF THE NEW KINGDOM

Ramses' successor, Merneptah (1232–1222 B.C.), struggled to arouse a fighting spirit again in Egypt. He had to fend off on the east and the north the attacks of the Peoples of the Sea, and the encroachments of the Libyans on the west and subdue rebellious Palestine. He succeeded for the moment, but during the reign of Ramses III (1182–1151 B.C., the second king of the Twentieth Dynasty), Syria was lost to the Peoples of the Sea. The Achaean and Hittite civilizations were falling. Egypt was saved, but its fate was sealed. Enclosed within its borders and governed by a line of weak Ramses, the country fell into its natural parts. The priests of Amon grasped the government for themselves and ruled Upper Egypt from Thebes, while the Twenty-first Dynasty ruled in the north from Tanis (1085 B.C.).

Egypt's days as a great power were over. It suffered slow eclipse and, after one final spurt (page 168), incorporation into other empires. Having advanced the progress of man by achievements in government, in art, in literature, in religion, Egypt was worn out. The spirit that had carried the Egyptians forward did not adjust to new times and new circumstances. Egypt remained hidebound by conservatism and by the weight of the past. It could not resist strong enemies pressing on its borders.

Libyan and Kushite rulers established themselves in power, and for the next four hundred years the country remained weak and small.

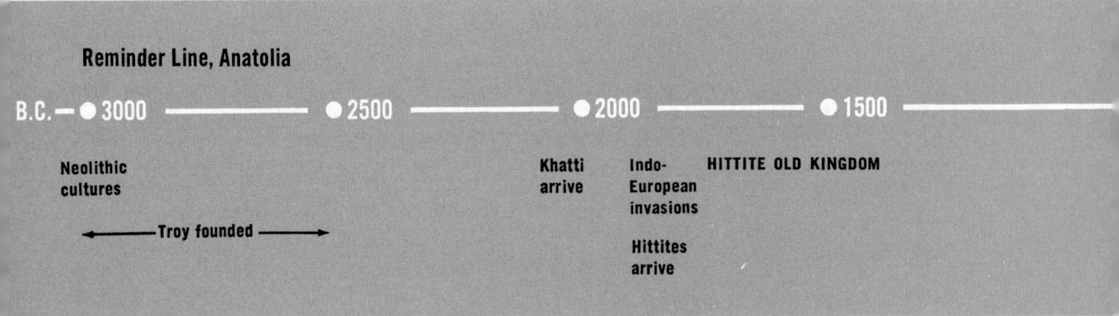

ANATOLIA: THE HITTITE EMPIRE AND WESTERN ASIA

For some 150 years following the successful raid against Babylon (page 113) the Hittite kingdom suffered a decline. Palace murders, the collapse of the Hittite federation, and constant dangers from abroad threatened to wipe out the country. The Hurrians attacked, and the Mitanni blocked expansion to the south. Order was briefly restored around 1525 B.C., but then conditions again worsened. Between 1460 B.C. and 1440 B.C. the reigning king saved his country by negotiating a treaty with Thutmose III of Egypt, who had been drawn into western Asia to restore the prestige of Egypt, which was suffering at the hands of the Mitanni.

In the middle of the fifteenth century B.C. the Mitanni (page 120) had the most powerful state in western Asia. Their horse-breeding kings held sway over the rising nation of the Assyrians to the east and over the Hurrians on the north. Extending their power from the Euphrates across the plains of Syria, the Mitanni absorbed territories previously held by the Egyptians, doing so while their diplomats were drawing Egypt into a friendly alliance (page 121). The Hittites, finding their alliance with the Egyptians dissolving, lost their Syrian lands to the Mitanni, who repeatedly attacked them and burned the Hittite capital at Hattusas.

The alliance of the Mitanni and the Egyptians was carefully preserved by Amonhotep III, who preferred diplomacy to war and kept Egyptian gold flowing to Tushratta of Mitanni in return for his good will and to maintain Egyptian influence in Asia. When Amonhotep was in his last illness and Egyptian doctors had exhausted their knowledge of medicine, Tushratta ordered the statue of the chief goddess of his subjects, the Assyrians, to be carried all the way to Egypt because she had a great reputation for healing. But the goddess failed, Amonhotep died, and Ikhnaten

Hittite warriors. A bas relief of running warriors from Yazilikaya, a rock-sanctuary near the ancient capital of Hattusas. Each warrior carries a sword and wears a high ribbed cap, shoes with upturned toes, and a garment with a short skirt tied with a belt. The Hittites were the first ancient people to learn to make iron, but they did not have the technological skill to make it in any quantity. Such skill did not develop until after 1000 B.C.

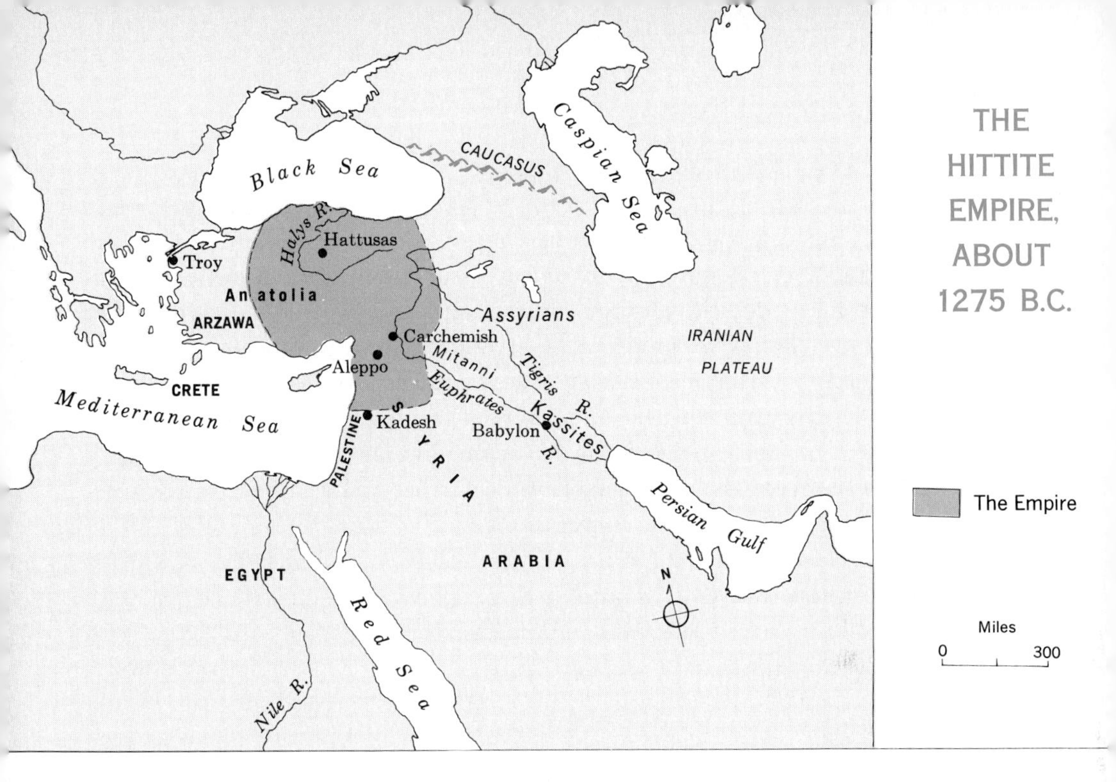

came to the throne. He turned his back on his father's allies (page 122) and ceased the gold payments through which Tushratta had maintained his control over his restless subjects. The Hittites used the Egyptian weakness to act. Under Suppiluliumas, the Hittite Great King, the upheavals that had plagued the Hittites ended.

Suppiluliumas (1375–1335 B.C.) ranks with the great soldier-kings of history. After strengthening the new fortifications of Hattusas and crushing several rebellions among the Hittite federated states, he turned his attention abroad. Taking advantage of Ikhnaten's abandonment of his allies, Suppiluliumas invaded Mitanni, defeated its army, and sacked its capital. He then led his armies west to northern Syria, which he overran. Intermittent warfare brought him back many times to Syria, until by 1340 B.C. Hittite control was firmly established. Suppiluliumas created two provinces in Syria, making one son king of Aleppo and another king of Carchemish.

The Hittite empire under Suppiluliumas and his son was at the peak of its power. Hittite influence replaced Egyptian in western Asia.

The tide of history for the Mitanni had turned. Mitanni was reduced to the status of a minor state and eventually was incorporated into the expanding state of the Assyrians, who were free to take control of the whole upper Euphrates Valley.

LAST DAYS OF THE HITTITE EMPIRE

Recovering from the disastrous state of affairs brought about by Ikhnaten's religious preoccupation, the Egyptians set out, in the thirteenth century B.C. under Seti I and Ramses II, to regain their Asian lands. War broke out between Egypt and the Hittites, and the Hittite Great King claimed a great victory over Ramses II in the battle of Kadesh (page 127). But the Hittites considered the Assyrians, whose power in the Fertile Crescent was growing, a more serious threat to their security than any danger from Egypt, so they negotiated a nonaggression treaty with Ramses (page 127). Friendly relations between the two empires were further strengthened by the marriage of a Hittite princess to Ramses.

Power and prosperity for the Hittites followed, but it lasted only fifty years. As the thirteenth century B.C. drew to a close, the Hittites were attacked on all sides. Dark days and the destruction of their civilization were ahead for the Hittites.

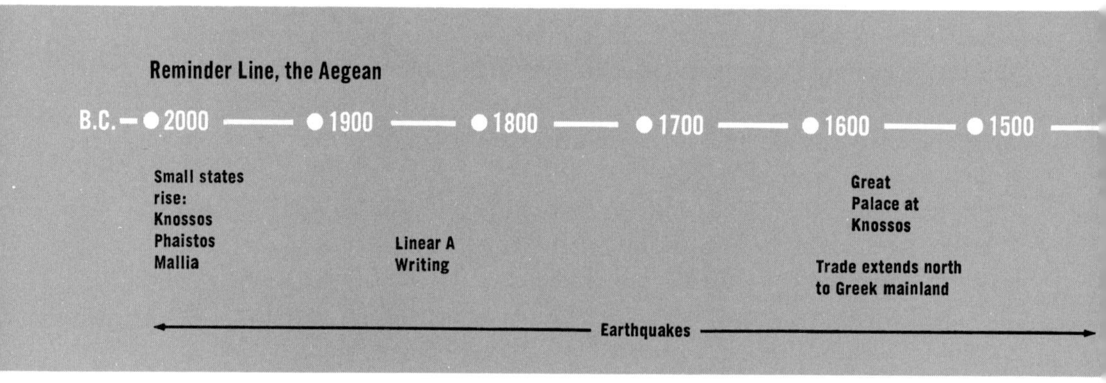

THE AEGEAN WORLD

In the sixteenth century B.C. Crete reached its greatest height. Knossos, as we have seen (page 114), was the leader among the Cretan cities. Whether a certain priest-king of Knossos, whom legend calls Minos, was ruler of the whole of Crete or whether, as seems more likely in the light of later Cretan and Greek customs, he reigned only over Knossos, we do not know.

THE LABYRINTH AT KNOSSOS

After a severe earthquake in 1600 B.C. the royal palace at Knossos was rebuilt in its final magnificence (page 115). This beautiful palace was known as the Labyrinth.

The most sacred symbol in Cretan religion was the *labrys* (double axe). It was placed in the hands of the Mother Goddess, in the hands of her son, and between the horns of the sacred bull, probably as a sign of life and of authority. The Cretans made labryses in sizes ranging from the tiny ones worn at a person's throat to those twenty feet high that stood in the palace throne room. Hundreds have been found lying in sacred caves and mountain sanctuaries, left as gifts to the gods. One grave-pit at Knossos was dug in labrys shape so that the dead were buried within the sacred sign. The sanctuary of the Mother Goddess was in the palace at Knossos. The chief priestess and the priest-king also lived there. As a result, the sacred sign appeared in so many places that the whole structure became known as the *Labyrinthos* (from the Greek, House of Labrys).

The Labyrinth at Knossos and the palaces in other Cretan cities surrounded large open paved courtyards in which bull games and other ritual dances could be viewed by spectators from the numerous verandas, porches, and windows. The dances followed intricate lines and were probably presided over by a priestess dressed as the Mother Goddess (and called on such occasions *Ariadne*—The Most Holy) and by the priest-king, the Minos. The maze of the dance and the multitude of palace rooms, which included many storerooms underground, were later confused by the Athenians into a legend of a labyrinth or maze in which lurked a half-man, half-bull, the Minotaur, ready to devour young Greeks (pages 11 and 135). The Minos wore a god bull mask during certain religious ceremonies, which may have been the germ of truth at the center of the legend. Many centuries after Knossos had been covered by the earth, dances and children's games were played all over the Greek and Roman world on pavements marked off with a maze of intricate lines that the children sometimes called the "Labyrinth" and sometimes "Troy-town."

THE ARTS OF CRETE

Cretan arts were not limited to pottery and fresco painting (page 114). Particularly appealing are the gold and ivory carvings at which the Cretans excelled. They inlaid bronze with gold, ivory, and precious stones. Tiny seals, used in place of signatures, were engraved in gold, bronze, and in such semiprecious stones or jewels as amethyst, chalcedony, jasper and rock crystal and in hard, durable polished rock such as basalt. Among their semiprecious materials were carnelian brought all the long way from Britain and amber from the distant Baltic Sea. Some of the seals had a small hole in a ridge on the back so that they could be worn as ornaments around the neck or wrist, like the Sumerian seals (page 65).

Luxurious swords and daggers with beautifully carved or jewel-inlaid handles were made for the great court nobles. Ceremonial swords of state, some over five feet long, were too magnificent and large for use in war and must have been borne before the king in processions as a symbol of royal authority. Smaller ones, for use in actual combat, were turned out not only in the palace workshops in Crete but also in quantity in mainland Greece and on such islands as Rhodes.

CRETAN INFLUENCE ON THE GREEK MAINLAND

On the Greek peninsula at this time there was a general adoption of Cretan arts, costumes, religion, and crafts, especially at the urban centers of Mycenae, Tiryns, and Pylos. These towns had been founded by the Achaeans, Indo-European peoples who had settled on the Greek peninsula around 1900 B.C. following the waves of migrations at the beginning of the

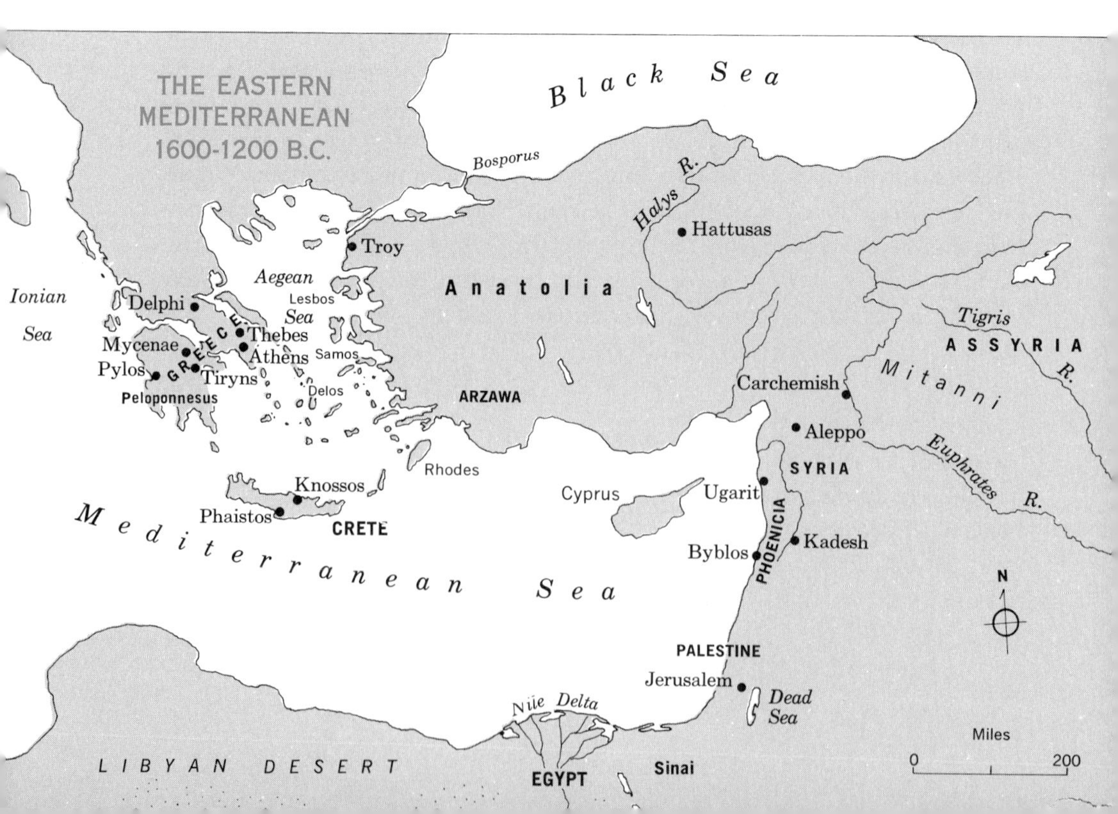

second millennium B.C. (see map, page 101). Above the Peloponnesus, Cretan influence showed itself chiefly at Athens and Delphi, but these towns had very little importance at this time. Athenian legends centuries later recalled the power of the Cretan Minos over the waters near Athens and told how children had been sent as hostages to Knossos. Whether there was a political "Minoan" empire that included Greece at this time or whether Cretan influence was exercised through trade alone is a matter of controversy. There were dozens of ports around the Mediterranean named Minos, which shows at least that the prestige of the priest-king of Knossos was very great, regardless of how much historic truth lies hidden in the tales of the Minotaur and the Labyrinth.

Of the mainland towns the most important was Mycenae, which in the sixteenth century B.C. began the steady rise to wealth and power that made it, by 1350 B.C., the leader of the Aegean world. The princes at Mycenae and Tiryns built palaces with light wells and wall frescoes in the Cretan manner. Men adopted the kilts and women the flounced dresses and elaborate hair styles of the court at Knossos. Cretan signets were used to sign official tablets. Local kings played the Cretan game of draughts. The religious cult of the Cretan Mother Goddess, with her sacred symbols of the dove, the pillar, the horns of consecration on the altar, and the labrys, was introduced at Mycenae.

The Mycenaeans did not imitate the Cretans in all things. The great fortifications around Mycenae and the other mainland cities, always built on a high hill with a view of all the surrounding approaches; the abundance of weapons; and the introduction of battle scenes with human figures in wall decorations were all alien to Cretan custom. As to the clean-shaven priest-kings of Knossos and the bearded warrior-kings of Mycenae and Tiryns, we have no proof of political control of one by the other.

The Mycenaeans were apt pupils in seafaring commerce. During the sixteenth century B.C. they developed their own trade with the Aegean islands and Anatolia. With the Cretans they sailed to Sicily and Italy.

RIVALRY OF MYCENAE AND KNOSSOS IN THE FIFTEENTH CENTURY B.C.

Mycenae increased steadily in trade and wealth until by 1500 B.C. it challenged Knossos as an equal. The good relations between the two cities then ended. Mycenaean colonies were planted at Rhodes and Cyprus in direct competition with the older Cretan settlements there.

About 1470 B.C. earthquake damage led to the rebuilding of parts of Knossos once again. A throne room like those at Mycenae and Tiryns was

The Lion Gate at Mycenae. Unlike the Minoan cities, the cities on the Hellenic mainland were strongly fortified. Mycenae was surrounded by huge walls. These so impressed the later Hellenes they attributed them to the Cyclopes, a mythical race of one-eyed giants. The Lion Gate was the main entrance to the town. It was an enormous portal, over ten feet in height, in which a triangular slab of stone was carved into two guardian lions opposing each other on either side of a column. The enormous size of the stones of the wall dwarf a present-day tourist.

built in the Labyrinth. About the same time Crete developed its first standing army, for which it hired African mercenary soldiers. The position of teacher and pupil between Knossos and Mycenae had been reversed.

The Fall of Knossos. By 1450 B.C. Knossos was ruling a centralized kingdom that included all of Crete. By 1350 B.C. Knossos was no more. How or when Knossos fell is not known, but it may be that the rulers in Knossos in 1450 B.C. were not Cretans at all but Achaeans, already enthroned following their first overseas expansion. We do know that by 1400 B.C. the Mycenaean Achaeans had wiped out the Cretan colony in Cyprus and had, for the first time, established direct trading connections between mainland Greece, Syria, and Egypt.

The date of the final fall of Knossos is hotly debated. Around 1400 B.C. a violent earthquake and tidal wave devastated the eastern Mediterranean. That may have caused the city's destruction. Some historians insist, however, that Knossos fell to invasion.

MYCENAE'S GREAT CENTURY

From about 1350 to nearly 1200 B.C. the Mycenaean Achaeans were the leaders of the Aegean world. We have no proof of a closely organized Mycenaean political empire, but there is no doubt that the same architecture, art, crafts, and language were shared by the Greek mainland, Crete, the Aegean islands, and Troy, and that the styles and patterns were set by Mycenae. The chief cities or city-states in the Achaean world were Mycenae, Tiryns, Pylos, Athens, and Thebes on the Greek mainland and Troy and Knossos overseas.

Troy was located in a corner of northwestern Anatolia called the Troad. On this excellent site trade routes from east, west, north, and south converged. As early as the middle of the third millennium B.C. a city existed on the site. Ten more rose and fell. The sixth Troy of 1300 B.C. was a civilized community, developing into a great city and carrying on friendly relations with the people of central Greece across the Aegean and with the Hittites to the southeast. But just as Mycenae could not tolerate the power of Knossos and may very well have overthrown that city, it turned on Troy as the chief rival member of the community. Between 1300 and 1290 B.C. Troy VI fell to the Achaeans in the first of two Trojan Wars, either or both of which may have contributed to the story told later in Homer's *Iliad* (page 203).

Northward Mycenaean trade extended at least as far as the upper valley of the Danube River. Eastward and southward its sailors were active on the coasts of Anatolia, Syria-Palestine, Egypt, and Libya, and Mycenaeans probably settled permanently in Syria (1400 B.C.).

DECLINE OF MYCENAE AND THE ACHAEAN WORLD

Mycenaean leadership among the Achaean cities did not go uncontested, as the Trojan Wars testify. The Achaeans of Mycenae and its neighbors destroyed and looted one another, and with constant warfare the arts of peace were neglected. Mycenaean civilization steadily declined in quality. The great centralized workshops that had produced goods for the whole Mediterranean were the first to go. Their place was taken by traveling tinkers who wandered from town to town making objects as they went. By 1200 B.C. there were no more luxurious weapons and vases, indicating that the highly civilized and sophisticated customers of the great days of Knossos and Mycenae no longer existed. As constant warfare within the Aegean world weakened the cities, half-civilized Indo-European warriors called Dorians, living until then in the Danube region to the north, sharpened their iron swords and took the wilderness trails to the south. A weakening civilization lay ready for them to loot and pillage. For the Cretan-Mycenaean civilization, as for the Hittite and the Egyptian, the end of the Bronze Age was drawing near.

Reminder Line, China

B.C.— ● 3000 —— ● 2000 —— ● 1800 —— ● 1600 ——

3000: Neolithic cultures spread into China from west and southwest

2000–1800: Five traditional emperors

Wheeled cart
Writing
Metals

1600: Legendary Hsia dynasty

CHINA: THE SHANG ERA, C. 1600–1000 B.C.

According to Chinese tradition the Shang dynasty followed the Hsia, lasting from approximately 1600–1000 B.C. (Some scholars give the dates 1765–1122 B.C., others 1523–1027 B.C.) Unlike the Hsia dynasty, however, the Shang period has archaeological evidence to give substance to the memory of the Chinese people.

THE SHANG CAPITAL: AN-YANG

Sometime after 1600 B.C., a great city by the name of An-Yang rose on a branch of the Hwang Ho (Yellow River) in north China. Like the civilized cities of the Fertile Crescent and the Mediterranean, An-Yang was surrounded by rich farmlands, and close cooperation existed between the farmers and the craftsmen of the city.

An-Yang was divided into districts like the cities of Egypt and Babylonia. Each district was assigned to a different craft, and the bronzemakers, the smiths, the potters, and the weavers had their homes and shops in a specific location.

Twenty-five miles away lay hills with minerals, stone, and timber. From the surrounding farms came wheat and rice, paid for by seashells imported from the distant coast. Livestock included pigs, dogs, cattle, water buffalo, sheep, goats, and horses. Silkworms were first raised during the Shang era, and poultry was raised.

The Shang people were enthusiastic hunters. From the forested hills they brought in deer, antelope, wild boar, foxes, bears, and occasionally an elephant, tiger, or rhinoceros (the latter are no longer found in north China). Even whalebones have been found at An-Yang, but it is not known whether the whole animal or only its bones were brought from the sea. The Shang hunters and soldiers fought with bows and arrows, spears, battle-axes, and daggers. The chieftains were distinguished in battle by their plumed bronze helmets.

Not much is known of the government of Shang China. The ruler of Shang might have been only a local ruler, or he might have been overlord of dependent nobles, called vassals, in surrounding states. Whatever the situation, warfare seems to have been constant. The An-Yang kings were buried in the style of the Early Dynastic Sumerians fifteen hundred years earlier. Weapons, tools, pottery, ornaments, and sacrificed human beings were placed in the grave. In one royal grave, for example, twenty-four women and seventeen men of the court lay near the king, with horses, chariots, soldiers, and dogs nearby to give him companionship in the world of the dead.

Offerings of many kinds were made to spirits believed to fill the world and to the royal ancestors. To the spirits of the dead, of the air, the earth, fire, water, trees, and the wind were offered flowers, fruits, vegetables, wine, animals, and household objects. They were wafted to the next world by burning, a burial custom the Chinese still follow.

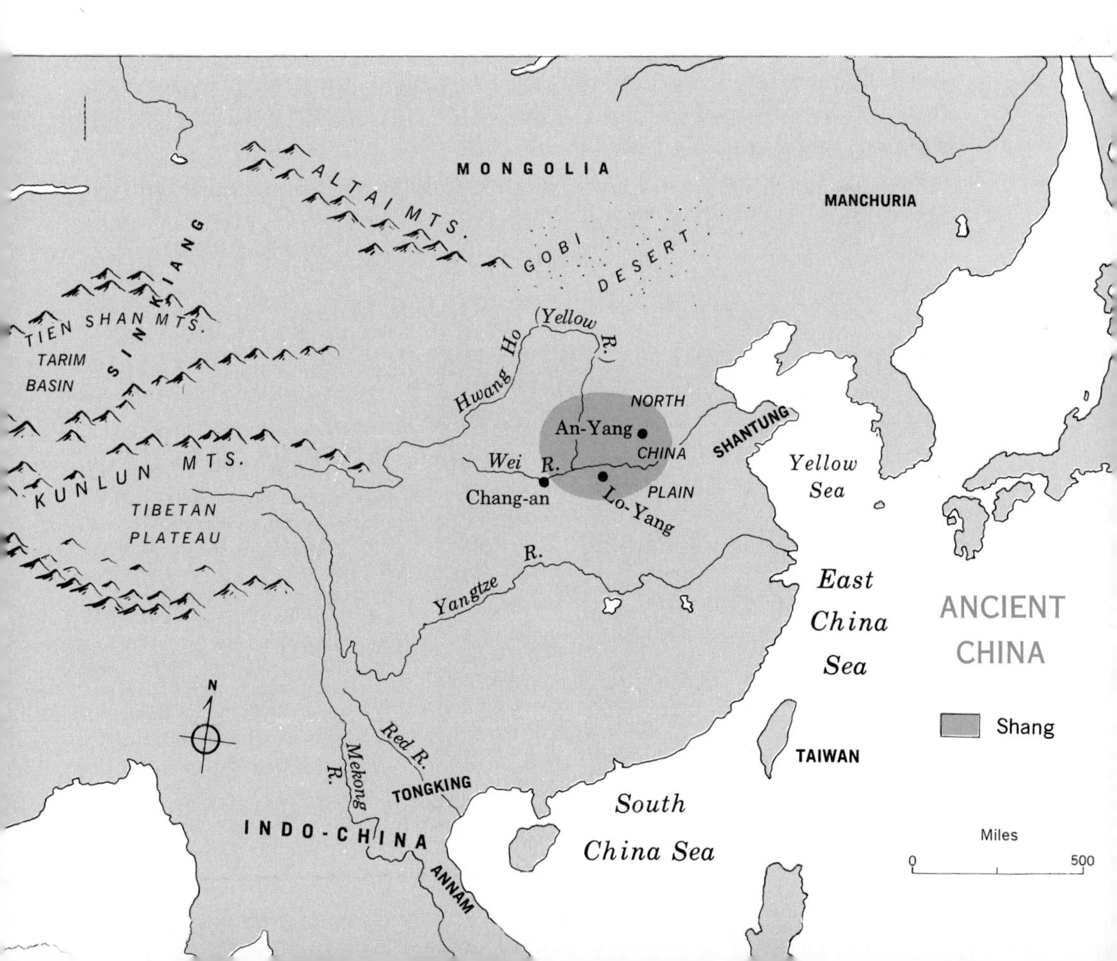

SHANG ARTS

During the Shang era bronze casting reached a high level of excellence. Prototypes of designs that were native to the Chinese, such as the dragon, made their first appearance, and the square corners and angular designs of bronze receptacles copied earlier works carved in wood. Bronze receptacles seem to have been ceremonial and have been found in quantities in the tombs.

Shang stone carving was as magnificent as their bronze casting. Objects were carved in marble and limestone in sizes ranging from tiny miniatures to figures larger than life. Artists carved birds, animals, and imaginary monsters from jade, from earliest days the national stone. Jewelers also worked in jade and in shell, bone, ivory, precious stones, and metals. Their skill in combining materials, such as bronze inlaid with turquoise, was equal to the Cretan technique of inlaying bronze swords with ivory and gold, a marvel of western art of the same period.

Chinese music developed along a different line from that of Egypt and the Fertile Crescent. In the Middle East the harp or flute served as a background and accompaniment for the sung melody. In China, music was created by striking together many different chimes, bells (which they were the first to invent), and drums, so that no single line of melody predominated. The differences in eastern and western music that began in the Bronze Age have continued to the present time.

Only in north China did civilization appear. South from the Hwang Ho Valley and the civilized Shang people the cultures of the rest of China remained primitive. In south China and Indo-China neolithic life continued.

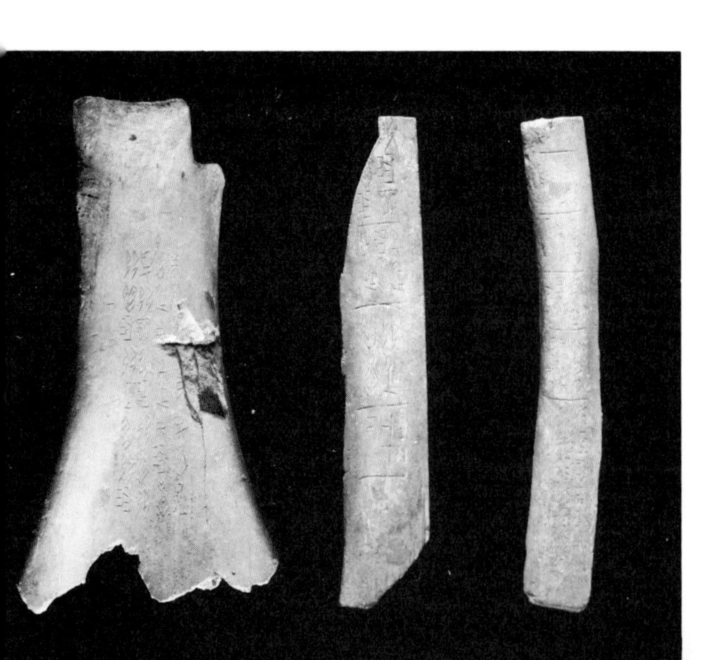

Oracle bones. One of our principal sources for Chinese history comes from the so-called oracle bones. These were animal bones used by soothsayers to predict the future. When heated the bones cracked. The cracks were interpreted and the message was written on the bone. These bones are from the Shang period. On the left is a scapula; it has four columns of writing with eight characters in each.

❁ ❁ ❁

The four centuries from 1600–1200 B.C. marked the high tide of the Mediterranean Bronze Age and the establishment of the first historical period in China. During these four hundred years ancient civilized man in the west had established three important empires: the Egyptian, the Hittite, and the sea-borne one of the Cretans and Greeks. He had established communications with his fellows throughout the eastern Mediterranean world, and he had reached new peaks in the arts, in government, and in providing himself with the luxuries and comforts that mark civilized life. Still, internal decay and decline set in. Invaders from the partly civilized border areas were once again on the move around 1200 B.C. They attacked, using new weapons of iron. The great civilizations of the Bronze Age could not resist them. During the disruptions of the next three hundred years, the foundations were laid for the new Iron Age ahead.

Outside Eurasia, the world progressed only slowly into the neolithic, or stayed paleolithic.

People, Places, and Terms

Ahmose	Mitanni	Mycenae
Hatshepsut	Minos	Akhetaten
Thutmose III	Suppiluliumas	Troy
Amonhotep III	Mycenaeans	An-Yang
Ikhnaten	Shangs	
Aten		Labyrinth
Ramses II	Aegean	*labrys*

Mastering the Reading

1. What groups and problems challenged and curtailed Egypt's expansionist mood? What accomplishments during the Eighteenth Dynasty made it a Golden Age?
2. In what ways was Ikhnaten's reign unsuccessful? What established patterns did he reject? For what is Ramses II famous?
3. What role did the Mitanni play in the affairs of neighboring empires? of the Hittites?
4. How was Mycenae similar to but different from Crete in culture and history?
5. What aspects of the culture of Shang dynasty China were different from the other civilized areas of the time?

Interpreting the Text

1. How did Ahmose and Thutmose III expand the empire? What role did Harmhab play?
2. Treaties were a new device of the Imperial Age of Bronze. How effective were they?

Exploring Beyond the Text

1. In what ways had the Hyksos stimulated the Egyptians to gain an empire?
2. Act out a meeting at the judgment seat of Osiris and portray Hatshepsut, Thutmose III, and Ramses II; each trying to show why his accomplishments were more worthy than those of the others. Read in other sources to back up your arguments.
3. Have several classmates prepare reports on a description of the palaces of Knossos, religious practices of the Cretans, and the significance of the *labrys*. Have others read and report on the Greek myth of Theseus including the Seven Maidens and Seven Youths, the Bull-Leaping, the Minotaur, and Ariadne.
4. Recent findings by archaeologists concern volcanic eruptions in the Aegean. These, they think, may relate to the downfall of Knossos. A later tidal wave created eruptions that may, they theorize, have extended to the area crossed by Moses and his band of Hebrews. Research these theories. They make good reading and give a clearer understanding of how the historian gets his information from many scientists working together.
5. The culture of the Hittites is an example of cross-cultural exchange. Read and report on the ways that the Hittites shared ideas, customs, and symbols with many of their neighbors.

8

Collapse of the Bronze Age

1200–900 B.C.

Between 1200 and 900 B.C. disaster came to the Bronze Age civilizations and their partly civilized neighbors. The destruction of the urban centers of culture was added to the confusion of invasions and migrations of many people seeking new homes. Among the most important of these were the Dorians, who attacked Greece and the islands of the Aegean, and the Peoples of the Sea, who fell on Syria-Palestine and Egypt. Still other invaders attacked the Hittites. Semitic nomads were also on the move. Mingling with the local populations in Syria and Palestine, and temporarily unhindered by the neighboring great powers that were in collapse, the Phoenicians, Arameans, and Hebrews, created flourishing states at the crossroads of the Middle East. In the Far East nomads moved on the civilized center of Shang and destroyed it.

HUMANITY UPROOTED

The climate of Europe was colder and rainier during the period 1200–1000 B.C. than it had been for many centuries. There is a probability that this climatic change was world-wide. Farming suffered, adding hunger to the misery of cold. Excessive rainfall resulted in flooding in many regions. Uncivilized tribes, whose populations had been increasing during the centuries of plenty, had to hunt for new homes or perish in the old ones.

From central and northern Europe, from the steppes of the Caspian Sea, from the desert lands of Arabia, from the wide expanse of central Asia, these tribes, carrying weapons made of iron, spread out in all directions. Some dispossessed neighboring tribes whose lands seemed to promise more food than their own, while others looted the rich cities of the Hittites, the Achaeans, the Egyptians, and the Shang. The peoples dispossessed by the first attackers were in turn displaced themselves. For some, such as the Achaeans, displacement meant wandering to find somewhere new to settle where war could not reach them, or swelling the ranks of the invaders.

AEGEAN TURMOIL

Down through the Balkan peninsula in eastern Europe came tribesmen of Indo-European descent who are known as Dorians. The Dorians were the uncivilized cousins of the Achaeans, who had preceded them into Greece several centuries earlier (page 134). During the great days of Mycenae, Achaean traders had introduced the Dorians along the Danube River to the weapons and ornaments of civilization. The Dorian tribesmen now burst into the Mediterranean borderlands, determined to take the spoils of civilization for themselves. They fought their way down to the western side of Greece to Pylos in the south, which they burned and looted. Marching east and north, they put to the torch and sword Mycenae and Tiryns and dozens of smaller towns, such as Athens. Some of the conquered Achaeans saved themselves from slaughter by joining the Dorians.

Taking possession of Achaean ships and sailors, the Dorians sailed to Crete, where they wiped out Knossos. Homeless Cretans swelled the navy of the Dorians. One by one the islands of the Aegean fell to the invaders, and their displaced inhabitants joined the raiders.

THE FALL OF THE HITTITE EMPIRE

By 1200 B.C. the Hittites were hard pressed. They were attacked on the north and east by warlike tribes coming over from Greece and down through the Caucasus Mountains from north of the Black and Caspian seas. The Hittites were overwhelmed. Hittite civilization ceased to exist, and it was so completely wiped from memory that it remained unknown until the twentieth century A.D. Asia Minor returned to an uncivilized state for about four hundred years.

THE PEOPLES OF THE SEA IN SYRIA-PALESTINE

A new group of migrating tribes hit the coast of Syria-Palestine. An Egyptian record stated: "The isles and the peoples of the sea are in turmoil." The city-states of Syria-Palestine fell, but Ramses III, rousing Egypt, defeated the invaders in a combined land and sea battle and saved his country. Some of the invaders then returned to northern Syria, where they set up a number of small neo-Hittite states. Others settled along the coast and became the Philistines. Still others, having ships at their command, sailed westward in the Mediterranean seeking new lands to conquer. Sardinia is probably named after the Sardana, while the seafarers whom we will meet as Etruscans in western Italy may possibly be the Turshoi.

SMALLER STATES OF SYRIA-PALESTINE

The land of Palestine along the eastern end of the Mediterranean is a narrow fertile coast backed by mountains beyond which lie the broad grasslands of the area known as Syria. On the slopes of the Lebanon and Anti-Lebanon mountains were the famous cedars and other hardwoods. Farmlands supported independent cities, which flourished along the coast as far north as Phoenicia, from which wool, woven into beautiful textiles, was traded throughout the Mediterranean world.

The eastern end of the Mediterranean is at the crossroads of the Middle East. This area played the part of middleman between the lands of the Mediterranean and those to the east. Throughout history the cities of Syria-Palestine transmitted the culture of one area to another. Travelers, traders, and, later, ambassadors from many lands rested and refreshed themselves and carried on business as they passed through. Syria-Palestine also served as the land bridge over which marched the armies of Egypt and Mesopotamia. Its strategic location attracted the eyes of its stronger neighbors, but its independent-minded rulers were never able to remain united for any length of time. In large measure the fate of Syria-Palestine reflected the fortunes of the powerful states surrounding it. When they were strong, Syria-Palestine

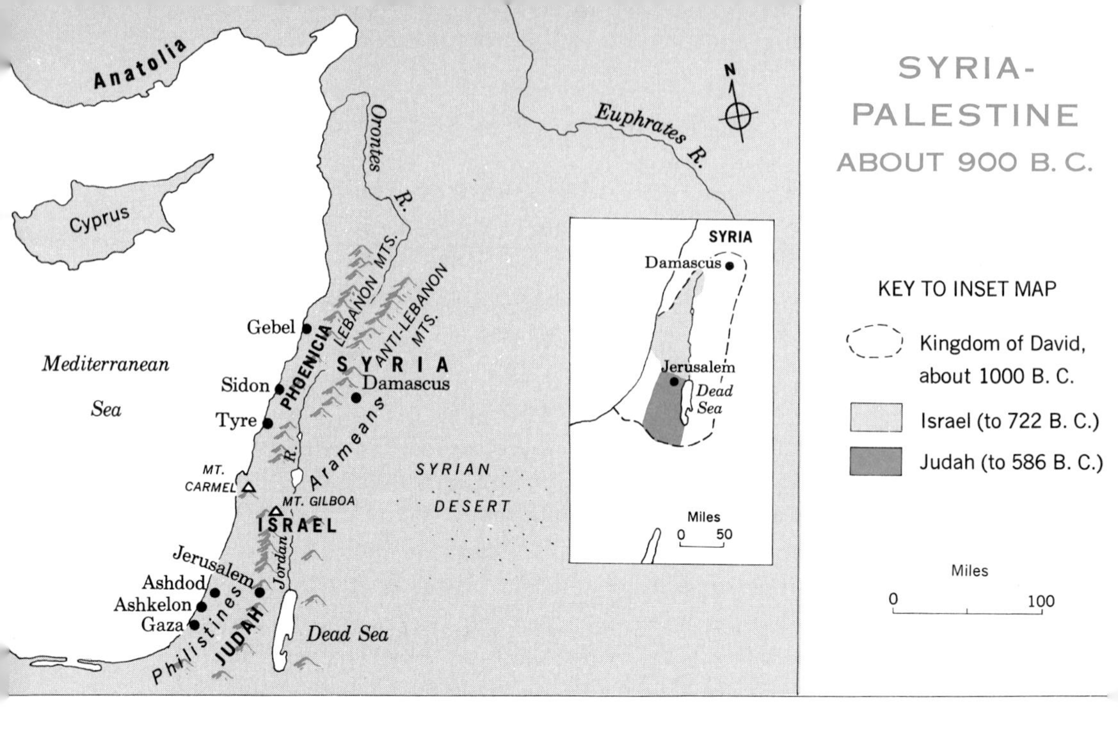

paid tribute, but when the great powers were weak, the cities were able to carry on an independent and thriving commercial life in the increasingly extensive trade of the region.

Unlike their big neighbors, the city-states of the coast and inland were not obliterated or isolated by the movements and invasions that occurred at the end of the Bronze Age. The newcomers were absorbed, and new groupings arose that dominated the area independently of great foreign powers from around 1200 to 900 B.C.

The peoples of Syria-Palestine were of mixed origins, though largely of Semitic roots. The native people, the Canaanites, were villagers and townsmen of mixed ancestry. They were descended from Semites who had come in from the Arabian desert in earlier times and from Hyksos, Hittites, and Egyptians who had settled permanently during periods of occupation. In addition to the Canaanites, three new peoples became important: the Phoenicians, the Arameans, and the Hebrews.

THE PHOENICIANS

By 1200 B.C. the Phoenicians had held the Syrian coast from Mount Carmel northward for a hundred miles for an unknown period. Their own traditions told of an original home eastward across the desert, perhaps in Babylonia, but recent studies suggest that they originated in the desert region between Egypt and Palestine.

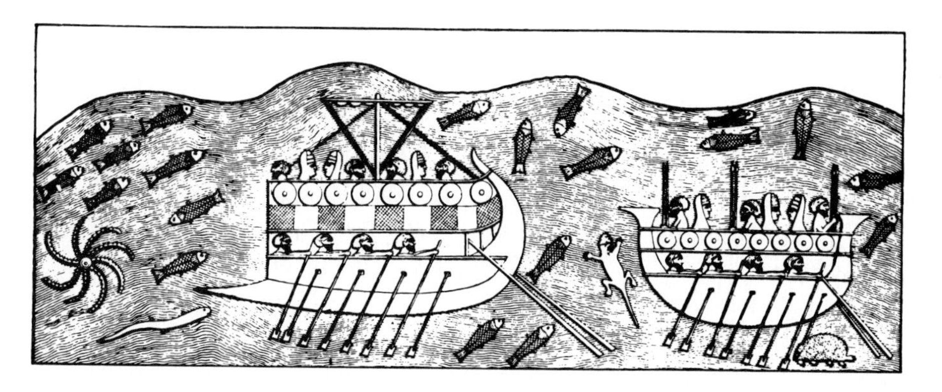

Phoenician ships. We have very few representations of the ships of the Phoenicians, the most important seafarers of the early first millennium B.C. This Assyrian relief, however, is believed to show two kinds of Phoenician ships. On the left, the ship is single-masted and furnished with beaked prow and incurving stern. The other is mastless, and prow and stern are similar. Both are rowed by two banks of oars. In the water are starfish, eel, a turtle, and an alligator, depicted from above rather than sideways.

After settling on the seacoast the Phoenicians learned to fish and to sail boats. Abandoning their desert ways, they became townspeople. Their chief ports were Gebel, Tyre, and Sidon. In the years before 1200 B.C. the Phoenicians kept to the shores of the eastern Mediterranean and to a coastal trade with Egypt. They were barred from exploring farther out in the sea by the ships of Crete and Mycenae.

The Phoenician ports were in the line of march of the Peoples of the Sea as they swept toward Egypt. Phoenicia was ravaged, and its towns went up in flames. That is why in Phoenician tradition every city has two founding dates, one after the Phoenicians came from the desert and another following the invasion of the Peoples of the Sea.

The dispersal of the Peoples of the Sea after their defeat on the border of Egypt and the disappearance of Cretan and Mycenaean sea power opened the Mediterranean to Phoenician exploration. The Phoenicians became the greatest traders and explorers of the Early Iron Age. First the sailors of Sidon and later those of Tyre ventured through the waters of the Aegean and then the Mediterranean. Famous for their seaworthy boats and for their skill in navigating by the stars, the Phoenicians carried the goods they made or traded throughout the Mediterranean and beyond the Strait of Gibraltar as far west as Cape Verde and the Azore Islands. In their travels they established overseas posts at strategic points. One of them, Carthage in North Africa, rose to dominate the western Mediterranean.

Phoenicia was famous for its beautiful textiles, dyed the rare "royal" purple, and for its great glassware industry. But the chief contribution of the Phoenicians was an indirect one: the diffusion of the alphabet, which they carried far and wide in trade. While the Phoenician alphabet's origin is obscure, Phoenician writing seems to have been influenced by Egyptian hieratic and by early Syrian efforts to evolve consonants. An alphabet of 22 consonants, but no vowels, was finally adopted. The Arameans (see below) carried a version of the Phoenician alphabet to Babylonia, from where it passed to Persia and eventually to India. From the Phoenicians it went west, and the Hellenes of Greece added vowels. They passed the new combination on to the Etruscans and Romans, from whom it came at last to all the countries of western Europe.

The Phoenicians were friends of the Hebrews, who were now in Canaan. Together the Hebrews and Phoenicians waged war against the Philistine ports of Ashdod, Ashkelon, and Gaza. In the tenth century B.C. Hiram, king of Tyre, cooperated with the Hebrew king, Solomon, to send joint Phoenician-Hebrew trading expeditions to the Red Sea and eastern Africa.

The Phoenicians maintained their independence until 850 B.C., when they were conquered by the Assyrians. Even after their conquest they maintained their supreme position on the seas. The Phoenicians were the foremost navigators and middlemen in trade until the supremacy of Athens in the fifth century B.C.

THE ARAMEANS

While the Phoenicians were creating seaports along the western slopes of the Lebanon mountains, the eastern slopes were settled by another Semitic tribe from Arabia, the Arameans. Another related tribe, the Chaldeans, pushed into Babylonia (page 169), and still other kinsmen, the Hebrews, moved into Canaan. The Aramean town of Damascus became the principal caravan center of western Asia.

The great historical importance of the Arameans was their adaptation of the alphabet to their own language and the spread of their language throughout the Middle East. Aramaic became the one language spoken by traders of all countries between the Mediterranean and India and between the Black Sea and Arabia. It remained in commercial use long after the Arameans themselves fell to the Assyrians in 732 B.C. For a thousand years Greeks, Hindus, Romans, and Persians carried on business with each other in Aramaic, and Christian writers used it in the first centuries A.D.

THE HEBREWS

Our only source of information about the Hebrews before they settled in Palestine is the collection of tribal tales handed down orally for many centuries that now appear in the Old Testament. They probably contain some truth, as do the legends of other ancient nations. It must be remembered, however, that they were told around the campfires in the desert to entertain and inspire their hearers, as well as to inform them about their ancestors. Their accuracy as history, therefore, is open to question.

According to their legends, the ancestor of the Hebrew nomads was an Aramean named Abraham. Abraham brought his family from "Ur of the Chaldees" across the desert from the Euphrates Valley into the back country of Palestine, probably about the time of Hammurabi in Babylon (1750 B.C.). Abraham's grandson Jacob, who was also called Israel, wandered with his family and flocks into the Sinai region and took up permanent residence on the outskirts of Egypt. Some of the Hebrew legends describe the Hebrews as living in the midst of the Egyptians and sharing the lives of the Egyptian peasants. The most ancient Hebrew tradition says that they continued to form a separate community, raising sheep and goats not in the Nile Valley but in a separate region called the land of Goshen. The stories describe how the Hebrew tribesmen were recruited to work on the building of the storage centers for grain at the cities of Pithom and Per-Ramses. Then, angered by their treatment at the hands of Egyptian contractors, they were inspired by Moses to leave Egypt and return to their ancestral nomadic lives in the neighborhood of Sinai. (Some scholars believe the Habiru [page 122], who we know were hired by Ramses II, were not the Hebrews but another nomadic people. These other nomadic people are thought to have left Egypt and joined up with the Hebrews in Sinai. The traditions of the two then intermingled to form the story of Moses and the pharaoh that we read of in the Bible.) Not a word about these events or the existence of Moses has been found in Egyptian records, although students have eagerly searched Egyptian writings ever since the Egyptian hieroglyphics were deciphered. It is highly probable, however, that Moses did exist and was chiefly responsible for the conversion of the Hebrews to the worship of Yahweh, the thunder god of Sinai. But the stories of Moses' appearance before Pharaoh and the drowning of the Egyptian ruler in pursuit of the fleeing Hebrews do not merit the same probability.

From Moses the Hebrews apparently accepted the teaching that Yahweh was the same as the *elohim* (tribal gods) originally worshiped by Abraham,

Isaac, and Jacob. When this particular Hebrew group entered Canaan, along with other Hebrew tribes who had not had the Egyptian experience, they brought with them an unshakable faith in the god Yahweh. They believed that Yahweh, with whom they had made a covenant, or binding agreement, to obey, was more powerful than all the gods of Egypt and all the *baals* (gods) worshiped by the Canaanites. As a symbol of their god the Hebrews carried with them a chest called the Ark, containing some totem or holy object the nature of which has never been revealed.

The Hebrews did not all enter Palestine at one time. Different tribes filtered in from Arabia and from Sinai over a period of two or three centuries. For a long time they were limited to the more mountainous regions where the Canaanites had not established towns or that they had not found suitable for agriculture. These areas provided forage for the Hebrew sheep and goats. Archaeology supports tradition in telling that there were periods of peaceful relations between the Hebrews and the more civilized Canaanites, from whom they eventually learned urban ways and the practices of civilization. Eventually the two peoples blended into one, but while they shared Canaanite arts and crafts, the Hebrews maintained their language and religion, which became the heritage of the blended people who are called thereafter Israelites. (Three names that are sometimes confused are *Hebrew*, which refers both to the language and to the people while they were nomadic tribesmen before they entered Palestine; *Israelite*, which describes the people after they had settled in Palestine and absorbed the Canaanites and other desert tribes into one people; and *Jew*, which refers to the people of Judah [see below] after their return from the exile in Babylon in 516 B.C. The last known is religious rather than national.)

With the coming of the Peoples of the Sea, the Israelites fell for a time under the control of the Philistines, the remnants of the great force that remained on the coast of Palestine after the other Peoples of the Sea had departed. The Philistines were warlike and possessed superior weapons. It seems that they were physically big. On Egyptian monuments they are drawn larger than the Egyptians, and the Israelite tradition stamps them as huge in the legend of Goliath, the "giant" from Gath, who was killed with a slingshot by David.

The struggle against the Philistines united the Israelites, who were both pastoral and urbanized, into one people. Their government was that of a tribal kingship, and Saul was the first king.

The Kingdom of Israel. Saul continued to live on his farm. He had no palace or elaborate court, no tax system, no regular procedure for raising armies. During his reign the country was occupied with the war against the Philistines, with the annexation of Canaanite towns that were still independent, and with war against nomadic Arameans who were founding states to the north in Syria. The Philistines defeated Saul on Mt. Gilboa, and his work in unifying the Israelites was temporarily undone.

David and Solomon. After the death of Saul and following a period of disorder, the tribal elders gave the kingship to David, a son-in-law of Saul and one of his chief captains. War was resumed against the Philistines, who were forced back into their cities. The Israelites controlled the rest of Palestine. David captured the Canaanite city of Jerusalem and made it the capital of his kingdom (see map, page 146). He took up residence in the fortress, Zion, which dominated the rest of Jerusalem, and this part of the city was henceforth known as the City of David. There, with the aid of Phoenician architects, David built a royal palace.

The unity of David's kingdom was twice threatened. First, the urbanized part of Palestine, which lay north of Jerusalem, declared itself independent, and David had to reconquer it. Second, during David's old age the court divided into factions over the succession to the throne. Plots were hatched in which David's sons took part. On his death the throne passed, with some opposition, to his tenth son, Solomon.

Although he was not able to preserve all the territory ruled by his father, Solomon tried by other means to increase the fame of his little kingdom. He sent many trading expeditions that brought back gold, silver, and ivory. He made many foreign marriages. Although Egypt had declined from its former position as a great world power, Solomon gained much international prestige by securing a daughter of a pharaoh as a bride. He commissioned luxurious new palaces, hoping to rival the splendor of those in Egypt and Phoenicia, and he built the first national temple of the Israelite state. The cost of the temple was more than the tiny kingdom could comfortably bear. Open resentment was expressed about the taxes needed to support it, especially by the northern urban centers that had already shown a lack of enthusiasm for events in Jerusalem during the reign of David. The temple, therefore, did not stimulate national unity in the way that the rebuilt temple was to do many centuries later.

The Collapse of the United Kingdom. In future years the Jews looked back with pride at Solomon, his temple, his trading expeditions and visits from such famous personages as the Ethiopian Queen of Sheba. This built up a picture of magnificence and importance that, in reality, was greatly exaggerated. While the wise sayings of many centuries that were later

Solomon's Temple. A reconstruction of the first temple as scholars imagine it looked. The temple is somewhat Egyptian in style, but it is also Phoenician for the king of Tyre helped Solomon to plan it. The temple seems to have been an appendage to a luxurious palace with throne room, guard houses, stables, and women's quarters.

lumped together and attributed to him may have reflected a popular belief in Solomon's wisdom, his personal extravagance and his political sharpness were not admired in his own time. The country seethed on the edge of rebellion, and on Solomon's death ten of the twelve tribes refused to give allegiance to his son. Henceforth the Israelites were divided into two rival states, Israel and Judah, at war with each other and with their neighbors and torn within by dissension.

Israel, the northern state, fell to the Assyrians in the eighth century B.C., and the Israelites (the "Ten Lost Tribes") vanished forever. Judah fell to Babylon a century later, and though its people returned to Palestine, they never regained their former unity or power.

The great contribution of the Israelites lay not in government or empire but in the growth and development of their religion, which is discussed in Chapter 15. As a people they were able to separate their identity as a national group from their identity as a special religious community, and so they were able to survive while their neighbors were absorbed into the empires that followed.

MIGRATIONS IN ASIA

Europe and the Mediterranean were not the only scenes of upheaval. During the same centuries several waves of Indo-Europeans poured southward out of central and western Asia. The Iranians, whose name was henceforth to be given to the plateau they seized, were not absorbed into the original native population as their Hurrian and Mitanni predecessors had been. They retained their own language and customs and were first known to the world as two separate groups, the Medes and Persians.

Other Indo-Europeans, kinsmen of the Iranians, seized lands farther east and eventually swept into India. They were the Aryans, the people who, with the original inhabitants, built civilization anew on the Indian subcontinent.

In China, meanwhile, the half-civilized Chou (pronounced *jo*) people were on the warpath from central Asia, overthrowing the Shang civilization and destroying the capital city of An-Yang about 1030 B.C. In central Siberia other tribes seized lands. Migrations and upheaval extended all the way from the Atlantic Ocean to the Pacific in both the central zones of civilization and the Neolithic zones surrounding them.

❦ ❦ ❦

The world from 1200 to 900 B.C. was one of nations uprooted, tribes on the march, civilizations collapsing. Mankind lost the knowledge that had distinguished the Bronze Age empires and, except in Syria-Palestine, there was a return to ignorance, lawlessness, the simple economy, and the smaller populations that characterize primitive life. The civilized areas of the world received a tremendous shake-up, which brought to an end the Bronze Age.

In the collapse of the great powers of the eastern Mediterranean, three Semitic people seized the opportunity to establish themselves in Syria and Palestine. The seagoing Phoenicians and the nomadic Arameans developed wide commercial contracts, acting as the middlemen between East and West. They advanced civilization by spreading their alphabet through a language that became the *lingua franca* of the Middle East, the meeting place of East and West. The Hebrews, the founders of one of the West's three great religions, established themselves politically and became settled and civilized. These little states carried on the traditions of the past and yet made important new cultural contributions of their own.

During the era that lay ahead, the Near East once again served as the cradle and crossroads of civilization, drawing the Aegean and Anatolia into contact with the east. First the Assyrians, then the new Babylonian people called the Chaldeans, and finally the Persians were to create greater and greater empires that would eventually unify the lands from the Mediterranean to India.

People, Places, and Terms

Dorians	Jacob	Sidon
Peoples of the Sea	Moses	Carthage
Etruscans	Saul	Jerusalem
Canaanites	Philistines	Israel
Phoenicians	David	Judah
Arameans	Solomon	
Israelites	Chous	Aramaic
Jews		covenant
Hebrews	Etruria	ark
Yahweh	Gebel	*lingua franca*
Abraham	Tyre	

Mastering the Reading

1. Where and how did climate influence the migratory patterns of nomadic tribes? What were the consequences of these migrations for each of the Bronze Age civilizations?
2. What advantages in resources and location did Syria-Palestine offer?
3. Why are the Phoenicians and Arameans called "transmitters of culture"? How did Aramaic become an international language?
4. In their stories and legends how did the Hebrews account for their origin? their migrations? their presence in Egypt?
5. What historical changes are reflected in the names "Hebrew," "Israelite," and "Jew"?
6. In what ways were the Aryans, Iranians, and Chous like the Dorians?

Interpreting the Text

1. How can you explain the survival of the Phoenicians, Arameans, and Hebrews in the aggressive arena of the Fertile Crescent?
2. The term "Dark Age" is often used to describe the period following the Dorian invasions. Why and for whom was this a Dark Age?

Exploring Beyond the Text

1. Unlike other Fertile Crescent peoples, the Hebrews had a tradition of Patriarchs and Judges rather than kings. In I Samuel, Chapter 8 the arguments for and against having a king are presented. From your knowledge of other kings of the Fertile Crescent, would you agree with Samuel or not? Why did the Hebrews want a king? Defend your position.
2. Demonstrate the changes in the alphabet from the alphabet of the Phoenicians to the alphabet of the Hebrews and the modern West.
3. Read about the Phoenician production of purple dye, and their production of paper at Byblos. Share your findings with the class.

4. Write a character sketch of Saul, of David, or of Solomon. How did each represent his time and the needs and progress of his people?

Working with the Map

1. Why would Damascus be a crossroad for trade?
2. On an outline map of the eastern Mediterranean, trace the routes of the uncivilized invaders who brought the Bronze Age civilizations to an end.

Looking Back to First Civilizations

Starting in the great river valleys of the Middle East, man created his first civilizations in Mesopotamia and Egypt and, shortly after, in India. Further ventures in civilization were made in Crete, Anatolia, and China.

As the effects of civilizations were felt by surrounding peoples, the Neolithic Revolution spread into adjoining areas. When a civilization had a period of weakness, however, it was subject to attack by people still living a neolithic life. In both west and east, such attacks brought to an end the Bronze Age in the years between 1200 and 1000 B.C. The Indian civilization had already vanished. The Bronze Age style of life was not strong enough to resist attack by invaders carrying new weapons and appearing in great numbers.

In those areas where civilization was not strongly rooted, the people slipped back into an uncivilized condition. New beginnings had to be made in the ages ahead. Such was the case in India, in Anatolia, and in the Aegean world. In the Middle East, however, civilization was already two thousand years old. It reasserted itself successfully in the new age ahead, and the Middle East became the crossroads between east and west.

Some Questions to Answer

1. "All civilizations have a culture, but all cultures are not civilizations." Analyze this statement and discuss it with good illustrations.
2. What were some of the religious ideas and symbols shared by all people in this period? What were some symbols that were unique to individual groups? Why did some men worship the sun, or the river, or thunder, while others did not?

FIRST CIVILIZATIONS, 3600-1000 B.C.

	MESOPOTAMIA	EGYPT	SYRIA-PALESTINE
3600-2800 B.C. COPPER-STONE AGE	Settled villages Agriculture Writing Urbanization Sumerian cities	Pre-dynastic period Unification Dynasties 1 and 2	Settled villages Agriculture Metal working
2800-2000 B.C. EARLY BRONZE AGE	Primacy of Ur Warfare Unification of Sargon Third Dynasty of Ur Invasions	Old Kingdom, Dynasties 3-6 Pyramids Nobles become independent Border raids First Intermediate Period	Urbanization Trade with Egypt and Mesopotamia Invasions
2000-1600 B.C. MIDDLE BRONZE AGE	Amorites Hammurabi's empire Invasions by Hittites and Kassites	Middle Kingdom, Dynasties 11 and 12 Powerful nobles Hyksos invasion Second Intermediate Period	Amorites Hyksos
1600-1200 B.C. IMPERIAL AGE OF BRONZE	Kassite rule Mitanni Rise of Assyria	New Kingdom, Dynasties 18-20 Thutmose III extends Egypt to its greatest extent Hatshepsut Amonhotep III Ikhnaten Ramses II and the treaty with the Hittites	Egyptian control Mitanni Hittite control Independent cities
1200-900 B.C.	Invasions	Ramses III saves Egypt from Peoples of the Sea Raids from Libya, Nubia Collapse of New Kingdom Egypt divides: foreign kings and priests govern the Two Lands	Invasions by Peoples of the Sea and Semitic tribesmen Hebrews, Arameans, and Phoenicians Small independent states

ANATOLIA	AEGEAN	INDIA	CHINA
Settled villages Agriculture Metal working	Mountain settlements Newcomers reach Crete Agriculture Metals Seaborn trade		Paleolithic
Urbanization The Khatti Invasions	Growth of eastern ports and grainlands Trade with Egypt, Fertile Crescent, Sicily, and Italy	Indus Valley civilization Urbanization Agriculture Trade with Mesopotamia and Egypt	Neolithic Revolution spreads into China Agriculture Pottery Metal working
Hittites Hittite Old Kingdom Hittites invade Babylon Dynastic confusion	Small states rise at Knossos, Mallia, and Phaistos Linear A Achaeans settle Greece	Civilization declines Invasions	City-kingdoms in north China Five Emperors Hsia dynasty Bronze
Collapse of Old Kingdom Clashes with Mitanni and Egyptians Suppiluliumas revives Hittite power	Knossos at its height Cretan influence on Greek mainland Rise of Mycenae Knossos falls	Aryan invasions Loss of civilized skills	Shang dynasty and An-Yang Arts flourish: bronze, stone, and jade
Trojan wars Invasions from the north and east Hittites overwhelmed Collapse of civilization in Asia Minor	Dorian invasions Collapse of Mycenaean civilization	Small village communities Agriculture Warfare	Invasions by the Chou Overthrow of the Shang dynasty

3. From Egypt in the west to India in the east, towns and cities appeared in the Bronze Age. What did towns offer? What inventions and advances were made as a result of the existence of cities? What dangers and disadvantages were created as a result of the Urban Revolution?
4. In what ways may geography influence culture and civilization?

Using Documents as Evidence

Hammurabi, the king of Babylon, issued one of the best known of the ancient codes of law in about 1750 B.C. A part of the Code follows.

THE CODE OF HAMMURABI

If a man brings an accusation against a man, and charges him with a . . . crime punishable by death but cannot prove it, he, the accuser, shall be put to death.

If a man, in a case pending judgment, bears false or threatening witness, or does not establish the testimony that he has given, if that case is a case involving life, that man shall be put to death.

If a man steal the property of a god [of a temple] or palace, that man shall be put to death; and he who receives from his hand the stolen property shall also be put to death.

If a man aid a male or female slave of the palace, or a male or female slave of a freeman to escape from the city gate, he shall be put to death.

If a man rent a field for cultivation and does not produce any grain in the field, they shall call him to account because he has not performed the work required on the field, and he shall give to the owner of the field grain on the basis of the adjacent fields.

If a man neglect to strengthen his dike and does not strengthen it, and a break be made in his dike and the water carry away the nearby land, the man in whose dike the break has been made shall restore the grain that he has damaged.

If he is not able to restore the grain, they shall sell him and his goods, and the farmers whose grain the water has carried away shall share in the results of the sale.

If a merchant gives money to an agent as a favor, and the latter meet with a reverse where he goes, he shall return the principal of the money to the merchant.

If a wine-seller . . . makes the measure for drink smaller than the measure for grain [that is, cheats], they shall call the wine-seller to account, and they shall throw her into the water.

If outlaws meet in the house of a wine-seller, and she does not arrest these outlaws and bring them to the palace, that wine-seller shall be put to death.

If a wife has not been a careful housewife and has roamed around and has neglected her house and has belittled her husband, they shall throw that woman into the water.

If a man destroys the eye of another man, they shall destroy his eye.

If a man breaks a man's bone, they shall break his bone.

If a man destroys the eye of a freeman or breaks the bone of a freeman, he shall pay one mina of silver.

If a man destroys the eye of a man's slave or breaks the bone of a man's slave, he shall pay one half his price.

If a physician operates on a man for a severe wound with a bronze lance and causes the man's death; or opens an abscess near the eye of a man with a bronze lance and destroys the man's eye, they shall cut off his fingers.

If a physician operates on the slave of a freeman for a severe wound with a bronze lance and causes his death, he shall restore [replace him with] a slave of equal value.

If a builder builds a house for a man and does not make its construction firm, and the house that he has built collapses and causes the death of the owner of the house, that builder shall be put to death.

Losing an eye as punishment for causing the loss of another person's eye, if it involved an equal, probably seems severe to most people today. But you should ask, "Was it usual or unusual in the world at that time?" That is, the historian must establish a *frame of reference*. Concepts of punishment and of equality before the law have changed over the many centuries since the Code was issued, and still differ from culture to culture. For example, in some parts of the world today, stealing is punished by amputation; in others by a fine.

You can analyze the Code of Hammurabi in many ways. From the internal evidence in the Code itself, how many classes were there in the society of that time and place? Was each class treated the same way in terms of punishment? Were the punishments equally severe?

❦ ❦ ❦

The ancient Egyptians believed in an afterlife for the soul. Copies of *The Book of the Dead* were placed in tombs to guide the soul after death as it sought a favorable judgment from the gods. Here is a part of that writing.

THE BOOK OF THE DEAD

Hail unto you, ye lords of Truth! Hail to thee, great god, lord of Truth and Justice! I have come before thee, my master. . . . For I know thee, I know thy name, I know the names of the forty-two gods who are with thee in the Hall of the Two Truths, living on the remains of sinners . . . in that day when account is rendered before Onnopris, the true of voice. . . . I have not committed iniquity against men! I have not oppressed the poor! . . . I have not laid labor upon any free man beyond that which he agreed upon for himself! . . . I have not committed that which is an abomination to the gods! I have not caused the slave to be ill-treated by his master! I have not starved any man, I have not made any to weep, I have not assassinated any man . . . and I have not committed treason against any! I have in no way diminished the supplies of temples! . . . I have not taken away the loaves and the wrappings of the dead! . . . I have not blasphemed [insulted the gods]! I have in no way curtailed the sacred revenues! I have not pulled down the scale of the balance! I have not falsified the beam of the balance! [I have not cheated in measuring.] I have not taken away the milk from the mouths of sucklings! I have not lassoed cattle on their pastures! I have not taken with nets the birds of the gods! I have not fished in their ponds! . . . I have not cut off a water channel in its course! I have not put out the fire in its time! I have not defrauded the Nine Gods of the choice parts of victims! I have not ejected the oxen of the gods! I am pure! I am pure! I am pure! . . . There is no crime against me in this land of the Double Truth! Since I know the names of the gods who are with thee in the Hall of the Double Truth, save thou me from them!

The Book of the Dead contains important evidence about Egyptian life and culture. What information can you find in this document about Egypt's economy? About Egyptians' religious beliefs? What were some of the actions that were considered to be crimes in ancient Egypt?

PART 3

Man Tries Again: The Early Iron Age

1000-350 B.C.

From 1000–350 B.C., man rebuilt his societies after the Bronze Age collapsed. City-states appeared in the beginning of the Iron Age just as they had in the Early Bronze Age. These city-states were created around the Mediterranean Sea by peoples newly civilized: the Phoenicians and Carthaginians, the Etruscans, the Hellenes, and in India and China by invaders establishing local control. The idea of empire survived only in the Middle East. There, where the roots of civilization were deep, successive empires developed, each greater in extent and higher in achievement than the one before it. These reached their peak in the Persian Empire.

In the west, the chief centers of civilization in the Early Iron Age were no longer in the river valleys. Civilizations moved north—to Greece and Italy and North Africa in the Mediterranean; to the Fertile Crescent, Syria, and Palestine in the Middle East. Agriculture no longer depended on river water brought to the fields by irrigation. Because of new techniques, farming could exist in lands watered only by rain. The continuing change in climate caused by the retreat of the glaciers also made northern regions more temperate and therefore more hospitable to civilized life. By contrast, the drying up of the Sahara cut off the peoples of Africa from contact with the lands on the Mediterranean. This condemned the Africans to an inhospitable land where few dared venture and in which they were isolated from stimulating exchange with other peoples.

Two other important developments that distinguished the Early Iron Age were the use of the alphabet and the invention of coinage. The first greatly increased literacy and thereby improved the position of the common man; the second facilitated trade and exchange and brought to power a new social group: the commercial class. This class was to have particular importance in Hellas, where commerce was necessary to maintain a population that was too big for the resources of the land.

The widespread use of iron, after which the new age was named, distinguished the third millennium of civilization from the first two. The Hittites had not known how to work iron in any quantity. Wandering smiths, however, who could easily learn the techniques of smelting iron, turned out tools and weapons for their customers on the spot, and so knowledge of ironworking spread. By 1200 B.C., perhaps earlier, neolithic peoples surrounding the civilized centers had iron weapons. With these they attacked the civilized peoples, who had continued to use bronze.

Finally, in the Early Iron Age men everywhere had new thoughts about man's relation to the gods. Several outstanding religious thinkers lived at this time. Their ideas did not die out when the Early Iron Age drew to a close but continued to influence succeeding generations.

9

Empires in the Fertile Crescent

1000–350 B.C.

Out of the primitive conditions into which men had fallen during the collapse of the Bronze Age societies, it was necessary to make fresh beginnings to establish government, law and order, literacy, and urban life. This was easier to do in the Fertile Crescent, where civilization was millennia old, than in Asia Minor or Greece or China, where cultures were not so firmly rooted in the past. In the Near East, the Assyrians, who held a key position in Upper Mesopotamia, unified the Fertile Crescent and created the first great empire of the Iron Age. When Assyria was no longer able to maintain rule over its vassal states, Egypt and Babylon once again gained independence. But their independence did not last, for with the rise of the Medes and Persians, a new empire was forged that drew together the lands of the Middle East from as far west as the Aegean to as far east as the Indus River.

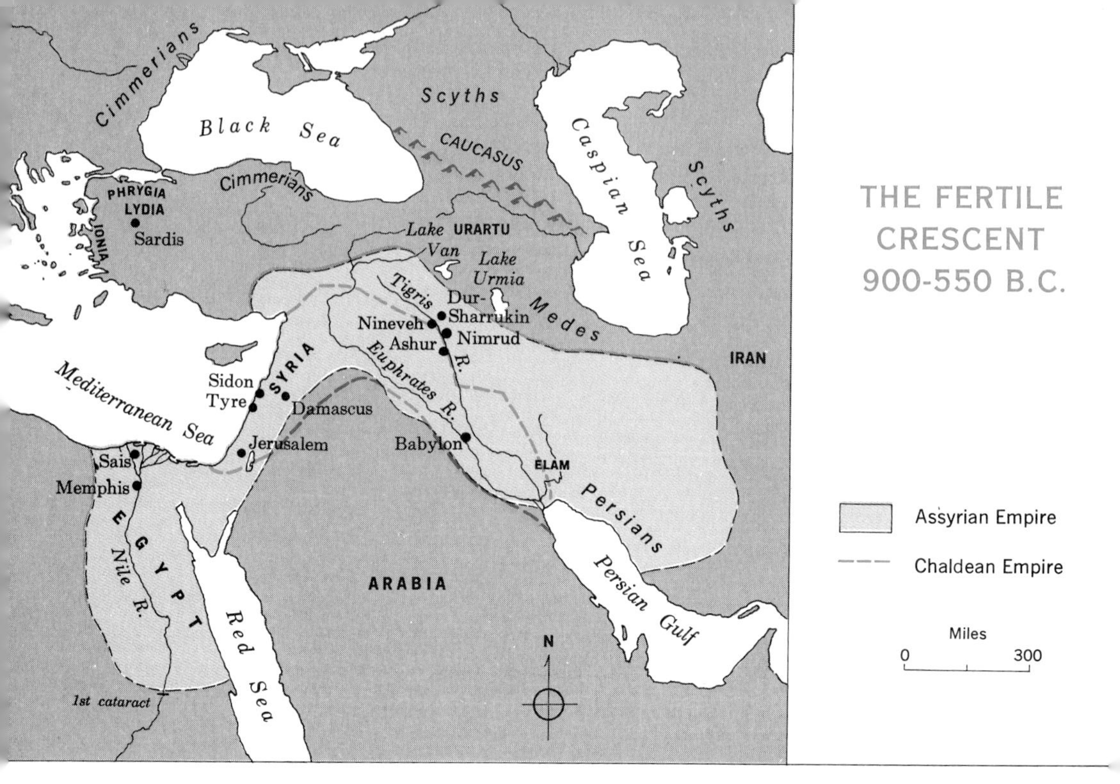

ASSYRIA

Assyria, which lay in the plains around the upper Tigris and Euphrates, had first emerged as a growing nation in the last centuries of the Bronze Age (page 132). Then it had suffered from the general collapse of the eleventh and tenth centuries B.C. and had lapsed into obscurity. Around 900 B.C. it was overshadowed by Urartu, a city-state to the north, which had denied it supplies of iron and horses, both of which were now vital to military success. But the Assyrians had one advantage. They held the most important trade routes of the Middle East.

Along these routes, the Assyrians built the four cities of Ashur, Nimrud, Dur-Sharrukin (Khorsabad), and Nineveh. The cities lay along the route coming up the Tigris from Babylon, and each was also on east-west routes between Iran and the Mediterranean. Making full use of the meeting points of caravan and river trade, the Assyrians brought in horses from the breeding grounds of the Medes in Iran and supplies of iron, copper, and lapis lazuli from Iran and Baluchistan. The Assyrians mounted their army on horseback and equipped it with iron weapons. Their advantages, combined with energy and determination to overcome all obstacles, made the Assyrians so effective that between 745 and 612 B.C. they were able to conquer the whole Fertile Crescent and the valley of the Nile, uniting them in one empire for the first time in history.

THE CIVILIZATION OF THE ASSYRIANS

The Assyrians were excellent organizers. Their army and their government reflected this. They organized their empire so successfully that many of its features were later adopted by the Persians and the Romans.

The Assyrian Empire was divided into provinces, each of which was ruled by a governor, a chief judge, and a treasurer or tax-collector. These three officials were separately responsible to the Assyrian king, so there was no chance of forming conspiracies against the central government. The tax receipts were not paid to the governor by the tax collector but were paid into the national treasury. The governor then received whatever amounts the king thought appropriate. Justice also was independent of the executive and the treasury.

A second practice of Assyria was to deport rebellious groups from their own homes to other parts of the empire, where, uprooted, they would be unable to organize effective conspiracies. The best-known instance of this policy concerned the Kingdom of Israel (page 152). King Sargon II (722–705 B.C.) of Assyria razed the capital and all the other large towns of Israel and deported its upper classes to destinations now unknown. The space left vacant by these "Ten Lost Tribes" was filled with non-Israelite exiles from Syria and Babylon who had been causing trouble for the Assyrian government. Such a policy, while brutal, increased the exchange and assimilation of ideas.

Assyria brought under one rule territories that had previously been separate. It considered itself the heir of Babylon and Sumer. As such it reflected the culture of these regions. It used iron, first introduced by the Hittites, and the horse, which had been Indo-European. Irrigation and engineering techniques were taken over from Urartu. In architecture the vault, arch, and dome—elements used by all the Bronze Age civilizations—were repeated in magnificent palaces. Assyrian religion was like that of Sumer and Babylonia except that the Assyrians called their national god Ashur. The cuneiform of Sumer and Babylonia was not allowed to perish. In great libraries, especially in Nineveh, the ancient writings of the Fertile Crescent in the Bronze Age were recovered and copied. In many cases, Assyrian copies of Sumerian and Babylonian writings are the only ones that exist

Assyrian warfare. "Hamanu, Elam's royal city, I besieged, I captured . . . I destroyed it, I devastated it, I burned it with fire." The Assyrians were formidable foes, they had impressive siege tactics, and they loved to boast of their successes. Here, the troops of King Assurbanipal scale Hamanu's fortifications with a ladder and advance unharmed while the Elamites tumble into the water below to drown and be eaten by the fish.

today. The talent of the Assyrians in organizing and preserving knowledge was one of their most important contributions to civilization.

The Assyrians were not just copyists. In the military field, besides mounting a cavalry and equipping their army with iron, they perfected the art of siege warfare, which was largely an Assyrian invention, and devised a new chariot that held three men. The Assyrian army was divided into corps of infantry, chariotry, and engineers, reflecting that same talent for organization with which the empire was established. The Assyrians were the first nation in the world to write history in the form of royal annals depicting in detail the exploits of their kings.

In sculpture the Assyrians built upon the techniques of Babylonian art and then went on to create their own. In portraying animals, the Assyrians achieved a realism surpassing all others in the ancient world. They were fond of hunting scenes, in which they skillfully portrayed wounded animals, and battle scenes, in which they showed horses full of life and energy. They were not without imagination as well as realism in their art. The royal palaces had imposing grand stairs lined with sphinxes twenty feet tall. Unlike the Egyptian sphinx, which had the head of a king on the body of a lion, the Assyrian sphinx had the crowned head of a king on the body of a bull with the wings of an eagle. The interpretation of these tremendous images is anybody's guess.

THE FALL OF ASSYRIA

The lands Assyria had conquered were restless and rebellious. In addition, the Assyrians had to devote much manpower to the defense of the civilized parts of the Middle East from the harassment of the Cimmerians and Scythians to the north, who were a constant threat. Assyria's fighting men were citizen-soldiers, chiefly farmers, who formed the basis of the population. Agriculture and herding had always remained in Assyrian hands, while commerce and trade were carried on by the Arameans and Phoenicians. Eventually the Assyrian farmers were too few in number to keep up the farms and also furnish troops. As this fact became apparent, Assyria's neighbors, greedy for the riches of royal Nineveh, combined with the rebel states to overthrow the empire. In 612 B.C., Nineveh was razed. The ruins of the destroyed and abandoned capital were in time covered with wind-blown dirt, and only the name of the capital survived as a hated symbol of a hated conquering state. The Arameans sought the protection of the Chaldeans of Babylon, who took control of the Fertile Crescent, and of the Medes, whose powerful, newly independent state rose in the Iranian highland to the east of Mesopotamia.

TEMPORARY END OF FERTILE CRESCENT UNITY

Following the fall of Assyria, three states contested for control of the Middle East. These states were Egypt, Chaldea (Babylon), and Media.

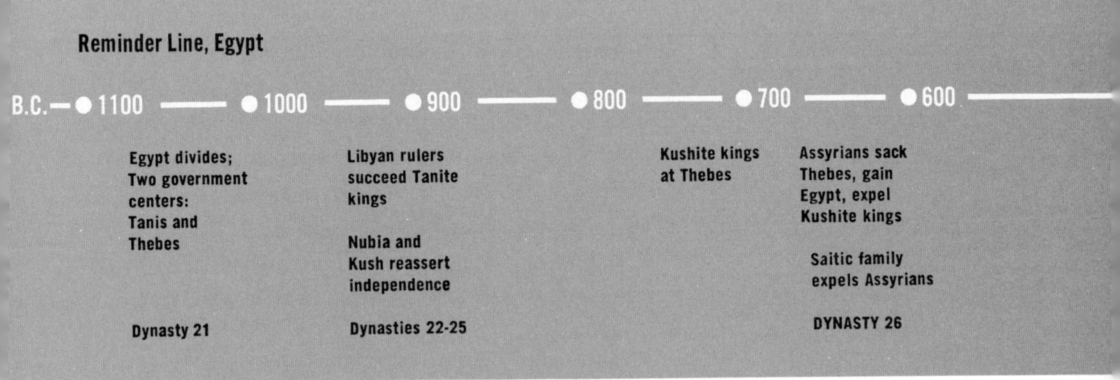

EGYPT UNDER THE TWENTY-SIXTH DYNASTY, 664–525 B.C.

The Assyrian control of Egypt lasted only a few decades. The fall of Assyria freed all the territories brought under Assyrian control. In Egypt a new dynasty had already established itself.

Twenty-Sixth Dynasty Egypt is often called Saite Egypt because its founder, Psammetichus, came from Sais, in the Nile delta. Psammetichus' father had been put in power by the Assyrians, but by 651 B.C. he had thrown off Assyrian control. By peaceful diplomacy, Psammetichus persuaded the local rulers of the various districts of Upper Egypt to accept his rule, and with the aid of hired soldiers from Greece, Libya, and Syria, he added a strip of the Syrian coast to his kingdom. Thus, he once again gave Egypt a foothold in the Fertile Crescent. The reign of Psammetichus (663–609 B.C.) proved to be the most prosperous that Egypt enjoyed in the Early Iron Age. His successor, Necho II (609–595 B.C.), taking advantage of the turmoil in the Fertile Crescent following the destruction of Nineveh, defeated and killed Josiah, King of Judah, thus gaining Jerusalem. Necho carried the Egyptian banners victoriously to the Euphrates River. To maintain his position, he tried to establish a friendly relationship with the crushed Assyrians, but he was foiled by their weakness and by the prompt counteraction of the Chaldean king of Babylon, Nebuchadnezzar. Necho then gave up interference in Fertile Crescent affairs and concentrated on improving conditions at home in Egypt. He began to dredge the Wadi Tumilat to connect the Nile with the Red Sea and reputedly sponsored a voyage of Phoenician sailors around Africa. Necho II and Psammetichus II built up a powerful navy so that Egypt ranked among the important naval powers of the Early Iron Age in the eastern Mediterranean.

The prosperity of Saite Egypt was reflected in monuments, temples, and tombs that went back two thousand years for their inspiration to the works of the Old Kingdom. The sculptures were particularly successful in capturing the spirit of dignified realism that was a mark of the art of the former age, and the portraits were true to life and skillfully executed. Geometry, algebra, and medicine were advanced beyond the Bronze Age achievements. Egyptian surgeons of this period were probably the most skillful of any in the world. They knew how to sterilize wounds by using fire, how to close wounds by taping and stitching, how to set broken bones, and how to successfully treat eye infections.

Saitic Egypt was ancient Egypt's last burst of glory under native kings. The pharaohs of the Twenty-Sixth Dynasty fought bravely to save Egypt when the Persians attacked, but they did not succeed. Egypt fell to Persia in 525 B.C. Not until the Hellenistic Ptolemies in the third century B.C. did it regain its former prosperity (page 329), and then Egypt was under foreign rule.

Reminder Line, Mesopotamia

B.C. — ● 1700 — ● 1500 — ● 1300 — ● 1100 — ● 900 — ● 700 — ● 500 —

Kassites attack Babylon

Kassites control Babylonia

Mitanni control northern Mesopotamia

Aramean infiltration

Rise of Assyria

Assyrians control Babylonia

THE CHALDEAN, OR SECOND BABYLONIAN EMPIRE, 612–539 B.C.

The Chaldean, or Second Babylonian Empire, controlled all the Fertile Crescent except for Nineveh and the northern part of Assyria, which had been seized by the Iranian Medes (see map, page 171). The middle classes and the peasants were descendants of the former Babylonians of the Bronze Age, but the ruling class were Chaldeans. They were Semites from Arabia who had infiltrated Babylonia, just as the Akkadians and the Amorites had done in earlier times. Once settled, the Akkadians had created the kingdom of Sumer-Akkad; the Amorites had established the Amorite Empire of Babylon; now the Chaldeans, repeating the pattern, produced the Chaldean, or Second Babylonian, Empire.

The most famous Chaldean king was Nebuchadnezzar (605–562 B.C.). During his reign, Babylon succeeded Nineveh as the world's most magnificent city. The walls fortifying the city were rebuilt and made more massive. They were pierced by tremendous gateways with outer and inner sections dominated by great towers manned by soldiers. The great Ishtar gate, named for one of Babylon's chief goddesses, was the most famous. The Ishtar Gate gleamed with a covering of lovely blue tiles on which lines of animals depicted in various colors were shown in a royal procession. It opened on the Sacred Way, an impressive broad avenue that led to the city's chief *ziggurat*, a huge, seven-staged mountain of a building. Near the ziggurat was the royal palace and the Hanging Gardens, a ziggurat-shaped structure upon whose many levels were laid tons of earth planted with flowering vegetation. It was built to please Nebuchadnezzar's queen, who was from Media and who had grown homesick for her native mountains in the midst of the flat Babylonian plain. The ancients considered the Hanging Gardens of Babylon one of the Seven Wonders of the ancient world.

The Ishtar Gate. Opening on the Sacred Way, the gate was a blaze of color: a background of turquoise and dark blue set off the animals colored in yellow, brown, and red. The animals were molded on a panel of clay. The panel was then cut up into separate bricks while soft, then glazed and fired, and then reassembled. On the left is a close-up of a mythical beast. The gate here is a reconstruction.

Nebuchadnezzar was more interested in fortifications and architecture than in science; he allowed science to be left to the priests. They tried to recover the knowledge held by the priests of Sumer-Akkad and Hammurabi's Babylonia, but unfortunately much had been permanently lost in the collapse of the Bronze Age and in the destruction of the libraries of Nineveh. Astronomy records were carefully kept, nevertheless, and progress was made in mathematics. The Chaldeans surpassed Saite Egypt in astronomy but lagged behind in medicine.

THE FALL OF THE CHALDEAN EMPIRE

Seven kings in all ruled the Chaldean Empire, but none of the others showed the executive or military skill of Nebuchadnezzar. Government became unstable as time went on; two of the later kings were assassinated. Religious, commercial, political, and racial cliques wrangled and fought among themselves. The last king was Belshazzar (556–539 B.C.) the ruler who supposedly saw magical writing suddenly appear on the wall during a banquet, foretelling the fall of Babylon.

Babylon did indeed fall (539 B.C.) and the collapse of the Chaldean Empire before the Persians was probably the speediest national fall in history. The whole episode took only a few days. Babylon received more lenient treatment from the Persians than it had given to Nineveh. Whereas the Assyrian capital had been wiped off the earth, Babylon was left standing and remained an important city for many centuries. It continued to flourish as a center for priestly studies in astronomy and divination and as one of the more important commercial centers of the Middle East.

THE KINGDOM OF MEDIA

Indo-European groups had entered Iran from the north and had spread through its great plateau and mountains for a thousand years before we hear of separate tribes, the "Medes" and the "Persians," in Assyrian records of about 835 B.C. By that time the Medes were living in the region around the southern end of the Caspian Sea and around Lake Urmia and were neighbors of Urartu and Assyria. The Persians had moved farther south along the Iranian plateau to lands near the Persian Gulf, and became neighbors of the Elamites and the Babylonians (see map, page 164).

During the ninth century B.C. the Medes were under the influence of Urartu and, at times, under its control. In the eighth century they were defeated by the Assyrians and suffered from raids of the Scythians. Then, during the late seventh century, Media rose to importance during the reign of Cyaxares (625–585 B.C.). The Scythians were expelled, and Median control was extended over the Persians to the south and over other peoples along the Caspian Sea's east coast. Cyaxares joined the Babylonians and Scythians in the invasion of Assyria and the overthrow of Nineveh in 612 B.C., taking Urartu and northern Assyria as Media's share of the spoils (see map, page 172).

Media's day of glory was short. In 550 B.C., Cyaxares' successor was overthrown by Cyaxares' vassal (and grandson) Cyrus of Persia.

THE ACHAEMENID EMPIRE OF PERSIA, 550–331 B.C.

The lands of the Middle East, which had divided into quarreling rival states after the overthrow of Nineveh, were reunited in a single empire by the Persians. The Persians also conquered lands outside the Fertile Crescent.

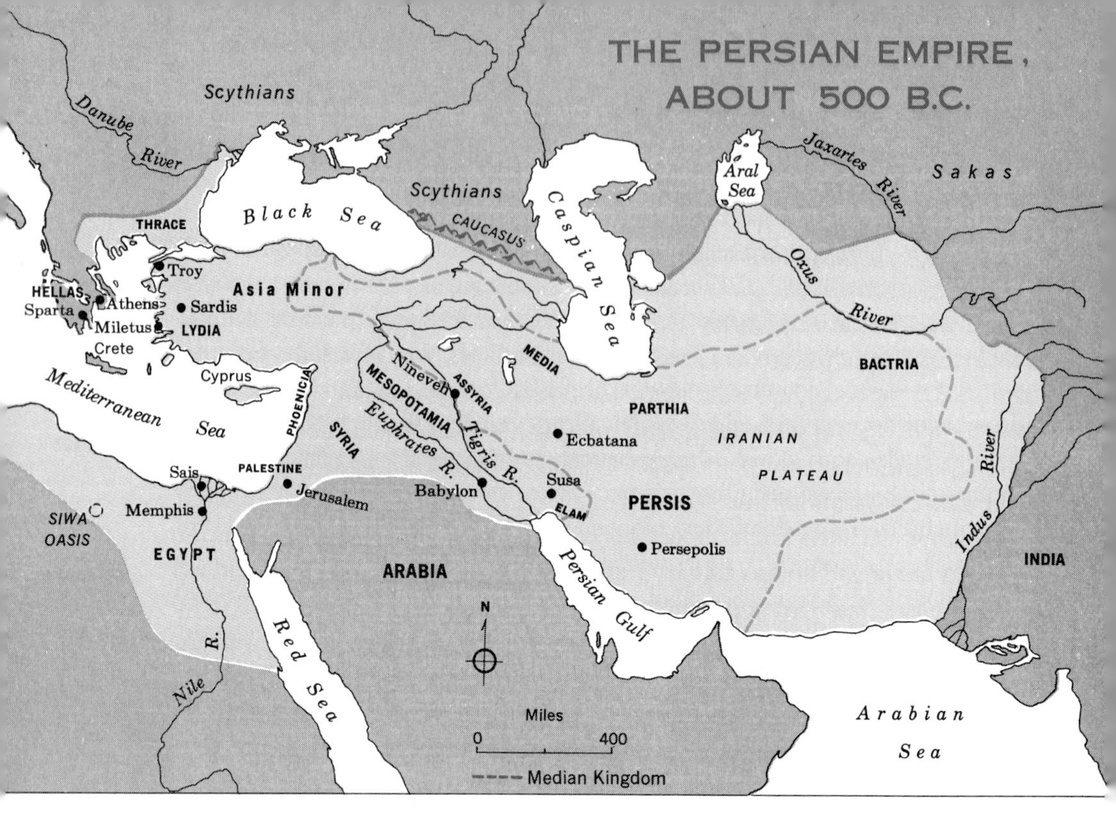

Eventually the Persian Empire stretched from Europe and North Africa to India. This great empire included Egypt, Palestine and Phoenicia, Syria, Asia Minor, Mesopotamia, Iran (Persia), northwest India, and, to the west, Thrace. The Persian Empire thus became the largest territorial state in world history up to that time. The Persians improved on the techniques of imperial rule they had adopted from the Assyrians and handed them on to Alexander the Great and the Romans. During the two centuries of Achaemenid rule, the people of the Early Iron Age in the Middle East reached a new high point in the development of civilization.

THE ACHAEMENID FAMILY BEFORE THE PERSIAN EMPIRE

About 700 B.C. an Iranian prince, Achaemenes, rose to prominence by winning leadership over the tribe called the Persians. Slowly, during some four centuries, the Persians became civilized by contact with such states as Urartu and Assyria. They were rugged mountain people of simple virtues who were taught "to ride, to shoot the bow, and to speak the truth." Their greatest glory was to serve the king. By the time of Achaemenes, the Persians had spread south to the Persian Gulf and were under the control of the closely related Medes. During the period of the Median kingdom, the Achaemenid family continued to rule the Persians as vassal or puppet kings of the Medes. In 550 B.C. the kingship of the Persians passed to the Achaemenid Cyrus II (Kurash II), often called Cyrus the Great, who was to become one of the most famous men in the history of the world. (Persian spellings will appear in parentheses. We are more familiar with the Greek spellings.)

CYRUS (KURASH) THE GREAT, 550–530 B.C.

In 550 B.C. Cyrus led a revolt of the Persians. He overthrew the Medes and combined the two kingdoms. Ruling from the Median capital Ecbatana (Hamadan), he proclaimed himself Great King of the Medes and the Persians and inaugurated the Achaemenid Empire of Persia.

Cyrus immediately proceeded to expand the limits of his kingdom. In 546 B.C. he defeated Croesus, the fabulously rich king of Lydia in western Anatolia, and captured the important trading center and capital of Sardis.

The Lydian kingdom had begun to grow in the eighth century after the defeat of the Phrygians, the uncivilized tribesmen who had overthrown the Hittites and established a loose kingdom in the north of Asia Minor. Lydia had become very wealthy by virtue of its excellent location on trade routes tying east and west and from the natural resources of Anatolia (page 111). Wool was woven into cloth by the Hellenes (Greeks) who, fleeing the Dorian invaders, had settled along that part of the coast of Asia Minor called Ionia. Very successful commercial relations were established between the Hellenes and the Lydians. In order to facilitate these relations coinage was invented in the sixth century B.C. by either Lydian or Ionian traders. Croesus, whose name is synonymous with wealth ("rich as Croesus"), issued the world's first gold coins.

Having conquered Lydia, Cyrus proceeded to capture the Ionian cities (546–540 B.C.). These conquests carried the Persian Empire all the way to the Aegean Sea, farther west than the empire of the Assyrians. In the years that followed, Cyrus was accepted as their ruler by many of the cities in Elam and Babylonia without fighting. In 539 B.C. he attacked Babylon itself. The city fell in a few days, and Cyrus annexed the whole of the Chaldean Empire, including Syria-Palestine.

Wherever possible Cyrus let the conquered nations follow their own local laws and customs. He presented himself to them not as a foreign conqueror but as the lawful successor to their own national rulers. In Persia he was

"Cyrus of Anshan, the Achaemenid"; in Media, "Great King, King of Kings"; in Babylon, "King of Babylon, King of the Lands." One of his first acts after occupying Babylon was to order the return to each nation of the national gods, which the Chaldeans had brought to Babylon as a sign of their conquests. Since the Jewish religion did not permit statues to be made of their god, Yahweh, Cyrus gave permission for the Jews in exile in Babylon to return to Palestine if they wished, and in place of returning a god's statue they were to be permitted to rebuild the temple in Jerusalem. In gratitude the Jews called Cyrus "The Anointed of the Lord." The Phoenicians placed their fleets at his disposal as a sign of their loyalty, and the Ionian Hellenes (Greeks) settled in Anatolia wrote of him in glowing terms. This policy of local cultural independence won for Cyrus the admiration of many people, and he came to be regarded as that rare being, a ruler with despotic power moved by a concern for all mankind. Believers in the brotherhood of man sometimes trace this ideal back to Cyrus. In all fairness, however, it must be realized that Cyrus' toleration was not put to a real test, for before he had a chance to organize his empire, he died in battle in the east fighting against the wild Scythians (Sakas) (530 B.C.).

CAMBYSES (KANBUJIYA) EXTENDS THE EMPIRE INTO AFRICA, 530–521 B.C.

In the last years of his reign, Cyrus was aided by his eldest son Cambyses, who acted for him as regent over Babylon and aided him in making plans for the conquest of Egypt, which was trying to interfere in the affairs of Palestine. The death of Cyrus brought revolts inspired by various claimants to the throne. This was to be a pattern that was repeated throughout Persian history. Less tolerant than his father, Cambyses rapidly suppressed all opposition and then turned to the Egyptian campaign his father had planned.

Cambyses invaded Egypt when the pharaoh had just died and a new, inexperienced ruler was on the throne. The Egyptian cause also suffered from the desertion of hired Hellenic soldiers. Cambyses captured Memphis and then put to death the pharaoh, bringing to an end the Saite (Twenty-Sixth) dynasty of Egypt.

Following the defeat of Egypt, the Hellenic cities on the African coast west of Egypt fell to Cambyses without fighting. With the Hellenes of Anatolia already part of the Persian Empire, two thirds of the Hellenes were under Persian rule. This two thirds included most of the commercial and cultural leadership of the Hellenic world. It was not long before Persian attention was turned to the Hellenic homeland.

At first, Cambyses had not intended to limit his African expansion, but an invasion of Ethiopia proved impossible because of the Nile swamps and the deserts, and a plan to capture the North African city of Carthage had to be given up when the Phoenicians refused to use their navy against a Phoenician daughter-city.

In Egypt, Cambyses followed his father's example of appearing as the lawful successor to the pharaohs by dressing for public ceremonies in Egyptian regalia and using the ancient Egyptian titles, Son of Re and Osiris. He placed Egyptians in some of the high government posts and permitted Hellenic traders from outside the Persian Empire to come into Egypt as freely as they had in the days of the Saitic pharaohs. Cambyses' behavior in Egypt was important because it set a pattern that was later followed by Alexander the Great, who has sometimes been given credit for it.

News of a rebellion in Babylon prompted Cambyses to return home. He died of an infected wound on the way.

THE EMPIRE AT ITS PEAK UNDER DARIUS (DARAYAVAUSH), 521–486 B.C.

During Cambyses' Egyptian campaign, a certain Darius, 28 years old and a distant cousin of the king, served as an officer in the famous Persian royal bodyguard, the "Ten Thousand Immortals," which had the reputation of being the finest body of soldiers in the known world. On the death of Cambyses, Darius claimed the kingship and was supported in his claim by the Immortals. He led the troops back to Babylon, where he slew the rebel who had claimed the throne from Cambyses. For two more years there were revolts in every part of the empire. In crushing them Darius' greatest support came from six young Persians from noble families. Darius and they became known as the "Seven" and linked their families together by intermarriage. As long as the Persian Empire lasted, the descendants of these families were given special privileges, such as preferment at court and the right to rule their estates as semi-independent princes. These privileges later proved to be a serious threat to the unity of the empire and the power of the king, and contributed, eventually, to the dangerous weakening of Persia.

Darius extended the boundaries of the Persian Empire to include lands never previously held by any one state of the Fertile Crescent. Eastward he swept across the mountains into India and held the Indus Valley. There he ordered the exploration of a sea route from India to Egypt in order to increase the ocean-borne trade of his empire. All these ventures in central Asia and India were pioneer ventures later to be imitated by Alexander the Great. Darius then visited Egypt and ordered the reopening of the Wadi Tumilat, whose dredging had been started by the pharaohs of Egypt's Twenty-Sixth Dynasty. To round out the world's greatest empire, Darius next launched an attack on the Scythian tribes in Europe near the mouth of the Danube and along the northern coast of the Black Sea. This venture was intended to serve a double purpose. It would end the Scythian raids on Anatolia, and it would cut off the European Hellenes from the grain supplies of the Black Sea farms, the timber of the Balkan Mountains, and the silver mines of Thrace. Both grain and timber were vital to the existence of the Greek cities, especially Athens, and Thrace was their chief source of silver. The Persian army crossed into Europe, reached the Danube, and turned eastward. In the wide plains of southern Russia it was unable to come to grips with the Scythians, who burned their villages and avoided direct battle. The campaign, however, brought Thrace into the Persian Empire. For the first time in history an Asiatic state had a foothold in Europe.

GOVERNMENT OF THE PERSIAN EMPIRE

Darius gave the Persian Empire the organization and administrative apparatus it badly needed but that his predecessors had been too busy to create. He followed the example set by the Assyrians and divided his empire into a group of provinces, each with its satrap (royal governor), military commander, and treasurer, who reported separately and directly to the Great King. In addition to these Assyrian-type officials, Darius created royal inspectors called sometimes the "Eyes" and sometimes the "Ears" of the king. The inspectors made unexpected visits to the provinces, examining official records and sitting as judges to hear complaints from the local people against the regular provincial officials. The inspectors had their own army contingents with them, so they could act against the military commander of a province if it became necessary. This system proved so effective in preventing corruption, rebellious plotting, and unwarranted harshness that it was copied in ancient, medieval, and even modern times by other peoples.

Under Darius, Persian judges were appointed for life. They could be removed from office only if found guilty of taking bribes or of distorting the law, in which cases they were subjected to brutal torture and execution.

Having life tenure freed the judges from the need of seeking reappointment and enabled them to dispense justice without being influenced by political pressures.

As members of the ruling nation, the Persians under Darius were given a special status. They paid no taxes, and administrators and generals were chosen from the ranks of their nobility. The subject nations paid taxes, some in food, raw materials, textiles, and manufactures and the rest in a fixed amount of gold and silver. They also were obliged to support the local garrisons and to provide quotas of troops and horses for the army. Seacoast provinces such as Phoenicia and the Hellenic cities of Anatolia and Egypt also provided squadrons of ships for the royal navy. In time of war the armies were fed by the provinces through which they passed.

RELIGION IN THE EMPIRE

Darius permitted local practices of the subject peoples to continue with the same toleration shown by Cyrus. He himself was a follower of Persia's most famous religious reformer, Zoroaster (or Zarathustra) (page 300). The Persians, like other Indo-European peoples, worshiped many gods and identified some of them with the forces of nature. Religious rites were performed at altars set up in the open country away from the temples, although they did have temples holding a sacred fire.

Originally distinct from the Persian religion, but finally interwoven with it, were the activities of a priestly brotherhood, the Magi. The Magi had been the priestly caste of the early Iranian settlers, and later they accepted the religion of Zoroaster. They took over the direction of the sacrifices where they still continued, interpreted dreams and omens, were guardians of the royal tombs, and taught young men. The Persians originally buried their dead and continued to do so in some instances, but, following the precepts of Zoroaster, the Magi taught them to expose dead bodies to be devoured by vultures and wild animals, a practice still followed by the Parsees of modern India, who are descendents of the Zoroastrians. Magi rituals were made more exciting to the people through the distribution of an intoxicating drink, *haoma*, the formula for which was a closely guarded Magi secret. The Magi resembled in many ways another Indo-European priestly brotherhood, the Druids, who were active in western Europe and Britain (page 279). The two groups kept their secrets so well that almost everything about them is still a mystery.

THE IONIAN REVOLT, 499–493 B.C.

The Persian Empire had grown progressively stronger through the reigns of Cyrus, Cambyses, and Darius, but before the death of Darius an event occurred that foreshadowed serious trouble for the fourth of the great Persian kings, Xerxes. The event was the revolt of the Ionian cities along the coast of Asia Minor.

On the Persian side of the Aegean Sea (Asia Minor), the chief Ionian city was Miletus, although there were many others of great importance. On the European side of the Aegean (Hellas), the chief Ionian city was Athens. The Ionians on both sides of the sea had a strong sense of kinship with each other, a feeling that was stronger than the political ties that bound the Asiatic Ionians to Persia.

About 510 B.C. the two Hellenic cities of Athens and Sparta both had anti-Persian politicians in power, a situation that rarely occurred. Under the prompting of Athens and Sparta, Miletus revolted against its Persian rulers and persuaded the other Ionian cities in Persian Anatolia to join them. A small fleet of Athenian ships went to help in the revolt, and the allies burned Sardis, the capital of the province. In reprisal, Persia destroyed Miletus in 495 B.C. and crushed the other rebel cities within the next two years. The Asiatic Ionian cities, which until then had surpassed all the other Hellenic cities in wealth, were so ruined that they did not recover for two hundred years.

Once the revolt was over, Darius determined to punish Athens and Sparta for their part in stirring it up. In 492 B.C. he sent his son-in-law into Europe with a large army. Darius expected a quick and easy victory. The first setback came when the fleet, advancing along the Greek coast side by side with the Persian army, was destroyed in a storm. Not until 490 B.C. were fresh ships provided, and the Persians tried again (see map, page 180). The fleet set out across the Aegean and put ashore at Marathon, a few miles from Athens. The heavily armed Athenians, led by their citizen-general Miltiades, charged the far more numerous but lightly-armed Persians and beat them. The Persians retreated to their ships and sailed along the coast to Athens, while the Hellenes marched overland during the night and were waiting for them the next day. The Persians lost heart when they saw the stalwart victors of Marathon and sailed away. The news of the victory at Marathon had meanwhile been carried to Athens by a runner who died of a heart attack after delivering the news. From this great exploit comes our word "marathon."

The victory at Marathon was a great one for the Hellenes. Its importance lay in the tremendous boost it gave to their morale when they discovered that they could challenge the most powerful empire in the world and win. Marathon became enshrined in Athenian patriotic legend, and the city celebrated it by permitting the soldiers who died at Marathon to be buried there instead of returning their bodies to Athens, as was the custom.

Athens was saved for the moment from further Persian attack by a revolt that broke out in Egypt. Darius recalled his troops in order to put down this more serious trouble within his empire. Then in 486 B.C. Darius died with Egypt still in rebellion and Athens still unpunished. The Babylonians seized on the death of Darius as an opportunity to try to overthrow their Persian rulers. Xerxes came to his father's throne in the midst of widespread rebellion.

XERXES (KHSHAYARSHA), LAST OF THE GREAT ACHAEMENIDS, 485–465 B.C.

The new ruler, son of Darius, was known to his Hellenic enemies by the oddly spelled name of Xerxes. In Persian it was Khshayarsha. (The Hebrew version, which appears in the Bible, is Ahashueras.) Xerxes put down the revolts in Egypt and Babylon, the two wealthiest and most civilized places of the empire, and in 480 B.C. he turned to the unfinished business in Hellas.

War with Greece Continues. Xerxes ordered out the might of the whole Persian Empire for his attempt to conquer European Hellas. His failure was not so spectacular to his subjects as it appeared to later generations. Nearly 200,000 soldiers from twenty-nine provinces and nations subject to Persia were assembled. (The Athenians declared the number to be five million!) Persia's navy, made up of contingents from Egypt, Phoenicia, and the Hellenic ports of Asia, included twelve hundred large warships, called triremes, and three thousand smaller craft.

Xerxes led the army in person, and his brothers held important army and navy commands. Among those present in the host were Hellenes from the eastern Aegean, and none excited more comment than Artemisia, Queen of Halicarnassus, who, with a little squadron of five ships, was in the forefront of the fighting and outspoken in the councils of war. Before leaving Asia, Xerxes stopped at Troy. He sacrificed to the gods, and proclaimed his venture as a new "Trojan War" to right the wrongs done to the Asiatics by the Europeans eight centuries earlier.

The great army crossed the straits into Europe without incident and passed through Thrace and Macedonia while their navy patrolled the coast. The Hellenes of the northern Aegean submitted promptly to the Persian king, sending him earth and water as the token of their submission. Then violent storms wrecked a fifth of the Persian fleet, and the army was temporarily halted at the narrow pass of Thermopylae, where, because of the nature of the land, large numbers of soldiers could not be brought into action at the same time. Sparta had rushed a token force of three hundred soldiers to Thermopylae, but its main army remained at home. Thebes had sent four hundred, and the little town of Thespiae had sent its total manpower of eight hundred men. When the Persians learned from a traitor of a path around the pass by means of which they could attack the Hellenes from the rear as well as the front, Leonidas, the Spartan commander, gave his forces the option of leaving or chancing a fight. The Thebans abandoned the pass. Leonidas, his three hundred men, and the eight hundred Thespians were annihilated by the Persians. The bravery and loyalty of Leonidas and the three hundred Spartans was later immortalized by Hellenic poets and orators, but that of the poor Thespians was forgotten.

As the Persian host entered the district of Attica, the Athenians abandoned their city and took refuge on the nearby island of Salamis. There they watched the smoke and flames of their homes light the eastern horizon. The Persians had avenged the burning of Sardis by putting Athens to the torch. Already Hellas as far west as Delphi had surrendered to Xerxes, including the important city of Thebes, which had gone over to the Persians without a struggle.

But all was not lost. Tricked by the Athenian leader Themistocles (page 224) into engaging the Athenian navy in the narrow waters at Salamis, where superior numbers of ships could not be brought into action all at once, the Imperial Navy suffered a resounding defeat under the eyes of Xerxes. The Great King watched the battle from a silver-footed throne raised on a hillside near the bay, and when he saw his forces defeated, he feared that the Athenian fleet would cut the supply lines of his gigantic army. With winter storms at hand, Xerxes ordered his troops to withdraw to Asia, leaving fifty thousand soldiers to winter in the northern part of Hellas.

The following year (479 B.C.) the Persian army laid Attica and the ruins of Athens waste for a second time. But as the army withdrew northward, it was followed by the united forces of the Athenians and Spartans. At Plataea the Persians suffered defeat at Hellenic hands. At the same time, across the Aegean Sea at Mycale near Miletus, the Hellenic allies met part of the Persian fleet in another victory that wrested control of the Aegean Sea from Persia and helped pave the way for the rising seapower of Athens.

The war was over, though the contestants did not realize it, and no peace treaty was negotiated. Xerxes had the world's largest empire to administer, and, having punished Athens as his father had wished, he saw no need to continue to carry on a war for the sake of annexing another province or two. From the viewpoint of the Athenians and Spartans, however, the importance of Marathon and Thermopylae, Salamis, Plataea, and Mycale could not be overstated. They had survived against the world's greatest power, although Athens was burned to the ground, and they had created a legend that inspired the Hellenes for centuries.

For the remainder of his reign, Xerxes devoted himself to peaceful pursuits, giving much time to the beautifying of his capital at Susa and the completion of the city of Persepolis, which Darius had started. Workmen were brought to Persepolis from Egypt, Babylonia, Assyria, and the Hellenic cities so that the royal architects could take full advantage of the

The Palace at Persepolis. Left, the audience hall and behind it, the palace of Darius. The hall stands on a raised terrace approached by a broad stairway whose steps were shallow enough for a horseman to ride up them comfortably. The carvings along the grand staircases leading to the audience hall have as their theme the visit of the courtiers of all nations to the king for the festival of the New Year. Right, Median dignitaries come to pay their respects. The older capital at Susa remained the winter residence of the Persian kings.

artistic and architectural skills of all. The cluster of palaces, staircases, halls, and buildings was constructed on a vast terrace covered with carvings. The marble and granite buildings were made beautiful by the lavish use of gold-leaf on the capitals of the hundreds of tall columns. The roofs of the buildings glittered with gold, silver, and colored tiles. Although Xerxes died before Persepolis was finished, he made it rank, with Nineveh, Babylon, Egyptian Thebes, and Rome, among the great imperial capital cities of all time.

DECLINE OF ACHAEMENID PERSIA

The Persians had been fortunate in the ability of the first four Achaemenid kings: Cyrus, Cambyses, Darius, and Xerxes. The kings who followed them lacked the energy to take the field at the head of their troops and the capacity to understand and halt the weakening of the Empire that occurred. Their reigns were marked by plots, rebellion, and assassinations with which they seemed unable to cope. They abandoned the policy of religious toleration in an effort to consolidate the empire, and this repression led to revolts by all the subject peoples. Egypt was a constant source of disturbance. It revolted with Athenian aid in 465 B.C., with the Medians in 424 B.C., and with the Phoenicians in 404 B.C. The third revolt was successful, and both Egypt and Phoenicia kept their independence for fifty years until the reign of the able Artaxerxes III (below). As far as Greece was concerned, the kings relied principally on bribes of gold to win friends among Persia's neighbors, the Hellenes of Thebes, Athens, and

Sparta. Persian gold continued to influence the politics of the Hellenic city-states until the empire was conquered by Alexander.

TEMPORARY RECOVERY UNDER ARTAXERXES III, 359–338 B.C.

In Artaxerxes III the Persians had a ruler who was clever, determined and ruthless enough to try to restore the past glories of the Achaemenids. He put an end to palace revolts and court plots by the simple expedient of slaughtering his dozens of brothers and sisters. He crushed the last of the rebel satraps by taking the field and leading the army in person. When Phoenician Sidon tried to rebel anew, he made an example of it by burning the entire city and its whole population. He visited rebellious Egypt with an army, drove its new pharaoh into exile in Ethiopia, and forced all the cities of the Nile to tear down their walls and fortifications. Justice was reinstituted in the empire, and the rightful claims of the poorer classes were listened to.

Artaxerxes III then turned to Hellas. He warned Athens to withdraw the ships and men on loan to the Hellenes of Asia and to Egypt or face another Persian invasion. The Athenians found themselves friendless in a world that held two threats: the renewed power of Persia and the rising strength of Macedon. Athenian opinion was divided on what to do. The great orator Demosthenes tried to persuade them to forget their ancient grudge against Persia because Philip of Macedon (page 319) was the most dangerous ruler on the Hellenic horizon. This argument won the day, and an alliance was signed with the Persians. But it proved fruitless. At the moment when all promised well for the empire, the Great King was poisoned (338 B.C.). His successor lacked the union and strength needed for the empire to survive the coming struggle with Macedon. It was only a question of time before Alexander the Great would strike at Persia and bring the Achaemenid Empire down in ruins (page 325).

❦ ❦ ❦

The Iron Age opened with the civilized world prostrate from the invasions and upheavals of attacking migratory tribes. In the Fertile Crescent, however, new empires soon arose, building on the basis of the civilizations of the past. The first was that of the Assyrians. Although Assyria failed in its attempt to dominate the Fertile Crescent, and independent states were able once again to assert themselves, the Assyrian Empire was soon followed by the Median and Achaemenid empires. The success of the Persians in bringing almost all the civilized world under their control was due in great measure to the first four Great Kings of the dynasty: Cyrus (Kurash), Cambyses (Kanbujiya), Darius (Darayavaush), and Xerxes (Khshayarsha). They extended the power of Persia from the Indus to the European continent. Only about one third of the Hellenic cities, those in European Hellas, Sicily, and southern Italy, managed to defy Persian might and remained free on the edge of western civilization.

People, Places, and Terms

Chaldeans	Nineveh	Salamis
Nebuchadnezzar	Ecbatana	Plataea
Achaemenids	Persepolis	Mycale
Cyrus the Great	Media	
Cambyses	Lydia	vassal
Darius	Persia	Saite Egypt
Xerxes	Hellas	Second Babylon
Zoroaster	Ionia	Hanging Gardens
the Magi	Athens	marathon
Leonidas	Miletus	satrapy
Themistocles	Sparta	trireme
	Marathon	siege
Urartu	Thermopylae	Persian Wars

Mastering the Reading

1. List all the means that Assyria used to weld the Fertile Crescent into one empire. What aspects of other cultures did Assyria preserve or adapt? What was uniquely Assyrian?
2. Under what conditions did Saite Egypt recover power? In what fields did it gain fame?
3. Why were the Chaldeans justified in calling themselves the Second Babylonians?
4. What relationship did the Medes have to the Persians before and after 550 B.C.? In what ways did Cyrus live up to his title "the Great"? Why is Cambyses renowned? How did Darius rule his empire?
5. What caused the conflict between Hellas and Persia?

Interpreting the Text

1. What factors enabled the little Hellenic states to defeat the vast Persian Empire at Marathon?
2. What were some of the contributions of the Persians to civilization?

Exploring Beyond the Text

1. The Greek historian Herodotus wrote much about Persian customs and exploits. How does he describe Persian dealings with foreigners and their successes? Is his view unbiased? Why or why not?
2. Xerxes built a beautiful Persian capital at Persepolis. Describe his capital and Persian contributions to art and architecture as revealed by the ruins.
3. How were the struggles of the Hellenes against the Persians similar to those of the American colonies against the British? How did the struggles differ?

Working with the Map

1. What modern-day countries were included in the Persian empire of Cyrus? of Darius?
2. Was Nineveh a good location for the capital of Assyria? Was Persepolis a good location for Persia's capital? What were the advantages and disadvantages of each?

10

City-States of the Sea Peoples

1000–500 B.C.

Between 1000 and 500 B.C. new peoples living around the Mediterranean Sea became civilized. They organized themselves into city-states that were both like, and yet different from, those of the ancient Middle East. Three of these peoples came to have particular significance: the Carthaginians, the Etruscans, and the Hellenes. All three were mixtures of older settlers and new invaders, the iron-welding barbarians that had swept into the Mediterranean world at the end of the second millennium B.C. The North African based Carthaginians were related to the Phoenicians. Carthage was founded by Phoenicians hoping to escape from the Assyrian sweep to the sea. The Etruscans, perhaps descended from Peoples of the Sea who had drifted west to Italy after their defeat by the Egyptians, developed a flourishing civilization that extended its power over the central part of the Italian peninsula and edged down to the south. The Greek Hellenes, after a Dark Age in which the civilization and exploits of the Myceneans were only dimly remembered in the songs of wandering poets and minstrels, coalesced into a new people and laid the foundations for a civilization that had a spectacular flowering.

Developing independently, yet coming into touch with each other through trade and raids, all three of these peoples crossed paths in the western Mediterranean. There each of them planted colonies that had strong ties to the mother countries. Conflict was inevitable. It resulted in a clash that by 550 B.C. left Carthage the strongest power in the west.

THE NATURE OF THE SEA PEOPLES

Each of the sea peoples developed independently, with individual characteristics and patterns of living that grew out of their geographical and historical circumstances. The Hellenes were particularly fortunate. They were close enough to the civilized east to be in touch with it and yet far enough away to be outside its immediate concern. Hellas, like Crete, was able to develop a civilization that borrowed what it needed and yet could modify what it borrowed free from outside pressure to conform to any special pattern. By the fifth century B.C., when the Persians turned their attention to the Aegean Sea, the Hellenes were already an ordered society with a special point of view.

All the sea peoples nevertheless had much in common. The most important were their forms of living, their cities and its peoples, their homes, food, and clothing.

THE ETRUSCANS

The origin of the Etruscans is still a mystery. When and how they reached Italy, and how they gained control of the land, is not yet known. Ancient scholars were also in disagreement. Herodotus (page 239) stated they came from Lydia. The urban style of life they introduced into Italy, the eastern design of their ships, and their art styles, which reveal Middle Eastern influences, support the theory of Middle Eastern origin (page 145). Herodotus was contradicted by the historian Dionysius of Halicarnassus, who insisted that they were native to Italy. Modern scholarship has reached no conclusion. Whoever they were, the Hellenes called them Tyrrhenoi or Tyrsenoi, and this name survives in that of the Tyrrhenian Sea. The later Romans called them Etruscans and their country Etruria. In modern times this region is known as Tuscany.

The Setting. Italy is a peninsula some 700 miles in length but not more than 125 miles wide except in the Po River Valley. The peninsula juts down into the Mediterranean, dividing it into an eastern and a western half.

In the west, Italy is a land rich in good soil, fertilized by the ash of the volcanoes that lie along the west side of the Apennine Mountains (see map, page 254). They cut across the northern part of the peninsula and extend south to the toe of the boot. Along the east coast the mountains are so close to the sea that there is little room for agriculture. Invaders were always attracted to the more fertile west coast, which faced the uncivilized areas of the western Mediterranean rather than the settled lands of the Near East.

To the north lies the Po Valley. It is a fertile plain about two hundred miles wide. The Po Valley is partially cut off from central Italy by the Apennines. It was controlled by the Etruscans until they were expelled by the barbarian Celts (Gauls). The Romans, once they gained the Po region, named the Po Valley, Cisalpine Gaul (Gaul on the Italian side of the Alps), to distinguish it from Transalpine Gaul, those extensive regions where the barbarians dwelt on the other side of the mountains.

To the south lie southern Italy and Sicily. Settlers from the Aegean early discovered these agreeable lands, and the Hellenes were one of many invaders who over the centuries attempted to conquer and control southern Italy. Only in the south was Italy influenced by the more civilized east.

Italy was favored with many natural resources. Good soil was the most important. The land demanded hard work, however, as it was subject to flood and erosion. Cattle were raised not only on the sandy slopes of the east coast but also in the south. They gave their name to the land, *Vitelia*, Land of Cattle, from which the Hellenes derived the name Italy. A variable climate encouraged the production of many different kinds of food. There was copper and tin to make bronze, iron deposits for weapons, timber and stone for building, and clay for the potter. The three main provinces of the west, Etruria, Campania, and Latium, were each watered by a good river.

The beautiful and productive land of Italy attracted invaders from the third millennium B.C. The Etruscans were not the final masters of the land. They were, however, its most important occupants for some four hundred years, until the rise of Rome in the fifth century B.C.

The Growth of Etruria. By 700 B.C. the Etruscans had formed a loose league of twelve cities for common worship in a yearly festival. In the sixth century B.C. the Etruscan search for trade led them to settle sites as far south as the Bay of Naples, where they founded Capua and Pompeii. Further ex-

An Etruscan tomb painting. A naked page serves guests reclining on couches. The men, wearing mantles, are dark; the women entertaining them are light. On the outside, an Etruscan tomb was a circular mound carved out of rock and covered with earth. Several entrances led to underground corridors, off of which were tomb chambers with walls covered by paintings.

pansion in this direction was halted by the Hellenes, who were settling southern Italy and had reached the bay, where they founded Neapolis, the "New City," which we now call Naples. After southern expansion was halted, the Etruscans turned northward across the Apennines to the rich valley of the Po, where they founded dozens of prosperous towns. One of them, Adria, gave its name to the Adriatic Sea. Although they were rivals of the Hellenes, the Etruscans traded with them, and Etruscan art and religion showed strong Hellenic influences. The Hellenic cities were their chief link with the more civilized societies of the Middle East.

The Etruscans decorated the walls of their underground tombs with scenes from their daily lives, and these pictures are our principle source of information about these people. Men and women were social equals, and in these centuries of Etruscan prosperity, life was apparently happy, for the tomb scenes are of banquets, games, dancing, and singing. Only in the later decline of Etruria and its eventual conquest by Rome did the tomb scenes become gloomy and despondent, filled with pictures of forbidding evil creatures of the world of the dead.

The Etruscans were apparently a people concerned with material wealth and things of an everyday, practical nature. They developed a thriving civilization based on commerce and trade and supported by agriculture. They were not only excellent sailors and skilled traders but were also famous for their skill in farming and as horse breeders. The Etruscan farmlands flourished under irrigation, with dams and terracing constructed for drainage. Horses were raised on ranches where the soil was not good enough for agriculture. The many forests of Etruria provided hardwood and pine for shipbuilders, and great fleets of cargo ships plowed the seas. Also the immensely rich iron deposits on the island of Elba were developed, as were the tin and copper ores of mainland Etruria. Etruscan bronze and iron objects were skillfully and beautifully made, and they were in demand throughout the Mediterranean. The general level of prosperity was so high that not only the nobility but also a large commercial class were able to afford beautiful clothing of linen and wool, fine jewelry and tableware, and comfortable home furnishings.

The Etruscans, however, never developed a political organization that went beyond their loose religious federation. They were therefore unable to unite successfully to resist Roman expansion in the following centuries. Though conquered by the Romans, the Etruscans remained a distinct group in the population. They were wealthy, respected, and believed to be particularly gifted in soothsaying, a talent much admired and sought after by the Romans.

THE CARTHAGINIANS

In the year 814 B.C. the Phoenician city of Tyre sent out a group of settlers to build a new port near the older base at Utica in Africa (see map, page 207). The new city was to provide refuge should Tyre's citizens wish to flee from the advancing Assyrians. The result was Carthage (Kart Hadasht—New Capital). Carthage was admirably situated at the junction of the eastern and the western Mediterranean. This location offered Carthage superb opportunities for trade. In addition, Carthage possessed the largest harbor in North Africa, and it was surrounded by fertile farmlands. Today, modern Tunis occupies the same site.

Legends tell that the leader of the Carthaginian settlers was Princess Elissa or Dido, sister of the King of Tyre, and that her death was offered as a sacrifice to assure the favor of the gods for the new city. Roman legends recount that she died for love of Rome's legendary founder, the Trojan Aeneas, who visited her on his way to Italy after the burning of Troy (page 209). Such stories are the only glimpses we have of Carthage's early centuries.

Tyre, Sidon, and the other Phoenician cities of western Asia fell to the Persians about 540 B.C. The Phoenician colonies around the Mediterranean—Gades in Spain, Utica, Carthage, and many more smaller ones on the African coast—were too weak to assert themselves when they were first cut off from aid from Phoenicia. The Hellenes seized the opportunity to establish rival colonies on the African coast between Egypt and Carthage (Cyrene) and in Italy and Spain (page 207).

Eventually, seeing that it had to either defend itself without aid from Tyre or be overrun by the Hellenes, Carthage rallied all the Phoenician colonies from Gades to Malta. In exchange for the use of its army and navy, Carthage was given the right to dictate the political and economic affairs of the Phoenician colonies. So, while the eastern Phoenicians were absorbed into the empires of the Fertile Crescent (page 148), the western Phoenicians became subjects of a Carthaginian sea empire. Carthage established friendly relations with the Persian Empire and sent embassies to the courts of Darius and Xerxes. It was prepared to take its place as a power in the Mediterranean.

THE HELLENES

The people who called themselves "Hellenes" are known in English as "Greeks." Hellas had no recognized boundaries like those of the nation of Greece today. The language of the Hellene was his distinguishing mark. Regardless of physical type, if he spoke Hellenic he was an Hellene; those who spoke other languages were all lumped together as *Barbaroi* or Jabberers. The word *barbarian* originally showed the contempt of the Hellene for anyone who could not speak his language and, since language is a reflection of thought, did not think as he did.

The Hellenic People. The Hellenes were a mixed people descending from two main groups of ancestors who differed physically and culturally. One branch came from the Bronze Age sea peoples, including the peoples of Crete, Cyprus, and Phoenicia, most of whom were distinguished by rather delicate, small bone structure, coppery skins that easily took on brownish-red tones when exposed to the sun, and large dark eyes. The other ancestral group was the Indo-Europeans who came in successive waves into the Mediterranean area from the north. They included the Achaeans, and later the Dorians who had helped bring the Cretan-Mycenaean civilization to ruin at the end of the Bronze Age. The Indo-Europeans were bigger, taller, and brawnier than the original Mediterranean settlers, and many of them had red or blonde hair and blue or gray eyes.

The Mediterranean side of Hellenic ancestry was strongly reflected in the customs and dialects of the Ionians. Miletus on the east coast of the Aegean and Athens on the Hellenic mainland were outstanding centers of Ionian culture, although there were dozens of other important Ionian cities. Of all the Hellenes, the Ionians were the most gifted in commerce, colonization, art, and philosophy, and their dialect was noteworthy for its beauty and flexibility. Quite different were the Dorians, who were settled chiefly in the Peloponnesus. Their main city was Sparta. They were much more conservative than the Ionians. They looked with disfavor on change or experiment. They planted few colonies, were very slow to adapt their government to changing times, disliked all "foreign" ways or ideas. They spoke a dialect, much more Indo-European in origin than Ionian was, that did not lend itself well to poetry, heroic tales, philosophy, or science. The mutual dislike of the Ionians and the Dorians expressed itself in commercial competition, athletic rivalry, and eventually in bitter warfare.

Besides the Ionians and Dorians other groups lived in Hellas, among whom were the Aeolians. These others made much less of an impact on Hellenic history.

The Hellenic Setting. The Hellenic mainland is a spur of land that juts down from the larger projection of land that today is called the Balkan peninsula. It is a small country with a ragged coastline surrounded on three sides by the Aegean Sea. Hundreds of islands dot the Aegean's surface, and they served as steppingstones for invaders, sailors, merchants, and envoys traveling east and west between European Hellas and the states of western Asia.

The islands were settled earlier than the mainland. Some of the smaller ones were rocky and barren, but many of the larger ones had much to offer settlers. The long history of Crete bears witness to this, as do the remains on Lesbos, Samos, Delos, and the Cyclades. The climate, moderated by the sea, was warm and balmy. The air was clear and bracing, crops grew well, and though metals were scarce, timber for ships and stone for building were abundant. The landscape was beautiful; the islands were very green, the sky and water were a deep blue, and the sun was strong and brilliant.

Many of the same advantages lay on the mainland. It too was a beautiful land surrounded by the sparkling sea and warmed by a brilliant sun. The tangy air was conducive to the rise of an energetic people. The mainland soil, however, was poor, and there were few rivers. None were navigable, which made communications more difficult in a land broken up by mountain ranges.

The mainland is quite small, only about 250 miles long and about 150 miles wide. It is divided into two distinct parts separated by a narrow strip of land known as the Isthmus of Corinth. The southern portion is the Peloponnesus. There, in that part known as Laconia, the Dorian invaders founded the city of Sparta. Gradually Sparta extended its sway over the native

inhabitants of neighboring Messinia, who were forced to remain tied to the land for several centuries. These people were called *helots*. The helots grew the food the Spartans ate, thus enabling the Spartans to concentrate on soldiering. Messinia and Laconia together formed Lacedaemon, so the Spartans are often called the Lacedaemons. By the close of the sixth century B.C., Sparta had extended its influence over the rest of the Peloponnesus and was able to establish a strong confederacy known as the Peloponnesian League. The members of the League furnished troops and looked to Sparta for guidance and protection. Corinth was an influential member of this league and the second most important city in the south.

The most famous place in the Peloponnesus was Olympia. There the great games to honor Zeus, "father of gods and men," were held every four years in midsummer. The Olympic Games were the greatest games in Hellas, but others were also held at Delphi (the Phythian Games) to honor Apollo, god of light, healing, and music, and on the Isthmus of Corinth to honor the sea god Poseidon.

The first Olympic Games known historically were held in 776 B.C. A sacred truce protected the site of the Olympics and all persons traveling to and from Olympia even in time of war. The prize in the contests was only a crown of wild olive leaves, but it was regarded as the greatest honor a man could receive. In addition, victors were often honored by their home city by being sculpted or by being given money.

To the north of the Isthmus of Corinth lay Attica, the home of Athens. Long before 500 B.C. the little city-states of Attica, hardly more than villages, had transferred their allegiance to Athens, and their members had become Athenian citizens. Such an arrangement did not take place everywhere. In Boeotia, for example, the villages simply united into a league under the leadership of Thebes. Aeolian Thebes was the most prominent city in Boeotia and, as we shall see, was the leader of Hellas for a short time (page 231). Delphi lay on the slopes of Mount Parnassus in Phocis. There the famous oracle of Delphi gave advice to all who sought it (page 297). Still further to the north, in Thessaly, stood Mount Olympus, the home of the gods, the peak ten thousand feet high that the Hellenes thought was the loftiest in the world.

Although good land for cultivation was scarce in ancient Hellas, there was clay for the potter, stone, and timber. The olive tree and vine provided staples for the diet, oil for cooking, light, and soap, and commodities for export in exchange for grain. The surrounding sea made communications easier; no spot on the mainland was more than two days from the sea. But the sea makes one look outward. Indeed, the sea eventually turned the minds of the Hellenes to overseas commerce and trade; and because good land was scarce and the sea was close, it was natural for the Hellenes to leave Hellas and seek new homes elsewhere (page 206 and 333).

THE MEDITERRANEAN CITY-STATE

The political unit that appeared after the collapse of the Bronze Age in the Mediterranean was the city-state. City-states had existed, as we have seen, before the first millennium B.C. In Sumer, for example, each little town was a city-state, ruled by the priests in the name of the city's god. The city-states of the sea peoples differed from those of the Middle Easteners. In the first place, none were the possession of a god. They were made by men for men. In the second place, the city-state was not expandable. Its form of government did not lend itself to controlling subject people. It was governed by the citizens, and when other peoples were conquered, they were killed or enslaved. But also, the city-state, as it developed in Hellas, was not expandable because its citizens did not wish it to be. Let us pause for a moment to see why this was so. It will tell us something about the Hellenes and why their history turned out as it did.

The Hellenic city-state, or *polis* as they called it, was not much of a city in the modern sense, and not exactly a state either. It was closest to what we would call a community, and the word includes the meanings of both "people" and "area." The idea of community is important because for a community to remain a community, it must be limited in size. Only three Hellenic cities had more than twenty thousand citizens (two in Sicily and Athens), and the ideal size was thought to be about half this.

Being small, the affairs of the *polis* were the affairs of those living in it, and the business of the *polis* became the business of every citizen. The citizen pursued not only his political life there, but also his social, intellectual, and cultural ones as well. To live in such a community naturaly molded and formed the individual, and it was considered the purpose of the *polis* to do so. When Aristotle says that "Man is a creature who lives in a *polis*," what he means is that this particular framework is the only one in which man can truly develop his human capacities. For the Hellene it was this that distinguished him from all others; he thought himself the only man who truly knew how to live, and to live truly, he had to live in a *polis*. We can see, then, in the development of the Hellenic city-state, that it was not only geography that kept the Greeks separate, but also a frame of mind that valued independence for the qualities it fostered in human life.

GOVERNMENT

In the early first millennium B.C. the city-states were governed by kings. These kings were leaders in war and religion and acted as judges. There were many local differences in the kings' power and length of rule. In some cities there were royal dynasties that lasted for a century or more, and the kingship passed from father to son. In others, the kings were elected by the nobles from among their own number. In some places the king, once elected, held the position for the rest of his life. In other places a new king was elected after a certain number of years. In Sparta, for example, two kings reigned at once. Every ninth year of the kings' reigns, men called *ephors* made a careful search for omens from the gods that would indicate whether the kings should be allowed to rule for another nine years. If the tokens from the gods were unfavorable, one or both would be deposed and the place filled by other nobles. In the land of the Etruscans and in early Rome, the king was elected for life by an assembly of the citizens and was confirmed in his post by the senate of family heads. The kings depended on the cooperation of the powerful nobles and only rarely called on the people to support them.

In the years from 750 to 500 B.C. many of the city-states changed their forms of government. In some, the nobles grew strong enough to overthrow the kings. They formed an *aristocracy*, the rule of the nobles. Thebes had an aristocratic government. The nobles derived their power and wealth from the agricultural lands. Where wealth came from commerce and trade, men possessing such wealth, who were called *oligarchs*, sometimes gained control of the government and formed an *oligarchy*, a "rule by the few." Carthage was an oligarchy. In many cities aristocrats and oligarchs struggled for power, and clashes, sometimes violent, occurred. Such struggles paved the way for the rise of usurpers called *tyrants*. The tyrant was a ruler who seized power from kings, aristocrats, or oligarchs. The student must be careful, however, not to read modern meaning into the ancient word *tyranny*. The original word had none of the modern meaning of oppression or cruelty. Tyrants, nevertheless, were illegal in that none of the law codes provided for the existence of one-man rule. Athens, as we shall see, came for a time under the rule of tyrants.

Sometimes tyrants were installed in power by the use of force, sometimes peaceably through popular acclaim. To be effective against the wealthy landed aristocrats and the commercially wealthy oligarchs, a tyrant had to have a large percentage of the citizens willing to accept his rule. In order to gain their support the tyrant lavished money on public works and on beautifying their cities. He also secured the support of many poor citizens by providing free theaters, elaborate civic festivals, and free allotments of food and olive oil to the needy.

Thus several types of government existed among the sea peoples, and some changed their form of government while others did not. We will study two in more detail, that of Sparta (page 221) and that of Athens (page 218).

THE LAYOUT OF THE CITY

The Mediterranean city-states were physically much alike. Each included a central small city and as much countryside as could be seen from the

The Acropolis of Athens. The high, rocky part of the city served as a fortress during the early years of Athenian history. Called the High Citadel by the Athenians, it was later covered with shrines and public buildings dedicated to the gods. The buildings whose ruins still crown the Acropolis today were largely the work of the fifth century B.C. statesman Pericles. In the foreground is the Parthenon, dedicated to Athena; to the left, the gateway, or Propylaea; and behind the Parthenon is the Erechtheum, a shrine dedicated to a legendary Athenian king.

center of town to the surrounding hills or the sea. The city was located close enough to the sea for a keen-eyed watchman to sight the landing of pirates on the distant shore, and far enough away to warn the people to take refuge with their flocks and herds within the city walls. Many Iron Age cities, like those of the Cretans and the Mycenaeans, were from three to ten miles from the sea for reasons of safety, even though the citizens lived partly by sea commerce and partly by raids against others.

For easier defense and for a longer view of the distant sea, the central part of the city was located on a hilltop, the steeper the better. Within the city was an open space where the citizens could meet to trade and to discuss civic affairs. For lack of space and convenience this area could not be on the heights. It was near or at the foot of the high place, and in time it came to be surrounded by temples, the theater, and other public buildings. Thus the Forum laid out by the Etruscans in Rome lay at the foot of the Capitol citadel, and the Agora (market) in Athens was near the

Acropolis (*acro*—top, highest; *polis*—city). There the rulers harangued the assembled citizens on questions of peace and war.

CITIZENS OF THE CITY-STATE

The inhabitants of the Early Iron Age city-state believed that a vital unity bound each city to its citizens and its gods. No individual could have any personal rights that might weaken this unity.

If the gods were believed to demand the death of one's children in the fires of the ritual to Moloch, then burn to death they must so that Carthage would be safe.

If the strength of the citizens as a whole demanded that weak or crippled babies be abandoned to starve or to be devoured by wolves, then die they must so that Sparta would be strong.

If the economic welfare of the city required that all creditors lose the money they had lent out, as happened once in Athens, then the public cancellation of all debts was not considered an injustice to those whose life savings were wiped out.

If the city's peace seemed to be disturbed by the actions of a citizen, then he must be *ostracized* (exiled). This exile lasted for ten years even though he had broken no law or done no wrong, and though such an exile cut him off from the city, the gods, and the friends who made life livable for him.

What would seem to us to be grave injustice to an individual was considered right and proper to the sea peoples, if by such an action the well-being of the city, its gods, or its citizens was in any way improved. Modern democracy stresses the rights of individuals; ancient democracy saw only the right of the triple unity of the city, the citizens, and the gods. The patriotism of an Hellene, of a Carthaginian, or of an Etruscan was not directed toward a nation, as with us, but toward this triple unity.

Only the citizens shared in the unity of the city-state. Many others did not. Left out were the noncitizens and slaves, both of whom existed in great numbers in all the city-states.

NONCITIZENS OF THE CITY-STATES

As the city-states increased in population and prosperity in the eighth and seventh centuries B.C., increasing numbers of noncitizens appeared in all the cities. Traders came to take advantage of expanding commerce, and their descendents often remained permanently in the city of adoption.

Skilled artisans moved from one city to another as opportunities developed for them to use their crafts. Athens went out of its way to encourage the immigration of foreign artists and such skilled craftsmen as cabinetmakers and vasemakers. Ostracized exiles waited in alien cities for the day when they might return to their homes. Neighboring tribes that had been conquered but not reduced to slavery lived within the territories of the city-state but without the rights of citizens.

None of these noncitizens, even when they came to live in the city at the request of the government, could share in the unity of the city, its gods, and its brotherhood of citizens. Nor could their children, though born in the city, claim citizenship through birth. One was a citizen only if one's parents were citizens. There was no such thing as "naturalization" whereby a person could acquire citizenship in a new country. The payment of taxes and service in the army, which we look upon as duties, were regarded by the sea peoples as precious rights. They were part of a total body of rights that included the right to worship the local gods and thereby receive divine protection and the right to sue in court and thereby receive the protection of the city's laws.

SLAVES

Slavery existed in every civilized state in the world during the early Iron Age, as it had during the Bronze Age. To a modern student, slavery hardly seems a step upward in human progress. In its beginnings, however, it was the alternative to death. The savage code of primitive, uncivilized warfare had taught that the defeated should be killed.

Civilized men came to realize that if citizens were to wage war for their city and if warfare were to be continual, as it was in some cases, somebody had to stay home to raise the food and produce the goods needed by the society while the citizen-soldiers were serving in the army. Instead of slaying the conquered, therefore, the victors brought home a few captives and put them to work tilling the soil, herding the animals, or working in the house. Educated slaves came to be clerks of the master's accounts, or tutors of the master's children, or handmaidens of the master's wife. The punishment for bad behavior was the whip, or torture, or, for more serious offenses, crucifixion. Crucifixion, the most prolonged way of causing death, was considered too degrading for citizens, although they too might be crucified for the worst of crimes, such as deliberate murder or jeopardizing the lives of comrades by desertion in the presence of the enemy.

Warfare was the chief source of slaves but not the only one. Criminals sentenced to die might have their sentence commuted to slavery. Men who refused to be drafted into the army, thieves caught in the act, the children of slaves, and, in some cities, debtors, swelled the number of slaves. Finally, since the father of the family had the power of life and death over his descendants, he could, in some cities, sell his children or grandchildren into slavery. This last practice was more apt to occur during times of financial difficulty or famine. At such a time the parents might feel that it was better that children should live as slaves than die of starvation in freedom. Such an attitude existed in other parts of the world, notably in China.

Thus the city-states of the Early Iron Age were populated by a group of citizens, large numbers of noncitizens who were free but not sharers in the laws, and large numbers of slaves, all living in communities that had no written constitutions but that had traditions and customs interpreted in the early centuries by kings.

HOMES AND FOOD OF THE SEA PEOPLES

The homes of the sea peoples, even the wealthiest, contained much less furniture than we are accustomed to in modern times. The one object

Women weaving. Left, two women pass the shuttle through the loom in a sixth-century B.C. "black figured" Hellenic hydria, or vase for carrying water. Below, a reproduction of the scenes on the hydria: the women preparing the wool, weighing it, and examining the finished product.

common to every household was the jar. It could be any size up to five feet in height. In poorer homes the entire furnishings consisted of a few such jars put to a surprising variety of uses. Some served as cupboards for food, clothing, or blankets, while others held liquids—wine, oil, or the entire water supply for drinking, cooking, and bathing. In all households could be found the brazier for cooking, and terra cotta (literally, cooked earth) lamps with a wick floating in fat or oil. Rush matting covered the floor in poor homes, carpets in rich ones.

Richer people owned chests for storing jewels and materials not easily kept in jars. If the family owned only one chest, the father would use it for his bed with a carpet for mattress. On his death, the chest might serve as his coffin. Ceremonial couches decorated with gold, silver, or bronze were used at the banquets of the very rich. The guests reclined leaning on one elbow while eating. In some societies it was thought proper for only the men guests to lie while women sat upright in chairs. Reclining at banquets was popular especially among the Etruscans, from whom the Romans copied the practice and spread it wherever Roman power took root.

The Mediterranean peoples lived chiefly on bread, wine, fish (fresh or salted), cabbage, chickpeas, and fruits. They cooked in olive oil, as their descendants do today. Meat was a rarity in the ordinary diet. Most people had it only on holy days, when animals were sacrificed to the gods; the parts not burned on the altar were distributed among the people. In such a way certain meats came to be associated with particular religious festivals; eating a goose or a suckling pig during the Roman holy days of the Saturnalia (page 267), around December 25, for example, a custom that passed to Christian countries descended from the Roman Empire. Dietary differences arose out of these religious associations. Present-day Europeans and Americans have an aversion to eating horses, although the Iron Age gods and traditions originally associated with this animal are completely unknown to millions whose eating habits are involved.

HELLAS: CULTURAL GROWTH UNDER IONIAN LEADERSHIP, 750-500 B.C.

The Ionians surpassed the other Hellenes in several ways. Their textiles and metals had a market throughout the Mediterranean, and their beautiful dyes competed with those of the Phoenicians. They were also particularly gifted intellectually.

PHILOSOPHY AND SCIENCE

During the seventh and sixth centuries B.C. a few bold thinkers calling themselves "philosophers"—lovers of wisdom—sought a natural origin for things rather than accepting the belief that the gods regulated the seasons and sent the thunderstorms. Miletus produced the first of the great Hellenic philosophers, Thales (c. 600 B.C.), who was one of the great astronomers and mathematicians of his time. According to legend, his prediction of a famous eclipse in 585 B.C. so startled two contending armies that they laid down their arms and refused to continue fighting. Thales thought that the substance basic to all creation was water, because he found that moisture was necessary to the growth of all living things. Thales was proved wrong, but his method—to seek knowledge and postulate theories—has continued ever since.

The island of Samos produced another great thinker, the mathematician Pythagoras, who went to live in the southern Italian town of Croton. Pythagoras discovered the mathematical laws describing the relation of the strings of the lyre to the pitch of the tone. He is credited with proving the famous theorem, that bears his name. The theorem proves that the square of the hypotenuse of a right-angled triangle is equal to the sum of the squares of the other two sides.

LANGUAGE AND LITERATURE

The most renowned figure during these centuries was Homer, another Ionian. The accomplisments of Thales and other Ionians were nothing to the ancient Hellenes when compared to the works of Homer. Although Homer presumably lived about 850 B.C., his works had spread throughout Hellas by 750 B.C. They exercised great influence on Hellenic language, literature, and thought, for they were carried by the Ionian colonizers to all parts of the Mediterranean during the migrations of 750–550 B.C. (page 206).

The Question of Homer. Was there ever such a person as Homer? Were the great epics attributed to him the work of one man, or of two men, or of groups of minstrels? These are questions that have been debated for the last two hundred years.

Homer is thought to have been a blind poet born in Asiatic Ionia between 900 and 800 B.C. He created two great poems of book length, the *Iliad* and the *Odyssey*. The *Iliad* tells of the events in a war between men who seem to be the Mycenaeans and their allies against the city of Troy. The objects described in Homer's epic—the wall of Troy, the palaces, the shields embossed with pictures—have been classified by archaeologists as belonging to the thirteenth and twelfth centuries B.C. Their descriptions must have been handed down by a series of poets through the three or four hundred years following the collapse of the Bronze Age and the beginning of the Early Iron Age. The political and economic life and the social conditions described by Homer, however, seem to be those of the ninth century, in which he lived. Religious ideas, stories of the gods, and customs surrounding burial of heroes appear to be a mixture of the old and new.

The second poem, the *Odyssey*, tells of the wonderful adventures that befell Odysseus (Ulysses) on his way home from the Trojan War. He toured the whole Mediterranean on the way, encountering all kinds of marvels, including a one-eyed man-eating giant and a seductive witch who turned men into pigs. The locations of whirlpools and islands that appear in the *Odyssey* can be traced today, and the geography is accurate. The material probably was collected during the Early Iron Age Hellenic probes of the western Mediterranean.

The *Iliad* and the *Odyssey* gave all the Hellenes a model of beautiful and grammatical language that influenced the style and nature of Hellenic literature for generations. The two poems also created the Hellenes' image of their gods, for in his work Homer included the tales and adventures of those gods recognized by all the Greeks. The same gods and the same language were two very important factors unifying the people. These, together with blood ties and customs, worked to counteract the geographical and political forces that tended to divide the Hellenes from each other.

Hesiod. Homer glorified the gods and the heroes whose traditions had come down from the Mycenean Age. The common man did not appear in Homer. The Mycenean Age had been essentially an aristocratic one in which power and wealth lay in the hands of kings and nobles. But the day of the common man was close in the future, and his voice was heard for the first time in the writings of the poet Hesiod. Hesiod sang his songs around 750 B.C. He lived on a farm at the foot of Mt. Helicon in Boeotia, and he found the peasant life of the fields bitter and miserable. His greatest poem, *Works and Days*, gives us a vivid picture of the woes of a farmer's life. Hesiod cried out against social injustice, against the cruelty and oppression of the nobles. The glorious kings of Homer were "gift-devouring" tyrants to Hesiod, and he warned that their greed and injustice would bring down the wrath of the gods. In Hesiod, Zeus, the king of the gods, is not only the carefree deity described in Homer but also has attributes of justice. Hesiod wrote, "For the animal kingdom Zeus has ordained the law that fish and beast and bird shall devour one another, for justice dwells not among them; but to mankind Zeus has given justice, which is by far the best."

Lyric poetry. Homer's *Iliad* and *Odyssey* are epics, that is, long narrative poems dealing with large and noble themes. In the seventh century B.C. a new form of poetry originated among the Ionians but was most beautifully expressed by two Aeolians, the poetess Sappho and the poet Pindar. The new form was the lyric, a short poem accompanied by the music of the lute. In the lyric, the poet could express his individual longings and emotions in a way that was not possible in the longer and more cumbersome epic.

"Violet-weaving, pure, softly smiling Sappho" lived on the island of Lesbos around 600 B.C. Her poems, of which we have many fragments but few complete works, were famous throughout antiquity. She was accorded a place among poets by the Hellenes that they never gave to any other woman, and she is today considered one of the world's greatest lyric poets.

Pindar, a native of Thebes, was world famous in his lifetime and was called on by many states and provinces to compose odes for special occasions. His only surviving poems are the *Epinikia*, written in honor of the victorious athletes at the Great Games. It is a pity that we do not still have the music that was written to accompany these lyrics, for it would no doubt add much to their proper appreciation.

HELLENIC RELIGION

In the years following the collapse of the Bronze Age, the Hellenes were polytheistic, that is, they worshiped many gods. Every tree, every flower, the weeds, sky, earth—each was inhabited by a spirit.

Certain of the gods were universal to all the Hellenes. Gradually the most important ones were grouped together into a council that met on snow-covered Mt. Olympus in Thessaly. These gods were pictured in human form, and they resembled human beings in every way except that they had superhuman powers and immortality.

Zeus was the king of the gods. He was represented by the storm and the lightning. The rainbow and eagle were his messengers, the thunder was his voice. Hera was his wife, the embodiment of wifely and motherly virtue. She was closely associated with the rites of marriage. Athena, the patron goddess of Athens, sprang full-grown from the head of Zeus. She embodied wisdom and virtue. Apollo, the great god of the sun, light, music, and healing, the ideal of manly beauty had a sister, Artemis, a huntress, the goddess of the woods and the moon. Aphrodite, born out of the sea foam,

Zeus. A Roman statuette of the king of the gods, whom the Romans called Jupiter. In his left hand he may have held a thunderbolt. The worship of Zeus probably came to Hellas with the Achaeans, Indo-Europeans who worshiped male sky gods. According to the later Greek myths, Zeus had several brothers and sisters. He drew lots for the rule of the universe with his brothers, Poseidon and Hades. Poseidon became lord of the seas, Hades accepted the rule of the underworld, while Zeus became god of the sky and thereby lord of the universe.

was the goddess of love and beauty, while Demeter, the great Earth Mother, watched over seed-time and harvest. Poseidon, brother of Zeus, ruled the waters; Ares was the god of war and battle. Dionysus was the god of spring and the vine; Hermes carried the messages of the gods, and Hephaestus was their smith. Hades ruled the underworld, the world of the dead.

Besides the Olympic gods, the gods whose exploits Homer had fixed forever in the minds of the Hellenes, there were many local gods presiding over household and daily activities who were closely associated with the immediate locality. In addition, nymphs and satyrs lived in the mountains, forests, seas, and streams. The Nine Muses presided over music, dancing, poetry, song, science, and history. The Fates ruled human destiny, while the Furies pursued those who murdered or committed sacrilege.

Worship was not a private affair in ancient Hellas; it was the concern of the whole community. The gods were honored at an open altar in ceremonies that had been handed down for generations. Prayers and hymns were said, choruses were sung, and sacrifices of meat and wine were offered. The gods were also honored in special festivals, of which the great games at Olympia were the most famous (page 193). The worship of the gods was part of one's civic duty. Atheism was not nonbelief but nonparticipation.

Because religion and worship were so much an affair of state, and participation in religious festivals and games was a responsibility as well as an honor, private feelings had little room for expression. In time the mystery religions arose to fill this need. The person who wished to belong to the religion took part in a sacred procession and sacrifice and in greatest secrecy participated in the enactment of a highly emotional ritual performance in which his feelings were aroused and swept up. Men and women, freemen and slaves, were followers of the mystery religions. Three gained great importance: the Eleusinian Mysteries associated with Demeter, the Dionysian Mysteries, and those developed by the followers of Orpheus, a mythical minstrel and wandering poet.

The Hellenic idea of life after death was dismal in the extreme. In the shadowy underworld of Hades, life was always gloomy and gray. Everyone went to Hades in Homer's Greece, but later poets sang of the Isles of the Blessed in the Elysian Fields at the western end of earth, where great heroes lived happily throughout eternity. They also spoke of Tartarus, a prison house locked by gates of bronze and iron, as far below Hades as earth is of heaven, for evil souls who had committed great crimes. Not until the mystery religions grew more elaborate and important was the hope of salvation held out to the ordinary man.

THE SEA PEOPLES IN THE WESTERN MEDITERRANEAN, 750–500 B.C.

One of the characteristics of a developing civilization is an increase in population. Under certain conditions it is possible for these increased numbers to find places for themselves in cities, which grow bigger to accommodate them. But neither the temperament of the Hellenes nor the geography of Hellas lent itself to the growth of giant cities. In Hellas the growing population could seek a livelihood in only two occupations, farming and commerce. Both required the Hellenes to move into new and hitherto unsettled areas. The Ionians, more flexible in their thinking and more willing to adapt to change, far outstripped the Dorians and Aeolians in the tremendous colonizing movement that took place over some two hundred years, from 750 to 550 B.C.

HELLENIC COLONIZATION

After 750 B.C. hundreds of tiny new city-states came into being. Although practically every Hellenic city produced at least one such new "colony,"

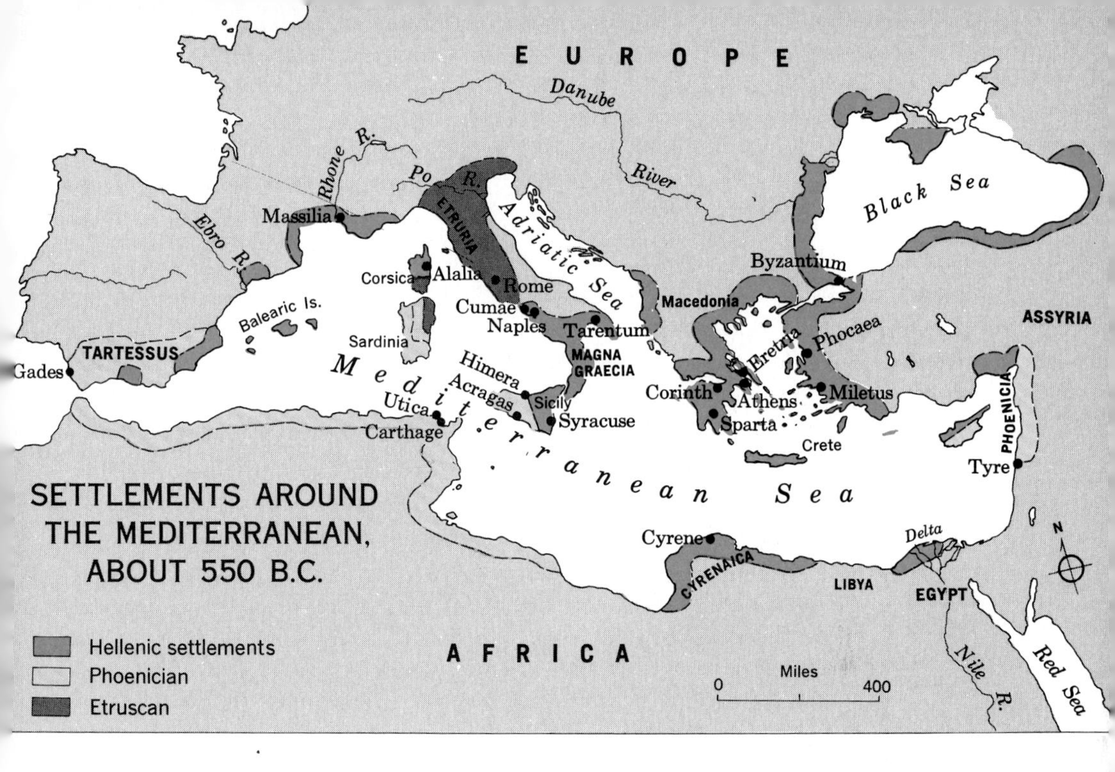

the record belongs to Miletus. Its pioneers built forty new towns around the Black Sea alone, and these in turn sent out men to found forty more, so that Miletus rightfully claimed the parentage of eighty city-states. The Black Sea region was developing into a grain-growing region, rivaling the rich productivity of the Nile wheatfields. The hardy Hellenic frontiersmen settled the Bosphorus, including a little town that grew into the mighty city of Constantinople. All the thinly settled lands of the northern Aegean were penetrated, and the ways of civilization were carried north on the Greek mainland into the back country to the crude Macedonians, who were destined to play a great part in the history of the Hellenes.

Africa offered few opportunities to the colonizing Hellenes, though thousands of their traders were made welcome by the pharaohs of the Twenty-sixth (Saite) Dynasty in Egypt. Naturally the Egyptians could not allow the Hellenes to be self-governing on Egyptian soil. Cyrene was the only important Hellenic colony planted in North Africa. Northwest Africa was dominated by Carthage. Carthage was hostile to Hellenic settlers, although it was willing to trade with their home cities.

Sicily and southern Italy as far north as Naples were another matter. Hundreds of Hellenic colonies took root there. Some of them, like Syracuse in Sicily, became richer and more mighty than most of the Hellenic cities at home. So many Hellenes came to Southern Italy that the region became known as Magna Graecia, "Great Greece." Sardinia and Corsica also looked inviting to the Hellenes, but Etruscan settlers were violently hostile. The Hellenes moved on to southern France, where they founded many places still in existence today, including Massilia (Marseilles) and Monaecus (Monaco). Sites in eastern Spain rounded out the Hellenic colonial areas.

Hellenic colonies differed from those of modern nations in that they were completely independent of the mother state. They were never governed by men sent out by the mother country. Nevertheless, since the first settlers of a colony came as a group from a single city, selected their location with the help of suggestions from the oracle of their home city's chief god, spoke the same dialect of Greek as the mother city, and carried on its particular customs and folkways, there were strong ties of sentiment binding the two states together. Such ties were more effective in leading colonies to take action on behalf of the mother state than actual political control might have been.

Since Hellas was wherever there were Hellenes, the Hellas of the year 600 B.C. extended from the Black Sea to Spain and was at least four times as large as the original Hellas of the ninth century B.C.

As the Hellenes were not alone in colonizing, it was inevitable that conflicts would arise with the Etruscans and the Carthagians, who were also interested in acquiring new lands for settlement and trade.

The first major conflict between the rivals took place off the island of Corsica at Alalia in 535 B.C. The Carthaginians aided the Etruscans against the Hellenes in the first major sea battle known historically in the western Mediterranean. The Hellenes won but were driven from Corsica. During the next thirty years, Carthage gained control of southern Spain and closed the Straits of Gibraltar to Hellenic ships. Then, by expelling the Hellenes from Cyrene, Carthage dominated the whole of North Africa from the Atlantic to Egypt. As a result, by 500 B.C. Carthage was dominant in the western Mediterranean, while the Hellenes were caught in a gigantic economic squeeze between the Persians in the east (page 178) and the Carthaginians in the west. In Italy the Etruscans controlled the Tyrrhenian Sea, extended their control over the Romans, and pressed on Magna Graecia.

EARLY ROME

When a nation emerges from an inferior position as a dependency of another, it has happened that it rewrites its history to affirm its new freedom and to lessen the importance of its previous rulers. This nationalistic distortion of history has occurred in both ancient and modern times. The way the Romans wrote their history is a case in point.

ROMAN REJECTION OF ITS ETRUSCAN PAST

Two peoples made early Rome: the civilized Etruscans from Etruria and Italic peoples of mixed native and Indo-European descent. The Etruscans were the civilizing element. It was they who turned the rural villages of Rome into a city and taught the rural Latins and Sabines architecture, fortifications, trade, writing, and city life. When the Romans overthrew the last Etruscan king of Rome in 509 B.C., they recreated their history by telling legends in which Rome had been founded by the Latin Romulus (below), and in which Latin folk heroes were magnified. Actual events were falsified, for example, the conquest of Rome by Porsenna, the Lars (king) of Clusium. As the Romans told it, the Etruscan king's army was halted by a Roman hero, Horatius, at the Tiber bridge. The Etruscan king fled back to Clusium, abandoning all his army supplies, which were seized and distributed among the Romans. Actually, Porsenna did not flee at all but captured Rome and razed its walls to the ground. Because of distress among the conquered Romans he distributed free supplies of food. For centuries "Porsenna's supplies" was the name of relief supplies given out by the Roman government. Tradition might falsify the record, but it could not eradicate the words and the historical fact they symbolized from Roman usage.

In actual fact, records of Rome's early history are very scanty. What evidence we have comes from archaeological excavations rather than historical writings, for the Romans were not aware of their history until they had risen to supremacy in the eastern Mediterranean and needed to explain themselves to the peoples they conquered. Their traditions, however, tied early Rome to the civilized Middle East. According to the Roman historians Vergil and Livy, the Trojan hero Aeneas, fleeing from the fall of Troy, eventually made his way to the western coast of Italy. There he married the daughter of a king of Latium and had a son, Ascanius, who founded Alba Longa (page 210). Rhea, a descendant of Ascanius, was loved by the war god Mars and bore him twin sons, Romulus and Remus. A wicked uncle set the twins adrift on the Tiber River, but they were cast ashore near the Palatine hill, nursed by a she-wolf, and raised by a shepherd. Upon reaching manhood, Romulus and Remus decided to build a new city on the Palatine. In marking out the boundaries, they quarreled, whereupon Romulus slew

The Capitoline Wolf. An Etruscan sculpture of a she-wolf that came to be identified with the wolf that nourished the legendary Romulus and Remus, whose figures were added many centuries later during the Renaissance. The wolf, in Roman times, was placed on the Capitoline Hill in Rome and dedicated to Jupiter.

Remus and became the sole founder of Rome, traditionally, in 753 B.C. The legend relates the history of the early kings of Rome, the last three of whom (page 211) were probably Etruscan.

Such legends, while usually of doubtful historical accuracy, are nevertheless of great interest to the historian because they show what a people thought was important about themselves, their origins, and those with whom they wished to be associated (in the case of the Romans, to the people of the more civilized and cultured Middle East). They further reveal customs, beliefs, and practices that help us understand social life, religion, and the contacts a particular people had with those who influenced their development.

ROME GROWS

The first settlement on the Tiber was a tiny village of a few Latin herdsmen. They lived on two or three of the hills overlooking the marshy area that later became the Forum and joined with other villages close by in worshiping the god Jupiter on a nearby hill called the Alban Mount. Often these villages were attacked by hostile neighbors, and soon they seem to have united under the leadership of Alba Longa, a more important village close to the Alban Mount.

Each family had a cattle yard and a vegetable garden near its cabin, which had walls of mud mixed with straw held up by a wooden frame. The low places were often flooded and were unhealthy. Writing was still unknown, and metals were rare, although some bronze and a little iron was brought in by Etruscan traders.

Eventually a union was formed between the Latins and the Sabine peoples living on their hills by the Tiber. Then sometime around 600 B.C. both came under the control of the civilized, well-armed Etruscans.

ROME BECOMES A CITY

With the Etruscans in command, the cluster of Latin-Sabine villages grew and expanded into a city-state with the Etruscan name, Roma. The Etruscans introduced engineering; they built the great sewer, the Cloaca Maxima, which still exists. They drained the central swamp and there laid out the Forum, the meeting and marketplace of the new city. The Etruscan engineers constructed Rome's first city walls and erected its first stone houses and temples. The rulers introduced writing and metal crafts and made the young city an important trading center. Tradition has it that Rome was by then the most important community in Latium, though it may not have become so until after 500 B.C.

It is probable that the Etruscan kings of Rome did not belong to a single dynasty, although the last three were from Tarquinia, were known as the Tarquins, and were said to have been father, son, and son-in-law.

Rome played no part in the expansion of the Etruscans southward in Italy to the Bay of Naples, nor in the Etruscan alliance with Carthage against the Hellenes (page 208). Its affairs were still limited and local under the guidance of the Etruscans.

❦ ❦ ❦

During the Early Iron Age, civilization reached out into the Mediterranean, and new societies arose in the lands that had been Neolithic in the previous millennium. Civilization in ancient Hellas gradually emerged out of the chaos of the Bronze Age invasions. It was stimulated by the increasing contacts of an expanding population with the more civilized Middle East and developed from such contacts its own distinctive patterns and styles of living within a period of about two centuries. Hellenic expansion to the west was checked by the Carthaginians and the Etruscans, other sea peoples whose growth and development in this period made them major powers in the western Mediterranean. Trade and settlement by the Hellenes brought the civilizing influence of the east into the Italian peninsula, forming the link between the old centers of civilization and the newer ones, while Hellenic and Carthaginian colonies founded in Spain and France brought the far western Mediterranean into the orbit of civilization for the first time.

In the years ahead, the sea peoples of the Mediterranean would engage in further conflict that would remove the Etruscans from the stage of history entirely and make way for the rise of the power that would dominate the Mediterranean for centuries—Rome.

People, Places, and Terms

Etruscans	Aeolians	Delphi	aristocracy
Carthaginians	Lacedaemons	Thebes	oligarchy
Thales		Bosphorus	tyranny
Pythagoras	Tuscany	Etruria	lyric
Homer	Apennines	Latium	philosophy
Hesiod	Po Valley		mystery religion
Sappho	Peloponnesus	peninsula	colony
Pindar	Olympia	city-state	forum
Ionians	Laconia	*polis*	oracle
Dorians	Attica	helot	*Barbaroi*

Mastering the Reading

1. Although the Etruscans disappeared as a distinct group by 500 B.C., what practices and knowledge did they pass on to the Romans and Latins? How was Carthage founded? What were some differences between the Dorians and the Ionians?
2. What was the physical appearance of a Mediterranean city-state? Describe the different groups that lived in the city-state. How did their rights differ?
3. What was the relationship of a Hellene to his *polis?* How did the Mediterranean city-state differ from the city-kingdom of Sumer?
4. How did the actual founding of Rome differ from the ancient legend about it?

Interpreting the Text

1. What part did geography and climate play in internal unity, occupations, intellectual development, and expansion for each of the Sea Peoples?
2. Why were Homer and his epics honored by the Hellenes? What effect did Homer's epics have on the Hellenic religion?

Exploring Beyond the Text

Ancient Words in Modern English. Polis has many forms in English. List words in English that have been derived from *polis* and see what their meanings are. Add these words and their meanings to your glossary:

citadel	forum	oligarchy
acropolis	aristocracy	philosophy

Working with the Map

On a blank map trace the probable movement of the sea peoples to their eventual homelands. Then trace their colonization routes. In what spots did they become rivals? Why?

11

Hellas: Rise to Greatness and Failure to Unify

500–350 B.C.

In 480 B.C., the Great King Xerxes, sitting on his silver-footed throne, had seen his navy ignominiously defeated by the Hellenes at Salamis. Before Salamis, the desperate defense of Thermopylae, at which the Spartans under Leonidas had won undying glory, had shown the Persians that the conquest of Greece would be no easy matter. It was not until the defeats at Plataea and Mycale in 479 B.C., however, that the Persians were convinced that Hellas was not worth the fight.

The effect of their victory on the Hellenes was profound. They had withstood the mightiest power of the world and won. They were confirmed in their feeling of superiority to the barbarians, men who lived in a huge empire governed by a despot, not free men like the Hellenes, who lived in a self-contained *polis* governed by its citizens. Little Athens had proved its worthiness by the use of a navy that had brought decisive victory; its men could take an equal place alongside the disciplined Spartan warriors. By the time of the Persian Wars, Athens had been ready to play a more important part on the Hellenic stage. Under the tremendous impact of the Persian victories, nothing seemed too much for it to accomplish, nothing seemed beyond possibility.

But the prosperity and growth that Athens achieved, its very success, held the seeds of destruction. No Hellenic state liked to see another too powerful, too confident. The Peloponnesian Wars were the tragic result of Hellenic rivalry. In order to prosper and grow, the city-states had to unify. This they would not do alone. Philip of Macedon, coming to the throne in 359 B.C., understood this quite well.

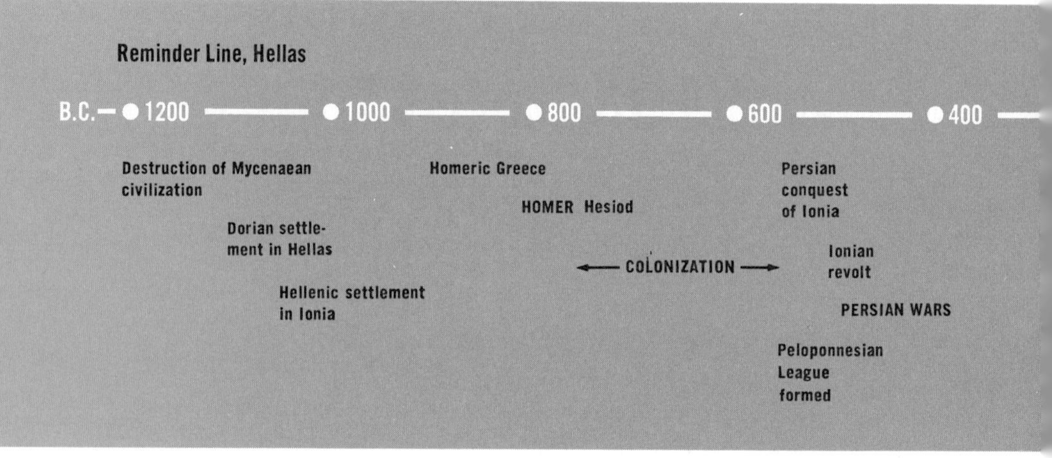

THE SUPREMACY OF ATHENS, 479–404 B.C.

The glorious victories over the Persians left the Hellenes confident and aggressive. Of no state was this more true than Athens, whose navy had been so decisive in the wars. No other state in Hellas except Sparta was in a position to challenge it. As long as Athens concentrated on commercial ventures through the power of its navy, Sparta, which was agricultural and land-based with a strong army, did not feel that their interests clashed. But rivalry was natural among the Hellenic states. When Athens gained power very rapidly through wealth gained by its navy, Athens aroused the fears and suspicions of its neighbors. Conflict broke out, producing the disasters of the Peloponnesian Wars.

THE DELIAN LEAGUE

After the Athenian victories at Salamis and Mycale (page 181), the Ionian Hellenes with Aegean ports were receptive to the idea of a permanent alliance against Persia. More than 160 island and coastal towns sent delegates to meet on Delos, an island sacred to Apollo. There they formed the League of Delos, or the Delian League, in 477 B.C. Delos was the central meeting place and held the treasury under the guardianship of the god Apollo. Each ally was to subscribe either goods or money to a fund for mutual defense. Shipbuilding members supplied vessels for a league navy, while smaller states made an annual money payment ("tribute").

From the beginning Athens dominated the league. Each state was bound by separate treaties to Athens. The officers of the league and the commanders of the league navy were all Athenians. The other states soon found, however, that once they were in the confederacy Athens could prevent them, by force if necessary, from withdrawing. In 454 B.C., under the pretext of guarding the treasury better, it was taken to Athens. Thereafter, the annual payments were collected by Athens and were spent on strengthening and beautifying the city and on building the "Long Walls," which lay between Athens and its port at Piraeus. The joint fleet became the Athenian navy. The Delian League had become a tool in an Athenian Aegean empire. This empire had grave consequences for the Hellenes.

THE ATHENIAN WAY OF LIFE

To the free-born Athenian, his *polis* was the center of his life—his country, his church, his business, his club, his home. He took part in its government, he honored its gods, and fought and sometimes died for it. Its honor and glory were his. Its common good was greater than any individual concern. The *polis* provided the mold in which he was formed and the ideals that would guide his conduct as an adult.

ATHENIAN EDUCATION

In order to become a worthy citizen of the *polis*, the Athenian was given an education intended to develop all sides of a man's nature: mental, moral, and physical. Education, in the mind of the Athenian, was the means to self-cultivation and worthy citizenship. A properly educated man was expected to take part in the affairs of the *polis;* limiting oneself to money-making was considered unworthy of a free-born Hellene. Though there was no system of free public education in Hellas, it was customary for all male children to receive at least the rudiments of education. Many private schools existed for this purpose.

School scene. In front of two seated older boys, two Athenian students study music and writing. On the left, the student learns to play the double flute by first listening. In the center, another boy sees his composition, written on a tablet, corrected with a stylus. To the right sits the *paedagogus*. This "red-figured" vase was made in Athens about 480 B.C.

Both boys and girls were under the direction and guidance of their mother until the age of seven. Usually there was a slave woman or a foreigner to help care for them. At eight the boy passed into the hands of a *paedagogus*, a slave who attended him everywhere and saw that he had the proper companions and learned the right manners.

From eight to eighteen a boy was given his formal education. His subjects were music, grammar, and gymnastics, which included jumping, hurling the discus, throwing the javelin, running, wrestling, swimming, and diving. The boys practiced naked, first smearing themselves with oil, which was scraped off after the practice was finished—the Hellenic equivalent of our shower. Musical education taught a boy to play the seven-stringed lyre and to sing to its accompaniment. These necessary social accomplishments were also intended to provide personal pleasure and to improve one's moral nature. Grammar included not only learning to write but also studying the national literature. The student read the works of Homer, parts of Hesiod, Aesop's fables, and popular compositions. He learned poetry by heart, and it was said that many Hellenes could recite the *Iliad* and *Odyssey* from memory.

Girls in ancient Hellas were given little formal education, but they were taught how to manage the house and the slaves, how to care for the children, and how to weave. An Athenian girl married between fourteen and sixteen a man her parents selected. Her life thereafter was quite separate from that of her husband. She did not leave the house except on rare occasions to attend a special religious festival, and she was then always accompanied. Her husband even did the marketing. She lived in a separate wing of the house and did not attend her husband's feasts or entertainments. She had no legal rights, nor any political ones, and if she was divorced her husband kept the children.

ATHENIAN CITIZENSHIP

At eighteen the Athenian man took the Ephebic oath, in which he swore to defend his city and its gods. He received his armor and spent the next two years in military training. From his twentieth year he was called on for active service, which might lead him from the Black Sea to Sicily or from Macedonia to Egypt—wherever the foreign policy of the state might send him. Military service was clearly the first and most important obligation of the citizen of Athens.

The Athenian citizen had several political responsibilities. He could vote in the Assembly if he had been present since the opening of the session and had heard all the speeches. He might even speak in the assembly if he had completed his military service, was married, was a landholder, had never thrown his shield away in battle, had completed all the obligations due his parents, and was not a debtor to the state. After the age of thirty he might, twice in his lifetime, be chosen by lot to serve as a member of the Council of Five Hundred, the *boule,* which managed Assembly meetings, supervised the army, navy, and state finances, and received foreign ambassadors. At the end of a year of service in the boule he had to stand public examination of all of his actions, particularly if he had been responsible for public money. (The Athenians seemed to have assumed that all men are dishonest if given a chance.) The Athenian citizen might also be chosen by lot to serve as one of the six thousand jurymen. Juries numbered from 201 to 2001 members. There were no judges nor lawyers. Each man pleaded his own case, and the jury then handed down the verdict.

The Athenian citizen also had religious duties. There were more than sixty days set aside in Athens for religious festivals. These festivals were marked by contests in music, oratory, athletics, and dramatics. If a citizen was wealthy, he might be given the special honor of paying all the costs of such a day of ritual. This was held to be a great honor because it supposedly brought the donor the favor of the gods. In actual fact such a custom was so expensive that to be honored more than once or twice would bankrupt all but the richest men.

Last, the citizen might be elected to serve as one of the Ten Generals who led the armed forces of Athens. Their duties included guiding the Assembly in its deliberations and executing its orders. Leading the armed forces was a dubious honor because those who lost battles were tried and exiled or executed (page 229). All public duties poorly carried out brought reprisal. Any citizen convicted of giving the Assembly bad advice was severely punished, as was anyone who was found guilty three times of advocating change in existing laws. Some historians have thought that it was severity peculiar to Sparta that led to the execution of a musician who dared to add another string to his harp, but such a punishment was equally possible in Athens for advocating change in any accepted ritual, political or religious.

THE GROWTH OF ATHENIAN DEMOCRACY

Monarchy was the earliest form of Athenian government. It gave way to an aristocratic form of rule and later to rule by tyrants. Athenian democracy only developed in gradual stages, and the process took about 150 years. The first step was the codification of law by Draco, c. 621 B.C. Draco's code was very severe, written "not in ink, but blood." The death penalty was given for nearly every offense. Still, Draco's code was a popular victory for the people, who were protected by laws that were specific and no longer open to interpretation by aristocratic judges.

The work of Draco was continued by Solon, c. 594 B.C., a man celebrated by his fellows as one of the wisest men of the day. Solon was given the powers of a dictator to effect the reforms that he said were necessary in a society that was being corrupted by greed and injustice. The Attic peasants who had fallen into debt and had therefore been sold into slavery were set free. Enslavement for debt was forever abolished. Solon limited the amount of land a noble might hold, restored lands to debtors who had lost them, and brought back to Athens debtors who had been sold abroad. He also performed a great service for Athenian agriculture and commerce by encouraging the production of wine and olive oil, which were very much in demand for export and which could be grown far more easily than grain in Attica's thin and rocky soil. He attracted foreign craftsmen to Athens, where they were promised citizenship, and he decreed that every man had to teach his son a trade. Then Solon passed legislation that admitted all citizens, even the poorest ones, to the Assembly. The admission of all citizens to the Assembly gave the average man a greater and more direct share in his government.

The next steps in the development of Athenian democracy were brought about by Pisistratus, c. 560 B.C., a nephew of Solon. Pisistratus gained supreme power as a tyrant by seizing power in a very crafty way. One day he appeared covered with blood in the marketplace. He said that he had been attacked and asked for a bodyguard. Now Pisistratus was very popular at Athens, having served well in war and having a pleasant and engaging personality. Furthermore, he was noted for his championship of the poor against the rich. He was given bodyguards armed with clubs. Quietly increasing their number, Pisistratus armed them all with spears and seized the Acropolis. This enabled him to gain control of the city and then of the government.

Pisistratus was removed from office a couple of times before he finally established himself firmly in power. Then he encouraged commerce by entering into alliances with neighboring cities. He aided agriculture by dividing up the estates of exiled noblemen among the poor farmers instead of letting it lie unused. He broadened the cultural life of the city by making the festivals more important. He added to their status by incorporating readings from the works of Homer into the Panathenaic Festival honoring Athena, and he gave new scope to the festival of Dionysus by encouraging a more elaborate performance that eventually led to the development of tragic drama (page 235). At the same time he brought artists and craftsmen to Athens to beautify the city and enhance its prestige, thus cultivating the taste, intelligence, and pride of the Athenians. These cultural additions to Athenian life, in which everyone participated, wove the lives of the noble and the common man ever more closely together, and helped to make one body of the Athenian citizens.

Cleisthenes, around 508 B.C., took the final step in creating the form of government that Athens was to maintain for the next two centuries. Cleisthenes revised the constitution by reorganizing the people into new voting groups that each contained a cross section of the population: farmers, artisans, and noblemen. Thus no one group of the citizenry would be able to outweigh another. He decreed that all must come together to vote in one place, in Athens. Then he made the Assembly the only legislative body, to which the magistrates were responsible, and he made the Assembly the final court of appeals. Finally, he introduced the system of ostracism (page 198) which enabled the people to oust tyrants and those politicians who lost popular favor (page 224).

Athens alone among the hundreds of Hellenic cities developed democracy. Athenian democracy, however, was quite unlike modern democracy. In actual practice it swung between oligarchy and tyranny (page 196). With a population of about 300,000, Athenian democracy placed the vote and the privilege of holding office in the hands of probably not more than twenty thousand people. One hundred thousand slaves, fifty thousand metics or noncitizens, all women and girls, and males under the age of 18, were excluded from participation in the democracy.

We can see, then, that Athenian democracy differed basically from American democracy. Rule in Athens was not by the majority but by a small minority (the citizens). The individual had no rights as an individual because all rights were vested in the state. Nevertheless, Athens had a democracy in theory though it did not always function as such in fact. This democracy was the first in the ancient world, and it created the concepts that were basic to the formation of our democratic republican form of government.

THE ATHENIAN DAY

The Athenian day started early. The Athenian gentleman usually arose at dawn, adjusted his tunic (a sleeveless undergarment of linen or wool), draped the mantle that had served as his blanket comfortably around him; ate no breakfast though he might have a little bread dipped in wine, and stepped forth. There was much to occupy his day. In the morning he attended the Assembly or law courts; in the afternoon he went to performances in the theater or to religious festivals. At all times he loved to gather with his friends to discuss public or private matters in the marketplace or at the gymnasium. He had a light meal at noon, after which he rested from the heat. His main meal was at sunset. This he shared with his wife or children if he had no guests. The Hellenes were frugal in their habits, temperate in drink as in food (page 20). Occasionally a rich man would serve special dainties, such as fruits and nuts. After the evening meal, the Athenian retired, for he got up early, and there was little artificial light to encourage keeping late hours.

THE SPARTAN WAY OF LIFE

The Spartans created quite a different society from the Athenian, one that had reached its final form by about 600 B.C. The Spartans attributed their laws to Lycurgus, a probably mythical figure who was said to have lived in the ninth century B.C. When the Spartans finally established a form of government and society that suited them, they saw no reason to change it so their society did not continue to evolve, as did the Athenian.

SPARTAN GOVERNMENT

Sparta was a military state under the leadership of two kings elected to office for nine years (page 195). Twenty-eight elders advised the kings, and decisions were ratified by shouting, the loudest shouts winning, in a popular assembly of all free Spartans. But the real management of civic affairs lay in the hands of the five *ephors*, or overseers, who were elected annually. Not only did they guide the deliberations of the Council and Assembly and closely watch the actions of the kings in war and peace, but they also superintended the education of the children and kept a paternal eye on everyone's private life. In addition, they supervised the helots, the pre-Dorian population the Spartans had enslaved (page 193).

Sparta had a standing army, the only such army in Hellas. Because of this army Sparta was easily the greatest military power among the Hellenic city-states. When military prowess was needed during the Persian invasions, the Hellenic forces rallied around the Peloponnesian League (page 193). Sparta was, in fact, not a city at all but a military camp of five villages. The Spartans were so sure of their warlike skills that they never surrounded their village with walls.

SPARTAN EDUCATION

Nowhere else in Hellas was the life of the individual so subordinate to the state. From earliest childhood, the Spartan's duty to his *polis* was instilled in him. Spartan education had one aim: to produce good soldiers and obedient citizens. To further this aim, the Spartan boy left home at seven and was educated by the *polis*. He lived in barracks, slept on a bed of bushes, went barefoot, and wore only one garment in winter and summer. He learned to endure hardships without complaint; he fended for himself, even stealing food when hungry. When caught, he was whipped—not for stealing but for getting caught. He was taught to express himself in the

Leonidas and a Draped Warrior. The bust on the left was found in Sparta and dates from the early fifth century B.C. It may well represent the Spartan king who fell at Thermopylae. The bronze warrior, right, was made in the sixth century B.C. Both warriors wear the war helmet, which, among the Hellenes, covered the face as well as the head.

briefest speech possible. Our word, *laconic* (meaning "very few words") is derived from the word Laconia, the name of the region containing Sparta.

At the age of twenty, the Spartan youth became a warrior. He continued to live in barracks, bringing with him his share of food, wine, and the iron bars that constituted Spartan money. His meals consisted of a thick black broth, sometimes a little cheese and a few vegetables, but rarely meat; his wine was mixed with water. Neither riches nor poverty was his. At thirty he became a full citizen and a member of the popular assembly. He then was obliged to marry to raise children for the state, but still he ate in the barracks, and attended the drill ground and the gymnasium. He had no home life until he was sixty, when he became an elder and retired from public service. Only then was he freed from the strict, harsh discipline of a soldier's life.

Women in Sparta were taught to be faithful and uncomplaining wives and mothers. Girls were given little formal education. They were taught gymnastics in order to be strong and healthy mothers; they were trained to be obedient, courageous, and modest in manner and behavior. Above all they were taught loyalty to the state. A Spartan mother did not tell her son to come back safely from battle. Handing him the heavy round shield on which his body would be carried home if he was killed and which he would have to drop if he fled, her words were, "Come back with your shield or on it." The bravery and discipline of Spartan men and women were famous throughout Hellas.

THE SPARTAN CHARACTER

The Spartan way of life had grown out of the need to control the helots. Having worked out their institutions to their own satisfaction, the Spartans discouraged change. The result was that Spartan society was immobile. Foreign visitors bringing new ideas were frowned on, and coinage, which would have made the exchange of goods easier, was forbidden. The simplest life, that which is most suited to the military, was the only acceptable one. Life was stern, as befitted a soldier, and rigidly regimented. "A Spartan's life is so unpleasant," quipped an Athenian, "that it is no wonder he throws it away so lightly in battle."

Yet for all its harshness, the Hellenes admired the Spartan way of life. The Hellenes valued a properly organized society, a *polis* that succeeded in its purpose of molding and forming the individual. Sparta was so organized that it accomplished what it set out to do, namely, to produce the best soldiers in Hellas. But beyond this, the Spartans had also created an ideal, the fulfillment of which made one proud to be a Spartan. The other Hellenes acknowledged this, and a little story illustrates it. An old man at the Olympic Games could not find himself a seat, and his search had provoked the jeers of the crowd. Coming to where the Spartans were sitting, he was offered a seat by all the young men and several of the old ones, whereupon the crowd applauded, and the old man, sighing, said, "All the Hellenes *know* what is right, but only the Spartans *do* it." The Spartans had imposed on their lives a certain pattern and had given up much for it. It was a way of life that was restricted in what it offered and what it sought to accomplish, and it was brutal and cruel. It did not, in itself, appeal to the other Hellenes. They saw nonetheless that it represented a standard of human excellence within a given framework. This was Sparta's creation and contribution: "not things in words and stones, but men."

RIVALRY BETWEEN ATHENS AND SPARTA

The success of Athens in repulsing the Persians (page 181) was due in large measure to Themistocles (c. 492 B.C.). Brilliant, persuasive, and imaginative, Themistocles embodied qualities that were typical of Athenian political leaders. He was strongly anti-Spartan. This antagonized the aristocrats and oligarchs, who feared that he would lead Athens into a war with the strongest Hellenic state in land fighting. But Themistocles was no fool. Realizing the strength of Sparta on land, he determined to make Athens invincible on the water.

In 483 B.C., between the attacks of Darius and Xerxes, rich new veins of ore were discovered in the state-owned silver mines. Themistocles, against loud opposition, persuaded the Athenians to spend all the new wealth on ships. The Athenian navy, as we have seen (page 181), turned out to be one of the decisive factors in defeating the Persians and in making Athens an equal of Sparta.

Themistocles' successor in leading Athens was Cimon, the son of Miltiades, the victor of Marathon (page 178). He was an aristocrat and allied by marriage to merchants of great wealth. He was elected as one of the Ten Generals each year from 476 to 462 B.C. He pursued a policy of war against Persia and friendship with Sparta. His victories in the former made him popular. His Spartan policy, however, was resented by many Athenians who harbored the ancient antagonism of Ionian against Dorian. When Sparta rudely dismissed an Athenian military force sent to aid them against Messinia (page 193), Athenian resentment was vented on Cimon, and he was ostracized in 461 B.C. The democratic party that next came to power was headed by Pericles, one of the most famous Athenians of all.

PERICLES, 460–429 B.C.

From 460 B.C. until his death in 429 B.C., Pericles dominated Athenian affairs. For sixteen consecutive years he was elected one of the Ten Generals. Periclean policy was to continue democratic reforms at home, extend Athenian power in central and northern Greece on land, and strengthen Athenian

THE CONFLICT BETWEEN HELLAS AND PERSIA

546-540 B.C.	Conquest of the Ionian cities by Cyrus.
499 B.C.	Ionian Revolt—the revolt of the Ionian cities of Asia Minor against Persia.
493 B.C.	Miletus destroyed and the Ionian cities crushed.
492-479 B.C.	THE PERSIAN WARS
492 B.C.	Darius' first expedition against Hellas and the destruction of the Persian fleet.
490 B.C.	Darius' second expedition against Hellas.
	The Persians defeated at Marathon by the Athenians led by Miltiades. The Persians sail home.
486 B.C.	Death of Darius.
483 B.C.	Themistocles persuades Athenians to spend new silver wealth on ships.
480-479 B.C.	Xerxes' expedition against Hellas.
480 B.C.	Persians defeat Leonidas at Thermopylae.
	Persians advance on Athens and burn it. Athenians retreat to Salamis in the bay of Attica where their navy, under the leadership of Themistocles, defeats the Persian fleet.
479 B.C.	Persians lay Attica waste but suffer defeat at Plataea by the combined Hellenic forces.
	Persian navy defeated by the Hellenic allies at Mycale near Miletus.
	War is over though no peace treaty is signed.

control of the Delian League. There was no fixed policy with regard to Persia.

The Periclean program was not successful in foreign affairs. Athenian support of Persia's foes brought disaster. Though peace with Persia followed in 448 B.C., it resulted in limiting Athenian naval activities to Aegean waters. In 445 B.C. the mainland states won back their freedom from Athens. Still, tribute from the Delian League, income from the silver mines and from taxes, and wealth from peacetime commerce poured into Athens. The next fifteen years of peace were spent by Pericles in making Athens the cultural leader of the world, and the creator of a Golden Age (see Chapter 12).

By 431 B.C. Athens had become the most populous city-state in Hellas. In the city and neighboring Attica there were at least 150,000 Athenians, some 50,000 aliens, and more than 100,000 slaves. The League, which had

Pericles. Aristocrat, warrior, statesman, and orator, Pericles gave his name to the golden age of Athens. In character he was grave, studious, and reserved. Although he did not speak often before the people, when he did "persuasion sat on his lips, such was his charm." Pericles' two domestic aims were to extend democracy and to make Athens the cultural and artistic center of the world. Both these aims were interrupted by the Peloponnesian Wars. In this Roman copy of a fifth century B.C. bust, Pericles wears his war helmet pushed back.

become Athens' empire, had a population of two million. It was engaged in flourishing commerce in waters made safe by the Athenian navy. In fifty years Athens had grown from a comparatively unimportant town to one with no equal in Hellas, and its people knew it.

HATRED TOWARD ATHENS

Athens now ran afoul of some of the most deep-rooted feelings in the Hellenic mind. One was the belief in individualism and the supremacy of the single city-state. In opposing the Persian Empire, Athens had appeared to be the champion of Hellenic individualism. Now this champion of liberty had become the oppressor. Each act of suppression against a Delian confederate deepened the fear of former friends and foes alike throughout Hellas that Athens was trying to establish its rule over its allies. This fear was made worse by Athenian boasts of ruthless acts. Other states lived in constant fear and resentment of what Athens would do next. Slowly the other states turned more and more to Sparta as their best hope of maintaining independence.

Another attitude that cost Athens dear was the ancient antagonism between Dorian and Ionian, which was rooted in differences of character. To the Ionian the Dorian was dull, slow-moving, artistocratic, old-fashioned. To the Dorian the Ionian was undependable, unstable, flippant, gabby, shallow. In lining up on the side of Ionian Athens or of Dorian Sparta, the Hellenes were dividing into two hostile camps in which emotion was fast replacing reason.

By 432 B.C. the Hellenes had divided into two political groups, each sure that its own way of life was the only good one and that it was endangered by those with a different philosophy. With this deep unreasoning hatred at work, Hellas had reached a point at which any minor incident could be the spark to set its world aflame.

THE HELLENIC WORLD WAR (PELOPONNESIAN WARS)

In 432 B.C. Athens barred the ships of Megara, her little Dorian neighbor, from all the ports of the Delian League. Meeting at Sparta, delegates from the city-states heard Corinth denounce Athens for aggression and criticize Sparta for her indifference to the wrongs Athens was inflicting on innocent states. The Spartan delegates replied that they did not seek war but that if Athens violated treaties, the rest of the Hellenes had a moral duty to preserve their liberties against the aggressor. Athens felt, of course, that it could not allow others to jeopardize its sacred right to do what it wanted with its own affairs. Both sides thus took a stand on high moral grounds. Each made it plain that it was a peace-loving people plunging into war in the cause of liberty. This may have been the first time in world history that propaganda of this kind was used; it was certainly not the last.

In Athens, Pericles decided against settling the problem by compromise. In financial resources Sparta was no match for Athens. Athens had a large reserve fund and could count on tribute from the Delian League. Let Sparta march on land; Athens would hold the sea. How could an elephant hurt a whale? The war must end in stalemate.

THE FIRST PHASE, 431–421 B.C.

The first phase of the war ended, as Pericles had foreseen, in a stalemate. While Spartan troops attacked Attica, the Athenian navy won victories along the coast of the Peloponnesus. What Pericles had not foreseen was Persian gold pouring into the Spartan war chest, the plague, his own death, and the unusual savagery with which both sides fought. Crowded for weeks into the walled city while Spartan troops ravaged the countryside, the population of Attica lived in conditions of filth in which pestilence ran riot. One out of every three persons died. The epidemic was no respector of persons or of rank. Slave and master, poor and rich, old and young alike perished. Having lost his two sons, Pericles himself was struck down by plague in 429 B.C.

Exhausted by the fighting, in 421 B.C. the adversaries signed a peace treaty. In the treaty each side agreed to give up all its captured territory and its prisoners, and the peace lasted fifty years.

THE SECOND PERIOD, 421–412 B.C.

Although neither side carried out the terms of the peace agreement, for seven years Athens and Sparta did not invade each other's territory. None of the hatred abated during the ensuing "cold war" period. It would still take only a spark to relight the fires of open conflict.

The spark was provided by Alcibiades, a nephew of Pericles. Handsome, clever, daring, conceited, and apparently lacking in any sense of right and wrong, Alcibiades' aims seem to have been solely self-gratification and self-advancement. Elected General in 420 B.C., he began at once to rebuild the war party in Athens. In 416 B.C. he persuaded Athens to attack, without provocation, the little Dorian island of Melos; the Athenians killed the entire male population and sold the women and children into slavery. Then a more grandiose scheme caught Alcibiades' fancy. His plan was nothing less than to extend the Athenian empire into the western Mediterranean by conquering the great Dorian city of Syracuse in Sicily (page 252).

In 415 B.C. Athens assembled a fleet the like of which had not been seen in Hellas since the Persian Wars. Twenty-seven thousand men sailed in 134 great triremes and 130 cargo vessels, the cost of which drained the Athenian treasury. The night before the fleet sailed, unknown persons mutilated the busts of Hermes that stood before the doorways of Athenian houses and were thought to be the guardians of peace and order. This act of vandalism filled the Athenians with superstitious horror and fear. In the days that followed, rumors spread through Athens that Alcibiades had been the instigator of the impiety. Messengers were sent after him to recall him to the city to answer the accusation of sacrilege. Instead of obeying, Alcibiades fled to Sparta, where he revealed the secret plans for the Athenian attack on Syracuse. With high hopes of victory, Sparta at once sent a force to aid Syracuse and to resume the war on the mainland. Two years of fighting in Sicily ended in the annihilation of the Athenian forces in Sicilian waters and turned the tide against the Athenians.

THE THIRD PERIOD, 412–404 B.C.

For eight years more the war dragged on. Athens' empire crumbled, and Sparta built a navy with the aid of gold from Persia. In 406 B.C. Athens won its last victory fighting near the Arginusae Islands to keep open the grain route from the Black Sea. But many ships were damaged, and many sailors lost their lives. So Athens celebrated her victory by executing, contrary to law, six of her victorious generals for losing the ships and men. When her enemies proposed an armistice, the Athenians rejected the offer. To the other Hellenes it seemed a clear demonstration of the saying, "The gods first drive insane those whom they wish to destroy."

In 405 B.C. the last Athenian ships in the north were destroyed in the battle of Aegospotami; another Spartan army invaded Attica, and a Spartan fleet blockaded the harbor of Piraeus. By 404 B.C. Athens was starved into unconditional surrender.

An oligarchic group of thirty men was set up in power in Athens by Lysander, the victorious Spartan general; all exiles were recalled, and the Thirty Tyrants then instituted an eight-month reign of terror during which political hatred was expressed by systematic murder. A popular uprising finally saved the Athenians and restored democracy.

HELLAS AT THE CLOSE OF THE HELLENIC WORLD WAR

The evil consequences of the Hellenic World War were shared by the victors and the vanquished. The Ionian cities of Asia fell back under Persian control. The Delian island states were under the control of Sparta, and, without the commercial outlet Athens had provided, their markets and economies were ruined. The one city that obtained some profit from the war was Thebes. Thebes had invaded Attica several times and had purchased, at low rates, the war spoils the Spartans had seized. Liberty for Hellas, for which Sparta had urged the Greeks to declare war on Athens, proved to be as unreal under the Spartans as it had been under the Athenians.

SUPREMACY OF SPARTA AND THEBES, 404–362 B.C.

The Hellenic World War ended with all political parties and leading cities discredited. Democracy at home had led to despotism abroad. Oligarchy had shown itself equally inhuman and unscrupulous. If Athenian democracy could produce an Alcibiades, Spartan oligarchic conservatism could match him with its Lysander. This man was equally insolent and ambitious, clever and charming, and had no morals or sense of public responsibility.

SUPREMACY OF SPARTA, 404–371 B.C.

The Sparta that had been the champion of liberty now became the oppressor, repeating the tyrannies of Athens after the Persian Wars. Opposition from any other Hellenic state was met with war. Within nine years Sparta's former allies had turned against it, and open conflict followed.

Persian gold, which had aided Sparta in crushing Athens, was diverted by the Great King to the Athenians in order to encourage Hellenic rivalry and disorder. With Persian aid, the port at Piraeus and its defenses were rebuilt. Athens again began to rise. When Sparta threatened an invasion of Persia, more of the Great King's gold made Athens an open ally of Persia, and the Spartan king was obliged to abandon his campaign at the height of his success. With Athens strong enough to oppose Sparta but not strong enough to defeat it, the two cities were once more at a stalemate. At this juncture they were ordered to send ambassadors to Susa to receive the orders of the Great King.

What could have been more humiliating to the Hellenes than to have to submit their affairs to the arbitration of the barbarian king, whose ancestor they had so gloriously defeated?

THE PEACE OF THE GREAT KING, 387 B.C.

Under the terms of the Great King's peace, the Ionian Hellenes of Asia were legally returned to the Persian Empire. Sparta received just enough Persian gold to allow it to enforce the peace in Hellas.

In the ten years that followed, everyone violated the peace. Sparta used its position to carry out its own aggressive policies. In 377 B.C. Athens called on all Hellenic states and all foreign nations except Persia to join it in overthrowing Spartan despotism. This Second Athenian League was set up in defiance of the Great King's prohibition. When the allies found Athens once more encroaching on their independence, the league dissolved.

Obviously neither Athens nor Sparta had learned anything from the disastrous experience of the Peloponnesian Wars and their aftermath.

Finally, in 371 B.C., a new peace conference was called by Sparta. All the Hellenic governments, including those in Sicily and Italy, were represented. Other participants were Macedon and Persia. At this first great peace conference in world history, a plan for general disarmament was proposed, and it was agreed that peaceful means (sanctions) would be used to oppose any aggressor; all commercial and diplomatic relations with an aggressor would be broken. The project suddenly collapsed when Sparta refused to allow Thebes to sign the treaty for the other Boeotian states, with which it was allied. The Theban delegations departed in a rage.

Persian gold was diverted to Thebes. When Epaminondas of Thebes defeated Sparta in the battlefield of Leuctra in 371 B.C., Sparta's day of supremacy was ended forever.

THE BATTLE OF LEUCTRA, 371 B.C.

The battle of Leuctra was important not only because it ended Spartan supremacy over the Hellenic states, but also because it was significant in the development of the famous and formidable Macedonian phalanx that Alexander the Great led to conquer the east.

Before Leuctra the Hellenes had followed a very simple method of fighting. A continuous line of troops surrounded the *hoplites*, the heavily armed infantry, who stood in the center. The flanks were covered by cavalry, and lightly armed soldiers skirmished in front until the opposing forces met, whereupon they engaged in hand to hand combat.

Epaminondas, the Theban commander, devised a new technique. He massed his best hoplites fifty men deep on the left wing and threw them with terrific force on the Spartan right flank. The enemy, drawn up eight men deep in the usual fashion, could not stand the onslaught. Their troops gave way, and the fight was won. This tactic of concentrating an attack of solidly massed men at one point on the enemy's lines was the most successful military tactic the Hellenes devised until Philip of Macedon improved on it some 25 years later (page 319).

SUPREMACY OF THEBES, 371–362 B.C.

For nine years Epaminondas of Thebes dominated Hellenic affairs. Following the defeat of Sparta, civil war immediately swept the Peloponnesian peninsula. Epaminondas invaded the Peloponnesus, and, though he threatened unwalled Sparta, he contented himself with restoring freedom to

Messenia. But the Greek states were no more willing to see the supremacy of Thebes than they had been to acknowledge the supremacy of Athens or Sparta. These two states buried their differences and, in alliance with other disgruntled cities, faced the Thebans at Mantinea in 362 B.C. Though each side claimed the victory, Epaminondas was killed, and the Theban day of glory was over. No state was strong enough to dominate the others, yet all were unwilling to cooperate on the basis of equality. From the north, Philip of Macedon regarded this state of affairs with the highest satisfaction.

Hellas was deeply weakened by the conflicts of the Peloponnesian Wars. They proved that the fifth-century B.C. *polis* was not capable of developing to govern a larger unit than itself and that the Hellenic love of independence overrode all other considerations. Neither Sparta nor Thebes had any greater success in satisfying the needs and ambitions of the Hellenes than the Athenians. It was evident that only an outside force would be capable of imposing a unity on the fiercely individualistic city-states of Hellas. The Macedonians, Hellas's neighbors to the north, were not unaware of this. Philip II came to the Macedonian throne in 359 B.C. His reign opened a new era for Hellas.

People, Places, and Terms

Themistocles
Draco
Solon
Pisistratus
Cleisthenes
Lycurgus
Cimon
Pericles
Alcibiades

Epaminondas

Latium
Leuctra
Mantinea
Macedonia
Delos

Peloponnesian League

Delian League
lot
ostracism
ephor
boule
Ten Generals
hoplite
Peloponnesian Wars

Mastering the Reading

1. What were the responsibilities of an Athenian citizen?
2. Step by step, how did each of the following men help democratize Athens: Draco? Solon? Pisistratus? Cleisthenes?
3. Compare the Athenian and the Spartan "ways of life."
4. What did the Delian League contribute to Athenian development? Why was it disliked?

5. List at least three reasons for the Peloponnesian Wars. What was the outcome of each?
6. Why did Sparta fail as the new leader of the Hellenes? How did Thebes fare under the leadership of Epaminondas, and then after his death?

Interpreting the Text

1. In what ways would you agree with the topic sentence of paragraph three, page 214, that ". . . the prosperity and growth that Athens achieved, its very success, held the seeds of destruction"?
2. What are the differences in method and principle between electing a person and choosing him by lot? Which offices in Athens were chosen by lot? by election? Why the difference?
3. Prepare to debate the proposition: Athens was not a democracy.

Exploring Beyond the Text

1. Each of the following men was admired at one time or another by the Athenians:

Miltiades	Pericles	Alcibiades
Themistocles	Solon	

   Do outside reading and then determine what qualities and qualifications each had that made him popular with the Assembly. Why were some ostracized? Were the Athenians justified in so doing? What does this tell us about the men and the citizenry?
2. *Ancient Words in Modern English.* Many of the following words have changed in meaning over the years. What were their historical meanings? What are their current meanings? Add these words and their meanings to your glossary:

draconian	spartan	democracy
laconic	solons	pedagogue

12

The Flowering of the Hellenic Mind

500–350 B.C.

In the long story of man's development, there have been times when geniuses have appeared in much greater number than is usual under ordinary circumstances. Such a blossoming of the human potential may occur in one small locality, or it may take place over a whole continent. It may happen within the span of a single generation, or it may flourish for a generation or two. Why it takes place when it does, and where it does, is a matter for endless speculation. Perhaps some great event stimulates the imaginations of thoughtful men. Perhaps expanding economic conditions provide part of the answer, or perhaps the ideas and actions of a few creative personalities start a chain reaction that stimulates others to use their abilities to the fullest. Perhaps all these must appear together. Certainly such a blossoming has a great deal to do with the particular environment, but whatever the reasons may be, the historical fact is that such periods exist. One such occurred in Hellas between the end of the Persian Wars and the coming of Alexander the Great, approximately 480–335 B.C.

IONIAN LEADERSHIP

The whole Hellenic world shared in the creativity of the times, but Attica, with Athens as its heart, was preeminent. Ionians had taken the lead in Hellenic poetry and philosophy in the eighth and seventh centuries B.C. (page 193). Just as the Ionians had seemed more flexible, imaginative, and daring than the other Hellenic peoples at that time, so they surpassed them once again. But whereas in the earlier time the center of Ionian culture had been on the Asiatic coast of the Aegean around Miletus, now it lay on the European side, in Attica. The heart of Attica was Athens. Athens not only gave birth to many geniuses but also drew to itself the artists and thinkers of the rest of Hellas. Pericles, the great Athenian statesman (page 224), said truly, "The magnitude of our city draws the produce of the world into our harbour," and "We provide means for the mind to refresh itself from business. We celebrate competitions and sacrifices all the year round . . . The admiration of the present and succeeding ages will be ours . . . As a city we are the school of Hellas."

In Chapter 10 (page 198) we saw that there was a unity between the citizens, their city, and their gods. In this unity the arts served the state and the gods rather than private individuals or private enterprise, as in our world today. Poems and plays were presented to government committees, which decided which ones were to be offered for competition before the public. Theaters and temples were built to honor the gods and glorify the *polis*, and religious and civic statues were commissioned. When public funds were insufficient to meet expenses, wealthy citizens held it a great honor to be chosen to take turns paying the costs (page 218).

The atmosphere of Athens was exciting and challenging, and the Athenians responded to it with a burst of creativity. Let us turn first to the development of the drama.

THE THEATER AND DRAMA

Drama in ancient Hellas had its roots in religious ceremonies (page 205). Among these were those performed around an altar to the god Dionysus during his festivals in midwinter and spring. On a round floor, or *orchestra*, in the center of which stood the altar, a choral group sang and recited in verse. On one side of the dancing floor there was a tent (*skene*), used as a dressing room for the performers. Later it became a building that served as an architectural background for the presentation. Even after the drama had developed, there was no curtain and no scenery.

In the early days of the drama, the chorus created the entire action. Then speeches for one actor gradually evolved. During the age of Pericles, a second actor was introduced by Aeschylus, (see below), the first great Athenian dramatist, and later Sophocles (see below) added a third actor and a painted canvas covering the skene. The three actors played all the parts, the women's as well as the men's. The chorus numbered fifteen men for tragedy and twenty-four for comedy.

The actors wore elaborate costumes, masks carved to portray the character or emotion represented, and high-heeled, thick-soled boots of crimson leather, which gave the actors added height so they could be more easily seen above the chorus. Musical accompaniment was played on a kind of reed pipe or flute called the aulos.

Hellenic plays were always performed out of doors in the brilliant sunshine. At first they were given in the marketplace, but because space was limited the performances soon moved to a convenient hillside. There thousands of citizens attended the drama seated in an amphitheater with sloping tiers of seats that rose in arcs above the choral pit behind the seats of the judges and leading dignitaries. The performances of tragedy occupied the last three days of the Dionysiac festival, beginning in the early morning

The theater at Epidaurus in Argolis. A horizontal gangway divides the horseshoe-shaped *theatron*, or viewing area, in half. Thirty-four rows of steeply banked seats occupy the lower two; twenty-one rows fill the upper. Fifteen thousand people could be accommodated. Built in the fourth century B.C., the theater is well preserved, and the acoustics are excellent. The ancient Hellenic plays are still performed here before present-day audiences.

and lasting until dark. The performances of comedy lasted one day. At the end of the festival a prize was awarded to the poet and chorus whose presentation was judged to have been of the highest excellence. All citizens were expected to attend, and the Athenian government considered the drama so important a means of indoctrinating the public with moral and religious ideas that a law was passed requiring that tickets, paid for by the state, be given free to those who could not pay the small admission fee.

Tragedy, so closely related to religion, was the first branch of the drama to attain artistic excellence. Comedy did not originate until after the Persian Wars, but the earliest comedies we have are those of Aristophanes, who lived some fifty years later.

The theater held a very important place in Hellenic life for more than one reason. Not only did it serve as a means of informing the public with moral and religious ideas, but after the creation of comedy it also became a vehicle for dealing with the leading personages and questions of the day. It was the newspaper, cartoon, and television of Hellas.

AESCHYLUS

Aeschylus (525–456 B.C.) was the first of the three great tragic poets regarded as supreme by the Athenians. The other two were Sophocles and Euripides, and in the hands of these creative geniuses the drama became a great literary form.

Aeschylus lived through the Persian Wars and wrote of them in his play *The Persians*. It is the only existing Hellenic tragedy that takes its theme from history rather than from mythology. The first ghost scene in theatrical history takes place in this play when the spirit of Darius comes to warn the Persians of their doom. In *Prometheus Bound*, the story of the god who brought mankind fire against the will of Zeus, and the *Oresteia* trilogy (a group of three related plays), based on a legend of murder and retribution, Aeschylus deals with the problems of suffering, virtue, and the workings of divine justice. He is considered a most powerful tragedian because of the greatness of his imagination, the beauty of his language, and his profoundly religious themes. In all of his plays he builds suspense to the breaking point, creating an intense emotional impact on his audience.

Although Aeschylus is deservedly called the Father of Greek Tragedy and devoted his mature life to drama, in his own mind the most significant event of his life was his part in the battles against the Persians. The inscription he asked to have placed on his tombstone made no mention of the theater or the many prizes he had won, but gave only his name and the sentence, "The famed grove of Marathon and the long-haired Mede will testify to his bravery." Aeschylus wrote about ninety plays, of which only seven have been completely preserved.

SOPHOCLES

Of all the tragic poets, Sophocles (c. 496–406 B.C.) was the most admired by his contemporaries. As a young man he won the prize against Aeschylus, and until his death he was the leading poet of Athens. The perfection of his style and form and his beautiful balance of choral and dramatic action led Aristotle to describe *Oedipus the King,* one in a trilogy of plays about Oedipus and his children, as the perfect tragedy.

Sophocles' plays are on a more worldly level than those of Aeschylus. They are more concerned with human conduct and the effect of life on a man's character and soul. The characters of Sophocles are marked by grandeur and nobility of character and action. In *Antigone*, part of the *Oedipus* trilogy, heroic self-sacrifice and sisterly devotion to a higher law of heaven that has been contradicted by an earthly decree are masterfully presented. Of more than a hundred plays of Sophocles, we have only seven.

EURIPIDES

Euripides (480–406 B.C.) was a contemporary of Sophocles, but unlike his older peer, he held aloof from civic life and devoted all his attention to his plays. He made changes in technique, used more varied costumes and varying meters in his verse. These changes, and his themes, which questioned accepted beliefs and traditions, especially those concerning the Olympic gods, offended the conservatives of his day. The result was that his plays won fewer competitions than those of Aeschylus and Sophocles. Nevertheless, his fame spread around the Mediterranean, and we are told that after the disaster of Alcibiades' expedition against Syracuse (page 229), the Sicilians granted freedom to all prisoners who could recite lines from Euripides.

In the plays of Euripides the characters act and talk like ordinary human beings; they are not the ideal figures depicted by Sophocles and Aeschylus. "I draw men as they ought to be," said Sophocles. "Euripides draws them as they are." The human qualities in Euripides' plays, his sympathy for women and the oppressed, as in the *Medea* and *The Trojan Women,* his tenderness, and the introduction of romantic themes gave his plays great appeal. They were well known throughout the Roman world long after his death. Nineteen of his ninety-two plays survive.

ARISTOPHANES AND COMEDY

Comedy seems to have originated from simple satiric exhibitions given at country festivals, and it had a great deal more freedom of expression and form than did tragedy. Neither the gods nor men were sacred to the writers of comedy. Local events and personalities were their favorite subjects.

Aristophanes (c. 450–388 B.C.) is the greatest master of comedy whose works have come down to us. He was a brilliant satirist and a truly excellent poet. In *The Knights* he baldly attacks Cleon, who succeeded Pericles in Athens; in *The Clouds* he criticizes the philosophy of the Sophists (page 249) and its practitioners, and Socrates; in *The Wasps* he makes fun of the law courts and the Hellenic delight in trying law cases; and in *The Frogs* he savagely criticizes Euripides and his new techniques and attitudes.

Not many writers have had Aristophanes' skill in puncturing sham and pretense with a few well-chosen words. His plays were extremely popular and seem to have had a strong effect on his audience. Indeed, it is believed that his attack on Socrates influenced public opinion against the philosopher (page 306). Only eleven of Aristophanes' plays are extant.

HISTORICAL PROSE

Until the fifth century B.C. history as we know it had never been written. All civilizations had kept records of their kings, had written down legends of the gods, and had recorded myths, genealogies, and local events. But history is more than this. It is not only the record of events but an interpretation of them. It was not until the fifth century B.C. that there appeared in Hellas the first true historians, men who attempted to inquire into the facts and to interpret the meaning and significance of events. The first of these true historians was Herodotus.

HERODOTUS

Herodotus (484–425 B.C.) was a native of Asia Minor. As a young man he got into political trouble and took himself to Athens. There he mingled with all the great men of his day and participated in the brilliant life of the

Athenian *polis*. At a time when traveling was not easy or customary, Herodotus visited Babylonia, Egypt, Italy, Sicily, and the Black Sea. He collected a great fund of knowledge on all sorts of subjects—governments, religions, customs, legends and tales—and all this he fitted into *The Histories*. Herodotus' method was not to diligently sift fact from fiction but to give us the facts when he had them and stories and legends, told in a most entertaining and informative manner, when he didn't. Taking as his main theme the great struggle between the Hellenes and the Persians, Herodotus set out to contrast the character and civilization of the two contending powers and to show how the arrogance of Xerxes in attacking the Hellenes had brought the wrath of the gods down on the Persian forces. Herodotus did not expect to find only rational explanations for the affairs of men, and used the will of the gods to help explain the outcome of events. Nevertheless, Herodotus is justly called the Father of History, for he tried to report factually where he could, to search for the truth as carefully as possible, and to explain the meaning of events as he understood them.

THUCYDIDES

Herodotus set himself the task of writing the history of the Persian Wars, a great conflict in which the hearts and minds of a whole people and two civilizations were caught up. The Athenian Thucydides (455–400 B.C.), the historian of the Peloponnesian Wars, had a lesser theme. His history merely recounts the details of a war betweeen the small city-states of Hellas. But Thucydides attempted to write history in a new way, to write only of those things that "I either saw myself or learned from others of whom I made the most careful and particular inquiry." In other words, he attempted to present only the facts, not fanciful if delightful stories as well. He also tried to show the relationship of cause and event and to illustrate that the outcome was the work of men, not of gods. Thucydides talked with eye witnesses, he gathered evidence, and then he formed conclusions. Although he was an Athenian general, no bias mars his work. If writing a fair and accurate account of events is the first business of the historian, to Thucydides goes the honor of being the first such writer of history.

XENOPHON

Thucydides' history ends abruptly in 411 B.C. We do not know why, but the task of completion was taken on by a younger contemporary,

Xenophon (434–354 B.C.). Xenophon was a man of a wide range of interests, and his writing has a fresh, personal style and a simple, lively tone. Besides the *Hellenica*, he wrote the *Anabasis*, or *March Upcountry*, a personal memoir of his career as a young soldier of fortune during a Persian revolt (page 320). Another work was a recollection of Socrates, which expressed his deep admiration for the philosopher. Xenophon was as much a journalist and biographer as an historian, and pieces on hunting, cavalry, estate management, and education illustrate his concerns when he lived the life of a country gentleman outside Sparta, a *polis* he admired. Xenophon was much esteemed during his lifetime for his literary style, but to us he does not have the depth of analysis or the powers of interpretation of his predecessor, Thucydides.

ARCHITECTURE, SCULPTURE, PAINTING, AND THE MINOR ARTS

The Hellenes possessed a wonderful sense of the beautiful, and all they created is distinguished by it. For the Hellenes the beautiful was part of everyday life; it was not set aside for special occasions or confined to objects of particular merit. Everything they touched reflected their superb artistic sense: not only the major arts of architecture, sculpture, and painting, but all the minor ones as well—furniture, vases, coins, jewelry, household objects.

The beauty of Hellenic art lies in its clarity and simplicity. Things are never out of proportion, there is never too much ornamentation or decoration, the scale and sense of balance are just right. What we are led to feel is the harmony among all the parts; that they fit together and complement each other in a way that no other people has surpassed.

During the Persian Wars the citizens of Athens, seeing their homes, and the temples and statues on the Acropolis, go up in flames, had vowed to leave the ruins as a reminder of the war. But after a peace treaty was signed with the Persians (448 B.C.), and with the money that came to the city through the Delian League, Pericles (page 225) decided to make Athens the most beautiful city of Hellas. Many new buildings were designed for the Acropolis. New statues were commissioned, and artists and craftsmen flocked to Athens. The new achievements in the visual arts were to be as remarkable as those in theater and literature.

ARCHITECTURE AND SCULPTURE: THE FIRST PHASE

The chief architectural expression of the Hellenes was the temple, the home of the god. It was usually built of limestone or white marble. When limestone was used, it was coated with white stucco in order to give it the appearance of marble. The Hellenes, unlike the peoples of the Middle East, never used sun-baked brick. Neither did they use the arch or the dome, both of which had been invented in Babylonia.

Hellenic temples were oblong structures with a pitched roof and a flat ceiling supported by rows of columns. They had doors but no windows. All decoration was on the outside; the interior was perfectly plain. The beauty of a Greek temple lay in its harmonious proportions and faultless symmetry. Straight lines were avoided. The columns were closer together at the ends of the rows than in the middle, and each column swelled slightly in the middle and tapered at the ends. The columns were built to lean inward toward the center of the building. Even the basement and steps have a slight convexity. Such subtleties, which produced the impression that the building had perfect symmetry, delighted the Hellenic mind.

Many of the most impressive Hellenic temple ruins are in southern Italy and Sicily, though the single best preserved temple is the Temple of Hephaestus at Athens, formerly known as the Theseum. In spite of many examples, one, even though nearly totally destroyed, is universally hailed as embodying the best spirit of the age. This building exemplifies the combination of architectural and sculptural genius which has never been surpassed; it is the Parthenon, the temple of Athena Parthenos, Athena the Virgin, on the Acropolis of Athens.

The architects of the Parthenon were Callicrates and Ictinus. Its sculptor was Phidias, who superintended all the works of art erected at Athens during the administration of Pericles and worked closely with the Parthenon architects. The building, including even the roof tiles, was entirely of marble and stood 227 feet long, 101 feet wide, and 65 feet high. The oblong central building (*cella*) was surrounded on all sides by rows of tall columns. The cella was divided into two chambers. The larger contained the statue of the goddess, the smaller was used as a storage room for the chests of temple treasure. The whole temple was colored and gilded on the inside and the outside. The great triangular pediments over the front and rear entrances were faced with groups of statuary. That above the east entrance told the story of the birth of Athena from the forehead of Zeus. That over the west entrance showed the contest between Athena and Poseidon, God

The Parthenon. Begun in 447 B.C. and completed within fifteen years, the Parthenon is the supreme example of the Doric form of Hellenic architecture. To acquire the marble needed for the temple, stone blocks quarried by slaves were slid down the mountainside in chutes. They were hauled to the building site in wagons drawn by teams of oxen. Workmen assigned by the state to build the temple were divided into teams with different jobs. Upon completion, the entire building was polished with oil and grinding stones. In 426 A.D., the Parthenon was converted into a Christian church, and about 1460 A.D., the Turks turned it into a mosque. The central part of the building was destroyed in 1687 when the Venetians used it as a powder magazine, which exploded.

of the Sea, for control of Attica and Athens. In this contest Athena had offered the Athenians the first olive tree and the gift of wisdom; Poseidon had offered them the horse and the power of the sea. The decision had gone to Athena, who became the patron of the city, although Poseidon continued to be held in great respect, for it was thought that he caused the mighty earthquakes that so often shook the eastern Mediterranean. Two borders, or friezes, encircled the roof of the temple. The outside one showed a legendary battle between the Athenians and the Centaurs, mythical creatures who were half man and half horse. The frieze around the cella showed the procession in which the citizens of Athens wound up the Acropolis to honor their patron goddess by presenting her with a new robe.

Inside the Parthenon's cella stood a great statue of Athena by Phidias. It was forty feet tall, made of a wooden core plated with ivory for the fleshy parts and with gold for the remaining. Outside the temple rose another statue of Athena, also by Phidias. Seventy feet from the base to the tip of the spear held by the goddess, the statue glittered in the sun and was the first sign of the city to be seen far out at sea by sailors homeward bound.

The chief subjects of Hellenic sculpture were the gods and the heroes: statesmen, generals, and athletes. The Hellenes limited themselves in the subjects they sculpted, devoting most of their skill to the human figure, but in this form they were never surpassed. From the earliest days they used wood; at all periods they used terra cotta for smaller works; they also used gold and ivory, both of which were rare and precious. The most common material for larger works was bronze, but marble was the favorite. It was of many hues and shades, quite unlike the whiter, more severe Italic marbles of later times. Statues were carved both in the round and in relief, and both styles were used in temple decoration.

Very few original sculptures from ancient Hellas remain. Marble was turned into mortar, or used for building, or ruined by neglect; bronze was melted down, gold and ivory have vanished, and wood and terra cotta are too fragile to last through the centuries. Most of what we have are Roman copies made several centuries later and mass produced (page 457). Yet even these are of such quality that we can only admire what must have been and regret that we do not have more.

Phidias was the greatest sculptor of the fifth century B.C. Besides the two Athenas for the Parthenon, of which the gold and ivory one was by his own hand, he conceived all the figures of the temple, which were executed under his direction. He also carved the gigantic statue of Zeus at Olympia, his most famous work. This enormous seated figure, some sixty feet high, was of ivory and gold. Zeus, it was said, could not stand up without going through the roof. The statue was classed by the ancients as one of the Seven Wonders of the World. Phidias' figures were awe-inspiring, of calm majesty and heroic dignity.

Two other sculptors of this period, Myron and Polycleitus, rank close to Phidias. Myron did his best work in bronze, but we have no originals, only Roman copies in marble and of very few subjects. The Discobolus (Discus Thrower) shows an athlete at the moment when his body is tensed to throw the metal plate. It is likely that this was created to commemorate an event of the Great Games. Polycleitus of Argos rivaled

Phidias in grandeur of conception and skill in execution. His favorite subjects were athletes, men rather than gods, such as his excellent statue to the Doryphorus (Spear Bearer). Though Polycleitus made this statue in bronze, we have only a Roman marble copy. In works such as the Disobolus and the Doryphorus, all the stiffness that had marked earlier Hellenic statues, created under the influence of Egyptian models, had disappeared and the classical style of the fifth century B.C. has emerged in which the human body was portrayed in all its natural grace and beauty.

ARCHITECTURE AND SCULPTURE: THE SECOND PHASE

The Age of Pericles was followed by the tragic Peloponnesian Wars. These wars had a profound effect on the attitude of the Hellenes. Steadily the age became more materialistic as the individual lost faith in the ideal of the *polis* and came to be more concerned with himself and his personal problems. There was a lowering of ideals from the level of the divine to that of the merely human, and the full effects of the change were clearly demonstrated in art and literature. Temples were commissioned, but no longer did they represent civic pride combined with a firm belief in the majesty of the gods and the heroic spirit of man. The new age was questioning, restless, and distracted. Its ideals had been shattered by the disasters of the war and the lack of security in life. It is typical that the fourth century B.C.'s most famous architectural achievement was a tomb. The greatest artists of Hellas were summoned by Queen Artemesia of Caria, in Asia Minor, to decorate the burial monument of her brother-husband, Mausolus. This monument to an individual reflects a new trend in Hellenic art in which a man, rather than Man, is glorified. The structure was so splendid that the ancients accounted it as one of the Seven Wonders, and every magnificent tomb since has been called a mausoleum.

Among the famous artists invited to decorate the Mausoleum at Halicarnassus was Scopas, one of the greatest sculptors of the fourth century B.C. Few of his works have survived, and it is chiefly from ancient writers that we know of the new spirit that characterized his art: one of violent emotion, which seems to reflect the spirit of turmoil of his times. Scopas originated styles in sculpture that were dominant in the Hellenistic Age that followed Alexander the Great.

Both Scopas and his contemporary, the equally great Praxiteles, reflected the individualism of the period and its greater attention to emotion. But where Scopas' figures reflect despair, agitation, and anguish, Praxiteles

The Hermes of Praxiteles. Hermes, messenger of the gods, gazes at the baby Dionysius, who may be reaching for a bunch of grapes. Praxiteles has sculpted the marble so carefully that it seems to be, rather than represent, real flesh. Hermes is not a heroic figure here, but one of charm and grace. Unlike other statues by Praxiteles, this one was apparently a minor work, for it was not mentioned by the sculptor's contemporaries.

turned to the softer side of life, to indolence and contemplation and even humor. Praxiteles sculpted many of the gods, but his purpose was not to show divine majesty, as Phidias had done. Instead he showed the grace and charm of the human form, especially of the female, and his gods and goddesses, though still beautiful, look completely human. His Hermes, discovered in modern times at Olympia, is the only statue known to us to be certainly the original work of one of the great Hellenic masters. His Aphrodite of Cnidus set the style for portraying the goddess of love for centuries.

PAINTING AND THE MINOR ARTS

Like all Mediterranean people, ancient and modern, the Hellenes loved bright colors. They used them on temples and statuary and the walls of their homes. Brightly colored murals were very common, and paintings on wooden tablets and stone were also popular. Only watercolors were used, as oils were unknown.

The greatest painter of the Periclean Age was Polygnotus. His work showed the same heroic feeling and civic spirit that characterized the sculpture and architecture of his day. Using only four colors, red, white, yellow, and black, with little shading or perspective, he covered walls with monumental scenes of sweeping grandeur: the Sack of Troy, the Battle of Marathon, and the legend of the descent of Odysseus to Hades. We have so few remains of Hellenic painting that we must accept the opinion of the ancients themselves as to its quality, but from their reports, Hellenic painting enjoyed a high reputation.

Painting on vases we may judge for ourselves. Many have been unearthed. They have revealed much of what we know about life in Hellas. Because jars were put to a great many uses (page 201), they came in many sizes and shapes. In decorating them the craftsman had to organize his design to fit the space he wished to fill, and the great skill with which he did so raised the craft of vase painting into an art.

Vase painting had a long tradition, and it had reached its height before the fifth century B.C. The earliest jars, the so-called black-figured, bore shapes painted in black over the red glazed surface of the earthenware jar (see photo, page 200). These gave way to the red-figured vases, in which the background was black and the figures were in the natural color of the pot (see photo, page 216). By the fifth century B.C. the quality of painting on pots had declined. It seems likely that the major arts occupied the talents of the most skilled artists and craftsmen. So the decorations on vases no longer were of the beauty and originality of the eighth century B.C., when Corinth was the center of the craft, or of the seventh and sixth centuries B.C., when Athenian black- and red-figured designs reached their peak.

Two other minor arts in which the Hellenes excelled were gem engraving and coinage. Intaglios, pieces on which the design has been hollowed out, and cameos, stones with a design in relief, were very popular, and great efforts were made to execute them well. Hellenic coins are particularly lovely and skillfully designed and made. Each city struck its own, most often of silver, occasionally of bronze, and sometimes of gold for special occasions. Those of Sicily are considered unusually fine.

We have no examples of Hellenic furniture, but the simplicity and wonderful sense of balance and design characteristic of all Hellenic art can be seen in pictorial representations on the vases.

Hellenic coins. Top, the head of the goddess Persephone, surrounded by dolphins; and on the obverse below, a horse chariot: from Syracuse, fourth century B.C. Then, the head of Athena; and on the obverse below, the owl and the olive branch, the symbols of Athena: from Athens, fifth to third centuries B.C. Both coins are silver. The earliest coins were copper or iron bits called *obols.* Six of them made a handful; in Greek, a *drachma.* Both coins pictured here, two times larger than the actual coins, are *tetradrachmas,* or four-drachma pieces. By 600 B.C., those Aegean states engaged in trade had begun to mint coins—a monopoly carefully guarded by the state rulers.

SOPHISM

With the rise of democracy in Athens, public office was opened to men of all ranks. Not all were skilled in argument and in impressing the Assembly with the force of their reason. Special skills were needed. To teach these special skills, people calling themselves Sophists, "men of wisdom" arose to provide training in how to use words effectively in speech and writing and to give lessons on society and government to provide the aspiring candidate with a background that gave substance to argument. The Sophists traveled from city to city giving demonstrations of their skills and impressing their viewers with the subtlety of their thought. They took in pupils for a fee and were particularly at home in the intellectual atmosphere of Athens.

Corax, a Sicilian (c. 450 B.C.) was said to have been the inventor of rhetoric, but the most famous Sophist was Protagoras (c. 485 to 410 B.C.) To him is attributed the famous maxim that man is the measure of all things. By this the Sophists meant that there are no eternal truths and virtues and that man's reason or intellect is the only acceptable standard by which we may judge the world around us. The Sophists, in questioning accepted traditions and beliefs, attracted the rich young men of Athens, who had been demoralized by the moral upheavals of the Peloponnesian Wars. The public at large, however, particularly the conservatives and the poor, disapproved of the Sophists. They accused them of teaching cleverness rather than virtue, of showing how to make the worse cause seem the better, of proving that black is white and white is black. Today a Sophist has come to mean one who knows how to make others believe what he does not believe himself.

Yet many of the Sophists were very intelligent men. They were not philosophers because they dealt only with practical subjects, not speculative ones, but they helped spread and popularize new ideas on morals and religion and politics. The Sophists were really the college professors of antiquity, and by the fourth century B.C. they were a firm fixture in the intellectual life of Hellas.

In the fifth and fourth centuries B.C. the Hellenic civilization attained heights that few peoples before or since have achieved. It was a remarkable flowering of native genius in many fields, and it reflected an age of idealism that was not to last but that set standards for generations to come.

People and Terms

Aeschylus	Callicrates	Polygnotus	minor arts
Sophocles	Ictinus	Protagoras	pediment
Euripides	Phidias		cella
Aristophanes	Myron	tragedy	frieze
Herodotus	Polycleitus	comedy	mausoleum
Thucydides	Scopas	trilogy	intaglio
Xenophon	Praxitales	terra cotta	cameo

Mastering the Reading

1. Why was Athens the center of creativity in the Periclean Age? What connection did religion have with drama? Describe the theater and the actors. Who attended the theater? Why?
2. Why is Aeschylus called the Father of Greek Tragedy? What innovations did Sophocles make? How did Euripides differ from the other playwrights? Why did Hellenic audiences love Aristophanes' plays?
3. What was new about history as written by the Hellenes? What was Herodotus' contribution to the writing of history? Why might Thucydides be called a better historian than Herodotus or Xenophon?
4. What concepts of beauty and perfection are revealed in the Greek arts? How did the works of Phidias differ from those of Polycleitus and Myon?
5. What major changes of theme and technique in architecture and sculpture took place during the Peloponnesian Wars? Why? How does Scopas' work show this? Praxiteles' work?
6. Who were the Sophists? Why did they become important in the fifth century B.C.? What gave some a bad reputation?

Interpreting the Text

1. Does Hellenic drama, sculpture, or architecture bear out Protagoras' view that "man is the measure of all things"?
2. What contributions to drama and theater did the early Greeks make that still exist today in practice or in theater language?

Exploring Beyond the Text

1. Write a brief biography of one of the artists of fifth century B.C. Athens to read to the class. Use pictures to illustrate your talk. Show how the artist carried out the current theories or art.
2. The English poet John Milton described Athen as ". . . the eye of Greece, Mother of the Arts and eloquence . . ." What do you think he meant by this?
3. During the Golden Age, Pericles delivered a funeral oration. Compare it to Lincoln's Gettysburg Address. How do they differ? How does each represent the speaker's own period?

13

Conflict in the Western Mediterranean and the Rise of Rome

500–350 B.C.

While Hellas was achieving greatness and failing to unify, the states in the western Mediterranean were prospering. Expansion continued to bring them into conflict with each other, for they were also influenced by affairs in the mother cities. The Peloponnesian Wars raged as far west as Sicily, where the conflict caught up the colonies and settlements of the western Mediterranean and promoted the rivalries of the Hellenes and the Carthaginians. Only Rome, to the north, having overthrown the Etruscans, was too busy protecting itself from destruction and creating its own pattern of life to be concerned with events beyond its borders. Rome's succcss would have a decisive effect on the future of Italy and the western Mediterranean.

Reminder Line, the western Mediterranean

B.C.—● 1100 —— ● 900 —— ● 700 —— ● 500 ——

Etruscans established in Italy

ROME founded

Rome under Etruscan rule

Phoenician and Hellenic colonization in the Mediterranean; Magna Graecia

Carthage founded

Battle of Alalia

THE COLONIES IN THE WESTERN MEDITERRANEAN

During the fifth to third centuries B.C. the settlements in Italy and Sicily founded by the Carthaginians and Hellenes were hotly fought over by the Mediterranean powers. The Etruscans fell behind, a poor fourth contender, for Roman power was growing and expanding, and the Etruscans found themselves hard-pressed by their aggressive neighbors (page 258). In 509 B.C. the Latin town of Rome, and other Latin settlements south of the Tiber revolted against the Etruscans, and in 474 B.C. the Etruscans were driven from the Bay of Naples by the Hellenes. These events marked the turning point of Etruscan history. Henceforth their power steadily declined.

At the beginning of the fifth century B.C. Carthage was the chief power in the western Mediterranean. It had possessions along the African coast west from Hellenic Cyrene to the Atlantic. A Carthaginian admiral, Hanno, had even made a journey around the west coast of Africa as far south as the Gulf of Guinea in an unsuccessful attempt to set up a water route for African gold to reach Carthage. It had a foothold in southern Spain and in Sardinia and Corsica. It decided that the time had come to extend its sway over Sicily.

By the beginning of the fifth century B.C. the Greek cities in Magna Graecia had all come under the rule of tyrants. The most clever and cunning of them was Gelon, who had united all of southeastern Sicily under the rule of Syracuse. Syracuse was allied to the second important Sicilian city, Acragas, which could be counted on to support Syracuse should the Carthaginians invade.

Carthage attacked in 480 B.C., just as Xerxes was mounting his great expedition against the Hellenes in the east (page 179). The Athenians were victorious in their homeland, and the Syracusans were victorious in Sicily at Himera. After a fierce and long battle, at the end of which legend says the Carthaginian leader threw himself as a living sacrifice into the flames on the altar of Moloch, the Hellenes won a complete victory. The defeat at Himera was one of the most important events in the first five centuries of Carthaginian history. With the Athenian navy dominating the eastern Mediterranean and the Syracusan navy controlling the central Mediterranean, Carthage was cut off from its contacts with both Phoenicia and its ally Etruria; its very existence seemed threatened. In reaction to the crisis, the people overthrew the kings, and an oligarchy seized control for the next two hundred years. Sicily remained Hellenic for another 75 years.

In 409 B.C., four years after Alciabiades' disastrous expedition against Syracuse (page 228), the Carthaginians determined to avenge their defeat at Himera. They attacked Himera, broke down its walls, plundered its temples, and massacred or sold into slavery all its inhabitants. Their success inspired them to try to conquer the whole island. Acragas fell in 406 B.C., but in 405 B.C. Dionysius of Syracuse (405–367 B.C.) bought a breathing space for his city by agreeing to peace with Carthage and surrendering two thirds of Sicily to the African state. He used the peace thus acquired to refortify Syracuse, to put down local opposition to his tyranny, and to hire Italian mercenary troops. This done, he forced the other Hellenic cities of eastern Sicily to accept his rule.

In 398 B.C., Dionysius attacked the Carthaginians and drove them from central Sicily. During the next five years, he took over the hitherto unconquered mountainous regions and assumed the title King of Sicily.

In 391 B.C. Dionysius invaded Italy. In four years he conquered the "toe" of the peninsula and made alliances with the cities all along the southwestern coast. He envisioned an empire that would eventually embrace all Italy. The Etruscans were steadily losing ground, Rome had just been sacked by the Gauls (page 259), who were raiding the whole peninsula, and the mountain tribes were preparing for war. Italy seemed ripe for the picking.

But before Dionysius could complete his Italian operations, Carthage struck again and he was badly beaten. Before he could recover from his losses he died (367 B.C.). The great Syracusan empire crumbled as quickly as it had risen. The bases in Italy and Dalmatia slipped from the incompetent hands of his son, and the Hellenes in Sicily overthrew the overlordship of Syracuse.

One final tyrant, Timoleon, a Corinthian, defeated Carthage (344 B.C.) and brought peace and prosperity to the island. His wise conduct fostered

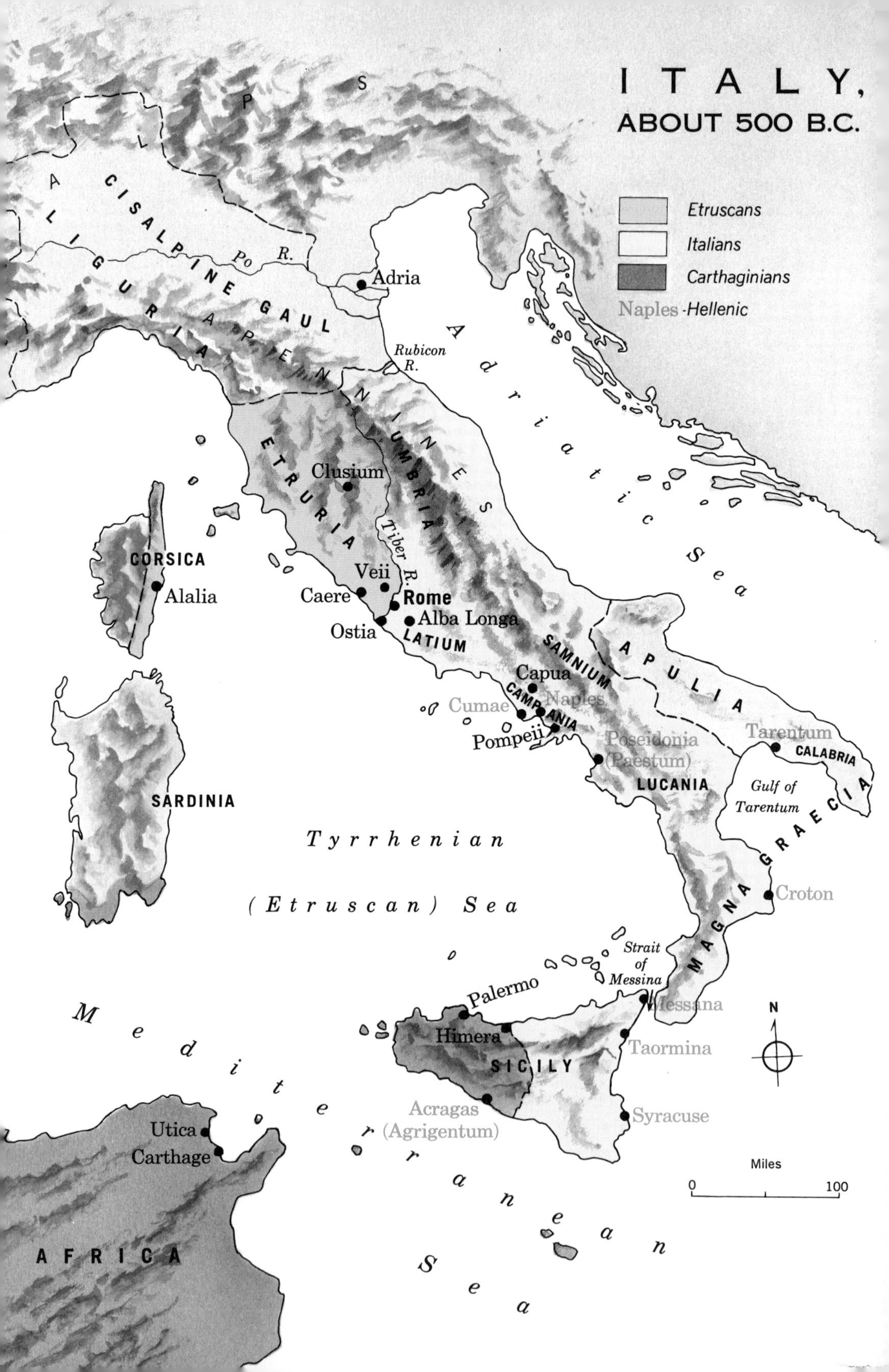

ITALY, ABOUT 500 B.C.
Etruscans
Italians
Carthaginians
Naples -Hellenic
ALPS
CISALPINE GAUL
LIGURIA
Po R.
Adria
APPENNINES
Rubicon R.
Adriatic Sea
ETRURIA
UMBRIA
Clusium
Tiber R.
CORSICA
Alalia
Veii
Caere
Rome
Alba Longa
Ostia
LATIUM
SAMNIUM
APULIA
Capua
Naples
CAMPANIA
Cumae
Pompeii
Poseidonia (Paestum)
Tarentum
CALABRIA
LUCANIA
Gulf of Tarentum
SARDINIA
Tyrrhenian (Etruscan) Sea
MAGNA GRAECIA
Croton
Strait of Messina
Palermo
Messana
Himera
SICILY
Taormina
Mediterranean Sea
Acragas (Agrigentum)
Syracuse
Utica
Carthage
AFRICA
N
Miles
0
100

democracy and attracted colonists, but his successors could not maintain his policies. Carthage gradually reestablished its sway over much of the island, while the Hellenes had to content themselves with Magna Graecia. No victor had yet emerged in the western Mediterranean.

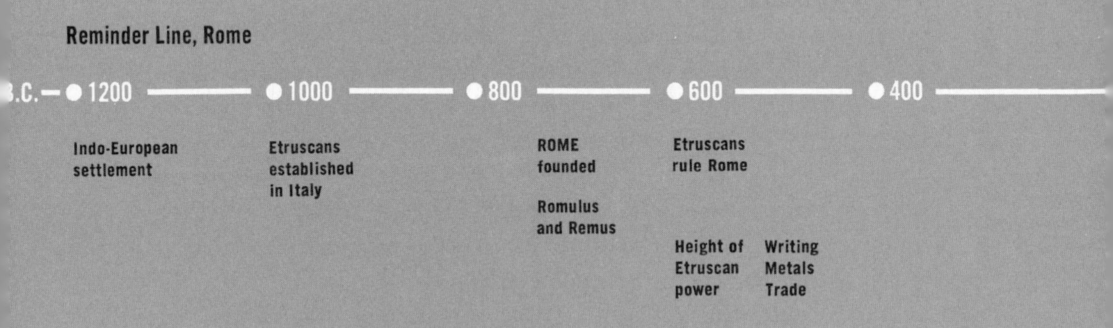

ROME: THE FOUNDING OF THE REPUBLIC AND THE CONQUEST OF LATIUM

In 509 B.C. the Latin communities in Latium rose in revolt against their Etruscan overlords. Rome, as the chief Etruscan stronghold in Latium, was attacked by the rebels. The Etruscans were eventually defeated and their royal family driven into exile. Antiroyal sentiment remained a powerful force in Roman thinking for many centuries.

ROME BECOMES A REPUBLIC

With the kings in exile, the citizens of Rome set up a republican form of government. They elected two heads of state called *consuls*, each serving a one-year term. Having two chief executives was a safeguard against either making himself king. Religious duties were carried out by a council, the chief of which was *Pontifex Maximus*. This means Great Bridge-Builder and indicates a close connection in the minds of the people between mathematics, magic, engineering, and religion. Financial affairs were controlled by two elected officials called *quaestors*.

The citizens met in two assemblies. All citizens belonged to both. One, formed during the early days of the Republic, was the *Comitia Centuriata*. In this assembly the men, as citizen-soldiers, were grouped into companies, or centuries, of one hundred men each. The Comitia Centuriata elected the consuls and quaestors and had the power to declare peace and war. The other assembly was the *Comitia Curiata*. It elected the Pontifex Maximus and debated religious matters. The heads of families formed a separate body called the Senate (*senex*—old man), which had originally given the king advice when called upon to do so. This body now became the chief law-making body of the republic, and the assemblies were called together only to ratify its decisions.

In its earliest days the Roman state seems to have been divided between patricians, who were descended from the founding fathers (Fathers—*patres*, hence "patrician"), and commoners called plebeians. The plebeians were poor residents of Rome whose villages had been absorbed in the growing city but who had not been compensated when their lands were taken in. Other plebeians were laborers, craftsmen, and traders, some of them wealthy. Many had lived in Rome for generations. The plebs also included former patricians who had become criminals because they had failed to pay their debts, had refused military services, or had committed other offenses.

Government was entirely in patrician hands. The patricians paid the taxes and controlled the army. They made the laws, and the courts were run by them and for them only. A plebeian could secure legal advice or a legal judgment only by attaching himself to a willing patrician, in which case he was called the patrician's *client*. He made gifts to his *patron* in return for the patrician watching over his affairs, and helping him secure a job. Plebeian marriages had no legal standing in Roman law, so their children's inheritance was never safe. A marriage between a patrician and a plebeian caused the former to lose his status as a patrician.

Having won freedom from the Etruscans, the Roman patricians had no intention of sharing government with the plebs. This state of affairs caused much unrest in Rome, and for the next two hundred years the plebs struggled for reforms in a contest often referred to as the Struggle Between the Orders.

REFORM OF THE REPUBLIC

The work of the plebs and their wealth were essential to the prosperity of Rome. Particularly important were their services in fighting in the army. As the years went by the plebs demanded a share in the government. They wanted changes in the laws concerning ownership of lands previously public property and in those concerning debt, as well as in other matters. Their appeals went unanswered for fourteen years. In desperation, in 494 B.C., the plebs marched out of Rome, threatening to found a city of their own elsewhere. This First Secession of the Plebs forced the patricians' hand. The plebs were given an assembly of their own, the *Concilium Plebis Tributum,* or Tribal Assembly, that could make laws binding on them. The Tribal Assembly was presided over by two (later ten) annually elected officers called *tribunes.* A tribune could veto any act of a consul if pleb interests were involved. A tribune's person was declared sacred so he would not suffer from assault, and his door had to remain unlocked at all times in case a plebeian in distress needed help.

By these changes Rome really had two governments, one of and for patricians, the other of and for plebeians. Such a state of affairs could not work well. The plebs continued to agitate. In 367 B.C. they won a great victory. Under the Lician-Sextian laws, at least one consul had to be a plebeian, thus making the lowest-born citizen eligible for the highest office of the state. Furthermore, since former consuls were admitted to the Senate, plebeians could now become senators. Eventually they were able to hold all the various magistracies, and finally they could be members of the sacred college of pontiffs, the governing religious body.

While the fight for political equality was continuing, clamor about the laws had led to the appointment of a ten-man committee (*Decemvirate*) to codify and publish a legal code. In the past the laws had been interpreted and administered according to the memories and prejudices of patrician judges. By 450 B.C. the laws were arranged in a code. They were inscribed on twelve wooden tablets and set up in the Forum for all to see. These laws, the Twelve Tables, were the beginning of what was to be one of Rome's greatest contributions to western civilization, its legal system (page 449).

In 445 B.C. social reforms were effected. The right of intermarriage between the two classes was granted. Plebs received equal legal status with patricians in business contracts and in military service. A new army post was created. Six military tribunes (not to be confused with the civilian tribunes) were to aid the consuls in war, and this office was open to plebs and patricians alike. In 421 B.C. the number of quaestors was increased to four, two from each class. Thus in less than two hundred years Rome was on its way to integrating its people into one body of citizens enjoying equal rights politically, legally, and socially.

ROME CONQUERS ITS NEIGHBORS

While the Roman Republic was struggling with the problems of developing and organizing a successful government and society, life in Italy in the hundred years following 500 B.C. was influenced by two factors, the decline of Etruscan power and tribal unrest, which caused migrations and invasions.

Tribal Unrest. When the Etruscans were unable to crush the Latin revolt in 509 B.C., their less civilized mountain neighbors seized the opportunity to break into the lowlands. Under tribal standards of bull, bear, boar, or wolf, the clans swept down from the Apennine peaks. Other tribes fled before the raiders or were wiped out. For over a century this turmoil lasted. When it was ended, the tribal and political composition of Italy had been permanently altered.

Rome found itself facea with possible destruction. From 504 to 450 B.C. attacks by the Sabines and other surrounding tribes were constant. In addition, Rome was threatened by its former masters from north of the Tiber. The Etruscan city of Veii clashed with Rome over the right to control the lower Tiber valley as an access to the sea. The other Etruscan cities stood back and allowed Veii to struggle alone. Had they united to help one another drive away the mountain tribes and to reconquer Rome, the course of world history might have been altered. But like the Hellenes, the Etruscans were strongly individualistic, and their personal jealousies proved stronger than their fear of outsiders. A century of dispute was to follow. In the end, Rome not only crushed Veii but also picked off the other Etruscan centers one by one (see below).

Etruscan Decline. In 493 B.C. the Senate sought an alliance with the Latin towns in Latium. It argued that neither Rome nor they would survive if they depended on their own resources but that together they might stem the tide of invasion. The alliance that resulted lasted for nearly 150 years. Under their treaty Rome undertook to defend itself and the Latins from the Etruscans, while the Latin League promised to defend itself and Rome from the mountaineers to the east and south.

Three generations of peace followed. Rome was given time to build an army against the day when diplomacy should fail and war again become necessary. In 418 B.C. the Romans took to the field. In the next 25 years they successively crushed the surrounding tribes in their mountain fastnesses and beseiged, pillaged, and reduced to a small village once-proud Veii. The whole of the south of Etruria quickly fell to Roman might. The original cities of Etruria were hemmed in by mountaineers on the east, by Romans on the south, by Celts on the north, and by Hellenes on the west, where the islands of Elba and Corsica had fallen to the Syracusans. The loss of Elba and Corsica were vital because Etruria depended on the rich iron ore deposits of Elba and the timber of Corsica.

On the day in 509 B.C. when Rome had exiled its Etruscan king and proclaimed a republic, the city and its surrounding lands amounted to about 390 square miles. A century later, as a result of successful diplomacy and then war, the city had not only been able to survive against serious odds, but had increased its holdings to more than eight hundred square miles.

THE SACK OF ROME, 390 B.C.

While Rome had been wrestling with the Etruscans and the mountain tribes, tribes of Gauls (Celts) had been settling in northern Italy in the fertile plains of the Po River. Cisalpine Gaul, as it came to be called, became a land of mixed Celtic and Etruscan culture. Many Gauls, too restless to settle in farming villages, formed marauding bands that terrorized the whole of Italy or acted as mercenaries (hired troops) of other peoples.

In 390 B.C. the Gauls attacked Rome, and Rome's allies and subject peoples seized this opportunity to declare their independence. For a second time Rome seemed doomed. The Etruscan cities declared war, and even Rome's century-old ally Caere joined in the attack. The members of the Latin League split up on the question of what stand to take, and at least half joined the onslaught. Rome was crushed. The Gauls sacked the city, stripping its temples and homes. Many buildings were put to the torch, and over the city on the sacred heights of the Capitoline hill, Gallic victory fires roared to the sky.

ROMAN RECOVERY

When the Gauls had departed from the ruined city, the survivors faced a major problem. Should they abandon the site of Rome and found a new home elsewhere? The Tiber River was not an important one for the transport of goods, and it flooded dangerously in the rainy season. Sometimes it shrank to almost nothing in dry weather. There were no large areas of productive farmlands nearby; there were no mineral deposits. If Rome was to be at the mercy of enemies from north, east, and south, perhaps it would be wiser to seek a spot more easily defended. But the Romans decided not. They had struggled for centuries on this spot, and they refused to be disheartened by a defeat. They had loyalty to the graves of their ancestors, ancestors whose faces were portrayed in the masks hanging in the entrance hall of every patrician Roman home. They felt bound by their faith in the gods of Rome. It was true that Jupiter was worshiped in many places, but Roman Jupiter could only be properly worshiped by Roman priests at Rome on the Capitol. In addition, Rome had certain advantages in location. It lay far enough inland to be safe from pirate raids and was surrounded by hills. It had become the marketplace of Latium, for it lay on the only navigable stream in Italy, and it controlled the north-south trade routes between Etruria and Campania. So the Romans determined to rebuild their city where the fates had decreed, on the Tiber hills.

From 387 to 338 B.C. war against the Gauls and the Etruscans and the mountain tribes continued. By 350 B.C. the Gauls had been expelled from central Italy. Between 340 and 338 B.C. the members of the Latin League demanded independence but the Romans refused, and in the fighting that followed the league cities were defeated. The league was disbanded, but Rome gave citizenship to those towns closest to it, partial citizenship to those further away, and made alliances with the rest. This fair settlement served as the basis of a new confederacy that supported Rome staunchly in the great trials against the Samnites that lay ahead (page 352).

Outside Italy, Rome turned again to extending its contacts. Friendly relations were established with the Hellenic port of Massilia, which served as entrance to the rich Rhone Valley of southern Gaul. In addition to being a commercial city of the first importance, Massilia was also a major naval base. Through friendship with Massilia, Rome had acquired as an ally one of the two most powerful Hellenic cities in the west. Rome also negotiated a treaty with Carthage under which Roman ships were to be allowed to take on food and water and to be repaired in Carthaginian ports. In return Rome agreed not to trade in Africa west of Carthage or in Carthaginian southern Spain. That Carthage was willing to make such a treaty with Rome testifies to Rome's growing importance in Mediterranean affairs.

By 350 B.C. Rome's territory had increased to 2,300 square miles. In fighting against overwhelming odds and suffering invasion and ruin, Rome had not only survived but had even increased its strength.

ROMAN INSTITUTIONS

By 350 B.C. Rome had evolved a form of government and had organized and strengthened its way of life. Both were still subject to change as new needs and pressures required solution, but by 350 B.C. the shape of Roman institutions was visible. They were proved both strong and flexible as Rome grew from a small city-state into a power extending over all of the Mediterranean.

THE STATE

The Roman state after the expulsion of the kings was a republic, what the Romans called a *respublica*, a thing (*res*) of the people (*publica*). In theory if not always in fact, Roman citizens, acting together in their assemblies, made the laws, elected their officials, and decided questions of war and peace.

The Consuls. At the head of the state were the two consuls elected by the assembly. They enjoyed equal power for their year's term. They were supreme at home and on the battlefield; at home they alternated power with each other by the month and on the battlefield by the day. A consul had the power of life and death over a citizen in the field. But by the Valerian Law of Appeal (c. 300 B.C. or earlier?), no citizen at home could be scourged or executed except by orders of a dictator without having the right to make an appeal to the Centuriate Assembly (page 255). Each consul could veto the acts of the other, the negative vote prevailing. If one consul said go, and the other said stay, they stayed. This check upon unlimited power prevented either from using his power unlawfully. A consul could not be reelected to power until ten years had passed, though if he were on the battlefield, he could complete the campaign by serving "in the place of the consul," *proconsule.*

The Dictator. The Romans understood that at times when grave danger threatened and immediate action was needed, one man or both might be incapacitated, or two men might prevent each other from functioning effectively. In such a case they appointed a dictator. The consuls proposed him on the advice of the Senate, gave him their authority, and put the property and lives of the people at his disposal. He had absolute power for a period not to exceed six months. Many dictators served for less. If we believe Roman tradition, one of the briefest dictatorships was that of Cincinnatus. Cincinnatus had served the state well as senator and consul, and in his old age had retired to his little farm. When the Senate received the news that an army with its consul had been trapped by the foe in a narrow pass, they sent a message to Cincinnatus. "Put on your toga," it said, "to hear the words of the Senate." They wished to appoint him dictator. Cincinnatus, whom the messenger found plowing his fields, accepted the command, organized an army, defeated the enemy within sixteen days, celebrated a splendid triumph (page 269), and then willingly laid down his power to return to private life.

The Assemblies. We have seen that Rome had three popular assemblies, the Comitia Curiata, the Comitia Centuriata, and last, the Tribal Assembly (pages 255 to 257). The first one had been formed under the monarchy, but gradually its position was taken by the Centuriate Assembly. Then in 287 B.C., under the Hortensian Law, the Tribal Assembly was permitted to make laws binding on all the people. After this law was passed, the Tribal Assembly became the principal assembly of Rome.

In all the assemblies, the citizens met only when they were summoned by a magistrate (he had to have military powers to summon the Centuriate Assembly). Voting was by group rather than by individual, and the assemblies could not initiate legislation but could only discuss and amend measures presented to it by the magistrates. Thus Roman citizens were limited in what they could accomplish in their assemblies. They did elect the state officials, but in legislation they had only the power to say yes or no to measures presented to them, and voting by block limited the power they might have had as individuals. In every case they were very much under the control of the officiating magistrates, the consuls and the tribunes.

The Senate. As we have seen (page 256), the Senate was originally an advisory body to the king. By the third century B.C. it had three hundred members, chosen for life by the consuls and later by the censors (page 264) from among the leading families. Vacancies in the ranks of the Senate were filled by former consuls and by the higher magistrates after they had fulfilled their year's term. Although in the early days of the Republic the senators had been patricians only, the composition of the Senate was widened in the fourth century B.C. when the plebeians gained admission through election to the consulship and the magistracies (page 257). Thus everyone who had served his country as statesman, general, or diplomat came to sit in the Senate, and so their experience and talent were not lost to the state. Furthermore, the plebeian tribunes, who at first had been allowed merely to sit outside the Senate door and listen to its deliberation and then to shout *Veto* (I forbid) if a measure was proposed that displeased them, were finally empowered not only to sit in the Senate but also to convoke it and present legislation for its consideration.

The Senate House in the Roman Forum. A reconstruction of the meeting place of the senators, the real rulers of Rome. During Rome's rise to power in Italy and the Mediterranean, the energy and skill with which they governed the state made them seem, in the words of an admiring foe, "an assembly of kings."

The Senate was the leading administrative body of the Republic. It controlled finances and raised taxes, directed public works and the functions of the state religion, conducted wars and appointed commands, received ambassadors, made treaties and alliances, administered conquered territory, and could suspend personal liberties and declare martial law in an emergency. Until the passage of the Hortensian Law in 287 B.C., it could veto the acts of the assembly.

The Senate's power, which was never clearly stated, was by custom and tradition rather than by law. The Romans had great respect for custom and tradition, and this respect was enhanced by the senators' experience and family prestige. The Romans seemed to feel that political ability passed from generation to generation and preferred to elect as consul, and to the other magistracies, a man whose family had occupied such positions in the past. Furthermore, no magistrate expecting to enter the Senate as a junior member was likely to oppose its advice during his years in office. On the contrary, he sought the Senate's advice and was disposed to follow its suggestions as to what legislation to present to the assembly. In this way, the magistrates were the mouthpiece of the senators, and the Senate was in fact the real governing body of Rome.

The Magistracies. Several grades of magistrates existed in the Roman Republic. These offices were created as the state grew during the fifth and fourth centuries B.C.

The lowest officials, the quaestors (page 255) at first had been assistants to the consuls, by whom they were appointed. In time they were elected by the assembly. Besides attending to the treasury, they handled criminal cases and presentations of appeals before the people. The *aediles,* originally plebeians only, aided the tribunes. Gradually their responsibilities in handling the affairs of the public market, games, streets, and buildings increased, and two more aedileships were created for patricians. The two higher magistrates were the *praetors,* who were judges in civil cases, and the consuls. Beyond the consulship only one office remained, that of the censorship. It was the business of the two censors to make a count of the people and to assess property for taxation. Beyond this, the censors, like the Spartan ephors (page 221), kept an eye on the conduct of the Romans and could expel a senator for immorality or deprive a citizen of his vote for misbehavior. The censors were usually former consuls elected for five years, but generally they completed their work in eighteen months. The most important plebeian magistrates were the tribunes, who could veto even a consul's actions.

All magistrates had *potestas,* authority, but only the praetors and consuls had *imperium,* the right to issue commands and the power of life and death. The highest magistrates were truly masters, as the term *magistratus* implies. They were accompanied, like the kings of old, by attendants called *lictors,* who bore a bundle of elm rods, the *fasces,* which symbolized the power of scourging. Outside the city limits the *fasces* surrounded an axe to remind those who might forget that the magistrate had the power of life and death there. The praetors and consuls wore robes bordered with purple and sat on ivory chairs while fulfilling their duties.

Yet the powers of the magistrates, while great, were not unlimited. The strength of the Roman system lay in its checks and balances. Every office except the dictator's was filled by more than one person, and this sharing of power served to limit excesses. All terms of office were for one year only, and a candidate had to allow time to elapse before he could present himself for office again. Finally, a man was expected to pass through the various offices in regular order. This was called the *cursum honorum*, the career of honors. A successful politician went from quaestor to aedile (to tribune if a plebeian) to praetor to consul. If a man fulfilled these offices with honor and glory, he might be elected censor to cap his career. Such a system encouraged only the most talented and experienced men to reach the top. Such officials, combining their services with those of the senators, gave to Roman government a breadth and strength that other states lacked.

When a Roman citizen wanted to follow a political career, he entered the army, where he remained a junior officer for some ten years (page 268). No citizen could become a magistrate without this experience. Then he posted notice of his candidacy with the proper official and went among the people dressed in white (*candidatus*) to ask for their votes. He was forbidden to bribe but could curry favor with the public by giving banquets and sponsoring public games.

Not every citizen could hold office in Rome. Certain occupations were considered unworthy. Actors, for example, and gladiators were disqualified from ever holding office. To be a magistrate was deemed a great honor and was a position of authority and power. Yet though the power of the Roman magistrate was great, it was still subject to the checks and balances within the system and beyond this to the greater if unwritten power that was held by the Senate.

RELIGION

Religion was a very powerful influence in the life of the early Romans. They believed that everything in nature and the world around them had a spirit, or *numen*. These *numina* would be influenced for good or ill by proper sacrifices. The Romans, legalistically minded, thought of the relationship as being somewhat like that of a contract: if religious duties were properly performed, the gods would confer the requested aid. Hence ritual was very important in Roman religion.

In the early days, the *numina* did not take personal form. But as time passed, especially after the Romans came into touch with the Hellenes, many did turn into anthropomorphic gods with characteristics and names. The most important of them reflected the Roman occupations of agriculture and war. Jupiter, like the Greek Zeus, ruled the heavens and sent sun and rain to sustain the crops. Jupiter's temple on the Capitoline hill was where the youth went to sacrifice on reaching manhood, where the magistrates made offerings before taking up their duties, where the victorious general went to lay the trophies of his conquests. The protectress of the sacred fire, like that of the hearth fire in each Roman house, was Vesta, whose round temple lay at the south end of the Forum. The sacred fire was cared for by six young women of noble birth, the Vestal Virgins, who lived nearby in a special dwelling. It was their duty to keep the fire burning at all times. If by accident it went out, a "pure" flame had to be relit by striking a spark with flint, or by rubbing two sticks together. Janus was the spirit of the door, whose two faces looked to the past and the future. The entrance to the Forum was a shrine to Janus, which was shut in peace and open in war. Mars was the god of war. His sacred animal was the wolf, his symbols were spears and shields, and his altar was in the Campus Martius, where the army

A Roman temple. This little circular temple built in the first century B.C. near the banks of the Tiber River still has its original columns, but the roof is a reconstruction. The style of the columns is Hellenic, but the design of the roof is thought to have originated from the roofs of the huts in which the earliest Romans lived.

assembled to march forth to battle. The Romans, a military people, named the first month of the year *Mars* (March) in his honor. Hellenic gods taken over by the Romans were Apollo, who came from Cumae; Asclepius, the god of healing (and the Hellenic name for Imhotep, page 89) via Egypt; and Hercules. Other gods were identified with their Greek counterparts: Juno, the wife of Jupiter, was identified with Hera; Neptune, a river god, with Poseidon; Ceres, the Earth Mother, with Demeter. Minerva, an Etruscan goddess, was identified with Athena. Many minor gods existed who retained their nonanthropomorphic forms. Among these were Health, Fortune, and Peace. Particularly important were the spirits supervising agricultural activities like hoeing, plowing, and sowing. The early Romans had many agricultural festivals to propitiate these spirits.

In order to determine the will of the gods as successfully as possible, the Romans were very careful to observe omens like the flash of lightning and the roll of thunder; and from the Etruscans they learned the art of divination, looking for signs in the number and flight of birds and in the entrails of animals. Divination of this kind was called "taking the auspices," and no event took place before the gods had indicated a favorable auspice.

Roman priests were chosen, like the magistrates, from among the people. They were grouped in "colleges" with special responsibilities. One college had charge of the auspices, another took care of the Sibylline Books (page 296), the Vestal Virgins cared for the sacred fire, and, as we have seen, the college of pontiffs (page 255) had overall charge of religious matters.

Many festivals were celebrated during the year. The Saturnalia was the finest; it lasted for seven days in December and honored Saturn, god of sowing. No war was declared or battle fought, no punishment was inflicted, children were excused from school, and rich and poor alike gave themselves up to feasting, revelry, and exchanging gifts. There were more than one hundred holy days in the Roman year, and though the citizen was supposed to do no work, exceptions had to be made when so many crowded the calendar. Nevertheless, in the early Republic the celebration of a festival was a religious ceremony in which all citizens were expected to take part. It united them in a common endeavor and fostered honor and respect for the gods and the state.

THE ARMY

The army was the backbone of Roman society. It was the instrument that made possible the conquest of Rome's neighbors, and it also strongly influenced the political development of the state. Without the presence of the plebeians in its ranks, Rome's army could not have existed, and, as we have seen (page 256), the plebeians made use of this fact to win for themselves political rights and equality with the patricians. The Roman army was the most effective fighting machine in the ancient world, and the Romans used it to extend Rome's sway around the Mediterranean.

All citizens between the ages of 17 and 46 were liable for military duty. In the early days of the Republic, the army was made up of landowning citizens only—tough, hardy farmers who knew how to fight and how to obey orders. They were not paid for their services, receiving only the booty captured from the enemy as their reward. When the long fight against the Veii made winter campaigns necessary, a system of pay was introduced, and the soldiers no longer returned home after the summer fighting to till their fields. Instead, they were kept under arms for a year or more and were trained in fighting and tactics.

The Roman fighting unit was the *legion.* An army consisted of one or more legions. A legion had three thousand heavily armed infantry, twelve hundred lightly armed infantry, and three hundred cavalry. After the conquest of Italy, Rome called upon its allies (page 355) to furnish troops, chiefly cavalry. These auxiliaries, as they were called, were separate from the legions and at least as numerous. The auxiliaries were loyal to Rome and fought bravely alongside the legionnaires. They were far more reliable than the mercenaries that formed a large part of the armies of Carthage and some of the Hellenic states and Persia.

Until he was 46, a man was classed as a Junior and was subject to call to active duty whenever he was needed. After reaching 46, or after completing at least sixteen campaigns in the infantry or ten in the cavalry, he became a Senior and was enrolled in the reserve, subject to call only if necessary to defend the city from attack.

The heavily armed infantry was divided into companies called *maniples.* The maniple was an open formation apparently adopted from the Samnites after the disaster at the Caudine Forks (page 352). The Romans had fought in the Hellenic phalanx formation (page 319), but the maniple proved far more flexible. The maniples were drawn up in three lines; first were the recruits, then the more experienced men, finally the veterans. Each line was several ranks deep, spaced checkerboard fashion so that the vacant spaces in one line were covered by the men in the line behind. The lightly armed soldiers were placed equally among the heavily armed soldiers, and the cavalry was on the wings.

Each man in the maniple, standing about eight feet away from his neighbor, carried a short sword, a javelin, and a shield (the last two also adopted from the Samnites), and wore armor consisting of a bronze breastplate and greaves (leg coverings). When the battle began, the light troops moved to the front to throw their javelins and harass the enemy. The companies of the first line then threw their spears from a distance of about ten to twenty paces, and then, wielding their formidable short swords, they dashed forward into the enemy ranks. This maneuver was like a volley of fire followed by a bayonet charge. If the charge was unsuccessful, the soldiers fell back through the gaps in the line and their places were taken by the more seasoned troops. Should these fail too, the veterans of the third line stood ready to deal the final blow.

Each legion had a medical corps, with orderlies and bandagers (named after their bandage boxes), and if a man was wounded, he was given professional attention and not simply left to die. Hospitals were set up in permanent locations. Pitch and turpentine were used as antiseptics; medicines were various herbs. Surgeons were highly skilled in amputation and knew how to remove foreign substances from wounds.

Discipline was very strict in the Roman army, and punishments were severe. Demotion in rank, loss of pay, hard labor, and a cut in rations were penalties for lesser offenses. Flogging was common. Cutting off the right hand was the penalty for desertion. Desertion or mutiny in the face of the enemy called for death by crucifixion. If unidentified members of a unit were found guilty of an offense, the unit was *decimated*, that is, each tenth man was executed. Sentries found asleep at their posts were stoned to death. Any officer who through kindness condoned faults that endangered the security of the army was considered weak and unfit to command by his legionnaires.

But discipline alone does not make good soldiers. Rewards for courage and bravery were presented in the presence of the entire army. Promotions, money prizes, and decorations were bestowed while all the men looked on. The most honored decoration was the civic crown of oak leaves, which was awarded to a man who saved the life of a fellow soldier on the battlefield or who was first to scale his enemies' walls or enter their camp. Victorious generals were offered a huge parade and procession in Rome called a *triumph*. While the populace lined the streets, the conqueror, clad in a purple toga and holding a laurel branch to symbolize his victory, was drawn to the Capitoline hill in a four-horse chariot. In front of him walked the magistrates and senators, and behind him were his troops, singing a triumphal hymn. Wagons of booty and captives bound in chains were displayed for the public. Reaching the Temple of Jupiter, the general laid his laurel branch on Jupiter's knees as a thank offering for his victory. While the people rejoiced, the captives were taken away and strangled in the underground prison of the Capitoline. The Romans were not known for tempering justice with mercy.

One of the outstanding features of the Roman military system was the fortified camps that the soldiers built wherever they halted. Even if they stopped for a single night, the troops laid out a square enclosure, fortified by a ditch, an earthen mound, and a palisade made of stakes, which they carried with them. This camp formed a little city neatly laid out in streets with four gates, the headquarters of the general, and a forum. Within its walls the soldiers were safe from surprise attack; they had a sure refuge in time of defeat; and if they did not choose to fight, it enabled them to sit quietly until a more opportune moment presented itself. These fortified camps played a major role in the success of the army, especially as the Romans moved farther and farther away from home into enemy territory.

Such was the army that sometimes lost a battle but always won the war. The spirit of its fighting men, its discipline and the subordination of the personal good to the greater good of the whole, its formidable short swords, flexible legion, and fortified camps, proved an invincible combination to those who opposed Rome's rise to power.

THE FAMILY

The basic unit of Roman society was the family. The state was only an enlarged family in the early days, and its practices grew out of those first formed within the family group.

When we think of a family, we understand it to be mother, father, and children. The Roman *familias* was broader than this. It included not only the parents and children but also the sons' wives and their families, the slaves, and the clients (page 256), whose position was hereditary. When a daughter married, she passed into the household of her husband.

The father, the *pater familias,* had complete authority over the members of his family, much as the magistrates had authority over the citizens. He could sell his wife into slavery or divorce her, if he chose. His new-born children were placed at his feet while he decided whether they should be exposed to die if weak, or raised. If they misbehaved, he could punish them with banishment, slavery, or even death.

The father's authority, however, was limited by custom. People frowned on a man who sold a married son into slavery or who exposed a son or first-born daughter. Before a *pater familias* could condemn his child to death, he had to submit his decision to a family council. The Roman matron might have few legal rights, but she enjoyed enormous respect and prestige in the home and in society. Unlike the Athenian wife (page 217), she could leave her home to make visits and to attend the games, the theater, and the courts with her husband. In the streets, a path was cleared for her, and anyone who insulted her was deemed worthy of death. In society her position was honored, and in the home she was mistress as her husband was master.

A Roman usually bore three names. The first, the *praenomen*, corresponds to our first name. In the earliest days, Roman parents often called their children by number, Primus, Secundus, Tertius. The second name, the *nomen*, was the clan name, while the third name, the *cognomen*, was the name of the particular family in the clan and was added in later centuries. For example, in Gaius Julius Caesar, Gaius was the praenomen, Julius was the nomen of the Julian clan, and Caesar was the cognomen of his family.

In the early days of the Republic, the main occupation of the citizen was farming or herding. Cincinnatus, you recall (page 261), on receiving the summons to be dictator, was occupied in plowing his fields. There were no great inequalities of wealth; while no one was very rich, few were very poor. Each household was largely self-sufficient. The women made the clothes from flax or wool. For themselves they made the stola and the outer garment called the pella, and for the men they made the tunic and wrap-around toga. Utensils were made of wood and clay. Whatever else was needed was obtained by barter in the markets held every nine days.

A Roman and His Wife. Affectionately holding hands, a Roman and his wife are portrayed with dignity and simplicity in a tomb sculpture of the first century B.C. The Romans were not always called Romans. Their oldest name was *Quirites*. This was later changed to *Romani*, a word derived from the name of their city.

Until the fourth century B.C. the Romans did not use coins but lumps of bronze. Gradually these lumps assumed fixed weights and were stamped with the figure of an ox or some other device. The use of bronze indicates that silver and gold were rare and precious, and the slowness of the Romans to adopt coinage, which was used by the Hellenes in Naples, suggests a lack of interest in commerce.

The father had full charge of the family estate, as he did of his household. It was his pride to manage it so well that when he died it was more prosperous than when he had inherited it. The family was not only a social unit but an economic one as well.

Just as the institutions of the state grew out of those of the family, so the state religion was built on that of the family. Within the family group the father was honored as chief priest; his home was the temple, and his hearth was the altar. Family worship took place every day at meal times, when the father threw a little food and wine into the flames of the hearth as an offering to the gods. The chief gods were the guardian deities, the Lares and Penates. The Lares protected the fields, and the Penates watched over the family stores. Vesta, the spirit of the hearth, and Janus, the guardian of the doorway, were other important household deities (page 266). The family ancestors were also honored. The ancestors were souls called *manes*, or pure ones. The Roman family included not only the living members but these dead ancestral spirits as well.

The education of the children was in the hands of the family. A mother taught her daughter household management, how to prepare food and cook, and how to make the clothes. A father instructed his sons in the practical necessities of life: reading, writing, and arithmetic, the Twelve Tables, and managing affairs. Beyond this he taught them the proper conduct, the qualities of *virtus, dignitas, gravitas* (page 346), and the stern virtues of respect for custom, tradition, the gods, and authority. The Romans revered the laws and traditions and honored those in authority, whether the *pater familias* or the magistrates. The Roman boy learned how to obey before he grew up to command, and as an adult he was expected to bring to bear in his public conduct the same virtues he displayed in governing his household.

The Roman family was the mold in which the character of the Roman was formed, much as the *polis* formed the character of the Athenian (page 215). The Roman poet Vergil described it thus: "We carry our children to the streams and harden them in the bitter, icy water; as boys they spend wakeful nights over the chase and tire out the whirlwind; but in manhood, unwearied by toil and trained to poverty, they subdue the soil with their plows or shake towns in war." Such training produced men who were tough, stern, and hard, abstemious in food and drink, of strong will, vigorous, and harsh. They were narrow in their outlook and slow to act, severe to those under their authority, but also strong in the noble virtues of dignity, courage, and bravery. They were willing to obey as well as to command, and they kept their word when they gave it. For such men the good of the state came above personal considerations, so they willingly left their homes and families when called upon to do so and endured sufferings and hardships without complaint. In their hearts the Romans believed that they were fit to rule their neighbors and that it was their destiny to do so.

* * *

While the Hellenes were failing to unify in the eastern Mediterranean, the Romans were consolidating their gains over Latium and developing a satisfactory form of government in the western Mediterranean. In 500 B.C. the Romans were a very minor people in the Mediterranean world. By 350 B.C., they had organized their republic, defeated their immediate enemies, and replaced the Etruscans as the main power in central Italy. As Etruria had felt the bite of the Roman sword, so would the colonies and city-states around the Mediterranean who were unable to resolve their quarrels or to eliminate each other as rivals.

Rome was ready to expand south. The fate of the western Mediterranean was decided not by the Carthaginians or the Hellenes but by the Romans. The fate of the eastern Mediterranean also lay in Roman hands.

People, Places, and Terms

Gelon
Dionysius of Syracuse

Tiber River
Veii
Elba
Corsica
Po River
Cisalpine Gaul

Transalpine Gaul
Massilia
Himera

republic
pontifex maximus
consul
assembly
senate

patrician
plebeian
veto
dictator
client
patron
auxiliary
triumph
magistrate

Mastering the Reading

1. How and why did Sicily and its large city-state, Syracuse, take part in the rivalry for control in the western Mediterranean?

2. What Roman offices and legislative bodies were created immediately after 509 B.C.? How did the patricians control the plebeians? What did the First Secession of the Plebs accomplish? What changes in Roman institutions between 450 and 367 B.C. gave more power to the plebs?
3. What reasons were there for the Romans to abandon their city after 390 B.C.? Why did they decide to stay? How did they make their position secure between 390 and 338 B.C.?
4. What was the function of each of the following: Comitia Curiata? Comitia Centuriata? In what ways was the Senate designed to attract the most intelligent and experienced people? What were the leading magistracies and what were their duties?
5. What were the outstanding features of the Roman army?

Interpreting the Text

1. Chart the *cursus honorum* of a patrician youth. Do the same for a plebeian youth. Indicate what power and responsibility the Roman law would give them at each stage.
2. What is the meaning of *republic?* Why is the United States called a democratic-republic rather than a republic? What countries today are republics, not democratic-republics?

Exploring Beyond the Text

1. Read some of the laws codified in the Twelve Tables. How do they differ from and resemble Hammurabi's Code? How do they contrast with Judeo-Christian Law as in the Ten Commandments? What do the laws reveal about Roman concerns?
2. Read Polybius' description of the workings of the Roman government. What was his tone as he described it? Did he prefer the Greek form that had been used in Athens?
3. *Ancient Words in Modern English.* Add these words and their meanings to your glossary:

republic	senate	patrician
plebeian	imperious	census

Working with the Map

What major changes in territorial possessions took place in the Mediterranean between 800 B.C. and 500 B.C.? Between 500 B.C. and 350 B.C. what strategic areas changed hands? By 350 B.C. what rivals for the Mediterranean existed? Where?

14

The Early Iron Age in Europe and Asia

1000–300 B.C.

In the Early Iron Age great empires arose in the Fertile Crescent, while in the Mediterranean the growth of city-states repeated the Middle Eastern historical pattern of the previous millennium. When we look at northern Europe and Asia at this same time, we find civilization expanding in the west to touch the barbarian Celts, who nevertheless remained tribal in organization. In the east we find civilization reviving in India and China after attack by chariot-riding, iron-wielding barbarians—the eastern branch of the Indo-Europeans, the same people from whom the Celts were descended. Much of the history of the Celts, the Indians, and the Chinese is lost, and we must reconstruct what happened from archaeological remains and literary allusions. Dates are, therefore, vague.

THE CELTS OR GAULS

The names Celts, Gauls, and Galatians apply to a language group that looms on the edges of civilization after 1000 B.C. By this time these people were already racially mixed. The Romans and Hellenes pictured the Celts as tall, heavy, red- or blond-haired people, but there is also a Celtic type in western Europe and the British Isles today that is short, slender, and dark haired.

THE ORIGIN OF THE CELTS

The Celts probably emerged as a distinct group somewhere in central Europe. From there they pushed westward into lands previously settled by the Iberians and Ligurians (Spain, France, the Riviera). The language of the Celts is Indo-European, and has characteristics in common with Germanic on the one hand and Italic on the other. Celtic is related more distantly to Hellenic, Slavic, Hittite, Iranian, and Sanskrit.

In time the Celts came to the Atlantic coast and were concentrated in the extreme western area by the pressure of Germanic expansion from central Europe. The strongest traces of the Celts today are in the western lands that were their last refuge: Brittany, Ireland, Wales, Cornwall, and northern Scotland. They eventually blended with the local people, but in corners of the British Isles their language is heard in Welsh, Scottish Gaelic, and Irish Gaelic. The medieval kingdom of Scotland was their last independent state until the creation of the Irish Free State in the twentieth century. Ireland is peopled by a very mixed population largely descended from Celtic ancestors.

THE HALSTATT OR EARLY CELTIC PERIOD, 800–400 B.C.

In the Early Iron Age, or Halstatt Period, the Celts centered in the district between the Moselle and Danube rivers, the region that today comprises western and southern Germany. They lived on high ground in rugged spots that in more civilized times have reverted to forest and brush lands. Their villages were strongly fortified, and near each were the large barrows (mounds) used as common tombs. These Celts were pastoral people who kept herds of goats. Cows were scarce, and one of the most common themes of Celtic legends is that of raids for cattle. The villages were connected by deeply rutted roads along which men drove small four-wheeled chariots, which were often buried with their owners. Men's razors were also buried in their graves. The shaved cheek was the mark of a warrior, although they did wear heavy mustaches. It was apparently thought that the dead would wish to continue to be clean-shaven in the next world. The Celts first fought with short bronze daggers and later with long iron ones carried in wooden sheaths. For protection they used round shields made of leather and wood. They cremated their dead and placed the ashes in urns, which were buried in the barrows.

THE LA TÈNE, OR LATER CELTIC, PERIOD

In less than a single century, beginning around 500 B.C., dramatic changes took place among the Celts. They improved the plow—an advance that enabled them to cut through the heavy soils that until then had been unusable. Farming replaced stock-breeding and this change meant increased food supplies and therefore greatly increased the population. Migrating families or tribes began to march from their homelands in western and southern Germany to the northwest or the south in search of land. Those who moved south came into contact with the civilization of the Hellenes and Etruscans and quickly adopted techniques of civilization from them. New lands between the villages were settled, and most of the people became peaceful farmers. Gradually they abandoned the Halstatt forts and left their new farm villages unfortified.

In addition, a religious revolution seems to have occurred among the Celts at this time. They gave up cremation and burial in the community barrow and began to lay bodies in individual oblong graves, with or without coffins. The careful alignment of the body east and west, with the head always to the west, indicates a new religious motivation that scholars cannot now explain.

The crafts of the new era were a continuation of those of the Halstatt, but decorations on clothing, jewelry, pottery, and weapons were copied from Hellenic and Etruscan models. Hellenic goods were brought north through the Balkans in the east and from Massilia in the west. From Etruscan models, Celts in northern Italy fashioned gold crowns shaped like masses of leaves, collars with egg-shaped pendants, and bracelets like coiled snakes. The Celts also adopted the Etruscan custom of placing in the tombs kitchen utensils, lamps, and spits. They cleaned their bodies by first rubbing them with oil and then scraping the old skin away with Mediterranean strigils (skin scrapers). The Celts developed their dagger into a cutting sword and improved the Etruscan shield to provide better body protection.

Celtic metal work: above, a mirror, below, a helmet. Metal working was the chief Celtic industry, and in designing objects the Celts were noted for their love of spiral decorative patterns, which included geometrical shapes and flowing plant and animal designs. Both these objects are in bronze and from Britain. The helmet was made in the first century B.C., the mirror in the first century A.D.

CELTIC FAMILIES

Family life centered around the hearth, on which the fire was the actual as well as the symbolic center of family welfare. There centered the worship of the ancestors. The father of the family was the head of the household and had the power of life and death over the members of the family. In some Celtic tribes the father's power over a boy lasted as with the Romans, until the parent's death. In others it terminated when the boy reached military age, fourteen, at which time he passed under the authority of the chief to whom he was presented for war service.

Usually there was one matron in a family, that is, the head wife, but there were also rented wives, concubines, and female slaves. The children of any of these women might be recognized as legal offspring if the master so wished.

As a rule, Celtic warriors did not take many prisoners, so there were few slaves. During their earlier history the Celts had been head-hunters, believing that the mystery of life was located in a man's head. Heads were brought home from battle to guard the palisades around the family enclosure. According to tradition, the heads of a country's greatest kings were buried on the frontiers or in the country's chief fortress so that they could serve as permanent guardians of the land. This head worship continued here and there among the Celts throughout the Early Iron Age. Certain spots, such as the Hill of Tara in Ireland and the site of the present Tower of London in Britain, were famed among the Celts as places where the heads of great chieftains had been buried. Thus a brave enemy in battle was more apt to have his head brought home as a trophy than to have himself brought back as a slave.

Celtic women often wore trousers. Among some tribes, such as the Belgae (among whose descendants are the Belgians), which probably meant "Trouser Men," the men also wore trousers. Other Celtic men wore mantles, and later they wore the short kilt that survives today in Scotland.

CELTIC RELIGION: DRUIDISM

The institution that bound together the Celts from the different parts of Europe into one group was Druidism. Its origin is unknown. According to Julius Caesar, Druidism started in Britain. The British Druids appropriated the thousand-year-old temple at Stonehenge, but it had already fallen into decay when they came, and its original use had already been forgotten.

The ancient Druids seem to have resembled priests of other Indo-European religions, most noticeably the Brahmins of India (page 282). This is not surprising when we consider that the Celts and the Aryans were the extreme branches of the same nomadic peoples from the plains of central Europe. Caesar was correct, however, in surmising that Britain was where the Druids were the most powerful, for the mystic lore from Britain was highly respected by the Celts on the continent.

The ancients associated the name of Druid with *dryads,* which were the spirits of the oak trees venerated in Druidic rites. Recent scholars prefer to derive the word from one meaning "wise men." Whatever the source of the word, the oak tree was important in Druidic lore. The mistletoe that grows attached to oaks was sacred, and the cutting of the mistletoe with a golden knife shaped like the crescent moon was a principal feature of the ceremonies at the end of December when rituals were performed to keep the sun from dying and to prevent the days from getting shorter. The Druids ate the acorns of the oak in the belief that they would give them the power to prophesy.

The Druids performed ceremonies publicly as well as in secret. At one time their rituals probably included human sacrifice. A white bull was slain at the cutting of the mistletoe, and its entrails were examined for omens of the future.

Druids acted as judges in lawsuits involving murder, inheritance, and property disputes. Each king had a Druid to act as his political and judicial adviser. The Druid of the legendary King Arthur was the famous Merlin. Druids were teachers. They taught the young by oral instruction, telling them the legends of the people, and the religious and moral doctrines of Druidism. The Druids had some knowledge of astronomy, of physics, and of botany, the last of which was used in their medicinal lore.

The Druids brought new members into their brotherhood by selecting and training gifted children, although in some cases there seem to have been families of Druids also. Occasionally a woman became a Druidess, but we do not know whether this was because she showed a natural capacity for magic, or because she was trained in the profession, or both.

Besides the Druids, among the respected advisers of kings were the bards, the poets who had memorized the legends of the past and sang of the great heroes and gods of former ages.

CELTIC POLITICAL INSTITUTIONS

What we know about Celtic political institutions comes to us from later sources, after the first century A.D., but we may presume that the institutions evident then had roots in much earlier times.

The Celtic "kingdoms" must be understood as small tribal unities and the "kings" as tribal chiefs. Ireland had five kings, each ruling a section of the country. The strongest of the five occupied the office of "High King" as well. Wales had a cluster of four kings, and Gaul probably had a similar system.

Within each kingdom people were grouped by descent from a common ancestor or by living on lands claimed by such a kinship group. In some cases these tribal groupings were originally identified by animal totems. By Roman times the original animal worship had long been lost, but its former existence was shown by the food taboos, which differed from tribe to tribe. Thus the people of Clanna Coneely might not eat seal, although other Irish did. "Coneely" means "seal," and legend says that the founders of this tribe were turned into seals in ancient days.

In the years following 300 B.C., the Celts expanded over Europe and into Asia Minor (page 336). In no case were they able to successfully establish lasting states of their own but merged with the local peoples wherever they settled. Only on the western rim of Europe, along the Atlantic coast in France and the British Isles, did the Celtic part of the population remain strong enough to perpetuate in a small degree its language and folk traditions.

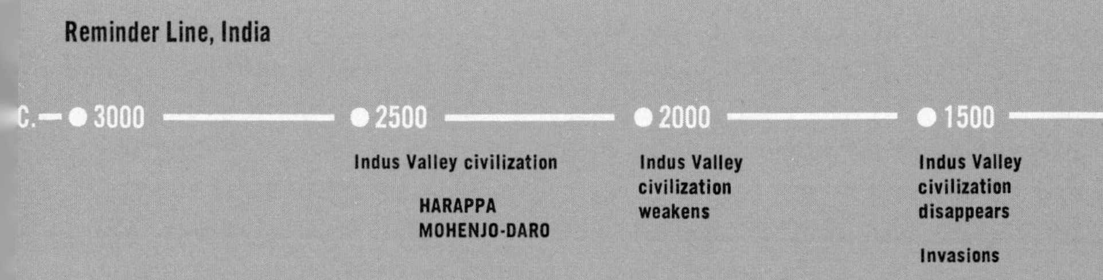

INDIA'S VEDIC AGE

Records are very few for the millennium between 2000 and 1000 B.C. in India. All we know is that there were many invasions from north and west of the subcontinent. The most important were those of the Aryans, who came from central Asia and Iran perhaps about 1500 B.C.

The Aryans were generally tall, long-headed people with blond hair and straight noses, differing sharply from the local population. They were a warrior people who rode chariots and spoke Sanskrit, an Indo-European, language. Sweeping down in several waves of invasion over perhaps three hundred years, they conquered the small darker-skinned natives. Gradually they settled down in the valleys of the Indus and the Ganges rivers, while bands pushed farther south as the need arose for new pasture lands for their cattle.

In central and southern India lived the Dravidians, a very dark, flat-nosed, short people who had inhabited this region from neolithic times. The

Aryans and the native population of the north were unable to penetrate far into the central and southern plateau lands of the Dravidians, but they kept trying, and warfare was constant all through the Early Iron Age.

EARLY IRON AGE LITERATURE OF NORTHERN INDIA

What we know of Indian life between 1500 B.C. and about 500 B.C. comes to us from the religious poems called the *Vedas*. This period in Indian history is therefore known as the Vedic Age. Because the *Vedas* were transmitted orally for many generations before they were written down, sometimes it is hard to know what is a true picture of the earlier times and what reflects the period in which the texts were set down. The people came to believe the *Vedas* were inspired by the gods, and even the arrangement of words was supposed to carry magic power.

Over the centuries, from about 1200 to 800 B.C., four collections of the *Vedas* appeared. The oldest, the *Rig Veda*, a collection of sacred hymns for the sacrifice and instructions for the priestly ritual, was entirely Aryan in origin. It also tells us of Aryan gods and heroes. From the *Rig Veda* we have a picture of warrior kings sweeping down on their unsuspecting foes and vanquishing them. The kings seemed to have performed the function of priests as well as of war leaders. They drank soma, an intoxicating brew that was offered to the gods. These gods represented the spirits of natural forces and elements, like those of other Indo-European peoples. The spirit of the *Rig Veda* is one of strength and joy. The Aryans were still tribal and only gradually settled in villages, which they fortified with walls against raids. The next two *Vedas* are more a mixture of Aryan and native Indian ideas and traditions, while the last *Veda*, in which magic is very important in ritual, appears to include what are probably Dravidian concepts. The *Vedas* therefore reflect a mixing of social and racial elements in the Early Iron Age.

In the eighth and seventh centuries B.C., prose commentaries on the *Vedas* called *Brahmanas* appeared. They were filled with regulations for religious worship and made the position of the priest (*Brahmin*) all-important in conducting the proper rituals. Indeed, the Brahmins insisted that performing the perfect ritual could compel the gods to grant the wish. The priests naturally became very important and powerful in society, as they held the key to the will of the gods. But not all men were satisfied with the role the Brahmins had assumed for themselves. As early as the eighth century B.C. men began to think more deeply about the nature of god and man, and they concluded that not ritual but private contemplation was the road to salvation. Between 800 and 400 B.C. such thinkers produced the body of philosophic speculation called the *Upanishads*, a mystical interpretation of the union of the individual soul with a nonanthropomorphic world soul that they called *Brahman* (not to be confused with the caste of Brahmins, see below). Riches, health, and long life were not the objects to be sought on earth. Instead, the object was to escape from the endless round of rebirths the Indians believed each soul went through, and to return to Brahman, from whom all things have come. The Brahmin priests had no place in such a scheme until they reconciled the new way with the old one by saying that the path of the *Upanishads* was suitable for the end of life, after one had observed ceremonial sacrifices, raised a family, and attained an honorable place in society. By such a reconciliation the Brahmins maintained their role in Indian society by incorporating into the Brahmanical religion new thought that might have undermined their influence and authority.

Two other works of literature help fill the gaps in Indian records. They are the two great epic poems, the *Mahabharata* and the *Ramayana*, which probably existed in earliest forms by the fourth century B.C. The *Mahabharata* is the tale of a war between families in which the gods take part, and the *Ramayana* is the epic of the great hero Rama and his faithful wife Sita. As did the *Iliad* and *Odyssey* of Homer, these two Indian epics established a literary style and fashioned a picture of what the gods were like and what constituted ideal behavior for heroic men and good women.

THE CASTE SYSTEM

One of the distinctive features of Indian civilization has been the caste system. Whether it was brought to India by the invading Aryans or whether it had native roots is not clear at this time. We do know that when the Aryans came into India, they held themselves apart from the native population, and that by 500 B.C. four classes or castes existed. Members of the different castes could not marry each other, or even eat with each other, and had to observe strict rules in their behavior toward each other.

In descending order the castes were those of the priestly *Brahmins*, the warrior and ruler *Kshatriyas* (note the resemblance to the Persian word *shah*), the *Vaishya* craftsmen, traders, herders, and farmers, and the *Shudras*, whose first purpose was to serve the castes above them. The three higher castes were considered Aryan and were much the same in composition as

Caste in India. The system of caste continues to exist in India today. The government, however, does not recognize untouchability. Here, in the south Indian city of Madras, a former untouchable carries out a job that may be performed by a number of different castes.

the social groupings of other Indo-European peoples. The Shudras were formed from the native population and from mixtures of the natives with the Aryans. The dark-skinned Dravidians formed the greatest number of *outcastes* or untouchables, who were outside the caste system entirely. The outcastes performed the most menial duties, and their touch or even their shadow was felt to pollute a caste member.

As the centuries went by, the four castes were subdivided into the thousands of subcastes that exist in India today. Even the outcastes subdivided themselves and became just as rigid in their dealings with the lowest group of all, the *Pariahs*, who washed the dead, as were members of the castes. Some subcastes were created out of a single occupation, some were of racial origin. Some came into existence because of geographical dispersion, others were connected with the worship of some highly specialized religious cult. Each of these many castes and subcastes had its own rigid rules of dress and behavior, which a person had to adhere to if he wished to maintain his place in society. One could recognize his fellow caste members by a sign painted on the forehead, as well as by the way in which a turban was folded or a cloak was worn. A person found in his caste the meaning and purpose of his entire life, and a person who "lost his caste" retained no place at all in Indian society.

In time the Indians came to believe that caste had been established by the gods. Here is how a late hymn in the *Rig Veda* expresses it:

> When (the gods) divided the Man, into
> how many parts did they divide him?
> What was his mouth, what were his arms,
> what were his thighs and feet called?
> The Brahmin was his mouth, of his arms
> were made the warriors.
> His thighs became the Vaishya, of his
> feet the Shudra was born.

Caste was supported by the theory of reincarnation, which holds that both good and evil in life are rewarded by rebirth into a higher or lower caste according to one's deeds (the doctrine of *karma*). A man is a Brahmin because he led a good life in his previous incarnation. But he also has to maintain his caste by his character and behavior, or he will be reborn lower in the social order or even outside it as a bug or worm. The idea of reincarnation gave a logical explanation to the differences in social position and served to justify the system of caste.

INDIAN WOMEN IN THE VEDIC AGE

The epic poems present contradictory pictures of the lives of Indian women in India's Early Iron Age, and it is not certain which versions are from the earliest period and which were added later. Though women were kept very much in the background, the mother was greatly respected and the faithful wife was admired. A girl in the higher castes received some education and was taught to dance and sing. Child marriages occurred but were not so common as in later times. The bride might select the groom herself from a group brought together for the purpose, and the marriage arrangements were completed by the payment of a bride price. Also, a survival from less civilized times, the bride could be forcefully abducted by the bridegroom. On marriage she entered her husband's home, where she might find herself one of several wives. Usually she did not own property in her own right. On her husband's death the widow committed a symbolic act of suicide, *suttee*, but this practice was carried out symbolically, not in fact, as suttee was in later times.

INDIAN CIVILIZATION REESTABLISHES ITSELF

By the seventh century B.C. the darkness that surrounded the Early Iron Age began to lift a little. Northern India in the Ganges plain and the

Himalaya foothills of the Punjab was divided into many tiny kingdoms. They were ruled by descendants of the Aryans who waged continual war among themselves and with the Dravidian peoples to the south. Gradually the small states were absorbed into the larger states. By 450 B.C. India's northern kingdoms were united into the single state of Magadha. In the fourth century B.C. the Nanda family gained the throne. The first king and conqueror of the family was said to have been the son of a barber of the Shudra caste, which showed that the caste system could still be broken by an aggressive man who wished to fight his way to power.

In the sixth century B.C. the growing kingdom of Magadha had come in close contact with the Persian Empire. In 516 B.C. Darius I of Persia extended the conquests of his predecessor in Baluchistan eastward into India and annexed the Indus Valley, making it a satrapy of the Achaemenid Empire (page 175). The Persians introduced writing, using a variation of the

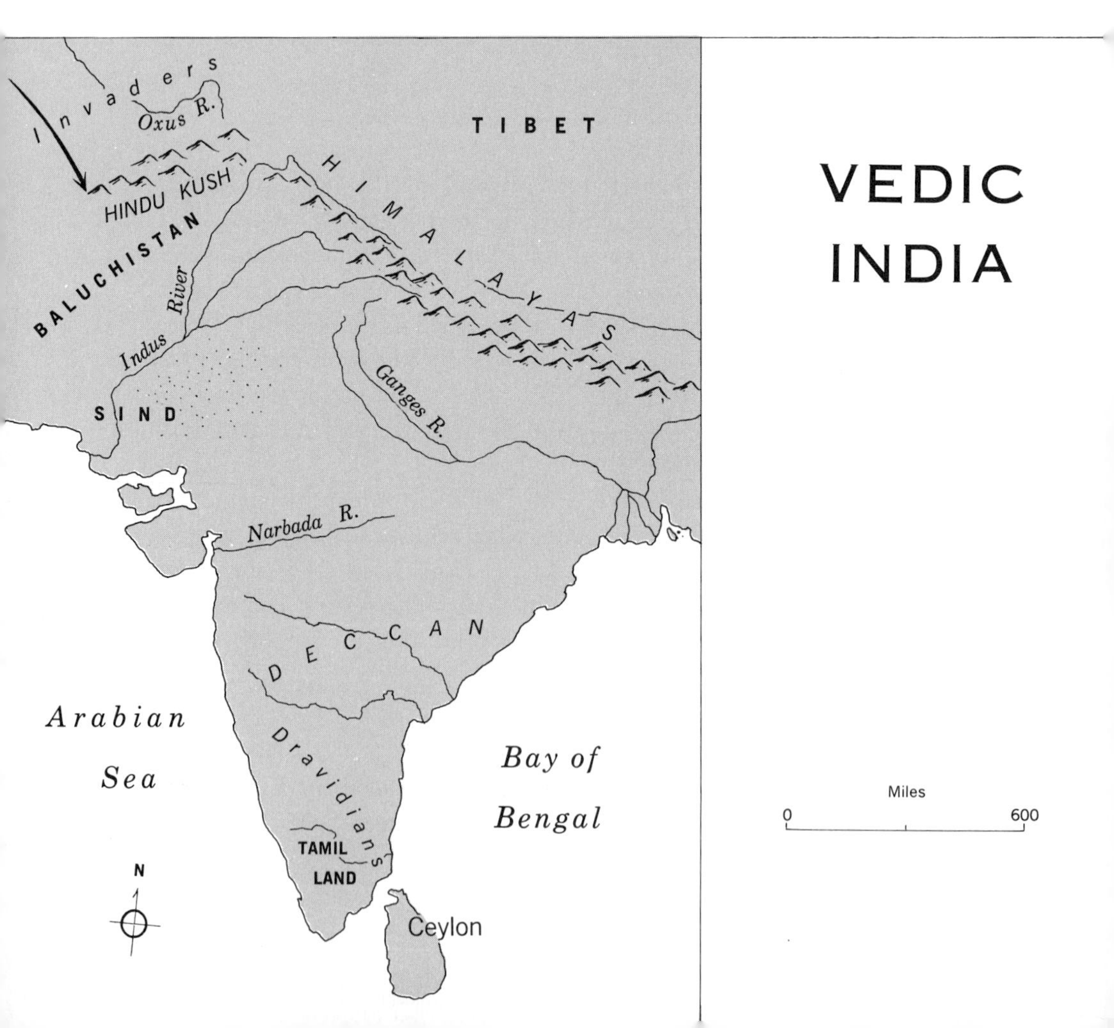

Aramaean alphabet, which became one of the two principal alphabets of India. Darius ordered a fleet of ships built on the Indus River to explore a sea route from India to Egypt. These ships were the first to ply again the sea route that in the following centuries was used by Arab traders in the great exchange of goods between India and the Hellenes and Romans. Indian merchants sailed into Persian waters, and one exotic traveler was the Indian peacock, which sailed west to Greece at this time.

In 327 B.C. Alexander the Great of Macedon entered India after overthrowing the Achaemenid Empire of Persia (page 327). When Alexander proposed to march beyond the Persian satrapy of northwest India eastward into the Ganges Valley, his army, weary of war, mutinied. Alexander returned to Babylon and died in 323 B.C. but his successor, Seleucus, again invaded northwest India in 305 B.C. Seleucus, however, was unable to establish a permanent Hellenic kingdom there. In the long run of India's history, the empires of Alexander and Seleucus left little permanent mark. The native Magadha kingdom, by contrast, became an empire that ruled most of the subcontinent.

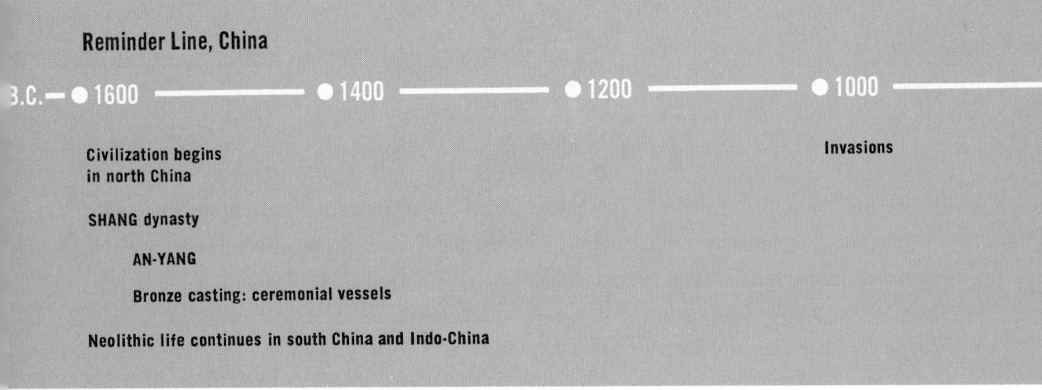

CHOU CHINA

The use of the phrase "Chou dynasty" must not mislead us into thinking that we have precise knowledge of the first millennium B.C. in China. On the contrary, our information for the early part of this period is very vague. But certain outlines in the growth of the Chinese civilization are clear. During the Chou period (1051–256 B.C.), Chinese culture expanded to cover a much greater geographical territory than it had formerly occupied. The earliest Chinese civilization occupied the North China Plain. During the early Chou it extended over the valley of the Wei River and around some of the bordering mountains in what is now modern Shantung province. By the close of the Chou, civilization reached into present-day Shansi, Shensi, Szechwan, and parts of the Yangtze Valley.

At the same time that civilization was spreading, the central political authorities were losing control to rival princes, who waged war continually. This warfare does not seem to have inhibited the growth of Chinese culture and life. On the contrary, art flourished and beautiful bronzes like those of the Shang period were created (page 140); merchants carried on commerce and trade using coins rather than cowrie shells (page 138); and the classics of Chinese literature were composed. Not least, the schools of thought that have influenced China until our own day appeared (see Chapter 15), and, indeed, the late Chou was one of the most intellectually stimulating periods of Chinese history. Although the records are not complete, we are able to detect many fundamentals of Chinese civilization making their first appearance during the Chou dynasty.

THE WESTERN CHOU, 1051–771 B.C.

The first Chou appeared in the Wei River Valley. Whether they were Chinese or aliens from farther west is debated. If they were strangers, then they were quick to adopt the religious and social ideas of the Shang, whom they conquered about 1027 B.C.

For a short time the conquering Chou king, Wu, and a few of his immediate successors may have exercised some real authority. This is uncertain, but if so, a kind of land-holding arrangement known as *feudalism* soon took its place. Warrior nobles held large estates by force, and landless peasants lived in villages on these estates for protection from invasion and raids. The land included in the Chou feudalistic society extended from the Yangtze River on the south to the Hwang Ho in the north.

By the eighth century B.C. the Chou region was checkered with hundreds of land holdings. Their rulers openly defied the Chou "rulers." A revolt in 841 B.C. overthrew the king, Chou Li, and placed his young son on the throne under the regency of a council of nobles. When the boy king ended the regency and assumed the throne in his own right in 827 B.C., he faced both rebellious nobles and constant war with the barbarians on his western frontiers. These dates of 841 and 827 B.C. are the earliest dates in Chinese history that we know with any certainty. Civilization had reestablished itself to the point where there was literature, mathematics, and record keeping.

In 771 B.C. rebel nobles, acting with non-Chinese barbarian invaders, invaded the capital and killed the Chou king. The center of Chou government, such as it was, was moved to Lo-Yang in the valley of the small Lo River. The period from then until 500 B.C. is known as the Middle Chou. The succeeding two centuries are called the Eastern Chou.

THE MIDDLE AND EASTERN CHOU, 771–256 B.C.

The splintering of China into many small feudal states continued at an ever greater and more ruthless pace. The more aggressive states absorbed their weaker neighbors until only a few dozen territories remained. These territories formed a cluster under the loose control of the Chou kings. Together they were called the "Center." Around the Center was a great ring of frontier nations. Larger, more powerful, and less cultured than the interior states, they paid less attention to the claims of the Chou overlords and in fact were independent. Surrounding the great ring of frontier states were the uncivilized tribes of the mountains and the desert. They eyed with envy the farmlands and towns of the civilized ring and seized every opportunity to break across the frontier to harass and kill and steal.

Against the barbarians and the nomads nothing but the most savage fighting was effective. But among their own civilized states of the Center and of the Ring, constant warfare produced an elaborate code of chivalry among the upper classes. In one record we hear of a wagonload of provisions sent as a gesture of defiance to an invading army, as much as to say, "We can

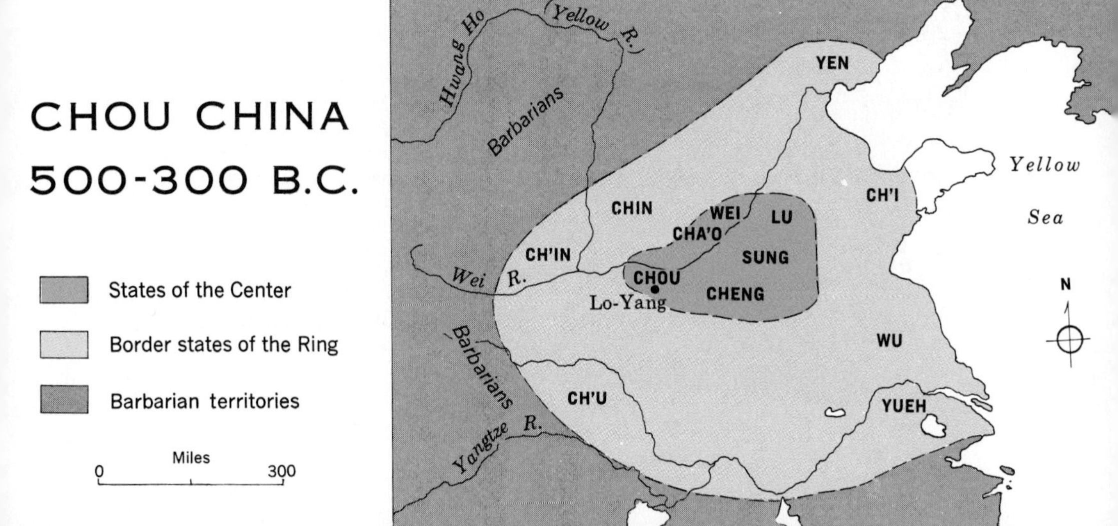

afford to feed you and still whip you on the battlefield." Warriors sometimes exchanged weapons with each other and then continued the interrupted fighting, or refused to kill an overthrown opponent who had shown unusual bravery. War in such cases resembled the tournaments in which the upper classes showed their skill in swordsmanship, archery, and chariot riding.

CHOU RELIGION

The religion of Chou China was a combination of the worship of the gods of nature with the cult of ancestor worship. The principal Chinese deity was called "Heaven" and seems to have been anthropomorphic. Heaven granted rule over earth to a specially selected person, the king, who called himself the Son of Heaven. The Chou kings thus claimed to be intermediaries between the gods and the people. In addition to its altar to Heaven, each community had a mound of earth known as the "Altar of the Land," which was considered the most sacred spot in the village or town. There were worshiped the various gods and goddesses of earth.

The state, like the family, was thought to have ancestors. These ancestors were the great kings and emperors of by-gone days. The ancestral spirits of the state were worshiped in special temples raised in the various capital cities. When a state was conquered in war, the Altars of the Land and the

A ceremonial vessel of the Kuei type. Chinese ritual vessels such as this one from the early Chou were originally patterned on pottery vessels used for food. Kuei-shaped vessels are round, they often have a massive square stand at their base, lobed handles representing birds or animals, and a lid, missing here. The method by which the bronze was cast has been lost. Whether metallurgy originated in China or was imported is debated. Certainly the styles and decorations on the bronze vessels are native to the Chinese, and this suggests a local origin.

ancestral temples were destroyed by the victors as a sign that the power of the preceding rulers had come to an end.

As in the western world, there were special sacrifices and rituals at certain seasons. The most solemn ceremonies were those of spring and autumn, when, it was believed, the gods intervened more directly in the affairs of men. The human sacrifices of the Shang seem to have been abandoned. Instead, burnt offerings of flowers, fruits, the best of the harvest, and the pick of the herds were offered to the gods and emphasized the importance of the occasion. Family ceremonies were led by the father; state rituals were performed by the king or emperor or by his specially designated representatives. There was no class of priests corresponding to the Celtic Druids, the Persian Magi, or the Indian Brahmins.

ACHIEVEMENTS OF THE CHOU AGE

By the sixth century B.C., canal building and swamp drainage made it possible to farm many square miles of marshlands that had formerly been useless. The Chinese used fertilizer to improve their crops, improved the plow to help their farming, and domesticated mules and donkeys to lighten the burden of the peasants. There was a corresponding increase in population, and many cities grew where the arts of civilization flourished. The Chinese codified more of their laws, adopted coins as a medium of exchange, and replaced bronze with iron for common tools and weapons.

The late Chou was a period of intellectual ferment in which the Chinese tried to understand the relationship of man to man and man to society, a subject of the most fundamental interest to the Chinese throughout their history. It was the age of the Master K'ung, known to the west as Confucius (page 305), the sage whose thought had such a profound impact on the development of the Chinese civilization. Several of the most important works of Chinese literature are attributed to the late Chou period. Just as the Early Iron Age of the Hellenes is depicted in the poems of Homer and the Vedic Age in India in the hymns to the gods, so we learn of Chinese customs and traditions from the writings of the Chou. Among the greatest of these is the *Shu Ching*, the Classic of History, and the *Ch'un Ch'iu*, the Spring and Autumn Annals, both historical documents of various periods and many authors. In poetry we have the anthology called *Shih Ching*, Classic of Poetry; in ritual the *Li Chi*, the Record of Rites; and from the professional diviners the *I Ching*, or Record of Forecasts. These books, the Five Classics, are extremely important because they were the basic texts studied by generations of scholar-bureaucrats until the twentieth century.

THE END OF THE CHOU PERIOD

In the fourth century B.C., the states of China entered into alliances with each other on a temporary basis. Eventually two permanent leagues emerged. The *Lien-heng* (West to East League), dominated by the northern state of Ch'in, coalesced into a single unified state. In the south, along the Yangtze Valley, rose the *Ho-tsong* (North to South League), led by the state of Ch'u. The states of Ch'u were organized into a confederacy in which each maintained its separate identity. The struggle between the ideas of confederation and those of unification became a battle between Ch'in and Ch'u for leadership of China. Ch'in won, and the prince of Ch'in took the title of king in 325 B.C. Until 256 B.C., however, other Chou princes still claimed their ancient overlordship of China.

❦ ❦ ❦

Outside the Mediterranean, world civilization was growing in the east and in the northwestern part of Europe. The Celtic culture never became urban or literate. Nevertheless, the Celts had an increasing impact on their civilized neighbors, from whom they were borrowing what appealed to them to enhance their own way of life. In China and India, after periods of barbarian invasion and a consequent decline in culture, civilized life re-established itself. We see a trend toward the organization of larger political units which in India led to the establishment of the Magadha kingdom, and in China to that of Ch'in. In the years ahead, the trend continued, and the basic institutions of religion and society, which we have seen slowly emerging at this time, fully developed.

People, Places, and Terms

Celts	La Tène	Brahmin
Gauls	Stonehenge	Nirvana
Galatians	Lo-Yang	reincarnation
Druids		caste system
Aryans	Ch'in	asceticism
Dravidians	Chou	bard
	anthropomorphic	Kshatriya
Ireland	Heaven	Vaishya
Scotland	Brahman	Shudra
Halstatt	dryads	*Vedas*

Mastering the Reading

1. What patterns of Celtic culture were distinctly Celtic? How did the Mediterranean Sea peoples influence the Celts during the La Tène period? What were the chief characteristics of Druidism? What happened to the Celts' identity as they expanded?
2. What do we know about the Aryans? Why is the Vedic Period so named? Why are the *Vedas* an important part of the social as well as the religious history of India? How did the *Upanishads* force a change in the thinking of the Brahmins?
3. What were the "Center" and the "Ring" in Chou China? How did formalized warfare evolve? What was the significance of ancestors to the family and the state? Under the Chous what progress was made in agriculture and literature?

Interpreting the Text

1. What arguments might a Shudra father give his son if the son wished to rebel against his caste position?
2. What proof might an anthropologist use to show that the Celts and the Aryans were originally related?

Exploring Beyond the Text

1. Homer's *Odyssey* and the Indian *Ramayana* have much in common. What parallels can you find?
2. The Indian word *rajah* can be related to other Indo-European words for *king* or *royalty*. Can you think of or discover others in Latin, Italian, French?
3. Although officially outlawed in India, the caste system still has a grip on Indian thought and life. What are some of India's health, food, social and technical problems that exist today because of the caste system? Why is it so slow to end?

Working with the Map

1. After looking at a map of the geographical features of the Indian subcontinent in an atlas, make a list of the geographical features of northen India that made it attractive to invaders.
2. Draw a topographical map showing the routes of invaders into both India and China during the Early Iron Age.

15

Search for Truth and Justice

1000–350 B.C.

After the collapse of the Bronze Age civilizations, the people of the Early Iron Age had to begin again to build society. Ignorance, primitive economies, uprooted people, and a general loss of law and order characterized society. In the preceding six chapters our view of the revival of civilization has been primarily political and economic because the establishment of government and law, and the search for ways to earn a living, are fundamental to any people. Now let us turn back to follow another kind of development, one just as crucial to our understanding of mankind—the development of human beliefs.

CHANGES IN RELIGIOUS THINKING

In the beginning of the Early Iron Age, the gods were numerous. Polytheism, the worship of many gods, continued. There were still gods for each force in nature, each activity, and each object in the world. Even though the Hebrews believed by 1000 B.C. that their own tribal god had a special relationship with them, they did not deny that other gods existed for other people.

As time passed during the Iron Age, the number of gods was gradually reduced to a pantheon, or group, of usually twelve or thirteen greater gods surrounded by other lesser ones. The gods of Olympus, for example, were a pantheon. Sometimes two or three of these gods were supreme, but there was a growing tendency to emphasize the importance of a single god or goddess over the others.

The gods of most civilizations seem to have had common attributes and functions. For example, everywhere there was a god who spoke in the thunder and who hurled the lightning, although he bore many names—Zeus in Hellas, Jupiter in Rome, Tin in Etruria, and Taranis among the Celtic people along the Atlantic coast. The goddess of love and beauty reigned everywhere, under such names as Venus in Rome, Aphrodite in Hellas, and Astarte in Carthage.

While goddesses were still widely worshiped, the male gods of the Indo-Europeans rose in importance. More and more the goddesses became simply wives and daughters of the male gods. The great day of the supreme Mother Goddess was past. Sky gods took first place over earth gods.

Another change came with representation of the gods. Anthropomorphic (human-shaped) gods replaced the animal-shaped older gods. Although some of the latter have survived to this day—for instance, the Indian god of wisdom, Ganesha, is still shown with an elephant head on a human body—by the ninth century B.C. a god might take on an animal form but only temporarily. Generally the gods were now visualized in human form. They were thought to be larger than human beings, more beautiful, or more frightful, as the case might be. Whatever qualities, bad or good, a man might have, the gods had them in greater degree. If a man could be tricky, a god could be trickier; if a man could steal, a god could be a greater thief.

While some of the gods were changing from animal to human forms, others were coming to be thought of as having no body at all. In India, Brahman was conceived as formless, while the Hebrews' tribal god, Yahweh, was also conceived as being beyond any physical representation.

FATE AND CONSEQUENCES—THE PUZZLE OF INJUSTICE

In the early Iron Age people began to give new answers to age-old problems that have puzzled man since the beginning of time. Two such problems concern the question of injustice. If the gods are really powerful, how can injustice be explained? Why are injustice and suffering allowed?

Different answers were suggested. In Hellas and India the idea grew that every action of a god or man has results. Neither god nor man can escape the law of consequences. Ignorance of what he has done or later regret for having done it cannot alter the events that result from every action. Even if the Hellenic god Zeus were all-powerful, he would still be bound by this law of the universe. Therefore, an action or a fate that might seem unjust may really be the inevitable consequence of some previous action. The Hebrews expressed this same thought when they said that the sins of the father would be paid for by his descendants down to the seventh generation.

The Persians answered the problem of injustice by their belief that the world is the scene of battle between two equal powers, evil and good (page 300). Whichever power received the most aid from mankind would eventually triumph in the world. While this did not prevent evil from existing in the world, it gave the Persians a reason for acting on the side of good during their lives.

Still another answer to the puzzle of the cause of suffering and injustice existed among the Hebrews. They believed that many of the evils that befell them might be punishment sent by Yahweh because they had not been obedient and faithful to him as their chosen god.

COMMUNICATIONS WITH THE GODS

All the Iron Age peoples believed that men could communicate with the gods. Such communications from gods to men might be by omens, by dreams and visions, or through persons "possessed" by a divine spirit. Persons with epilepsy, an affliction the ancients knew little about, were thought to be possessed when they foamed at the mouth or raved, and they were regarded with superstitious awe all over the civilized world. Iron Age people tried to discover the intentions of the gods by many different methods.

Books of Prophecy. The first Tarquin king of Rome was believed to have purchased from a *sibyl* (prophetess) at Cumae several books written in antique Greek that were supposed to foretell, in mysterious language, the entire future of Rome. Known as the Sibylline Books, they were guarded as Rome's chief treasure for a thousand years, and whenever the city faced a crisis the Books were consulted for advice. They were finally destroyed by Christians about 400 A.D.

Casting of Lots. A cluster of sticks or arrows of various lengths, sometimes inscribed, were shaken in a holder until one fell out. The *Urim* and *Thummim* used by Hebrew priests in the early tribal days may have been of this nature. They are not mentioned in later writings, but when the Hebrews ceased to use them is not known.

Observation of Birds and Animals. The behavior of birds and animals was believed to be more sensitive to divine impulse than that of human beings. The twelve ravens that flew by Romulus during the legendary founding of Rome, were universally interpreted by the Romans as foretelling that Rome would last for twelve hundred years.

Dreams. Sleeping in holy places and observing rituals were believed to induce dreams of divine origin. The Assyrians and Egyptians thought that interpreting such dreams was a science that could be taught, while the Hebrews believed that the ability to interpret dreams was a personal gift from Yahweh. At the shrines dedicated to Asclepius, the god of healing and medicine, the Hellenes interpreted dreams to help the sick.

Oracular Shrines. At special places that they particularly favored, the gods were thought to make their wishes known through oracles. The oracle was both the messenger of the god and the speaker. The most famous shrine in the Mediterranean world was at Delphi, which the Hellenes believed was the center of the earth. There for centuries private persons and ambassadors

Delphi, the ruins of a *tholos* or round building. The oldest oracle in Hellas was that of Zeus at Dordona in Epirus, where priests interpreted the will of the king of the gods by the rustling of the leaves on a sacred oak tree. Apollo's shrine at Delphi, however, was the most renowned. An ancient myth related how Apollo had come to Delphi, slain the dragon Pytho guarding the place, and had made it his own. The Delphic oracle's predictions served, on the whole, as a moderating influence on the affairs of the Hellenes and their neighbors.

of governments came from the Hellenic world, and occasionally from the Etruscans, Persians, or Egyptians, to ask questions of the god Apollo. The answers to the questions were spoken in delirium by the Pythia, the priestess of the shrine. The mutterings of the Pythia were so obscure that they had to be written down and then interpreted by the priests, who delivered the answers to inquirers in verse. Since these priests talked with the best educated and most informed persons from all parts of the civilized world, they possessed extraordinary amounts of information of all kinds—political, geographical, personal. The priestly interpretations of the Pythia's mumblings were no doubt based on this wide knowledge of conditions in the world, which might explain the great reputation this particular oracle enjoyed for foretelling events accurately. (Apollo, however, was not always right. The most famous example of wrong-guessing at Delphi came during the Persian invasion, when the oracle foretold that the Persians would be successful.)

Omens and Portents. The ancient lore of Sumer and Babylonia was widely studied in the Iron Age by all the peoples of the Mediterranean; some of it seems to have penetrated as far as China and India. The heavens were scanned nightly for the appearance of signs such as comets or meteors. The entrails of animals were examined after sacrificial slaughter (page 106). The sound of thunder was carefully noted since the direction it came from indicated which gods were speaking and what kind of message they were sending. The Romans in particular made much of such lore. They had inherited it from the Etruscans, who might have brought it with them from their earlier home in the east.

THE GREAT RELIGIOUS TEACHERS, 700–400 B.C.

As the Early Iron Age moved into the sixth and fifth centuries B.C., several men appeared in many parts of the civilized world who had enormous effect on man's religious development. These great religious reformers and teachers include the Hebrew prophets, Buddha and Mahavira in India, K'ung Fu-Tzu (Confucius) in China, and Zoroaster in Persia. Never before or since has such a great cluster of religious thinkers appeared at the same time. Through their teachings the idea of monotheism, the concept that there is only one god, maker and creator of the universe, slowly emerged, and new ideas were postulated on the nature of truth and justice in the world.

TEACHERS AND PROPHETS AMONG THE HEBREWS

On Solomon's death (c. 935 B.C.) the Hebrew kingdom had split into two states. Ten of the tribes formed the more settled and commercial state of Israel, while the remaining two tribes, more pastoral and agricultural, became the state of Judah. In the ninth century B.C. the shadow of rising Assyria fell across the Middle East and encompassed the Phoenicians (page 148). Then in 735 B.C. Israel was attacked by Assyria and in 722 B.C. was destroyed; its ten tribes were deported to unknown destinations (page 152). Judah escaped destruction for a time by signing a treaty of alliance with Assyria in 735 B.C., but it was conquered by Chaldea in 586 B.C. At this time the skilled and educated part of Judah's population was exiled to Babylon, where it remained until it was freed by Cyrus the Persian. Three hundred fifty years of calamity and the loss of the greater part of its population would have disheartened almost any nation. But not the Hebrews, for in the years after there arose among them, one after the other, fifteen great prophets. These men called the Hebrews to new obedience to Yahweh and the Covenant, to more righteous living and to have courage against their fears. The three known as the "major prophets" are Isaiah, Jeremiah, and Ezekiel. Each of them reflected tragic events in the destruction of the Hebrew states.

Isaiah (742–687 B.C.) appeared in the time of Israel's conquest and Judah's subjugation to Assyria. He attacked social injustice and urged the Jews to righteousness in their public and private lives so that they might enjoy Yahweh's blessing. "Cease to do evil, learn to do good; seek justice, correct oppression; defend the fatherless," he said, speaking as the oracle of "The Holy One of Israel."

Jeremiah (627–580 B.C.) claimed to be the voice of Yahweh as Jerusalem fell to the Chaldeans and its leaders were exiled to Babylon. He urged the exiles to keep their faith and to look beyond the exile to a better time in the future, saying for Yahweh, "I will restore Israel to his pasture, and he shall feed on Mt. Carmel and in Bashan . . . In those days and in that time iniquity will be looked for in Israel and there shall be none, and sin will be sought in Judah and none will be found."

Ezekiel (593–563 B.C.) shared in the Babylonian exile, assuring the deportees that Yahweh was still with them. His message was of the integrity of the individual and of each man's personal responsibility to Yahweh. "The son shall not suffer for the iniquity of the father nor the father for the iniquity of the son; the righteousness of the good man shall be only upon himself, and the wickedness of the bad man shall be only upon himself."

The other twelve prophets are called "minor" only because few of their writings have survived. They were not minor in the sense of having had something less important to say. The twelve, beginning with Amos and ending with Malachi, taught from 760 B.C. to about 400 B.C. Typical was Amos (c. 760 B.C.), who taught that ritual in the temple was less important than justice among men. He wrote, "Thus says the Lord God, 'I take no delight in your assemblies, your burnt offerings I will not accept, your peace offerings I will not look upon . . . But let justice roll down like waters, and righteousness like an ever flowing stream.' "

Under the leadership of the prophets, the Jews changed slowly from being *monolatrists*, believing in one god for themselves but accepting the existence of other gods for other people, to being *monotheists*, holding that Yahweh was the one God of all men. But they still believed that as Jews they had a special relationship to God, that they were the Children of the Covenant, the agreement between Yahweh and mankind.

ZOROASTER AND THE PERSIANS

Sometime in the sixth century B.C. the greatest Persian religious teacher, Zoroaster or Zarathustra, appeared. The precise dates of his life are in dispute and the facts of his life unknown. Zoroaster reacted against the excessive rituals of the Persian religion (page 177) and especially against the sacrifice of living creatures. He taught kindness to both humans and animals and forbade the ancient practice of animal sacrifice. To him the earth, fire, and water were sacred, and they must not be polluted. The dead, therefore, were not to be buried, burned, or drowned, but were to be exposed in structures open to the sky known as Towers of Silence. After the body had decayed or vultures had removed the flesh, the bones were collected and placed in stone tombs or caves.

Zoroaster believed that the universe was the scene of a mighty war between two divine forces. On one side was the all-powerful god Ahuramazda, creator and upholder of the universe. Originally an Iranian sky god like those of the other Indo-European peoples, Ahuramazda was defined by Zoroaster as the personification of goodness and light. Ahuramazda wages constant war with Ahriman, the personification of darkness and evil, and his demon hosts. Each human being must choose the side he will serve. In the end truth will prevail and the forces of good triumph, but Zoroaster taught that men must face the consequences of their choice. After death those who have served Ahuramazda will be rewarded with eternal blessedness, while all others will suffer eternal misery. In emphasizing human individual responsibility for a good and moral life, Zoroaster was like the Hebrew prophets, the Indian teachers (below), and the Hellenic poets and philosophers (page 306).

SIDDARTHA GAUTAMA, THE BUDDHA, 563–483 B.C.

At the time that Zoroaster lived in Persia and the prophets were preaching in Israel, one of the world's greatest religious figures lived in India. This man was Siddartha Gautama, also known as Sakya Muni (The Wise Man of the Sakya clan) or, as he became, the Buddha. The Buddha's intention was not to found a new religion but to reform the old one. Brahmanism had become rigid and inflexible; it followed the letter but not the spirit of its precepts, and India was ripe for the teachings of a man who would revitalize the ancient religion of the Brahmins.

Siddartha was the son of a rajah or petty king in the north of India. Early in his life he had shown signs of a restless and speculative temperament. His father, concerned for the boy's health and well-being, built him a splendid palace filled with luxuries where he would be shielded from the harshness and misery of life. At sixteen the young prince married a beautiful princess. But Siddartha was not happy. One day, according to legend, he went out with his faithful charioteer Channa. Suddenly they saw an old man, bent and trembling with age. Siddartha knew nothing of age. "What is wrong with this man?" he asked. "He is old," said Channa. "Such is the way of life. To that we all must come." Shortly after they saw a man greatly afflicted with a loathsome disease. "Such is the way of life," Channa repeated. While pondering the things he had seen, Siddartha came upon a funeral procession and saw the corpse lying on the bier. Once again Channa said, "Such is the way of life." Horrified at the contrast between the life he knew and the realities of the world, Siddartha determined to leave home, wife, and the little son who had just been born to search for the meaning of life. In the dead of night so none would stop him, Siddartha left his palace and exchanged his silken robes for those of a beggar he met on the road. That night in the 29th year of the life of the Buddha is known as the Blessed Night of the Great Renunciation.

For some time Siddartha wandered about India listening and studying with wise men. Then he settled down to a life of meditation. Several years were devoted to the self-denial of a hermit's life, which brought him to the verge of starvation. Still he could not find the answers to his questions. Finally he decided that truth was not to be found in the extreme of ascetism. In desperation he settled himself beneath a fig tree, determined to stay there quietly in its shade until he discovered the answer he was seeking. He meditated for 49 days and then the answer finally burst on him. Misery and suffering are the lot of mankind because men are filled with selfish desires. One could relieve one's sufferings only by ridding oneself of these desires and their attendant evils: greed, jealousy, and self-concern. One should live for the welfare of others, in compassion and love, seeking goodness, truth, and salvation by following Buddha's precepts. These teachings are known as the Four Noble Truths. Buddha said that happiness was to be found in avoiding all extremes—too much food was as bad as too little, too much concentration on one's self was as bad as too little.

Buddha accepted the Brahmanical idea of reincarnation, which held that each soul inhabits a series of bodies, animal as well as human, and that the sins of one existence are punished by having to live the following life on a lower plane. But Buddha taught that it was possible to be free of this endless chain of lives (and suffering) and to enter what he called *Nirvana*. To attain Nirvana, Buddha laid out a series of precepts called the Noble Eightfold Path. These precepts included right views, right aspirations, right meditation, and right action. In Nirvana, all desires cease, and there is perfect freedom and peace.

The moment at which Siddartha understood the mysteries of life he became the Buddha, the Enlightened One, and the revelation he experienced is called the Enlightenment. He was 35 years of age. Satisfied with the answers he had discovered, he taught his message to all who would listen until he died at the age of eighty. Upon his death, his body was cremated and his ashes and bones were divided and enshrined.

Buddhist monks. Every monk had to follow a strict discipline once he entered a monastery and became an *arhat*, or disciple of the Buddha. He had to wear a yellow robe, keep his head shaved, beg for his food, and meditate daily. Buddhist monks today follow the same practice. The monks here are receiving gifts of food from a family.

Buddha's followers founded monastic communities where his disciples could follow the teachings of the Four Noble Truths. But, in spite of three great councils of Buddhist leaders in 543 B.C., 443 B.C., and 270 B.C., all of which tried to develop Buddha's ideas into a single system, Buddha's followers divided early into a number of sects. These sects had contrasting ideas picked up from various other religious bodies. Thus the Buddhism of India came to be different from that of Tibet, where it absorbed the devil worship of that country, and both were different from the Buddhism that finally swept across Southeast Asia, China, and Japan. Ironically, Buddhism died out in Buddha's own country (page 489), but it did leave its mark on the Brahmanical religion that came to be Hinduism.

VARDHAMANA MAHAVIRA AND JAINISM

Contemporary with the Buddha there lived another great Indian teacher, who was called Vardhamana Mahavira. Mahavira was born at Magadha, on the western Ganges. Like the Buddha, he was of the ruling warrior caste, and like Siddartha he married and had children. Also like Siddartha, he abandoned his high social position and became a pilgrim and a hermit. At the age of 42 enlightenment came to him, and he spent the next thirty years preaching his religion, Jainism, throughout India.

Accepting Indian belief in the endless wheel of rebirth, Mahavira taught that one could escape it by following a five-fold rule of poverty, chastity, honesty, truth, and, most important of all, nonviolence (*ahimsa*) against all things. His followers carried his rules to a greater extreme than he himself did; they were even careful to strike no stone carelessly in passing because even stones felt pain. Agriculture was impossible for the Jains because it involved tearing up the ground and killing insects. Food must be eaten raw because fire, too, had a soul and must not be abused. The sacredness of life included all things, even lice and rats.

When Mahavira died, his followers claimed that he was the last of a series of holy men, or conquerors, whom they called *jinas*. It is from the jinas that Jainism, the Religion of the Conquerors, received its name.

Jainism and Buddhism were alike in that they both accepted karma (page 285), reincarnation, and Nirvana and alike in that both rebelled against the rigid caste system of India, blood sacrifice, and the importance of priests. They differed in that Buddha advocated moderation and the avoidance of extremes, while Mahavira believed asectism was the road to salvation. Perhaps because of its extreme views, Jainism never became one of the world's more popular religions; as did Buddhism; nor did it spread outside India. But Jainism survived nonetheless and today has nearly two million followers.

Neither Buddhism nor Jainism succeeded in replacing Brahmanism in India, but both introduced new concepts of morality and of humaneness, as had the messages of Zoroaster and the Hebrew prophets.

GREAT TEACHERS IN CHINA

In the same century as Mahavira, Buddha, and Zoroaster there lived in China two of her greatest teachers, K'ung Fu-Tzu (K'ung the Great Teacher), known in the western world by the Latinized form of his name, Confucius, and Lao-Tzu, the founder of the philosophy of Taoism. The teachings of both these men had a lasting effect on Chinese civilization.

Lao-Tzu. Lao-Tzu (born 604 B.C.?) is supposed to have been the court librarian in the state of Chou. His profession was indicated by his name, which means "Old Scholar."

Lao-Tzu believed that it was possible to achieve happiness by following the Path or Way, which is called *Tao.* Tao is the impersonal force that permeates and controls the universe. In order to be in harmony with the Tao, men should seek quiet and contemplate nature. As the Tao controls heaven, so heaven controls earth, and earth—nature—controls men. This harmonious relationship has been disturbed by men, who in making laws to regulate government and society seek to impose their designs on the Tao. Laws, according to Lao-Tzu, only encourage people to break them. The way to achieve harmony with the Tao is to do everything by doing nothing, to escape into passivity and contemplation, to live a life that has as little ceremony and regulation as possible. Lao-Tzu scorned wealth and ambition. He abhorred those who tried to advance themselves by seeking power and position. Men should rid themselves of such desires in order to achieve balance and poise with nature. "He who overcomes others is strong; he who overcomes himself is mighty." The best life is the simplest. Men, said Lao-Tzu, should live in villages close enough to each other to hear the cock's crow but far enough away for the owner of the cock to remain unknown. The best government for the Taoist is the one that leaves men free to work out their lives for themselves.

Tradition says that Lao-Tzu taught for many years until the day he set off for the western mountains, never to return. According to legend, as he passed the last gate guarding the boundary of Chou, the gatekeeper asked him to write down his wisdom so that it would not be lost to mankind. The result was the *Tao Te Ching*, which became the holy book of Taoism. Some scholars think that the *Tao Te Ching* may have been written by the followers of Lao-Tzu a couple of centuries later in order to refute the teachings of Confucius. Indeed, that Lao-Tzu lived at all is questionable since we have no real facts about his life.

Lao-Tzu's philosophy appealed to the poor in China, who saw in the way of Tao a means of achieving peace and happiness without worldly goods. Taoism, however, was not to remain a philosophy advocating a simple life in harmony with nature. Lao-Tzu's followers turned his teachings into a religion with priests, temples, and idols. Magic and superstition became important, and people bought strange potions like powdered dragon's teeth to help them find the happiness they wanted to achieve without worldly success. Lao-Tzu himself became a god.

Since its founding, Taoism has been one of the two main forces in Chinese thought. The second is Confucianism, the philosophy taught by Lao-Tzu's younger contemporary, K'ung Fu-Tzu.

K'ung Fu-Tzu, 551–479 B.C. Like Lao-Tzu, K'ung Fu-Tzu, known as Confucius, was a philosopher and sage. He taught not about the gods but about the proper way to live. Like the teachings of Buddha and Zoroaster, those of Confucius were oral and are known to us only through records written long after his death.

Confucius said that the qualities of a good man are manly virtue, self-control, and formal politeness that comes from both the heart and the brain. Manly virtue is reflected in self-respect based on a sense of one's own dignity and of human brotherhood. Self-control is necessary to maintain one's public and private dignity and is shown by presenting a calm and pleasant appearance on all occasions. Formal politeness comes in the ritual and ceremony Confucius thought essential to smooth the relations between parents and children, husbands and wives, rulers and subjects, man and woman. Confucius believed that historically the state had grown out of the institutions of the family. These two social units reflect each other, he said. The parent in one corresponds to the ruler in the other, as does the son to the subject. Respect and obedience within the family and honor and loyalty within the state are the outcomes of proper behavior. All are strengthened by the observance of ritual, which prescribes what correct conduct is. For example, bowing to elders reinforces an attitude of respect to elders. Confucius summed up his principles by saying that one should never do to others what one would not like others to do to oneself.

Confucius opposed the use of force by rulers or parents, saying, "Govern by moral force, keep order by ritual, the people and your sons will come to you of their own accord." To children and citizens he said, "Never disobey. While your elders live, serve them according to ritual; when they die, bury them according to ritual and sacrifice to them according to ritual." It will be noted that Confucius differed from Zoroaster, Buddha, and the Hebrew prophets in believing that ritual was the solution to the problems of human relations and injustice.

THE HELLENIC PHILOSOPHERS, 450–350 B.C.

Confucius had pointed the way toward resolving the problems of right and wrong without introducing questions of divinity or the immortality of the soul; in other words, he had followed the path of philosophy instead of that of religion in his search for truth. Some western thinkers also followed this path. The greatest philosophers to appear in the Mediterranean world at the end of the Early Iron Age were among the Hellenes. Of them the famous sequence of teachers and pupils—Socrates, Plato, and Aristotle—are the greatest.

SOCRATES, 470–399 B.C.

Socrates, son of a poor Athenian stonecutter, left no writings of his own and is known to us only through the sometimes disagreeing descriptions of his pupils Plato and Xenophon. Like Confucius, Socrates had little sympathy with mystic speculations. He taught that the first step toward virtue and a good life is for a man to know himself as he really is, without self delusion, and to behave accordingly. His teaching method consisted of continually asking questions that forced his hearers to clarify for themselves the vague terms they were using, such as *goodness*, *evil*, *courage*, and *fear*, and to realize the difference between what they really knew and what was only opinion. He spent his days walking and talking in public places, surrounded by young people who enjoyed hearing questioned all the things their elders held sacred. Socrates' short body, large bald head, and homely features were hardly those of the ideal Hellenic man, but regardless of his appearance, Socrates was thought to be the wisest man of his day. Eventually the Athenian government came to identify Socrates with the irresponsible behavior of many young Athenians in the period of moral

Socrates. Socrates' schooling had been very limited, but when the Delphic oracle proclaimed him to be the wisest of men, he was encouraged to give up his trade as a stone carver and devote his life to the pursuit of thought. The great Hellenic philosopher had a short stature, snub nose, and square head, features that did not appeal to the Athenians.

confusion following the Peloponnesian Wars. He was tried on charges of atheism (page 205) and of corrupting youth and was condemned to die by drinking hemlock.

According to Plato, who later wrote it from memory, Socrates' final speech before the judges ended, "When my own sons are grown up, I would ask you, my judges, to punish them; and I would have you trouble them as I have troubled you, if they seem to care about riches or anything more than about virtue; or if they pretend to be something when they are really nothing, then reprove them, as I have reproved you, for not caring about that which they ought to care, and for thinking that they are something when they are really nothing. And if you do this then both I and my sons will have received justice at your hands. The hour of parting has come; let us go our way, I to die, and you to live. And which is the better way, only the God knows." Then Socrates, refusing to escape from his prison cell, took the hemlock and calmly discoursed on the immortality of the soul while waiting for death.

PLATO, 427–347 B.C.

Plato, the most famous of Socrates' disciples, differed from his teacher by being aristocratic, handsome, and wealthy. How much the teachings of the master and pupil may have differed cannot be known because most of what is attributed to Socrates comes to us through Plato's writings. Unlike Socrates, the pupil wrote many books. They took the form of dialogues, conversations in which answers emerge from the opposing opinions of various speakers. Many of Plato's 24 dialogues were written in the Academia, a school much like our modern universities but conducted in a public "garden." In Plato's Academia, philosophy, science, and mathematics were taught, and women as well as men were students.

Throughout his discussions, which touched on every aspect of relations among men, Plato expressed a desire to see righteousness triumph. Justice is central to his philosophy. The greatest fact of the universe, he taught, is that it is a system of perfect and eternal "Ideas." Every object known to man is only an imperfect reflection of these Ideas. Man himself, for example, is a poor distorted reflection of the perfect, eternal, ideal "Man." Gods, as man sees them, are partial and fragmentary glimpses of the greater eternal "Divine." Men should train and clarify their minds so they can see more truly the eternal, ideal truths that underlie the universe. If all men do this, justice and righteousness on earth will come ever closer to the Ideal.

Plato was 28 when Socrates was executed, and the close association between them made the younger man the object of suspicion by the political leaders of Athens. So he wandered abroad for twelve years studying in Egypt and Italy; he even went to live in Syracuse. Some argue that his thinking shows that he must also have been in Palestine and India, but his travels for the most part are veiled in mystery. At the age of forty he came home to Athens to open his famous Academia. Among his pupils was one who was also to rank as one of the great thinkers of all time, Aristotle.

ARISTOTLE, 384–322 B.C.

Called "The Stagirite" after his birthplace in Macedonian Stagira, Aristotle was born into a family that had provided physicians for the Macedonian kings. His boyhood is reported to have been reckless, which was apt to be true of the youth of all Macedonians, but little is really known of his early years, including those during which he studied under Plato. Whether he studied for eight years or twenty, as different scholars contend, he emerged as a thinker who idolized Plato at the same time that he quarreled with him on the nature of philosophic truth.

On Plato's death Aristotle went on his own travels, in the course of which he married a king's daughter in Anatolia. Her dowry enriched him so that he did not need to worry about earning a living. In 343 B.C. Aristotle accepted an invitation to teach "sweetness and wisdom" to the thirteen-year-old Prince Alexander of Macedon (page 321). Aristotle taught Alexander until the death of Alexander's father, Philip. Alexander thereupon became king of Macedon and set out to conquer the world. Before departing he gave Aristotle, as a token of his regard, eight hundred talents (equal to several million dollars in modern purchasing power) for scientific equipment and research. He also ordered experts with his army to collect specimens of plants and animals in the countries they conquered and to send them back to Aristotle for study.

Aristotle returned to Athens and established his own school, the *Lyceum*, named after a nearby temple of the god Apollo Lyceus. There he assembled his botanical and biological collections. Never before had so much money or such wide resources been put to the service of scientific inquiry. The number of books in which Aristotle reported his scientific observations varied, according to different sources, between four hundred and a thousand. They included studies in logic, aesthetics, politics, and philosophy, as well as science.

Aristotle's scientific studies were made without the aid of clocks, thermometers, barometers, telescopes, microscopes, or chemical analysis, none of which had yet been invented. Therefore he incorporated much that was unsound and untrue, but in spite of this his encyclopedic writings became the fountainhead of scientific thinking for almost two thousand years.

On the question of righteousness Aristotle taught that the highest human good is the life of reason, which is attained through the practice of the "Golden Mean," that is, moderation in all things. The Buddha, too, taught that extremes are bad regardless of their cause or purpose. Overdoing is as evil as underdoing or not doing. Courage is better than extremes of either rashness or cowardice, liberality is better than extravagance or stinginess, moderation is better than gluttony or self-starvation. Self-control, friendship based on equality, and self-reliance are the marks of a virtuous man. The virtuous man "is his own best friend and takes delight in privacy, whereas the man of no virtue or ability is his own worst enemy and is afraid to be alone with himself."

In the period 1000–350 B.C. mankind entered into new ventures of the mind. Four great religions were born from these inquiries: Buddhism, Zoroastrianism, Jainism, and Judaism. In Hellas and China philosophers proposed new systems of how man should deal with man, and in Hellas the first steps toward scientific research were made in the school of Aristotle. The riddles of the existence of evil were not solved, nor was there even the beginning of agreement on how to secure justice among men. But the achievements of thought were so widespread and of such quality that the Early Iron Age is marked forever as a time of great intellectual accomplishment far beyond the attainments of the Bronze Age.

People, Places, and Terms

Isaiah
Jeremiah
Ezekiel
Amos
Zoroaster
Gautama Buddha
Mahavira
Lao-Tzu
Socrates
Plato

Ahuramazda
Aristotle

Delphi
Magadha

major prophets
minor prophets
pantheon
monolatry

Buddhism
Nirvana
Noble Eightfold Path
Jainism
ahimsa
Jina
Tao
dialogue
lyceum
sibyl

Mastering the Reading

1. What answers were given to the question, Why is there evil and injustice? What forms of communication did man use to reach the gods?
2. Why did the prophets advocate social justice? What is the difference between monolatry and monotheism?
3. How did Zoroastrianism offer hope to every man?
4. What were the Four Noble Truths of Buddhism? In what ways was Jainism similar to Buddhism? How did the path to Nirvana differ in the two religions?

5. What did Lao-Tzu dislike about governments? According to Taoism, how does man achieve happiness? How did Taoism conflict with Confucianism?
6. What were the principles involved in Confucius' code of conduct? Why is he called a philosopher, not a religious leader?
7. Why were Socrates, Plato, and Aristotle considered the great Hellenic philosophers?

Interpreting the Text

What Judeo-Christian concepts concerning man's relationship to man and to God began to take shape during the time of the prophets and Zoroaster?

Exploring Beyond the Text

1. Dr. Martin Luther King credits the Indian leader Mahatma Gandhi with influencing him in the use of non-violent, passive resistance. Where did Gandhi get his ideas?
2. Make a study of the modern use of names of gods and goddesses in advertisements. What must the consumer know about each of the gods or goddesses in order to understand what the ad and product stand for?

Looking Back to the Early Iron Age

Civilization revived after the collapse of the Bronze Age and spread during the Early Iron Age. It reached new territories in the west on the European continent; it reappeared and continued along new lines in India and China. At the same time, the first links between east and west were created by the Achaemenid Empire of Persia.

Four distinct civilizations established themselves in this period: the Hellenic, the Indian, the Chinese, and the Middle Eastern which was a synthesis of the old cultures of Egypt and Mesopotamia and the new contributions made by the Iron Age peoples of the Fertile Crescent. Each civilization had its individual style of life, political and social organization, and religious formulations. In the age ahead, these four civilizations would be brought into permanent contact with each other as the result of the campaigns of Alexander the Great. His conquests, first in Europe and then in the Middle East and central Asia, opened a new chapter in the relationships of the peoples of the Eurasian continent.

MAN TRIES AGAIN, THE EARLY IRON AGE, 1000-350 B.C.

	MESOPOTAMIA	EGYPT	SYRIA-PALESTINE	ANATOLIA
1000-800 B.C.	Assyrians rise to power	Two governments: Tanis and Thebes Libyan rulers succeed Tanite kings	Phoenician cities Hebrew kingdom Israel, Judah	Invasions Hellenic settlement in Ionia Urartu controls Anatolia
800-600 B.C.	Assyrians control Fertile Crescent and gain Egypt	Kushite kings at Thebes Assyrians conquer Egypt	Assyrian conquest; Israel falls	Phrygians establish loose kingdom Kingdom of Lydia Ionian cities Coinage invented
600-400 B.C.	Kingdom of Media New Babylonian (Chaldean) Empire Rise of Persians Persian Empire	Saitic family expels Assyrians; inaugurates 26th Dynasty Persian conquest	Chaldean conquest; Judah falls Persian conquest Judaeans return to Palestine; have religious but not political freedom	Croesus king of Lydia Persian conquest

Some Questions to Answer

1. Who were some of the empire builders of the Early Iron Age and how did their motivations, methods, and locations differ from those of the empire builders of the Bronze Age?
2. Measuring the stages of development of man by the materials he relied on (stone, copper, bronze, etc.) is only one of several ways of designating the ages of man. What other systems can you think of? How do each of these systems break down and measure man's development from ancient times to the present?
3. List as many great personalities from the Early Iron Age as you can. Include men from India, China, Persia, Israel, and Hellas. Then try to

AEGEAN	MEDITERRANEAN	INDIA	CHINA
"Dark Age" Dorian settlement Ionian migration	Etruscans established in Italy Carthage founded	Vedic Age	Western Chou Feudalism
Homeric Greece Homer, Hesiod Colonization Spartans conquer Messenia Age of Tyrants	Rome founded Colonization by Phoenicians and Hellenes	Tiny kingdoms in north India	Middle Chou
Cleisthenes' reforms in Athens Ionian revolt Persian Wars Supremacy of Athens Delian League Socrates Peloponnesian Wars	Rome under Etruscan rule Conflict between colonizing powers; Carthage gains supremacy Rome frees itself from Etruscan rule; sets up Republic; sacked by the Gauls Hellenes and Carthaginians fight for Sicily	Rise of Magadha Buddha and Mahavira Persians invade Indus Valley	Coinage Iron Lao-Tzu (?) and Confucius Eastern Chou Conflict between states of The Center and states of The Ring

think of some who lived during the Bronze Age in Egypt, Sumer, and Babylon. What was the occupation of most of them? Did the people from Iron Age Hellas and Iron Age Israel have the same occupations as those from Bronze Age Egypt, Sumer, and Babylon? Why? What other patterns do you see? What conclusions might you draw from your lists about these cultures? Why must you be cautious?

4. What reasons can you give to explain why the arts, literature, religious ideas, and philosophy flourished in many different parts of the world from 650 to 400 B.C.? What similarities and differences existed among them? Why?
5. What are some of the characteristics that distinguish the Hellenic, Indian, Chinese, and Middle Eastern styles of life?

Using Documents as Evidence

Pericles was the famed leader of Athens in its period of greatest glory. Thucydides, one of the greatest historians of all times, reported Pericles' words at a public funeral for the men of Athens who had died in a war against Sparta in 431 B.C.

THE FUNERAL ORATION FOR NATIONAL HEROES

Our form of government does not enter into rivalry with the institutions of others. We do not copy our neighbors but are an example to them. It is true that we are called a democracy, for the administration is in the hands of the many and not of the few. . . . The law secures equal justice to all alike in their private disputes, but the claim of excellence is also recognized. When a citizen is in any way distinguished, he is preferred for the public service. . . .

And we have not forgotten to provide for our weary spirits many relaxations from toil. We have regular games and sacrifices throughout the year. . . . Because of the greatness of our city, the fruits of the whole earth flow in upon us. . . .

Then, again, our military training is in many respects superior to that of our adversaries. Our city is thrown open to the world, and we never expel a foreigner or prevent him from seeing or learning anything of which the secret if revealed to an enemy might profit him. . . . And in the matter of education, whereas they from early youth are always undergoing laborious exercises that are to make them brave, we live at ease and yet are equally ready to face the perils that they face. . . .

We are lovers of the beautiful, yet simple in our tastes, and we cultivate the mind without loss of manliness. Wealth we employ, not for talk and ostentation, but when there is a real use for it. . . . We alone regard a man who takes no interest in public affairs not as a harmless but as a useless character. . . . To sum up: I say that Athens is the school of Hellas. . . . There are mighty monuments of our power that will make us the wonder of this and of succeeding ages. For we have compelled every land and every sea to open a path for our valor. . . . Such is the city for whose sake these men nobly fought and died. . . .

In reading this document, you should try to determine what parts are fact and what parts are opinion. It is clearly a *fact* that Athens fought a war with Sparta in 431 B.C. But it is Pericles' *opinion* that "because of the greatness of our city [Athens], the fruits of the whole earth flow in. . . ."

Place Pericles' words in context by answering the following questions on the basis of what you have read in the text. Were all of the men of Athens citizens? Which groups were excluded? Did women have a role in politics? Were similar restrictions common in other societies of that time?

PART 4

The Growth of Civilization

350-30 B.C.

Alexander the Great was born in 355 B.C. In eleven years he marched across nearly all the civilized world and by 323 B.C., the year of his death, he had opened up central Asia to the peoples of the eastern Mediterranean. His conquests enlarged the knowledge of the world to civilized people and his armies passed Hellenic ideas and ways of life to peoples from Asia Minor to central Asia.

Alexander was the first of several outstanding rulers to live in the period from 350 to 30 B.C. This period had many great empire builders, politicians, and military geniuses. Under their guidance, Rome grew from a power in central Italy to the conqueror of the Mediterranean. Nearly half the Indian subcontinent was united under one dynasty. China reorganized and expanded its territory north, south, and west into an empire that pushed into the lands of the barbarians.

During this period, the civilized areas increased their territories to such an extent that they bordered on each other across Eurasia. Great empires appeared in the west, the Middle East and Asia. At the same time, civilization continued to spread to the barbarians, who, through trade and raids, absorbed the arts and techniques of civilization.

16

The Rise of Macedon and the Empire of Alexander the Great

350–300 B.C.

Macedonia was a region larger than any of the Hellenic states. It extended from Thrace on the east to the borders of Epirus and Thessaly on the south. From its forested mountainsides came the timber, pitch, and turpentine needed for Hellenic ships; and from the narrow valleys and broad fertile plain opening on the coast of the Aegean came wool, leather, and wheat.

The people of Macedonia were a mixture of tribes descended from native inhabitants and the Dorian invaders who had swept south centuries before. The Macedonian royal family claimed descent from the Dorian princes of Argos in the Peloponnesus, and their claim was acknowledged by the Hellenes, who allowed a Macedonian king to take part in the Olympic Games—a privilege not extended to foreigners. The people of Macedonia spoke a different dialect from the Hellenes, however, and only the nobles considered themselves to be Greek. The rest of the population thought of themselves as a separate and distinctive people, the Macedonians.

The inhabitants of southern Macedonia gradually learned farming, gathered in towns, and traded with the Hellenic colonists who had settled along the peninsula of Chalcidice (see map, page 193). Following the Persian Wars the kings of Macedon invited the Hellenes to visit their court. Artists and poets spread Hellenic culture while friendly trade relations were established between the city-states and Macedon.

In the early fourth century B.C. many Hellenes still looked on the Macedonians as illiterate and vulgar peasant farmers and herders. But they were mistaken to underestimate the abilities of these rugged northerners. The Macedonians were ready to unite into a national state, the first in the Aegean area, and to play a greater part on the world stage. Philip II provided the leadership necessary to accomplish this.

THE REIGN OF PHILIP II, 359–336 B.C.

Philip II of Macedon became king at the age of 23. He was not a stranger to the Hellenes. For three years he had been a hostage at Thebes, where he had studied the military ideas of the great Epaminondas (page 231). He had also keenly observed the weaknesses and rivalries of the Hellenes and had made plans accordingly. On his return to Macedonia, he set himself the tasks of reorganizing the army, and of increasing the state income by seizing nearby gold mines in Thrace. This would provide him with the cash necessary to build his army, bribe his opponents, and build a fleet once he had gained an outlet on the Aegean Sea. He acquired this outlet by conquering the Hellenic towns on the peninsula of Chalcidice. He wanted to make a strong, united Macedon the leader of Hellas, and he had the ambition, the talent, and the will to do it. "Philip," said an Athenian orator, "to gain empire and power, had an eye knocked out, his collarbone broken, his arm and leg maimed; he abandoned to fortune any part of his body she cared to take, so that honor and glory might be the portion of the rest."

Philip's greatest contribution to the success of the Macedonians was the reorganization of the Macedonian army. He recruited his troops on a territorial basis and banded them into regiments with special titles and battle honors. Leadership was provided by the nobles, who were formed into a special cavalry corps known as the "King's Companions." They gave their loyalty and that of their kinsmen and troops to Philip personally. Philip then took the basic idea of Epaminondas (page 231), that of massing the troops in a solid column, called the *phalanx*. But Philip improved on the basic idea by leaving enough space between the files of the phalanx to allow quick and easy movement. The body of men in the center was flanked on each wing by cavalry. This cavalry Philip used as an attacking force, and trained it to move as a single unit. The combined force of infantry and cavalry fought together as one mass.

The Macedonian phalanx, which Alexander wielded for world conquest, was an invincible force. Each man bore a huge lance, 24 feet in length. While the phalanx advanced to engage the enemy, the cavalry rode into the enemy's flanks. This reliance on mass cavalry attack was something new in warfare. Supporting these tactics were curious engines called *catapults*, which could pitch ammunition some three hundred yards, and battering rams, each protected by a little house within which men operated the machine that beat down the walls surrounding a besieged city. Unlike the Hellenes, Philip did not confine sieges to blockades but attacked as well. He also was willing to fight at all seasons, not just in summer.

With his newly organized and well-disciplined army united by a common spirit and by new techniques, Philip was fully prepared to pursue his plans.

There was only one sign that anyone in Hellas was aware of the peril growing in the north. The orator Demosthenes, in a series of famous speeches against Philip known as *The Philippics*, begged the Athenians to beware of the danger Philip posed to Hellenic independence. Demosthenes was opposed by Isocrates, the leader of a pro-Macedonian party that approved of Philip's plan to form a union of the Hellenic city-states.

The position of Isocrates' party may seem strange without stopping for a moment to have a glimpse back to the past and Hellas' relations with Persia. Some fifty years earlier the Hellenes had directly witnessed an upheaval in Persia caused by a revolt of the satraps. The Hellenes had become involved when Cyrus the Younger, satrap in Asia Minor in 401 B.C., decided that he wished to be king. He set about collecting a great army to help him with his plans. As was customary, he invited mercenaries to join his forces, among them some thirteen thousand Hellenic troops at loose ends after the Peloponnesian Wars. These troops marched into the heart of the Persian domains and were victorious in the battle of Cunaxa near Babylon. But they were left leaderless when Cyrus was killed, the native soldiers fled, and their generals were murdered. What to do? The Hellenes, having marched into Mesopotamia to reach Cunaxa, found themselves stranded deep in enemy country with no commanders and no guide to show them the way back.

Discipline and training came to the rescue. The remaining ten thousand men organized themselves into a city-state, drew up laws, and elected new leaders, of whom one was the Athenian historian Xenophon (page 240). Then they began a retreat northward along the Tigris River. The enemy dogged their footsteps, harassing them at every turn; but the Hellenes passed through the plains and reached the mountains of Armenia. Keeping up their courage through snow and freezing weather, hunger and fatigue, they finally glimpsed the Black Sea. A great shout went up and passed from rank to rank: *thalassa, thalassa,* the sea, the sea. Now these bone-weary soldiers knew the march was won. A few days later they were home, and Xenophon sat down to write of their trials in a little book called *Anabasis* (military expedition). Xenophon's *Anabasis* became a textbook for generations of Hellenic schoolboys. It showed that a hardy band of disciplined Hellenic soldiers could meet the might of the Persian Empire, defeat it, and return home in safety. The March of the Ten Thousand had exposed a weakness in mighty Persia and gave the Hellenes the idea that Asia Minor might be a field for new conquest and settlement. This, however, would not be possible unless the city-states of Hellas joined forces to defeat the Persians. Isocrates believed that Philip might be just the man to unite the Hellenes and carry out such a plan, and Philip did all he could to foster such a view.

The Athenians, meanwhile, could not make up their minds whose position to support: Isocrates' or Demosthenes'. While the Athenians waited to see how events would develop, Philip copied a Persian technique of acquiring support by secretly financing pro-Macedonian parties in the major cities of Hellas by suitable gifts of gold.

It was not long before Philip's policies paid off, and he was able to obtain a foothold in central Greece. Between 356 and 346 B.C. a quarrel broke out between Thebes and Phocis over the sacred shrine of Apollo. The Thebans called on Philip for help. He was only too glad to support the Theban cause, for it enabled him to pose as the champion of Apollo. In return for his services, Philip was admitted to the inner councils of the Hellenes.

Philip's maneuverings began to alarm the Athenians. When he appeared in Greece at the head of an army in 338 B.C., the Athenians called on the Thebans to form a defensive alliance. The Thebans were persuaded to put aside their quarrels with Athens (Athens had been an ally of Phocis), and the two joined forces. The adversaries met at Chaeronea in Boeotia. Though the citizen-soldiers of Hellas fought bravely, the well-drilled and seasoned Macedonians won. Philip's tactics had made him master of Greece.

Philip now proceeded to think about conquering Asia Minor. A congress of the Hellenes voted him the necessary ships and men for the undertaking and placed him in command of the allied forces. But it was not Philip's fate to lead the Macedonians east. While celebrating a daughter's marriage, he was struck down by an assassin's dagger. The task of conquering the Persians fell to Philip's son Alexander.

ALEXANDER THE GREAT

Few men in the history of mankind have captured the world's imagination as did Alexander of Macedon. His death at the age of 33 ended eleven years of war during which he never lost a battle while overthrowing the greatest empire the world had yet seen, Achaemenid Persia. Under his successors, the east and the Middle East were organized into a cluster of kingdoms that evolved a mixture of Hellenic ideas and customs with those of the Orient, the cultural synthesis that we call Hellenistic. What the world would have been like had Alexander lived is much debated. By dying early he escaped the consequences of any mistakes he had made, and so his reputation glittered the more gloriously.

THE BACKGROUND AND PERSONALITY OF ALEXANDER

What is actually known about Alexander is but a drop in the flood of romantic fictions that collected around his name as soon as he died. For over a thousand years stories of the marvelous *Iskander* (founder of ancient cities) enthralled listeners around the campfires of nomads from central Asia to inner Arabia.

Alexander was the son of the astute soldier and politician Philip II, but his heredity was colored also by his mother, the violent and strange princess Olympias of Epirus (now Albania). Her savage nature was only thinly cloaked by the manners of civilization. One of her notions was that the pet snake that shared her bed incarnated a god, and she may have given the young Alexander the idea that his father was the god, not Philip.

As unruly as his mother, Alexander was sometimes out of favor with his father. Nevertheless, Philip provided his son with the best education possible, for he not only trained him in all the arts of war but also persuaded the great philosopher Aristotle (page 309) to be Alexander's tutor. Aristotle found Alexander to be a receptive student and instilled in him a love of all things Hellenic. Alexander was fond of saying that while he owed his life to his father, he owed to Aristotle the knowledge of how to live it well.

In appearance Alexander was ruddy of complexion and wore his hair in a bushy mane brushed back from his forehead. His habit of being clean shaven set the style in the Mediterranean world for the next four hundred years. His eyes were large and expressive, and his physical beauty appealed to the Hellenes. The strength and vigor of his physique made observers forget that he was only of medium height.

Alexander soon developed into a splendid athlete. He was bold and fearless with his rough riding companions, and when he tamed the horse Bucephalus (Beautiful Head, from the white blaze on his black forehead), his father is reputed to have told his son to seek a kingdom "suited to your powers; Macedonia is too small for you." Whether he would have any conquests left to make worried Alexander when Philip won victory after

Alexander the Great. Alexander was born while Philip was campaigning. The Hellenes, who loved coincidences, liked to believe that Philip received three messages at once: that one of his generals had just defeated the Illyrians; that his race horse had won a victory at the Olympic Games; and that at Pella, the Macedonian capital, a son had been born, the future Alexander III. Another legend told how the Temple of Diana at Ephesus, one of the Seven Wonders of the ancient world, had burned down the night of Alexander's birth, because, so it was said, the goddess was preoccupied with bringing Alexander into the world.

victory. "My father," he said to his companions, "will get ahead of us in everything; he will leave no great task for me to share with you."

At the age of eighteen Alexander fought at Chaeronea. Philip, dealing lightly with Athens for its part in the war, sent Alexander with a military escort to carry home the ashes of the cremated Athenian soldiers. This was the only time that the prince was to set foot in the cultural center of Hellas.

In these years Alexander gathered around himself friends of whom Philip disapproved and whom he banished. After his father's death Alexander recalled them, and their fame is associated with his for the rest of his career. These companions were Nearchus, his admiral; Harpalus, his treasurer; and Ptolemy, one of his generals. His closest companion was Hephaestaion. Hephaestaion and Bucephalus were with Alexander through ten of his eleven years of campaigning in Asia, and their deaths seem to have been among the few things that the conqueror ever regretted.

THE LEADERSHIP OF GREECE

Alexander became king of Macedon at twenty. Before embarking on the war against Persia, for which his father had made all the plans, the young king guaranteed that Europe would be quiet in his rear. He marched south into Greece in the autumn of 336 B.C. and without opposition reached Corinth, where he summoned the Hellenic city-states to a conference. All except Sparta answered his summons and agreed to his wish to be elected commander, in his father's place, of an all-Hellenic attack on Persia. The following spring Alexander marched north into the Balkan peninsula into the lands that today are Yugoslavia, Bulgaria, and Rumania. There he destroyed all opposition from the half-civilized tribes, but rumors of his death reached Greece and touched off an anti-Macedonian rising headed by the city of Thebes. Marching three hundred miles in two weeks, Alexander arrived before Thebes and demanded its surrender. When the Thebans elected to fight, Alexander attacked the city and completely destroyed it except for the house where the poet Pindar had lived. All surviving Thebans were sold into slavery. With this vivid example of the punishment for rebellion before them, balanced by Alexander's respect for Hellenic culture, the Hellenic cities accepted Alexander as their leader once again. Hellas would offer no further trouble during Alexander's absence in Asia.

THE MACEDONIAN ARMY

Alexander started his campaigns in Asia at the head of the best-organized, best-equipped fighting force the world had yet seen. He had adopted his father's army and had the loyal support of his generals. He maintained the honor guard of the King's Companions and organized corps of quartermasters, engineers, well-diggers, scientists and poets and historians. By the standards of the time Alexander's army was not a large force, but it was extremely well trained and coordinated.

Alexander's army consisted of about thirty thousand footsoldiers and five thousand cavalry. The latest infantry equipment included helmets, breastplates (cuirasses), leg armor (greaves), shields, swords, and sarissas. The last was a long, heavy spear with a hooked end on the blade. The cavalry used blankets in place of saddles and, like all ancient horsemen, the Macedonians rode without stirrups.

Once engaged in battle, commands were given by word of mouth, trumpets, flags, and smoke signals. The troops were clothed and fed by the army. A soldier's food was bread, olives, salted fish, and dried or salted meat. No organized hospital service existed until introduced by the Romans (page 269).

After the conquest of Persia, soldiers were recruited in the regions that produced the most warlike men, and they were trained to fight in the Macedonian manner beside the Macedonian recruits. During the first eight years of campaigning, recruits were sent out from Macedonia alone.

The fleet that sailed along the shore paralleling the marching army consisted of 180 ships. Alexander lacked, however, the most powerful Hellenic navy, the Athenian, which did not send any ships as Athens remained neutral in the coming war. Its sympathies were divided between the anti-Persians and the even more outspoken anti-Macedonians.

As the commander-in-chief, Alexander considered his proper place to be the forefront of the march and battle. He was many times wounded: on the neck, head, shoulder, and thigh in the early battles of the war. In the later campaigns he suffered several more injuries, a broken leg, and a pierced lung. He had dysentery and fever several times before the last fatal fever. But aside from his military prowess and daring, perhaps not the least of Alexander's gifts was his ability to inspire confidence in his generals and men, and to hold their support even through the most difficult trials.

CONQUEST OF ASIA MINOR AND EGYPT

Alexander planned to occupy the whole coast of the eastern Mediterranean before striking inland at the heart of Persia. This would enable him to hold the important naval bases from which an attack might otherwise be launched on Macedonia while he was engaged in Asia. It took him four years to occupy the coast. In 334 B.C., after sacrificing to the gods on the site of ancient Troy, the site of battle of his legendary ancestor Achilles, he won his first engagement against the Persians at the Granicus River. Asia Minor lay open to invasion. Alexander marched to inland Gordium, where a famous incident occurred. In one of Gordium's temples, a knot that seemed to have no beginning or end was tied on a chariot shaft. It had been prophesied that whoever untied the knot would become master of the world. In a characteristically impatient gesture, Alexander cut the knot with his sword. Gordium was an important station on the royal road running through the heart of Persia to its distant capital at Susa. Instead of following the road, Alexander kept to his original plan of destroying Persian sea power, and he continued down to Syria and Phoenicia. Meanwhile, Darius III had regrouped his forces and had advanced to the narrow pass at Issus. Once again the superior Persian forces were ineffective. Alexander defeated the Persian army, though Darius escaped. Again refusing to be diverted from his plan to occupy the whole Mediterranean coast, Alexander did not follow Darius into Persia but continued into Phoenicia. Tyre, the center of Persian naval power, fell after a seven-month siege, and enfeebled Egypt became Alexander's in the autumn of 332 B.C.

While wintering in Egypt, Alexander laid the foundation of the first of the more than sixty cities named after himself that he built across the former Persian Empire. Alexandria in Egypt became the greatest port in the Mediterranean (page 334). During his Egyptian visit Alexander followed the example of the Persian kings; as he had done at Troy, he sacrificed to the gods of Egypt and had himself hailed as the son of Egyptian god Amon.

CONQUEST OF MESOPOTAMIA AND PERSIA

With Persian naval power effectively smashed and the eastern Mediterranean safely in his hands, Alexander marched out of Egypt in 331 B.C. through Palestine and Syria and turned eastward to the Euphrates. At Gaugamela in Assyria he once again met the Persian host. The great battle that took place there decided the fate of the Persian Empire. All the might and splendor of the Persian forces were aligned against Alexander. The Macedonians, however, proved invincible. After a bitter fight, the Persians were routed, and though Darius once again escaped, Alexander found the great Persian Empire his for the taking. Babylon surrendered without a fight, and Alexander gave his troops a month's leave, which he and they spent in drunken carousing. He permitted the Babylonians to rebuild all the temples that had been destroyed after their last revolt against the Persians, and he sacrificed to Marduk and the other Babylonian gods according to rites directed by the Chaldean priests. He appointed a Persian who had fought well against him earlier to be his satrap over Babylon, but he kept the posts of military commandant and supervisor of the treasury in Macedonian hands, a practice he followed in other places.

After Babylon Alexander seized Susa, the administrative capital of the Persian Empire, which had a royal treasure in gold worth $60,000,000. Among the many royal treasures were jars of water from the Danube and the Nile, which Persian monarchs had brought back with them as symbols of their conquests, and 250,000 pounds of royal purple dye whose colors were still fresh after two hundred years in storage. The bronze statues of two Athenian heroes, seized when Xerxes had burned Athens, were found in the treasury and returned, at Alexander's command, to Athens.

In January, 330 B.C., a month's march through wild mountains brought Alexander and his troops, strengthened by fresh recruits from Macedonia, to Persepolis. There were the tombs of the Achaemenid kings and their greatest palaces. The treasury held over $155,000,000 in gold that the Persian monarchs had withdrawn from circulation. To carry away the loot of furniture and other wealth of the fallen city took twenty thousand mules and five thousand camels. To dramatize the fact that Achaemenid rule had ended and as a token of Hellenic revenge for the Persian burning of Athens, Alexander ordered the palace at Persepolis burned to the ground.

CONQUEST OF CENTRAL ASIA AND NORTHWEST INDIA

Alexander was not content with the riches of the Persian Empire. He could not bear to rest while there were conquests still to be made. Between 330 and 324 B.C. he continued to march east, winning victory after victory until his exhausted troops would go no farther. In these six years he marched through the Iranian plateau, beyond the Oxus and Jaxartes rivers to the Indus, and attempted to continue on to the valley of the Ganges.

The conquest of central Asia and India started in March, 330 B.C. Alexander resumed his pursuit of Darius, who had sent his harem and baggage train north to the Caspian shore. Darius himself planned to withdraw eastward into Bactria in central Asia. Darius burned everything behind him in a scorched-earth policy. When Alexander drew near, the Bactrians stabbed Darius and fled. Shocked at the murder, Alexander pun-

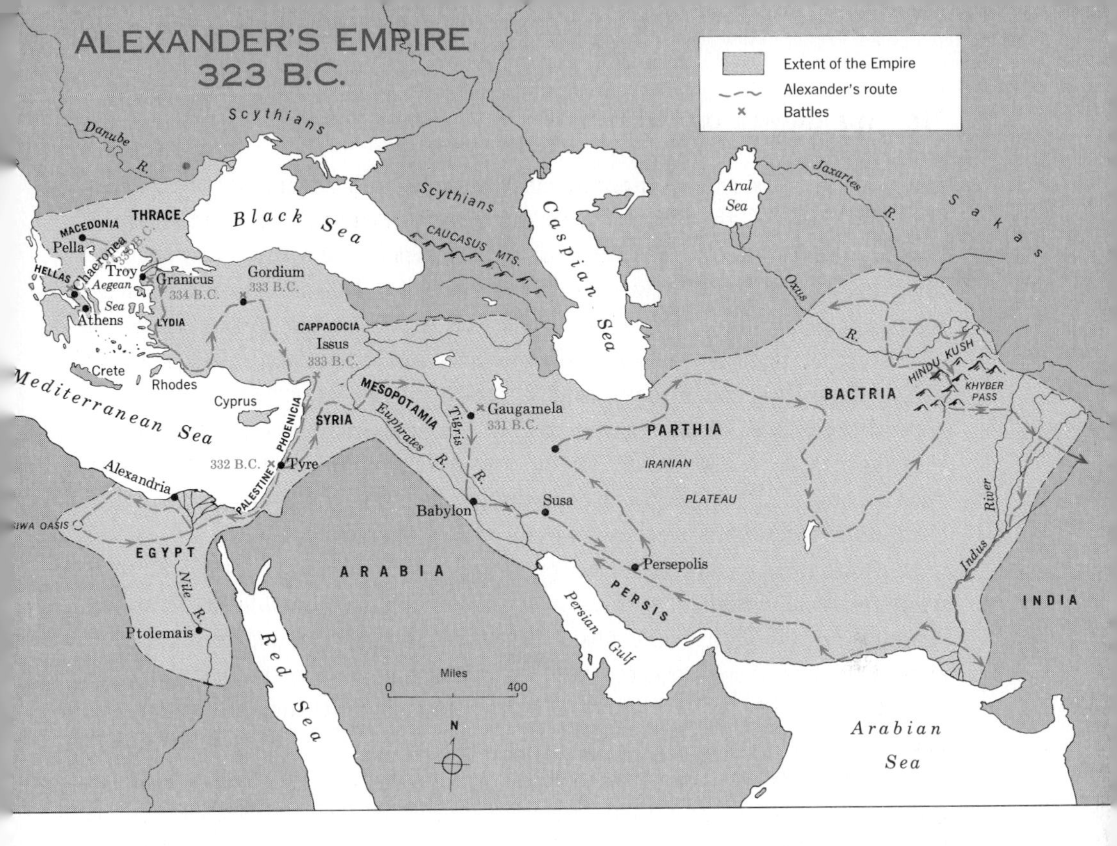

ished the assassins and sent Darius' body to his family, to whom he had offered protection. The death of the Persian monarch was interpreted by the Macedonian troops as meaning that the war was over and that they could return home. When the troops came to realize that they were to march still farther into Asia, they mutinied. It was only by an impassioned speech that Alexander temporarily rewon the support of his soldiers, but shortly thereafter a plot against his life came to light. The trial and executions of the friends and generals who were involved in the plot made it clear to Alexander that his plans were beyond the scope of his followers and that his dream would be fulfilled only at great cost.

In 327 B.C. Alexander followed the path of the Persian conquerors of earlier times and passed through Afghanistan and the Khyber Pass down into India. In the Indus Valley a huge Indian army, supported by large contingents of elephants and cavalry, was defeated in the most severe fighting of the entire campaign. Having no idea of the great expanse of India that lay to the east and south, Alexander started to push on. But his army was completely exhausted by their marches through some of the most rugged mountains and most barren deserts on earth. For six years they had been increasingly homesick for Macedonia, particularly when passing through parts of the world they had never heard of before. When the monsoon rains set in, the army mutinied. Alexander was forced to abandon his plans to conquer the world and turn back to Babylon. While he went overland, his admiral, Nearchus, organized a fleet to go by sea from the Indus to the Persian Gulf. Arriving in Babylon in 324 B.C., Alexander set about organizing his conquests and making plans to expand his empire over the western Mediterranean to the Atlantic. In Babylon, a year later, he caught a fever. As he lay dying, the Macedonian army, man by man, filed by his bed to bid their commander farewell. On June 13, 323 B.C. Alexander succumbed to his illness. He was 33 years old.

In the ancient world Alexander acquired fame attained by few other men. Modern evaluation of his character finds much that could be improved. There is no doubt that militarily he excelled both in the long-term strategy necessary to win a prolonged war and in the immediate tactics necessary to win on the battlefield. There is no evidence of his peacetime capability. Many scholars have seen in Alexander the builder of a world in which Europeans and Orientals would cooperate. They believe that he was the proponent of the brotherhood of man and think that had he lived he would have been able to accomplish such an intermingling of east and west. These beliefs, however, cannot be validated. Nevertheless, the immediate result of Alexander's conquests was to open up the lands of the Persian Empire to the influence of the west, and to break down the barriers that had isolated the east from the Mediterranean.

THE SUCCESSORS TO ALEXANDER

Upon Alexander's death, his empire fell apart. He did not leave behind him a son of age, as had Philip, trained in the arts of war and statesmanship. Dissension immediately broke out among the ambitious generals of the army, and there was no one force to keep them together. The generals proclaimed allegiance to the unborn child of Alexander's Persian wife, but the soldiers favored Alexander's half-brother, the subnormal Philip III. Between 323 B.C., the year of Alexander's death, and 310 B.C., the year of the assassination of his son, Alexander IV, Alexander's wife, half-brother, sister, sister-in-law. nephew, and mother were all murdered, along with several of his generals, in the intrigues and scramble for empire. The empire itself fared little better.

THE NEW DYNASTS, THE DIADOCHI

Out of the fragments of the empire arose three great kingdoms that maintained their independence until the rise of Roman power in the Middle East. These were Macedon, Egypt, and Syria.

Ptolemy established the Kingdom of Egypt, ruling from the great new city of Alexandria, where the conqueror lay entombed. This kingdom included part of North Africa, the island of Cyprus, and, until captured by Syria, several cities along the coast of Syria-Palestine. Ptolemy's dynasty endured longer than any of the other Diadochi (successors), coming to an end only with the suicide of the famous Cleopatra VII three centuries later. Ptolemic Egypt became rich and prosperous, and with its strong navy and military strength, it became a leading center of civilization once again.

Seleucus reigned over a huge territory that in the beginning stretched from the Aegean Sea to the Indus River. Subsequent losses reduced this territory to Syria proper, the Tigris-Euphrates Valley, Media and parts of Anatolia. India was lost when Seleucus returned it to native Indian rulers in exchange for five hundred war elephants, while the provinces of Iran fell back under the rule of native princes until the rise of the Parthian kingdom. Under the Seleucid dynasty, Babylon enjoyed the last revival of the ancient Mesopotamian culture on the banks of the Tigris and Euphrates.

The descendants of Antigonus, another of Alexander's generals, had to settle for Macedonia. The Macedonian (Antigonid) kingdom also laid claim to the Hellenic city-states and the islands of the Aegean Sea. Macedon was a strong state by virtue of its natural resources and its hardy population.

For some fifty years, Alexander's generals and their descendants jockeyed among themselves, and warfare was continual. Macedon and Egypt battled over control of the Aegean; Macedon and Syria fought over Asia Minor and Thrace; Syria and Egypt were rivals in western Asia. In Greece the Hellenic city-states had lost out. They had attempted to maintain their independence after Alexander's death by forming two leagues. These leagues never included all the city-states, and, as usual, rivalry within them diminished their strength. Sparta would not join the Achaean League of the Peloponnesian states unless the Spartan king, Cleomenes, was made commander-in-chief. The league members refused and, fearful of Spartan power, called in the Macedonians to back up their decision. Henceforth Macedon controlled the league. Athens held aloof from the Aetolian

League, which had been formed by the states of central Greece, but neither it nor the members of that league were strong enough to outweigh the Macedonians in political power. Hellas, divided and weak, declined in importance, and only Athens maintained its position through its continued cultural supremacy.

Until Alexander's time, the Persian Empire was largely unknown territory. Travelers from the west had visited Persepolis and Babylon, but the lands to the east were only vaguely defined, and there was no knowledge at all of the Indian subcontinent or China. In the wake of the Macedonians came colonists, merchants, artists, philosophers, and scientists. They were especially important in western Asia, where the cultures of Hellas and the east merged into the synthesis known as Hellenistic, and which the Romans later built on when they created a new empire binding the west to the Middle East.

People, Places, and Terms

Philip II	the Diadochi	Granicus River	Hellenistic
Alexander		Issus	levy
Xenophon	Macedonia	Tyre	commissary
Epaminondas	Chalcidice	Alexandria	quarter-master
Ptolemy	Chaeronea		Ptolemaic
Seleucus	Gordium	phalanx	*Anabasis*
Antigonus	Gaugamela	catapult	

Mastering the Reading

1. How did the Hellenes regard their Macedonian neighbors? How did Philip II prepare Macedon to gain control of the Hellenes?
2. What were the chief arguments of Demosthenes and Isocrates? While they and all the Athenians debated, what action did Philip take?
3. Why did Alexander's personality and appearance appeal to the Hellenes?
4. What were Alexander's most important victories between 334 and 330 B.C.?
5. What happened to Alexander's plans for India? What were the territories of the Diadochi? How did they fare?

Interpreting the Text

1. Aristotle defined a tragic hero of a drama as one who meets a bad end because of a flaw in his own character. How might he have defined the character of his old student, Alexander?
2. What did Alexander leave as a legacy to the world?
3. What psychological and organizational techniques did he employ to conquer and control such diverse groups as the Hellenes on the one hand and the Egyptians or the Syrians, on the other?

Exploring Beyond the Text

1. Prepare a meeting of the Panhellenic council to discuss the question, Should Philip II of Macedon be chosen head of the Hellenes? Prepare arguments, and show what animosities existed among the Hellenes. Use *The Philippics* and other sources in preparation.
2. "Alexander was as much influenced by Aristotle as he was by his father, Philip." Discuss this statement and defend your opinion.
3. Read in several sources, including Plutarch's *Lives*, about Alexander. How would you evaluate him as a youth? leader? conqueror? soldier?

Working with the Map

1. Draw a map showing the resources of Greece and Macedonia. Which had the most important resources for ancient peoples? What geographical and climatic factors were responsible? How?
2. Compare the map of Alexander's empire (page 327) with that of the Persian empire (page 172). What areas were held by both? only by Persia? only by Alexander?

17

The Hellenistic Age

300–30 B.C.

The Hellenistic period lasted for about two and a half centuries after the death of Alexander the Great. During the early part of this period, from roughly 300 to 200 B.C., it was an age of great prosperity and growth. Many new cities were founded by the Hellenes, and trade and commerce prospered. Hellenic life and thought spread over the eastern Mediterranean and mingled with the older ideas of the Near East. A cultural unity resulted that broke down the barriers that had separated the peoples of the eastern Mediterranean.

After 200 B.C. a decline set in which coincided with the expansion of Rome in the west and Parthia in the east. In the end the Hellenistic kingdoms that had arisen and flourished during the period were swept away, but not before the work of Hellenization had been accomplished and a new vigor, energy, and unity had infused the Mediterranean world.

THE HELLENIZATION PROCESS

Throughout their history, the Hellenes had left their homeland to found new settlements where favorable commercial and agricultural opportunities beckoned. During the seventh to fifth centuries B.C., migration from the Aegean had been principally to the western Mediterranean, until the Hellenes came into conflict with the Etruscans and Carthaginians. Now these migrations were directed primarily into Asia Minor. There, more than eighty new Hellenic towns were established. Another cluster arose in Syria, and two, Alexandria and Ptolemais, were founded in Egypt. Other settlements were made throughout the east as far as India.

Wherever they went, the Hellenes left their mark. They brought with them their language and their ideas, their methods of laying out cities and building, their system of education. Many were administrators and officials in the Hellenistic kingdoms, where socially they formed the upper classes. Others were soldiers, teachers and scholars, traders, tourists, colonists, artists. All these forms of contact and exchange passed Hellenic culture and ways to the native inhabitants. The primary diffusion of Hellenic culture, however, was through the founding of new cities.

HELLENISTIC CENTERS

The political unit of Hellas had been the city-state. The new cities were also city-states, but they differed from earlier city-states in several respects.

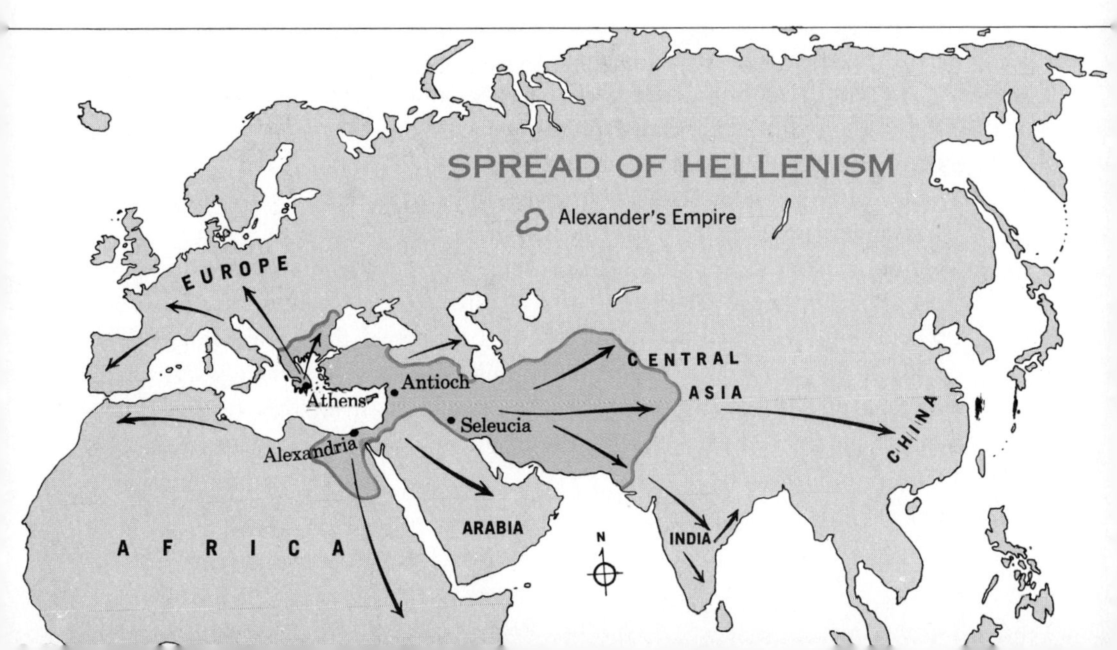

Usually they were not free and independent but paid taxes and tribute to the ruler. They were administered by a governor appointed by the king rather than by public assemblies. The population was more mixed than that of the Hellenic city-states. The Hellenes formed a privileged group within the population. They lived separately from both the natives and other foreigners as living quarters were in sections based on nationality.

In style the new cities were a mixture of Hellenic and Near Eastern. Greek order and logic produced cities that were neatly laid out with broad avenues. Many streets were paved. Good water supplies existed, and there were public centers of every sort like those in Hellas: markets, gymnasiums, theaters, and the new institutions of the age, libraries. Architecturally the new cities combined Hellenic and non-Hellenic elements; the Near Eastern round arch and vault and the Hellenic column were especially popular.

Many of the new cities became the greatest of their region. Others, further removed from the centers of administration, were garrison towns or outposts along the frontier. In all cases they were the seats of Hellenic influence wherever they were established.

ALEXANDRIA

Of the many cities founded and settled by the Hellenes, the foremost was Alexandria, established by the Iskander in 332 B.C. Alexandria was the meeting place of the world in the third century B.C. It had a population estimated at more than half a million, one that reflected the cosmopolitan nature of the Hellenistic world. Natives rubbed shoulders with soldiers, traders and merchants, scholars, and government officials from Hellas, Italy, Sicily, and western Asia. Many thousands of Jews, attracted to the city by its wealth and opportunities, lived in a special quarter, and a motley native quarter was full of beggars by day and thieves by night.

Alexandria lay on a strip of flat, sandy land between Lake Mareotis and the sea. A wide mole (causeway) connected the mainland with the island of Pharos, which separated two well-protected harbors; Lake Mareotis also had a harbor connected with the Nile. While little of Ptolemaic or Roman Alexandria remains, descriptions that have come down to us indicate the enormous impression it made on contemporaries. The most famous structure was the lighthouse on Pharos, one of the Seven Wonders of the ancient world. Four hundred feet high, it had a perpetual fire whose reflection in a metal mirror could be seen twenty miles out to sea. Alexander lay in the mausoleum (the acquisition of his body had been a great feather in the cap of the first Ptolemy), while the famous library and museum (page 340) attracted scholars from all over the Mediterranean to work under the patronage of the kings. The city itself, in contrast to the sandy, barren waste on which it lay, was beautiful. It was laid out in gridiron fashion with regular blocks and two one-hundred-foot-wide central avenues at right angles to one another. At night torches blazed along their entire length, and they were lined with colonades and imposing public buildings, theaters, and temples.

The city was magnificently located. Asia, Africa, and Europe lay within easy access. For over two thousand years Alexandria's continuing commercial prosperity testified to the excellence of its site.

ANTIOCH AND SELEUCIA

While Alexandria was the greatest of the Hellenistic cities, Antioch, the splendid and luxurious capital of the Seleucids, became one of the great cities in western Asia. In addition to a good location between the Mediterranean and the Euphrates, the city profited from the luxuries of the south Arabian trade, which the Seleucid kings had managed to capture from local merchants. The city was laid out in the gridiron fashion of Alexandria and had two quarters, one for the Syrians and Jews, and the other for the ruling caste of Hellenes. Antioch had a fine climate, close to both the hills and the waters of the Orontes River. About five miles south was a beautiful resort whose gardens, springs, and groves attracted travelers from many lands and was very much admired throughout Roman times. The city grew and prospered until the sixth century A.D., when it was laid in ruins by repeated earthquakes.

The Seleucids founded other towns that, in addition to Antioch, had an Hellenic population on which they could rely and that also served as defense outposts for the empire. The most important was Seleucia on the Tigris, for it was at the end of the caravan routes from India and Iran. It too became rich and prosperous, taking the place of Babylon as the foremost city of Mesopotamia. Besides Alexandria, both Antioch and Seleucia had populations of over half a million.

PERGAMUM

Besides the major Hellenistic kingdoms of the Ptolemies, the Seleucids, and the Antigonids, several other little kingdoms managed to establish themselves and keep their independence in the eastern Mediterranean (see map, page 330). Prominent among them was Pergamum in northwest Asia Minor. Pergamum occupied the rich agricultural land immediately around the capital city. It controlled a number of Hellenic cities whose respect and gratitude it had earned some fifty years after the death of Alexander. At that time, the Celtic Gauls had swept into northern Hellas, burning and ravishing the land, and had then passed over to Asia Minor, where they established their own kingdom. Pergamum heroically resisted the invaders. The Hellenic cities located on the coast accepted the rule of the kings of Pergamum and became outlets for a flourishing trade in local products. The city became very prosperous, and its rulers beautified it with architecture and sculpture until it rivaled Athens. The most famous sculptures commemorated the victory over the Gauls. In a series of very moving works that gained much popularity in Roman times, the artist showed with realism and pathos the suffering of the Gallic warriors in defeat. Crowning the heights of the Pergamum acropolis was the Great Altar of Zeus, and close by were a palace and a theater. In addition, Pergamum had an excellent

The Dying Gaul. The wounded warrior, at the point of death, supports himself on his arm, which is weakening as his life ebbs away. The physical details of the statue—the carefully carved mustache, matted hair, and strands of the gold necklace (all of which portray a barbarian rather than a Hellene), the tough muscles, and the drops of blood on his side—are typical of the realistic qualities of Hellenistic art. The emotional quality of that same art is reflected in the spirit of the statue. With great restraint, the artist has put into physical form the idea that the figure protrays: "the defeat that kills the spirit rather than the pain of physical violence that destroys the flesh."

library. Here scholars pursued their labors using the skins of animals, for export of Egyptian papyrus to Pergamum was forbidden because the Ptolemies feared that Pergamum's library would rival Alexandria's. This parchment (originally *pergament*) proved far more indestructible than papyrus and was widely used by the Romans and through the Middle Ages until the invention of paper.

Pergamum maintained its independence until the arrival of the Romans in the affairs of the eastern Mediterranean. The Pergamum king allied himself with this new power of the west, and when he died, in 133 B.C., he bequeathed his kingdom to Rome (page 369).

RHODES

The island of Rhodes lies south of Anatolia at the crossroads of the Aegean and southeastern Mediterranean. The island's excellent location favored the growth of commerce between Asia Minor and the European mainland. Around 400 B.C. the island's three little villages decided to form one city at the head of the island, where there were two magnificent harbors. By the end of the fourth century B.C., Rhodian merchants were well established in trade, wine being their special commodity. During the Hellenistic period, Rhodes became the clearing house for all trade between east and west. Rhodian merchants acted as bankers, provided loans, extended credit and facilities for reshipment of goods. These activities would not have been possible if Rhodes had not followed a policy of freedom of the seas. The islanders had built up a strong navy that kept the sea clear of pirates and maintained its neutrality. In the wars of succession following Alexander's death, the navy had saved the island from incorporation into the Macedonian kingdom. Since that time, Rhodian rights had been fully respected. (To celebrate their victory, the Rhodians had built an enormous statue to honor the patron god of the island, the sun god Helios. One hundred and twenty-five feet high, it straddled the entrance to the harbor. Unfortunately, it stood only a few years before a great earthquake leveled it, but its colossal size had so impressed its viewers that it was classed among the Seven Wonders of the ancient world.)

All ships entering Rhodes were taxed at 2 per cent of the value of their cargoes. This revenue, added to monies received from control of lands in southwest Asia Minor, made Rhodes very wealthy. Its rulers, like those of Pergamum, attracted artists from all over the Hellenistic world to beautify their city. It is said that no fewer than three thousand statues adorned the streets and public buildings. Two of the most famous Hellenistic sculptures were made by artists from Rhodes: the violent and emotional group showing Laocoön and his sons struggling to free themselves from the coils of snakes, and the magnificent Victory of Samothrace, which commemorated the Rhodian naval victory over the Antigonid Antiochus III.

Rhodes also had a famous school of philosophy, where many Romans, including Julius Caesar and Cicero, studied oratory and writing. Not least, Rhodes developed maritime laws that were widely consulted and much respected; later they were incorporated into Roman law. The esteem in which Rhodes was held is reflected in the list of those who came to its aid after the great earthquake of 227 B.C. Sicily, Egypt, the kingdoms in Asia Minor including the Seleucids, and various cities of the Aegean and Black seas all made gifts to help its recovery.

Rhodian supremacy, however, was not to last. Around 167 B.C. it came into conflict with Rome by supporting the Macedonians in a territorial quarrel (page 369). The victorious Romans penalized the island by taking away its Asia Minor possessions. Rhodes passed from the scene as a strong commercial post in the Mediterranean.

Until the arrival of the Romans disrupted trade and commerce, all the new Hellenistic cities benefited from the prosperity of the times. The supremacy of Athens had given way to a new situation in which the Hellenes successfully transplanted their way of life to many different places and became cosmopolitan citizens of a larger world.

The harbor at Rhodes. An old fortress now guards the harbor where the Colossus of Rhodes once stood. Rhodes, now part of Greece, passed to the Roman Empire in the East (Byzantium) when the barbarians conquered the western empire. It regained some of its commercial importance in the fourteenth century A.D. when it was occupied by the Knights of St. John of Jerusalem.

TRADE AND COMMERCE

The activity that made so many of the new cities artistic and commercial centers had been fostered by the gold found by Alexander when he captured the Persian treasury. For many years the Achaemenid kings of Persia had withdrawn from circulation the masses of gold and silver that poured into Susa as tribute from the various parts of their widespread empire. When Alexander released this great accumulation, it acted as a powerful stimulus to trade. The bullion was made into coin, a medium of exchange far superior to the bulk of goods used in trading in kind, and coins came into general use for the first time in history. Furthermore, the removal of former political barriers proved an even more powerful incentive to the free flow of goods between Europe and Asia. The Hellenistic kings did not let their political rivalries interfere with economic exchange. On the contrary, travel by sea increased, new trade routes were opened up to south Arabia and to east Africa, and long caravan routes connected Mesopotamia with Iran, Bactria, India, and, by the first century B.C. extended to China. The volume of trade was far greater during the early Hellenistic Age than it had been when the Athenian empire was at its peak. Indeed, the third century B.C. was one of the most prosperous in ancient history.

LANGUAGE AND THE NEW LEARNING

Increased economic and cultural contacts resulted in a new unity throughout the Mediterranean that was recognized when a new word was coined to identify the eastern Mediterranean world. It was labeled the *Ecumene* (the inhabited world). Acting as a binding agent for the Ecumene was a new dialect, the *Koiné*, a language that was basically Attic Greek but that had added words from other Hellenic dialects and from the oriental languages. The Koiné became an effective means of communication for the populations from Sicily to Iran. Using the Koiné, Hellenic speakers not only carried on trade but also spread the culture of Hellas to Lydians, Egyptians, Syrians, Persians, Medes, Babylonians, Arameans, and Jews. New schools sprang up everywhere to teach the new language and with it the literature and drama of Hellas. In the libraries of the new cities scholars of the Hellenistic Age copied the great classical masterpieces of the Hellenic Age in Koiné and brought them to wider audiences than could possibly have been reached by Attic Greek.

The best example of the Koiné in existence today is the *Septuagint*, a translation of the Old Testament into Koiné made in the third century B.C. for the Koiné-speaking Jews of Alexandria. In the first century A.D. the New Testament of the Christians, which included the letters of Paul, the account of the acts of the Apostles, and the Gospel of St. Luke, were also written in the Koiné. Both the Jewish and the Christian scriptures thus became intelligible to an audience of many nations.

Every group of people around the Mediterranean contributed to Hellenistic literature and science in the Koiné. Egypt produced Euclid, the father of geometry; Ptolemy, the geographer; and the poet Callimachus. Syracuse produced Archimedes, the physicist, and Theocritus, the poet. Arcadia in Hellas produced the historian Polybius, and Boeotia the biographer Plutarch. Although Athens retained its importance in philosophy, the center of learning rested in Alexandria in Egypt. Until commercialized parchment was invented in Pergamum, Egyptian papyrus was the principal writing material, and for a time Alexandria almost had a monopoly in making inexpensive books. Alexandrian scholars used slaves to copy the manuscripts.

Alexandria's library was the most famous in the world. The idea of a library had probably come from Assyria or Babylon, and libraries appeared in all the dynastic capital cities. There were particularly fine ones in Antioch and Pergamum. But the Alexandrian library outshone them all. Founded by Ptolemy I and organized by Ptolemy II, it had some 700,000 works of science, philosophy, religion, and literature. Editing and translating were an important part of the work of the library staff. Alexandria also boasted the Museum, named for the Muses. It was not a place for exhibition, as museums are today, but an institution for research and study. It had botanical and zoological gardens, an astronomical observatory, and galleries of art. It was manned by an association of scholars who received yearly pensions (fatted fowls in a coop, an envious rival called them). The Museum quickly took the leading place among such Hellenistic institutions of learning as the Garden of Epicurus and the Stoa (Porch) of Zeno (page 345).

Many machines were invented by the scientists of the Museum. The Romans adopted one, the hydraulic organ, for use in great amphitheaters, which they built in all the large centers of their empire. In this organ wind pressure was applied by means of a water compressor and pistons instead of bellows, while the pipes were played by a simple kind of keyboard. Its loud, penetrating tone made the instrument very effective for outdoor entertainments like the gladiatorial combats and races the Romans enjoyed.

Education spread during the Hellenistic Age. Many cities supported public schools to which wealthy citizens could make donations. Physical education, reading, writing, and mathematics were the chief subjects taught between the ages of seven and fourteen. For those who could afford to continue their schooling between the ages of fourteen and eighteen, the curriculum included geometry, music, and the works of Homer, Euripides, Plato, Menander, and Theocritus (page 342). The culmination of education came in the gymnasium, where young men of high social station studied philosophy and military techniques. A small number might continue after the gymnasium by studying with famous philosophers or scientists. Athens and Rhodes were famous for their schools of philosophy, Pergamum and Cos (page 348) for medicine, and the Museum at Alexandria in Egypt for scientific research.

HELLENISTIC LITERATURE

All branches of Hellenistic learning were represented in the literature of the period. Writers produced drama, poetry, histories, biographies, scientific works, treatises on mathematics and astronomy, philosophy, and religion. Scholars concentrated in the cities, for there they were supported by the state and were inspired by others of the same interests and occupation. Because education was more widespread, not only did a much bigger reading public exist but wealthy men collected books for their own personal use. Writing became a recognized profession. The names of more than eleven hundred Hellenistic authors have come down to us, but the bulk of their writings has long since disappeared.

Drama was more popular than ever before. Traveling groups of actors went from city to city to perform, and every city worthy of the name had its own theater. Many new kinds of plays were written. The most famous were those of the New Comedy. A school of New Comedy flourished in Athens, and Menander was its leading author. Menander wrote comedies of manners in beautifully turned phrases. His work was not profound, but it was full of good quotations: "Those whom the gods love die young" and "Conscience makes cowards of even the bravest men." Menander saw the world as full of amusing, trivial persons whom he made stock characters in his plays: the bullying father, the lovesick teenager, the gabby soldier back from the wars. Compared with the great comedy writer Aristophanes (page 239), Menander seems shallow. His comedies were meant only to amuse, not to persuade or to reform like those of his greater predecessor. But the audiences of his own day loved his work, and he was imitated and sometimes copied directly by other well-known authors such as the Romans Plautus and Terence.

Mimes were another extremely popular form of dramatic entertainment. They were sketches of daily life, often coarse in subject and language, and they appealed particularly to the common people. Tragedies were also written, but they did not have the breadth and depth of those of earlier times. Most have not survived.

Hellenistic poetry was highly polished and elegant, though it was sometimes artificial in subject and style. The poets experimented with new forms. The *idyll* was a short piece, a little picture complete in itself. The most admired of the idyllic writers was Callimachus of Cyrene, who was a librarian and scholar as well as a poet. He is best remembered for his poem on the death of a friend:

> They told me, Heraclitus, they told me you were dead,
> They brought me bitter news to hear and bitter tears to shed.
> I wept as I remembered how often you and I
> Had tired the sun with talking and sent him down the sky.
>
> And now that you are lying, my dear old Carian* guest,
> A handful of grey ashes, long long ago at rest,
> Still are thy pleasant voices, thy nightingales awake,
> For Death, he taketh all away, but them he cannot take.

Another famous poet was Theocritus of Syracuse. He was perhaps the greatest writer of pastoral idylls in antiquity; he sang the songs of the shepherd, the fisherman, and the peasant. He was copied by as great a writer as the eminent Roman Vergil. Particularly popular also were the miniature epics, which usually told of one episode in the struggles of gods and men. Callimachus was a leading writer of epics as well as idylls.

In prose writing, historiography was the most significant. Unfortunately, none of the many histories of the two generations following Alexander have survived. A few can be glimpsed at second hand through later writers who copied them. Manetho, who was an Egyptian priest (page 71), and Berossus, a Babylonian priest, wrote the histories of their respective countries, but little more than fragments of their lists of kings have survived. Contemporary events were more fully recorded. Ptolemy of Egypt was the first general or king in history to write an account of his campaigns. His

* Caria was on the coast of Asia Minor, below Ionia.

history of Alexander was based on Alexander's official journal and other records, to which he added his own first-hand observations. Two other close associates of Alexander also wrote about him; Nearchus described naval affairs, and Aristobulus described Alexander and wrote of the geography of his wars. A very important history of Alexander's successors was written by Hieronymous of Cardia. Much of his material was used later by Plutarch in his *Parallel Lives of the Greeks and the Romans* (page 456), and so has not been totally lost.

Of writers who described the times following Alexander, Polybius of Megalopolis in Hellas is the first. Polybius (201–120 B.C.) wrote of the expansion of Roman power throughout the Mediterranean. He was a native of Arcadia, one of the states of the Achaean League (page 329), and had been prominent in its affairs. Taken as a hostage to Rome, he came to enjoy the friendship of many prominent Romans who recognized his education and talents (page 375). He understood the importance of Rome's success and sought to explain Roman character and purpose to his Hellenistic readers. Of the forty books of his *Histories*, only five and a few fragments remain, but they show Polybius to be a skilled, thoughtful, and conscientious writer who deserves to rank high among ancient writers of history.

HELLENISTIC PHILOSOPHY

During the Hellenistic Age, there was a breakdown in the close relationship between the gods, the city-state, and the citizens (page 198). As the city-states were conquered or absorbed into kingdoms and empires, men felt themselves turning into little cogs in a vast machinery in which they had no control over the collective life of the state. The interests of the individual increasingly turned inward, to concern with a personal happiness that could be attained by leading "the good life." Several schools of philosophy attempted to define the good life. The most important were those of the Cynics, Epicurus, and Zeno.

DIOGENES AND CYNICISM

To the Cynics, virtue was the only good, vice the only evil. Virtue is knowledge, the knowledge of one's self. Beyond this, nothing is important. The ties of society are meaningless; wealth, social position, fame, honor, and material possessions all hold second place to endurance, the power to accept what comes.

The most famous Cynic was Diogenes, who passed through the sunlit streets of Athens holding a lighted lamp seeking, he said, an honest man. Diogenes lived in a large earthenware jar or tub, getting along on bread and water and a bag full of beans. When Alexander the Great asked him what he most desired, Diogenes replied that he wished Alexander would step aside and stop blocking out the sunlight.

The Cynic message of endurance, combined with scorn for the vanities and comforts of the world, appealed to the common people. It alienated the rich and intellectual, however, who were offended by the Cynic disregard for the material needs of life.

EPICURUS AND EPICUREANISM

Epicurus was born in 342 B.C. of poor Athenian parents. At the age of 35 he started his own school in Athens, where his students included his three brothers, many friends, their children and slaves. The group met for discussions in a garden belonging to Epicurus, and thus the Garden is forever associated with Epicurus as is the Academy with Plato and the Lyceum with Aristotle.

Epicurus met with uncomplaining courage the constant illness and pain that beset him throughout life. It is possibly because of this suffering that his philosophy held the absence of pain to be the greatest good. The absence of pain is happiness, he said, and happiness is the supreme good. Other philosophers, rivals of Epicurus, falsified his teaching, perhaps because the quest for personal happiness can so easily lead to self-indulgence. To them is due the impression, which has never died, that Epicurus taught that good is excessive pleasure, including gluttony and drunkenness. Epicurus' actual teachings must be understood in terms of the conditions under which he taught. His statement that the pleasure of the stomach is the root of all good is better understood when one knows that he and his students in the Garden lived principally on bread and water. They considered they had a real feast when they could afford a bit of the cheese that was common fare for Athens' poorest people. Friendship was also held to be a great good, and Epicurus used as an example of this quality the tenderness he and other adults felt for children.

To Epicurus evil was bodily pain, which must and can be endured. Bodily suffering should be endured if it made possible the higher pleasures of the mind. The greatest enemy of the mind is fear, which is also evil. Epicurus said that religion was evil when it taught fear of death, of punishment after death, and of the dreadful loneliness of souls wandering for eternity through a woeful wilderness beyond Lethe, the river of forgetfulness. Epicurus admitted the existence of gods but thought that they did not concern themselves with the affairs of men.

The Epicurean philosophy failed to appeal to the masses of the people because it was too intellectual. For the next five centuries it remained the belief of only a small number of educated persons.

ZENO AND STOICISM

A rival of the Epicurean philosophy was that of Zeno, who was born on Cyprus of Phoenician parents soon after 350 B.C. Business affairs took him to Athens, where he also studied philosophy, but he did not identify himself with any of the established schools. Although he greatly admired the stories of Socrates, especially those in which he calmly faced death, Zeno rejected many of Plato's ideas. Zeno's own school was called the Stoa (porch) after the place where his followers met. His teachings at the Stoa became known as *Stoic*.

Stoicism tried to mold the character by the principles of right conduct, in order to enable it to meet with fortitude the difficulties of this world. To the true Stoic such things as possessions, wealth, and health were merely incidental to living the good life. The good life, and therefore happiness, came from right conduct, which meant making the will conform to the laws of nature, laws that were rational and just.

Stoicism taught that the course of nature was decreed by a Divine Lawgiver, God, or Zeus, but he was distinguished from the Zeus of the popular religion. This supreme Stoic God, whose essence was fire, was the soul of the world, and each man had within himself a spark of the Divine Fire. Because they shared in this divinity, men should love one another. There could be no place for chance in the order of nature created by God. The course of history was thought to be determined by natural laws and was believed to be moving to a climax in which the world would be destroyed by fire. A recreation would follow, and another of the endless cycles God has instituted would begin.

Stoicism appealed less to the Hellenes than it did to their neighbors to the east and west. It was very popular at first in Syria and later in Rome. Its principles appealed especially to people in positions of responsibility. Nearly all the Hellenistic rulers identified themselves with Stoicism. Its success with the Romans was due partly to the similarity of some of its teachings to ideas respected by the Romans: *virtus*, or manliness; *dignitas*, which forbade any excessive display of emotion; and *gravitas*, which opposed flippancy and silliness (page 272).

Whereas Epicureanism remained unchanged with the passing of time, Stoicism continued to grow as a body of beliefs. Under Zeno's successors, it became a religion in which the right conduct became obedience to the will of God. In Rome, Stoicism was further developed by Seneca, philosopher advisor to the emperor Nero (page 432), and by an emperor, Marcus Aurelius (page 438).

Satisfying as Stoicism was to men of sober, dignified, responsible character, it represented a way of life and an ideal too lofty and self-denying for the mass of people.

HELLENISTIC SCIENCE

Before the Hellenistic Age, philosophy and science had not been distinguished from each other. The early philosophers were also observers of nature who tried to explain the phenomena of the world around them other than by the will of the gods (page 202). Aristotle, for example, was both a philosopher and a scientist. His studies of the habits and anatomy of animals laid the foundations for the science of zoology, and his successor Theophrastus, who studied and classified plants, may be said to have started the science of botany.

Both men were greatly aided in their work by the animals and plants sent back to Hellas by the trained observers taken along by Alexander on his conquest of the east. Alexander's enthusiasm for science was shared by the Ptolemies of Egypt. At Alexandria's Museum, many of the scholars were scientists, and the Museum was the center of Hellenistic scientific studies.

Great advances were made, particularly in the fields of mathematics, astronomy, medicine, and geography. Although Hellenic mathematics and medicine had been well grounded before Alexander's time, the first century after his death witnessed a great spurt in new scientific endeavors. The Hellenistic Age became one of the few truly important periods in scientific thinking during ancient times.

The union of Babylonian and Hellenic knowledge gave rise to a new astronomy. The procession of the equinoxes, the true length of the solar year and the lunar month, the revolution of Mercury and Venus around the sun and the possibility that the earth might do likewise, and the greater size of the sun as compared with the earth are a few examples of Hellenistic anticipation of facts accepted by modern astronomers. Aristarchus of Samos concluded that the earth moved around the sun, but as his facts did not accord with the conclusions and opinions of others (he was even accused of impiety), his theories were rejected.

Geometry kept pace with astronomy. Many men were active simultaneously in both fields. Euclid, who worked in Alexandria, wrote a textbook on plane and solid geometry called the *Elements* that remained the standard work in the field until the twentieth century. It was used in turn by the Greeks, the Romans, the Arabs, and medieval and modern mathematicians. Trigonometry, the measurement of angles, was founded during this period.

The greatest Hellenistic scientist was Archimedes of Syracuse (c. 287–212 B.C.). Unlike most scientists of his day, who were theoreticians only and considered practical applications beneath their dignity, Archimedes was both a theoretician and a genius in practical mechanics. He put his science to work when the Romans attacked Syracuse by creating war machines that delayed the capture of the city. He invented the double pulley, and his water screw was used in irrigation projects and to pump water out of mines. Archimedes advanced the study of geometry and came close to calculating the true value of *pi*, the ratio of the circumference of a circle to its diameter. He discovered the law of specific gravity, which we call Archimedes' Principle, after observing the displacement of his bath water one day in the public gymnasium. *Eureka!* (I have found it!) he shouted as he dashed home naked. His knowledge of levers led him to state, "Give me a fulcrum on which to rest and I will move the earth." Slave labor, however, was too common and too cheap in the ancient world for much attention to be given to machines, and technology had to wait until modern times for its full flowering.

Among geographers Eratosthenes of Cyrene (275–200 B.C.) was outstanding. His estimate of the size of the earth, based on calculations of the angles of shadows in two cities located seven hundred miles apart in Egypt, came within two hundred miles of the circumference as conceived by modern scientists. Eratosthenes taught that Europe, Asia, and Africa was one land mass surrounded by a great ocean, and that one should be able to reach India from Spain by sailing south around Africa. He also taught that Asia could be reached by sailing west from Spain, thus anticipating both Vasco da Gama and Christopher Columbus. He thought that the Atlantic Ocean might be divided by a north-south land mass, as it is, in fact, by the Americas.

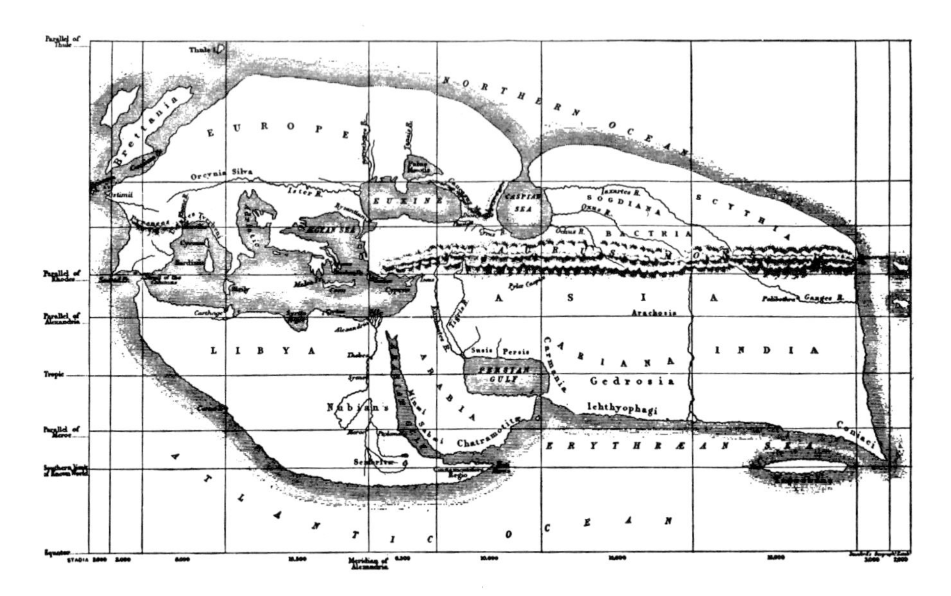

The map of Eratosthenes. In the third century B.C., man's idea of the world was limited. The existence of the Americas and China was unknown, while India's shape was mostly a matter of speculation. Nevertheless this map represents a considerable advance in man's thinking about Eurasia—an advance largely due to information brought back by men traveling with Alexander the Great.

Many new medical advances were made in Hellenistic times. The famous medical school founded by the "father of medicine," Hippocrates (c. 450 B.C.), around the sanctuary of Asclepius, the god of healing (page 267), continued to flourish on the island of Cos, while in Alexandria new studies were made in anatomy and physiology. Herophilus of Chalcedon (c. 300 B.C.) discovered the nerves and their connections with the brain and spinal cord. He distinguished the cerebrum and cerebellum as separate parts of the brain. He maintained that the arteries carried blood and not air, as others supposed. He derived arterial pulsation from the heart and anticipated the discovery of the circulation of the blood. Herophilus' ideas were all lost upon the collapse of the classical civilization and were not reconsidered until seventeen hundred years later.

Alexandrian physicians used drugs, primarily opium, for anaesthetics. Most cities maintained a public physician, and the royal courts each had doctors in residence. Popular medicine, however, was still largely based on superstitions and magical spells.

Not all the sciences fared well. Chemistry remained unknown, physics made little advance, and botany remained at the point where Aristotle and

Theophrastus left it. Interest in zoology was confined to zoos for the amusement of the public. The Athenian zoo boasted a tiger brought all the way from India. Ptolemy II's zoo at Alexandria is known in some detail. It contained lions, tigers, leopards and lynxes, water buffaloes from India and Africa, wild donkeys from Arabia, a giraffe, a rhinoceros, and a polar bear. In its reptile house was a forty-foot-long python. The aviary sheltered parrots, peacocks, pheasants, and many African birds.

For more than a century after Alexander the Great, the Hellenistic kingdoms flourished. Despite political rivalries, the eastern Mediterranean world was drawn into a new cultural and economic unity. New cities based on a mixture of Hellenic and Near Eastern models in government, architecture, and way of life spread Hellenic ideas. Developments in science were outstanding. A new language, the Koiné, and a new learning broadened the horizons of people living in the Ecumene and produced a new cosmopolitan outlook where the luxuries of a vastly increased trade and commerce found a ready market. But new powers were rising outside the Hellenistic world: Parthia in the east and Rome in the west. During the second and first centuries B.C., while Mesopotamia fell to the Parthians, Rome's presence was increasingly felt in the eastern Mediterranean. The energy the Hellenes had displayed in moving out into the Middle East was waning. Rome, strong and full of vitality, was to step in where Greece left off.

People, Places, and Terms

Menander	Herophilus	Pergamum
Callimachus	Manetho	Rhodes
Theocritus	Berossus	
Polybius	Hieronymus	Hellenization
Plutarch	Epicurus	diffusion
Theophrastus	Zeno	assimilation
Aristarchus	Diogenes	parchment
Euclid		*Ecumene*
Ptolemy	Alexandria	*Koiné*
Archimedes	Antioch	mime
Eratosthenes	Seleucia	idyll
Hippocrates	Cos	cosmopolitan

Mastering the Reading

1. What characteristics did the new Hellenistic cities have in common? What were some of their unique features? What were some of the unifying forces at work in the Hellenistic world?
2. How did the writing of the time represent the mood of the Hellenistic Age in style, form, and subject matter? How did the writing of history change?
3. What questions were the philosophers asking and trying to answer? How did the Cynics, the Epicureans, and the Stoics explain and define life? Who was satisfied by their answers? Why?
4. What scientific advances were of special importance? Which sciences were emphasized? Which were neglected?

Interpreting the Text

1. Describe a day in the life of an Alexandrian. Show how his horizons were broadened during the Hellenistic Age.
2. That the release of the hoarded Persian gold stimulated trade is easy to understand, but how this gold triggered artistic, scientific, poetic and drama development is not so obvious. How can this connection be explained?

Exploring Beyond the Text

Explore some of the famous personalities of the times showing how they were true "Hellenistic" men.

Working with the Map

To understand more fully the wide extent of Hellenistic culture, make a list of artists and writers, philosophers, and scientists of the period and mark their native lands on a map of the Hellenistic world. To which, if any, Hellenistic kingdom did each of their cities or provinces belong?

18

Rome: Expansion Over the Mediterranean

338–133 B.C.

In the two hundred years between the middle fourth century B.C. and the middle second century B.C., Rome grew from a small city-state in central Italy to a major power in the Mediterranean world. Such a phenomenal growth came about in gradual steps. First the Romans had to gain control of the Italian peninsula and devise a system of governing the peoples they had conquered. Then three wars with Carthage followed that left them in control of the western Mediterranean. Immediately, alliances and obligations drew them east and involved them in the affairs of the Hellenistic kingdoms, while westward they moved into Spain and Africa. Such a rapid expansion had profound effects on Roman society and the Roman character.

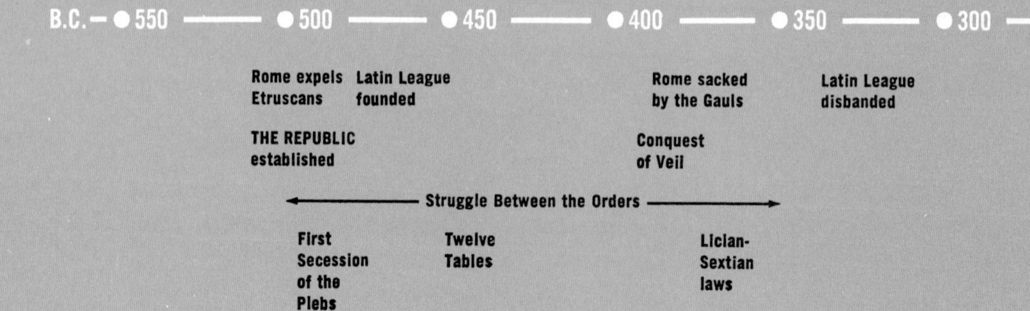

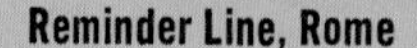

CONQUEST OF CENTRAL AND SOUTHERN ITALY, 338–265 B.C.

Between 500 and 338 B.C., Rome had successfully defeated its immediate neighbors and weakened the Etruscans. It had withstood the burning of Rome by the Gauls and the uprising among the members of the Latin League. Now it had to face its most formidable foe, the Samnites, rugged mountaineers who wanted the fertile fields of the Campania, into which the Romans were pushing.

THE SAMNITE WARS, 327–290 B.C.

We have no reliable account of the three wars between the Romans and the Samnites. Roman historians, writing of the events in later centuries, described glowingly the patriotic exploits of the Romans. No account, however, could gloss over a great disaster that befell the Roman troops at the Caudine Forks, a pass in the Apennines, in 321 B.C. An army of forty thousand men suffered ambush and defeat. Pontius, the Samnite commander, made the Romans pass "under the yoke," the deepest humiliation that could be inflicted. Each man, unarmed and with only his shirt on, had to run between two upright spears upon which a third rested, so his head was forced down. The consuls solemnly promised peace, but the Senate refused to honor it because it had not been ratified by the Assembly. Naked and in chains, the consuls were surrendered to the enemy, and the fight went on.

Peace was finally made in 304 B.C., but it did not last. It only allowed the Romans a breathing spell to gather strength to meet a great coalition formed against them by the Samnites, the Etruscans, the Gauls, and another Italic people, the Umbrians. Their combined forces attacked Rome in 300 B.C. Neither side was victorious until a decisive battle took place in Umbria at Sentinum in 295 B.C. The consul Decius sacrificed himself by plunging into the thick of battle to inspire his troops, and they won the day. Though deserted by their allies, the Samnites hung on for another five years. They were finally defeated by the consul Marius Curius Dentatus. Curius, like Cincinnatus (page 261) and Decius, was a proud figure in Roman tradition. He had celebrated three triumphs but still lived simply on his farm. To him one day, before their final defeat, came envoys from the Samnites. They offered him rich bribes. Curius looked at them with scorn. "Go tell the Samnites," he said, "that Curius counts it glory not to possess wealth but to rule over those who do."

The defeat of the Samnites left Rome supreme in central Italy. Besides Samnium, Rome annexed Etruria in 283 B.C,. and the Gauls were pushed back beyond the Rubicon River. Roman rule extended from the Po Valley to the region of Magna Graecia.

THE CONQUEST OF MAGNA GRAECIA, 281–270 B.C.

The Hellenic cities of the south were not prospering. They had been weakened by the constant warfare between Carthage and the Hellenic states (page 252). Only Tarentum continued to flourish because of its excellent harbor and prosperous trade and commerce.

When a conflict arose between Tarentum and Rome, the Romans decided to send an army south. The people of Tarentum, realizing that they could not face Rome alone, called on Pyrrhus, king of Epirus, to come to their aid. He, the finest soldier of his age, answered their appeal. Pyrrhus was a cousin of Alexander the Great and had visions of an empire in the west like the one his cousin had created in the east. His plan was to unite the Italians and the Sicilian Hellenes and then to subdue Carthage.

Pyrrhus descended on Italy with twenty thousand mercenary soldiers. He also brought with him twenty huge war elephants, an innovation in Italian warfare. The Romans were twice defeated. Pyrrhus, however, though he won the battles lost so many men that such a victory has been called ever since a "Pyrrhic victory." He asked for peace but was turned down by the proud words of the censor Appius Claudius: "Rome never makes terms of peace with a victorious enemy on Italian soil." Wearying of the struggle, Pyrrhus crossed over to Sicily to aid his countrymen against the Carthaginians, but the desertion of his allies, who were not interested in his ideas of

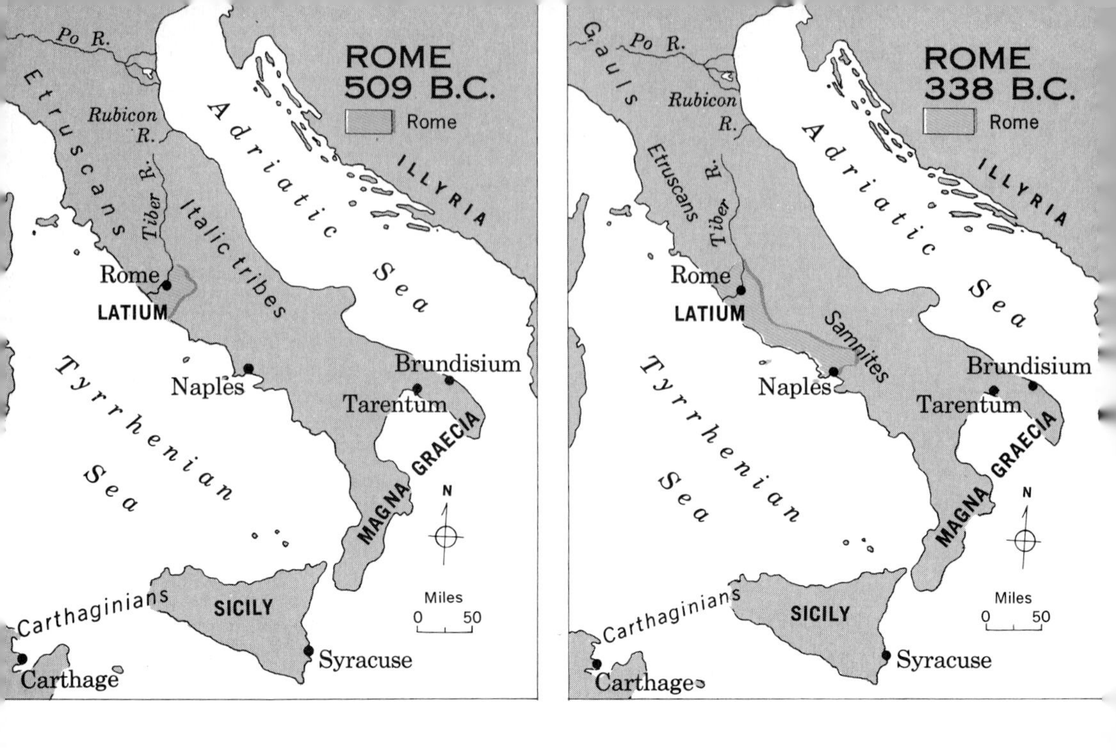

empire, forced his return. A crushing defeat followed, and Pyrrhus returned home. Tarentum capitulated, and by 265 B.C. Rome had established its rule over all of southern Italy. The Romans, whose territory extended to the toe of the Italian boot, were now face to face with the Carthaginians in Sicily.

THE ORGANIZATION OF ITALY

Following their military successes, the Romans entered into alliances and agreements with the peoples they had conquered. The Latin League (page 258) was extended into an Italian one, which was to be one of Rome's most successful political achievements. The confederacy was composed of many small states each tied to Rome by individual treaty. The separate alliances granted various rights and privileges depending on individual circumstances. The strength of these ties, which were severely strained in the wars against Carthage, were to testify to the success of the Roman method.

THE CONFEDERACY: THE ALLIES

Rome had two classes of allies. The first were the Latin allies. There were several kinds: cities, conquered territory, and colonies. The largest were the colonies. They had been planted all over Italy and formed self-governing

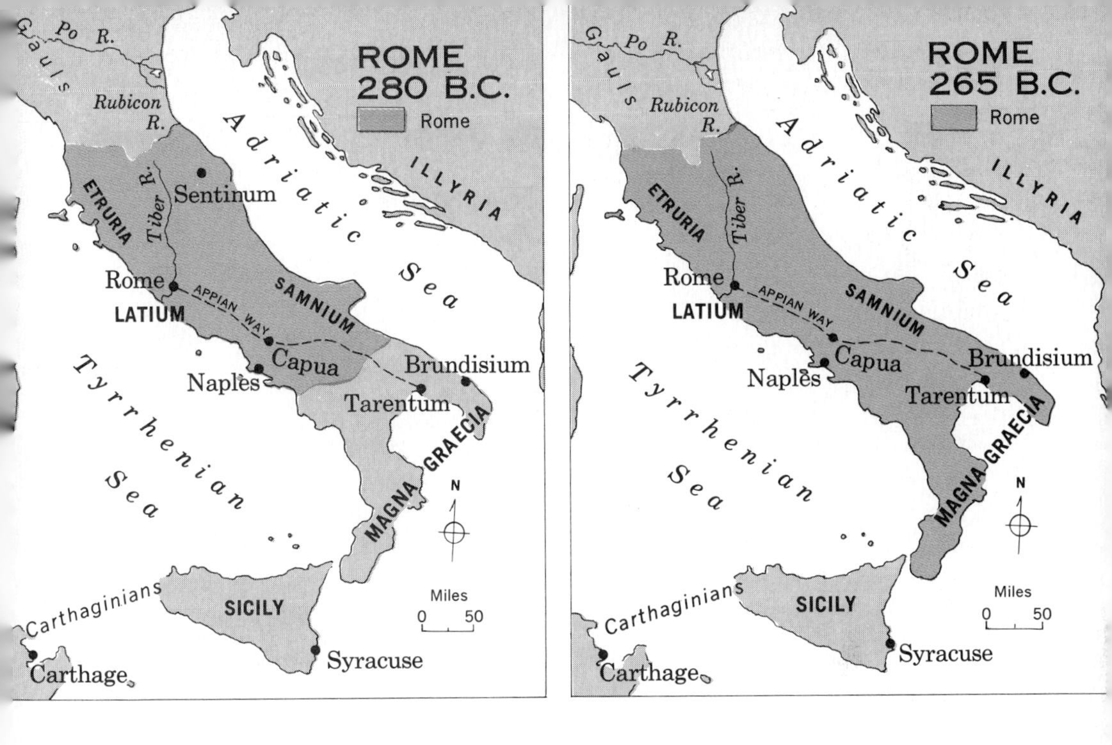

states—miniature Romes. Founded by Romans (who gave up their citizenship) as well as Latins, and therefore closest to the Romans in language, custom, and sympathy, the Latin colonies were a means of extending the Latin language and civilization up and down the peninsula and of relieving overpopulation and poverty at home.

The second class of allies were the Italians. Like the Latins, they were bound to Rome by individual agreements. They, too, were self-governing, keeping their local customs and laws. Both Latin and Italian allies were expected to furnish troops for the army or ships and crews. They did not pay taxes or tribute, but they gave up the right to declare war, determine strategy, or make peace.

THE CONFEDERACY: THE CITIZENS

Rome also had two classes of citizens. The full citizens lived in Rome and in surrounding towns and villages that had been granted citizenship because of their strategic value to Rome. Special settlements of military colonies were also granted full citizenship. Each of these was founded by three hundred land-hungry families as a garrison town. Towns of full citizenship were subject to Roman magistrates, and their inhabitants could vote in Roman elections and present themselves as candidates for office.

The second class of citizens were called *cives sine suffragio*, citizens without voting rights and lived in communities, or *municipia* (municipalities).

The Via Appia, or Appian Way. One of the most famous of the Roman roads still exists today. Roman roads were built with great care, as straight and level as possible, from eleven to fifteen feet wide. Milestones marked the way and also doubled as aids in mounting horseback. Other roads binding Italy together were the Latin Way to southern Italy, the Flaminian Way and the Aemilian Way to the Po Valley and north, and the Aurelian Way to the northwest.

They were self-governing, furthermore, their inhabitants could not vote or hold office in Rome. Most of these towns were in Latium, Campania, and Etruria. The system of municipalities was Rome's method of preparing for citizenship those who they felt were not ready for it at the moment, but would be eventually. Those who had only partial citizenship looked forward to the day when they would gain full citizenship. The system worked so well that by 150 B.C. half citizenship had nearly totally disappeared.

ROMAN IMPROVEMENTS

As the Romans advanced through Italy, they built bridges, drained swamps, and cleared land. Prosperity increased in the wake of Roman conquest. The Romans also built a system of roads to facilitate troop movements and dispatches of supplies and official messages. The most famous of these roads was the Appian Way (Via Appia), built in 312 B.C. and named after the censor Appius Claudius (page 353). It ran from Rome to Capua and later was extended to Brundisium. Though built for military purposes, the roads proved to be a boon to travelers and merchants. They brought outlying districts into closer touch encouraging commerce and trade, and so helping to Romanize the Italian people.

Though the Romans never made peace except on their own terms, and though they were determined to be master in every situation, they dealt wisely with their foes. By making alliances and agreements that fit each particular situation, they gained the loyalty of the Italian people and were able to create a patriotic interest in a common welfare. This bound together the peoples of Italy and fostered a common "Italian" nationality of which everyone was more and more aware.

THE CONTEST BETWEEN ROME AND CARTHAGE, 264–201 B.C.

Rome's conquest of Italy made it one of the five major powers of the Mediterranean world. The others were the Hellenistic kingdoms of the eastern Mediterranean—Syria, Egypt, and Macedon, heirs to Alexander the Great (page 329)—and in the west, Carthage.

At the time of the conflict between Rome and Carthage, Carthage had a republican form of government with a senate, popular assembly, and two elected officials, much like the Roman consuls, called *suffetes*. The real power in Carthage was the senate. It was in the hands of a few wealthy aristocrats who formed an oligarchy. The Carthaginian state also had a large number of slaves; tenant farmers called serfs attached to the land, and poor freemen who tilled the rich farmlands along the African coast.

Until Roman power reached the toe of the Italian boot, Rome, as heir to the Etruscans, had had several alliances with the Carthaginians (page 260). Carthage was a commercial power. It had colonies spread around the western Mediterranean and a large fleet, which was its strength in war. Its troops were mercenaries skilled in the various military arts: African infantrymen and Numidian (African) horsemen who rode without saddles and shot their arrows in full gallop; Gauls; hardy Spanish tribesmen; and slingers from the Balearic Islands, who were expert in casting and flinging lead balls. The money Carthage received from trade gave it ample funds to pay its troops. Rome, by contrast, was a land power. It had never been interested in trade or commerce, but it did expect to have political sway over the peoples of Italy. Its resources were a unified homeland and citizen-soldiers who fought for love of country.

Carthage was allied to Numidia, but the tie that bound them, like those with its other dependencies, was one of ruler and ruled, quite different from the tie that linked the members of the Italian confederacy. Carthaginian soldiers were brave, but they fought for money, not patriotism. Carthage's commercial empire included not only the North African coast west of Cyrene but also settlements in Sicily, Sardinia, Corsica, and southern Spain, and ports in Malta and the Balearic Islands. This was a far flung empire, not compact like the Italian peninsula.

Rome did not have the wealth that Carthage possessed. It had no fleet or tribute from its allies (page 355). But Rome was able to call on its allies for troops, and it could command more soldiers than any other Mediterranean power. It also had great natural resources in the produce of the land. Rome, ambitious to be a land power, felt that it must defend its frontiers at all costs and accept the responsibility of coming to the aid of its allies. Carthage, a sea power, had to protect its sources of supply and increase its markets where it could.

Each power was strong where the other was weak. Each was subject to ambitions and fears that were easily magnified. Their conflict was inevitable. The struggle between them, which lasted more than 125 years, is known as the Punic (Phoenician) Wars. There were three such wars. They were the most famous contests in the history of the ancient west, they were recorded in some detail by the historians Livy and Polybius (page 343), and they ended in the destruction of Carthage.

THE FIRST PUNIC WAR, 264–241 B.C.

The control of Sicily was the object of the First Punic War. Neither Hellenes nor Carthaginians had been able to conquer and then hold the entire island. In the third century B.C. the Carthaginians had made steady gains (page 255). With the defeat of Pyrrhus, it seemed possible that Sicily would fall to Carthage.

The Romans were aroused by the fear that Carthage, having gained Sicily, would move into Italy. Rome needed a pretext to prevent this. Fear for its territory, as well as desire to gain new ones, prompted it to act when the opportunity arose.

In 264 B.C. the town of Messana in Sicily became the base of a gang of mercenary soldiers and pirates. Besieged by both Hellenes and Carthaginians, the Messanans sent to Rome for help. Rome, fully realizing the importance of the step it was taking, decided to go to the aid of Messana. The Romans sent troops south, saved Messana, and then gained the allegiance of Syracuse. The Romans met with success after success as they captured Carthaginian towns in the interior of Sicily. The cities on the coast presented a more difficult problem. They were impossible to subdue, for they were constantly supplied by Carthaginian ships.

With characteristic energy, the Romans decided to build a fleet. Finding a shipwrecked Carthaginian quinquereme, a ship rowed by five men on each

A Roman galley. Left, the enemy. Right, the Roman warship. The corvus is down, and over it the troops pass to board the enemy ship. The galley here is a trireme, or three-banked ship.

oar, the Romans studied it carefully and set to work. The legionnaires sat on benches along the shore learning to row in the sand. In two months time, we are told, the Romans had 120 ships. Now the Romans knew that their soldier-sailors would be less skilled than the Carthaginians, so they thought up a scheme to compensate for this. Each of their ships had a drawbridge called a *crow* (corvus). At the end of the crow was a huge spike. When the enemy ship drew near, the drawbridge was dropped with such force that the spike fastened onto the enemy deck. Then the legionnaires rushed into the enemy ranks to engage in hand-to-hand combat. This clever device enabled the Romans to win a great victory off Mylae in the north of Sicily (260 B.C.). The Carthaginians lost half their fleet, but even more important, the Romans had acquired the sea power that was essential if they were to gain control of the Mediterranean.

Following this victory, the Romans decided to carry the war to Africa, the Carthaginian homeland. Building another large fleet, they again defeated their enemy and cleared the seas. They landed a force on African soil under the command of the consul Regulus (256 B.C.). Regulus won a battle but then decided not to capture Carthage or make peace but to wait instead over the winter for fresh troops and the consul who was to replace him. Meanwhile, the Carthaginians entrusted their troops to a wandering soldier of fortune named Xanthippus. Xanthippus, a Spartan, trained the Carthaginian mercenaries in the phalanx formation and taught them how to make the best use of their cavalry and war elephants on level territory. Then he tempted Regulus to battle before reinforcements had arrived. The Carthaginians won an overwhelming victory, and Regulus was captured.

Several years later, after the Carthaginians had suffered a bad defeat in Sicily, they sent Regulus to Rome to arrange for an exchange of prisoners and to urge the Romans to end the war. It was understood that he would be freed if he succeeded but that he would return to Carthage if he did not. Entering the Senate, where there was a strong sentiment in favor of peace, Regulus began to speak. His words were strong and full of conviction. But instead of telling the Senators to ransom the prisoners and end the war, he urged them to fight on. Then, keeping his eyes on the ground so he would not see his grieving wife and children, he returned to Carthage to suffer crucifixion and death. His bravery did not go unavenged, for two Carthaginian admirals were tortured in revenge, but Regulus' conduct illustrated to furture generations what the Romans meant by devotion to country.

The war dragged on. The Romans were twice defeated in naval engagements and in Sicily fared no better. They could not defeat a new Carthaginian general sent out against them (247 B.C.). This was Hamilcar, surnamed Barca (lightning). His genius for guerrilla warfare—he would sweep down on the Roman troops and then pull back to hideout where the enemy could not reach him—prevented the Romans from winning, but his attacks were not major enough to bring the Carthaginians victory. Polybius compared the contestants to two well-bred gamecocks "which fight to the last gasp. You may see them often, when too weak to use their wings, yet full of pluck to the end, striking again and again." Finally, patriotic citizens in Rome contributed from their own pockets the money for a new fleet of two hundred warships. This fleet won a complete victory near the Aegates Islands off Sicily (242 B.C.). Carthage, without money because of the loss of its trade, could no longer pay its mercenaries or build a new fleet. It sued for peace in 241 B.C. By the terms of the treaty Carthage agreed to abandon Sicily, to pay an indemnity, and to return all prisoners without ransom. After 24 years, the First Punic War was over, and Rome was the victor.

THE INTERVAL BETWEEN THE WARS

As soon as Carthage surrendered to Rome, the mercenaries who formed its armies mutinied. For three years Carthage was caught up in a terrible life-and-death struggle. It took all the great military talent of Hamilcar Barca for Carthage to survive. At the beginning of the mutiny, Rome had aided Carthage by sending supplies. Then, when Roman aid against the Carthaginians was requested by Sardinia, Rome changed its policy. It went to the aid of Sardinia and declared war against Carthage. Unable to accept the challenge, Carthage had to give up Corsica and Sardinia, which it bitterly resented. The Tyrrhenian Sea became a Roman lake with the three great islands of Sicily, Sardinia, and Corsica in Roman hands.

While Rome was strengthening its position in the south, it was also extending its frontiers in the east and north. Across the Adriatic Sea from Italy a partially civilized people, the Illyrians, lived by raiding towns on the mainland and by piracy at sea. Now that Rome held sway over southern Italy, the south Italian towns appealed to Rome for protection. Rome sent a fleet and troops against the Illyrians in 229 B.C. and again in 220 B.C. The victorious Romans established permanent bases on the Illyrian coast, and many of the Hellenic cities entered into an alliance. This brought Rome into direct and unfriendly contact with the Macedonian kingdom (page 329), which had designs on the cities of Hellas, and paved the way for Rome's later involvement in the affairs of the Hellenistic states.

In the north, the Romans defeated the Gauls who were living in the Po Valley. For fifty years the Gauls had ceased their raids into Italy and had been living quietly above the Rubicon River. Then in 225 B.C. they were joined by other Gallic tribes from beyond the Alps and invaded central Italy. After several years of fighting they were pushed out of the Po Valley, which was settled by colonies and traversed by a military road. Rome was now safe on its northern, eastern, and southern frontiers and controlled Italy from the Alps to the sea. It could await further developments with Carthage secure in the knowledge that it had no enemies at its front or rear.

Carthage, too, was trying to regain its losses. It turned to Spain, where it already had several settlements (page 170). It hoped that Spain's rich iron and silver mines and its hardy fighters would enable it to establish a new empire and provide resources against a future war with Rome. On Hamilcar Barca's death in 229 B.C., his son-in-law Hasdrubal continued his policies, conquering the east coast of Spain as far as the Ebro River. He founded New Carthage (Cartegena) as the future Punic capital in Spain. The Barca family acted like kings there. Carthage permitted this partly because of the great popularity of the family but more because their successes were reflected by quantities of Spanish silver flowing into the treasury of Carthage.

As Hasdrubal drove north, the Hellenic town of Massilia became alarmed and invoked its ancient alliance with Rome (page 260). Rome sent an embassy to Spain. It concluded a treaty with Hasdrubal in which he agreed to halt his northward expansion at the Ebro. The Romans returned home satisfied. They regarded Carthaginian expansion in Spain with a tolerant eye because Carthage was using some of its Spanish revenues to pay the war indemnity. Furthermore, as war with the Gauls was imminent (above, page 361), Rome needed peace on its other frontiers.

On Hasdrubal's death in 221 B.C. his brother-in-law (and Hamilcar Barca's son) Hannibal, 25 years old, became the Carthaginian commander. Disregarding Hasdrubal's treaty with Rome, Hannibal moved north of the Ebro River and also attacked Rome's ally Saguntum in 219 B.C. Rome demanded that Carthage depose Hannibal and surrender him to Rome. The Carthaginians refused, and Rome declared war.

The First Punic War had been a struggle for commercial supremacy in the Mediterranean. The Second Punic War was a fight for national survival, and it centered around the great Carthaginian general, Hannibal.

HANNIBAL

The personality of Hannibal is known to us only through his enemies. Though they were hardly in a position to evaluate him fairly, one Roman, the historian Livy, has left us a description of the Carthaginian that gives us some idea of his qualities: "His courage in meeting dangers and his prudence in the midst of them were extreme. Toil could neither exhaust his body nor subdue his mind, and he could endure hunger and cold alike. He ate and drank no more than nature demanded. Working day and night, he thought of sleep only when there was nothing else to do; then, wrapping himself in his military cloak, he would lie on the ground among the watchers and the outposts of the army. He was the first to enter battle and the last to leave the field."

The soldiers eagerly welcomed Hannibal as their leader, "for they imagined Hamilcar in his youth was restored to them; they noticed the same vigor in his frame, the same animation in his eyes, the same features and expression of the face . . ." He was a man fit to be the idol of his soldiers. He was a born leader of men, understanding well the psychology of his troops and that of his enemy. He was a brilliant military tactician who knew how to place his troops and take advantage of the terrain of the country. His great skills as a military commander have placed him in the rank of Alexander the Great, and his tactics have been studied with profit down to our own day.

Hannibal had been with his father in Spain all through his earliest years. Perhaps the story is true that Hamilcar Barca, never forgiving Rome for its treachery in seizing Sardinia and Corsica, had made the nine-year-old Hannibal swear undying enmity to Rome before the Carthaginian god Moloch. The tragedy of Hannibal was that his devotion and patriotism to his country, which never failed, only left Carthage weaker than when he found it, and that with all his genius, he made no mark on the future course of history.

THE SECOND PUNIC WAR, 218–201 B.C.

As naval master of the western Mediterranean, Rome intended to wage war in Africa and Spain, far from its own shores. A consul was immediately dispatched with an army to Sicily to protect the grain shipments to Rome, and another was ordered to Massilia to tie Hannibal down so he could not return to Africa to the defense of Carthage. But Rome reckoned without the genius of young Hannibal, whose bold movements immediately upset all calculations.

Hannibal in Italy. In the spring of 218 B.C. Hannibal crossed the Pyrenees from Spain into Gaul with an army of Spaniards and Africans and a contingent of war elephants. Hannibal thought an offensive war was the best way to defend Carthage and the possessions in Spain. His idea was to invade Italy, where he counted on being welcomed by the turbulent Gauls, still smarting under their recent defeat, and by Rome's allies, who, he thought, were anxious to be freed from the Roman yoke. Bypassing Massilia, where the Roman consul was posted with his army, Hannibal plunged into the Alps. Bringing not only infantry and cavalry but also a corps of elephants through the Alpine heights, where the people were hostile, there were no roads, and trails were overlaid with ice and snow, staggers the imagination. After a five-month march, the Carthaginian general had lost half his men and most of his elephants. He arrived in Italy with about twenty thousand men and six thousand cavalry, expecting to face a foe that could muster to its defense half a million men.

In northern Italy, after two victories at the Ticinus and Trebia rivers, Hannibal was warmly received by the Gauls. They furnished much needed troops for his army. In the spring of 217 B.C., now blinded in one eye by an inflammation that had not healed, Hannibal wiped out a whole Roman army and its consul at the battle of Lake Trasimene, one of the worst defeats that Rome ever suffered.

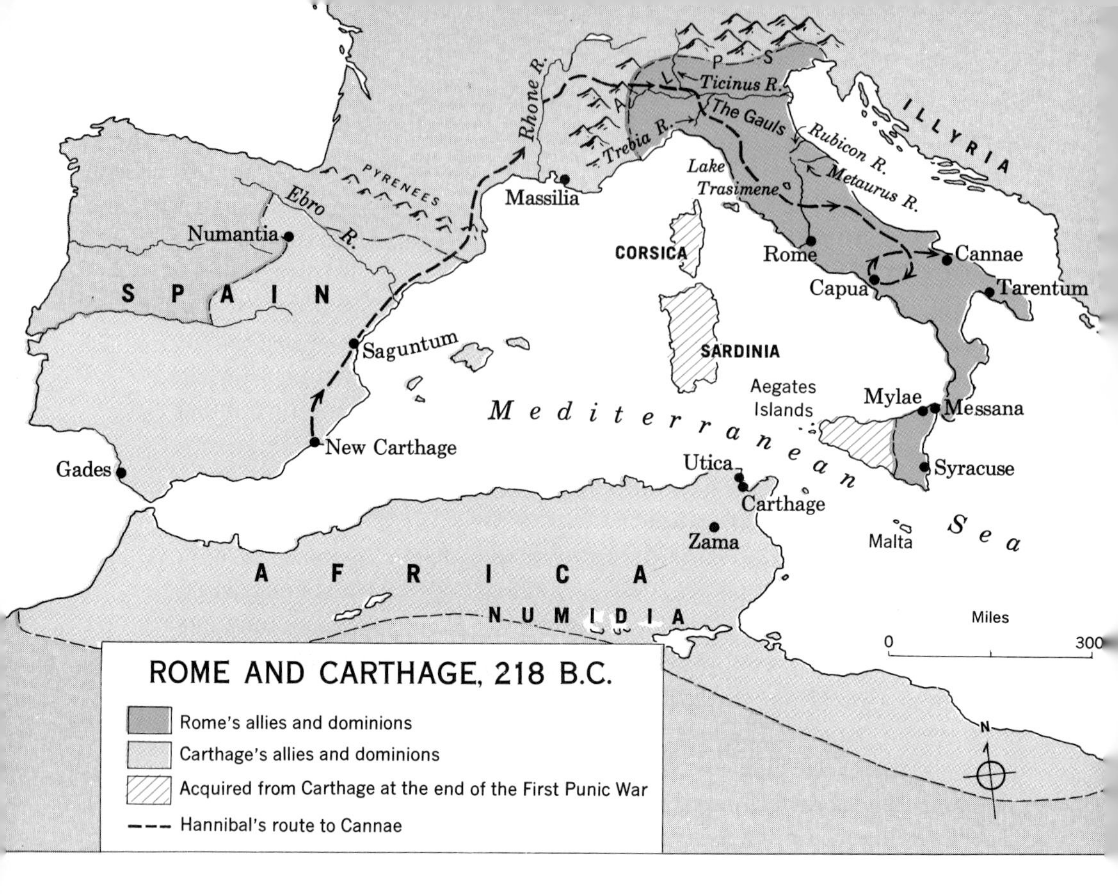

Hannibal found the road to Rome open before him. But he could not risk besieging the city without the necessary catapults and rams, equipment that he did not have. Instead he concentrated on gaining the alliance of the Italians. He set Italian prisoners free and sent them home with the news that if they joined his forces, he would liberate their cities. Not a single city accepted his invitation.

The Romans met the disaster of Lake Trasimene by appointing a dictator, Quintus Fabius Maximus. This cautious man refused, in spite of popular clamor, to chance a head-on collision with Hannibal. He recognized the superiority of Hannibal's tactics and the advantage the superb Numidian cavalry gave his foe, so he decided to dog Hannibal's footsteps instead. By hovering near Hannibal, Fabius hoped to cut off the Carthaginian parties foraging for food and to weary the enemy by keeping him constantly in a state of alert. This would give Rome precious time to raise and train a new army. Such a policy earned for Fabius the title *Cunctator* (Delayer), and such holding tactics have been known as Fabian tactics ever since.

A year later, in 216 B.C., Rome had trained ninety thousand fresh troops and sent them into the field under the new consuls of that year. They were told to find Hannibal and force a battle, for the people were weary of Fabius' tactics. The result was the greatest defeat in Roman history. At Cannae, Hannibal, although greatly outnumbered, annihilated the Roman army. How he accomplished this is extremely interesting to the student of military tactics. Hannibal had about fifty thousand men; his opponent had eighty thousand. Hannibal's superiority lay in his cavalry, the best in the world. This he posted on the wings. The infantry was placed in the center. The center was weak and was intended to draw the Roman troops in. It gave way before the Roman advance, a solid-column mass attack that the Romans had expected would gain them a quick victory. Instead of crushing the enemy, the Roman soldiers found themselves surrounded on both flanks and taken in the rear by the cavalry. The legions were attacked on three sides, the sun shone in their eyes, a strong wind blew the dust in their faces, and they were huddled so close together that they could not even draw, let alone wield, their swords. The result was a hideous butchery and the loss of nearly the entire army.

The battle of Cannae marked the high point of Hannibal's career. He had matched swords with the Romans four times, and each time he had won. He had proved that he could conquer with a much smaller force than his opponent and live successfully off the land. His victory at Cannae had serious consequences for Rome. Its allies, till then so faithful, began to show interest in supporting Hannibal. Even the Latin colonies were reluctant to send fresh troops. Philip V, the king of Macedon, made a treaty with Hannibal. The Sicilian cities, headed by Syracuse, came over to his side. Capua opened its gates to him, and Tarentum declared for him.

As Hannibal moved south, the Romans realized they would have to resume the delaying tactics of Fabius. By calling up boys and old men, they put together still one more army. The Romans then hung on Hannibal's flanks with smaller forces called up from each region. When not engaged in skirmishes, these troops forced deserting allies back to their Roman allegiance. They captured Syracuse after a siege of two years and then regained Capua and Tarentum. These victories among the Italian Hellenes enabled the Romans to keep the Macedonian king in check (page 368).

With dwindling forces, Hannibal awaited reinforcements from his brother, also called Hasdrubal, from Spain. Hannibal's first notice that his brother had crossed the Alps came on a day in 207 B.C. when Hasdrubal's severed head was hurled into Hannibal's camp. The Romans had intercepted messengers sent to Hannibal telling him of his brother's coming. Hastily they had put together an army, met Hasdrubal on his march south, and destroyed his

A war elephant and its driver. Elephants at first threw the Romans into a panic, but eventually they learned to fight against them, and on occasion to use them. In the turret on the elephant's back, much bigger in life than portrayed here, at least fifteen soldiers could be accommodated.

army at the Metaurus River. This was the last battle of the Punic Wars fought on the Italian peninsula.

Until 203 B.C. Hannibal remained in southern Italy. Then, after fifteen years on Italian soil, he returned to Carthage. A Roman army under Publius Cornelius Scipio had landed in Africa.

Scipio in Spain. Scipio, the most famous member of a famous family, had fought at Cannae at the age of eighteen and had been one of its few survivors. In 210 B.C. he had been sent to Spain to wage war against Hasdrubal. Myths sprang up around Scipio so that it is often difficult for us to know how much of what is told of him is true. His soldiers spread the story that he was the son of the god Jupiter and recounted miracles in which the gods held back a river so that Scipio's troops could cross without difficulty. Scipio reorganized the troops that had been badly beaten by the Carthaginians in 211 B.C., and in 209 B.C. he attacked New Carthage. He quickly captured the city. Its loss was not only a severe blow to Carthaginian prestige, but it also cut off the flow of silver to Carthage. In 208 B.C. Scipio defeated Hasdrubal, but the Carthaginian general slipped away with the remnants of his troops, leading them from Spain across southern Gaul and the Alps to Italy, where he was slain. Scipio's final victory in Spain came in 206 B.C., when he defeated an army led by Hannibal's youngest brother, Mago. When the city of Gades (Cadiz) deserted Carthage to join Rome, the Carthaginian empire in Spain was gone.

Scipio and Hannibal at Zama. In 204 B.C. Scipio had led a Roman army into Africa. He had no success until he was able to secure the aid of the Numidians, until then allies of Carthage and their chief source of horses and cavalry. The Carthaginians sued for peace, an armistice was granted, and Hannibal was called home. But his presence renewed Carthaginian hopes, and they broke the armistice. The two great generals, Scipio and Hannibal, faced each other near Zama in 202 B.C. Due partly to the presence in the Roman army of large numbers of Numidian cavalry, and partly to the retreat of Carthaginian mercenaries at a crucial moment, Scipio won the battle. This great victory earned him the title of "Africanus." It was the only battle that Hannibal lost, and we are told that if he had beaten Scipio, Hannibal would have ranked himself above Alexander the Great and Pyrrhus as a military leader.

Results of the Second Punic War. Carthage had already lost Spain. It was now stripped of all its African possessions, was forced to surrender all but ten ships and all war elephants, and was forbidden to engage in any future wars without Rome's permission. Carthage's Numidian neighbor was organized into a Roman allied state to hold Carthage in check.

Italy too suffered very heavily from the Second Punic War. The losses in manpower were enormous. The rural population had almost entirely vanished, fields lay untilled, the land had returned to wilderness, and many cities had lost their prosperity. Particularly heavy losses had been sustained in southern Italy, where Hannibal had ravaged the land for fifteen years. In order to prosecute the war, the government had had to take liberties with the constitution, appointing military commanders of talent, such as Scipio, to commands year after year through the device of proconsulships (page 261). Inflation and the rise in grain prices because of the disruption in agriculture added further to the trials of the Roman people. Yet the war had called forth all their best qualities—courage, devotion to country, and self-sacrifice. Though the war had drained their resources and severely reduced their manpower, their conduct had been steadfast. It aroused the admiration of generations to come.

ROMAN EXPANSION IN THE EASTERN MEDITERRANEAN, 200–133 B.C.

Until Pyrrhus had descended on Italy in response to the appeal from Tarentum (278 B.C.), the Romans had had little interest in the affairs of the eastern Mediterranean. Then the war against the Illyrians (229–219 B.C.) had won it the gratitude of the Hellenes but brought it into conflict with Philip V of Macedon. He had entered into an alliance with Hannibal (page 365), attacked Roman outposts in Illyria, and threatened an invasion of Italy. This conflict with Philip (the First Macedonian War, 215–206 B.C.) had important consequences. It aroused Roman fears that they might suffer an attack from the east. Once again the extension of Roman boundaries and alliances brought it into new potential conflicts.

Although the people were exhausted after the victory over Carthage, there were men in Rome whose pride had been swelled by the excitement and successes of the Punic Wars. They overrode the general reluctance for further war, played on fears of a possible Macedonian invasion, and created an atmosphere in which the Senate decided to chastise Philip V for his help to Hannibal.

A pretext for a fight with the Macedonians was easy to find. Philip V was an ambitious ruler. When Rhodes and Pergamum appealed to Rome for help against him, the Romans were quick to respond. Under the consul Flamininus, the Romans met the Macedonians at Cynocephalae (Dog's Head) in Macedon (197 B.C.). It was a contest of phalanx against legion, and the legionnaires won. Because Rome did not feel ready to annex additional territory at this time, Philip was allowed to keep his kingdom. But he had to give up his Hellenic possessions and pay a heavy indemnity. Macedon became a dependent Roman ally.

The Romans then declared the freedom of Hellas at the Isthmian Games at Corinth the following year (196 B.C.). The victor of Cynocephalae, the consul Flamininus, was nearly killed by the Hellenic demonstrations of joy. But though the Hellenes had won their freedom from Macedon, their constant quarrels did not cease. Rome was their new arbiter, and as the Hellenes learned, their liberty had its limits.

No sooner had the Romans liberated the Hellenes than a new threat appeared. Antiochus III, called the Great, of Syria, was expanding the boundaries of his kingdom and wished to add some of the Macedonian possessions that the Romans had freed. Antiochus found some allies among disgruntled Hellenes. He overran Asia Minor and invaded Thrace. The Romans, however, forced him out of Europe and into Asia Minor, where they defeated him in a great battle at Magnesia in Lydia in 190 B.C. Antiochus had to give up all his possessions in Asia Minor west of the border formed by the Halys River and the Taurus Mountains and pay a huge indemnity. The Romans left the states of Asia Minor free, as they had

Macedon. The Seleucid kingdom was confined to Palestine-Syria, Mesopotamia, and Cilicia, and it was told to stay out of Egypt, which the Romans wished to protect because of its grain shipments.

Rome was now fully involved in the affairs of the eastern Mediterranean. Soon again a new outbreak of hostilities disrupted the peace.

Perseus, son of Philip V of Macedon, harbored a deep resentment against the Romans. He had not forgotten his father's humiliation at their hands. He decided to look around among the Hellenic city-states for new partners to join him in an alliance against Rome. Before his plans matured, the Romans took to the field against him. The two forces met at Pydna in southern Macedonia in 168 B.C. Once again phalanx was pitted against legion; once again the legion proved its superiority. Perseus fled but was later captured. Macedonia became a province of Rome in 148 B.C.

The Romans had treated the city-states of Hellas leniently up to the victory of Pydna. Now they sought revenge against those states that had allied themselves with Perseus. Cities were looted, and their inhabitants were sold into slavery. Shiploads of furniture, works of art, and metals were sent to Rome to adorn the city and furnish the houses of wealthy Romans. One thousand hostages, among them the historian Polybius (page 343), were taken to Italy, where they languished for sixteen years. Finally, through the efforts of Polybius, who had come to know many influential Romans, they were allowed to return home. Resentful of the cruel words of the censor Cato ("It is only a question whether a parcel of worn-out Greeks shall be carried to their graves here or in Achaea [Hellas]"), they inflamed the passions of their countrymen upon their return, and the Achaean League (page 329) rashly declared war. Roman vengence was swift and fell on Corinth, the capital of the league. Corinth was one of the most beautiful cities in the world and was commercially very prosperous. The Romans sacked it and burned it to the ground in 146 B.C. Not only vengeance but also fear of commercial competition instigated this ruthless act. The Romans were not sure enough of their power to brook any rival, and Carthage suffered the same fate the same year (page 370). The other Hellenic city-states remained independent allies of Rome but lost some of their self-governing privileges. About one-hundred years later they were transformed into the province of Achaea with a rebuilt Corinth as its capital.

Further to the east the Romans had ruined the island of Rhodes (page 338) by creating the free port of Delos and then depriving Rhodes of its Asia Minor possessions for attempting to mediate in the quarrel with Perseus. In 133 B.C. the Romans accepted the kingdom of Pergamum from its last king (page 337). Pergamum, along with the Hellenic cities of Asia Minor, formed the rich province of Asia (129 B.C.). The Romans now controlled a good portion of the eastern Mediterranean. Parts of Asia Minor, Syria, Palestine, and Egypt were still independent, but Syria was subject to the will of Rome. In the next hundred years these areas too were conquered.

ROMAN EXPANSION IN THE WESTERN MEDITERRANEAN, 200–133 B.C.

While the Romans were extending their rule over the eastern Mediterranean, they had not been idle in the west. The Gauls were punished for their aid to Hannibal. Cisalpine Gaul was recovered between 198 and 191 B.C., new Latin colonies were established, and the area was crossed by new roads. In Spain, Roman rule was fiercely contested. Scipio's victories had pushed out the Carthaginians, but the barbarian Spaniards were not willing to accept the Romans in their place. The Spaniards were wild and independent, and in their mountain strongholds they put up a long and terrible struggle to maintain their independence (154–133 B.C.). Five times Viriathus, a chieftain of Lusitania, defeated the Roman armies. Spain raised such fears in Rome that levies were hard to raise. Finally the Romans paid for the assassination of Viriathus. Still desperate, they resorted to treachery and treaty violations to put down other native resistance. The final struggle centered at Numantia, an unwalled city in northern Spain. It was starved into submission in 133 B.C. Its fall ended Spanish resistance but the heroic conduct of its defenders is still celebrated in Spain.

A process of Romanization rapidly followed. Many colonists settled in Spain. The legionnaires acquired land and wives and intermingled with the population. Rome arrived with the sword, as in Italy, but it stayed to bring civilization in its wake. It repeated the process in Gaul, Britain, and among the barbarians of northern Europe.

THE THIRD PUNIC WAR, 149–146 B.C.

The greatest problem of all in the west was Carthage. After Zama (page 364), Hannibal had reorganized his city. With awe and fear, Rome watched its rival once more regain prosperity and commercial power. In 195 B.C. the Romans demanded Hannibal's surrender, but the Carthaginians, unwilling to sacrifice their hero, exiled him. He sailed to Syria and sought refuge at the court of Antiochus III the Great (page 368). The Romans continued to hound him, and when Antiochus' fleet was destroyed by the Romans, Hannibal fled to Bithynia, a kingdom in Asia Minor. The Romans sent a delegation to Bithynia demanding Hannibal's surrender. To avoid capture, Hannibal committed suicide in his 63rd year (183 B.C.).

Carthage's revival continued to haunt the Romans. It aroused the jealousy of Roman agricultural and commercial interests and made the land-hungry envious. After Cato the Censor (page 369) visited Carthage and saw its prosperity with his own eyes, he ended every speech in the Senate with the chilling words, "Carthage must be destroyed."

Under the treaty ending the Second Punic War, Carthage had been forbidden to wage war, even in self-defense, without Roman permission (page 367). Bordering Carthage on the south, and extending from the Atlantic past Carthage and hundreds of miles toward Egypt, lay the kingdom of Numidia, an ally of Rome. Its king, Masinissa, continually encroached on Carthaginian territory. Each time Carthage appealed to Rome, the Romans sent a commission to investigate; the commission secretly encouraged Masinissa and ruled in his favor. Masinissa intended to seize Carthage itself, but at this point Rome's interests differed from its ally's. A union of the great Punic port and the Numidian kingdom would create a state more powerful than the original Carthage, and there was no guarantee that such a state would not then rival Rome. So Rome watched for an excuse to destroy Carthage and at the same time prevent Masinissa from annexing the land. The chance came in 150 B.C.

For fifty years Carthage had faithfully observed all the terms of its treaty with Rome. Then in 150 B.C. it was driven to desperation by Masinissa's attacks and took up arms in defense against him. At the same time Carthage asked for Roman assistance and reaffirmed its desire to abide by its treaty obligations.

In a secret session the Roman Senate voted for the complete destruction of Carthage. Knowing that an announcement of this decision would arouse resistance in Africa, the vote was kept undercover. When the Carthaginian ambassadors arrived and asked what Rome wished, they were told "to give satisfaction to the Roman People." A second embassy was sent from Carthage to ask for a clearer statement of what was expected. This embassy was dismissed with the single statement, "You know well enough." In a new secret session the Senate voted to dispatch a Roman army to Africa. Not knowing Rome's plans, Carthage sent a third embassy and placed itself completely at Rome's command. It was now told to surrender three

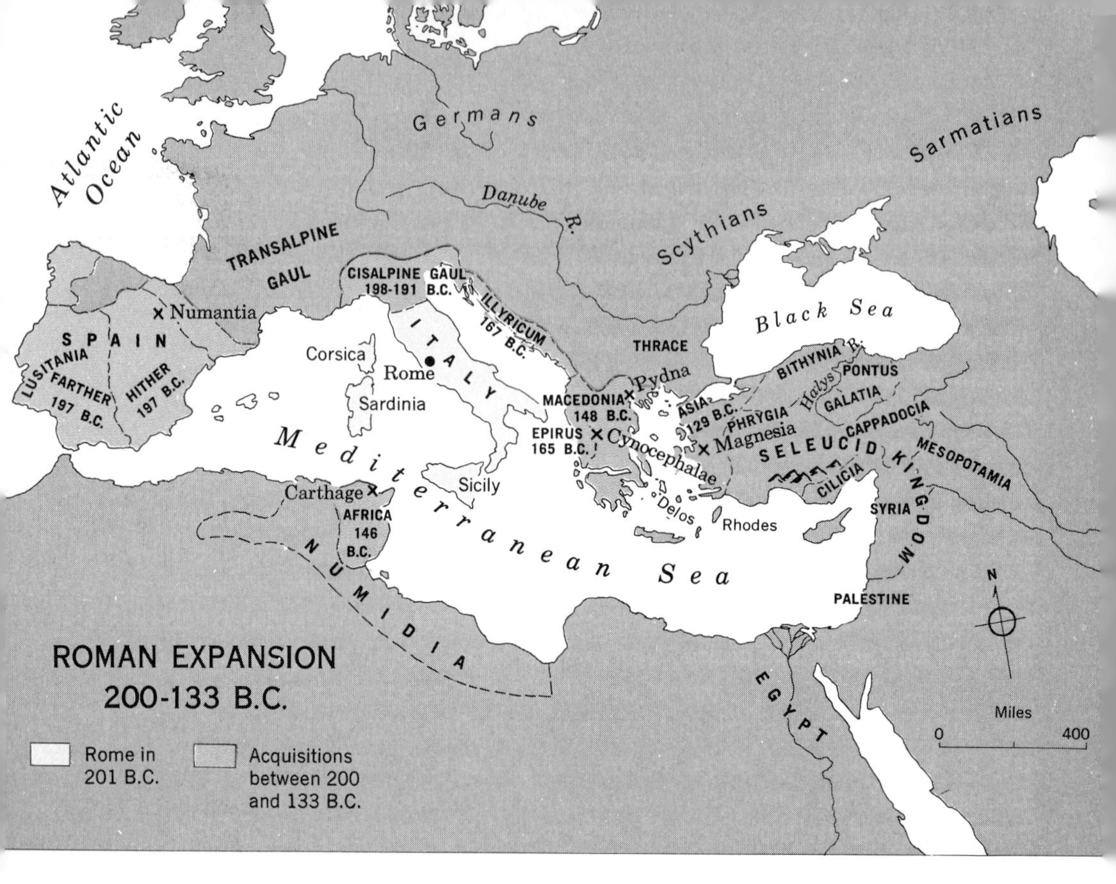

hundred hostages and then to wait further orders. The Roman consuls refused to make any statement until they could land an army in Africa.

In spite of their dismay at Rome's warlike preparations, the Carthaginians offered no resistance to the Roman navy and army when they arrived. The consuls ordered Carthage to hand over all weapons of any kind and all machines that could be used in war. Two hundred thousand swords and spears and two thousand catapults and other machines were accordingly surrendered. With Carthage completely defenseless, the consuls revealed their last orders. The entire population of Carthage was to leave the city permanently and to scatter at least ten miles inland from the sea. To a great city whose entire livelihood rested on sea commerce, this was recognized as the death sentence it was intended to be. The Carthaginians decided to resist. Without equipment, they barricaded themselves in their city and fought with whatever they could improvise. Lead and iron were torn from the public buildings and temples to make armor, while women cut off their hair and twisted it into ropes for catapults and bowstrings. It took three years of merciless, continual attack for the Romans to starve out the

the Carthaginians. Carthage was then razed to the ground, and the site was declared accursed. The land was plowed up with salt to symbolize its return to open fields, and all its remaining inhabitants, some fifty thousand, were sold into slavery. The inland region around it was organized into the Roman province of Africa. The Romans dignified the whole treacherous and disgraceful episode with the name of the "Third Punic War."

PROVINCIAL RULE

The Roman provincial system came into being when Sicily, which had been acquired at the end of the First Punic War (241 B.C.), was organized in 227 B.C. as Rome's first province. By 133 B.C., other provinces were Sardinia and Corsica, Hither and Further Spain, Illyricum, Macedonia, Epirus, Achaea, Africa, and, in 129 B.C., Asia.

The status of each province was determined by a victorious general and ten senators specially appointed to assist him. Their efforts were subject to the later approval of the Senate. A few communities were allies, like those of the Italian confederacy. Others, by special act of the Roman government, were free. The largest majority by far were tax-paying dependencies. They were under the jurisdiction of a governor, a Roman magistrate. He was either a praetor or consul especially appointed by the Senate to serve abroad, and he was called proconsul or propraetor. A province was allowed to follow its own laws and customs and had its local officials and popular assembly, subject to the governor. Even if it had wished to do so, Rome did not have the men to manage the internal affairs of each community it conquered. Foreign affairs were conducted by Rome.

The governor was appointed for a term of twelve months, and he received no salary. His duties were primarily military and judicial. He commanded the army, whose duty was to protect the provincial boundaries, and he judged cases involving Roman citizens. The governor was also expected to keep the peace, law, and order, and to arrange for the payment of taxes. These were either a fixed sum or 10 per cent of the annual produce of the province. In neither case were they exorbitant. They were usually similar to what had always been collected. At the end of his term, the governor could be called up to account for his year in office upon his return.

The system of administrating the provinces was just in theory, but it did not work out justly in practice. The primary reason for this was that the provinces were looked on as rich plums to be squeezed for all they were worth. They were plundered by victorious generals and soldiers. Their governors, unpaid, looked on them as the source of their future fortune. Governors established levies, accepted bribes and presents, and even confiscated lands to enrich themselves at public expense; and a really grasping governor, it was said, might leave his province with three fortunes: the first to pay off the enormous debts he had acquired in Rome in order to be elected to a magistracy, the second to pay off his judges should he have to stand trial upon his return home, and the third to enable him to live richly ever after. Even if a governor had the best intentions upon taking office, it was difficult, during a twelve-month term, to correct existing abuses.

The worst abuse was in the system of taxation. The collection of taxes was in the hands of private collectors called *publicans*. They wrung all they could from the wretched people, paid the stipulated amount to the government, and then kept the rest for themselves. These publicans were so greedy and the abuses of the provincial system became so flagrant that they created a scandal in Rome (page 392). Little, however, was done to correct the system. Rome, so successful in organizing the confederacy, was unable to transpose its success abroad. Not until the Empire were the abuses in the provinces corrected. The governors remained virtually independent. Many of them were appointed on the basis of favoritism, without regard to ability or honesty. If they were tried upon retirement from office, their judges were magistrates who themselves hoped to be governors one day. Furthermore, the provincials had no system of representation in Rome. If they complained, they had little chance of redress at the hands of a Senate, now open to bribery and that, in any case, had only the vaguest idea of provincial affairs. The crux of the matter was that the Romans did not have the same attitude toward the provinces that they had toward the Italian territories. These they had treated as equals or allies. The provinces, on the contrary, were merely subjects whose main function was to pay tribute. As the Romans increased their territories, they came to enjoy the rewards of loot and plunder which poured into Rome. They considered the benefits of peace and order, a uniform system of law, and a standard coinage, all of which followed in the wake of Roman conquest, enough for the provincials.

ROMAN SOCIETY AFTER THE PUNIC WARS

The Roman of the early Republic had been a small farmer, honest, stern, moral, celebrated for his conservative, old-fashioned ways. Such men worked hard on their little farms, fought bravely in the legions, and honored the family and state gods. Cincinnatus was such a man (page 261), as were Curius Dentatus (page 353) and Regulus (page 360).

The Roman wars of conquest transformed the character of the Romans and of their civilization. Contact with the east, and specifically with the Hellenistic world, wrought these changes. The Romans came into extended touch with the Hellenes for the first time in Sicily during the First Punic War. Then the conflicts with Macedon and Syria exposed the Romans to further Hellenistic influence. Roman soldiers saw the beauties of Hellenistic art and architecture; they attended the theater, were introduced to Hellenic prose and poetry, listened to the intricacies of philosophic discussions, and heard about new religions. The enormous wealth that poured into Rome from booty and the provinces made it possible to have luxuries from the east that were new to the thrifty Romans—beautiful statues for the temples, galleries of paintings in their houses, silk and gold for their clothes. Prisoners of war were brought to Rome to serve as slaves in the fields, where they displaced the free workers, and in the household. Often far more learned and cultivated than their masters, they passed on their learning as tutors and secretaries to wealthy Romans and as rhetoricians, philosophers, and doctors. Such a man was the historian Polybius, a hostage from the wars in Hellas (page 369). He was the tutor and friend of Scipio Aemilianus, conqueror of Carthage. The Scipios were famous *philhellenes* (lovers of things Greek). Scipio Aemilianus gathered about him a group of able and cultured Hellenes who did much to popularize Hellenic literature and philosophy in Rome.

Such changes excited the opposition of those who clung to the time-honored virtues and who saw danger in the way Roman traditions were being overwhelmed by Hellenistic ones. Cato the Censor was the foremost spokesman of this group. He lived during the period following the Second Punic War. Next to his father's farm stood the modest cottage of Curius Dentatus (page 353), a constant reminder of the old-fashioned Roman ways and their simple virtues. Cato practiced what he preached during his years in the Senate. He "worked with his slaves, in winter wearing a coarse coat without sleeves, in summer nothing but his tunic; and he used to sit at meals with them, eating the same loaf and drinking the same wine." In vain did he expel dissolute members of the Senate, establish laws providing that a woman could wear no more than one ounce of gold on her person, and limiting the number of guests a man could have for dinner and the amount of money he could spend on it. The "customs of the fathers" were not able to stand up under the impact of eastern influence.

Particularly unfortunate was the effect of this influence on the Roman religion, the basis of the Roman moral character. The Romans incorporated Hellenic gods in their pantheon (page 267), but they lost faith in deities who had human weaknesses. With the old belief in the ancestral gods undermined by Hellenic philosophic speculations and the new gods unacceptable, a vacuum was created that was filled for many of the poorer people by the mystery religions (page 206), which were introduced to Rome at this time. Among them was the cult of Dionysus (page 206) and that of Cybele, the Great Mother of Asia Minor. These were suppressed in 186 B.C. because of the extremes of some of their rituals, but they had a strong emotional appeal in Rome, as they had in Hellas. In the long run it was as impossible to keep them out as it was to outlaw the introduction of luxuries and refinements.

The influence of the Greek east had many positive effects. Rome lost its provincialism. Its exposure to the higher culture of the east refined its tastes and raised its standard of living. It became a cosmopolitan city, more sophisticated intellectually, and physically more beautiful. "Captive Greece captured her conqueror rude," wrote the poet Horace. Rome had abandoned its old ways and was entering new paths as befitted its position as ruler of much of the Mediterranean world.

❦ ❦ ❦

In two hundred years Rome had risen to be first a local power in Italy, then one of the five powers in the Mediterranean, and finally the foremost power. In conquering the peoples of Italy, it had woven them into a confederacy that inspired their loyalty and support during the devastating years of the Punic Wars. The Romans, victorious over their Carthaginian rivals, then pushed east and west in further conquests as alliances and treaties involved them in conflicts in the Hellenistic and barbarian worlds. Such extensions of the Roman horizons changed the Roman character and the quality of their society. It produced far-reaching changes in their government, and these in turn had profound effects on the Mediterranean world.

People, Places, and Terms

Samnites
Pyrrhus
Hamilcar Barca
Hannibal
Fabius the *Cunctator*

Scipio Africanus
Cato the Censor

Campania
Tarentum
Epirus

Cannae
Zama
Illyria
Corinth

mercenary

guerilla warfare
indemnity
punic
publican
philhellene
proscription

Mastering the Reading

1. How did Rome gain control of the peninsula of Italy? What working relationships did Rome establish with its allies? What differences existed in full and half citizenship? How did Rome stimulate a sense of Roman identity even among former enemies?
2. What caused the Roman-Carthaginian rivalry? What was achieved in the First Punic War? What footholds did Rome gain between the First and Second Punic wars? What were the results of the Second Punic War?
3. With what consequences did each of these men draw Rome into Eastern Mediterranean affairs: Philip V? Antiochus III? Perseus? How did Rome become involved with the Hellenic states? What was the outcome?
4. What were some of the underlying flaws in the Roman provincial system? In what ways did Rome profit from contact with more advanced cultures? Why did the solid, conservative Republican consider such contact a threat?

Interpreting the Text

1. How many examples of Roman "practicality, ingenuity, and adaptability" can you find as Rome grew from a small town into mistress of the Mediterranean world?
2. Do you agree with Horace that "Captive Greece captured her conqueror rude"?

Exploring Beyond the Text

Any of the following would make fascinating reading: Roman military tactics; Hannibal, Scipio, or Fabius as seen through the eyes of Polybius, Livy, and Plutarch (how and why they differ in interpretation); the art of diplomacy as practiced by Rome.

Working with the Map

1. Judging from the series of maps on pages 355 and 364, why would you say that the Punic Wars were inevitable?
2. Compare the maps on pages 372, 391, and 436. What peoples had the Romans absorbed during their expansion?

19

Rome: The Passing of the Republic

133–30 B.C.

The Romans had gained an empire after building the fleet that won them mastery over the Carthaginians. Now they had to face the problems of expanding the machinery of a city-state government to rule such an empire and of adjusting to new political and social needs brought about by their conquests.

This was not an easy matter. Continual warfare had dislocated Roman society. No longer were few rich, few poor, as in the days of the early Republic. Many farmers had been killed and their property ruined or confiscated. Others, returning from the wars and finding the land devastated or their homes gone, drifted poverty-stricken into Rome, where they had no means of support. Not only did their condition seriously weaken the economy, but the decline in the small landowning class also made it difficult to raise men for the army, as property was still a qualification for service. A whole class in Roman society was on the verge of disappearing, a class that had been the backbone of the Republic and that had produced the men who had created the Roman state.

While the farmers were turning into a city mob, "preferring to clap their hands at the circus to working in their fields and vineyards," other groups were growing richer. During the war against Hannibal, the senators had been forbidden by law to engage in commerce. Their services were needed to govern the Republic during the crisis. They turned their wealth into land. Buying up large tracts, they worked them with gangs of slaves who flooded the market from conquered territories. The senators—learned, pleasant, agreeable, and good company—were very often more interested in their individual needs and pleasures than with the concerns of the Republic.

Furthermore, the senators, who had always been the real governing body of the Republic, now found their authority challenged by a group with interests different from their own. Because the senatorial class had been excluded from conducting the business of Rome, a new group of propertied men called knights (*equites*) arose to do so. Into their hands fell the lucrative contracts for building the houses to shelter the city poor, for laying out the new military roads, for making loans to the provincials. The knights became prosperous and wished to share in the political and social privileges of the senators. And, like many of the senators, they had lost the virtues of honesty and patriotism on which the older Romans had prided themselves. Too often open to bribery in politics and loose in morals, they were made of very different stuff from their stern ancestors. They represented a new class that had to be integrated into a new Roman society.

The rival needs and ambitions of the different social groups at home, the demands of an empire on a government designed to rule a city-state, and the failure of the senatorial class to cope with these problems, produced a political revolution that ended the republican form of government in Rome. This change, not planned but gradually inevitable, took about one hundred years. Many very able men were responsible for it. The first of these were the two Gracchi brothers, Tiberius and Gaius. They came forward with a program they hoped would bolster the Republic by helping the sagging economy of Italy.

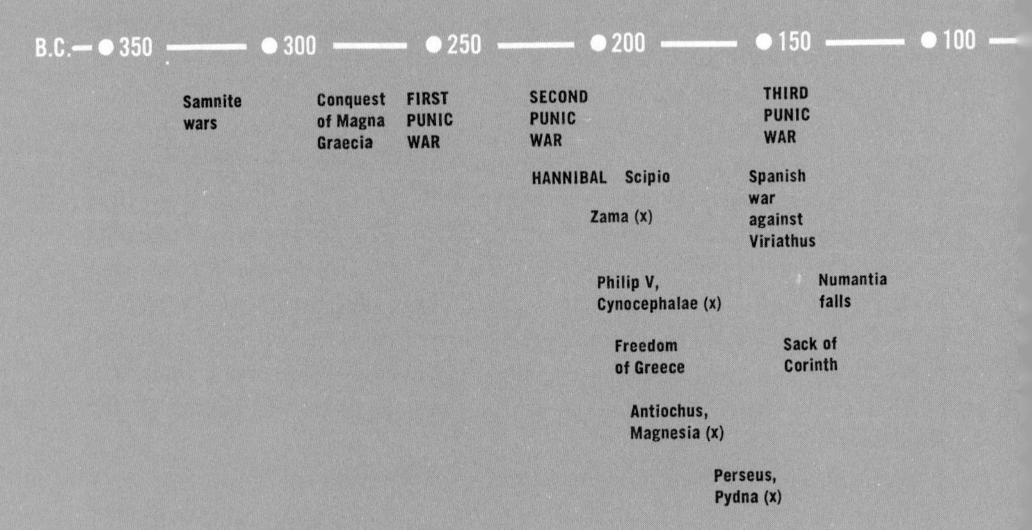

THE REFORMERS, 133–78 B.C.

During the third and second centuries B.C., a new aristocracy had arisen in Rome after the plebeians had gained social equality with the patricians (page 257). This new aristocracy was composed of the patricians and those wealthier plebeians who had won election to the higher magistracies and had then entered the Senate. Such men were "known" or "distinguished," called by the Romans *nobile*. All their descendants thereafter shared this distinction.

THE GRACCHI AND AGRICULTURAL REFORM

The father of Tiberius and Gaius Gracchus was a *nobile*. He had served his country as a consul and proconsul and had been elected Censor (page 264). Their mother, Julia, was a patrician, the daughter of Scipio Africanus, the conqueror of Hannibal. She called her boys her "jewels" and taught them to love their country above all else. Tiberius, after having served honorably with the army in Spain, decided to seek political office as one of the ten tribunes of the people. He was elected in 133 B.C., the same year the revolt in Spain ended and Asia was acquired (page 370).

Tiberius immediately proposed a series of agrarian reforms. His program was to reclaim the public lands, largely in the hands of the rich, and divide them into tracts for the poor. The government was to advance money for the purchase of livestock and equipment. This proposition aroused the opposition of the senators and the wealthy knights. The senators promptly pressured another tribune to veto the measure. Tiberius then took matters into his own hands. He had the veto overruled by instructing the Assembly to remove the offending tribune from office. While not exactly illegal, this act was contrary to custom and therefore not entirely legal. But Tiberius prevailed, and the law was passed. Tiberius then offered himself for reelection, again contrary to custom, because he wished to be sure his reforms were carried through. But a riot erupted on the day of the election. Tiberius and three hundred of his followers were murdered, and their bodies were flung into the Tiber.

Such a display of violence shocked the people. The land commission that had been set up was therefore allowed to continue its work, and the census rolls reveal the names of many new landholders. In the meantime, other matters occupied the public's attention and passions cooled. Gaius Gracchus decided the time was ripe to stand for election to continue his brother's work.

Gaius was elected tribune in 123 B.C. In the ten-year interval between his brother's magistracy and his own, the tribunate was opened to reelection. Gaius intended to use this position to effect his reforms by controlling the assembly year after year through reelection. This would make the tribunate and the assembly the real governing force in Rome. Gaius understood that he needed the support of both the people (*populares*) and the knights (*equites*) to accomplish this. His proposals, therefore, were far more sweeping than his brother's.

Gaius' primary aims were the relief of the poor by the continuation of Tiberius' land act, the establishment of commercial colonies both at home and overseas, and a grain dole. As he also pushed through an extensive public-works program, the grain dole was presumably intended as a stopgap to provide for the people until they could do so for themselves. He pleased the knights by enacting a measure by which juries were selected from their number, a privilege formerly reserved to senators, and by placing the collection of provincial taxes in their hands. But then he lost the support of both knights and people when he proposed that the Italian allies be given Latin rights and the Latins full citizenship. These were privileges jealously guarded and rarely granted, and both knights and people were afraid that the enrollment of a large number of new citizens would infringe on their privileges.

A Roman farmer. A stooping farmer walks to market, carrying his goods and taking his cow with him. He passes houses and roadside shrines. By the first century B.C., when this relief was carved, small farmers were in serious trouble. Few could compete with rich property owners working large tracts of land with slave labor.

In this measure Gaius was farsighted. He realized, as had one or two magistrates before him, that the success of any program depended on making one nation of all the Italian people with Rome as their capital. The time to do so, however, was not ripe. Gaius failed to be reelected tribune for a third term in 121 B.C., and on a pretext the Senate declared him a public enemy. Rather than suffer the disgrace of a trial, he committed suicide by the hand of a slave.

The Gracchi are controversial figures in the history of Rome. Some scholars look on them as heroes who tried to reform the Republic before it was too late; others regard them as destroyers of the Roman way of life who used the untutored mob as a support for reform and demoralized the people with a dole. Unwittingly, perhaps, the agricultural reforms of Tiberius Gracchus provoked a conflict between the interests of the poor and those of the rich. The unwritten power of the Senate had been openly challenged, and such a challenge had to be solved for the state to function effectively. The people had a program, a cause, and two martyrs whose memorials, springing up all over Rome, kept the issues alive in the public mind. The knights had had a taste of political power and wished to increase it to advance their interests. So the agricultural issues on which the Gracchi had based their reforms were lost in the larger ones of how and by whom the Romans were to be governed. Thus the reforms of the Gracchi are considered the first step in the revolution that led to the downfall of the Republic.

In the careers of the Gracchi, violence twice prevented the constitution from functioning properly. It seemed that violence was to be a new instrument of power. This new instrument was given visible form under the leadership of Gaius Marius, a new popular leader on the political scene.

MARIUS AND THE NEW ARMY

Marius was a "new man," one who had risen to power through his own efforts and abilities. His plebeian origin made him an outsider to the aristocrats. They distrusted him, though he had married the patrician Julia (page 393). Marius, in turn, had little use for the nobility. "Compare me, the 'new man,' my fellow citizens," he said, "with those proud nobles. What they know from lectures and books, I have myself seen, myself done. They despise me for an upstart, I despise their worthlessness. They can taunt me with my social position, I them with their infamies. My own belief is that men are born equal and alike: nobility is achieved by bravery."

Jugurtha and the Gauls. Marius made his money as a government contractor. He acquired enough property to become a knight and then started his political career as a tribune. He was elected consul in 107 B.C. upon promising to conclude the lingering war against Jugurtha, a Numidian who had illegally seized the throne of that Roman ally. During Jugurtha's campaigns many Roman and Italian merchants in Africa had been killed, and public opinion was aroused. Marius disposed of Jugurtha with the help of a young lieutenant named Sulla, who captured the wily African by treachery. Marius returned to Rome to celebrate a triumph in which Jugurtha appeared in chains, and immediately a new threat engaged his attention. Two Celtic tribes, the Cimbri and the Teutones, had pressed on the province of Narbonensis, the Rhone lands forming the southeastern part of Transalpine Gaul (see map, page 391). In 105 B.C. they routed a Roman army in a battle nearly as catastrophic as Cannae. The passes over the Alps to Italy lay open. Panic gripped Rome, and all eyes turned to Marius. Hurrying north, he waited for the Celts. By some change in plan the Teutones had swept north to range through Gaul. Contrary to custom, Marius was reelected to the consulship four years in succession while waiting their return. Not until 102 B.C. did they turn south. Then Marius met and defeated them at Aquae Sextiae (Aix). The following spring the Cimbri, who had entered the Po Valley, met the same fate at Vercellae. For the moment the barbarians were contained, but their presence was to be a recurring problem in the following centuries.

Marius' Army. Italy had been saved not only by the skilled generalship of Marius, who had won over a barbarian force much larger than his own, but also by the fighting ability of the new army he had put together. The legion had been reorganized and was divided into ten *cohorts* of six hundred men, each subdivided into six *centuries* commanded by a *centurion.* The maniple arrangement (page 268) was given up, and all the men were drilled and trained alike to operate like clockwork. This army, unlike armies in the past, had been recruited from among the poor city dwellers without property. These men were enrolled as volunteers for a term of sixteen to twenty years, making them a professional fighting force.

Here was a solution to the problem of the depopulation of the countryside. Such an army was very different, however, from that of propertied citizen-soldiers fighting for love of country. In Marius' army the soldiers looked to their general for pay, promotion, and rewards. They owed their loyalty to him, not to the Senate or the state. Such soldiers might be the extra arm a man could use to establish and hold himself in power. A popular general could always look to his legionaires for support.

Marius returned in triumph to Rome and could then and there have made himself king. But he accepted another consulship instead and turned to domestic politics, hoping to advance the cause of the people. In this role he was unsuccessful. He neither pushed through true reform nor created a new place for himself in the government. Furthermore, when a disorder arose over the election of 99 B.C., Marius, in the end a solid citizen and a knight, supported the established order and the Senate against the people, and his supporters were killed. His political fortunes suffered an eclipse while those of Sulla, his former lieutenant in the war against Jugurtha, rose.

SULLA AND A NEW SENATE

Lucius Cornelius Sulla was an impoverished patrician endowed with a great many natural talents. To them were added a reputation for good fortune and his own belief in a lucky star that never failed him. In middle age his physical appearance was striking: "His eyes were an uncommonly pure and piercing blue, which the color of his face rendered still more terrible, as it was spotted with rough red blotches interspersed with white, a mulberry besprinkled with meal." Indulgence had left its mark on a strong constitution that had enjoyed all the pleasures of a cosmopolitan city.

Sulla had acquired his fortune by serving as governor of Cilicia in Asia Minor. His military career had included service against Jugurtha, and he had fought well against the Cimbri. Now another opportunity for him to further his career presented itself.

The Social War, 90–88 B.C. The Italian allies, discouraged by their repeated failures to be admitted to the franchise and to gain other citizenship rights, revolted. They set up their own state, called it Italia, and made Corfinium its capital. They established a form of government much like that of Rome, with consuls and a senate. They issued a coinage and offered citizenship to all those who joined them. Their armies, composed of veterans of Marius' army, were again and again successful in the field. Here was a very severe menace to Rome. The Romans, with fresh troubles brewing in the east (below), thought again and then offered citizenship to all who would return to their allegiance. Their policy of divide and conquer won the day. The Italian revolt collapsed, and in the years that followed, the Romans and Italians gradually blended into one people, citizens of a national state with Rome as its capital. This long overdue development had come about only as a result of a bloody war to gain for the allies what Rome could have granted them peaceably. Once again the Senate had failed to deal with a pressing need, and violence had resulted.

The Social War (from *socii*, allies) added luster to Sulla's star as he had won honor fighting in the south. It had also brought Marius back to popular favor, for he had fought well in the north. When the senatorial party won the election of 88 B.C., Sulla was given the consulship. He was promptly appointed to the command against Mithradates, king of Pontus in Asia Minor, who had seen a chance to add to his territory in the east while Rome was diverted by the Italian revolt. Sulla gathered an army and prepared to leave Italy.

Rivalry Between Marius and Sulla. Marius had watched Sulla's rise with disapproval and envy. No two men could have been more different: the one a hardy, simple, plain-spoken soldier, the other an elegant aristocrat whose polished manner and urbanity covered a cruel and unscrupulous nature, sharpened by want in youth and debauchery in age. The rivalry that followed between Marius and Sulla marked the extreme use of violence and proved to be another important step in the decline of the Republic. Each man used the army to support his claims to power, and their successors followed suit. For the next seventy years, Rome was shaken by a continuous series of fierce civil wars that put scores of legions in the fields, decimated families by bloody purges, and did not end until one man, Octavian, held the reins of power firmly in his hands.

The War Against Mithradates. When Marius' supporters heard that Sulla had been given the Mithradates command, they intrigued in the assembly to have it transferred to Marius. They were successful. Sulla, meanwhile, had not yet left Italy. When he heard what had happened, he turned back to Rome, entered the city illegally with his army behind him—the first time any commander had ever done so—punished his opponents, though opposition had melted in the face of his troops, and strengthened senatorial authority so the government would be safe while he was away. Marius fled to Africa, wondering whether the prophecy that he would serve seven consulships would ever be fulfilled.

Sulla sailed east in the spring of 87 B.C. He defeated Mithradates in two years and then so ravaged Hellas and the cities in Asia Minor for their part in supporting the king that they did not regain their prosperity for two hundred years. Sulla then concluded a peace with Mithradates, but he allowed the king to keep his kingdom as trouble was stirring in Rome.

No sooner had Sulla left Italy than the people, under a new leader, Cinna, recalled Marius. The aged soldier, a wounded elephant after his misfortunes, put together a new army and seized the city. A terrible massacre of all Sulla's supporters followed, as if Marius had gone mad. Marius was elected to his seventh consulship in 86 B.C., but, exhausted by his exertions, he died a few days later.

Civil War Between Marius and Sulla. Sulla in the meantime made preparations to return home. He first sent back a report to the Senate describing his campaigns, and then he declared grimly that he was coming home to punish his enemies. He landed at Brundisium in 83 B.C. with an army of loyal veterans who, rewarded by loot and booty from their campaigns, were ready to follow their general against all comers. The son of Marius had gathered an army, and for eighteen months war waged between the forces of the young Marius and those of Sulla. Two young men named Crassus and Pompey correctly assumed that Sulla's battle-trained troops would have the edge and raised armies on his behalf. Sulla's lucky star did not fail him. He won the final victory at the battle of the Colline Gate before Rome in 82 B.C., and the doors of the city were opened to him.

Sulla's vengeance against his enemies proved to be even more fantastic than Marius'. A veritable carnival of butchery followed, not only in Rome but throughout the cities of Italy, against those who found disfavor with Sulla or his friends. Several thousand people perished, and the memory of the Sullan proscriptions stayed long in Roman memory.

The Dictatorship of Sulla. Vengeance accomplished, Sulla turned his attention to the problems of government. He accepted the title of Perpetual Dictator, and Rome came under the rule of one man for an unlimited period for the first time since the expulsion of the kings.

Sulla tried to reestablish the traditional position of the Senate, which, though weakened and corrupt, he thought was preferable to that of the fickle urban poor. He attempted to establish by law the power and authority of the Senate that in earlier times had been accepted by custom and tradition. Though he did not succeed in this endeavor, he did make successful changes in the machinery of government. Among his most important measures was one to broaden the Senate by enlarging it to six hundred and including younger members of the propertied class (knights), many of whom were from the Italian cities; another was to bring more mature men into government by setting minimum age limits for the course of office (page 265). Sulla also made efforts to regulate the provincial governorships, and, in order to prevent future civil wars, he decreed that it was treasonable for provincial governors to lead their armies out of their provinces.

The succeeding years, which largely undid the work of Sulla, proved that it was too late to reform the Republic by reestablishing the power of the Senate, and that the question was simply who would replace Sulla in power. But the Perpetual Dictator, thinking his work accomplished, unexpectedly lay down his power in 79 B.C. to live out his life in luxury. He died one year later and was given a splendid state funeral. His epitaph read: "No friend ever did him a kindness, and no enemy a wrong, without being fully repaid."

THE REPUBLIC FAILS, 78–49 B.C.

In the thirty years following Sulla's death, four figures were continually at or near the center of the political stage. These four were Pompey, Crassus, Cicero, and Julius Caesar.

POMPEY THE GREAT

Gaeus Pompeius, known in English as Pompey, first came to the attention of the public when he raised an army to support Sulla's return to Rome (page 386). No Roman ever surpassed Pompey in the ability to arouse friendship, love, admiration, and approval. He was thought to resemble the fabled Alexander the Great in physical beauty and to excel all Romans in dignity and manliness.

Sulla rewarded Pompey for his support by sending him to Africa and Sicily to wipe out Marian opposition there. Successfully accomplishing this task, Pompey returned to Rome and demanded a triumph. This he received,

Pompey. Though an honorable gentleman and much admired, Pompey, we are told, was also vain and pompous. History has treated him harshly because he failed to achieve any positive good for the Republic.

as well as the further honor of the title of *Magnus*, the great, bestowed on the young man by the flattering Sulla.

Sertorius. After Sulla's death, trouble arose in Spain. Sertorius, the governor of the province, had been a supporter of Marius. A brave and dedicated man, he sympathized with the provincials and understood their desire to be equal with the Romans. He felt he represented the true government of Rome and made Spain the center of popular resistence to the Senate. Very skillfully he obtained the support of the Spaniards. He governed them fairly, educated the sons of prominent families in the Roman fashion, and treated all Spaniards as potential citizens. Sertorius defeated all the armies sent out by Rome against him. In desperation the Senate created a special command for Pompey, and though he had held no civil office, the senators sent him to Spain with the rank of proconsul. For seven years, 78 to 71 B.C., Pompey and Sertorius fought an indecisive war. Finally, Sertorius' forces were weakened by conflict between his Spanish allies and his Roman supporters, and he was murdered. Pompey defeated his remaining forces and regained Spain.

The Revolt of Spartacus. Hastening back to Rome once again victorious, Pompey stopped off to mop up the remnants of a great slave revolt that had been put down by Crassus. This revolt, led by a Thracian gladiator named Spartacus, had terrified Rome. Some seventy thousand slaves, outlaws, and poverty-stricken peasants had joined Spartacus in the crater of Mt. Vesuvius, then inactive, and had beaten back two armies sent against them. Spartacus had hoped to lead his followers out of Italy and north to freedom, but they refused to follow him and turned aside to plunder and ravage the countryside.

Crassus, the richest man in Rome, was given a special command to defeat them. He killed Spartacus in 71 B.C. and most of the rebel army was defeated; but a remnant fled north, and Pompey cut it off. This action enabled him to claim a share in Crassus' victory. Six thousand slaves were crucified along the Appian Way to serve as a warning to any future revolutionaries. Nevertheless, the success of Spartacus in raising such a mighty force testifies to the great dissatisfaction in the land and to the profound discontent among the poor.

Pompey and Crassus, Consuls. Two successful generals and two armies faced each other in Italy. Both men demanded triumphs and both wanted the consulship for 70 B.C. Pompey's demand was illegal, for he was not qualified either by age or by experience in government. But the Senate was in a weak position due to a scandal involving the mismanagement of Verres, the governor of Sicily (below, page 391), and could only hope to turn Pompey and Crassus against each other. Rivals they were, but fools they were not. The maneuver did not work, and the two of them together overawed the Senate and gained the consulships.

Pompey and Crassus had both been followers of Sulla. Crassus, like Pompey, had raised an army to support Sulla (page 386), and his great wealth had come from buying up the proscribed lands at low cost. Now both Pompey and Crassus turned against the Sullan constitution when they found the Senate standing in their way, and they sought support among the knights and the people. They pleased the people by restoring the rights of the tribunate, which Sulla had made a dead end office. They strengthened the position of the smaller propertied groups by giving them a place on the juries, which Sulla had once more returned to the senators.

The War Against the Pirates. The consulship over, Pompey looked around for a further opportunity to pursue his career. Since the chastisement of Rhodes (page 369), pirates roamed freely over the waters of the Mediterranean. They endangered the vital shipments of grain from Egypt to Rome, and generally lorded it over the seas with "gilded masts and purple sails and silvered oars, as if they reveled in their iniquity and preened themselves on it." When the Senate was fearful of giving Pompey the extraordinary powers he demanded for war on the pirates, the assembly passed a special law granting him a fleet of five hundred war ships, the right to use public funds and recruit soldiers and sailors by force if necessary, and command of the entire Mediterranean to a distance of fifty miles inland from the sea. The danger was real, and the public was fearful. Within three months Pompey repaid the people's confidence by crushing the pirates completely.

The Second War Against Mithradates. Pompey's great success against the pirates made him the natural selection to end another war begun by Mithradates of Pontus (page 385). The Senate had sent out an extremely capable and conscientious man, Lucullus, to deal with Mithradates. Lucullus, however, was not one to play politics. In his upright dealings with the provincials, he had antagonized both his soldiers, whom he prevented from excessive plundering, and the knights at home, who resented his tax measures and the financial adjustments he had made to relieve the provincials of the hideous burdens of debt and interest imposed by Sulla. The people and knights forced the Senate to turn Lucullus' command over to Pompey.

Pompey was given overall command of the east to make peace or war as he saw fit. For four years, from 66 to 63 B.C., he crossed and recrossed Asia Minor, remaking the map. Mithradates was defeated, and Pontus became a province. Other states in Asia Minor were reorganized. Marching into Syria, Pompey intervened in a civil war following the death of the last Seleucid and made Syria a province (64 B.C.). In Palestine, part of the independent kingdom of Judaea was annexed to Syria, and the rest became a Roman dependency under the rule of its high priest. By 62 B.C. all of the Middle East, with the exception of Egypt, was under Roman control or allied to it. Even Armenia was made into an ally to serve as a buffer state between the provinces of Asia Minor and the rising kingdom of Parthia to the east. The Roman frontier was at the Euphrates River. Having completed Sulla's work in the east, without Sulla's burden of tribute, Pompey made preparations to return home.

THE RISE OF CICERO

While Pompey was campaigning in the east, a new figure arose on the political scene in Rome. This was Marcus Tullius Cicero, a man from a knightly family of moderate wealth. Cicero, like Marius, was a "new man," facing all the obstacles the nobility could put in the path of one such as he. But Cicero was able to make his way in Rome by his exceptional social and intellectual gifts, his great capacity for friendship, and his brilliance as an orator. Trained in the law, he decided on a political career. He believed that the Senate was the rightful governing body of the state and that an

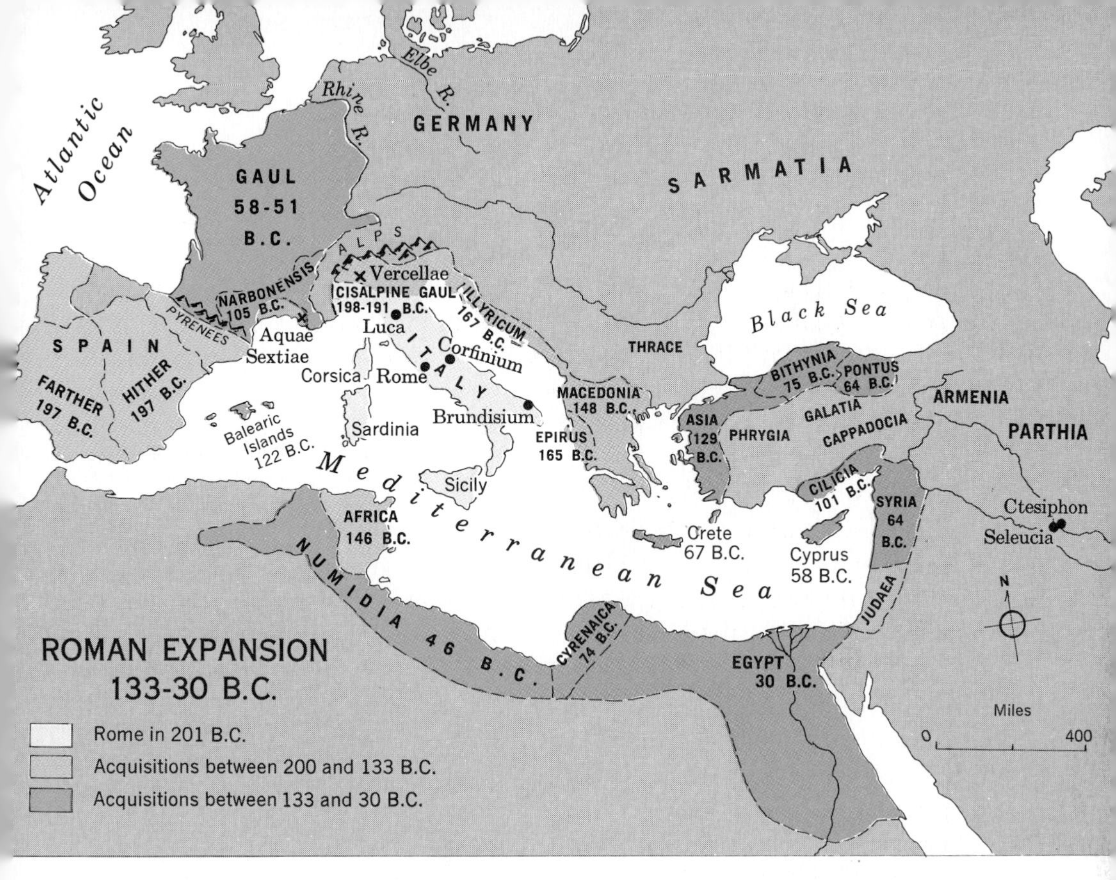

alliance between the senators and the knights, "the best men," would counterbalance the influence of a city mob that backed any man who provided enough "bread and circuses." In spite of the senators' suspicions, Cicero championed the senatorial cause.

Cicero's opportunity to make a name for himself came when the Sicilians, remembering that he had served them well as quaestor in 75 B.C., selected him to prosecute the shamelessly corrupt Verres, propraetor from 73 to 71 B.C.

The Trial of Verres. Verres' career is an apt contrast to that of Lucullus, and a good example of the misfortunes that too often attended Roman provincial rule in the last days of the Republic. During his years in office, Verres acquired a fortune of several millions of dollars by robbing the Sicilians right and left. He stole valuables and works of art as fast as his thieving fingers could grasp them; he disposed of all offices to the highest bidder; he compelled the farmers to give the greater part of their grain crop to him, which he then sold to increase his swelling fortune. His outrages were so excessive that all Cicero needed to do was to gather the

Cicero. Cicero was an outstanding figure in an age of exceptional men. Though he was extremely vain (his contemporaries reported that no one liked better to hear his own praises sung) he was without envy and did not begrudge his rivals their successes. Even his bitterest enemies acknowledged his abilities, and in the words of one of them, he was a man who loved his country well.

evidence, which he did with dispatch, and Verres fled into exile before the verdict of guilty was handed down. The prosecution of Verres established Cicero's reputation, and his career moved ahead.

The Conspiracy of Cataline. In 63 B.C. Cicero obtained the consulship. The year was marked by the discovery of a plot to seize Rome, murder the magistrates, and put the government into the hands of Cataline, a young noble without money but of vengeful character and ambitious disposition who had sought but missed the consulship. Cicero heard rumors of the plot, and in a series of famous speeches he exposed the machinations of the conspirators to an astonished Senate. The rebels were rounded up, and the death penalty, though illegal without trial, was voted by the Senate.

POMPEY'S REBUFF BY THE SENATE

It was now 62 B.C. Pompey was expected home. In the months preceding his return, Rome seethed with rumors. The Senate waited in terror of reprisals from the man whose excessive power they had opposed and who was now to land, they supposed, like another Sulla at the head of a victorious army, ready to punish his enemies and start another proscription. But, to the amazement of friends and enemies alike, Pompey left his army on landing in Italy and proceeded to Rome as a private citizen. He had no intention of playing the tyrant. Instead, he asked that his actions in Asia be formally declared legal and that his promise of land in the provinces to forty thousand of his veterans should be honored. Pompey apparently hoped that his enormous prestige alone would enable him to control the government, and to do so under the appearance of the old Republic. The Senate, however, humiliated him by examining each of his Asiatic actions in detail and refused his men their grants of land and money. This action turned Pompey away from the Senate and caused him once again to look around for new political support. This he found in an unexpected quarter.

CRASSUS AND JULIUS CAESAR

While Pompey was in the east, his rival Crassus had been active in politics. Realizing that any success Pompey gained would leave him outside the center of stage, Crassus sought support by furthering the career of a popular figure who would act as a counterweight to Pompey. His choice fell on Gaius Julius Caesar. Caesar was a member of an old but not rich patrician family. His father had favored the people's cause and his aunt Julia had married Marius. Caesar's first wife was the daughter of Marius' supporter Cinna (page 386), and his last wife was also allied to the democratic cause. Caesar, through expediency as much as through inclination, decided early in life to enter politics on the people's side, and Crassus realized that here was a person who, without fortune but of an ambitious and gifted temperament, might need support in a public career.

Caesar had managed to escape Sulla's proscriptions by absenting himself in Asia. On the death of Sulla he returned to Rome, where he won popular fame as a brilliant orator by the age of 22. With the help of Crassus' money, he lavished expenditures on public games and works and moved fast up the rung of magistracies, serving as quaestor in 68 B.C., as aedile in 65 B.C., and as praetor in 62 B.C. In 61 B.C. he went to Spain as propraetor and there acquired the money that enabled him to pay his debts, which even with Crassus' help amounted to a fortune. In 60 B.C. he was forty years old and the idol of the people.

Upon his return to Rome, Caesar realized that the Senate had antagonized Pompey. Caesar decided that the rivalry between Pompey and Crassus should be put aside for the moment because a union among the three of them would bring to each what each wanted. Accordingly, Caesar worked behind the scenes to unite the two men. He succeeded. The result was the unofficial political union known as the First Triumvirate. To the union Pompey brought his soldiers and prestige, Crassus his wealth, and Caesar his influence

Caesar. A striking portrait of the man whose influence on Rome was enduring. Caesar attempted to remodel the state according to its needs as he saw them, and his assassination not only cut off his projects but threw the Roman world into confusion.

over the city mob. The formation of this political ring set the stage for the last act in the fall of the Republic.

THE FIRST TRIUMVIRATE

As part of the triumvirs agreement, Caesar received the consulship in 59 B.C. He immediately set to work to pass legislation favorable to the triumvirs. Much of this legislation had to be forced through the Senate illegally. Pompey's treaties in the east were recognized, his men were given land, and Crassus' financial interests were protected. Caesar's relations with Pompey were strengthened by the marriage of his daughter Julia to the general. Caesar obtained for himself a five-year provincial command of Illyricum and Gaul, and in 58 B.C. the consulship having ended, he set forth to pursue his personal fortunes in the north.

Caesar in Gaul. In 58 B.C. Gaul was divided into three parts, as Caesar tells us in his justly famous campaign records, the *Commentaries.* Part of this territory had already been subjugated. Cisalpine Gaul, from the Rubicon River to the Alps, had been settled in the interval between the two Punic Wars (page 361). Transalpine Gaul between the Alps and the Pyrenees formed the province of Narbonensis, called by the Romans simply the Province (Provence). The rest of Transalpine Gaul, north and east to the Rhine River, was occupied by various Celtic tribes, loosely federated but very susceptible to the Roman practice of divide and conquer. Beyond the Rhine lay Germanic tribes. Their movements threatened to unsettle Gaul, and it was to contain them that Caesar made his conquests.

Caesar moved north from Narbonensis, and in the next seven years he conquered northern and western Gaul, pushing back the invaders and subduing the Celts. He entered Germany, building a bridge across the Rhine to do so. Twice he crossed over into Britain (55 and 54 B.C.), but his invasions were really no more than exploratory thrusts. These campaigns added to Rome's domains all the territory bounded by the Pyrenees, the Alps, the Rhine, and the Atlantic Ocean.

Caesar published his *Commentaries* in 49 B.C. They had a simple but forceful style, and Caesar cleverly used the third person so that he could write of himself dispassionately. The *Commentaries* made it plain that the man the author was writing about was a consummate general, well deserving the praises and respect of the Republic. They served as excellent propaganda at the crucial time when Caesar was seeking the consulship of 48 B.C. Without question, however, Caesar dealt well with the Gauls. He treated them leniently and his good sense rallied them to his standard and ensured their loyalty. Furthermore, like the Spaniards (page 370), the Gauls adopted the Latin language and Roman customs and laws, illustrating again how the Romans came with the sword but left civilization.

The Triumvirate Renewed. While Caesar was in Gaul, trouble was brewing in Rome. Pompey, fearful of Caesar's growing prestige, sought senatorial support and recalled Cicero, who had been banished for opposing the Triumvirate. Pompey also supported a rival faction to Caesar's in the assembly, and their quarrels produced anarchy in the streets. Caesar decided the triumvirs should meet and called a conference at Luca in 56 B.C. The three men decided that after all they were not ready to part company. They renewed their arrangements for another five years. Pompey and Crassus were also given commands: Pompey's in Spain, which he was to govern by lieutenants so he could keep an eye on things in Rome, Crassus' in Syria, where he planned to set out against the Parthians.

These arrangements did not hide the obvious fact that Pompey and Caesar's rival ambitions were on the road to collision. When Pompey's wife Julia died, and Crassus was killed by the Parthians, all links between the two men were broken. While fearful of Pompey, the Senate was even more fearful of Caesar. So it decided to back Pompey and it appointed him sole consul. The issue seemed settled. But Caesar by now had a loyal, well-trained army behind him. When he refused to disband it, and sought to gain the consulship for 48 B.C. while in Gaul, the Senate declared him a public enemy. Caesar had offered to compromise the issue; he offered to lay down his powers if Pompey would do the same. When Pompey refused, Caesar had no option. He well knew that if he came back to Rome as a private citizen, his enemies would try to destroy him for the illegal legislation he had passed during his consulship of 59 B.C. So, with his army, Caesar crossed the Rubicon River, the southern boundary of his province, making the famous remark, the die is cast. His illegal action started another civil war.

CAESAR RULES ROME, 49–44 B.C.

Caesar quickly marched to Rome. His fast action caught his enemies by surprise. His well-trained veterans were more than able to take on Pompey's untested Italian troops. Pompey decided to make his stand in the east, and Caesar was unable to prevent him from leaving Italy.

Caesar, having secured Rome, turned to Spain to destroy Pompey's forces there. He wanted to be sure of the west before he marched east. To his friends he remarked that "he was going against an army without a general, and would return against a general without an army." In only six weeks, Caesar crushed all opposition in Spain. He then returned to Rome to organize his forces to sail east.

The decisive battle between the two men took place in Thessaly at Pharsalus. Pompey's advisers, senators and knights anxious to return to Rome to share the spoils of Pompey's anticipated victory, urged him to battle. Pompey, complying, met disaster. Caesar's veterans, though outnumbered two to one, turned the tables and won the day. Pompey fled to Egypt and there was treacherously murdered by agents of the young Ptolemy. Caesar followed Pompey, and the murderers, hoping to find favor with Caesar, sent him Pompey's head, pickled in brine. Caesar, not ungenerous to his enemies, is said to have burst into tears.

In Egypt, Caesar was captivated by the charms of its lovely queen, Cleopatra. He established her claim to the Egyptian throne against that of her brother. Though still nominally independent, Egypt in fact became a dependent ally of Rome.

After dallying with Cleopatra for some months, Caesar marched up to Asia Minor to put down a revolt instigated by an ambitious son of Mithradates. He reported his quick victory with the laconic words: "I came, I saw, I conquered" (*veni, vidi, vici*). Then he returned to Rome, where Pompey's supporters were preparing to resist him.

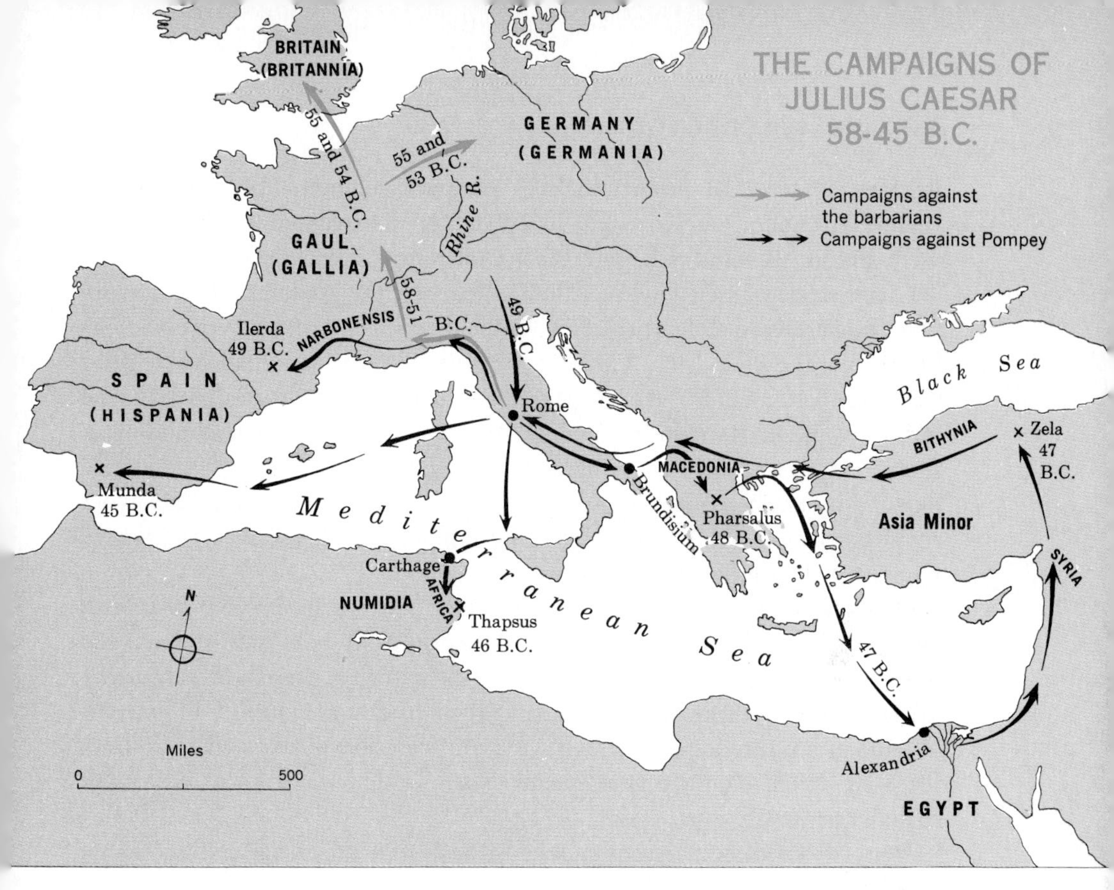

Pompey's followers made their first stand in Africa. The Pompeian forces were allied with Juba, king of Numidia. The alliance proved fruitless. At Thapsus in 46 B.C. Caesar routed their forces. A year later Caesar sailed to Spain, where new resistance had appeared. At Munda, in 45 B.C., he crushed the remaining Pompeian forces. This was his last battle. He returned to Rome victorious to receive the title of Father of his Country (*Pater Patriae*), and to govern the city his sword had won.

CAESAR'S REFORMS

When he returned to Rome in 45 B.C., Caesar found himself master of the Roman state. He had not planned to wreck the Republic. He had been drawn into civil war only when he found there was no alternative to political ruin. Now, unlike Sulla, he set about to reform the state, not merely to patch up a government that for several generations had proved itself worn out. Caesar saw quite clearly that Rome was ready for change, that the city-state of the forefathers was now an empire composed of many diverse peoples whose interests had to be brought into harmony with those of the

Romans. Caesar had proved himself a superb soldier and general and a resourceful politician. Now he proved himself a broadminded statesman as well, and in his reforms he laid the foundation for imperial rule.

Caesar made himself king in all but name, and the government he created was a monarchy in all but title. He became dictator and held other republican offices like the consulship. He held the title of *Imperator*, had his portrait stamped on coins, and had his statue placed with those of the kings of Rome in the temple of Romulus-Quirinus. Though he kept all the old republican forms, the Senate once again became merely an advisory body, the assemblies his mouthpiece, and magistrates and senators his appointees. He wore royal purple and the laurel wreath of triumph, and he received the Senate while seated to indicate his superiority.

Caesar wished to give the Roman world a better organization, to redress provincial misrule, to reestablish prosperity in both Italy and abroad, and to create a government in which the peoples of the empire might participate in the central government as well as in their local communities. He started his rule in a positive spirit. There were no proscriptions. His enemies were forgiven, much to their amazement. Then he entertained the city with splendid triumphs.

Many of Caesar's measures sought to deal with the social and economic distress of Italy. He restricted the monthly grain dole to those actually in need in an effort to make the capital city less attractive to an idle and shiftless mob. Colonies for the landless and the veterans were established overseas, notably at refounded Carthage and Corinth. Other measures were designed to improve agriculture in Italy, and one act limited the slave labor a great estate could use so that the poor would have work. Caesar made plans for a census of the population and resources of the Roman world, for the codification of the law, for the improvement of coinage, and for the reform of the calendar. Only the last was completed before his death, and Caesar's calendar, the Julian, based on the Egyptian with improvements by a Greek, is basically ours today.

Caesar's reforms in the provinces were equally as far reaching as those at home. He took into his own hands the appointment of provincial governors and held them strictly accountable. He reduced taxes and regularized the ways of collecting them. Roman citizenship was granted to communities in Sicily, Narbonensis, and Gaul, and many non-Italians were admitted to the Senate and to the legions. Caesar was attempting to break down the distinctions between Romans and provincials, to wipe out the disparities between the conquered and the conquerors.

THE CONSPIRACY AGAINST CAESAR

Caesar did not remain in power long. Many senators were alarmed when they realized that he had no intentions of restoring the Republic, and others feared that he intended to hand down his authority to an heir. Sixty of them plotted together to kill him. The ringleaders were Marcus Brutus and Gaius Cassius, the one an officer who had served Caesar in Gaul and the other a former supporter of Pompey. Caesar had been warned of a conspiracy against him, but he decided to disregard it, and on March 15 (the Ides of March), 44 B.C., he entered the Senate unarmed. He was surrounded by the conspirators and stabbed 23 times at the foot of the statue of Pompey. The citizens of Rome carried his body to the Forum and burnt it on a pyre, and his lieutenant, Mark Antony, gave the funeral oration.

The night before the assassination Caesar had been dining with friends. A discussion had come up on the subject of death and the question was asked, what kind of death is best? Caesar had answered, that which is least expected.

The figure of Julius Caesar looms large in history. The historian Suetonius tells us that, to the Romans Caesar "ranked among the gods, not only by formal decree, but in the belief of the people." His was a many-sided personality that could inspire passionate devotion and bend the will of others to do his way. His character was capable of change and development as it was stretched to meet new situations. He was not only a masterful politician and brilliant general, ranking with Alexander and Hannibal, but also a statesman who was generous in victory and farsighted in policy. At his death he was 56 years old, and many of his plans were incomplete. Yet his career captured the imagination of generations to come, and his name was a proud one to be borne not only by Romans but also by German kings (kaiser) and Russian emperors (czar).

At Caesar's death, Rome once again fell into chaos. Very quickly the conspirators realized that though the tyrant was dead, the tyranny still lived. The question was not how to restore the Republic but to whom Caesar's mantle would fall.

CAESAR'S HEIRS: ANTONY AND OCTAVIAN, 49–30 B.C.

The murderers of Caesar had thought of themselves as the liberators of the Republic. What they found out was that they had no support either from the rest of the Senate, which remained uncommitted, or from the people, who mourned a benefactor and leader. The conspirators quickly left Rome to save themselves; Brutus and Cassius went east to provinces that Caesar had assigned to them to govern. Mark Antony remained in Rome as Caesar's successor.

Antony soon found a rival on his hands. In his will, Caesar had made his grandnephew his adopted son and left him his immense fortune. This young man, eighteen years old, was Octavius. Against all advice he hurried to Rome, took his inheritance, and assumed the name of Gaius Julius Caesar Octavianus. Octavian, as we now call him, had displayed the talent that was to make him master of the Roman world. Next, capitalizing on the power of Caesar's name, Octavian quickly captured the affections of the people by distributing the legacies that Caesar had left them. Then he turned to the Senate and gave the impression that he sided with them against Mark Antony. Even Cicero was deceived and delivered powerful orations against the would-be usurper Antony.

Octavian, however, had other ambitions. Antagonized by the actions of the Senate, which tried to push him aside, he entered into an alliance with Mark Antony. The two men joined forces with Lepidus, one of Caesar's lieutenants, and marched on Rome with their legions. Together the three men formed the Second Triumvirate. They were voted dictatorial powers to govern Rome for five years.

THE SECOND TRIUMVIRATE

A terrible proscription followed, largely of rich people, whose wealth went to fill the empty coffers of the triumvirs. The most illustrious citizen to fall was Cicero, who paid with his life for his orations against Antony.

Having firmly established their rule in Rome, the triumvirs turned east to meet Brutus and Cassius. The issue was quickly decided. At two battles near Philippi in Macedonia, first Cassius and then Brutus fell. Antony and Octavian, victorious, proceeded to divide the empire between them. Octavian was to rule in the west and Antony in the east. Lepidus was given Africa.

This arrangement lasted ten years, during which time Lepidus was ignored. In Italy Octavian was successful in finding land for his veterans, in fostering agriculture, in putting down brigandage. His moderation toward his opponents and the success of his policies gained him popularity and support, and this support was skillfully fostered by propaganda extolling Octavian and disparaging Antony.

In the east, Antony fared badly. Falling in love with the fascinating Cleopatra, he willed to her and to her children by himself and Caesar some of Rome's richest provinces in the east on the excuse that they were originally Ptolemy lands. This did not please the Roman people; nor did Antony's action in divorcing Octavian's sister and marrying Cleopatra. Octavian saw his chance, and when Antony refused to abandon Cleopatra, he declared war on Egypt. The two forces met in the bay of Actium on the coast of Epirus in 31 B.C. Cleopatra managed to escape, and Antony, sensing defeat, followed her. Upon reaching Egypt, Antony committed suicide, and Cleopatra, not wishing to be led a captive in chains in Octavian's triumph, did so too. Octavian had himself crowned pharaoh, and Egypt became a Roman province. Then Octavian returned to Italy, master of the Roman world whose territories now included all the lands that touched on the Mediterranean Sea.

❦ ❦ ❦

The failure of the Senate to remedy the ills that were destroying the state was in part the result of a conflict between rich and poor that enabled personally ambitious leaders to rise to power by playing off different sides against each other. It was also in part the result of foreign warfare, which made special commands necessary and enabled successful generals, supported by their soldiers, to gain control of the government.

The passing of the Republic ended the rule of the Senate and the Roman people and transformed the city-state by the Tiber into an empire. Octavian's victory over his rival, Mark Antony, ushered in a new era in Roman history, that of the Principate.

People, Places, and Terms

the Gracchi	Verres	Pharsalus
Jugurtha	Crassus	
Mithradates	Cataline	*equites*
Sertorius	Caesar	*nobile*
Spartacus		*populares*
Lucullus	Rubicon River	triumvirate

Mastering the Reading

1. What new classes and class conflicts arose following the Punic Wars? How did Tiberius and Gaius Gracchus try to solve Rome's economic problems?

2. What were the highlights of the careers of each of these leaders: Marius? Sulla? Pompey? Cicero? How did each weaken the Republic but build the empire?
3. Why did Julius Caesar form the First Triumvirate? What changes in Roman government and social conditions did he make? What did the conspirators fear?
4. What means did Octavian use to become emperor?

Interpreting the Text

1. Was "constitutional" government good for Rome? Who benefited? Who suffered?
2. How did Marius, Sulla, and the Gracchi brothers contribute to the rise of one-man rule? What else destroyed Rome's republican form of government?
3. In what different ways and why did land cause contention in Rome, in Italy, and in other parts of the empire?

Exploring Beyond the Text

1. Compare the characterizations of the major figures in William Shakespeare's play *Julius Caesar* with historical interpretations. In what ways do they differ?
2. How had the make-up and role of the army changed since early republican days? What is the significance of this change?

Working with the Map

1. Follow the map of Caesar's campaigns (page 397) and make a list of the outstanding battles and their results.
2. How did the campaigns of Julius Caesar contribute to the expansion of the Roman Empire? What new peoples were added to the Roman Empire?

20

Kingdoms in the East

300–30 B.C.

In the years between 300 B.C. and 30 B.C. Rome gained supremacy in the west, and the flourishing Hellenistic kingdoms weakened. In the east, beyond Mesopotamia, the kingdom of Parthia was established by Iranian tribesmen who threw off Seleucid control and whose leaders claimed descent from the Achmaenid kings of Persia. Further to the east, in northern India, the Magadha kingdom became the great Mauryan Empire that controlled north India and much of south India too. Still further to the east, the states of Chou were united into the centralized kingdom of Ch'in and then grew into the great Eastern Han Empire.

The fate of all the peoples in the east was strongly influenced by the movement of the nomadic tribes who lived across the steppes of central Asia. When one tribe or collection of tribes defeated another, or when pasture lands dried up, or were cut off, or were acquired by another tribe, the nomads migrated. Sometimes they absorbed, sometimes they displaced those peoples into whose territory they moved. In the second century B.C. and again in the first century B.C., several such displacements occurred. Parthia and India lost parts of their territory to the Sakas, the eastern branch of the

Indo-European Scythian tribes whom we encountered earlier in south Europe and the northern part of Asia Minor (page 167). The Sakas were pushed south by other tribes defeated by the Hsiung Nu, a people of the Altaic (not Indo-European) linguistic family who may have been ancestors of the Huns. The Hsiung Nu, new on the stage of history, formed the first powerful confederation on the steppes. They pushed south and invaded China many times. The Chinese built the Great Wall to hold them back, but while the wall cut off their pasture lands, it did not prevent them from constantly attacking the fertile plains of north China in Ch'in and then Han times.

PARTHIA, BRIDGE BETWEEN EAST AND WEST, C. 250 B.C.–224 A.D.

To the east of Mesopotamia lay the lands that had formed the Persian Empire of the Achmaenids. They had fallen to Alexander the Great after the battle of Guagamela (page 325), and then, upon Alexander's death, they became part of the Hellenistic kingdom of the Seleucids (page 329).

The region known as Parthia (see map, page 327) soon fell away from Seleucid control. Around 250 B.C. two brothers named Arsaces and Tiridates inspired a revolt that ended in independence. The two brothers claimed descent from the Achmaenid kings and inaugurated a Parthian dynasty, the Arsacid, which gained strength and territory as the Hellenistic kingdoms weakened during the second century B.C.

In 141 B.C., under their greatest king, Arsaces VI Mithradates I (171–138 B.C.), the Parthians extended their rule over Mesopotamia. In the east their territory stretched all the way to the Indus and was bound in the north and south by the Oxus River and the Indian Ocean. But Parthian power did not stand uncontested. From the second century B.C. on, the Parthian boundaries fluctuated. In the east, nomadic peoples were on the move, and the Parthians were not always able to defend their frontiers successfully against them (page 412). In the west, the Romans were advancing into the eastern Mediterranean (page 367). When the Seleucid kingdom collapsed and Syria was made into a province by Pompey in 64 B.C. (page 390), Parthia and Rome were back to back. Each power fought for control of Mesopotamia and Armenia for the next three hundred years. Neither was successful in retaining its gains for long. The Euphrates River became the shifting boundary between them; it was the easternmost edge of the Roman Empire, the westernmost of the Parthian kingdom.

THE PARTHIAN STATE

The Parthian kingdom was a loosely organized monarchy. The king claimed the allegiance of a powerful group of nobles who formed his imperial council, governed the provinces in his name, and raised the armies. These nobles lived on great estates, much like tiny kingdoms, where hosts of serfs tilled the soil. Their most important duty was to guard their lands against the constant inroads of wandering nomads. The king did not always have firm control over his well-armed nobles.

The strength of the Parthian army was in its cavalry. The nobles formed the heavy cavalry. Both they and their horses were covered by scales of steel armor. Here was something new, and extremely effective, in military equipment. In order for the horses to bear the extra weight of armor, the Parthians had developed larger animals, possibly by feeding them alfalfa, a plant that could be harvested all year around. Their big, beautiful, horses were the envy of the surrounding peoples and were much in demand as far away as China, with whose court the Parthians were in touch (page 471).

The light cavalry were archers mounted on small, fast ponies. These bowmen's skill was legendary. One of their most deadly tactics was to pretend to flee and then shoot backwards over their shoulders at their pursuing, and unsuspecting, foes. Their unerring arrows seldom missed their mark and won the Parthians many victories.

The Parthians controlled the main trade routes between the Far East and the Mediterranean. The silk trade from China passed through their lands. It was a major source of conflict between the Parthians and the Romans, among whom silk was much in demand and who would have liked to control this traffic themselves. Along the route lay a number of Hellenistic cities populated by Hellenes, Jews, and Babylonians. The most important was Seleucia (page 335), right next to which the Parthians built their capital city of Ctesiphon. The kings of Parthia drew a large part of their income from taxing the profitable trade revenues of their cities.

The Hellenistic cities were in large measure self-governing (page 333), and they maintained their Greek culture even after coming under the control of the Parthians. The Parthian kings became Hellenized. They spoke Greek, issued coins with Hellenic inscriptions, attended performances of Hellenic tragedy, and added the title of *Philhellene* (Friend of the Greeks) to the Persian one of King of Kings.

The influence of Hellenism was confined to the cities, however. In the countryside the peasants and serfs followed their traditional way of life. Their religion was Zoroastrianism mixed with the lore of the Magi. Iranian-speaking nomads, constantly infiltrating the borders and settling down, adopted the dress and manner of the peasants, and so the native culture was maintained and enriched. Even the kings were not entirely Hellenized. They seem to have had a second council of "Magians and wise men" and wore their hair and beard in the Iranian manner.

THE DECLINE OF PARTHIA

After the Hellenistic kingdoms collapsed, Hellenic influence weakened while the native Iranian traditions grew stronger. A nationalistic revival was in the making, and it burst forth in 224 A.D. Ardashir, one of the king's nobles, succeeded in overthrowing his overlord and gained the support of the other nobles. The loose monarchy of the Parthian kings was unable to withstand this assault, and Ardashir founded a new Persian dynasty and kingdom, the Sassanian, into which Parthia was absorbed.

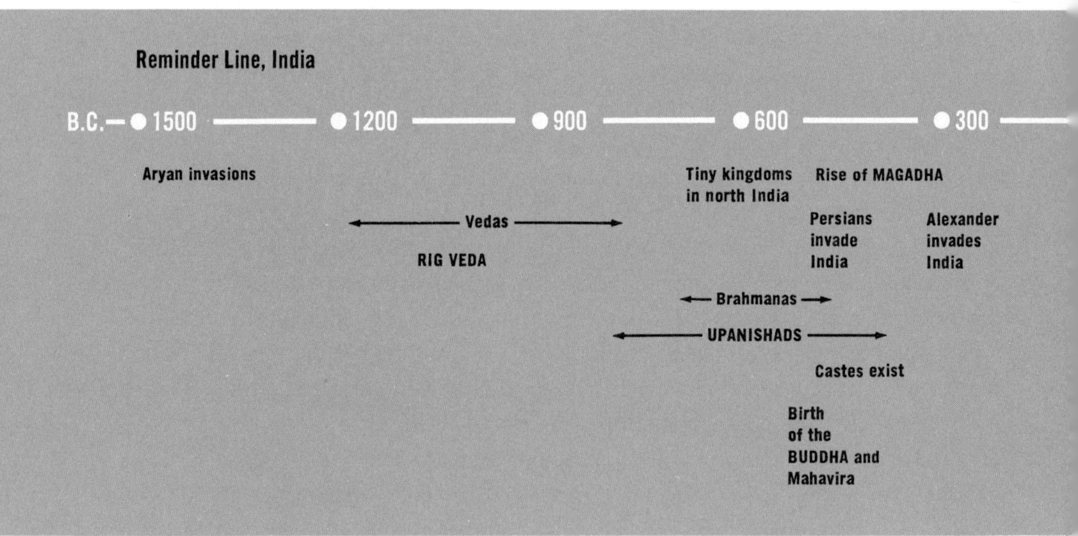

INDIA: THE EMPIRE OF MAURYA AND THE SOUTHERN KINGDOMS

In 327 B.C. Alexander the Great invaded northwest India. His campaign was ended, however, two years later by the mutiny of his soldiers, who refused to advance further into unknown lands. Alexander thereupon organized the Indus Valley into satrapies and returned to Babylon and death (page 328). Along the Ganges, to which Alexander had been denied the chance to advance, lay the Indian state of Magadha. In 322 B.C. the ruling dynasty was overthrown by the commander of the army, Chandragupta Maurya. For seventeen years Chandragupta built up his army. In 305 B.C. he struck at Alexander's heir in the northwest, Seleucus I, and forced him to surrender all his lands in India and Baluchistan. Chandragupta thereafter established the largest empire India had yet seen, the Maurya; at its height it extended from the Hindu Kush mountains on the west to present-day Burma in the east, encompassing the valleys of both the Indus and the Ganges rivers and extending into the Deccan (see map, page 412).

THE MAURYAN STATE, 321–184 B.C.

The Mauryan Empire was highly centralized. Each province was governed by a viceroy and a staff of district officers responsible to the king. The chief officials at the king's court had hereditary positions. A huge army was maintained. It was well paid, and its horses and military machines were provided by the government. Soldiers were carefully trained and kept in condition by regular drill. When not on active duty, the men were assigned to reserve regiments that were called up when war broke out.

Life in the Mauryan Empire was highly regulated and supervised. The people were registered by the state and were required to carry identification papers. Foreigners were obliged to have passports, and their travels around the country were closely watched. Spies of the state were everywhere. Soldiers, priests, actors, professional people, even children and beggars acted as informers. Secret agents were carefully trained in special schools where they learned such techniques of spying as writing in code. Punishment for crime was sudden and severe. An accused person might be arrested secretly and never seen again.

The fear that permeates a police state was not unknown in the king's own palace. Chandragupta lived in fear of assassination. His palace was a maze of secret passages, hidden stairways, and sliding panels by which the king moved unseen from room to room. Conferences with the highest officials were held in secrecy, and the time and place of meetings were constantly changed. No one was permitted in the king's presence without a permit. No food or drink passed the king's lips until it had been tasted in his presence by some other person.

The economy, too, was controlled by the government. Workers were organized into state supervised unions. Prices were fixed, and sales were regulated by the state. The road system, and the inns and the messengers of the postal service who sped along the highways, were supervised by the government.

Only religion was free in the Mauryan Empire. Brahmanism, Buddhism, and Jainism existed side by side.

Chandragupta was as dedicated a king as he had been a soldier, and he worked twelve or more hours every day on affairs of state. After 24 years of rule he felt his work was done. He handed the empire to his son, Bindusara, in 299 B.C., and according to tradition he spent the last two years of his life practicing the severe austerities of a Jain monk.

Little is known of Bindusara (299–274 B.C.) except that he extended the territory of the empire into the southern part of the Indian subcontinent, the Deccan. After a 25-year reign his son Ashoka (274–236 B.C.) succeeded him as the third and greatest of the Mauryas. Ashoka was one of the very great men in world history.

Ashoka, 274–236 B.C. (*?*). An Indian tradition states that Ashoka reached the throne by slaughtering all but one of his 99 brothers. This seems improbable from what we know of Ashoka, though such wholesale blood purges were only too common in oriental history. Other aspects of Ashoka's reign, however, are known to us in some detail from a series of royal decrees and records carved on rocks and on stone pillars during his reign. They reveal many events and describe the conditions that existed in the empire in his time.

Ashoka's first eight years as king passed smoothly. They were filled with hunting, feasting, dancing, and other pleasures and luxuries available to the ruler of a large and wealthy empire.

Then in 262 B.C. the king took up arms against the people of Kalinga, a region today called Orissa. In the war that followed, the province was devastated. One hundred fifty thousand prisoners were taken, another hundred thousand were slain, and several more hundreds of thousands perished of starvation and pestilence. The horrors of the Kalinga war made a deep and lasting impression on the victorious king. He published on a stone pillar his "profound sorrow and regret" for having caused the "slaughter, death, and captivity of the people" in the Kalinga war. Such a statement was certainly a highly unusual one for a victorious general to make, but Ashoka seems to have meant it. Never again did he lead the army into war. Even toward the uncivilized and troublesome hill tribes, the government followed a policy of moderation.

Ashoka had known of the Buddhist faith as a young man. Following the Kalinga campaign he was converted, and for the rest of his life he tried faithfully to follow Buddhist precepts. Forsaking war was his first step. Then he applied the Buddhist rule of kindness to animals as well as people. He went no more on the royal hunts in which he had once taken such delight. He ended his royal banquets by severely limiting the number of creatures slain for food. Many birds and animals were brought under royal protection, and it was forbidden to kill them for any reason. Ashoka founded the first hospital for animals in the world.

Ashoka realized that under a highly centralized and bureaucratic system like the Maurya, it was easy for the officials to treat the people harshly. He decreed that he would hear appeals from his people at all hours, "whether dining, or in my bedroom, or in my carriage or in the palace gardens." Special officials were appointed to promote piety among the people, to prevent unlawful punishment or imprisonment, to help the afflicted, and to increase religious tolerance in the empire.

The Expansion of Buddhism. Ashoka did not rest with applying Buddhist principles to his own life and to the rule of his kingdom. He used the full prestige of his position as emperor to foster the spread of Buddhism. When Ashoka came to the throne, Buddhism was only a minor religious cult limited to northern India. Ashoka sent out missionaries and supported Buddhist monasteries. During his lifetime Buddhism spread rapidly throughout the whole of India and was carried to the island of Ceylon.

Buddhism was brought to Ceylon by a group of Buddhist missionaries who went to that island on the invitation of King Tissa. One of the missionaries was a woman, and it is believed she was a relative of Ashoka. Her name was Sanghamitta, and she took with her a cutting of the tree under which the Buddha had sat when he was passing into the stage of enlightenment. The cutting was planted at Anuradhapura, then capital of Ceylon, and for many centuries it grew and flourished until destroyed in modern times. Anuradhapura became the brilliant capital of the Buddhist royal court of Ceylon. One of the sights of the mighty city was the dagoba or stupa (see below), the mound that enclosed a fragment of the Buddha's collarbone, a gift from Ashoka to Ceylon. The mission to Ceylon was highly successful, and the island became strongly Buddhist.

The Art of Maurya. Until Mauryan times wood had been the principal building material in India. Now stone was substituted for wood. Sandstone was most commonly used. It was polished brilliantly so that observers often thought that the huge stone columns on which Ashoka published his edicts were made of metal. These columns, weighing as much as fifty tons, were fifty feet tall and were carved in styles that showed both Persian and

Hellenistic influence. At the top of the column were animals carved with a unique combination of realism and idealism. The lion from the column at the city of Sarnath now appears on the state seal of modern India.

In Ashoka's reign cave-temples were dug out of solid cliffs to shelter communities of monks during the rainy seasons. In time the walls of these caves came to be covered entirely with paintings and sculptures.

The Buddhist stupa also developed under Ashoka. A stupa was originally a simple mound of earth piled over a Buddhist relic. In time it became a dome made of stone surrounded by a railing and with huge ornamented gateways opening to the north, south, east and west. A processional pathway wound around the stupa, recalling the processional ramps around the ziggurats of ancient Babylon. On top of the stupa dome rose a mast symbolizing the axis of the world, as the dome stood for the arch of heaven.

The End of the Maurya Empire. The last years of Ashoka were obscure. No records mentioning him exist after the last pillar inscription carved in 246 B.C. Tradition says that he lived another ten years and that he was placed under restraint by high officials who resented his generosity to religious groups. Whether or not this is true, it does not affect Ashoka's unique place in world history. As the ruler of a widespread empire that was well-organized and prosperous, with the world's largest armies at his command, Ashoka directed all the power in his hands against war and the forces of hatred. During his reign India was governed with benevolence and peace. Finally, through Ashoka's interest, Buddhism grew and expanded from a minor cult into one of India's two major religions.

The stupa at Sanchi. During the second century B.C., the stupa was rennovated and enlarged. On the gateways of the railing enclosing the shrine, the artist demonstrated his skill by carving elaborate figures and animals from mythology and from the popular cults acceptable to the Buddhists.

The Mauryan Empire broke up about fifty years after Ashoka's death. In the chaos that followed, the details of history have been lost. For some five hundred years northern India was divided. Civil wars within and invasions from without can be glimpsed in the confusion. Foreign conquerors established themselves in northwestern and northern India (see below). The Ganges Valley, which had been the core of the Mauryan Empire, declined in importance, while new kingdoms rose farther south in the Deccan plateau of central India and in the Tamil peninsula of the extreme south.

ANDHRA AND THE SOUTH INDIAN KINGDOMS

We do not know much about the kingdom of the Andhras (110 B.C.–225 A.D.) as records are very scanty. The Andhras were of Dravidian origin; at its height their kingdom stretched from sea to sea across central India; their language was Prakit, and their religion was that early Hinduism whose origins are lost in antiquity. The rulers of Andhra tolerated Buddhism, however, and some of its kings granted favors to the younger religion.

Other little kingdoms also existed in south India, Tamil Land, but we know hardly anything about them. Three were of particular importance: Chera (Kerala) on the southwest coast, Chola on the southeast coast, and Pandya on the southern tip (see map, page 412). Royal courts were maintained with elaborate ceremony. The villages were allowed considerable self-government. An assembly in each state was composed of delegates from the villages and was responsible for development of roads and irrigation projects. These little states were constantly at war, and no political unity was achieved among them.

BACTRIANS AND SAKAS IN NORTHWEST INDIA

In central Asia lay the independent Greek state of Bactria. Bactria, which lay between the Hindu Kush mountains and the Oxus River, had been part of the Persian Empire and then had been included in the empire of the Seleucids (see map, page 330). In the middle of the third century B.C. the Hellenic governor in Bactria broke away from Seleucid control and set up an independent kingdom. In the early second century B.C. (185 B.C.) the Bactrians invaded the Indian Punjab country and set up a Greek state in the northwestern corner of India. The weak successors of the Mauryans could do nothing to prevent this. But in the late second century B.C., Bactria itself was overwhelmed by the invasions of a nomadic people, the Sakas, and the Indo-Greek state fell.

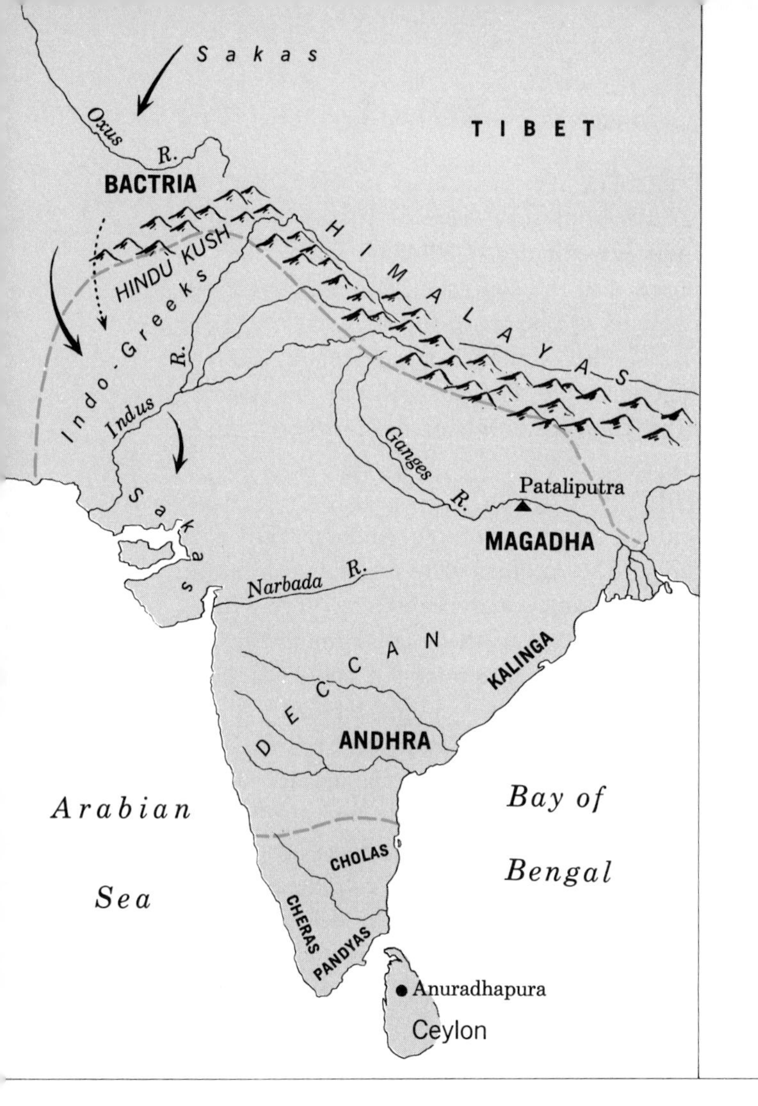

INDIA
300-30 B.C.

▲ Mauryan capital

Extent of Mauryan Empire

Miles
0 600

The Sakas (the Indian name for the Scythians) were one more of the seemingly endless peoples to come out of central Asia. In the second century B.C., during an upheaval of the nomadic peoples living in central Asia caused by the building of the Great Wall of China (page 414), the Sakas were pushed out of their pasture lands and turned south. They raided Bactria and Parthia, destroying the Bactrian kingdom in 135 B.C. Between 75 B.C. and 25 B.C. they overran the Indo-Greeks in northwest India and even reached the western edge of the Ganges plain. But they in turn were pushed out by other nomads invading India (page 465), and moved further south and into western India, where a much reduced Saka state lasted till the fifth century A.D.

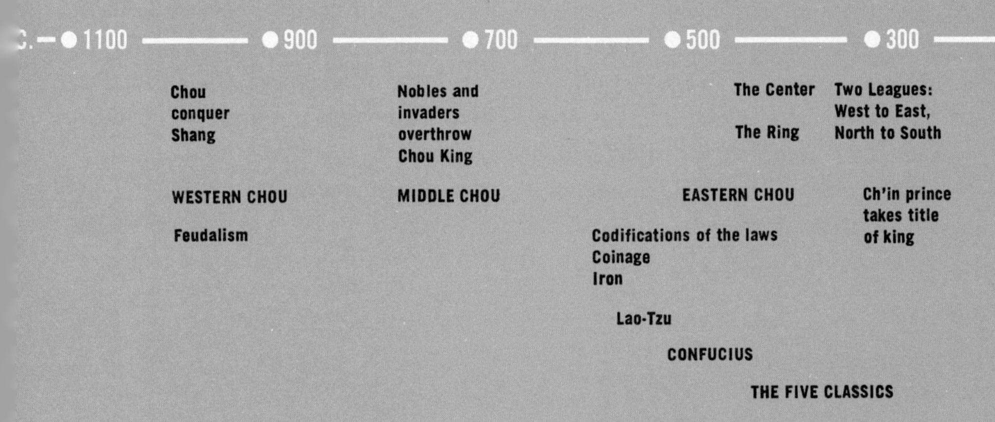

CHINA: THE CH'IN AND EARLY HAN EMPIRES

For several centuries the Chou had been emperors only in name, and kings of other states had ignored the unenforced claims of the Chou to Chinese overlordship. In 256 B.C. the last Chou "emperor" died. The title was revived in 221 B.C. by King Cheng of Ch'in, who assumed the title of Shih-Huang-Ti, meaning First Emperor.

CH'IN SHIH-HUANG-TI, UNIFIER OF CHINA, 247–210 B.C.

Shih-Huang-Ti became king of Ch'in in 247 B.C. at the age of thirteen. At the age of 25 he began to expand the frontiers of Ch'in. Between 230 and 221 B.C. he defeated and annexed all the other Chinese kingdoms.

Shih-Huang-Ti then set about reorganizing China. He abolished the boundary lines of the former kingdoms and divided the united land into 41 districts, each with a military governor, a civil governor, and a supervisor of the treasury. These three provincial officials were all responsible directly to the emperor, as in the Assyrian and Persian empires. With the abolition of the Chou feudal system, the land returned to private ownership.

Shih-Huang-Ti built a network of tree-lined highways, established a postal system, and standardized the writing system. He improved agriculture by constructing canals and had river channels deepened to encourage water transportation. The many different law codes were abolished in favor of one universal legal system. Money, weights, and measures were made uniform so that trade flourished across the empire. Even the width of roads and the axles of wagon wheels were standardized.

All these improvements, together with the establishment of a bureaucracy appointed and supervised by the emperor, bound the many regions of China into one economic and social unit. They laid the foundations for a remarkable achievement: the creation of a unified land with a system of government that outlasted invasions and disruptions for two thousand years.

Before Shih-Huang-Ti's time, walls of varying length had been built in the northern parts of China to contain the nomads on China's northern frontiers. These people, called by the Chinese Hsiung-Nu, had formed a

The Great Wall. In 214 B.C., Shih-Huang-Ti appointed a general to supervise the construction of the Great Wall. Workers were forced into service, transported to the area, and stationed along the proposed path of construction. Among their number were criminals and unfortunate scholars who were suspected of opposing the government. In all, 300,000 men, dying by the hundreds from the difficulties of the task and the attacks of the nomads, labored to build a wall 30 feet thick and 50 feet high. Watch towers were constructed at regular intervals along the wall, which wound inland some 1,500 miles. Today the wall's remains can still be seen north of Peking.

confederacy based in Mongolia. Shih-Huang-Ti ordered all barriers united into one "Great Wall of China," which stretched unbroken from the sea to more than a thousand miles inland. The Hsiung-Nu were expelled from the lands along the Yellow River to the other side of the Great Wall, which was strengthened by forts and army encampments at regular intervals. In the south, Shih-Huang-Ti marched into south China as far as the delta of the Red River (see map, page 416).

Throughout his empire Shih-Huang-Ti carved inscriptions on monuments, cliffs, and rocks, commemorating his actions. These, like the stone inscriptions of Ashoka of India (page 409), have provided us with a record of the events in Ch'in. Later tradition speaks of one of the most famous of these: the "burning of the books." When Shih-Huang-Ti determined to reorganize China, he knew that he would have to overturn former ways of doing things that were familiar and beloved by the people. He realized that many Chinese traditions were passed from generation to generation by the classic works of literature (page 291). Thinking that they might influence the people to oppose him, he had them collected throughout the kingdom and burned. Only certain works pertaining to medicine, agriculture, and law were spared, and one copy of each of the other books was kept for the royal archives. Nevertheless, though 460 scholars were put to death, many works were safely concealed, and Shih-Huang-Ti did not succeed entirely in his work of destruction.

The arts flourished during Shih-Huang-Ti's reign. A new style in bronze, distinct from that of the Chou, made its appearance. This style was characterized by motion. Certain of the designs in the new style were similar to designs of the nomads beyond the Great Wall. Some experts think that Greek ideas of design were imitated by the Scythians of the central Asian steppes and that they were then passed on by the nomads to the Ch'in artists in China.

Like Chandragupta, Shih-Huang-Ti worked every day from dawn to midnight on the mountains of reports that came to him from all parts of the empire. Also like Chandragupta, he was a tyrant who lived in constant fear of assassination. He remained hidden within a gigantic palace whose size and splendor made it a wonder of the world.

The death of Shih-Huang-Ti in 210 B.C. was followed by the temporary breakdown of the empire. Shih-Huang-Ti's son lacked the abilities of his father. After several years of anarchy, order was eventually restored, but in the turmoil the Ch'in dynasty was swept away, and a new line of rulers, the Han, installed themselves in power.

THE EARLY OR WESTERN HAN EMPIRE, 202 B.C.–9 A.D.

The Han Dynasty of China lasted for more than four hundred years. The Early or Western Han was contemporary with the Roman Republic from the end of the Second Punic War to the reign of Octavius Caesar (Augustus). It ended in confusion and a break in the succession. When the Han were restored to power, a new branch of the family known as the Later or Eastern Han reigned from 25 A.D. to 223 A.D. and was roughly contemporary with the Roman Principate. Thus at the two ends of the civilized world, two great empires, that of Rome and that of Han China, existed simultaneously.

During the first reigns of the Han Dynasty, from 202 to 141 B.C., the Hsiung-Nu invaded China five times. Twice there were civil wars in which local vassals revolted. These dangers were successfully met, the dynasty survived, and in 141 B.C., the greatest of the early Han emperors, Wu-Ti, came to the throne.

Emperor Han Wu-Ti (140–87 B.C.). Wu-Ti was sixteen years old when he became emperor. He grew into a man of tremendous energy, great courage, and high intelligence. He recalls Alexander the Great in the boldness of his temperament and in the devotion he aroused among his subordinates. He was an excellent administrator and had the intelligence to surround himself with wise counsellors, from whose suggestions he profited.

Han Wu-Ti ruled for 54 years. He was nicknamed the Martial Emperor. During his reign, the power of the Hsiung-Nu was temporarily broken. The Chinese marched into central Asia, establishing suzerainty and encircling

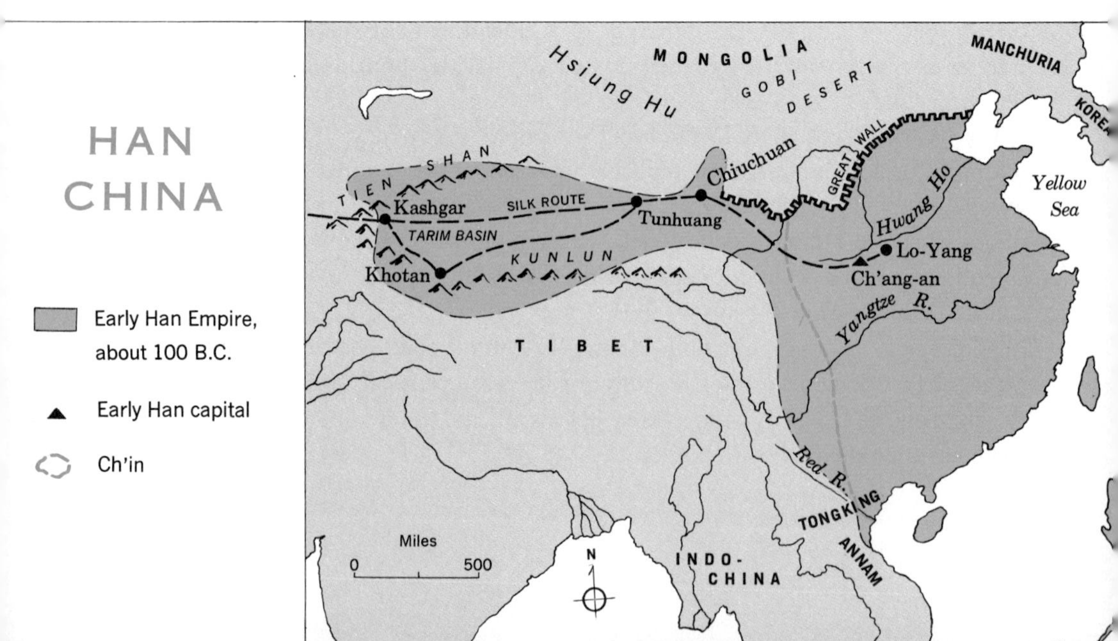

the nomads. This remarkable extension of power—the deserts of central Asia are enormous, cold, and barren—led to the establishment of a caravan route along the string of oases between China and the Jaxartes River. This became the famous Silk Route, the land passage over which trade and ideas flowed between east and west (see map, page 461).

Chinese expansion was not confined to the west. During the reign of Han Wu-Ti, the Chinese also colonized Manchuria and Korea; they annexed south China, and they exerted lordship over parts of Indo-China. To control these additions to the empire, imperial supervisors watched over the activities of vassal kings, and the Great Wall was repaired and maintained by a force of a hundred thousand men.

The greatest fortunes in Early Han China were made in salt, metalworking, and horse and sheep breeding. These activities were pursued on large estates, where slave labor was used. Slaves were owned both privately and publicly in Han China, but the slave population was probably not more than a fiftieth of the total population as compared with about half in the Hellenistic Mediterranean. The iron and salt industries did not remain in private hands for long. Wu Ti turned them into government monopolies as a profitable source of revenue.

Wu-Ti admired scholarship and surrounded himself with the finest scholars in the kingdom. He particularly favored the Confucianists. From this association of scholarship and government arose the Mandarin class, the scholar-officials who administered the Chinese empire under emperor after emperor until the Chinese republic was inaugurated in A.D. 1912. Under Han Wu-Ti Confucianism was officially accepted as the basis of the state (page 470).

❖ ❖ ❖

If an observer had looked down on the lands east of Mesopotamia in 300 B.C., he would have seen the warring state of Alexander's successor Seleucus attempting to hold the territory that formerly belonged to Persia but from which Parthia and Bactria would soon declare independence. He would have observed the kingdom of Magadha in the Ganges Valley and northwest India united in the great Mauryan Empire, and he would have seen the warring states of Chou China fighting each other and the nomads to the north.

If an observer had looked down on the east again in 30 B.C., he would have seen that the Seleucid kingdom no longer existed. Instead, he would have seen the loosely organized state of Parthia lying across the trade routes of central Asia and fighting against Rome for control of Mesopotamia. He would have noticed that northern India had many small states governed by Indians, Greeks, and people descended from the Saka nomads of the central Asian steppes, and that central India was united in the Andhra kingdom but that other small states existed further south. Finally, he would have seen that in China a unified kingdom was growing and expanding on western, northern, and southern frontiers.

People, Places, and Terms

Arsacid	Wu-Ti	Tamil
Chandragupta Maurya	Han	Bactria
Ashoka	Mauryan	Ch'in
Bactrians		
Sakas	Parthia	stupa
Shih-Huang-Ti	Deccan	mandarin

Mastering the Reading

1. How did the Arsacid Parthians reflect a blending of Hellenistic and Iranian culture?
2. How did Chandragupta and his grandson differ in the way they controlled their empire? Why is Ashoka considered an outstanding world figure? How did various nomadic tribes weaken the Parthians and the Mauryans?
3. What moves did Shih-Huang-Ti make to unite China? Under Han Wu-Ti, what changes were made in daily life, in government, and in the economy? How?

Interpreting the Text

1. How did the central Asiatic tribes influence China, India, and Mesopotamia?
2. What problems did Chandragupta and Shih-Huang-Ti have in common? How did some problems differ? Why?

Exploring Beyond the Text

1. Read Ashoka's Edict and find out more about his life. What prompted him to take his role as a benevolent, pacifist leader?
2. Discuss the following statement: "The Ch'in dynasty united China and left an indelible stamp on it."
3. What do today's leaders in Red China have in common with Shih-Huang-Ti?

Working with the Map

1. From the information on Magadha in this chapter, in Chapter 14, and in outside sources draw a map of India showing the growth of the kingdom and of other states existing in India at the same time.
2. Refer to the maps of Shang, Chou, and Han China on pages 139, 289, and 416. Then on your own map, show how the territory of China increased from Shang to Han times. Indicate the state of outlying territories as well; for example, those which were occupied by the barbarians, those which were neolithic, those which were subject to Chinese influence.

Looking Back to the Growth of Civilization

The east and the west became aware of each other following the conquests of Alexander the Great. This was the first result of Alexander's conquests. The second was that the Hellenic way of life encountered the Middle Eastern to form a new synthesis, that which we call Hellenistic.

In the west, Rome was strongly influenced by the Hellenistic way of life, particularly in cultural areas: art, education, religion, philosophy. This influence was lasting and spread from the Romans to the barbarians and so had a marked effect on the growth of western civilization. In the Middle East, the Hellenistic kingdoms brought together for the first time the peoples of Europe, Egypt, and the Near East. Such prosperity and cultural exchange resulted that the peoples of these areas thought of themselves as inhabiting only one world, the Ecumene. In central Asia, the Parthian kings were proud to be thought Hellenistic, while in Asia, the Indian rulers of Bactria had Hellenic origins and names.

The Hellenistic kingdoms, however, did not last. The Middle Eastern style of life reasserted itself, and the impact of Hellenism faded. By 30 B.C., Rome was master of the Mediterranean, having stepped in with vigor when the Hellenistic kingdoms were weakening. The Parthians turned back to their native Iranian heritage, while the Indo-Greeks were swept away. In central and south India, as in Han China, the native styles of life were strengthened and extended.

THE GROWTH OF CIVILIZATION, 350-30 B.C.

	MIDDLE EAST	AEGEAN	MEDITERRANEAN	INDIA	CHINA
400-300 B.C.	Alexander conquers Mesopotamia, Persia, Egypt, and Asia Minor	Rise of Macedon Plato and Aristotle Alexander conquers Hellas	Rome conquers the Samnites Dionysius of Syracuse gains Sicily, attacks Italy, but dies Sicily remains half Hellenic and half Carthaginian	Alexander invades the Indus Valley Chandragupta Maurya founds Mauryan dynasty	Eastern Chou weakens Rise of leagues: West to East (Ch'in) and North to South (Ch'u) Ch'in wins and its ruler takes title of king
300-200 B.C.	Hellenistic kingdoms of Seleucus and Ptolemy Height of Hellenistic kingdoms and cities Gallic invasion of Asia Minor	Macedonian kingdom of the Antigonids Achaean League of the Peloponnesian states Aetolian League of central Hellenic states Gauls invade Hellas	Rome conquers Magna Graecia First Punic War Rome acquires Sicily, Sardinia, and Corsica Second Punic War; Hannibal	Ashoka Buddhism spreads to Ceylon Tamil land "kingdoms" Bactrians revolt from Seleucus and become independent	Last Chou emperor dies Shih-Huang-Ti establishes Ch'in dynasty, unifies China, and contains barbarians
200-100 B.C.	Decline of Hellenistic kingdoms Parts of Asia Minor become Roman province of Asia Jewish state established in Palestine by Maccabees Parthian revolt from Seleucus; Arsacid dynasty Parthians gain Mesopotamia Sakas invade Parthia	Rome defeats Philip V of Macedon Freedom of Greece Rome defeats Antiochus and Perseus Sack of Corinth Macedonia becomes a province	Rome expands east in the Mediterranean and west to Spain Third Punic War; Carthage destroyed The Gracchi	Mauryan Empire collapses Bactrians invade north India and set up Indo-Greek state Sakas overrun Bactria and raid Parthia	Western Han dynasty Han Wu Ti Chinese expand into central Asia and annex south China
100-30 B.C.	Mithradatic wars against Rome Syria becomes a province; Palestine comes under Roman rule Egypt becomes a province		Reformers fail Civil wars Conquest of Gaul Dictatorship of Julius Caesar Octavian succeeds Caesar, defeats Antony, and rules Rome	Rise of Andhra in the Deccan Sakas invade north India and reach Ganges	Confucianism accepted as basis of the state

In both east and west, great empires had formed in this period. Civilized areas across Eurasia touched on each other. Barbarians, except in periods of weakness, no longer inhabited the hills and valleys between one civilization and the next. Men were aware of civilized societies other than their own. In the age ahead, this knowledge would be used to bring the civilizations of Eurasia into permanent contact on an international scale.

Some Questions to Answer

1. If Alexander the Great had lived longer, do you think he could have successfully united the ancient world from the Atlantic Ocean to India? What problems would he have faced?
2. Compare and contrast the visual and literary arts, the philosophies, and the scientific thought of fifth century B.C. Hellas with those of the Hellenistic world.
3. There were many reformers in the ancient world; some political, some social, some religious. Who were they and what reforms did they try to make? (Include in your list Ashoka, Amos, Plato, Confucius, the Gracchi brothers.)
4. Compare the Eurasian worlds of 500 B.C. and 30 B.C. What changes took place within the states and between the east and the west? Consider the extension of civilization, forms of government, communications.

Using Documents as Evidence

The Peloponnesian War (431–404 B.C.) weakened both Athens and Sparta and opened the way for Philip of Macedonia to extend his power over the Greek states. Demosthenes of Athens tried to arouse the Greeks to unite against the common danger. Part of one of Demosthenes' speeches of warning, delivered in 341 B.C., follows.

DEMOSTHENES DENOUNCED PHILIP OF MACEDONIA

That Philip, from a mean and inconsiderable origin, has advanced to greatness; that suspicion and factors divide all the Greeks; that it is more to be admired that he should become so powerful from what he was than that now, after adding such strength, he should accomplish all his ambitious schemes; these, and other like points that might be dwelt on, I choose to pass over. But there is one concession which, by the influence of your example, all men have made to him, which has heretofore been the cause of all the Grecian wars. And what is this? An absolute power to act as he pleases, thus to harass and plunder every state of Greece successively; to invade and to enslave their cities. . . .

All Hellas, all the barbarian world, is too narrow for this man's ambition. And though we Greeks see and hear all this, we send no embassies to each other, we express no resentment. But into such wretchedness are we sunk (beseiged within our several cities) that even to this day we have not been able to perform the least part of that which our interest or our duty demanded, to engage in any associations, or to form any confederacies; but look with unconcern on this man's growing power, each fondly imagining (so far as I can judge) that the time in which another is destroyed is gain to him, without ever consulting or acting for the cause of Greece, although no man can be ignorant that, like the regular periodic return of a fever or other disorder, he is coming on those who think themselves most remote from danger.

You are also sensible that whatever injuries the Greeks suffered by the Lacedaemonians, or by us, they suffered by the true sons of Greece. And one may consider it in this light. Suppose a lawful heir, born to riches, should in some instances be guilty of misconduct. He, indeed, lies open to the justest censure and reproach; yet it cannot be said that he has lavished a fortune to which he had no claim, no right of inheritance. But should a slave, should a pretended son, waste those possessions that really belonged to others, how much more heinous would it be thought. How much more worthy of resentment! And shall not Philip and his actions raise the same kind of indignation? He who is not only not Greek, no way allied to Hellas, but sprung from a part of the barbarian world unworthy to be named; a vile Macedonian, where formerly we could not find a slave fit to purchase.

What does Demosthenes see as the major cause of all the wars among the Greeks? Have the Greek states usually been united, or have they been attacked one after the other?

What evidence is there of Demosthenes' strong bias and prejudice against Philip? If Philip were Greek, is it probable that Demosthenes would have had such strong feelings against him? Can you think of other examples of similar biases and prejudices to demonstrate that conflicts within a group are considered by its members in a very different way from attacks by external enemies?

PART 5

Empires in the East and West

30 B.C. to the Barbarian Invasions

Empires and trade routes stretched across Eurasia in the first four hundred years A.D. The ancient civilizations, once isolated, grew and then came into touch with each other in the later years of the first millennium B.C. Now they entered into communications with each other.

Goods passed east and west. Over land and sea routes, international trade flourished. Ideas also were passed from one civilization to another as merchants, sailors, travelers crossed paths in the markets of the Middle East and central Asia.

Not everyone, however, benefited from the prosperity of these years. The economy of the ancient world was limited by its technology. Goods were made by hand and were relatively few in number. They were expensive. They were transported by animal power on land and by sail on water. Transportation was slow and risky. Not everyone could share in the wealth that existed. The poorer classes, drifting into the new cities from their villages, were without roots in the new environment, often without work, and without hope of improving their economic status. They had to seek meaning for their lives outside the framework of state and society. In ever greater numbers, they looked to a world beyond the grave where there was salvation for believers. New religions that offered them this hope—in the west, Christianity, in the east, Mahayana Buddhism and Hinduism—were established in this period.

Following the prosperous years of the first centuries A.D., a series of calamities struck the ancient world. The balance of strength that had existed between the barbarians and the civilized peoples was broken. All along the frontiers the barbarians struck. Multitudinous, vigorous, and strong, they attacked the civilized centers. Plague, famine, and economic collapse further disrupted society.

The barbarian invasions extended over a period of some three hundred years. Between 400 and 700 A.D., with one exception—Byzantium—the empires of Eurasia fell, and an era in man's history came to an end.

21

The Roman Principate

30 B.C.–180 A.D.

When Octavian returned from Egypt in 29 B.C., Rome was treated to a splendid triumph that lasted three days. The end of war was proclaimed when the doors of the Temple of Janus were closed for the first time in two hundred years (page 266). The populace was further gratified when taxes were canceled because so much booty from Egypt poured into the city.

The Romans were tired of war and were eager to support a man who would establish peace. Yet though the Republic was dead, the customs and traditions of the Republic remained very much alive in the hearts and minds of the people. Octavian was fully aware of this, and it was his genius to organize a government that preserved the outward forms of the Republic while the power rested with him. Octavian's compromise between monarchy and the republican form of government was an effective one, and it brought peace and stability to the Roman world for more than two hundred years.

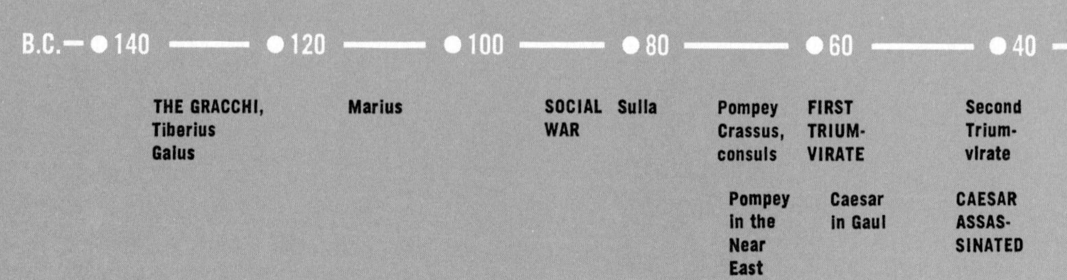

THE AGE OF AUGUSTUS, 27 B.C.–14 A.D.

Octavian's new form of government was called the Principate, a name that comes from *princeps*, or First Citizen. *Princeps* was Octavian's favorite title. He had received it from the Senate in 27 B.C. when he had laid down his powers and returned the rule of state to the Senate and the Roman people. Naturally he had no intention of leaving his projects incomplete, and obviously the senators knew this. Instead of accepting his resignation, they gratefully made Octavian First Citizen and furthermore bestowed on him the title of *Augustus*, meaning "revered and majestic one." These titles, plus that of *imperator*, commander, given him by his soldiers, turned Octavian the private citizen, into Augustus the emperor, and Rome in all but name into an empire.

THE REORGANIZATION OF THE STATE

Augustus admitted that he surpassed other men in prestige, but he was not altogether accurate in saying that he had no more power than his colleagues. He had held the consulship for several years, but knowing this was against custom, in 27 B.C. he accepted a proconsulship while retaining all the consular powers. He was made tribune for life, which brought him control of the assemblies, and he became Pontifex Maximus, which gave him the added power and prestige that came from heading the Roman religion. Of primary importance was Augustus' control of the army, and with it foreign policy, by obtaining special commands (as proconsul) to govern the provinces where the armies were stationed. In addition to these primary responsibilities, he directly controlled Egypt in order to supervise the grain supply, and he was in charge of administering the city of Rome.

In his person Augustus combined both civil and military rule. Yet all these jobs were given to Augustus by legal processes in which the people participated. Augustus always insisted that the Senate and the people were the source of sovereignty. The Principate was founded in law. In fact, Augustus did not rule by virtue of any specific office or decree but by the prestige that went with the title of *princeps*.

While Augustus held all real power through his various offices, the Senate, the assemblies, the magistracies and the *cursus honorum* (career of honors) and also the provincial governorships continued to function. This

Augustus. The emperor is shown addressing his troops. On his breastplate are mythical scenes indicating the empire's peace and harmony, and at his feet Cupid astride a dolphin symbolizes the family's claim to divine ancestry. The historian Suetonious has given us an interesting sketch of the *princeps:* He was a handsome man, retaining his good looks throughout life; he had a compact, well-knit figure, piercing eyes, and a character of firmness and restraint. Augustus disliked pomp and display and lived far more simply than many Roman nobles.

accorded with keeping the outward forms of the Republic. Augustus' relationship with the Senate was particularly sensitive. By his tact and consideration, he gained the support of the senatorial class. He formed a council of senators to help him prepare legislation, and all his decrees were ratified by the Senate. Though in fact Augustus' close counselors were the ones with whom he consulted, appearances were preserved, and the prestige of the Senate was acquired in support of the new government.

Other classes also supported the Principate. The knights continued to be the businessmen and bankers of Rome. At the same time, they came to occupy many important posts in the ever-expanding imperial administration. In the lower echelons of society, the people were kept happy by gladiatorial shows and chariot races paid for by the emperor, and grain was distributed free to the poor. The citizens, however, took less interest in attending the assemblies, while the provincials hardly ever came to Rome to cast their ballots. The *princeps* determined the laws and selected the candidates, and the people willingly accepted his rule.

The imperial administration came into being when the needs of empire forced Augustus to seek the help of men to serve him personally and then to act for him in various capacities in administering Rome and the imperial provinces. In time, all ranks of society were employed in this civil service. For the provincial governorships and the higher army commands, the *princeps* tapped the most experienced and trusted senators. For positions of secondary importance, he selected knights. As the imperial bureaucracy became bigger and more organized under Augustus' successors, it took on a life of its own and administered the empire when emperors were away fighting the barbarians or contesting for power with each other. The Senate became simply an advisory body, whose candidates were nominated by the *princeps* and whose advice the *princeps* took or ignored. The old magistracies also lost their importance. Yet to be a magistrate or senator was still a source of pride in Rome, proof that Augustus' reorganization had successfully combined the fact of monarchy with the traditions of the Republic.

FOREIGN POLICY

Augustus' foreign policy was defensive rather than offensive. He wished to acquire boundaries that could be maintained easily. Such a policy meant expansion in Europe to provide a secure boundary on the northeast. Caesar had expanded Roman territory to the Rhine River. Augustus wished to push it to the more easily defensible Elbe. Such an advance meant conquering the tribes of Germans who inhabited the forests, swamps, and marshes of central Europe. By 5 A.D. Tiberius, Augustus' stepson, had managed to reach the Elbe. Then in 9 A.D. a terrible revolt against the Roman general Varus resulted in a massacre in the Teutoberg Forest and the loss of three legions. This disaster was a great shock to the aging emperor, and in moments of discouragement, he could be heard murmuring, "Varus, Varus, give me back my legions." This first great victory in German history rolled back the legions to the Rhine, but other boundaries remained quiet. Augustus made the army a standing one, unlike those of the Republic, which were disbanded at the end of a campaign, and he set its strength at 25 legions.

REFORMS IN RELIGION AND SOCIETY

Augustus was not content merely to reorganize the government. Society had suffered badly from the stresses and strains of the previous century. The instability of life had undermined religion, morals, and family life (page 376). The emperor, by legislation and personal example, tried to remedy this. Marriages were encouraged, divorces were frowned on, and families with more than three children were excused from paying taxes. Loose living and ostentatious extravagance brought reprimand, and Augustus did not exempt his own family. Both his daughter and his granddaughter were banished for their licentious living. To promote religion, temples were built or refurbished, ancient sacrifices were revived, and the old festivals were celebrated with pomp and majesty. While personal faith can never be legislated, Augustus' religious reforms did inspire a true patriotism and loyalty in all classes, who were reminded of the brave deeds and noble traditions of their ancestors as they carried out the time-honored ceremonials.

Emperor Worship. Throughout Italy and the most Romanized provinces, the Principate was accepted favorably by people who were strongly rooted in the Republican tradition. In the east, however, where the divine monarchy was the more customary political expression, a new link with Rome was needed to secure the people's understanding and support. This new tie was the cult of emperor worship, in which citizens and noncitizens alike publicly paid homage to the *princeps* and through him to Rome. Such an idea might seem strange to us, and in Italy the emperor was not worshiped until after his death and his formal deification by the Senate. In the eastern provinces, however, temples were raised and priests sacrificed to the emperor's name even during his lifetime. This new cult proved very successful in providing a universal religion for an empire of many diverse peoples and traditions.

Augustus ruled for nearly fifty years. Shortly before his death, he composed a record of his deeds from the time he came to Rome in 44 B.C. *The Deeds of the Divine Augustus* summarized the conditions of the empire and contained the names of freedmen and slaves serving in the imperial bureaucracy from whom specific details could be obtained. Augustus also determined the succession. In theory the Principate was not hereditary, and Augustus' many separate powers returned at his death to the Senate and the people. Augustus tried to solve the problem of succession by taking under his patronage first one and then another member of his family. When all died or were killed, he turned to his stepson Tiberius, by then a middle-aged man, and conferred on him the powers of tribune and proconsul. Having these powers would guarantee Tiberius' acceptance as the next *princeps*. Such an arrangement was extremely informal. The problem of the succession remained to plague Augustus' successors.

By 14 A.D. Augustus was worn out. He was 76 years old. As he lay dying, he turned to his friends and said, "What think you of the comedy, my friends? Have I fairly played my part in it? If so, greet my exit with applause."

THE JULIO-CLAUDIAN CAESARS, 14–68 A.D.

The first four emperors who followed Augustus were related to him either directly or through his wife Livia. They are known as the Julio-Claudian Caesars. The name "Caesar" belonged to these rulers by right of descent or family adoption.

TIBERIUS, 14–37 A.D.

Tiberius became *princeps* at the age of 56 in 14 A.D. He was Augustus' last choice, and the knowledge that he had been publicly passed over in favor of others embittered him. His unhappy personal life (he had been forced to divorce a wife he loved and marry Augustus' daughter Julia) further reinforced his naturally aloof and austere temperament. His personality irritated the senators, to whom he was unwittingly tactless and brusque, and perhaps out of fear they did not respond to his genuine desire for them to share more in the government with him. Had they been willing to assume greater responsibility, the Principate might have been modified along the lines of the Republic.

Though personally unpopular, Tiberius proved to be an excellent administrator. The provinces were kept in order, mutiny in the legions was suppressed, and the northern frontier was stabilized at the Rhine. Tiberius filled the treasury by careful management, but he antagonized the people by refusing them a constant supply of free bread and circuses.

Tiberius' last years were spent on the island of Capri in the beautiful bay of Naples, where he retired after plots and accusations within his family further disrupted his public and private life. His responsibilities were delegated to the head of the Praetorian Guard, the military force that protected Italy and the *princeps*' person. This action humiliated the senators, for their dependence on Tiberius' orders was made evident. The Senate revenged itself by refusing Tiberius deification after his death, which came in 37 A.D.

GAIUS, CALLED CALIGULA, 37–41 A.D.

Gaius, born while his father was campaigning and nicknamed Caligula, Little Boot, by the troops was at first received enthusiastically. He was the son of a granddaughter of Augustus and a nephew of Tiberius. But the Senate's hopes for a good *princeps* were soon shattered. Caligula's personal excesses, combined with his power as emperor, apparently unbalanced his mind. He insisted that he and his sister be deified in their lifetime and appointed his horse to the Senate. His wild entertainments ran through Tiberius' surplus in a year, while his murders of people whose property he desired left no one safe. After four mad years, Caligula was assassinated by members of the Senate and the Praetorian Guard.

CLAUDIUS, 41–54 A.D.

In the interim following Caligula's death, the Senate debated about restoring the Republic. While they talked, the Praetorian Guard acted. They sought out Caligula's uncle Claudius, discovered him hiding behind a curtain in the imperial residence, and hailed him as emperor. Poor Claudius, shy and scholarly and most reluctant to be *princeps*, was not in a position to refuse, and neither was the Senate to reject him.

The unprepossessing Claudius turned out to be an excellent *princeps*. He understood the needs of the empire and the temperament of the legions. He realized that the provincial cities were playing an increasingly important role in the well-being of the empire, and he acknowledged their desire to share more in the government. Following the policy of Julius Caesar, Claudius gave citizenship to many provincials and even enrolled Gallic noblemen in the Senate. The imperial bureaucracy was enlarged, and Claudius organized it into separate departments for special affairs.

During Claudius' rule, the conquest of Britain was undertaken. The *princeps*, as *imperator*, visited the legions to reinforce their morale and took part in the closing phases of the invasion (44 A.D.). This extension of empire was not an easy task. The Celts of Britain were just as reluctant to accept Roman rule as had been their fellow tribesmen in Gaul, some of whom escaped to Britain and stirred up resistance there. In 61 A.D. there was a revolt under the queen Boadicea. She rallied her people, who slaughtered a legion and sacked Londinium (London). The Britons, however, did not succeed against the legions. The revolt was eventually crushed, Boadicea committed suicide, and the Romans brought the whole of southern England firmly under their control. By the end of the first century A.D., the west (Wales) and the north up to the Scottish Highlands were also conquered.

NERO, 54–68 A.D.

Nero was the great-great-grandson of Augustus. He fancied himself an artist and poet and appeared in public as an actor and singer and even as a charioteer in the circus. His talent as an artist is questionable, and his personal reputation has suffered as a result of his being accused of being the murderer of his mother. She, in turn, was charged with having murdered her husband Claudius. Nero was also accused of setting fire to Rome and strumming on his lyre about Troy while the city burned to inspire him, but this accusation seems to have been false. Nero, nevertheless, needed a scapegoat to blame for the disaster and picked the Christians, an obscure sect that refused to participate in the public worship and was hated and feared by the general public. The apostles Peter and Paul are supposed to have lost their lives in this first great persecution of Christianity, which, however, was confined to Rome.

Nero's rule came to an end when the Senate declared him a public enemy. The upper classes were scandalized by his public appearances and personal extravagances and feared for their lives and property. The final straw came when the legions revolted. Nero, finding it impossible to escape, had a faithful freedman stab him to death. His last words concerned not the empire but his frustrated talent. "What an artist," he exclaimed, "dies in me."

CONTEST FOR THE PRINCIPATE, 68–69 A.D.

On Nero's suicide, the line of Julio-Claudian emperors came to an ignoble end. Because no candidate could legally claim the throne, a break in the

Principate seemed inevitable. In the vacuum, the legions took matters into their own hands, and civil war ensued. Three generals were proclaimed emperor by their troops, but none could successfully establish himself in power. Finally Vespasian (Flavius Vespasianus), choice of the legions in the east, asserted his claim by capturing Egypt and controlling the grain supply. He established the line of Flavian Caesars, whose three members ruled from 69 to 96 A.D. The Flavians inaugurated the practice of using "Caesar" as a title, as it was not their family name.

The rule of Nero not only ended the rule of the Julio-Claudian families. It also brought to an end the monopoly of imperial offices by natives of the city of Rome. Most of the great Roman families had perished under persecution by Nero or in the wars of 68–69 A.D. Starting with Vespasian, the chief officers of the empire were drawn from the upper middle classes of Italy.

THE FLAVIAN CAESARS, 69–96 A.D.

VESPASIAN, 69–79 A.D.

Vespasian proved to be a strong ruler, one who reestablished the Principate along the lines laid down by Augustus. Working relations between the *princeps* and the Senate, flouted and mocked by Caligula and Nero, were reaffirmed. This was of great importance, for it was the basis upon which the reorganization of the Republic had been effected.

Vespasian knew the empire at first hand. He had helped conquer Britain for Claudius, and later had fought on the Rhine, in Syria, and in Egypt. Like Claudius, he understood that Rome was no longer only the Romans and the Italians, and he followed Claudius' policy of extending citizenship to new provinces. He further broadened this policy to include the provincials who served in the army. Vespasian also reorganized and stabilized the finances of the empire after Nero's extravagances.

Vespasian's reign was marked by a revolt of the Jews in Palestine. The Jews had always presented a difficult problem to their rulers, for they refused to worship state gods or follow the social and religious customs of their conquerors. Palestine had come under Roman rule during the conquests of Pompey in the Near East (page 390). The Jews were allowed religious freedom, but they had to pay taxes to Rome. In 64 A.D. the Jews revolted when the Roman governor confiscated money from the Temple for taxes that had fallen in arrears. The revolt lasted until 70 A.D., when Vespasian's son Titus sacked Jerusalem, destroyed the Temple, and bore off to Rome its treasures, still clearly depicted in a triumphal arch raised in the Forum to comemorate his victory. The Jews were forbidden to reconstruct the Temple. Much of their state was turned into public land and opened to colonists, and many Jewish towns were destroyed and their inhabitants sold as slaves.

TITUS AND DOMITIAN, 79–96 A.D.

Titus, "the light of the world," came to the throne when his father died. He was enormously popular with Senate and people alike, "the darling and delight of mankind." He ruled only two years before death overtook him. His brief reign was marked by the eruption of Mt. Vesuvius, on the bay of Naples, and the burial of the cities of Pompeii and Herculaneum under ashes and lava.

Titus was succeeded by his brother Domitian, an entirely different sort of person. Beset by fears and suspicions, Domitian terrorized Rome for

A street in Pompeii, right, and a child encased in pumice stone and ash, left. The eruption of Mt. Vesuvius in 79 A.D. completely buried two cities—their dwellings, temples, baths, fountains, fortifications, theaters, water systems, and their animals and people as they fled or hid or were caught up in the activities of everyday life. Ever since the eighteenth century, when the ruins of Pompeii were accidentally discovered, the excavations of these cities have revealed in wonderful detail the life of a Roman provincial city.

fifteen years until he was murdered by conspirators in his household. A tyrant at home and feared by the Senate, Domitian persecuted the Christians and Jews, which further blackened his name. But he governed the provinces well and chose able and honest men to administer them. Indeed, all the emperors following Augustus were honored in the provinces for the prosperity that followed upon the establishment of the Principate. While whispers of murder, gluttony, and debauchery were circulated by the anti-Caesar factions in Rome, the emperors were widely respected and loved abroad.

THE GOOD EMPERORS, 96–180 A.D.

Vespasian, like Augustus, had wanted the throne to go to the members of his family, and in order to confirm his wish he had associated his son Titus with him in rule. When Titus' brother Domitian was murdered, the problem of succession once again reappeared. The Senate acted by selecting an elderly and gentle senator, Nerva, to be the next *princeps*, hoping that he would be their willing tool. The army acquiesed on the understanding that Nerva would select his heir immediately. Nerva appointed as his colleague and successor a general, the forty-year-old Trajan, a man of ability and experience whom he then adopted. Here was an acceptable solution to the problem of the succession: the selection and adoption of the "best man" to succeed to the throne. This method was extremely successful for nearly one hundred years, perhaps because no *princeps* had a son until Marcus Aurelius. It satisfied both the tradition of the Roman upper classes of adopting sons to continue the family line and the desire for hereditary succession, more customary in the Near East.

With the accession of Nerva to the Principate, the era of the Good Emperors, also called the Antonines, begins. During this period, the empire reached its peak in prosperity and good government, and the *Pax Romana*, the great Roman peace inaugurated by Augustus, was maintained throughout the Mediterranean world.

Nerva reigned for only two years, and on his death, his adopted son, Trajan, succeeded him.

TRAJAN, 98–117 A.D

Trajan was born in Spain, which made him the first provincial to reach the throne. On his accession he was in early middle age, experienced in military affairs and administration, firm but not autocratic. He had the ability to inspire friendship and respect among his associates and subordinates alike.

Trajan was ranked by the Romans themselves with Augustus and Vespasian as one of Rome's greatest rulers. He was the only *princeps* to receive from the Senate the official title *Optimus* (the best).

During the rule of Trajan, the Roman Empire reached its greatest geographical extent. On the European frontier, the emperor fought several campaigns against the Dacians, a barbarian people who had coalesced into a kingdom north of the Danube during the reign of Domitian. Trajan defeated them and made their kingdom into the province of Dacia (modern Rumania). The new province, a thousand miles in circumference, was repopulated with settlers from all parts of the empire. In the east, Trajan pushed into Mesopotamia and annexed Armenia, but revolt flared in his wake, and his death interrupted reconquest. His successor, Hadrian, abandoned these eastern territories, realizing that the time had come to consolidate rather than expand the empire.

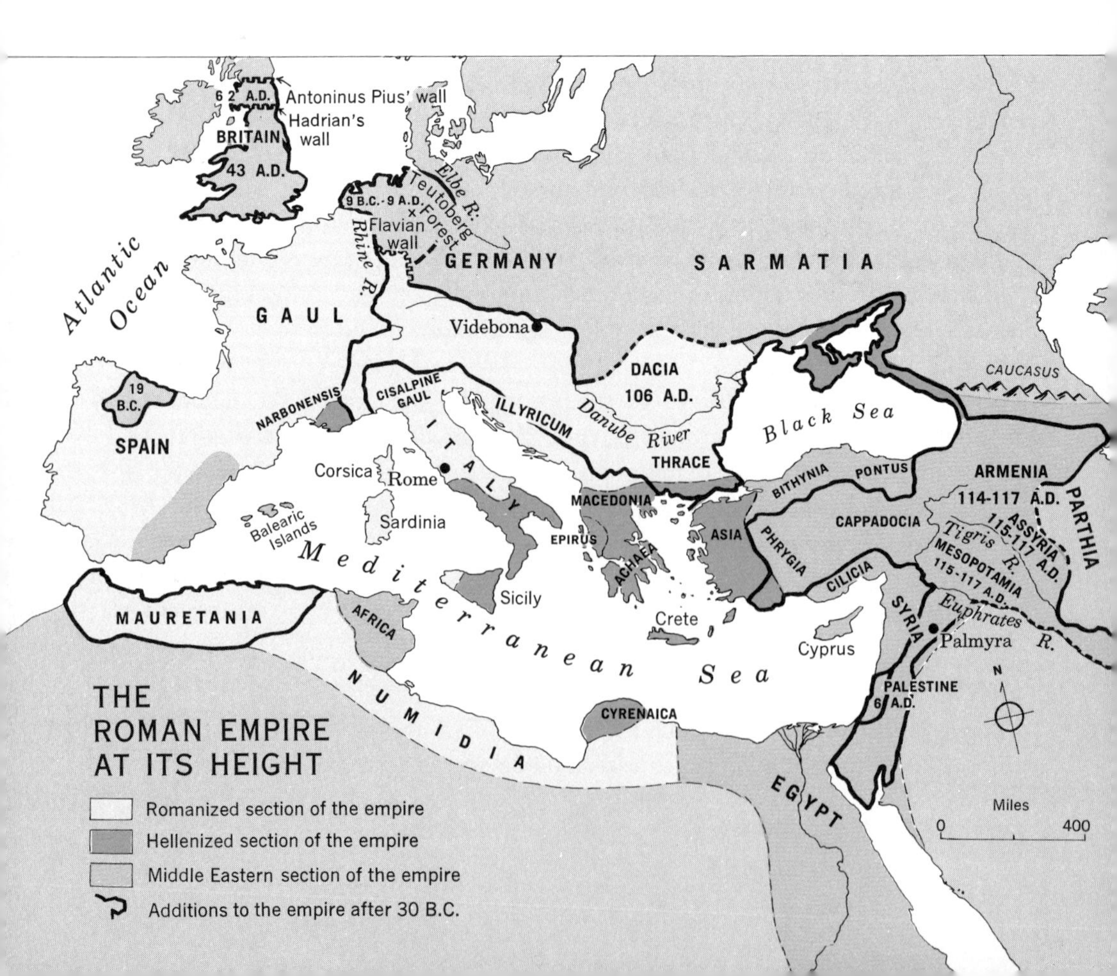

Trajan postponed the selection of a successor until his deathbed, when it was given out that he had adopted his cousin, the brilliant and versatile Hadrian.

HADRIAN, 117–138 A.D.

Like his predecessor, Hadrian was an excellent administrator, a brave soldier, and skilled in military affairs; but unlike his predecessor, he was a scholar and man of peace, not a conqueror. Hadrian maintained and defended the borders of the empire rather than attempting new conquests. He reorganized the army, and the generals devised a new formation that could better offset the wild charges of the barbarians. Permanent camps ringed the frontier. A great fortified wall was erected across Britain to protect the province from raids by the highlanders; another wall held Gaul's Rhine frontier against the Germans. Hadrian's decision to rebuild Jerusalem, which had lain in ruins since its destruction by Titus, brought on a new rebellion by the Jews, who were both angered at the thought of a Roman temple to Jupiter on the site of the ancient temple to Yahweh and anxious for political freedom. After the death of half a million rebels and their self-announced "messiah," Simon bar Kochba, Hadrian continued with his plans to rebuild Jerusalem. Though he permitted the surviving Jews freedom to worship in their own way, he did not allow them to live in the rebuilt colony.

Hadrian was in Rome only seven years of his twenty-one-year reign. Twice he took extensive tours through the empire, raising temples and theaters, aqueducts, and baths. His travels took him from Britain to Syria, but he particularly favored Hellas and the Near East, for he had had a Greek education. He was intensely interested in art and literature and was a gifted architect. In his old age he retired to the beautiful estate which he designed at Tivoli near Rome. There he constructed copies of those works of art that had pleased him most on his tours. His tomb, which he also designed and which was used as a fortress for a thousand years, still stands as the Castel Sant'Angelo near St. Peter's in Rome.

ANTONINUS, SURNAMED PIUS, 138–161 A.D.

Antoninus Pius, for 23 years, reaped the harvest of peace and security planted by the hardworking Trajan and Hadrian. No important wars or revolts called him abroad, and he was content to remain quietly in Italy, where affairs were tranquil. For many years he associated himself in rule with his adopted son, Marcus Aurelius, who succeeded him without incident.

MARCUS AURELIUS, 161–180 A.D.

When Marcus Aurelius came to the throne, the empire was outwardly healthy and strong. By the end of his reign, a combination of events had so undermined it socially and economically that it never completely recovered.

A philosopher by temperament, Marcus Aurelius was denied the quiet and serenity for which he yearned. From the beginning of his reign the peace and security of the Roman world was shattered. Three years of a major war with Parthia were followed by the appearance of a pestilence that, starting among the armies on the Parthian frontier, swept the whole empire, killing at least a fourth of its people. The plague was followed by famine and by incursions of barbarian tribes into the empire from across the Danube. The royal treasury was totally depleted, and the drop in population made it difficult to collect new taxes. Fighting manfully against all disasters, Marcus Aurelius was struck down by the plague at Videbona (Vienna).

Marcus Aurelius bore all difficulties with fortitude, for he had become a Stoic in his youth. In his little book the *Meditations*, written during the

Marcus Aurelius. This mounted (equestrian) statue shows the emperor as an all-conquering king. According to medieval records, a small figure of a conquered barbarian chieftain crouched under his horse's roof. Note that the emperor, like the Sassanian monarch depicted on the silver dish (page 463), rides without stirrups.

campaigns in the last part of his life, we see his acceptance of the role fate had thrust on him and his willingness to do his duty to the best of his ability. These *Meditations* are among the most moving works of literature to survive from the ancient world.

During the last year of his rule, Marcus Aurelius associated his son Commodus with him. This boy, who became the next emperor, was totally unfit to cope with the problems of the empire.

THE REIGN OF COMMODUS AND THE WEAKENING OF EMPIRE, 180–192 A.D.

Commodus was a disaster for the Principate. Had a Vespasian succeeded Marcus Aurelius, the empire might have been strengthened again, the barbarians contained, and the imperial finances restored. Commodus, who regarded himself as the reincarnation of Hercules and proposed to accept the consulship of 193 A.D. costumed in a gladiator's lionskin, thrust aside trusted advisers and insulted the Senate. He was strangled to death in his bath. The succession was thereby left undetermined, and civil war, as at the death of Nero, broke out.

With the death of Commodus, the chance for orderly reorganization of the Principate was lost. After two centuries of prosperity, the great age of the Roman Empire had come to an end. Future generations witnessed the transformation of the Principate into an undisguised autocracy, and the gathering strength of two new forces that would have a vital effect on European history: the barbarian tribes of the Germans and the religion of Christianity.

People, Places, and Terms

Augustus
Tiberius
Gaius
Claudius
Nero
the Julio-Claudians
the Flavians
Vespasian
Titus

Domitian
Nerva
Trajan
Hadrian
Antoninus Pius
Marcus Aurelius
Commodus

Mt. Vesuvius

Britannia
Pompeii
Herculaneum

Principate
princeps
Pax Romana
Imperator
diaspora

Mastering the Reading

1. What did each of Octavian's titles imply? Why did he wish to appear to preserve republican traditions? What changes in republican institutions did Augustus make? How did he reform Roman society? What did he do for the provinces? What did he do about succession?
2. For what personal characteristics, accomplishments or failures are each of the Julio-Claudian emperors remembered?
3. Why did Vespasian and Titus suppress the Jews and destroy their Temple?
4. How "good" were the "Good Emperors"?

Interpreting the Text

1. Which emperors did the most to make the *Pax Romana* a peaceful time for everyone? What groups did not find peace and prosperity in this period?
2. Was the Principate the best solution for the empire? Why or why not?

Exploring Beyond the Text

1. Titus reigned for only a short time, but much is remembered of his reign. Report on one of these topics: the dispersion of the Jews after the destruction of the Temple; the building of the Colosseum; Pompeii; the Arch of Titus; or Herculaneum.
2. Discuss the values and dangers of "one-man" rule using as examples the emperors from 30 B.C. to 180 A.D.
3. From Caesar to Marcus Aurelius the frontier and the barbarians caused concern and challenge. Trace the influence that they had on the empire.

Working with the Map

After the Punic Wars, Rome continued to expand until it reached its height about 117 A.D. Make an outline map showing Rome's possessions in 133 B.C., 30 B.C., and during the reign of Hadrian. Why was some territory lost? Using the maps on pages 372, 391, and 436, determine the general direction the expansion took during each phase.

22

The Mediterranean World During the Pax Romana

30 B.C.–180 A.D.

During the Principate, the Roman state was stabilized politically and prospered economically and culturally. While the empire was defended by the legions, the provinces flourished, cities multiplied and the populace benefitted from an extensive trade and a strong local self-government. The Roman Empire during the first and second centuries A.D. contained perhaps a hundred million people. They were bound together by a common loyalty to the imperial government and lived in peace with each other.

Rome's greatest contributions to civilization were in practical fields—law, engineering, government. The Principate nevertheless was a great age for architecture and literature and for achievement in many fields. Rome, now a magnificent city, was filled with monuments built by the emperors; it bustled with people, trade, and industry. It was truly an imperial city, the source and inspiration of a newly unified world.

THE FRONTIERS AND DEFENSE OF THE EMPIRE

With the annexation of Egypt by Augustus in 30 B.C., every country bordering the Mediterranean Sea was either allied to Rome or governed by it. In the west, the Mediterranean Sea had become what its name indicated, the center (*med*—middle) of the earth (*terra*). The Romans proudly called it *Mare Nostrum*, our sea. Over its waters, Roman galley ships patrolled the coast to keep the sea lanes free of pirates, and Romans engaged in commerce and trade over a water highway connecting such far flung points of the empire as Cartegena in Spain and the cities of Asia Minor.

The frontiers of this great empire were largely the natural ones of ocean, river, and desert. To the west lay the great Atlantic Ocean, to the north the Rhine and Danube rivers. To the south spread the Sahara, and to the east the grasslands of Syria and the Euphrates River. Behind these barriers, nomadic and barbarian tribes lived on uneasy terms with each other and with Rome. Along the Rhine and Danube lived the vigorous and warlike Germans. Primitive tribes inhabited the area beyond the great natural barrier of the Sahara, while in Arabia, nomads continued their centuries-old existence. In the east, where the barrier was weak, the boundary shifted constantly as various peoples attempted to gain control of Mesopotamia.

Where the natural barriers were vulnerable, the Roman legionnaires and a complex system of fortifications protected the empire. After the reign of Hadrian (page 437), the soldiers were stationed in permanent fortified camps located at strategic points along the long frontier. The number of legions was increased from 25 to 28 by Vespasian, and they were supplemented by as many auxiliary troops, such as cavalry and bowmen. Augustus kept the army largely Italian in composition, relying on its proven mettle and loyalty. Succeeding emperors increasingly recruited provincials as the Italians grew too soft for military life. The blood of the Roman army became very mixed, and in the Late Empire even barbarian. But during the Principate, Roman character and discipline prevailed, and a strong *esprit de corps* bound the soldiers to each other and inspired them with loyalty to their commander and to Rome.

The Roman legionnaire did not only fight. In the long intervals of peace during the Early Empire, he built the roads that linked all parts of the empire and that provided the means to move troops quickly to their posts. Without these roads, the defense of the empire over such long distances would have been impossible. The legionnaire also built aqueducts to carry water, bridges to span the rivers, and fortifications at weak points.

Legionnaires. In dress uniform with plumed helmets and ornate oval shields, these soldiers may be members of the Praetorian Guard, the 9,000 member force that guarded the emperor and the city of Rome. During the Early Empire the members of the Guard were Italians who enlisted for sixteen years; the regular troops were Roman citizens who enlisted for twenty years. By the end of the second century A.D., 400,000 troops guarded an empire of perhaps 100,000,000 people, covering over 3,500,000 square miles.

One such weak spot in the frontiers existed in the north of Britain. No natural barriers protected the legionnaires from the forays of the fierce Picts, who lived in the Scottish Highlands. Hadrian's wall (page 437) was extended by Antoninus Pius to the Clyde River, where it marked the limits of Roman expansion in Britain. Another vast fortification was erected by the Flavian emperors to protect the exposed angle between the Rhine and Danube rivers in central Europe. This was the spot that Augustus had hoped to protect by pushing the frontier to the Elbe, but the Roman defeat in the Teutoberg Forest (page 429) had blocked that plan permanently. The complex fortifications required enormous amounts of labor and years of work, but they were so well constructed that even today their ruins are imposing.

For nearly two hundred years, peace existed within the borders of the Roman Empire. This great *Pax Romana* was broken only twice, once in

68–69 A.D., after the suicide of Nero, and again after the murder of Commodus in 192 A.D. The boundaries of the empire were stable except for the additions of Britain and Dacia and the constant conflict in the Near East with the Parthians. There the boundary shifted, and Trajan's conquests were abandoned by Hadrian. While it is true that the peace was imposed by a conquering power rather than assumed freely by those under Rome's sway, it was accepted nonetheless gratefully as the provinces prospered. The "immense majesty of the Roman Peace," as one ancient writer described it, supported by the hardy legionnaires and a magnificent system of defense, was one of the most impressive achievements of the ancient world.

THE PROVINCES AND MUNICIPALITIES

At its height during the Early Empire, Rome had 45 provinces. Once the abuses of the Republican system of provincial rule had been corrected, these provinces were well governed. They were also protected from barbarian assaults, and they prospered through increased opportunities for commerce and trade. Under the emperors the imperial system worked well, for the Romans had finally learned how to unite and govern successfully the many peoples under their sway.

THE PROVINCES

Two types of provinces existed. The first were the imperial provinces—the newer and therefore less Romanized ones and those where the barbarian threat was the greatest. These provinces were under the jurisdiction of the emperors. The remaining provinces were administered by the senators. As senatorial influence declined during the Late Empire, the senators lost control of their provinces. By the end of the third century A.D., the Senate retained the rule of only those provinces that had the fewest people and the least wealth.

The provincial administration was thoroughly revised under the emperors. The imperial provinces were governed by men responsible to the emperor alone, and they were carefully selected by him for honesty and efficiency. Even the senatorial provinces had close supervision from the emperor, and their governors had to be personally acceptable to him. Gone was the absolute authority of the Republican proconsuls and propraetors. Now a superior at home checked closely on the governor's conduct and issued orders and instructions for his guidance. Taxes were properly regulated.

While the provincials still had to pay the equivalent of the old tribute in a land tax, the amount of the tax was based on a careful assessment of the inhabitants and the value of the property in the province.

One major reason for the success of the provincial administration was the excellence of the imperial bureaucracy (page 428). It encouraged talent. A senator who served well in one province could look forward to promotion to a more important one. Men of education and ambition in all classes were willing to serve the emperor because they knew their skills would be rewarded. The bureaucracy thus became professional. Experienced men replaced the incompetent amateurs of the Republic. The Roman genius for organization was nowhere better represented than in the smooth functioning of the civil service. By the fourth century A.D. it had become so efficient that it kept the empire going even under the most terrible and chaotic years of the Late Empire.

THE MUNICIPALITIES

The Roman Empire, in contrast to the older civilizations of the Near East, was marked by the growth and development of cities besides those of the capitals. The peace and prosperity of the first two centuries A.D. greatly encouraged the formation of new towns. Even in the remotest regions small cities were established. One hundred sixty cities lay beyond the Rhine; after Romanization Dacia boasted one hundred twenty, while in the province of Asia there were some five hundred.

A few of these cities were old ones, settled in the long years of the past. Others, especially in the Near East, were Hellenistic. A great many were Roman, outgrowths of the camps and colonies in which Roman soldiers and citizens had settled.

The largest city of the empire was Rome. Its population at its height may have been over a million. Next in size was Alexandria, the largest city in the Near East. Syracuse in Sicily held third place.

The cities were self-governing. In the Romanized provinces of the west, they had councils like the Senate, popular assemblies, and magistrates, who joined the council at the end of their term. The magistrates received no salary. They considered the honor of serving compensation enough. The cities were supported by rents from city-owned property, and these rents were usually high enough to make municipal taxes unnecessary.

Many of the emperors encouraged the growth of cities by passing special decrees for their benefit. One of the most famous of these was Trajan's. He made it possible for a *municipium* to receive bequests as if it were a

Gerasa. First colonized, historians believe, by veterans of the army under Alexander the Great, ancient Gerasa (modern Jarash in Jordan) rose to prosperity and importance as a Roman provincial city in the second century A.D. It was adorned with magnificent buildings, including a temple to Jupiter. From this temple, above, the colonnaded main street led to the Temple of Artemis, whose columns can be glimpsed in the distance. Archaeologists have excavated Gerasa extensively and have found it the best preserved Palestinian city of Roman times.

private person. Many men won the accolades of their contemporaries by taking advantage of this decree. Pliny the Younger, a Roman governor under Trajan, gave his home town of Como in the north of Italy a library, a temple, and endowments for charity. Other men, richer than Pliny, gave aqueducts, race courses, theaters.

The cities were a characteristic feature of the Roman Empire at its height. They suffered disastrously during the crises of the third and fourth centuries A.D. Their populations declined or fled when trade fell off, plague struck, and they were taxed beyond their capacity to pay. They shrank in size while the surrounding countryside once again arose in importance. This was to be the inheritance of the Middle Ages: not strong cities but a countryside of great estates whose defenses protected landless laborers.

COMMERCE, TRADE, AND INDUSTRY

The greatest era of commerce and trade in the ancient west was during the Early Empire. The prosperous world of the Principate became a great market for so many foreign commodities that the city by the Tiber became "golden Rome who possesses the mighty treasures of the conquered world."

While the sea routes were those used earlier by the Hellenes and Phoenicians, new avenues of trade by land were created by Rome's conquests. The annexation of Gaul and Britain, and the areas north and south of the Danube, increased the trade between northern and central Europe and the Mediterranean. Particularly in demand was the amber brought to Rome from around the Baltic Sea. The Amber Route followed the valleys of the Rhine, Danube, Vistula, and Elbe. Other imports from the north were furs and slaves from Germany, tin and leather from Britain, lumber from Gaul. From the west came wool from Spain. Following the conquest of Carthage, Rome reached into the heart of Africa as well as Europe. Two routes existed: one in the west across the Sahara, and one in the east by way of the Red Sea and East Africa. Caravan and ship cargoes carried ivory, gold dust, ostrich feathers, and all kinds of wild animals for the arenas of the larger cities of the empire. Frankincense, perfume oils, and precious stones came from distant Arabia. Even further afield, from faraway India, came pepper that was so much in demand special warehouses were maintained by the government to store it and insure the supply. Most of Rome's trade with India was not direct. Goods were usually transshipped by the Arabs of the Red Sea to Alexandria. India in turn was a transshipment center for goods destined for Rome from southeast Asia and China. From China came silk, much prized for luxurious garments. Though some goods came by way of the sea, others came overland via Parthia and the Silk Route (see map, page 461).

Rome paid for its goods with tribute collected in the form of taxes levied on the provinces. Rome never became a large manufacturing center. Her many articles of luxury—fine furniture, lace, glass, pottery—were chiefly for home use. Such a system of intake but no output is only possible in an empire built on conquest and supported by it. When goods were traded, the favored ones were pottery, glass, jewelry, and masses of coins of gold, silver, and copper. One of the benefits that Rome conferred on its empire was the use of an imperial currency to replace local ones of limited circulation. Another was to sweep away export and import duties. Free trade flourished among cities and provinces around the Mediterranean.

Rome's commerce was in the hands of thousands of traders, both merchants who invested monies and retail shopkeepers. Sometimes shopkeepers were slaves or freedmen. The slaves at Rome were not confined to household or agricultural duties. They were involved in many industrial occupations. Indeed, until the end of the empire, slavery remained one of the bases of the economic system. The laws, customs, and moral views of the people found nothing wrong with it. Steadily, however, it diminished in economic importance. Although the Roman of the Republic had been inclined to look on manual labor with contempt and on petty trade as unworthy of a citizen, his descendants had a less restricted view. The reduction in the number of wars during the *Pax Romana* meant a comparable reduction of the numbers of captives. Many owners found it profitable to give skilled slaves a share in the profits of their work. Sharing in the profits enabled more slaves to save enough money to purchase their freedom.

Besides tradesmen, Rome had many craftsmen, such as furriers, ropemakers, carpenters, ironworkers. These and more than 150 others, were organized into guilds (*collegia*). The *collegia* (page 454) were organized for social and religious purposes rather than to secure higher wages and better working conditions. The right to form clubs and societies was of ancient standing in Rome. Julius and Augustus Caesar had tried to abolish them on the grounds that they might become centers of political conspiracies. In spite of the ban, the number of associations steadily increased, and the government accepted the situation by licensing them.

Free laborers worked about six or seven hours a day beginning in the early morning, so they had the whole or most of every afternoon free. The number of holidays varied as new ones were added, or as rulers tried to restore more days to the pursuit of industry. Under Claudius there were 159 public holidays in the year, of which 93 were devoted to free entertainment of the crowd. Marcus Aurelius reduced holidays to 135, but a century later they had again increased to over 200, more than half the year.

Although commerce and industry flourished, agriculture as practiced by the small free farmer never reestablished itself. Most of the land remained in the hands of wealthy landowners who worked it by slave labor or rented it out to tenants. These tenants were the former owners or men too poor to furnish their own tools and stock. Such necessities were provided by the landlord, who received a percentage of the crops as his return. These tenants were known as *coloni*, and their lot was in many cases as unfortunate as that of the slaves. The law not only compelled them to work for their master a certain number of days each year but also forbade them to leave their plots to seek work elsewhere. This form of tenancy is called serfdom, and it became characteristic of Rome in the Late Empire. Serfdom had existed in Carthage, but it was the Romans who introduced it to Western Europe. Serfdom and large estates were to become the economic basis of the Middle Ages.

ROMAN LAW

The Romans were one of the most legally minded people in history. The development of their law was Rome's greatest and most enduring achievement. Roman law, formed during the Republic, was adapted to serve the needs of the empire. When the empire declined, it was carried forward into the legal systems of the Middle Ages, where it became the model for European and South American law codes until the twentieth century.

The earliest law was that of religious custom. The Romans called this *fas*. The pontiffs, in their capacity as advisers to the kings, determined the *fas*. Disputes between individuals were arbitrated by the king, who in the regal period was also a judge. The king's judgments were called *jus*, and they were first codified in the Twelve Tables (page 257).

The Twelve Tables were strict and harsh. They were also limited. As the little city-state by the Tiber grew, more detailed laws were needed to regulate a society that was growing more complex and more civilized. The Roman magistrates, particularly the praetors, were the source of this new law. The praetor's duty was to decide cases by interpreting the Twelve Tables and by applying their regulations to the dispute in question. When the praetor had to judge a case where the law was not clear or where it was not exactly suitable, he rendered an interpretation based on his opinion. This new ruling, if it worked, was then adopted by his successors. At the beginning of his term, each praetor issued an edict stating the principles he would use to guide him in administering the law. In this way, a body of law developed that could be changed to fit new needs and yet was based on the custom and traditions inherited from the forefathers.

The largest body of Roman law was the *jus civile*, or civil law. It applied to Romans only. After Roman rule was extended over the Mediterranean, disputes naturally arose between Romans and foreigners. In Rome, a new official, the praetor for foreigners, was appointed to listen to disputes between citizens and foreigners. In the provinces, the governors had the job of settling disputes between Romans and provincials. The opinions of both the praetors for foreigners and the governors together produced a new set of rules called the law of nations, or *jus gentium.* The development of the *jus gentium* indirectly affected the *jus civile.* In order to make fair rulings, the praetor for foreigners and the governors carefully studied the laws and customs of the conquered territories. Often they found that foreign laws and customs were applicable to Roman needs, so the praetors gradually incorporated them into the civil law. In such a way did the excellent maritime regulations of Rhodes become part of the Roman code.

As the law grew more complex, schools arose to train lawyers in the technicalities of their profession. Two such schools had appeared by the reign of Augustus, and they were later supplemented by several in the provinces. Lawyers advised the emperors, who became a new source of law by issuing edicts, while other jurists collected the written sources of the law. In the reign of Hadrian, these written sources were collected, edited, and, by order of the emperor, issued into one body of law called the Perpetual Edict. The Perpetual Edict was binding in every Roman court. Some four hundred years later, the emperor Justinian issued the most famous law code in western antiquity, and it was through this code, the *Corpus Juris Civilis*, the Body of Civil Law, that Roman law was passed on to us.

The Roman law was based on the concepts of justice and the rights of the individual. It is from the Romans that we inherited the belief that a man should not be accused anonymously, that he should not be penalized for what he thinks, that he should be considered innocent until he is proved guilty. Justice as defined by the Romans was "the steady and abiding purpose to give every man that which is his own." Remarkably, Rome's legal system, developed in a pagan society in which slave labor was common, turned out to be adaptable to the Christian society of the Middle Ages and then to the capitalist society of the post-seventeenth-century world, and so it came down to us.

LIFE IN THE CITY OF ROME DURING THE PRINCIPATE

Rome of the Principate was a crowded city in which palaces and slums existed side by side in utter confusion. Some 2,000 houses and 4,600 brick apartment buildings (*insulae*) rose from a maze of winding streets so narrow that wagons were forbidden to enter the city during daylight hours, when the streets were thronged with milling, jostling mobs. Wealthy men were carried about in litters, officers of the state were surrounded by guards who forced their way through the crowd. The only carts permitted in the streets in daytime were those of building contractors moving bricks, mortar, and beams to the site of yet more lofty tenements. During the night the streets, unlighted except by torches, were a bedlam of farm animals and produce wagons pouring in to restock the city's markets.

HOUSING

Private houses in Rome had no windows in the walls along the street. All rooms surrounded an inner courtyard, upon which the second and third stories looked down. Tenements were six and seven stories high and were solid blocks of rooms with no courtyard. Their windows overlooked the street, to the great danger and discomfort of passersby when refuse was discarded.

Lighting was by candle, torch, or open lamp with a wick floating in vegetable oil. Heating was by open fires in pans or braziers. Water was carried to the upper stories by hand. The first floor apartments, where wealthier persons lived, sometimes had water piped in. Fires were common, and they often swept whole sections of the city before they could be extinguished. From the time of Augustus a corps of fire-fighting watchmen was maintained, but it could do little to abate the everpresent terror of tenement dwellers of being burned alive. Arson was the most serious crime in the Roman calendar. When suspicion of setting fires fell on a person or a group, as it did on Christians after the Great Fire under Nero (page 432), no punishment was felt to be too severe for the guilty.

Another peril threatening the Roman in his tenement was the collapse of the structure. They were often built too high, with walls too thin, and on beams too slender, by contractors squeezing greater profits through such devices as using poorer cement. The roar of collapsing buildings and the screams of the victims were all too familiar sounds in Rome.

FURNITURE AND DECORATION

Roman houses and apartments contained little furniture. The principal, and sometimes the only, piece was the bed on which one slept or reclined for eating or receiving guests. Wealthy homes had an armchair (*thronus*) for the master or chief guest and possibly a reclining chair (*cathedra*) for the great lady. Everyone else sat on benches or folding stools. Chests were

Gladiators. In a fourth century A.D. mosaic (a design made by inlaying small bits of colored stone or glass), gladiators battle. They are dressed in breechcloths or in armor,

used to store bedding, cushions, clothing, eating utensils, and, in wealthy homes, jewelry. While glass was known to the Romans, it was not used in windows, which were shuttered by hangings of cloth or leather.

PUBLIC BATHS

Popular resorts for all people were the great public baths that had first appeared in Rome in the second century B.C. At the beginning of the Principate, there were 170 of them in the city, and the number increased as time went on. They had charged a small fee during the Republic, but by the time of the empire, philanthropists had assumed the costs so that the baths became free to the public. Magnificent new baths were built by Agrippa, friend of Augustus and governor of Britain, and by Nero, Titus, Trajan, and the Severi princes; those built by the last are known today as the Baths of Caracalla. Bath buildings included gymnasiums and rest rooms, swimming pools, hot and cold baths, libraries, promenades, gardens, and shops. From noon to sundown the baths, like the forums, the circuses, and the law courts, hummed with human activity.

ENTERTAINMENTS

Among entertainments the gladiatorial shows grew steadily in popularity. They were deeply rooted in the customs of the Etruscan past. In the arena

they fight with swords, spears, and tridents, and they carry shields. They are accompanied by musicians playing horns and the water organ, left.

the contest brought thousands of lions, tigers, elephants, bulls, and other animals from their jungle or desert homes in Africa and Asia to a bloody end side by side with the human prisoners and slaves pitted against them and each other. The dying agonies of beasts and humans delighted the screaming mobs.

Chariot races were so popular that to house them the great open-air theater known as the Circus Maximus was enlarged to hold 250,000 spectators. In the time of Augustus, 12 races a day were held. By the time of Caligula, 24 had become the standard offering. Victorious charioteers became popular heroes despite the fact that they were often slaves. Certain horses won a fame and popularity surpassing that of Rome's most popular rulers.

As time went on, the open air-theaters produced fewer and fewer of the great Greek tragedies and comedies that had been popular in the past. Plays gave way to pantomimes, ballets, and acrobatics, for which leading actors, like the charioteers, won a frenzied acclaim. It was not unusual for riots to rage between the admirers of rival star performers.

The laws of the Republic had fobidden gambling except on contests of a physical nature. In spite of this prohibition, gambling had always been rife among the Romans and continued to be so through the Principate. In addition to fortunes lost at the arenas and race tracks, many sums large and small were risked at dice games in the illegal gambling rooms secreted in the back rooms of inns and taverns.

FASHIONS

Other places popular with the crowds were the barbershops, where friends met to exchange the latest gossip while waiting their turns under the scissors, razor, or curling irons. From the days of Scipio Africanus and Sulla, Roman men had been clean-shaven and wore their hair short. These practices were continued by the rulers of the Principate from Augustus to Trajan and were copied by their subjects. In the time of Hadrian, however, men began to wear beards and to dress their hair long, sometimes in artificial curls.

Women's hair styles also became much more elaborate in the later Principate. They abandoned the smooth hair parted in the middle and gathered in a knot at the nape of the neck—a style characteristic of the old Republic—or the simple braids wound round the forehead as worn in the days of Augustus. Wigs were used to supplement or replace nature's own tresses. The great lady's hair was dressed at home, as was her elaborate make-up. When she visited the baths on the hours or days reserved for women, her slave carried with her the many jars and pots of ointments, creams, lotions, and colors necessary to restore the damage caused by steam and water.

A new practice at court in the days of Claudius was to enamel the teeth with powdered horn. Needless to say, such customs and expensive cosmetics were beyond the reach of the poorer women of the tenements, who aged rapidly and hideously once the brief bloom of their youth was past.

Outdoor life in Rome of the Principate was dominated by the men. Women in society might mingle with men at banquets or the races, following traditions from the Etruscans, but middle- and lower-class women conformed to the practices of Greece and the east and avoided public life. Even at Rome, public occupations were filled almost entirely by men. For example, the shopping for the family food was done by the husband, who went to the markets, basket on arm, as in Hellas.

THE COLLEGIA

One of the constant fears of the Roman was that he would be forgotten after death and that his ghost would wander in the cheerless otherworld without the consolation of a prayer, a memory, or a friendly thought from the living. Many of the *collegia* (page 448) provided banking services to finance funerals for their members and to support yearly memorial services and banquets in honor of the dead. The *collegia* maintained clubrooms (*scholae*), borrowing the name *schola* from the lounging room of the baths.

The *collegia* were run democratically. The officers were elected by a majority of all members, each of whom had one vote regardless of his social position or wealth. A slave could join if his master permitted, and once a member of the *collegium*, he had the same standing there as a free man.

Soldiers were strictly forbidden to join associations, although there is some evidence that this rule was relaxed for officers. The danger of treasonable plots lay behind the ban on military membership. In place of contributing to a *collegium*'s burial funds, the soldiers paid a regular sum into a special fund supervised by the army. When a donation was made by an emperor, as at the beginning of a new reign or any other time when the prince was seeking popularity with the army, half the gift was retained by the army in a special fund from which veterans received pensions, and the remainder was divided among the soldiers as an immediate gift.

THE WORLD OF THE MIND

EDUCATION

Roman education during the Principate followed the Hellenic system (page 215). Hellenic slaves and freedmen served as teachers for those who could afford them. Education remained a private affair in the early years. As in the Republic, the father taught his sons when he could not afford to hire teachers, and the young children were taught at home. Vespasian was the first prince to provide public funds for the salaries of *rhetors* (professors of oratory). Trajan paid for the education of five thousand poor boys. Hadrian provided pensions for poor teachers and endowed schools in the provinces, practices continued by the rulers who came after him.

At the age of thirteen, education at home ended, and the boy went to a school presided over by a *grammaticus* (teacher of grammar). There he studied public speaking, literature, arithmetic, geometry, music, and astronomy. At sixteen the pupil passed on to a rhetor. Under the rhetor's guidance, he studied oratory, a necessary skill for a career in law, politics, and the army. Those wishing and able to afford more advanced education, usually went to Greece to study.

LITERATURE

Writers in Greek and in Latin made the Principate one of the outstanding literary periods in world history. The Augustan era was noteworthy for a group of writers celebrating the Roman past. The history of the city from its beginnings was recounted by Livy (59 B.C.–17 A.D). In the epic poem, the *Aeneid*, Vergil (70–19 B.C.) traced the fortunes of the legendary Trojan hero who founded the Julian family in Italy (page 209). The poet Ovid (43 B.C.–17 A.D.) looked back to the myths of the legendary days of Greece and Rome. The great lyric poet of the day was Horace (65–8 B.C.).

These writers of the early Principate were followed by another outstanding group of writers, including the stoic philosopher and tragedian Seneca (4 B.C.–65 A.D.) and the epic historian Lucan (39–65 A.D.), Seneca's nephew. Both were provincials, the leaders of a Spanish school of literature. The low morals of the period of Nero were laid bare, and the upstart newly rich millionaires were ridiculed in *The Satyricon*, a book attributed to Petronius, whose death was ordered by his former friend, Nero, in 66 A.D. Pliny the Elder (23–79 A.D.) compiled current knowledge in natural science, and Pliny the Younger (62–113 A.D.) (page 446) reflected the life and events of his time in letters to various associates. Flavius Josephus (37–? A.D.) recorded the history of the Jewish revolt in 67 A.D., in which he had taken part. Quintilian (died 95 A.D.) wrote on the theory and practice of rhetoric. Quintilian was a Spaniard—the professor of oratory for whom Vespasian endowed a chair.

Under the "Good Emperors" the Principate produced its last great writers. Tacitus (55–116 A.D.) recorded the history of Rome and described life among the Celts and the Germans. The *Lives of the Twelve Caesars* (including Julius) were the subject of the historian Suetonius (75–150 A.D.), who repeated all the malicious gossip that was current. Plutarch (50–120 A.D.) more soberly compared the greatest Greeks with the greatest Romans in his justly famous *Parallel Lives of the Greeks and the Romans*. The romance sometimes called *The Golden Ass* by Apuleius (born 124 A.D.) remains the only surviving example of a Roman novel, with the exception of fragments of the work of Petronius mentioned above.

Some of the emperors found time to write amid the many demands on their attention. The historical works of Claudius have not survived, but an example of Hadrian's lyric poetry exists, and the book of meditations by Marcus Aurelius is still studied by students of philosophy.

PAINTING AND SCULPTURE

The emperors lent their prestige and patronage to the art of painting, and some of them, including Nero, Hadrian, Marcus Aurelius, and Alexander Severus, won acclaim as competent amateurs. In the days of Augustus, sculpture was the principal art. Copying the Greek originals for use in Roman homes and public places was a major industry. Many of the Greek statues are known to us today only because they were copied by the Romans. Masks and portrait busts of one's ancestors were sculpted and placed in the hallways of the home and carried in funeral processions. This custom, which had been derived from the Etruscans, has bequeathed to us Roman portraits that sought truthful rather than beautiful representations.

As the Principate grew older, painting increased in popularity until it replaced sculpture in the public affection. Painting was popular with all classes. Pictures were carried in the triumphal processions of victorious generals and were used in law courts to illustrate crimes.

❦ ❦ ❦

The age of the Roman Principate was one of prosperity and peace. The political and economic organization of the empire, protected by the bulwark of the legions, brought renewed strength and vigor to society. A multitude of remains testify to Rome's achievement: the ruins of basilicas, baths, and theaters, of roads, aqueducts, and bridges from Britain to Egypt; the works of poetry and prose; the portrait busts of persons of importance and of those now unknown. These things made clear to its citizens the majesty of imperial Rome and bear witness to the success of the Principate in fostering unity, wealth, and security during the first two centuries A.D.

People and Terms

Livy
Vergil
Ovid
Horace
Seneca
Lucan
the Plinys

Tacitus
Josephus
Plutarch

province
bureaucracy
municipality

collegia
serfdom
jus civile
jus gentium
fas
Pax Romana

Mastering the Reading

1. How did Rome gain allegiance from its subjects? What part did civil service reforms play in the provincial system?
2. How did the praetors help develop Roman law? What was the Perpetual Edict? What legal concepts of Roman law were passed on to us?
3. Why did a large number of municipalities develop? What part did slaves, artisans, and expanded trade play in creating their prosperity?
4. What were some typical attributes of a big city of the Principate? What places in a city offered special entertainment or service?

Exploring Beyond the Text

1. It has been said that the Twelve Tables were strict and harsh. Do you agree? Was this Roman law harsher than Hammurabi's Code?
2. Read a selection from a work by either Livy, Josephus, Plutarch, or Tacitus. How does your author reflect his background? What does his subject matter reveal about the reading tastes and the level of his readers?
3. *Ancient Words in Modern English.* Latin has given us many words. Add the following words and their meanings to your glossary:

collegia	scholae	municipium
principate	cathedra	

23

The East from the First Century A.D. to the Barbarian Invasions

During the first centuries of the new millennium A.D., while the Roman Empire was establishing itself in the west, the kingdoms of the east were enjoying periods of prosperity. All during these times, however, they were feeling the pressure of barbarian movement along the steppe frontier. After the third century A.D. this pressure proved more than every civilization could bear. Between the third and sixth centuries A.D. the Chinese and Indian empires fell to the barbarians, as Rome was to do in the west. Only the Sassanian Empire of Persia, successor to Parthia in central Asia, held the nomads back. Sassanian Persia fell too, but not to the steppe peoples from the north. Its conquerors were a new people erupting onto the scene of history, the Arab followers of Muhammad carrying the religion of Islam.

Reminder Line, Persia

B.C.— ● 600 —— ● 400 —— ● 200 —— ● 1 —— ● 200 —— A.D.

ACHAEMENID EMPIRE of Persia **Alexander**

Seleucus

ARSACID dynasty of Parthia Arsaces, Tiridates

Conquest of Mesopotamia

Ardashir's revolt

THE SASSANIAN EMPIRE OF PERSIA, 227–651 A.D.

During the first two centuries A.D., Parthia, with varying degrees of fortune, was the most important central Asian state. It lay on the crossroads of the Roman Empire to the west, the Kushan Empire of northern India, and the Chinese Han Empire to the east. Parthia's era of power drew to a close in the early third century A.D. In 208 A.D., a minor Persian noble named Ardashir came to the throne of the province of Persis (see map, page 172). In 227 A.D. he killed the Parthian king in battle, seized the capital of Ctesiphon, and proclaimed a new Persian Empire. This is usually called the Sassanid or Sassanian after Ardashir's grandfather, Sassan.

THE SASSANIAN STATE

Ardashir reigned from 227–240 A.D. His power, and that of his successors, was based on the support of the powerful Persian nobles. But whereas the Parthian kings had had trouble controlling the nobles (page 405), the Sassanian kings gained their allegiance by appealing to their pride and patriotism and by successfully harking back to the glories of the Achmaenid past. Sassanian kings not only wore traditional Persian dress and built great palaces in the Achmaenid style, but Ardashir successfully allied the throne with the Persian religion of Zoroastrianism. This religion was supported by a priesthood drawn from the ranks of the nobility and closely allied to it. The priesthood had judicial and administrative functions as well as religious ones. The strength of the new Sassanian Empire thus came from a strong nobility and a powerful priesthood that shared in the glories and achievements of the new state. Such support gave the throne the stability it did not

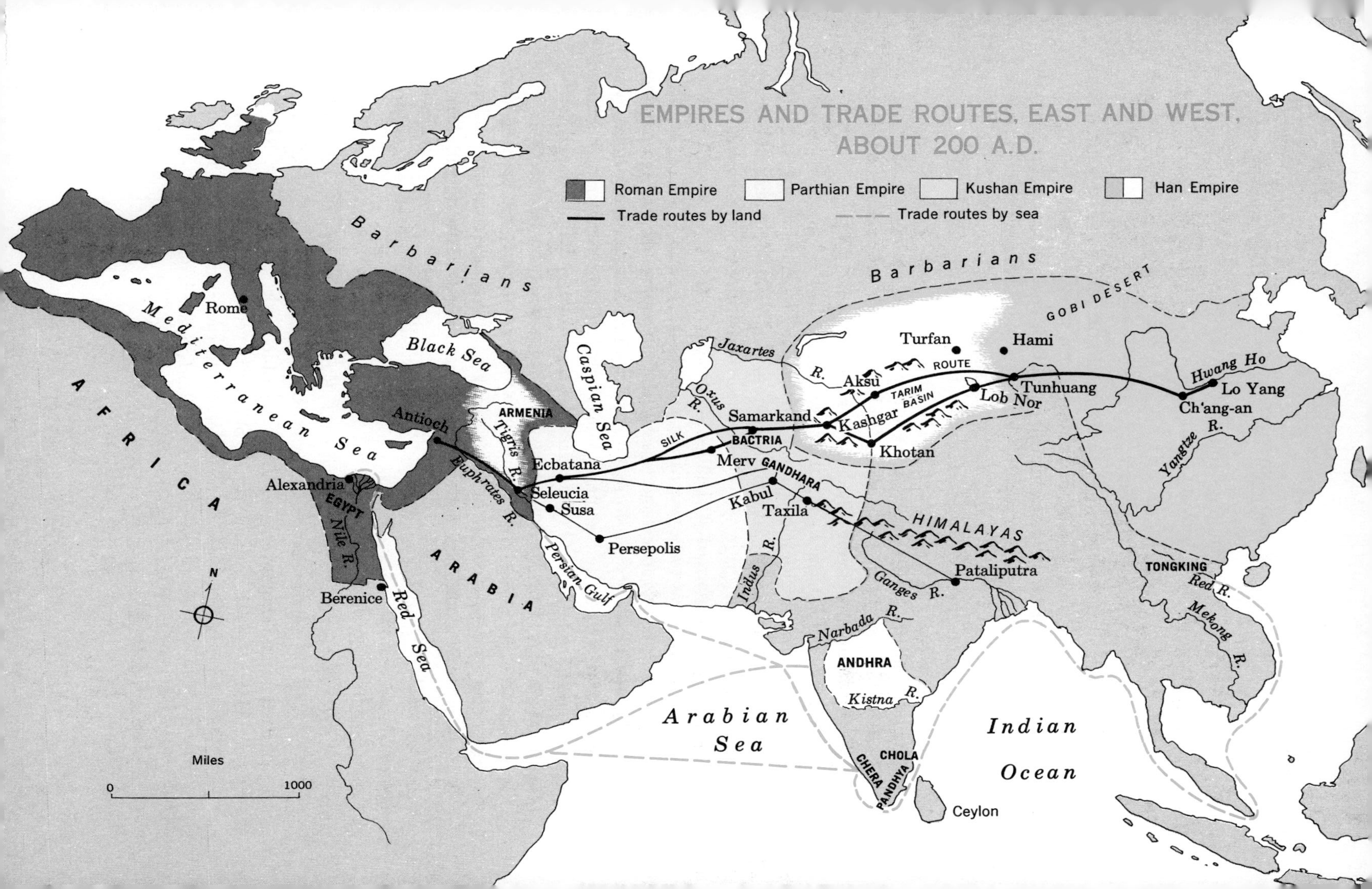
EMPIRES AND TRADE ROUTES, EAST AND WEST, ABOUT 200 A.D.
Roman Empire
Parthian Empire
Kushan Empire
Han Empire
Trade routes by land
Trade routes by sea
Barbarians
Barbarians
GOBI DESERT
Rome
Mediterranean Sea
Black Sea
Caspian Sea
AFRICA
ARABIA
Antioch
ARMENIA
Tigris R.
Euphrates R.
Ecbatana
Seleucia
Susa
Persepolis
Persian Gulf
Alexandria
EGYPT
Nile R.
Berenice
Red Sea
Jaxartes R.
Oxus R.
Samarkand
BACTRIA
SILK
ROUTE
Merv
GANDHARA
Kabul
Taxila
Indus R.
Turfan
Hami
Aksu
TARIM BASIN
Kashgar
Khotan
Lob Nor
Tunhuang
Hwang Ho
Lo Yang
Ch'ang-an
Yangtze R.
HIMALAYAS
Pataliputra
Ganges R.
Narbada R.
ANDHRA
Kistna R.
CHOLA
CHERA
PANDHYA
Ceylon
TONGKING
Red R.
Mekong R.
Arabian Sea
Indian Ocean
N
Miles
0
1000

have under the Parthian kings and enabled the Sassanian state to develop a rich culture and hold back its enemies.

A REVIVED ZOROASTRIANISM

The religion preached by Zoroaster had undergone many changes during Parthian times. Throughout the country, local shrines had attempted to preserve true doctrine and lore, but variations had inevitably crept in. Ardashir decided a new scripture was needed. The old traditions were therefore reorganized and unified into a new scripture, the *Avesta*. Though the revitalized religion became deep rooted in the countryside and among the great nobles, it never appealed to the people of the cities, where rival religions flourished. In the seventh century A.D. the Arabs conquered Persia and introduced Islam, the religion of Muhammad. Zoroastrianism and Sassanian culture, so closely allied, were swept away.

Though Zoroastrianism was the state religion of the Sassanians, other religions competed with it within the empire. The most important were those of two reformers, Mazdak (sixth century A.D.) and Mani (third century A.D.). Manicheism (page 486) had a great initial success in Persia and even received the support of Ardashir's son Shapur I (241–271 A.D.). It spread west, where it was to be one of the most formidable rivals of Christianity. Mazdakism had less appeal and was successfully suppressed. Foreign religions included Christianity (a form of Persian Christianity, Nestorianism, was carried from Persia and China to India) and Judaism. In the east, Buddhism remained firmly rooted in the territories that had formerly belonged to the Kushans. The king was usually careful to maintain an alliance with the Zoroastrian priesthood, but rival religions also encouraged the priesthood to maintain its position by supporting the king. Rival religions thus suffered heavy persecutions, Christianity especially after it was identified with Persia's rival, Rome.

FOREIGN AFFAIRS

Sassanian Persia was faced with the Kushan Empire based in northern India on the east and with first the Roman and then the eastern Roman empire of Byzantium on the west. Ardashir made gains against Rome in northern Mesopotamia and his son Shapur I even took the Roman emperor Valerian prisoner in 260 A.D. (page 496). In the east, Shapur I forced the Kushan lands in central Asia to pay tribute, and Shapur II (309–379 A.D.), one of Sassanian Persia's greatest monarchs, annexed these lands. Sassanian

A Sassanian monarch on a boar hunt. A Persian silver bowl from the fourth century A.D. shows a Sassanian king engaged in hunting a boar with bow and arrow and wearing armor. To ride and to shoot the bow (see text, page 172) were still marks of the Iranians. The bow and arrow, however, were never used in Europe though armor had passed to the west by 300 A.D. When the medieval armored knight acquired stirrups, missing here, he gained added leverage in fighting on horseback with sword and lance.

influence was extended as far east as China, and Sassanian culture passed to the oasis cities of the central Asian steppes.

To the north, the Sassanians, like the other peoples from Rome to China, faced the steppe nomads. The Sassanians, however, had far greater success in holding them back than did the Romans, Kushans, or Chinese. The most successful Sassanian force was the heavily armed cavalry, developed in Parthian times (page 405). For four hundred years it turned back enemy attack, and from Persia the technique of mounting armored riders on horseback spread first to the eastern Roman empire of Byzantium and then to Medieval Europe.

DECLINE OF SASSANIAN PERSIA

In the fifth century A.D., Sassanian Persia faced a number of serious difficulties. There was an increase in internal disorders brought on by famine, religious dissension, a bankrupt treasury, and failures in foreign wars. The aristocracy refused to accept the suzerainty of the king, rival nobles fought each other, and the country seemed doomed. But before the end there was a temporary respite under Chosroes (*Kos*-roy) I (531–579 A.D.). The aristocracy and clergy recognized Chosroes' authority. The economy was stabilized, villages were restored, canals, roads, and bridges were reopened. On the western front, the Sassanians won several victories against Byzantium; on the eastern front victories were gained against the White Huns, who had settled in Kushan territory. When Chosroes I died after nearly half a century of rule, he had won an enduring and deserved place in the affections of his people and in the traditions of Persia.

Chosroes is remembered as the last great Sassanian king. Under his successors Persian strength crumbled in disastrous wars against Byzantium, the line of kings came to an end through assassination, and the empire dissolved. The lives of the people fell into disorder. When the Arabs slew the last king of kings fleeing to the east in 651 A.D., Persia became part of the empire of the Muslims.

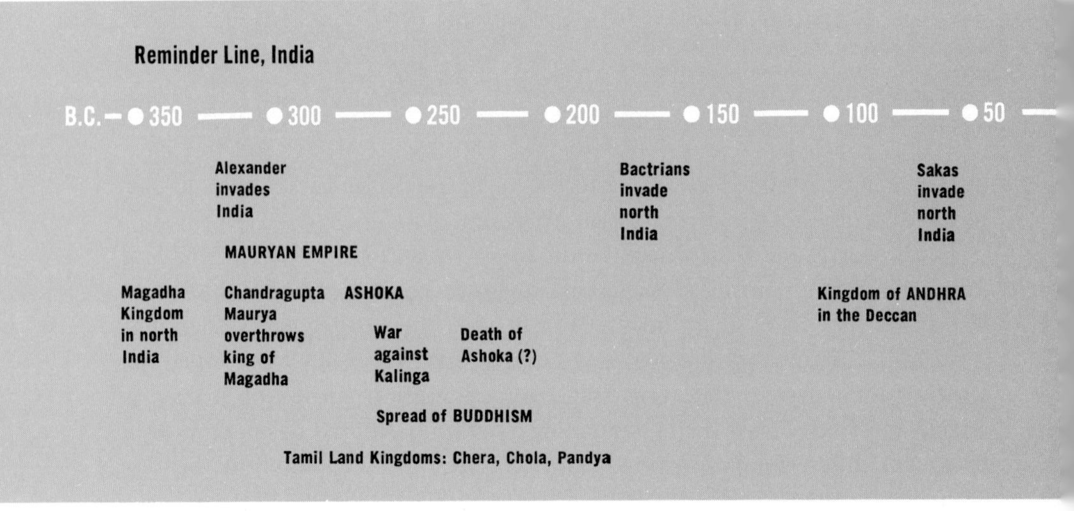

INDIA IN THE FIRST THREE CENTURIES A.D.

THE KUSHAN EMPIRE

One of the nomad groupings inhabiting the steppes of central Asia was a people of Iranian descent known (from Chinese records) as the Yueh-chi. When the Chinese built the Great Wall (third century B.C.), the Hsuing-Nu moved west seeking new pasture lands. They pressed on the Yueh-chi, who started the ripple of movement across the steppes that resulted in the overthrow of Bactria by the Sakas and the establishment of a Saka state in northwest India (page 412).

The Yueh-chi were destined to disrupt the Sakas once again. Sometime in the first century A.D., five Yueh-chi tribes were united under a chief named

Kujula Khadphises. He gained northern Baluchistan (Gandhara) and led his fellow tribesmen over the mountains into the Indian subcontinent. The Sakas were driven further south (page 412). These five Yueh-chi tribes are known as the Kushans.

Kanishka. The most important Kushan king may have been a grandson of Kujula. His name, Kanishka, is far more certain than the dates of his reign, which historians have placed as commencing anywhere from 78 to 144 A.D. Under Kanishka northern India was the center of religious and artistic developments. Though the Kushans worshiped tribal gods, the monarch himself is said to have been converted to Buddhism. Buddhism had been declining in the land of its birth, but under Kanishka's patronage it gained new converts, and missionary activity was greatly encouraged. Buddhism spread north to the oasis cities of central Asia, and from there eventually passed into China. New doctrines in Buddhism were officially recognized (page 487) and inspired Indian artists to create the first representations of the Buddha.

Although Kanishka embraced Buddhism, he was tolerant of other religions which existed in an empire astride the crossroads of Asia. On the coins minted during his reign appear, in addition to Buddhist symbols, the god Vishnu from Brahmanism, the god Mithras of the Iranians, and the hero Heracles of the Hellenes. Kanishka's gold coinage indicates the wide circulation of Roman coins in trade, for they duplicated Roman coins in design and weight.

Rome welcomed the rise of the Kushans as a way of keeping pressure on the Parthians with whom the Romans were often at war. Ships could go from Roman Egypt to northwest India and the Kushans. The routes bypassing Parthia had the disadvantage of being longer and more roundabout than the route from the Mediterranean to the Euphrates and then through Parthia. Consequently, the Romans used the Parthian route when relations with the Parthians were peaceful and fell back on the alternative routes otherwise. The Kushans themselves varied in their relations with Rome. In 99 A.D. they sent an embassy to Trajan, which was warmly received. At other times they were cool to Roman overtures, especially at times when they were engrossed in expanding their conquests in India.

The Kushan State Falls. As long as the Kushan western frontier was held by the Parthians, the Kushan state flourished. But in the early third century A.D., the Sassanid dynasty established itself in Parthia and forced the Kushans to pay tribute. Shortly afterwards the Kushan Empire broke into small fragments. Those in India were absorbed into a new Hindu empire, the

Left, a head of the Buddha. Right, a Hellenic head of Athena. The influence of Hellenism was strong on the artists who worked in the northwest of India, where the first images of the Buddha were made in Kushan times. This influence continued for several centuries. The head of the Buddha here shows a strong resemblance to the Hellenic bust of Athena in the treatment of the head, the expression, and the proportion of the features. The Buddha was made in the fifth century A.D. in Gandhara; the Athena, in the fifth century B.C. in Athens.

Gupta, while the western territories came under Persian control (page 462). A tiny unimportant Kushan state persisted at Kabul in Afghanistan until the fifth century A.D., when its name was wiped from the map.

THE DECCAN AND SOUTH INDIA

The power of the Andhras collapsed in the third century A.D. Local governors maintained independent rule over petty territories in the central part of the subcontinent for the next two hundred years.

Through the four centuries 200 B.C.–200 A.D., the Tamil states fought each other for control of the island of Ceylon. At the end of this period Ceylon won its independence from all the Tamil states, and its capital, Anuradhapura, became once more the great center of Buddhism that it had been in the days of Ashoka (page 409).

Trade and Colonization. In the first century A.D. the Tamils learned to take advantage of the southwest monsoon winds to make regular voyages to Arabia. They produced many of the things destined for the luxury classes of the Roman Empire, and Tamil Land cities served as way stations for other products coming from Southeast Asia and bound for the Mediterranean. Hordes of Roman gold coins have been unearthed in Chola, Chera, and Pandya, proving the extent of the Roman-bound trade in precious stones, pearls, ivory, spices, monkeys, tigers, parrots, and slave girls.

Colonists from the Tamil states as well as from more northerly Indian regions settled in large numbers along the eastern trade routes around the mouths of rivers in Burma, Siam, and Cambodia. These trade settlements eventually developed into native kingdoms. Other Indian centers were established in the islands of Indonesia. All of them carried Hinduism and Buddhism, and associated Indian customs and arts, eastward toward the Pacific.

INDIA UNTIL THE INVASIONS OF THE WHITE HUNS

The five centuries following the collapse of the Mauryan Empire (second century B.C. to third century A.D.) had been periods of invasion and new peoples in the north of India. Because historical records are scant, we really have only glimpses of Indo-Greek states, Sakas, Kushans. In the Deccan and Tamil Land, records are even more scarce, and the best evidence suggests that petty kingdoms and territories, with the exception of Andhra, waged war with each other constantly and with little success. The extreme south of India underwent much less mixing of races and cultures than did the north. The southern languages remained almost entirely the Dravidian

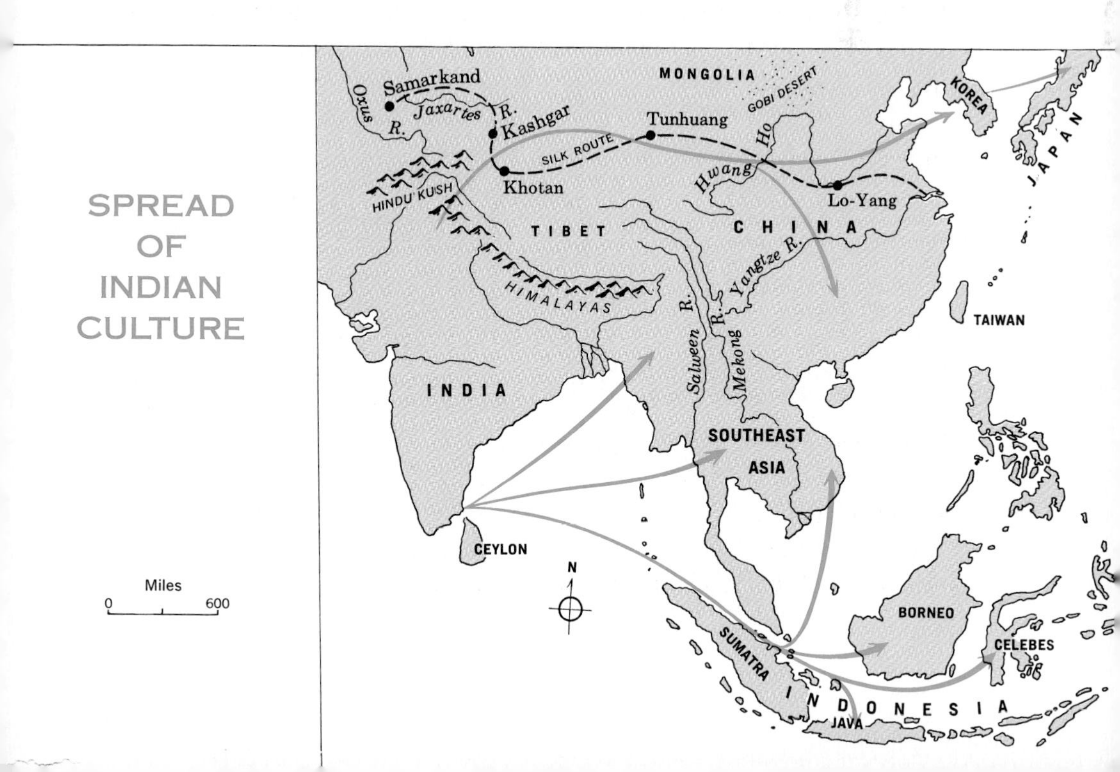

ones inherited from the prehistoric inhabitants, and such Vedic customs as penetrated from the north were diluted and adapted to Dravidian ways. The caste system, for example, in the Tamil states had no classes of Kshatriyas and Vaishyas, but only the top (Brahmin) and bottom (Shudra) castes.

In 320 A.D. a new dynasty established itself in the Ganges Valley and ruled over much of India for the next two hundred years. This great dynasty, the Gupta, saw a brilliant flowering of the Indian culture and the triumph of Brahmanism, modified by Buddhism and the Dravidian influence of Tamil Land into that new combination we know as Hinduism (page 489). But invaders from central Asia were ready to strike at India. In the sixth century A.D., Gupta India was destroyed by people known as the White Huns. They were probably related to the Huns who so terrified Rome in the fifth century A.D. (page 507) and to the nomads who descended on Han China (page 473). In India, the White Huns established themselves in the northwest, and their descendants became the warrior Rajputs who still live in the territory of the Punjab, controlling the passes from the mountains into the Ganges Valley. Independent states reestablished themselves throughout the Indian subcontinent.

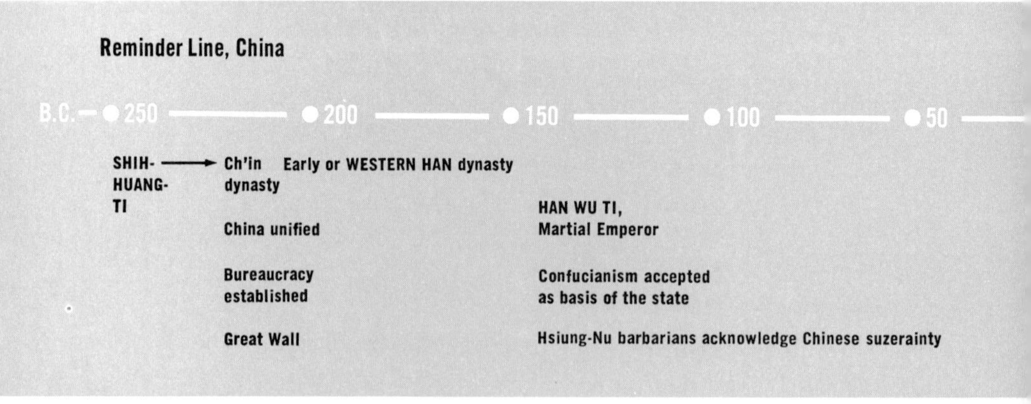

CHINA IN THE FIRST TWO CENTURIES A.D.

The decline of the Roman Republic in the last century B.C. was paralleled on the other side of the world by the decline of the Early Han dynasty. While Augustus was busy with the creation of the Roman Principate in the first years of the new millennium, the Early Han dynasty came to an end. The interval between the Early and Later Han dynasties was filled by the emperor Wang Mang, one of the most unusual rulers in Chinese history. He chose to call his dynasty the Hsin or "New," but he was destined to be its only member.

THE HSIN DYNASTY OF WANG MANG, 9–23 A.D.

In 9 A.D. the line of the Early Han emperors came to an end. At that time a certain Wang Mang, who was related to the imperial family through an aunt who had become empress, seized the throne. Wang Mang immediately inaugurated a number of very drastic social reforms. He nationalized the land and redistributed it in equal tracts to those who tilled it and then forbade its sale or purchase. He abolished slavery. He fixed state prices to protect the farmers and provided state loans without interest to those in need. Then he added to the state monopolies of salt and iron those of wine, timber, and wild products. Such a basic social reorganization could not help but arouse opposition. The land reforms brought down on Wang Mang the hatred of all the classes of Chinese who owned property. The anger of the peasantry was aroused by the state monopolies in the forests and fisheries. To make matters worse, the Hwang Ho overflowed its banks and inundated wide areas of northern China. Famine followed, and by 14 A.D. it was so severe that the peasants were driven to cannibalism. Gangs of desperate, starving men formed brigand gangs, painting their eyebrows red as a way of identifying themselves to one another. The Red Eyebrows received widespread support from the poorer people and were strong enough in 18 A.D. to defeat the regular army and to seize control of the eastern valley of the Hwang Ho. Border tribes reasserted control of outlying provinces.

At this point two princes of the Han family raised the standard of revolt. In 22 A.D. they stormed the imperial capital at Ch'ang-an. The unfortunate Wang Mang was abandoned by all his followers and was beheaded while sitting on his throne in full regalia. His attempts to bring about a better and happier society had failed. The Han prince who had overthrown Wang Mang was himself besieged in Ch'ang-an by the Red Eyebrows, who strangled him while looting the capital.

THE LATER OR EASTERN HAN DYNASTY, 25–220 A.D.

In 25 A.D. the second Han prince who had rebelled against Wang Mang proclaimed himself emperor. He opened his reign with a victory over the Red Eyebrows, crushing a force reported to number eighty thousand men and women. Thousands were slain, and the strongest of the survivors were recruited into the imperial army.

The capital was moved from the ravaged city of Ch'ang-an to the ancient capital of the Chou monarchs, Lo-Yang.

Confucianism the Basis of the State. The emperor Han Wu-Ti (page 416) had made Confucianism the official state ideology. During the Later Han, Confucianism gained complete acceptance as the foundation of society and state. A Confucian college that in 84 B.C. had only fifty students had thirty thousand in 170 A.D. K'ung Fu-tse was by then known simply as "The Master." Sacrifices in his honor were made compulsory throughout China. Confucius' *Analects* and the *Five Classics* (page 291), erroneously attributed to him, became the basis of the curriculum in school. From these schools thenceforth came the scholar-gentlemen who formed the bureaucracy that governed China under the direction of the emperor.

The acceptance of Confucianism had a significant effect on the history of China. On the negative side, the acceptance of one philosophy encouraged uniformity of intellectual thought. Such a policy meant the sacrifice of originality to conformity within the accepted tradition. Yet Confucianism unified China into a cultural whole. This cultural unity proved exceptionally strong. It held the country together even during centuries of political chaos and division. Nowhere in the west was there a comparable achievement.

Foreign Affairs. During the Later Han era, Chinese authority was once again established in central Asia. The Hsuing-Nu confederacy had been weakened by military defeat and internal struggles, and the Chinese took advantage of the state of affairs to seek alliances among the nomads to keep them at peace. Military success abroad always fluctuated, depending on the strength of the nomads relative to that of the emperors at home. Weakness in one meant gains for the other. The first aim of Chinese arms during the Han was to protect the caravan route to the west, a policy whose success was in large measure due to Pan Ch'ao, a general and man of action sent by the emperor to be agent in the west from 75 to 102 A.D. Pan Ch'ao came from a very distinguished family. His sister was the famous Pan Chao, China's greatest woman of letters, and his brother was Pan Ku, a notable historian. Pan Ch'ao extended Chinese influence into Sinkiang, and then in 97 A.D. he sent an embassy to open formal relations with the Parthians and the Romans. The Parthians received the embassy in a friendly manner but persuaded it to go no farther west and to give up the idea of reaching the Romans. The Parthians were thus able to preserve their place as middlemen on the trade routes between China and the Mediterranean. In the south, the boundaries were extended to Indo-China—to Tongking and northern Annam—

as during Ch'in. There Chinese manners and customs were gradually accepted by the local people.

Cultural Growth and Exchange During the Han. Across the steppes of central Asia, from oasis to oasis (see map, page 461), the Silk Route linked China with the west. The most important product traveling west was the fabric that gave its name to the route. The secret of making silk was kept by the Chinese until the end of ancient history. It was so much in demand that rolls of it were used as a substitute for coin in official exchanges with foreign courts. Paper was another important Chinese export. It was invented by a Chinese official between 75 and 114 A.D. Besides silk and paper, the Chinese exported furs, skins, and rhubarb, and the peach and apricot had reached Rome by the first century A.D. Traveling east came glass, Parthian horses (page 405), masses of Roman coins, precious stones, scented woods and pearls from India, and, by the first century B.C., the grape and alfalfa.

Diplomatic embassies followed the caravan routes. The Chinese knew of Rome, which they called Ta Ch'in, and in 166 A.D. merchants reached Lo-Yang claiming to have come from Ta Ch'in's emperor (Marcus Aurelius). Westward, however, no envoys apparently traveled beyond Parthia and the Persian Gulf (see above).

Besides the land route, trade was also carried on by sea. Ships leaving the Red Sea raised their sails when the southeast monsoon (from the Arabic

A Bactrian camel. The use of the two-humped (Bactrian) camel was essential to the silk trade, because only he could stand the passage over the enormous stretches of desert without water. The Bactrian camel had come to China perhaps by 500 B.C., and probably originated somewhere in central Asia. The bronze camel here is Iranian, about 800 B.C.

mauzin, season) started to blow, and they returned by the winter monsoon blowing across India. Although Arabs had known of the monsoons earlier, by the first century A.D. Hellenistic and Roman traders were confidently sailing across the Arabian Sea to ports on the west coast of south India (page 466). Goods proceeded from the Indian east coast across the Bay of Bengal to the Straits of Malacca, and then to Tongking (see map, page 461).

Ideas as well as goods traveled between east and west. They were particularly evident in the fields of religion and art. During the Han, Buddhism reached China, where it became one of the major religions of the country. Art styles in China reflected foreign influence. More lifelike figures of men and animals appeared. Animals were depicted in action, a trait typical of Scythian art. Bronze was still popular, especially fashioned into mirrors. The popularity of mirrors may have been due to the belief that the reflected image was related magically to the soul of the person reflected. Glazing pottery was invented, as was the first kind of porcelain ("China"). For the first time, the Chinese baked brick, which they used widely in making tombs.

Amusements of the Han. Juggling of balls and other objects was well known in China and seems to have been extremely popular. News of this apparently traveled west, for jugglers from Alexandria in Egypt are known to have made the enormous trek to China to perform before the Chinese court. Acrobats performed on the high wire and on the backs of horses. Dog races, cock fights, and bull fights entertained the crowd. Puppet shows were in existence perhaps since a much earlier time.

Amusements in which the people participated included hunting birds with trained hawks, archery, footraces, and tugs-of-war. Stilt walking and dancing were widespread. Football was a regular part of the physical-fitness program for soldiers.

Music continued to be popular with Chinese of all classes, and foreign instruments appeared in China. The lute, a four-stringed instrument with a round body and a long stringboard, was introduced into China from Greece via Parthia and central Asia. From southeastern Asia came a bamboo zither with fourteen strings.

The End of the Later Han. After 106 A.D. the throne was occupied by a succession of weak boy emperors who were puppets in the hands of their family and ministers. Their youth and inexperience fostered intrigue and dissension, and the line finally petered out. In 220 A.D. a new dynasty was formed in the north, another was founded in the west, while a member of the Han line fled south and maintained power there for nearly fifty years. This period of the Three Kingdoms lasted until 265 A.D. when China was briefly reunited for a few years under the Tsin dynasty. In 317 A.D., the last Tsin emperor surrendered to a barbarian chief and was put to death. Confusion and barbarian invasions ravaged the land, which remained in a state of weakness for nearly three hundred years.

Achievements of the Han. During the Han, China as it was to be politically, geographically, and culturally had come into being. The borders of the Chinese Empire had been marked out, the territory that was to be the China of the future had been entered. Although parts of this territory were lost at different times, they were being assimilated gradually. This talent at assimilation, a characteristic of the Chinese, ensured cultural unity among diverse traditions. The state had accepted an ideology, Confucianism, to support the emperor, who received a mandate from Heaven to govern his subjects with virtue. He was aided by a bureaucracy whose members were recruited henceforth from civil service examinations based on the Confucian writings. In China an imperial structure and a cultural unity had been established. They were so suited to the Chinese temperament that though they suffered attack and, in certain instances, marked modifications, the Chinese to the present century were still able to hark back in history some two thousand years to call themselves proudly *Han Jen*, the Men of Han.

From the third to the sixth centuries A.D., the lands of Asia underwent attack and collapse. Barbarian peoples, stretching across Eurasia from the Pacific to the Atlantic, occupied large areas of the civilized lands of India and China. They pressed on Persia and the eastern Roman empire of Byzantium, successor to Rome in the west. Yet the first two centuries of this period had been an era of relative strength and political stability in the east, as it was in the west. Trade flourished among all parts of the civilized world, and ideas as well as goods traveled over the caravan and sea routes connecting Rome with China. Each civilization was able to borrow what it needed from others, at the same time heightening its own form of culture. Such activity was particularly successful in China, whose way of life was laid on a firm foundation during the Han.

The intrusion of the barbarians, successful everywhere but in Persia, was repeated in the west. But other forces were at work that proved equally as important to the civilizations of the future as the barbarian invasions. These forces were those of the great religions taking shape in these same centuries. Their growth and spread had major impacts on both civilized and uncivilized peoples throughout Eurasia.

People and Terms

Sassanians	Wang Mang	Avesta
Ardashir	Red Eyebrows	Manicheism
Chosroes I	Pan Ch'ao	Nestorianism
Shapur	Tsins	nationalize
Kushans	Tamils	Zoroastrianism
Kanishka		ideology
the Gupta	steppe	suzerainty

Mastering the Reading

1. How did Zoroastrianism help the Sassanian kings control their empire? In what ways did Sassanian culture blend past cultures and the cultures of its neighbors?
2. Who were the Kushans and what was their history? What effect did Kanishka have on Buddhism?
3. What part did the Tamils play in the transition of culture? Who were the White Huns?
4. What revolutionary practices did Wang Mang try to introduce? What effect did the acceptance of Confucianism have on the history of China? How did its contacts with foreign countries in the Late Han period help China?

Interpreting the Text

1. Why were more contacts made between east and west during the first centuries A.D. than in any other period in ancient times? What ideas became widespread as a result?
2. Why did the Han era leave such a strong imprint on China?

Exploring Beyond the Text

Prepare a conversation between two merchants, one from the east, the other from the west. See how much information about life in China and Rome can be included.

Working with the Map

1. On an outline map, show which products went from one country to another across Eurasia. Follow the proper trade routes.
2. Show how the trade routes from southern India were important in spreading Indian culture throughout southeast Asia, and how those from northern India were equally important for China.
3. Compare the Han and Roman empires in 200 A.D. What similarities were there between them? What differences?

24

Development of Great World Faiths

In the first centuries A.D., religions that were to have a tremendous impact on men's lives arose in both east and west. No one could have foreseen this impact at the time. New religious leaders and new doctrines seldom attract attention except among a tiny number of faithful believers.

Each of the three religions of Christianity, Mahayana Buddhism, and Hinduism, offered men a doctrine in which a personal savior had a prominent role. Such a personal savior had great meaning to men living in times of upheaval that brought terrible uncertainties to individual lives. The knowledge that a firm belief in a savior assured salvation in the next life went far to help compensate for the miseries of this one.

Other faiths also captured the hearts and minds of men, though not to the extent of these three. In Persia, a crossroads, the religions of Mithras and Mani appeared. Mystery cults (page 206) had a number of faithful believers. Judaism broadened its teachings. Men everywhere found new solace for their lives.

RELIGIONS IN THE WEST

The first two centuries of the first millennium A.D. were years of prosperity and political stability in the west. The Mediterranean world was outwardly secure, prosperous, a good place to live.

But underneath the surface, men in every rank of society were seeking and questioning the meaning of life. They were wondering about the future and about death, about whether salvation existed.

Among the upper classes, faith in the old gods was weak. No longer were educated people willing to believe in the all too mortal gods of the Hellenes. Romans had never fully accepted the Olympian deities (page 376), and many had also become skeptical about the rituals of the Roman religion. The worship of the emperor, while it inspired unity and patriotism, offered no spiritual message. As a result, many Romans turned to the philosophy of Stoicism (page 345). The teachings of Seneca (page 345), and the lame Hellenic freedman Epictetus attracted many new believers to Stoicism. But Stoicism was not suited to all men. Its principles were too rigorous, too intellectual. The lower classes, poor and looked down on, with no hope for economic or social improvement, needed a more immediate, emotionally satisfying religion. In ever greater numbers they turned to mystery cults. The cult of the Great Mother Cybele (*Magna Mater*) from Asia Minor had entered Rome as early as 204 B.C. The worship of Isis from Egypt attracted many converts, especially women. The Hellenic mystery cults (page 206) reached Rome and survived as one of the last strongholds of paganism until the fourth century A.D. After the celebration of the mystery, the initiate possessed "sweeter hopes about death and about the whole of life." The mystery cults, however, did not emphasize moral instruction, and they made no calls on man to lead a righteous or upright life.

Superstition was common in all classes. Wonder-working shrines, such as that of Asclepius, were crowded, astrologers were consulted by the emperors, clever fakers performed miracles that an all-too-eager public was anxious to believe.

Neither the mystery religions, nor superstitions, nor philosophy answered the deepest needs of most men. Something else was sought, something that gave hope for a better life, that assured a future salvation, that provided moral guidance. A new religion if it answered all these needs, would find willing adherents among all conditions of men.

In the first centuries A.D. several new religions entered the Roman Empire. The religions of Mani and Mithras from Persia (pages 485 and 486) gained many faithful followers. Judaism had spread all over the Mediterranean world in the last centuries B.C. In the west, however, the religion of Christianity was to triumph. Christianity, with roots deep in Judaism, had won the Roman Empire by the fourth century A.D. Its success lay partly in the fact that Judaism helped prepare the Roman world for the ideas and the message of the Christians.

THE JEWISH STATE AND THE GROWTH OF JUDAISM

In the sixth century B.C., the Achmaenid emperor Cyrus had permitted the Hebrews exiled in Babylon to return to Palestine (page 174). In the region known as Judaea, the exiles established a theocratic state subject to a high priest. Jerusalem was its capital, and there the Jews, filled with fervor, rebuilt the Temple.

Although the Jews had religious freedom, Palestine remained a subject state in the Persian Empire. It was under the political jurisdiction of a governor. The day of political freedom had yet to come.

In the second century B.C., Jewish expectations were fulfilled. Under the high priest Mattathias and his five sons, the Maccabees, (from *Maccabaeus*, Hammer, the nickname given to the third son, Judah) the Jews threw off foreign rule after 25 years of struggle. In 143 B.C. they established an independent kindom. Their hard-won freedom did not last, however. Rome was moving into the Mediterranean, and Palestine came under Roman control in the first century B.C. (page 390). The Romans allowed the Jewish state semiautonomy under its own priests and their kings. But political and religious turmoil disrupted the peace. In 6 A.D., after the death of Herod the Great, the Romans made Palestine a province and sent a Roman magistrate, a procurator, to govern Judaea.

The Spoils of Jerusalem. In a scene carved in relief on the Arch of Titus, built to commemorate the Roman victory over the Jews, of 70 A.D., the treasures carried off from the Temple in Jerusalem are displayed in a triumphal procession in Rome. Though the relief is mutilated, the spoils, including a seven-branch candlestick, can still be clearly seen.

Peace did not follow. In 70 A.D., the destruction of Jerusalem by Titus (page 434) destroyed the Temple to Yahweh, while in 135 A.D. the rebellion of Simon bar Kochba (page 437) ended Jewish hopes of political independence. The Jews, no longer able to look to Jerusalem as the focus of their spiritual and political hopes, henceforth centered their life on the study of the Law and its interpretations.

The Law, the core of Judaism, is today found in the Pentateuch, the first five books of the Old Testament. During the years between the return from the Babylonian captivity (page 174) and the destruction of the Temple by Titus, the Law was written down. On the Sabbath, the people gathered together to hear readings of the Law in special meeting places called synagogues. Scribes studied the Law in schools attached to the synagogues. Their interpretations amplified it and made it applicable to particular cases, much the same way as the rulings of the Roman praetors interpreted the Twelve Tables (page 449). Especially famous and learned scribes, who were sometimes laymen, sometimes priests, were acknowledged as masters, or *rabbis*. The writing and interpretations of the scribes were later collected into the Mishna, which, along with other writings, formed the Talmud, the second great source of Judaism.

The Jews of the last century B.C. did not live exclusively in Palestine. Many had remained in Persia after Cyrus' decree, and their descendants formed prosperous communities in the cities of Parthia and later of Sassanian Persia. During the Hellenistic Age, Jews had settled in Alexandria and Syria (pages 334 and 335). When Rome unified the Mediterranean, Jews went to live in Africa, Spain, and Gaul. A large community was established in Rome.

Everywhere they lived, the Jews familiarized the non-Jews, or *Gentiles*, with their concept of the One God, the high ethical and moral principles of the Law, and their form of worship. They also spoke everywhere of their hopes for the coming of a Messiah. This Messiah whose advent was prophesied was to come from Yahweh, but there was no agreement as to who he would be or what he would do. Some said he would be of lowly birth, others that he would be of royal birth. He would reign gloriously, he would suffer and die in battle. He would be an earthly king, restoring Jewish independence for the next thousand years, he would inaugurate the spiritual kingdom of God on earth. The Gentiles did not know what to make of this difficult sect, full of theological disputations whose believers were unwilling to adapt themselves to Hellenic and Roman civilization. The Jews were looked on with suspicion by the common people, though religious toleration was the official Roman policy. There were only a few converts, for Judaism did not have the emotional appeal of the more popular mystery religions.

By the first century A.D., the Gentiles of the Mediterranean world were familiar with many Jewish ideas. When bands of people calling themselves Christians appeared, claiming the Messiah had come, people thought at first they were merely a new sect of Jews. But while some Jews joined the new faith, others did not. It soon became evident that Christianity was not a sect of Judaism but a new faith. Although it sprang from Judaic roots, the new faith found its believers not among the Jews but among the Gentiles.

CHRISTIANITY

The founder of the Christian religion was a man known historically as Jesus of Nazareth. Nothing is known of Jesus except from the writings of his followers, none of whom wrote during his lifetime. While Jesus lived, his teachings were overshadowed by other events and personalities that at the time seemed more important. What little is known of his childhood and early adult years working as a carpenter in Nazareth of Galilee is found in the first three gospels (Matthew, Mark, and Luke) which were written probably after the middle of the first century A.D. Jesus' short teaching ministry of about three years and his crucifixion under Pontius Pilate, procurator of Judaea, as a potential source of civil disturbance were lost in the turmoil of events stirring the Roman Empire and in the rumors and speculations of the Messianic expectations in Judaea. Thus, our sources on the life and teachings of Jesus come from men who held certain beliefs about the founder of their faith, as did those who wrote of other great religious leaders.

The Birth, Life, and Death of Jesus. The Gospel according to Matthew tells us that "Jesus was born in Bethlehem of Judaea in the reign of Herod the King." The year of his birth is in doubt, and we do not know the exact date. Perhaps Jesus was born in 3 B.C., perhaps 4 or 5 B.C. At any rate, his birth occurred during the reign of Augustus. His death, more certain because tradition has placed it on the eve of the Jewish festival of the Passover, probably took place on April 7, 30 A.D., while Tiberius ruled the Roman Empire.

The Apostles. During his ministry, Jesus was accompanied by a band of followers, twelve in number, called the Apostles (missioners.) It was they whom Jesus first converted and to whom he entrusted his teachings. It was they to whom the crucifixion came as a stunning blow, seemingly ending all their hopes. When, however, the Apostles came to believe that they had seen the risen Master, they were fired with new devotion and enthusiasm, believing that Jesus was truly the *Christos* (the Anointed), or the Messiah, foretold by the prophets.

The First Christians. For some ten years the little group of Jesus' followers lived in Jerusalem. They preached and sought converts zealously until they aroused such opposition that the Roman authorities feared the peace would be disturbed. The Apostle James was reputedly beheaded, while Peter, whom Jesus had designated as chief of the disciples (followers), was arrested but managed to escape. The group decided to carry the message of Jesus to the Jewish communities outside Judaea. Peter went to Antioch in Asia Minor, where one of the first Christian communities outside Jerusalem was founded, and then to Rome. Other disciples went to other parts of Palestine, to Syria, and to various regions of the Mediterranean.

The Message of Jesus. The central element in the teaching of Jesus repeated throughout the gospels and developed further by St. Paul, was that Jesus was the Son of God who had come to redeem man from sin. Thus, although born as man of the Virgin Mary, he identified himself with his Heavenly Father. Jesus also taught that men should love one another as God loved them. Brotherly love of man for man was more important in God's sight than social class or political power. No man was too poor or too outcast to deserve pity and aid. No man was too evil to be restored to the community of good men providing he repented of his past misdeeds. The belief in the immortality of the soul, in a final resurrection in an eternal paradise, in a God whose love for mankind was direct, personal and without limit, gave to the early Christians a tremendous joy and hope. This made them eager to spread their glad tidings (*gospel*) to others.

Soon there were Christian communities in Palestine, in Asia Minor, in Rome. All classes of society, but particularly the humble and downtrodden, turned in ever greater numbers to the new religion. "We are but of yesterday," wrote a convert, "yet we have filled cities, islands, towns, markets, the palace, the Senate, the forum. We have left to you [the pagans] only the temple of your gods."

Reasons for the Success of Christianity. Besides the powerful appeal of its message, there was another reason why Christianity succeeded in the Roman Empire. Although Judaism had helped to prepare the path for Christianity in the Gentile world, through the efforts of Paul, a convert to Christianity, the teachings of Jesus were broadened to appeal to the Gentiles.

Paul had been born Saul in a prosperous Jewish family in the city of Tarsus in Asia Minor. The people of Tarsus were Roman citizens, and Saul had been given a good education, studying Greek philosophy and Stoicism. He was, however, a firm believer in Judaism. He actively persecuted the Christians until he was converted by a vision of Jesus on the road to Damascus. Saul changed his name to Paul and then went out to preach. His education enabled him to understand his adversaries and made him an acceptable missionary to the Greek-speaking world. For thirty years he labored unceasingly in the cities of Asia Minor, Greece, Macedonia, and Italy. His deep spiritual insight as well as his great intellectual abilities had a powerful effect on his listeners, and he attracted many converts. His thinking also had a profound effect on the development of Christian theology. Paul's many letters (epistles) to the Christian communities that he founded are now part of the New Testament.

Paul, like Peter, reputedly met his death in Rome (page 432). Paul's work, however, had been accomplished. He had insisted that the message of Christianity was for all men, not just the Jews. This view was hotly disputed

The Conversion of St. Paul. Overwhelmed by a great light while traveling on the road to Damascus, Saul of Tarsus hears the words, "Saul, Saul, why persecutest thou me?" For three days, while recuperating from the blindness caused by the vision, he pondered the experience. Then, concluding that he had truly heard the voice of Jesus, Saul was converted to Christianity.

by other followers of Jesus. But Paul's view prevailed. Gradually, under his direction, Gentiles were accepted as converts to Christianity, and Jewish practices and beliefs were modified. Christians, for example, gave up observing the Sabbath on Saturday and changed it to Sunday, the first day of the week and the day of the resurrection of Jesus. Moreover they regarded God as a Trinity of God the Creator and Father, God the Savior and Son, and God the Holy Spirit and Comforter, three persons in one divine nature. Such changes clearly distinguished Christianity from Judaism.

There were still other reasons for the successful spread of Christianity. Its founder was a real person, unlike the mythical founders of the mystery religions. The life and personality of Jesus had fixed themselves in the hearts and minds of his followers, and he remained alive and vivid to them. This made his message more immediate and direct. By the work of Paul and the destruction of Jerusalem, Christianity was freed from a particular locality and a particular people and therefore could offer hope and salvation to all people everywhere. Indeed, Christianity spread to Mesopotamia and Persia, to India and even to China. It was carried north to the barbarians of Europe and the steppes. According to tradition, Thomas went to Parthia and India, and Andrew went to central Asia to preach to the Scythians. Finally, Christianity held fast to its beliefs and would not tolerate or compromise with its rivals. This gave it enormous appeal at a time when people were looking for a new source of strength and inspiration in a world filled with a "weariness for life," wars, and disasters (Chapter 25).

The Organization of the Church. On the Sabbath, the early Christians, like the Jews, gathered together to pray and worship in special meeting places. Such groups were the core of the first churches. The faithful sang hymns, listened to readings of the holy scripture, and partook of a sacrificial meal that commemorated the last supper of Jesus with his Apostles. This came to be called the *Eucharist* from the Greek word for thanksgiving. At first these meetings were in private houses, but when persecution started, the Christians met in underground chapels called catacombs. There they also buried their dead. All services were conducted by presbyters or priests, who also instructed the converts, and prepared them for baptism, their acceptance as full-fledged Christians. The chief priest was called bishop, which comes from the Greek word *episkopos*, overseer or guardian. There were also deacons who visited the sick and helped the poor and needy.

By the third century A.D., the episcopal system of deacon, priest, and bishop was well established for the Christian communities had expanded greatly. The bishops became the spokesmen for as well as the directors of their congregations. Believing themselves to be the heirs of the Apostles, they felt it was their duty to establish church doctrine when disputes arose, and they wrote and debated with each other. The most important bishops were those of Rome, Jerusalem, Antioch, Alexandria, and Constantinople, the cities with the largest congregations. The bishop of Rome claimed to be the chief of all the bishops. The position of the bishop of Rome was reinforced by his claim to be the successor of Peter, who had founded the church in Rome, by presiding in the capital of the empire, and by the unity of the church in Rome on questions of theology. Such unity did not exist among the churches in the Near East, where there was constant quarreling about doctrinal points.

The Persecutions. The Christian communities were expanding and organizing under the most difficult circumstances. The Christians suffered heavily for their beliefs and practices. Consciously, however, they set themselves

St. Peter. On his feast day, a statue of the first bishop of Rome is clothed in the magnificent robes and crown that represent his position as pope, or head of the Roman Catholic Church. The statue's toe has been worn smooth by the kisses of thousands of devout Roman Catholics.

apart from their neighbors. They refused to take part in the public worship, they participated in secret meetings, thus subjecting themselves to various rumors about their conduct, they never attended the public festivals. "Haters of mankind," the historian Tacitus said the people called them. Feared and harassed by their neighbors, the Christians suffered official state persecutions as well. Under Nero, Domitian, Marcus Aurelius, many Christians lost their lives. A last and terrible persecution in the early fourth century A.D. was carried out under Diocletian and Galerius (303–311 A.D.). But by this time, the Church was well organized, strong, and militant. It had thousands of converts who unflinchingly endured fire, the rack, and the hungry beasts in the circus, singing as they faced death. Such behavior, and the fervor and devotion of the Christian converts, deeply impressed the people. By the fourth century A.D., from one third to one tenth of the empire was Christian. The empire was, in fact, won. This fact was recognized in 313 A.D. when the emperor Constantine issued the Edict of Milan. This decree made Christianity an official religion, equal with others in the empire. Constantine then associated the Church with the state to gain Christian support, first by making it tax exempt and then by stepping into the midst of a great doctrinal controversy that had arisen in the Middle East.

Heresy and Triumph in the West. In 325 A.D. Constantine convened a council of theologians in Nicaea, a city in Asia Minor. The object of the meeting was to solve a dispute that had arisen over the nature of Christ. Arius, a priest of Alexandria, maintained that Christ had been created by God the Father and was therefore inferior to him. This point of view was disputed by Athanasius, another Alexandrian theologian. Athanasius held that Christ was not a created being but equal to God the Father in all ways. The dispute was resolved when the arguments of Athanasius were accepted by the Council and held to be *orthodox*, that is, religiously true. They were formulated as official church doctrine in the Nicene Creed and supported by the state. Arius was condemned as a heretic and his opinions as heresy. But missionaries believing Arius' view had gone among the barbarians, and many Germans were converted to Arianism. Constantine, indeed, apparently accepted Arius' arguments, for he was converted to Christianity on his deathbed by an Arian bishop. The conversion of the Germans to Arianism, however, made their assimilation with orthodox Christians more difficult after the Germans gained control of the western Roman Empire in the fifth century A.D.

The difficulties encountered in defining the person and nature of Jesus resulted in other divergent teachings which were condemned by later church councils. One of these, Nestorianism, penetrated Persia and even found adherents in India and China. The somewhat more numerous Monophysites included the Armenians, most of the Egyptians and Syrians, and later the Ethiopians.

In the west, the Church won its final victory by 395 A.D. under Theodosius, the last ruler of a united empire. By then Christianity had become the state religion. Henceforth, sacrifices to the Roman gods and the ancestors were forbidden, temples were closed, and the Delphic Oracle, the Eleusinian mysteries, the Olympic Games were abolished. Church and state institutions slowly merged, and the Christian clergy assumed secular as well as religious authority. The bishop of Rome took over the ancient title of Pontifex Maximus. When the barbarians overwhelmed the empire in the west, the Church was ready in experience and organization to assume many of the responsibilities the state had lost.

RELIGIONS IN THE EAST

While Christianity was gaining converts in the west, new religions and old religions in new forms were gaining believers in the east. The spread of Buddhism in Asia may be compared to the spread of Christianity in the Mediterranean world. Hinduism slowly triumphed in India, while from Persia, Manicheism and Mithraism spread west and posed a serious challenge to Christianity.

MITHRAISM

One of the most powerful of the new religions was that of the Persian Mithras, leader of the forces of Light for the god Ahuramazda. The worship of Mithras had its origins in Zoroastrianism. But Mithras was more than a solar deity in the army of Ahuramazda. He became a god of purity and truth, whose worshipers were cleansed of sin and promised immortal life if they faithfully partook in the rituals of the worship and successfully passed through the seven grades of initiation. The Mithraic worship took place underground in natural or artificial caves and cellars, for Mithras was represented as a youthful hero who was reborn each day at dawn from a rock. From the Asia Minor cult of the Great Mother Cybele the rite of the *taurobolium* was adopted. In this rite, the initiate entered a pit and bathed in the blood of a bull sacrificed on a platform above him. Thus was he purified of sin and reborn to eternal life. The worshipers of Mithras formed a secret society open to all men, rich or poor, slave or master. Mithraism was particularly popular among soldiers, fighters in the battles between men as were the followers of Mithras in the battles between good and evil. Temples to Mithras have been excavated in Britain, along the Rhine and Danube, in Syria and North Africa—wherever the legions of Rome had permanent headquarters. In the Roman Empire, Mithraism was Christianity's chief rival by the second century A.D.

MANICHEISM

In the third century A.D., the religion of Mani gained a strong foothold in Persia. Like Mithraism, it invaded the Roman Empire, and for a time it seemed that it might prove an even more serious rival to Christianity than Mithraism. Manicheism has sometimes been called a Christian heresy, because many Christians accepted it. One of the most notable early Christians, Augustine, adhered to it for nearly ten years. However, in addition to Christian elements, Manicheism also had aspects of Judaism, Buddhism, Babylonian philosophy, and especially of Zoroastrianism.

The prophet Mani began his public preaching at Ctesiphon, the Sassanian capital, in 242 A.D. At first he was protected by Shapur I and lived for a time at the royal court. It is possible that Shapur may have hoped that this religion would serve to unify his subjects, who were divided into Zoroastrians, Mithraists, Christians, Jews, and Buddhists (page 462). But Shapur died in 272 A.D., and with royal support withdrawn, Mani was seized by the Zoroastrian priesthood and crucified about 279 A.D. He was then flayed and his stuffed skin exposed as a trophy.

Like the Christians, the followers of Mani were severely persecuted; yet for a hundred years Manicheism spread from Persia westward to the Atlantic. It became popular particularly in North Africa.

Mani's Teachings. Mani taught that the world is the scene of a battle between a Kingdom of Light ruled by Yahweh and a Kingdom of Darkness ruled by Satan. Yahweh created the first man to help him in the battle, but Satan captured man. In this contest, man lost some of his particles of Light, which mixed with Darkness to produce the present world. Satan then created Adam and Eve out of the dust of the world, so they had in them both Light and Darkness. According to Mani, Yahweh then sent Jesus to redeem the descendants of Adam. When all men have been redeemed, they will become children of Light. The battle between the two kingdoms will end in the victory of Yahweh and the destruction of Satan and his Kingdom of Darkness.

Mani held that the divine message was always the same, no matter who preached it. It is men themselves, he said, who corrupt it. Mani left strict instructions that his writings were not to be corrupted by careless copying, so very little of his work remains. Yet, while Manicheism was suppressed in Persia, in the west it continued to gain men's adherence for many centuries. It seems to have appeared last during the Middle Ages in southern France as the Albigensian Heresy, against which the Church and the French government launched a crusade in 1209 A.D.

INDIA: MAHAYANA BUDDHISM AND THE EVOLUTION OF HINDUISM

For many centuries the religion of Buddha flourished in India. It had noble patrons like Ashoka, and it had thriving monastic communities. Splendid temples gave witness to its prosperity.

In the first century A.D., northwest India was conquered by the Kushans (page 465). Buddhism seems to have received the support of the Kushan kings, and the greatest king, Kanishka, is reputed to have become a convert. Buddhist missionaries were encouraged, and new doctrines, called Mahayana, were officially recognized.

Mahayana and Hinayana. For several centuries following the death of Buddha, it was accepted that if one truly wished to achieve Nirvana, one became an *arhat*, or disciple, and lived with one's fellow believers in a religious community. But the spiritual self-discipline of the Eightfold Path (page 302) was severe. Such a disciplined life did not appeal to every person. The average man did not wish to live in a monastic community. He wished to remain in the world. Above all, the average person felt the need for a personal savior or god to help him attain salvation. The rigorous demands of the self-salvation of the Four Noble Truths (page 302) were too difficult for him to follow alone.

To answer such needs, an important development took place within Buddhism. Certain followers of Buddha slowly came to accept the doctrine known as Mahayana, or the Greater (*maha*) Vehicle (*yana*—ship). The Mahayana teachings expanded the original doctrine of the Buddha to include divine saviors called *boddhisattvas.* The boddhisattva is a soul who has perfected itself and is ready to enter Nirvana but who decides not to do so in order to help suffering mankind. These saviors live a spiritual existence in heaven, where prayers from the faithful can reach them and from where they can help their petitioners.

The Mahayana teachings held out hope to the ordinary man that he too could reach heaven by becoming a boddhisattva. Buddha's instructions to "work out your own salvation with diligence" was replaced by the Mahayana doctrine of "have faith, say so often, and the Buddha will save you from the consequences of your sins." Mahayana doctrine taught that there is not only one Buddha but many. These Buddhas enter the world when they are needed to make truth known to mankind. In Mahayana, there are innumerable Buddhas and Boddhisattvas from the past and for the future who are deities and helpers to mankind.

Not every Buddhist accepted Mahayana doctrine. Those who believed in the traditional way of the arhat seeking Nirvana within the monastic community are said to follow Hinayana (Lesser Vehicle) and are called *Theravadin* Buddhists. The Theravadins lived primarily in south India and Ceylon. There they wrote their sacred texts in the language of Pali. The Mahayanist Buddhists, who had formulated their ideas in the north of India, used Sanskirt. Such language differences further distinguished Hinayana from Mahayana.

During the Kushan period, a Fourth Buddhist Council met, perhaps under the patronage of Kanishka. At this council the differences between Hinayana and Mahayana were formally recognized. Mahayana, indeed, by broadening the Buddha's doctrine, turned Buddhism into a world religion. From the north of India, Mahayana Buddhism spread into Tibet, where it mixed with the local worship to form Lamaism. Traders carried it into the caravan cities of the steppes, where rich merchants endowed splendid monasteries and temples. Missionaries brought it to China, where, after the fall of Han, it gained many converts in the times of turmoil of barbarian invasions. Settlers from China carried Mahayana to Korea and Japan.

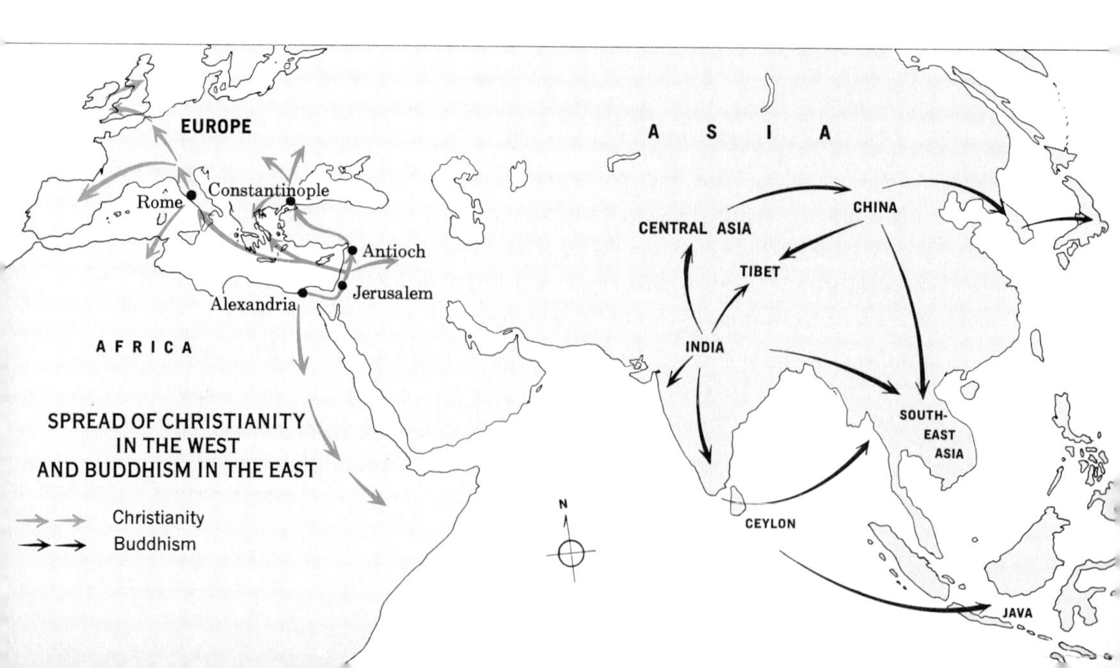

SPREAD OF CHRISTIANITY IN THE WEST AND BUDDHISM IN THE EAST

Hinayana also spread, but not over so wide a territory. It gained converts primarily in southeast Asia. Under the influence of Mahayana, Hinayana gradually modified the strictness of its doctrine to allow, for example, a layman to enter a monastery and become a monk for a short period of time rather than for his whole life.

Hinduism Emerges. While Buddhism was gaining converts throughout Asia, it was losing followers in the land of its birth. Buddhism had never replaced the Brahmanical religion entirely. It usually existed side by side with it. Brahmanical priests, for example, sometimes officiated at Buddhist marriages or funerals. Furthermore, as Buddhism spread over India, its monasteries grew wealthy and its lands extensive. The monks, rich and secluded, lost touch with the people.

In the south of India, the Brahmanical religion came into touch with Dravidian beliefs, native religions, and Buddhist teachings. From this meeting of faiths, the Brahmanical religion slowly evolved into something new, what we call *Hinduism* and what the people themselves call *Dharma.* Two ancient gods were gradually established as the primary ones in the Brahmanical pantheon. These two gods were Shiva and Vishnu. (In the Indus Valley civilization, a statue was discovered that might possibly represent a forerunner of Shiva, page 96.) Shiva and Vishnu were believed to exist in many guises. Vishnu, for example, was thought to be a savior god who assumes different forms to come to earth to help mankind. Once he came as a great boar to save the earth from sea monsters, once as a fish to rescue the first man from flood, once as the cow-herd Krishna, once as the hero Rama. Vishnu is supposed to have had nine such specific incarnations, or *avatars,* on earth. At other times Vishnu or Shiva was identified with a local god who fulfilled the needs of a particular set of worshipers. Thus the local god was thought to be Vishnu or Shiva in one of the greater god's innumerable appearances.

Buddhism had great difficulty in maintaining a separate identity in competition with such a religion. Buddha was easily absorbed into the Hindu pantheon. He became merely a specific savior or incarnation. Thus Mahayana Buddhism could offer nothing new to believers in a religion that already had innumerable gods and saviors. Hinduism even appealed to the most intellectual or philsophical believers. They considered Shiva and Vishnu to be manifestations of the great world soul, or Brahman, of the *Upanishads* (page 283). So Hinduism had something to offer to everyone, from the simplest peasant to the most sophisticated and educated person. Buddhism died out in India at the same time that it was gaining converts all over Asia, and in its

Shiva Nataraja, or Lord of the Dance. A representation of the god in the cosmic dance that both creates and destroys the world. In Shiva's upper right hand is a drum, signifying sound which sets the universe going. In his upper left hand is a tongue of flame, for fire is the destroyer of the world. Crushed beneath his foot is the dwarf of ignorance, which binds man to this world, while the foot poised above the dwarf signifies the release that is possible for the believer. Around Shiva's head is a halo of flames or light, the energy of wisdom. The god's face above his whirling limbs and torso remains calm and remote. As his body represents the rush and movement of time, so his expression signifies the immutability of eternity. Shiva Nataraja is one of the most famous manifestations of the god.

place Hinduism established itself as the religion of the vast majority of India's people.

❦ ❦ ❦

During the first centuries A.D., men everywhere sought new meaning in life and hope for salvation in the future. The three faiths of Christianity, Mahayana Buddhism, and Hinduism answered these needs in more successful ways than did competing religions.

In the west, Christianity's triumph meant the extinction of the old pagan faiths: the Roman religion, emperor worship, the mystery cults. Only the Jews remained faithful to the religion of their ancestors. In the east, Hinduism did not deny other religions. Its great strength lay in its ability to use them to enrich its own doctrines. Buddhism almost entirely disappeared from India, but it spread throughout Asia in the expanded doctrine of Mahayana. There it had as great an impact on the lives of millions of converts as had Hinduism in India and Christianity in the west.

No other religion except Islam, which appeared in a later period of history, captured men's allegiance as widely as did Christianity, Mahayana Buddhism, and Hinduism. These religions, unlike their competitors, did not die out but continued to influence the lives of men down to the present day.

People and Terms

Maccabees	Edict of Milan	heresy	catacomb
Jesus of Nazareth	Torah	Theravada	boddhisattva
Paul	synagogue	Mahayana	priest
the Apostles	rabbi	Hinayana	bishop
Shiva	Gentile	Hinduism	deacon
Vishnu	messiah	Dharma	arhat
	Talmud	orthodox	theology
Pentateuch	disciple	gospel	epistle

Mastering the Reading

1. Why did each of the following fail to keep men's faith: emperor worship? Stoicism? the Cybele cult? Isis cult? the mystery religions? Manicheism? Mithraism?
2. How did Judaism prepare many people to embrace Christianity? Why is there so little accurate information about the life of Jesus? What caused the rapid spread of Christianity?
3. How was the early Christian church organized? Why were the Christians persecuted? What were some of the early divisions of opinion and controversy in the Christian community?
4. What concepts of Mithraism and Manicheism were adapted to Christianity?
5. How did Mahayana Buddhism evolve? How did it differ from Theravadin Buddhism? Where and why did Mahayana Buddhism spread? Why was it rejected in the Buddha's own homeland?
6. What changes did Hinduism bring about in the old Brahmanism? Why was Hinduism more popular than the other religions in India?

Interpreting the Text

1. In what ways was the persecution of the Christians similar to that of the Jews? Why was the dispersion of the Jews from Jerusalem a deep religious blow?
2. What did the eastern religions have in common?

Exploring Beyond the Text

Compare some of the famous philosophers and religious leaders from ancient times. In what ways did each differ from the thinking of his times?

25

Crisis and Collapse in the Mediterranean

180–395 A.D.

The era of the Good Emperors had been brought to an end by the accession of Commodus in 180 A.D. Commodus had held the reins of power for twelve years. His lack of ability, coupled with the upheavals that had undermined the reign of Marcus Aurelius, brought to the surface many weaknesses that had lain hidden during the years of peace and prosperity. One such weakness was the growing independence of the army. The soldiers, off on the distant frontiers for long years of service, did not care much about what was happening in the provinces and Rome. Their interests lay in improving their lot by increased bonuses and privileges. Successful generals could hope to gain their soldiers' favor by attending to such interests, and the soldiers in turn supported their general's ambitions. The army and the Praetorian Guard in Rome were in the position of being able to make and unmake emperors, and an emperor selected by the army was aware of where his support lay. Another problem was the increasing dependence of provinces on the emperor. In seeking money, they also sought advice. This dependence decreased their sense of responsibility, which had been one of the strengths of the Early Empire. Still a third problem was the demands of the Roman populace for food and entertainments and the ever present threat that if they were curtailed, the government would be disrupted. There was a growing cleavage between the lives of the poor agricultural workers who drifted into the cities and those of the wealthy commercial and administrative classes.

Such problems, coupled with warfare, disease, and loss of revenue from a decreased population, set the stage for the third and fourth centuries. This period, called the Late Empire, begins with Septimius Severus and the Severan dynasty. The Late Empire was a period of decline just over two hundred years long. It falls roughly into two parts. The first part, from the death of Commodus until 284 A.D., was a century of military despotism, economic distress within the empire, and strain on the frontiers. The second part, commencing with the reign of Diocletian (284 A.D.), brought reforms and strengthened government, which however, could not keep the empire together. This century ended with the division of Rome into an eastern and a western half in 395 A.D., and the barbarian takeover of the Roman Empire in the west in the next century.

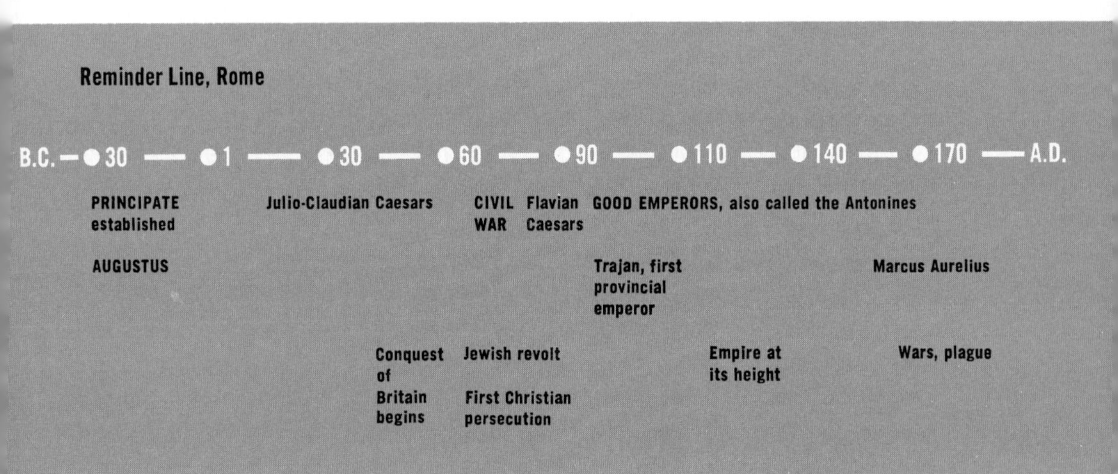

THE MILITARY MONARCHY OF THE SEVERANS, 197–235 A.D.

The murder of Marcus Aurelius' unfortunate son Commodus in 192 A.D. began five years of civil war. In return for lavish bribes, the Praetorian

Guard installed a candidate whom they murdered three months later because of his honesty and efficiency. The throne was then auctioned off to the highest bidder, a low point in the political history of Rome. The winner was a wealthy senator who promised to pay the Praetorians a thousand dollars each. He lasted only two months as the legions were also engaged in emperor-making. Those in Britain, in Syria, and on the Danube each nominated their own candidate, and not surprisingly the general leading the largest army, the Danubian, won. The winner, Septimius Severus, was from Leptis Magna in Africa. His nomination was confirmed by the Senate, and after finishing a short campaign against the Parthians, he arrived in Rome in 202 A.D. to claim his title.

Septimius Severus was a soldier and also a provincial; his interests favored the provinces and the army. During his administration both became of paramount importance in the empire. The emperor filled the Senate with his allies and friends until more than two thirds of the senators were non-Italian as well as non-Roman. At the same time, soldiers, now primarily provincials, rose through the ranks to become knights and then moved into the imperial bureaucracy. The Roman government, though still technically a civil administration, acquired a decidedly military tone. "The emperor and his council resembled a general and his staff, with the equestrian (knight) civil servants as their executive officers," wrote an ancient historian. The Principate was turning into a military autocracy.

The army was increased to 33 legions, and barbarians, led by Roman officers, were accepted as auxiliary troops. To keep the men happy, they were given increased rations and more pay and were allowed to keep their wives with them while in service. "Enrich the soldiers and scorn other men," Severus advised his son, mindful of how he had risen to the throne. In succeeding generations, such a policy weakened the army's vigor and immobilized the legions into standing garrisons. Defense of the empire came to rest on mammoth fortifications constructed not just at the weak spots but on all frontiers.

Septimius Severus was succeeded by a son known to history as Caracalla (a nickname derived from a Gallic cloak he wore). Caracalla, an unpleasant person, brutal, immoral, and a spendthrift, murdered his brother to secure the throne and then was murdered himself. Other Severan relatives of little merit followed him until the line came to an end in 235 A.D. with the assassination of the principled but weak Severus Alexander, the last emperor to rule with the "advice" of the Roman Senate.

MILITARY ANARCHY, 235–284 A.D.

With the death of Severus Alexander, the *Pax Romana* came to an end. In the preceding two hundred years, there had been revolts, rival claims to the throne, and disturbances of the peace, but all had been quelled successfully. Now, for the next fifty years, a dreary succession of "imperial phantoms" reigned an average of two and a half years, and civil war was constant. More than a hundred men claimed the imperial title, sometimes a half dozen or so at one time. Twenty-six were technically monarchs. "You

A German Barbarian. The Germans were not strangers to the Romans. Barbarians had entered the empire as invaders, colonists, and slaves from the time of Augustus. During the third century A.D., barbarians outnumbered Romans in the imperial armies, and when Julian was proclaimed emperor, his troops raised him on their shields, an ancient German custom. This German medallion, in bronze, is from the sixth century A.D.

little know," said one, "what a poor thing it is to be an emperor." Though many were able soldiers and administrators, none had the strength to acquire permanent support.

During this period of anarchy, the empire nearly collapsed. Though Septimius Severus was a good administrator and an able general, his talents did little more than stem the tide of troubles that threatened to engulf Rome. Wars on the frontiers were constant. To the north, the Germans along the Rhine were coalescing into the federations of the Franks and the Alemanni. Beyond the Danube, the eastern Germans began to move south, forming the nation of Goths and raiding the Danube lands. In 251 A.D. they defeated and killed the emperor Decius (249–251 A.D.), the first time a Roman emperor was killed by the barbarians. To the east, the newly revived Persian dynasty of the Sassanians (227 A.D.) contested with Rome for Mesopotamia. The greatest disgrace ever to befall Roman arms came when the Persians captured the emperor Valerian (253–260 A.D.). He was displayed at the Sassanian court as an object of ridicule, and a bas relief made at the time shows him used as a footstool by the Persian king. Legend has it that the unfortunate Roman was eventually slain and his skin tanned and stuffed to hang for centuries as a trophy in a Persian temple. Meanwhile, in Africa, border tribes raided the prosperous towns of the coast.

Money problems constantly plagued the empire. The population, decreasing because of war and disease, could no longer provide the required revenues. People fled to the countryside, or changed their social class to a lower one where the financial burdens were less. A terrible plague raged from 251 to 266 A.D., and for a time five thousand persons are supposed to have died daily in Rome, while Alexandria lost two thirds of its population. With the failure of local taxes to produce the revenues needed, officials in the community were made personally liable for the expense of public repairs and improvements. To be a magistrate, formerly an honor, was a serious handicap. Men with personal property tried to escape from the responsibilities of public office, so such posts were made obligatory. When Caracalla extended Roman citizenship in 212 A.D. to all freemen in the empire, the first purpose was to increase the number of persons liable for public office and taxation. As the prestige of Rome declined, so did the honor of its citizenship.

A soaring inflation further burdened the population. Money was debased, and the coinage became nothing but pieces of copper or lead with a thin wash of precious metal. In Egypt, still the empire's greatest producer of grain, the price of grain multiplied six thousand times in fifty years. As money lost its value, services in civilian life and in the army were paid for by goods and commodities. The consequent failure to exchange goods between regions hastened the economic slump. As trade fell off, the plight of the cities worsened, and the cycle became a downward spiral.

Trouble at home was compounded by revolts abroad. Under a weak emperor it was not difficult for an ambitious governor to throw off the authority of Rome. From the confused records of the period, it is impossible to know to what extent such revolts may or not have been attempts to break away from Roman rule. At one end of the empire, out in the Syrian desert at the junction of important caravan routes, Palmyra, "the city of Palms," successfully defended itself against the Persians; and as Roman power declined in the east, Palmyra extended its sway over Syria, Palestine, and Egypt. The beautiful Queen Zenobia, boasting of her descent from Cleopatra, ruled over this kingdom until the emperor Aurelian invaded Palmyra, captured Zenobia, and paraded her, laden with golden chains, in his triumphal procession in Rome. Aurelian also restored Gaul to the empire. Its governor and his successors had been recognized as legitimate rulers for some twelve years by Spain and Britain. Aurelian's accomplishments enabled him, not without justification, to call himself "restorer of the world."

Aurelian (270–275 A.D.) was the strongest emperor since Septimius Severus, yet he could not escape murder. Several emperors succeeded him in rapid succession until their assassinations removed all competition from the path of Diocles, an Illyrian who came to the throne in 284 A.D. With Diocles, the fortunes of the empire revived.

Toward the close of the third century A.D., no part of the Roman Empire had escaped the ravages of war, the plague, inflation, and the economic slump. The internal stresses and strains had been so great that the empire would never fully recover, but the reforms that Diocles inaugurated infused a new vigor into the tottering structure so that it endured in one piece for another hundred years.

RECONSTRUCTION OF THE EMPIRE UNDER DIOCLETIAN, 284–305 A.D.

Diocles' immediate predecessors had been a series of generals from Illyria, of whom Aurelian was the most outstanding. Legend tells that a Druid priestess had previously foretold to Diocles, also an Illyrian, that he would become emperor after killing a boar. Diocles had long made boar hunting his favorite sport. When a general named Aper (boar) slew the reigning emperor, Diocles is said to have remembered the prophecy and to have avenged the emperor and killed his boar (Aper) in one blow. Diocles then took the name of Diocletian and became the most successful of the Illyrian rebuilders of the empire.

THE TETRARCHY

Diocletian immediately set about reorganizing the government. He realized that the state had suffered badly from the disasters of the previous century and that it had become unwieldy. He saw that to administer such a vast and varied territory as well as guard the frontiers was more than any single man could do. He also realized that the succession had to be made secure by a new method. Selection by adoption, by the Senate, by the army, had all proved unsatisfactory.

Diocletian's reforms established two emperors, called *Augusti*, who shared the burdens of ruling and defending the empire. To assist them, Diocletian appointed two younger men, called Caesars, who would also be the heirs apparent. The succession would thus be secured by the automatic promotion of the Caesars into the positions of Augusti. This form of a four-way partnership government was known as a *tetrarchy*.

Diocletian selected as his Augustus a trusted lieutenant named Maximian. Maximian ruled the most important western provinces, while Diocletian kept for himself the more troublesome eastern ones of Asia, Asia Minor, Egypt, and Thrace. The empire was further divided into prefectures, each one under the rule of a Caesar or Augustus. Capital cities in the provinces were chosen for each of the prefectures. When Rome was not selected, its transformation from a city-state to the capital of an empire to the principal city of a province was complete. Though its prestige would never fail, its position as the central city of the Mediterranean world was gone. Emperors did not hesitate to issue their edicts from provincial cities or from military posts, where they were stationed to fight more easily against the barbarians.

Diocletian then reorganized the provinces to lessen the possibilities of revolt and independence. He made the existing 45 or so into some 100 smaller units, and then he centralized them into twelve dioceses, each governed by a *vicarius*, or vicar. A direct hierarchy existed from the lowest public official to the governors of the provinces, the vicars of the dioceses, the prefects of the prefectures, to the Augusti and the Caesars. The empire of the early years, characterized by self-governing municipalities, had become a highly organized, centralized monarchy.

The changes in the structure of the administration were accompanied by a frank abandonment of the fictions of the Principate. No longer did the emperor rule with the consent of the Senate and the Roman people. Diocletian never consulted the Senate and did not have it ratify his decisions. The Senate became the municipal council of Rome, the consuls its public officials. Where Augustus had attempted to conceal the power of the *princeps*, Diocletian aimed to display that of the autocrat. He proudly bore the title of *Dominus* (lord). The son of a slave, possibly of eastern origin, Diocletian had no nostalgia for the republican traditions of Rome. At court, many practices the Romans of the Republic would have scorned were now accepted. The emperor was treated as a god, he was approached on bended knee, and it was an honor to kiss his hand, foot, or the hem of his robe. In the Early Empire the emperor had been an *imperator*, the general of the army. Now he was openly a king and accorded the obsequious attitudes and prostrate forms of approach of the monarchies of the ancient Middle East and of Sassanian Persia.

The Palace of Diocletian at Split, Yugoslavia. Following his abdication, Diocletian built himself an enormous palace in his native province of Illyricum. It was laid out like a Roman camp (see text, page 270), and after the empire collapsed the town of Split grew up within its ruins. On the left is an interior view of the palace; on the right, a restaurant and buildings in a courtyard.

THE FAILURE OF THE TETRARCHY

As long as Diocletian presided over the Tetrarchy, the system worked well, chiefly because the other three rulers followed the lead of the system's founder. When the twenty years he had set as his term of office ended, and his health began to fail, Diocletian did an unprecedented thing: he retired, the only Roman emperor ever to do so, and obliged Maximian, the other Augustus, to do the same (305 A.D.). The former Caesars advanced to the rank of Augusti; two new men took their places as junior rulers. So far these events accorded with Diocletian's plan, but almost at once trouble developed. A young Illyrian, Constantine, hitherto the holder of only unimportant army posts, and suspected of being involved in plots at Diocletian's court, fled to Britain to join his father, the Augustus Constantius. Father and son waged a successful campaign against the Picts of Scotland, at the end of which Constantius died at York in July, 306 A.D.

Diocletian had not planned for sons to succeed their fathers in the Tetrarchy. He wished candidates to be sought among the most able men, regardless of their family ties. Furthermore, even if the imperial title were to be decided by heredity, Constantine would have been ineligible since he was the illegitimate son of Constantius and a concubine. Brushing all legalities aside, Constantine turned to the army, and the British legions hailed him as Augustus.

The example of Constantine as a usurper was followed by others. Within two years of Diocletian's abdication, six Augusti were competing with each other. The empire seemed in danger of drifting back to the chaos that had preceded the coming of Diocletian. By 313 A.D. natural death, suicide, and military defeat had reduced the contenders to two. Constantine held the west and Licinius the Near East until 324 A.D., when Constantine became the sole ruler of the empire. He retained control until his own death in 337 A.D.

CONSTANTINE AND THE NEW ROME, 305–337 A.D.

To signal his inauguration of a new era, in 330 A.D. Constantine created a new capital, which he named after himself, Constantinople, city of Constantine. It was on the site of the ancient town of Byzantium, present-day Istanbul. The emperor intended it to be the New Rome. Like the old Rome, the new city boasted seven hills, fourteen districts, palaces, a forum, hippodrome, baths, aqueducts, and a Senate House, where a second Senate went through the motions of debate. Constantine had several good reasons for removing the capital from Rome to Constantinople. Its harbor, the Golden Horn, extended four miles inland from the Bosphorus and was a natural crossroads of trade between Asia and Europe and between the Black Sea and the Mediterranean, as Troy had been in more ancient times. The New Rome not only balanced the old Rome as a great city in the eastern half of the empire, but it was more centrally located to deal with the most dangerous forces pressing on the Roman world: the barbarians above the Danube and the Persians. Above all, it was to be a city where the new religion, Christianity, could grow without the pagan associations of Rome.

Constantine adorned his new city with great magnificence. Many cities of the empire were stripped of their art treasures so that the new one would be worthy of its founder's idea of its importance. Thousands of statues were transported to embellish the palaces and public places. Likenesses of emperors from Rome mingled with those of Hellenic gods and goddesses from Greece and Asia Minor all over the new city. Many statues were mutilated, like the gigantic Apollo whose head was replaced with a portrait of Constantine himself.

Having recognized Christianity as a religion equal with the others of the empire by the Edict of Milan in 313 A.D. (page 484), Constantine and his mother, Helena, sponsored the building of many Christian churches. At Rome, one dedicated to Saint Peter was built on the site the present Saint Peter's now occupies, and another, dedicated to Saint Paul, was built outside Rome's walls. At Constantinople, Constantine's many donations included the Church of the Twelve Apostles, in which he was buried.

CONSTANTINE'S SUCCESSORS, 337–395 A.D.

Roman law never admitted in theory that the imperial power could be passed from one ruler to another by any system other than election or appointment. In practice, however, during the Principate inheritance had taken its place beside senatorial nomination in the cases of the Julio-Claudians, the Flavians, the Good Emperors, and the Severans. Rejecting Diocletian's system of promotions, Constantine turned to the hereditary practice. He planned to divide the empire among his three surviving sons and two of his nephews. The three sons quarreled, civil war broke out, and not until 350 A.D. did Constantius II become sole ruler. He died in 361 A.D., after a reign marked by the inroads of the Germans across the Rhine.

Constantius' cousin Julian, the only other survivor of the many relatives of the great Constantine, had been made Caesar in 335 A.D. at the age of 23. On the death of Constantius, Julian became sole emperor.

JULIAN THE APOSTATE, 361–363 A.D.

As Caesar, Julian had fought against the Germans of the Rhine. As emperor, he turned to war against the Persians. A man of great courage and devoted to his soldiers, he gave up the Christianity in which he had been reared and embraced the Mithraism that was so popular among the legionnaires (page 486). His desertion of Christianity was never forgiven by the Christians, who vilified his memory and gave him the label by which he is generally known, "The Apostate."

Julian ordered that temples appropriated by the Christians should be restored to their original pagan usages, withdrew government aid from Christian clergy, and forbade Christians to interpret the ancient pagan literature in the schools. His encouragement of the study of pagan writings gave temporary new life to the Hellenic aspects of classical culture. His attempts to revive paganism and to mold it into a monotheism similar to Christianity were defeated by the brevity of his life and the impossibility of breathing lasting life into worn-out forms.

Julian is a lonely figure in the politics of the fourth century A.D. His character fitted him to have been one of the Good Emperors had he been born in the time of Trajan and Hadrian. His respect for the ways of the Principate and the Republic, his attempts to limit the activities of informers, to treat justly the officials of the local governments to correct injustice in the application of the laws, and his unquestioned personal courage, recall the attitudes of the Antonines.

Resolved to rid the Roman Empire of its eastern problem by overthrowing Persia and placing a pro-Roman prince on its throne, Julian crossed the Euphrates in 363 A.D. at the head of 65,000 troops. After a victory at Ctesiphon, Julian marched up the Tigris expecting to meet reinforcements from his ally, the king of Armenia. The Persians, under Shapur I, blocked his advance. In a minor skirmish Julian was slain, possibly by a spear cast by one of his own soldiers, some of whom resented the emperor's encouragement of paganism. Julian was 32 years old.

FROM JULIAN TO THEODOSIUS, 363–395 A.D.

Following the death of Julian, the empire was once again divided. In the east, the incompetent Valens held the title of Augustus. His reign was

Ancient and modern Rome. The wall, attributed to the legendary king Servius Tullius, may have been built in the fourth century B.C., after the Gauls attacked. It contrasts interestingly with the present-day railroad station behind it. The catastrophes that afflicted Rome in the third century A.D. resulted in repairing such old walls and in building new ones to protect the city and the frontiers. No walls, however, were strong enough to keep out the barbarians.

marked by the settlement of a large number of Visigothic (western Gothic) peoples of Germanic origin within Roman territory. He lost his life fighting against them in 378 A.D. Theodosius I (379–395 A.D.), Valens' successor in the east, also had to deal with Goth incursions. He managed to come to terms with them just before they reached the walls of Constantinople. Under Theodosius, the empire was reunited for the last time under one ruler. At the same time Theodosius recognized Christianity as the state religion (page 485).

On the death of Theodosius at Milan in January, 395 A.D., the division of the empire, which had occurred in the past on a temporary basis, became lasting. The eastern empire, governed from Constantinople, went to Theodosius' son Arcadius (395–408 A.D.), and the western empire, ruled from Rome and Ravenna, went to his son Honorius (395–423 A.D.). The collapse of the empire in the west loomed in the century to come.

THE ROMAN STATE IN THE THIRD AND FOURTH CENTURIES A.D.

THE EMPEROR

In addition to the old titles of Augustus, *Imperator*, Proconsul and Tribune, the ruler now bore those of Lord (*Dominus*), Eternal Victor, and Eternal Triumpher. He and whatever belonged to him was "sacred" or "divine." Crowned with a diadem and robed in silk whose crimson-purple was the sacred royal purple of Phoenicia, encrusted with gold and jewels, surrounded by a numerous corps of palace officials, the emperor was treated like an idol in its temple. He was seldom seen by ordinary people, and the rare occasions when he appeared before them were arranged with the utmost pomp and ceremony.

THE CITIZENS

Below the nobility, the citizens of the empire were divided into two classes. First were the *honestiores*, which included senators, soldiers, and veterans. Members of this class could not be executed for crime without the emperor's consent and were exempt from penal servitude and from torture during judicial investigations. Other citizens belonged to the class of *humiliores* (the humble) and enjoyed none of these legal exemptions.

Government spying on the populace became a common thing. Arrests were made on the basis of rumors, anonymous accusations, unsupported charges of disloyalty or of political ambition. It was unsafe to tell one's own friends of one's dreams or to make jokes that could be interpreted as criticism of the government. Self-accusations and the doom of additional innocent persons became the products of the torture chamber.

SEPARATION OF CIVIL AND MILITARY CAREERS

Under the Republic and the Principate, the Roman's public career took him through an alternating succession of civilian and military steps (page 265 and 428). A constant identification of civil and military responsibilities applied all the way from the citizen-soldier at the bottom to the consul-general at the top. In a series of edicts of the Late Empire emperors, two important changes in these procedures were made. First, civil and military functions were completely separated. Men of senatorial or equestrian rank were barred from army service. Second, all military posts were made attainable through promotion within the ranks. The lowest soldier might some day, if worthy, attain a generalship. In the dark days to come, when barbarians increasingly manned the Roman armies, some of them, by means of this promotion system, would overshadow the emperor they were supposed to be serving.

THE ARMY

From Diocletian on, the empire no longer depended on voluntary enlistment of troops, the system in existence since Marius had introduced it four centuries earlier in the Republic. During the Late Empire, the provinces were divided into units, each of which had to supply a specified quota of soldiers. The first drafted were the sons of soldiers. Other men drafted to make up the quota could, if they were rich enough, hire substitutes when men were found willing to sell themselves.

At the head of the armies were the Masters of Troops and the Masters of Cavalry. Each was surrounded by his own band of subordinates, who gave him the loyalty and support that ought to have been given the emperor.

The acceptance of large numbers of barbarians into the army, and their rise to the highest position, was followed by the adoption of many barbarian military customs. Gothic dragon trumpets, for example, appeared in the Roman ranks.

TAXATION

As in the provinces, the productive land of the empire was divided into units for the assessment of taxes. The new taxes replaced the former land taxes and were to be paid in produce instead of in money. In addition to a tax on the farmland, there was an additional tax to be paid in produce on each unit of farm labor, a unit being either one man or two women. Taxes payable in money were levied on all trades and occupations other than farming. Persons of senatorial status were liable for compulsory gifts to the emperor and a special tax against their estates.

In addition to taxes in produce and in money, the citizenry was required to perform certain public services without payment. The imperial postal service and the provision of shelter and supplies for troops moving through their sector stripped many areas of horses and impoverished the inhabitants.

In order to make proper assessments, a correct census had to be taken. The census established under Diocletian was extremely thorough and very detailed. People were expected to remain in one spot so the censor could find them. They were discouraged from changing occupation, which would free them from paying their previous tax. The result was that the population gradually became fixed in location and in job: the serfs to the land, craftsmen to their trade, the sons of soldiers to the army, and so on throughout society. As men became fixed in occupation, social class became rigid as sons followed in their fathers' footsteps.

THE BUREAUCRACY

The bureaucracy expanded enormously under Diocletian and his successors. While the division of power and responsibility eased the burdens on each of the individual Augusti and Caesars, it meant that extra administrations had to be staffed and financed, several courts maintained with oriental pomp, and various capital cities supplied. The populace of both Rome and Constantinople had to be fed and entertained, and each had a

The Colosseum in Rome. The emperors were fond of building monuments to commemorate their reigns and their victories. This huge amphitheater, the largest in the empire, was begun by Vespasian, dedicated by Titus in 80 A.D., and completed by Domitian. It was decorated with marble, stucco, and metal. According to tradition, Christians as well as gladiators met their death here. The performances held at the Colosseum fell into disrepute as the empire became Christianized. Gladiatorial combats were forbidden after 404 A.D.; spectacles with beasts, after 523 A.D.

Senate acting as municipal council with respected rights and honors. The emperors indulged in vast building programs in which baths, amphitheaters, and palaces gave witness to the splendors of the empire. Such enormous drains on the treasury were compounded by the huge, increasing costs of maintaining the army. In addition to the garrison troops, a mobile force of about 200,000 men was kept in readiness to rush to action on a threatened frontier. The costs of maintaining the vastly increased bureaucracy and the ever-growing army in the end ruined the economy of the empire. It could not maintain itself; the burdens placed on it were too great.

From a society in which individualism had been strong within the ties of family and city loyalty, the ancient Mediterranean world became a rigid social and economic structure in which each man's occupation was determined from birth. Private enterprise died, invention ceased, industry, commerce, agriculture withered. The glittering imperial court presided over a world in which loyalty, enthusiasm, hope, courage, and willingness to sacrifice oneself for the state no longer existed. The only recourse for society was a reorganization and a fresh start. This was to be a process brought about by the barbarian takeover of the western empire.

THE COLLAPSE OF THE EMPIRE IN THE WEST

In the fifth century A.D., the Roman Empire in the west fell to the barbarians who had been pressing on the frontiers for the preceding two hundred years.

From above the Rhine and Danube rivers, German tribes swarmed into the empire. Under the Visigoth chief Alaric, the Germans sacked Rome for three days in 410 A.D. By the middle of the fifth century German kingdoms had been founded in North Africa by the Vandals, in Spain and southern Gaul by the Visigoths, and in northern Gaul, the Rhone Valley, and Britain by other tribes. Then from the east came an even greater threat: the Huns, steppe people from central Asia who had moved west to the Danube region. Their short, swarthy appearance and behavior—they lived on horseback, riding over the land like a whirlwind, leaving death and destruction in their wake—terrified their enemies. Under their great chief Attila, the Scourge of God, "a man born to agitate the nations, the fear of all the lands," the Huns formed a confederacy and moved as far west as Gaul, where in 451 A.D. they were defeated by combined German and Roman forces (the battle of Chalons). Notwithstanding their defeat, the Huns turned south to Italy, but when Attila died in 453 A.D., the confederacy broke up

The Hunnish terror having disappeared, Rome next suffered a fourteen-day sacking by the Vandals of North Africa, who sailed over the Mediterranean to the Tiber in 455 A.D. In their greed, the Vandals even carried off the gilded roof of the Capitol, thinking it was gold. By this time, however, the emperors in the west were figureheads. In 476 A.D., after the German chief Odoacer deposed the boy emperor Romulus Augustulus and was proclaimed king by his troops, he sent the imperial regalia back to Constantinople, indicating the reunion of the empire under one head. In return he accepted for himself the title of Patrician from the emperor in the east, but in fact Odoacer was king of an independent barbarian kingdom in Italy.

The empire in the west was now entirely in barbarian hands. Yet to those living at the time, 476 A.D. marked no significant date. Though the empire in the west was dead, the people did not know it. In the Near East that mixture of Hellenic, Hellenistic, and Christian that we call Byzantine would survive for another thousand years, and the people in the west thought of themselves as part of this eastern Roman Empire until Charlemagne was proclaimed Holy Roman Emperor in the west in 800 A.D.

❦ ❦ ❦

The period from 180 A.D. to 395 A.D. was one of decline in the west. The success of the barbarians against the legions in the fourth and fifth centuries A.D. merely underlined the fact that Rome was no longer able to sustain its old role in the Mediterranean. The barbarian success provided the framework for a basic reorganization of society. In the future, barbarians and Romans would mingle under the inspiration and guidance of the Christian Church to form a new civilization in history, that of the Middle Ages.

People, Places, and Terms

Septimius Severus	Licinius	Honorius	Constantinople
the Severans	Franks	Alaric	
Caracalla	Alemanni	Vandals	military autocracy
Dicius	Julian	Attila	Caesars
Valerian	the Apostate	Odoacer	Augusti
Zenobia	Goths		tetrarchy
Aurelian	Valens	Leptis Magna	Dominus
Diocletian	Theodosius	Palmyra	*honestiores*
Constantine	Arcadius	Illyria	*humiliores*

Mastering the Reading

1. What basic signs of decay were evident in the empire after 180 A.D.? How did Septimius Severus' accession to the throne and his reign exemplify the decay?
2. How did Diocletian solve the succession problem? Describe the government under Diocletian. How did it differ from government under the Principate?
3. What did Constantine do for Christianity? Why did he prefer Constantinople to Rome? How did he show this preference?
4. In addition to barbarian attacks, what internal troubles caused the weakening of the Roman Empire in the third and fourth centuries A.D.? How could barbarian tribes like the Goths and Vandals defeat the Western Empire?

Interpreting the Text

List as many concrete causes as possible for the decline of the once-great Roman Empire. What date would you give for the fall of Rome? Why?

Exploring Beyond the Text

What lessons can we learn by contrasting the economic, political, social, and intellectual life of the Roman Empire of Diocletian's time with that of the Principate? What changes would we have to make in order to create a *Pax Romana?* What pitfalls of the empire should we avoid? of the Principate?

Epilogue

All along the frontiers between 400 and 700 A.D. barbarians broke through the barriers of civilization and left death and destruction in their wake. To these attacks, the civilized societies responded differently. In the west the Roman Empire collapsed. The new civilization that developed had its roots in Rome, but it was also barbarian and above all, Christian. The Roman Empire in the East, Byzantium, continued for a thousand years, but it too fell to barbarians in the end. In the east, by contrast, China proved capable of reabsorbing its invaders. After some three hundred and fifty years of invasion and disorder, China was reunified and continued its civilization along the lines laid down by the Han.

EMPIRES IN THE EAST AND WEST, 30 B.C. to the Barbarian Invasions

	MIDDLE EAST	MEDITERRANEAN	INDIA	CHINA
1-100 A.D.	Jesus of Nazareth Parthians fight Romans for control of Mesopotamia and Armenia Palestine made into a province Jewish revolt, Temple destroyed	Principate; Augustus; the Early Empire Julio-Claudians Conquest of Britain Flavians Destruction of Pompeii and Herculaneum	Kujula Khadphises unites Yueh-chi tribes; invades India Kushans rule north India Kanishka; height of Kushan power Tamil states a center of trade west to Arabia and east to Indo-China	Wang Mang Eastern Han dynasty Chinese authority reestablished in central Asia Trade between east and west flourishes along the Silk Route
100-200 A.D.	Second Jewish revolt under Simon bar Kochba	"Good Emperors" Height of Early Empire Parthian wars, plague, economic difficulties	Buddhism splits into two major sects: Mahayana and Theravadin Kushan states weaken after death of Kanishka	Han dynasty weakens through rule of weak boy emperors
200-300 A.D.	Ardashir's revolt; Sassanian Persia Shapur I forces Kushans to pay tribute Mani	Severans End of Pax Romana Military anarchy; barbarian raids	Kushans pay tribute to Sassanians Andhra collapses	Han dynasty falls Three Kingdoms Brief reunification by Tsin
300-400 A.D.	Shapur II annexes Kushan lands in the west	Late Empire: Diocletian reforms the empire. Constantine builds new capital; recognizes Christianity Christianity state religion Division of the empire into eastern and western parts	Kushan empire dissolves; Indian lands absorbed into great Gupta Empire	Barbarian invasions Fall of Tsin China disunited for 300 years
400-700 A.D.	Internal weakening; revival under Chosroes I Wars against Byzantium Arab invasions and conquest; conversion of Persia to Islam	Barbarian invasions Romulus Augustulus, last Roman emperor in the west, deposed Barbarian kingdoms in the west	White Huns invade north India; destroy Gupta Empire Small states reestablish themselves north and south	

Between the eastern and western extremes of Eurasia, the other civilized states fared differently. The Sassanians fell to the Arabs and were converted to Islam. Persia was absorbed into the Islamic Empire. Islam created a new civilization. It had a distinctive style of life though it covered many diverse peoples. In India, no great empire arose to reunite the valleys of the Ganges and the Indus. Small states continued to exist side by side. Hinduism became the binding force in Indian society; the proper observance of caste duties was the first aim of the Indian.

The Eurasian world went through a tremendous upheaval in these three hundred years. It was comparable to the upheaval that had brought collapse to the Bronze Age civilizations. But, whereas the attacks of the Bronze Age invaders had brought several civilizations to an end, the new invaders disrupted but did not destroy civilization. Civilization was rooted firmly. It could be changed but not wiped out. The changes that the barbarians precipitated in the civilized centers, however, were profound. We may say that their attacks brought the ancient world to an end for new syntheses, with new or renewed ways of life, were in the making. One phase of man's history had closed.

Some Questions to Answer

1. Of all the empire builders of the ancient west, Rome was the most successful. What factors enabled Rome to succeed? Why was Rome unsuccessful in creating a unified world with all men living together in peace and harmony? Is such a goal impossible?
2. Although the western Roman Empire collapsed and broke up into many Teutonic kingdoms under chieftains, what Roman institutions and traditions remained to preserve the knowledge and experience gained by the ancient west?
3. Discuss the influence of the barbarians on the civilized centers. In what ways did the barbarians reveal weaknesses in the civilizations which they encountered?
4. Discuss the ways in which trade between east and west influenced the cultures of the countries taking part in the trade. What is the significance of these cultural exchanges?
5. In what ways were the Han and Roman empires similar and dissimilar in government, social organization, and military policy? How do you explain this?
6. What were some of the many legacies passed down from the ancient peoples to western civilization? to eastern civilization? to the civilizations between?

Using Documents as Evidence

Tacitus was a historian in Rome under the reign of Vespian. These comments of his on education were written in 75 A.D.

TACITUS COMMENTS ON ROMAN EDUCATION

The [Roman] infant, as soon as born, was not consigned to the mean dwelling of a hireling nurse but was reared and cherished in the bosom of its mother, whose highest praise it was to take care of her household affairs and attend to her children. It was customary, likewise, for each family to choose some elderly female relation of approved conduct, to whose charge the children were committed. In her presence . . . nothing was done against propriety and good manners. The hours of study and serious employment were settled by her direction; and . . . even the diversions of the children were conducted with modest reserve and good manners. . . .

In the present age, what is our practice? The infant is committed to a Greek chambermaid, and a slave or two, . . . generally the worst in the whole household. . . . From the idle tales and gross absurdities of these people, the tender and uninstructed mind is suffered to receive its earliest impressions. . . . Not one servant cares what he says or does in the presence of his young master. . . . The parents themselves . . . set them the first examples of luxury and immoral behavior. Thus our youth gradually acquire . . . a total disregard of that reverence they owe both to themselves and to others. . . . It seems as if a fondness for horses, actors, and gladiators, the peculiar and distinguishing folly of this our city, was impressed upon them even in the womb. . . . What opening is there left for the noble arts? Who talks of anything else in our houses? If we enter the schools, what other subjects of conversation do we hear among the boys? The preceptors [teachers] themselves choose no other topic more frequently to entertain their hearers; for it is not by establishing a strict discipline, nor by giving proofs of their genius, that this order of men gain pupils, but by fawning and flattery. . . . Sufficient pains are by no means taken in making them [children] acquainted with the best authors, or in giving them a proper notion of history. . . .

Which parts of Tacitus' comments are facts? Which parts express his opinions? What evidence does Tacitus cite to support his claim that Roman standards of education had declined? What main criticisms does Tacitus make of Roman teachers?

Glossary

A.D., *Anno Domini*, Latin for "In the year of the Lord." The Christian calendar dates events from the accepted date of Jesus' birth, the year 1 in the western calendar.

A.H., *Anno Hegirae*, Latin for "In the year of the Flight." The Muslim calendar dates events from Muhammad's flight from Mecca to Medina, 622 A.D. This is the year 1 in the Muslim calendar.

ANTHROPOLOGY, the study of man, his physical changes and his development and distribution over the ages (physical anthropology), and his customs, institutions, reactions to environment, etc. (cultural anthropology).

ANTHROPOMORPHISM, the attribution of human shape or characteristics to inanimate objects, animals, gods, or God.

ARCHAEOLOGY, the study of the material remains of human life and activities, such as fossils, bones, artifacts, and buildings.

ARISTOCRACY, (1) a small, privileged class whose position is usually based on inherited wealth and social position; (2) the nobility; (3) government by the nobility; (4) an élite, the best.

ARTIFACT, a product of human work such as tools, pottery, and clothing.

ASTROLOGY, the ancient art of foretelling the future by studying the location and movement of the sun, moon, and stars in the belief that they influence human behavior and events.

AUTOCRACY, government by a ruler, generally a hereditary monarch, who has absolute power, not limited by any other person or group of persons.

B.C., the letters for the words *Before Christ*. The Christian calendar dates all events before the birth of Jesus as B.C.

BARBARIAN, (1) originally used by the Hellenes to denote any foreigner who did not speak Greek; (2) the semi-civilized people on the frontiers; (3) today, someone who is uncivilized, ignorant, crude.

BRAHMIN, (1) a member of the highest Hindu caste, a priest; (2) today, a colloquial term for any person of a long established, upper class family; (3) also spelled Brahman, but not to be confused with the non-anthropomorphic world soul of Hinduism.

BUREAUCRACY, the body of appointed officials who carry out the instructions of an autocrat or of an elected government.

CASTE, the organization of society into hereditary classes and occupations based on birth, as found in India.

CATARACT, (1) a large waterfall; (2) in Egypt, the six rapids that block the Nile River between present-day Khartoum, Sudan, and the sea.

CITY-KINGDOM, a political unit in ancient Mesopotamia ruled by a king or priest that centered around the temple complex.

CITY-STATE, (1) a political unit in which the governing power rests in the hands of the free citizens; (2) a state consisting of an independent city and the territory under its control.

CIVILIZATION, a complex, advanced culture characterized by urban life, systematic political institutions, distinct social classes, economic specialization of occupation, metallurgy, writing, organized cooperation, record keeping, and leisure time for conscious development of the arts and the intellect.

CLAN, one of the earliest forms of social organization, in ancient times within a tribe, where several families claim descent, through either the father or the mother, from a common ancestor.

COLONY, (1) a company of people settled in a distant land who remain loyal to their native land; (2) a land and its people controlled by an outside power.

COVENANT, a contract or agreement between two or more people or between man and God, as in the Jewish and Christian religions.

CULT, (1) a system of religious worship or ritual; (2) today, attachment to a person or principle, not necessarily pertaining to religion.

CULTURAL DIFFUSION, the spread of customs, ideas, and practices from one group to others.

CULTURE, the way of life of a specific group in a given time and place; their habits, institutions, arts, ideas.

CUNEIFORM, (1) wedge-form; (2) symbols formed by a wedge-shaped point; (3) the writing of the ancient Mesopotamians.

DEMOTIC, one of the two simplified systems of Egyptian hieroglyphic writing, used for everyday purposes.

DICTATOR, (1) one who exercises supreme authority in a state; (2) in ancient Rome, a special official given full power to rule up to six months during an emergency.

DIVINATION, the art or practice of foreseeing and foretelling events through the study of stars, dreams, or organs of sacred animals.

DIVINE KINGSHIP, the rule by kings who are considered to be either gods, or related to the gods, or who are the gods' earthly representatives.

DOMESTICATE, to tame, either plants or animals, for agricultural purposes and for food.

DYNASTY, a series of rulers from the same family.

ECUMENE, (1) in Hellenistic times, the eastern Mediterranean, the "inhabited world," hence (2) today, the permanently, inhabited portion of the earth, the most densely inhabited portion of any region; (3) ecumenical—general, universal.

EMPIRE, a group of nations or territories conquered and controlled by one power.

ENSI, (1) a religious title in early Sumer; (2) the name of the ruler of a Sumarian city, originally the person who controlled the city's economic life.

FEDERATION, a union of two or more states for war, mutual protection, commerce, and the like.

FORUM, a marketplace and meeting place where legal and commercial affairs were conducted in ancient Rome, hence, (2) a meeting place for discussion of public issues.

GENTILE, (1) any person not a Jew; (2) specifically, in Roman times, the non-Jewish people of the Mediterranean.

GEOLOGY, the study of the earth's crust as revealed by the structure and formation of its layers, and rock types, and forms of life found as fossils.

GOSPEL, (1) a translation from the Greek meaning good news, glad tidings; (2) the first four books of the New Testament, which tell of the life and teachings of Jesus.

HERESY, (1) a religious belief opposed to the orthodox doctrines of a particular church or sect; hence, (2) any opinion opposed to official or established views.

HIERATIC, an abridged, cursive style of hieroglyphics used by Egyptian priests or religious writers.

HIEROGLYPHICS, (1) Greek for "sacred carvings"; (2) the writing of ancient Egypt; (3) a method of writing using hieroglyphs, a picture or symbol representing a work, syllable, or sound.

IDEOGRAM, a pictorial symbol of an idea or object.

INSTITUTION, (1) an established practice, law, custom; (2) an established organization or corporation.

KOINÉ, a dialect of Greek that became the international language of the Mediterranean world during Hellenistic and Roman times.

LABYRINTH, (1) in ancient Crete, the palace of the Minos; (2) today, a maze or intricate structure.

LUGAL, the name of the military and civil king in the Sumerian city-kingdoms who sometimes shared power with, and sometimes displaced, the priests (ensis).

MANDARIN, (1) the scholar-bureaucrat who served as an official of the Chinese state; (2) the dialect spoken by the officials and educated classes in China.

MERCENARY, (1) a soldier hired for pay to fight in a foreign army; (2) motivated by desire or greed for money and gain.

MONOGAMY, the practice of being married to only one person at a time, as opposed to polygamy.

MONOLATRY, the worship of one god though with the recognition of the existence of other gods.

MONOTHEISM, belief in the existence of only one god for everyone, everywhere.

MUNICIPALITY, a town, city, or other district having powers of local self-government.

MYSTERY RELIGIONS, ancient cults in which initiated members participated in secret rituals, known as mysteries, at shrines dedicated to a particular god.

NIRVANA, in Buddhism, the state in which all desires cease and there is perfect freedom and peace.

NOMAD, a wandering tribesman moving from place to place to find food for his animals or to hunt or forage.

OLIGARCHY, (1) a form of government in which a small number of persons are in control; (2) in the ancient Mediterranean world, government by a small number of persons whose wealth came from commerce.

ORACLE, (1) the revelation of a god or gods to the worshiper through the medium of a priest; (2) the priest who receives the revelation; (3) the place where the message is revealed.

ORTHODOX, conforming to the established doctrines or beliefs of a particular religion or institution.

Ostracism, (1) in ancient Athens, a method of banishment without trial or special accusation by means of a popular vote; hence, (2) the involuntary separation of a person from the group.

Patrician, (1) originally, a member of a family in ancient Rome that claimed descent from one of the city's founding fathers; hence (2) any person of high social rank; (3) noble, aristocratic.

Philology, (1) the study of language as a means of discovering how it reveals the history and culture of the people who use or used it, hence, linguistics; (2) the study of written records.

Philosophy, (1) originally, love of wisdom or learning; (2) in ancient Hellas, the search for truth and man's purpose in the world; (3) the underlying body of principles in any field of knowledge.

Plebeian, (1) a poor, or lower class, Roman, as opposed to a patrician, one who claimed descent from one of the city's founding families; (2) today, someone with vulgar, common, tastes.

Polis, (1) Greek for city, (2) to the Hellenes the definition of the city-state, including its political, cultural, social life.

Polygamy, the practice of having two or more mates at the same time, as opposed to monogamy.

Polytheism, belief in, or worship of, many gods.

Primitive, from the Latin *primus*, first; hence, in regard to culture, an early, simple, way of life, as opposed to a complex, civilized one.

Psychology, the social science that deals with the study of man's mind, emotions, and behavior.

Race, the classification of sub-groups within the human family according to physical characteristics.

Reincarnation, (1) the reappearance of the soul after death in another and different bodily form; (2) a belief of the Buddhist and Hindu religions.

Republic, a form of government in which the power rests in the electorate and is exercised by a presiding officer and representatives elected by the people. The electorate may consist of everyone (a democratic republic), or the landowners, or the members of a party (limited republic).

Savage, (1) barbarian, uncivilized; (2) in a state of nature, wild, untamed; (3) a person who is uncivilized and lacking advanced culture.

Serf, (1) a tenant farmer attached to the land whose tools and stock are provided by the landlord in return for a percentage of the crop.

Sociology, the social science that deals with the study of man and his relationship with individuals and groups.

Theocracy, (1) literally, government under the immediate direction of God, hence, (2) government by priests claiming to be representatives of God.

Totem, among primitive people, an animal or natural object, or its emblem, considered to be related by blood to a given family or clan.

Tribe, a closely-knit group of people, generally in a primitive or nomadic state, consisting of a series of families, clans, or generations, believed to be of common origin, bound together under a chief and sharing common language and customs.

Tyranny, (1) in ancient Hellas, a form of government by a tyrant, a usurper who seized power illegally; (2) government by a ruler who takes power by force and maintains an absolute control through force.

Index

Figures in italics are references to photos or captions.

Key to Pronunciation (based on pronunciation key in *Webster's New World Dictionary of the American Language, College Edition,* © 1959 by The World Publishing Company): **a** = *f*at; **ā** = *a*pe; **â** = b*a*re; **ä** = c*a*r; **e** = t*e*n; **ē** = *e*ven; **ê** = h*e*re; **e** = ov*e*r; **i** = *i*s; **ī** = b*i*te; **o** = l*o*t; **ō** = g*o*; **ô** = h*o*rn; **o͞o** = t*oo*l; **oo** = l*oo*k; **oi** = *oi*l; **ou** = *ou*t; **u** = *u*p; **ū** = *u*se; **u** = f*u*r; **g** = *g*et; **j** = *j*oy; **y** = *y*et; **ch** = *ch*in; **sh** = *sh*e; **th** = *th*in; *th* = *th*en; **zh** = lei*s*ure; ə = *a*go, compl*y*; ' = abl*e* (ā'b'l); **a** = French b*a*l (intermediate between [a] and [ä]); **ë** = French c*oeu*r (round the lips for [ô] and say [e]); **ö** = French f*eu,* German K*ö*nig (round the lips for [ō] and say [ā]); *n* = French mo*n* (vowel just before is pronounced through the nose); *o* = French c*o*q, German d*o*ch (between [ō] and [ô]); **ü** = French d*u*c, German gr*ü*n (round the lips for [o͞o] and say [ē]); **kh** = German do*ch,* Scottish lo*ch* (a guttural sound produced by arranging the speech organs as for [k] and allowing the breath to escape in a continuous stream, as in [h]); H = German i*ch* (intermediate between [kh] and English [h]).

ILLUSTRATION SOURCES

ALINARI-ART REFERENCE BUREAU, INC.: 189, 336, 392, 481. AMERICAN EXPORT LINES: 434 right. THE AMERICAN MUSEUM OF NATURAL HISTORY: 21, 27, 28. THE ART INSTITUTE OF CHICAGO: 290 (Gift of Hope S. Buckingham). Belzeaux, Pierre: 495 (Time-Life Books, Barbarian Europe, *© 1968 Time, Inc.). THE TRUSTEES OF THE BRITISH MUSEUM: 62, 72, 226, 278, 307. CONSULATE GENERAL OF INDIA, INFORMATION SERVICE: 410. MUSEUM OF FINE ARTS, Boston: 91. FOTORAPIDA, Terni, Italy: 322 (Capitoline Museum). AUGUSTA GOLDSTEIN: 499 right. GOVERNMENT OF INDIA TOURIST OFFICE, N.Y.: 490. HIRMER FOTOARCHIV MÜNCHEN: 166. IRAQ MUSEUM LIBRARY, Baghdad: 170 left. ITALIAN STATE TOURIST OFFICE: 506. LABORATÒRIO FOTOGRAFICO DELLA SOPRINTENDENZA ALLE ANTICHITA DELLA CAMPANIA: 366. LOUVRE, Paris: 443. JAN LUKAS: 115, 356, 434 left. MAGNUM PHOTOS, INC.: 38 (Leonard Freed), 414 (Rene Burri © 1968), 446 (George Rodger), 503 (Elliott Erwitt © 1966). MARBURG ART REFERENCE BUREAU: 70. THE METROPOLITAN MUSEUM OF ART: 11 (Harry Burton), 40 (left to right: Rogers Fund, 1907; Rogers Fund, 1915; The Theodore M. Davis Collection, Bequest of Theodore M. Davis, 1915; Rogers Fund, 1920, 1910, 1912, 1919), 65 (Bequest of W. Gedney Beatty, 1941), 84 (Museum Excavations of 1931–34, Rogers Fund, 1934), 86, 108 (Rogers Fund, 1945), 110 left (Museum Excavations of 1919–20, Rogers Fund, supplemented by contribution of Edward S. Harkness, 1920), 110 right (Gift of Edward S. Harkness, 1917), 123 (Museum Excavations, of 1928–29, Rogers Fund, 1930), 140 (Gift of Paul E. Manheim, 1967), 200 (Fletcher Fund, 1931), 205 (Rogers Fund, 1917), 248 (Gift of Edmund Kerper, 1952), 438, 471 (Rogers Fund, 1953). MONKMEYER PRESS PHOTO SERVICE: 302 (Fujihira). MUSÉES NATIONAUX: 105. MUSEO CIVICO ARCHEOLOGICO DI BOLOGNA: 466 right. THE NEW YORK PUBLIC LIBRARY: 147, 152, 359. NY CARLSBERG GLYPTOTHEK, Copenhagen: 388. THE ORIENTAL INSTITUTE OF THE UNIVERSITY OF CHICAGO: 59, 182. ANTHONY PACCIONE: 243, 266. PALERMO MUSEUM: 366. PEABODY MUSEUM, Harvard University: 348. PHOTO RESEARCHERS, INC.: 284 (Bradley Smith). JOSEPHINE POWELL: 130. RAPHO GUILLUMETTE PICTURES, INC.: Pierre Belzeaux, Time-Life Books, Barbarian Europe, © 1968 Time, Inc., 452–53; J. Allen Cash, 236; Dimitri, 297; Dr. George Gerster, 170 right; Leonard von Maft, 483; Bernard G. Silberstein, 136, 197, 338. RESIDENZMUSEEN MÜNCHEN, ANTIQUARIUM: 394. E. RICHTER: 477. From exhibition circulated by THE SMITHSONIAN INSTITUTION, courtesy of TURKISH EMBASSY and MUSEUM OF ARCHEOLOGY, Ankara: 42. THE SMITHSONIAN INSTITUTION, FREER GALLERY OF ART, Washington, D.C.: 463. SPARTA MUSEUM: 222 left. STAATLICHE ANTIKENSAMMLUNGEN UND GLYPTOTHEK, Munich: 382. STAATLICHE MUSEEN PREUSSISCHER KULTURBESITZ ANTIKENABTEILUNG, Berlin: 126, 216. NICK STOURNARAS: 246. UNESCO: 9 (Rex Keating). THE UNIVERSITY MUSEUM OF THE UNIVERSITY OF PHILADELPHIA: 80. VATICAN MUSEUM: 271, 427. THE VICTORIA AND ALBERT MUSEUM: 466 left. WADSWORTH ATHENEUM, Hartford: 222 right (E. Irving Blomstrann). ROGER WOOD: 66. YUGOSLAV STATE TOURIST OFFICE, N.Y.: 499 left.*

MAPS: Christie McFall